William T Brooke

Methodist Free Church Hymns

William T Brooke
Methodist Free Church Hymns
ISBN/EAN: 9783744780476

Printed in Europe, USA, Canada, Australia, Japan

Cover: Foto ©Thomas Meinert / pixelio.de

More available books at **www.hansebooks.com**

METHODIST FREE CHURCH

HYMNS.

O sing unto the Lord a new song.—*Psalm xcvi. 1.*

Be filled with the Spirit; speaking to yourselves in psalms and hymns and spiritual songs, singing and making melody in your heart to the Lord.—*Ephesians v. 18, 19.*

London:
ANDREW CROMBIE,
UNITED METHODIST FREE CHURCHES' BOOK ROOM,
119, SALISBURY SQUARE, FLEET STREET, E.C.
1889.

NEW AND ENLARGED EDITION.

[Entered at Stationers' Hall according to Act of Parliament.]

LONDON:
HAYMAN, CHRISTY AND LILLY, LTD., PRINTERS,
113, FARRINGDON ROAD, E.C.

2.—57.—90.

PREFACE.

BY a resolution of the Annual Assembly of 1884, it was decided that a hymn-book should be prepared to replace the one which has been used by the United Methodist Free Churches since 1860, and a Committee was appointed to give effect to the resolution. Several reasons made a new compilation desirable. The first was that, in recent years, many hymns have been published, whose fervour and poetic power have won the approval and acceptance of nearly all sections of the Christian Church. Other reasons were, the imperfect classification of the hymns in the book hitherto in use, and the fact that a considerable number of them had become obsolete, owing to their want of adaptation for public worship.

To introduce into the new volume the principal hymns that have enriched the literature and worship of the present day, and to avoid too large a compilation, it was necessary to consider well which of the hymns in the old collection should be omitted from the new. The Committee approached this part of its duty with no small anxiety, and has endeavoured to execute it with the greatest care. The object kept continually in view was to omit no hymn that had become familiar by use, or that, by other associations, had endeared itself to our Churches. In a few cases hymns that otherwise would have been excluded have on this account been retained. Archaic words or phrases in some of the hymns of the former book have been altered; and hymns that were too long have been shortened by the omission of one or two of the weaker verses, so that each hymn may be sung through without inconvenience.

In the selection of new hymns the compilers have spared no effort in searching for the best, the most poetical, but before all, the most spiritual of the productions of the poets of our own and other lands. No collection of hymns or sacred songs of any repute has escaped attention.

The principle which guided the Committee in the compilation of the book was to fulfil in the highest degree the purpose and conditions of Divine worship, and to afford fitting means for the outpouring of the heart in prayer, the up-lifting of the soul to nobler aims, holier aspirations and fuller consecration, and the realisation, through sacred song, of communion and fellowship with God.

Not less earnestly has the Committee endeavoured, in the inclusion of new hymns, to provide for the glad and grateful expression of praise. It is still, it will always be 'a good thing to give thanks unto the Lord.' In all ages praise has been the universal language of the children of God, and He reveals Himself in response, when they draw nigh to Him with songs of thanksgiving. Thus, at the dedication of the temple, 'when they lifted up their voices,' 'the glory of the Lord filled the House of God;' and 'the great multitude which no man can number,' with 'the voice of many waters,' sing the new song 'unto Him that sitteth upon the throne, and to the Lamb for ever and ever.'

The compilers have also striven, by the choice of suitable hymns, and through the classification and arrangement of the whole book, to stimulate the manifestation of practical Christianity, and to supply a medium for the devout utterance of the varied emotions and experiences of the Christian life. Many hymns are comprised, that, to those who are afflicted, and to those in suffering and sorrow, will be full of consolation, and will be welcome 'as the shadow of a great rock in a weary land.'

PREFACE.

An Evangelistic section for Mission Services, and a section for Travellers by Land and Sea, as well as one adapted to Services for the Young at times when the Sunday School Book cannot be used, have been provided, as have also sections for other special services and occasions. Indices of first lines, of authors' names and dates, of texts and subjects illustrated by the hymns, of hymns classified under one section but also suitable for others, or for use at special meetings or services, are appended to all but the cheaper editions. These indices make the contents of the book most easy of reference.

The thanks of the Committee are sincerely tendered to the authors and also to the publishers whose names are given below, for permitting, either without charge, or by purchase, the insertion in this book of original or of copyright hymns. Some hymns—the number is but small—that would also have been inserted, have had to be excluded because the right of publication could not be secured. The Committee has laboured diligently to ensure, as far as practicable, accuracy of versions and of authors' names and dates, and has had the advantage of passing this part of its work under the revision of Mr. W. T. Brooke, who is one of the foremost authorities on hymnology.

The compilers cannot expect to escape criticism; but those who judge of the book from outside the pale of Methodism, and who may be disposed to object to the retention of some hymns which, in their opinion, might have been spared, are reminded that this is a Methodist hymnal, prepared for Methodists who hold, in the main, those views of Christian truth and practice expounded by John Wesley.

From 'the thousand-voiced heart of the Church,' the hymns comprised in this collection have sprung. Though they have originated from minds whose doctrinal beliefs are wide asunder, they are animated by a catholicity of thought and love for the great verities of the Christian religion that have rejoiced and cheered the members of the Committee in their work, and have also strengthened the hope and intensified the prayer for the coming of that time when the whole Christian Church shall 'keep the unity of the Spirit in the bond of peace.'

RALPH ABERCROMBIE
SAMUEL SAXON BARTON
RICHARD CHEW
ANDREW CROMBIE
ALFRED JONES

JOSEPH KIRSOP
MARMADUKE MILLER
JOHN MYERS
THOMAS SNAPE
JOHN SWANN WITHINGTON

Committee.

April, 1889.

The following authors and proprietors have given permission to insert copyright hymns:

Rev. W. Hay Aitken, 258.
Rev. S. Baring-Gould, 569, 941.
Mr. Arthur H. Bateman (for the late Mr. Henry Bateman), 692.
Rev. C. S. Bere (for Miss Jane M. Campbell), 860.
Miss M. Betham-Edwards, 940.
Bishop E. H. Bickersteth, 12, 413, 437, 438, 735, 849, 891.
Rev. A. G. W Blunt, 816.
Rev. Dr. Horatius Bonar, 42, 52, 216, 221, 311, 315, 354, 406, 623, 646, 751.
Mrs. E. Baldwin Brown (for the late Rev. J. Baldwin Brown), 401.
Rev. R. Brown-Borthwick, 733.
Messrs. Burns and Oates (for the late Rev. F. W. Faber), 44, 97, 187, 273, 317, 320, 534, 578, 585, 614, 789, 793.

Mrs. Elisabeth Rundle Charles, 645, 667.
Mrs. B. E. Chater (for the late Rev. F. W. Goalby), 867.
Mrs. Conder (for the late Rev. G. W. Conder), 174.
Rev. George T. Coster, 890.
Miss Frances E. Cox, 115, 199, 546.
Rev. Henry J. Cummins (for the late Rev. J. J. Cummins), 219.
Messrs. Curwen & Co. (for Mrs. M. E. Shelly), 942.
Miss Sarah Doudney, 268.
Mrs. Elizabeth Downton (for the late Rev. Henry Downton), 684, 839.
Rev. John Ellerton, 78, 239, 252, 254, 255, 289, 717, 767, 790, 886, 943, 1039.
Miss E. E. S. Elliott, 934.

PREFACE.

Rev. Canon Furse (for the late Rev. J. S. B. Monsell), 62, 112, 185, 192, 203, 381, 436, 532, 551, 566, 618, 636, 780, 834, 853, 858, 863, 883.
Miss Gaskell (for the late Rev. W. Gaskell), 630, 644.
Mr. Thomas H. Gill, 3, 87, 966.
Mrs. Elizabeth Ayton Godwin, 382.
Mr. John B. Greenwood, 862.
H. L. L., 285, 499, 509, 515, 521, 550.
Rev. Newman Hall, 922.
Rev. Dr. Hannay (for E. S. A.), 864, 914.
The late Miss M. V. G. Havergal (for the late Miss F. R. Havergal), 54, 84, 125, 336, 414, 415, 426, 429, 504, 825, 831, 124.
Mr. J. T. Hayes (for the late Dr. J. M. Neale, from 'Hymns of the Eastern Church'), 90, 275, 568.
Rev J. Page Hopps, 502, 553, 843.
Bishop W. W. How, 55, 94, 300, 325, 492, 555, 638, 791, 839, 842, 843.
Miss Genevieve S. Irons, 326.
Rev. W. J. Irons, 305, 496, 787.
Rev. Ebenezer E. Jenkins, 904.
Rev. John Julian, 81.
Messrs. Kegan Paul, Trench & Co. (for the late Archbishop R. C. Trench), 513.
Rev. R. F. Littledale, 838.
Mrs. Lynch (for the late Rev. T. T. Lynch), 48, 91, 129, 282, 536, 652, 664, 666, 670, 721, 949.
Dr. George Macdonald, 617.
Mr. W. J. Mathams, 440.
Mrs. Mary F. Maude, 430.
Mr. Albert Midlane, 147, 920.
Rev. H. A. Mills (for the late Rev. Edward Caswall), 162, 288, 461.

Messrs. Morgan & Scott (for Miss C. E. Clephane, 103 (from 'Sacred Songs and Solos').
Mr. C. E. Mudie, 444.
Messrs. Thomas Nelson & Sons (for the late Rev. James D. Burns), 267, 449, 833.
Rev. Dr. J. H. Newman, 190, 487.
Messrs. Novello, Ewer & Co. (for the late Rev. S. Childs-Clarke), 855, (for the late Dr. J. M. Neale), 1036 ; (for the late Dr. Wm. J. Irons), 1040.
Messrs. Oliphant, Anderson & Ferrier (for the late Rev. R. M. McCheyne), 542.
Mr. W. H. Parker, 932.
Rev. E. H. Plumptre, 840, 877.
Rev. Francis Pott, 170.
Archdeacon Sir George Prevost (for the late Rev. Isaac Williams), 832.
Proprietors of Home Hymn Book, 270.
Mrs. Punshon (for the late Rev. William Morley Punshon), 270.
The late Mr. George Rawson, 2, 156, 153, 210, 278, 279, 280, 286, 287, 303, 686, 835, 882, 885, 946.
Mr. Frederick Sherlock, 957.
Messrs. Smith, Elder & Co. (for the late Miss Anne Bronte). 366, 952.
Rev. C. H. Spurgeon, 262.
Rev. Samuel J. Stone, 13, 584, 828.
Rev. T. A. Stowell, 925, 938 and for the late Rev. Hugh Stowell), 719, 929.
Rev. Godfrey Thring, 70, 89, 93, 128, 157, 198, 235, 265, 276, 654, 658, 848, 878, 894.
Rev. L. Tuttiett, 547.
Rev. Henry Twells, 251.
Miss Anna L. Waring, 217, 653.
Rev. Benjamin Waugh, 462.
Rev. Frederick Whitneld, 342, 465.
The late Mr. William Whiting, 888.

The following original hymns have been presented to the Committee :

Rev. Edward Boaden, 876, 955, 958. | Rev. Alfred Jones, 837.
Rev. Alfred Winfield, 850.

Permission to use copyright hymns has been purchased from the following :

Messrs. George Bell & Sons (for Miss A. A. Proctor), 186, 497, 665.
Mr. W. Chatterton Dix, 65, 308, 859, 889.
Messrs. Longman & Co. (for Miss C. Winkworth, from 'Lyra Germanica'), 30, 75, 193, 240, 821, 884.
Messrs. J. Masters & Co. (for Mrs. Cecil F. Alexander), 122, 264, 917, 923, 926 (and for Dr. J. M. Neale), 755, 785, 865.

Miss Annie Matheson, 935, 937.
Proprietors of Chorale Book (for Miss Catherine Winkworth), 283, 494.
Messrs. Raphael Tuck & Sons (for Miss Annie Matheson), 215.
Rev. Christopher Wordsworth (for the late Bishop Christopher Wordsworth), 74, 116, 178, 231, 274, 586, 832.

If any copyrights have been unintentionally infringed, the Committee sincerely apologise, and will be glad to acknowledge its obligation to authors or proprietors in a future edition of this Hymnal.

CONTENTS.

	HYMNS
GOD THE FATHER.	
His Nature and Perfections	1—13
His Works in Creation	14—23
His Providence	24—37
His Mercy and Grace	38—48
THE LORD JESUS CHRIST.	
His Divinity and Glory	49—63
His Incarnation and Advent	64—81
His Example and Teaching	82—94
His Passion and Death	95—110
His Resurrection and Ascension	111—122
His Intercession and Reign	123—128
THE HOLY SPIRIT.	
His Regenerating and Sanctifying Grace	129—147
His Work as Teacher and Comforter	148—159
THE HOLY TRINITY	160—170
DIVINE WORSHIP.	
Praise and Prayer	171—229
The Lord's Day	230—255
Morning	256—268
Evening	269—289
THE HOLY SCRIPTURES	290—305
THE GOSPEL MESSAGE	306—317
EVANGELISTIC SERVICES.	
Invitation to the Sinner	318—334
Exhortation to Repent	335—340
Salvation through Faith	341—351
Rejoicing in Forgiveness	352—363
THE CHRISTIAN LIFE.	
Contrition and Longing for God	364—398
Faith and Consecration	399—440
Adoption and Sonship	441—449
Love and Holiness	450—486
Light, Guidance and Growth	487—509
Thankfulness	510—516
Affliction and Resignation	517—560
Conflict and Courage	561—586
Watchfulness and Steadfastness	587—602
Declension and Recovery	603—613

	HYMNS
Humility	614—620
Prayer (See also Prayer Meetings)	621—637
Service and Giving	638—671
Hope and Joy	672—692
THE CHURCH OF CHRIST	
Character, Unity and Fellowship	693—702
Reception of Members	703—706
Recognition of Ministers	707—711
Prayer Meetings (See also Prayer)	712—721
Baptism	722—724
The Lord's Supper	725—737
Lovefeast	738—741
Watch-Night Service	742—745
Covenant Service	746—749
DEATH, RESURRECTION AND JUDGMENT	750—772
HEAVEN AND THE LIFE HEREAFTER	773—803
CHRISTIAN MISSIONS	804—823
NEW YEAR	824—833
SEASONS OF THE YEAR	834—845
FLOWER SERVICE	846—850
HARVEST THANKSGIVING	851—860
SPECIAL OCCASIONS.	
Marriage	861—862
Laying Foundation and Memorial Stones	863—866
Opening Services	867—876
Hospital Sunday and Benevolent Institutions	877—880
Burial of the Dead	881—887
TRAVELLERS BY LAND AND SEA	888—904
PARENTS AND FAMILY WORSHIP	905—911
SERVICES FOR THE YOUNG	912—944
PRIVATE DEVOTION	945—954
TEMPERANCE SERVICES	955—960
NATIONAL HYMNS	961—969
DISMISSAL HYMNS AND DOXOLOGIES	970—980
PSALMS AND CANTICLES	981—1042

CONTENTS.

PSALMS.

I.	941
VIII.	942
XVI.	983
XIX.	984
XXIII.	945
XXIV.	946
XXV.	947
XXVII.	988
XXXII.	949
XXXIV.	990
XXXIX.	991
XLII.	992
XLVI.	993
LI.	994
LXIII.	995
LXV.	996
LXVII.	997
LXXII.	998
LXXXIV.	999
LXXXIX.	1000
XC.	1001
XCI.	1002
XCV.	1003
XCVI.	1004
XCVIII.	1005
C.	1006
CIII.	1007
CXV.	1008
CXVI.	1009
CXVIII.	1010
CXXI.	1011
CXXII.	1012
CXXXVI.	1013
CXXXIX.	1014
CXLV.	1015
CXLVI.	1016

CANTICLES.

1 Chron. xxix.	1017
Isaiah xii.	1018
,, xxv.	1019
,, xl.	1020
,, lii.	1021
,, liii.	1022
,, lv.	1023
,, lx. & ix.	1024
Lamentations iii	1025
Habakkuk lii.	1026

SELECTIONS FROM THE NEW TESTAMENT.

Matthew v.	1027
Romans viii.	1028
1 Cor. xv.	1029
1 Cor. v., Rom. vi., 1 Cor. xv.	1030
Ephesians iii.	1031
Revelation i. & iv.	1032

ANCIENT HYMNS OF THE CHURCH.

Te Deum Laudamus	1033
Magnificat	1034
Benedictus	1035
Nunc Dimittis	1036
Gloria in Excelsis	1037
The strain upraise	1038
Sing Hallelujah forth	1039
Dies Iræ	1040
SANCTUS	1041
THE COMMANDMENTS	1042

INDICES.

SPECIAL INDEX OF SEASONS AND OCCASIONAL SERVICES.
ALPHABETICAL INDEX TO HYMNS.
AUTHORS AND TRANSLATORS.
SCRIPTURE TEXTS.
GENERAL INDEX OF SUBJECTS.

INDEX to find Hymns placed under the several Sections of this Hymnal which are suitable for the various Seasons of the Year, and for Special Services.

Ascension Day. 118-122, 125, 986.
Baptism: 702, 722-724, 905, 910.
Bazaars: 178, 429, 638, 645, 876.
Bible Society Meetings and Bible Classes: 3, 19, 28, 38, 144, 153-155, 196, 268, 290-305, 331, 338, 486, 511, 815, 821, 984.
Birthdays: 433, 954. See New Year, The.
Chapel Anniversaries: 134, 166, 170-173, 175, 185, 200, 208, 213, 231, 232, 241-244, 246-249, 300, 476, 480, 493, 515, 569, 573, 578, 587, 608, 673, 675, 858, 868, 870, 872, 873, 988, 995, 999, 1000, 1010, 1012, 1053, 1039, 1041.
Choir Anniversaries: 5, 170, 188, 200, 204, 205, 229, 238, 514, 1006, 1013, 1015.
Christmas: 61-67, 70-81, 676, 926, 934, 1034-1036.
Church Meetings: 137, 222, 493, 504, 633, 673, 677, 693-696, 698-703, 709, 713, 729.
Covenant Services: 142, 198, 221, 288, 353, 361, 362, 399, 405, 424-427, 429-432, 435, 437, 440, 454, 458, 640-642, 654, 657, 663, 668, 690, 746-749.
Easter: 50, 111-117.
Evangelical Alliance and Union Meetings: 126, 303, 578, 647, 652, 662, 684, 695, 639, 701, 703, 706, 729, 978.
Evangelistic Services: 38, 42, 48-51, 57, 58, 63, 85, 92, 95-110, 129-159, 179-182, 184, 197, 200, 221, 277, 297, 306-440, 442, 445, 452, 453, 463, 466, 468, 473, 476, 487, 569, 573, 578, 587-589, 592, 593, 603-613, 627, 628, 641, 657, 662, 668, 673, 675, 681-683, 685, 705, 706, 713-716, 719, 749, 762, 766, 770, 776, 780, 782, 796, 797, 799, 801, 802, 807, 924.
Evening: 36, 250-255, 269-289, 947.
Flower Services: 17, 21, 112, 174, 178, 200, 215, 516, 826, 834, 836, 837, 846-850, 912, 922, 923, 937, 1038.
Foundation and Memorial Stones: 863-866.
Funeral and Memorial Services: 115, 555, 559, 750-758, 767, 779, 791-795, 800, 881-887, 991, 1001, 1029.
Good Friday: 95-110, 190, 336, 353, 396, 416, 443, 461, 468, 520, 917.
Harvest Thanksgiving: 14, 17, 21, 116, 174, 176, 178, 184, 195, 298, 340, 662, 696, 770, 814, 826, 840-842, 851-860, 996, 1003.
Home: 192, 200, 221, 258, 260, 261, 270, 282, 304, 462, 516, 614, 905-911, 918, 920, 926, 930, 933, 934, 941, 943.
Hospitals and Benevolent Societies: 87, 91, 93, 94, 177, 645, 656, 846, 877-880, 935.
Lectures and Literary Societies: 3, 17, 18, 23, 45, 126, 176, 200, 303, 419, 462, 511, 513, 515, 516, 578, 581, 585, 602, 614, 650, 660, 662, 664, 666, 671, 717, 847, 848.
Lord's Day, The: 230-255.
Lord's Supper, The: 95-110, 353, 468, 520, 523, 725-737, 977, 1030.
Love-feasts: 180, 197, 341, 465, 467, 469, 483, 682, 683, 684, 704, 705, 706, 732, 738-741.
Messages: 861, 862.
Members, Services for the Reception of: 703-706
Ministers, Meetings of: 144, 484, 486, 504, 525, 588, 628, 637, 641, 644, 648, 649, 651-653, 658, 660, 662-664, 678, 707, 710.

Ministers, Recognition of: 476, 504, 646, 708-711, 814, 815, 1021.
Missions: 19, 49, 50, 56, 63, 72, 123, 124, 127, 128, 131, 145, 164, 165, 169, 172, 188, 218, 289, 306, 307, 309, 312, 316, 322, 334, 489, 569, 651, 662, 675, 676, 679, 804-822, 959, 997, 998, 1004, 1005, 1023, 1024.
Missionaries, Ministers and Friends, Departure of: 696, 738, 822, 823, 970, 974, 977.
Morning: 223, 256-268, 378, 470, 913.
Nation, Thanksgivings and Prayers for the: 41, 189, 193, 561, 578, 684, 808, 961-969, 993, 998, 1000, 1003, 1008, 1015-1017, 1019.
New Year, The: 3, 26, 33, 34, 490-494, 496, 497, 499, 501, 502, 509, 515, 552, 674, 692, 744, 745, 773, 774, 824-833.
Opening Services of Chapel or School: 867-874.
Organ Opening: 200, 875.
Peace Meetings: 72, 79, 676, 811, 961, 962, 965, 967.
Prayer Meetings: 213, 244, 601, 617, 621-637, 663, 700, 712-721. See Evangelistic Services.
Revivals: 130, 132, 133, 137, 139, 140, 144, 145, 147, 155, 214, 364, 378, 388, 393, 515, 603-605, 818.
Sabbath Day, The: See Lord's Day, The.
Sea, For Those at: 89, 91, 438, 491, 500, 544, 691, 888-904.
Seasons of the Year: 826, 831-845.
Sick Room: 30, 32, 90, 126, 186, 219, 229, 271, 274, 277, 503, 517-560, 774, 776, 781, 797, 952, 953.
Social Meetings: 17, 21, 31, 200, 652, 653, 660, 666.
Sunday-school Anniversaries: 169, 562, 569, 573, 662, 679, 858, 914, 916-926, 930, 931, 935-938, 940, 942, 982, 1038.
Teachers' Meetings: 504, 644, 646, 652, 662, 905-908, 910.
Temperance Meetings: 614, 645, 662, 664, 955-960.
Thank Offerings: 336, 435, 439, 414, 638, 643, 645.
Watch Night Services: 12, 24, 35, 487, 510, 521, 537, 587, 665, 742-745, 750, 751, 753-755, 764, 768, 771, 843.
Week Day Services: 221, 267, 436, 457, 502, 570, 601, 630, 644, 646, 648, 652, 658-661, 669-671, 717.
Whitsuntide. 129, 130, 132-139, 144, 149, 154-159, 464, 932.
Young, Services for the: 21, 29, 48, 51, 64, 67, 73, 74, 82, 103, 110, 111, 122, 125, 130, 134, 156, 159, 174, 176, 178, 179, 182, 184, 186, 192, 194, 195, 197, 198, 200, 210, 221, 223, 252, 255, 256, 259, 261, 269, 271-273, 275, 277, 279-281, 284, 289, 291, 294, 311, 316, 317, 331, 333, 339, 349, 351, 359, 364, 406, 407, 416, 419, 426, 429, 430, 437, 440, 449, 452, 461, 466, 487, 491, 492, 513, 516, 537, 541, 542, 545, 548, 562, 569, 573, 578, 584, 614, 618, 623, 627, 644, 652, 658, 662, 685, 749, 751, 752, 770, 776, 782, 785, 789, 793, 799, 805, 809, 811, 815, 824, 825, 831, 832, 838, 839, 842, 843, 845, 846-860, 880, 912-944, 959

METHODIST FREE CHURCH HYMNS.

God the Father.

HIS NATURE AND PERFECTIONS.

1 L.M.
The whole earth is full of His glory.
Isaiah vi. 3.

ETERNAL Power, whose high abode
 Becomes the grandeur of a God,
Infinite lengths beyond the bounds
Where stars revolve their little rounds!

2 Thee, while the first archangel sings,
 He hides his face behind his wings;
And ranks of shining thrones around
Fall worshipping, and spread the ground.

3 Lord, what shall earth and ashes do?
 We would adore our Maker too!
From sin and dust to Thee we cry,
The Great, the Holy, and the High.

4 Earth from afar hath heard Thy fame,
 And worms have learned to lisp Thy name;
But, O! the glories of Thy mind
Leave all our soaring thoughts behind!

5 God is in heaven, and men below;
 Be short our tunes, our words be few!
A solemn reverence checks our songs,
And praise sits silent on our tongues.
          Isaac Watts. 1706.

2 8.7.8.7.4.7.
Let them praise Thy great and terrible name; for it is holy.—Psalm xcix. 3.

GOD the Lord is King! before Him,
 Earth, with all thy nations, wait!
Where the cherubim adore Him,
Sitteth He in royal state:
  He is Holy:
Blessed, only Potentate!

2 God the Lord is King of Glory!
 Zion, tell the world His fame;
Ancient Israel, the story
Of His faithfulness proclaim!
  He is Holy:
Holy is His awful name!

3 In old times when dangers darkened,
 When, invoked by priest and seer,
To His people's cry He hearkened,
Answered them in all their fear;
  He is Holy:
As they called, they found Him near.

4 Laws divine to them were spoken
 From the pillar of the cloud;
Sacred precepts, quickly broken!
Fiercely then His vengeance flowed:
  He is Holy:
To the dust their hearts were bowed.

5 But their Father, God, forgave them
 When they sought His face once more,
Ever ready was to save them,
Tenderly did He restore:
  He is Holy:
We, too, will His grace implore.

6 God in Christ is all-forgiving,
 Waits His mercy to fulfil;
Come, exalt Him, all the living;
Come, ascend His Zion still!
  He is Holy:
Worship at His holy hill!
          George Rawson. 1857.

3 8.8.6. 8.8.6.
Your life is hid with Christ in God.
Colossians iii. 3.

LORD GOD, by whom all change is
  wrought,
By whom new things to birth are brought,
 In whom no change is known!
Whate'er Thou dost, whate'er Thou art,
Thy people still in Thee have part;
 Still, still Thou art our own.

2 Ancient of Days! we dwell in Thee;
 Out of Thine own eternity
  Our peace and joy are wrought;
We rest in our eternal God,
And make secure and sweet abode
 With Thee, who changest not.

GOD THE FATHER.

3 Each steadfast promise we possess;
Thine everlasting truth we bless,
　　Thine everlasting love;
The unfailing Helper close we clasp,
The everlasting arms we grasp,
　　Nor from the refuge move.

4 Spirit who makest all things new,
Thou leadest onward; we pursue
　　The heavenly march sublime.
'Neath Thy renewing fire we glow,
And still from strength to strength we go,
　　From height to height we climb.

5 Darkness and dread we leave behind,
New light, new glory still we find,
　　New realms divine possess:
New births of grace new raptures bring;
Triumphant, the new song we sing,
　　The great Renewer bless.

6 To Thee we rise, in Thee we rest;
We stay at home, we go in quest,
　　Still Thou art our abode.
The rapture swells, the wonder grows
As full on us new life still flows
　　From our unchanging God.
　　　　　　　　Thomas H. Gill. 1869.

4 *O give thanks unto the Lord; for He is good.*—Psalm cxviii. 1. 　8.8.8.8.8.8.

O GOD, of good the unfathomed Sea!
　Who would not give his heart to Thee,
　Who would not love Thee with His might?
O Jesus, Lover of mankind!
Who would not his whole soul and mind,
　With all his strength, to Thee unite?

2 Thou shin'st with everlasting rays;
Before the insufferable blaze
　Angels with both wings veil their eyes;
Yet, free as air Thy bounty streams
On all Thy works; Thy mercy's beams
　Diffusive, as Thy sun's, arise.

3 Astonished at Thy frowning brow,
Earth, hell, and heaven's strong pillars
　Terrible majesty is Thine!　[bow;
Who then can that vast love express,
Which bows Thee down to me, who less
　Than nothing am, till Thou art mine!

4 High throned on heaven's eternal hill,
In number, weight, and measure still
　Thou sweetly orderest all that is:
And yet Thou deign'st to come to me,
And guide my steps, that I, with Thee
　Enthroned, may reign in endless bliss.

5 Fountain of good, all blessing flows
From Thee; no want Thy fulness knows;
　What but Thyself canst Thou desire?
Yet, self-sufficient, as Thou art,
Thou dost desire my worthless heart:
　This, only this, dost Thou require.

6 O God, of good the unfathomed Sea!
Who would not give his heart to Thee,
　Who would not love Thee with his might?
O Jesus, Lover of mankind!
Who would not his whole soul and mind,
　With all his strength, to Thee unite?
　　　　　　　John Scheffler. 1657.
　　　　　　Tr. *John Wesley.* 1739.

5 *Awake up, my glory.*—Psalm lvii. 8. 　4.4.6. 4.4.6.

MY God, my King,
　Thy praise I'll sing,
My heart is all Thine own:
　My highest powers,
　My choicest hours,
I yield to Thee alone.

2 My voice, awake,
　Thy part to take,
My soul, the concert join;
　Till all around
　Shall catch the sound,
And mix their hymns with mine.

3 But man is weak
　Thy praise to speak;
Your God, ye angels, sing;
　'Tis yours to see,
　More near than we,
The glories of our King.

4 His truth and grace
　Fill time and space,
As large His honours be;
　Till all that live
　Their homage give,
And praise my God with me. Amen.
　　　　　　　　H. F. Lyte. 1834.

6 *Who is like Thee, glorious in holiness, fearful in praises, doing wonders?* 　L.M.
Exodus xv. 11.

O GOD, Thou bottomless abyss!
　Thee to perfection who can know?
O height immense! What words suffice
　Thy countless attributes to show?

2 Unfathomable depths Thou art;
　O plunge me in Thy mercy's sea!
Void of true wisdom is my heart;
　With love embrace, and cover me!

3 While Thee, all-infinite, I set
　By faith before my ravished eye,
My weakness bends beneath the weight;
　O'erpowered I sink, I faint, I die!

4 Eternity Thy fountain was,
　Which, like Thee, no beginning knew;
Thou wast ere time began his race,
　Ere glowed with stars the ethereal blue.

HIS NATURE AND PERFECTIONS.

5 Greatness unspeakable is Thine,
  Greatness, whose undiminished ray,
  When short-lived worlds are lost, shall shine
    When earth and heaven are fled away.

6 Unchangeable, all-perfect Lord,
  Essential life's unbounded sea,
  What lives and moves, lives by Thy word;
  It lives, and moves, and is from Thee.
      Ernst Lange. 1711.
      Tr. John Wesley. 1737.

7 L.M.
By the word of the Lord were the heavens made.—Psalm xxxiii. 6.

THY hand, O God, Thy forming skill,
  Firm fixed this universal chain;
Else empty barren darkness still
  Had held its unmolested reign.

2 Whate'er in earth, or sea, or sky,
  Or shuns or meets the wandering thought,
  Escapes or strikes the searching eye,
  By Thee was to perfection brought.

3 High is Thy power above all height,
  Whate'er Thy will decrees is done:
  Thy wisdom, equal to Thy might,
  Only to Thee, O God, is known.

4 Heaven's glory is Thy awful throne,
  Yet earth partakes Thy gracious sway:
  Vain man! thy wisdom folly own,
  Lost is thy reason's feeble ray.

5 What our dim eye could never see
  Is plain and naked to Thy sight;
  What thickest darkness veils, to Thee
  Shines clearly as the morning light.

6 In light Thou dwell'st; light that no shade,
    No variation, ever knew:
  Heaven, earth, and hell, stand all displayed
    And open to Thy piercing view.
      Ernst Lange. 1711.
      Tr. John Wesley. 1737.

8 L.M.
Thou art God alone.
Psalm lxxxvi. 10.

THOU, true and only God, lead'st forth
  The immortal armies of the sky;
Thou laugh'st to scorn the gods of earth;
Thou thunderest, and amazed they fly!

2 With downcast eye the angelic choir
  Appear before Thy awful face;
  Trembling they strike the golden lyre,
  And through heaven's vault resound Thy praise.

3 In earth, in heaven, in all Thou art;
  The conscious creature feels Thy nod,
  Whose forming hand on every part
  Impressed the image of its God.

4 Thine, Lord, is wisdom, Thine alone;
  Justice and truth before Thee stand
  Yet, nearer to Thy sacred throne,
  Mercy withholds Thy lifted hand.

5 Each evening shows Thy tender love,
  Each rising morn Thy plenteous grace;
  Thy wakened wrath doth slowly move,
  Thy willing mercy flies apace!

6 To Thy benign, indulgent care,
  Father, this light, this breath we owe;
  And all we have, and all we are,
  From Thee, great Source of Being, flow.
      Ernst Lange. 1711.
      Tr. John Wesley. 1737.

9 L.M.
All that is in the heaven and in the earth is Thine.—1 Chron. xx.x. 11.

PARENT of Good, Thy bounteous hand
  Incessant blessings down distils,
And all in air, or sea, or land,
  With plenteous food and gladness fills.

2 All things in Thee live, move, and are,
  Thy power infused doth all sustain
  Even those Thy daily favours share,
  Who thankless spurn Thy easy reign.

3 Thy sun Thou bidd'st his genial ray
  Alike on all impartial pour;
  To all, who hate or bless Thy sway,
  Thou bidd'st descend the fruitful shower.

4 Yet while, at length, who scorned Thy might
  Shall feel Thee a consuming fire,
  How sweet the joys, the crown how bright,
  Of those who to Thy love aspire!

5 All creatures praise the eternal Name!
  Ye hosts that to His court belong,
  Cherubic choirs, seraphic flames,
  Awake the everlasting song!

6 Thrice Holy! Thine the kingdom is,
  The power omnipotent is Thine;
  And when created nature dies,
  Thy never-ceasing glories shine.
      Ernst Lange. 1711.
      Tr. John Wesley. 1737.

10 S.G. 8.8.6.
God is Light.—1 John i. 5.

ETERNAL Light! Eternal Light!
  How pure the soul must be,
When, placed within Thy searching sight,
It shrinks not, but with calm delight
  Can live, and look on Thee!

2 The spirits that surround Thy throne
    May bear the burning bliss;
  But that is surely theirs alone,
  Since they have never, never known
    A fallen world like this.

GOD THE FATHER.

S O! how shall I, whose native sphere
  Is dark, whose mind is dim,
Before the ineffable appear,
  And on my naked spirit bear
    That uncreated beam?

4 There is a way for man to rise
  To that sublime abode:—
An offering and a sacrifice,
  A Holy Spirit's energies,
    An advocate with God:—

5 These, these prepare us for the sight
  Of holiness above;
The sons of ignorance and night
  May dwell in the Eternal Light,
    Through the Eternal Love.
      Thomas Binney. d. 1874.

11   C.M.
*O Lord, Thou hast searched me,
and known me.*—Psalm cxxxix. 1.

IN all my vast concerns with Thee,
  In vain my soul would try
To shun Thy presence, Lord, or flee
  The notice of Thine eye.

2 Thy all-surrounding sight **surveys**
  My rising and my rest,
My public walks, my private **ways**,
  The **secrets** of my breast.

3 My **thoughts lie** open to Thee, Lord,
  Before they're formed within;
And, ere my lips pronounce the word,
  Thou know'st the sense I mean.

4 O wondrous **knowledge, deep and high**!
  Where can **a creature hide**?
Within Thy circling arms I lie,
  Beset **on every side**.

5 So let Thy grace surround me still,
  And like a bulwark prove,
To guard my **soul** from every ill,
  Secured by sovereign love. Amen.
      Isaac Watts. 1719.

12   7.6. 7.6. D.
*Thou art the same, and Thy
years shall have no end.*—Psalm cii. 27.

O GOD, the Rock of Ages,
  Who evermore hast been,
What time the tempest rages,
  Our dwelling-place serene;
Before Thy first creations,
  O Lord, the same as now,
To endless generations
  The Everlasting Thou!

2 Our years are like the shadows
  On sunny hills that lie,
Or grasses in the meadows
  That blossom but to die;

A sleep, a dream, a story
  By strangers quickly told,
An unremaining glory
  Of things that soon are old.

3 O Thou, who canst not slumber,
  Whose light grows never pale,
Teach us aright to number
  Our years before they fail.
On us Thy mercy lighten,
  On us Thy goodness rest,
And let Thy Spirit brighten
  The hearts Thyself hast blest.

4 **Lord,** crown our faith's endeavour
  With beauty and with grace,
Till clothed in light for ever,
  We see Thee face to face
A joy no language measures;
  A fountain brimming o'er;
An endless flow **of** pleasures;
  An ocean without shore. Amen.
      Bishop E. H. Bickersteth. 1858.

13   8.8. 8.8. **8.8.**
*The Lord He is God; there is none
else beside Him.*—Deut. iv. 35.

NONE else but **Thee** for evermore,
  One, All, we dread, believe, adore;
Great earth and heaven **shall** have their day,
And, worn and old, shall pass away,
But Thou remainest on Thy throne,
Eternal, changeless, and alone!

2 **None else** we praise! in **every form**,
In peace of calm, and power of storm,
In simple flower, and mystic star,
In all around, and all afar,
In grandeur, beauty, truth, but Thee
None else we hear, none else we see.

3 **None else we love! for sweeter grace**
That made anew a ruined race;
The **heirs of** life, the lords of death,
With earliest voice and **latest** breath,
When days begin, when days are done,
Bless we the **Father** for the Son.

4 **None else we** trust! though flesh may fall,
Or heart may sink when foes assail,
Thou, **by** Thy Spirit, art our stay,
And peace that shall not pass away;
None else in life and death have we,
But **we** have **all in** all with Thee.

5 Yea, none but Thee all worlds confess,
And those redeemed ones numberless;
Father, with Son and Spirit, One,
And evermore beside Thee none,
Of all that is, has been, shall be,
We praise, love, trust none else but Thee!
            Amen.
      Samuel J. Stone. 1865.

HIS WORKS IN CREATION.

14 L.M.
It is good to sing praises unto our God.—Psalm cxlvii. 1.

PRAISE ye the Lord! 'tis good to raise
 Your hearts and voices in His praise;
His nature and His works invite
To make this duty **our** delight.

2 He formed the stars, those heavenly **flames**;
He counts their numbers, calls their **names**
His wisdom's vast, and knows no bound,
A deep where all **our** thoughts are **drowned**.

3 Sing to the Lord! exalt Him high,
Who spreads His clouds **along the sky**;
There He prepares **the fruitful rain**,
Nor lets the drops **descend in vain**.

4 He makes the grass **the hills** adorn,
And clothes the smiling hills with corn;
The beasts with food His hands supply,
And the young ravens when they cry.

5 What is the creature's skill or force?
The sprightly man, or warlike horse?
The piercing wit, the active limb?
All are too mean delights for Him.

6 But saints are lovely in His sight,
He views His children with delight;
He sees their hope, **He** knows their fear,
He looks and loves **His image** there.
 Isaac Watts. 1719.

15 7.7.7.7. D.
Whom have I in heaven but Thee!
Psalm lxxiii. 25.

LORD of earth! **Thy** forming hand
 Well this **glorious** frame hath planned;
Woods that wave and hills that **tower**,
Ocean rolling in its power;
Yet, amid this scene so fair,
Should I cease Thy smile to share,
What were all its joys to me?
Whom **have I** on **earth** but **Thee**?

2 Lord **of heaven! beyond our sight**
Rolls **a world of purer light**;
There, **in love's eternal reign**,
Parted friends **shall meet again**;
O that world **is passing fair!**
Yet, shouldst **Thou be absent there**,
What were all **its joys to me?**
Whom have I **in heaven but Thee?**

3 Lord of earth **and heaven! my breast**
Seeks in Thee its only rest;
I was lost, Thy accents mild
Homeward lured Thy wandering child;
O should once Thy smile divine
Cease upon my soul to shine,
What were heaven or earth to me?
Whom have I in each but Thee?
 Sir R. Grant. d. 1838.

16 S.M.
O come, let us sing unto the Lord.
Psalm xcv. 1.

COME, sound His praise abroad,
 And hymns of glory sing;
Jehovah is the sovereign God,
 The universal King.

2 **He** formed the deeps unknown;
 He gave the seas their bound;
The watery worlds are all His own,
 And all the solid ground.

3 Come, worship **at His** throne;
 Come, **bow** before **the** Lord;
We are His works, and not our own;
 He formed us by His word.

4 **To-day attend His** voice,
 Nor dare provoke His rod;
Come, as the people of His choice,
 And own your gracious God.
 Isaac Watts. 1719.

17 C.M.
Lift up your eyes on high, and behold who hath created these things.
Isaiah xl. 26.

THE God of **nature** and of grace
 In all His works appears;
His goodness through the earth we trace,
 His grandeur in the spheres.

2 Behold this fair and fertile globe,
 By Him in wisdom planned;
'Twas He who girded, like a robe,
 The ocean round the land.

3 Lift to the firmament **your eye**;
 Thither your path **pursue**;
His glory, boundless as the sky,
 O'erwhelms the wondering view.

4 He bows **the heavens,—the mountains stand**
 A highway for their God;
He walks amidst the desert-land,
 'Tis Eden where He trod.

5 The forests in His strength rejoice;
 Hark! on the evening breeze,
As once of old, the Lord God's voice
 Is heard among the trees.

6 In every stream His bounty flows,
 Diffusing joy and wealth;
In every breeze His Spirit blows,
 The breath of life and health.

7 His blessings fall **in plenteous showers**
 Upon the lap of earth,
That teems with foliage, fruit, and flowers,
 And rings with infant mirth.

8 If God hath made this world so fair,
 Where sin and death abound;
How beautiful beyond compare
 Will Paradise be found!
 James Montgomery. 1819.

GOD THE FATHER.

18 L.M.
The firmament showeth His handiwork.—Psalm xix. 1.

THE spacious firmament on high,
  With all the blue ethereal sky,
And spangled heavens, **a shining frame,**
Their great Original proclaim.

2 The unwearied sun, **from day to day,**
  Does his Creator's **power display;**
  And **publishes to every land**
  The **work of an Almighty hand.**

3 Soon as the evening shades prevail,
  The moon takes up the wondrous tale;
  And nightly **to** the listening earth
  Repeats the **story** of her birth:

4 Whilst **all the stars** that round her **burn,**
  And all the planets in their turn,
  Confirm the tidings as they roll,
  And spread the truth from pole to **pole.**

5 What though in solemn silence all
  Move round this dark, terrestrial ball;
  What though no real voice nor sound
  Amid their radiant orbs be found;

6 In reason's ear they all rejoice,
  And utter forth a glorious voice;
  For ever singing as they shine,
  The Hand that made us is divine.

Joseph Addison. 1712.

19 L.M.
The heavens declare the glory of God.—Psalm xix. 1.

THE heavens declare Thy glory, Lord,
  In every star Thy wisdom shines;
But when our eyes behold Thy word,
We read Thy name in fairer lines.

2 The rolling sun, the changing light,
  And night and day, Thy power confess;
  But the best volume Thou hast writ
  Reveals Thy **justice** and Thy grace.

3 Sun, moon, and stars convey Thy praise
  Round the whole earth, and never stand;
  So when Thy truth began its race,
  It touched, and glanced on every land.

4 Nor shall Thy spreading gospel rest,
  Till through the world Thy **truth has** run;
  Till Christ has all the nations **blest,**
  That see the light or feel the **sun.**

5 Great Sun of Righteousness, arise,
  Bless the dark world with heavenly light
  Thy gospel makes the simple wise;
  Thy laws are pure, Thy judgments right.

Isaac Watts. 1719.

20 6.6.6.6.8.8.
The Lord reigneth; let the earth rejoice.—Psalm xcvii. 1.

THE **Lord** Jehovah reigns,
  His throne is built on high;
The garments He assumes
  Are light and majesty;
His glories shine with beams so bright
No mortal eye can bear the sight.

2 The **thunders** of His hand
    Keep the wide world in awe;
  His wrath and justice stand
    To guard His holy law;
  And where His love resolves to bless,
  His truth confirms and seals the grace.

3 Through **all** His mighty **works**
    Surprising wisdom shines,
  Confounds the powers of hell,
    And breaks their dark designs
  Strong is His arm, and shall fulfil
  His great decrees, His sovereign will.

4 And can this sovereign King
    Of glory condescend?
  And will He write His name,
    My Father and my Friend?
  I love His name, I love His word;
  Join all my powers to praise the Lord!
Amen.
Isaac Watts. 1719.

21 7.7.7.7. D.
Every good gift . . . is from above.—James i. 17.

HAPPY man whom God doth aid!
  God our souls and bodies made;
God on us, in gracious showers,
Blessings every moment pours;
Compasses with angel-bands,
Bids them bear us in their hands;
Parents, friends, 'twas God bestowed,
Life, and all, descend from God.

2 He this flowery carpet spread,
  Made the earth on which we tread;
  God refreshes in the air,
  Covers with the clothes we wear,
  Feeds us with the food we eat,
  Cheers us by His light and heat,
  Makes His sun on us to shine;
  All our blessings are divine!

3 Give Him then, and ever give,
  Thanks for all that we receive!
  Man we for his kindness love,
  How much more our God above!
  Worthy Thou, our heavenly Lord,
  To be honoured and adored;
  God of all-creating grace,
  Take the everlasting praise! Amen.
Charles Wesley. 17??

HIS PROVIDENCE.

22 C.M.
Great is the mystery of godliness.
1 Timothy iii. 16.

FATHER, how wide Thy glory shines!
  How high Thy wonders rise!
Known through the earth by thousand signs,
  By thousands through the skies.

2 Those mighty orbs proclaim Thy power,
  Their motions speak Thy skill;
And on the wings of every hour
  We read Thy patience still.

3 Part of Thy name divinely stands
  On all Thy creatures writ;
They show the labour of Thy hands,
  Or impress of Thy feet.

4 But when we view Thy strange design
  To save rebellious worms,
Where justice and compassion join
  In their diviniest forms;

5 Here the whole Deity is known,
  Nor dares a creature guess
Which of the glories brightest shone,
  The justice, or the grace.

6 Now the full glories of the Lamb
  Adorn the heavenly plains;
Bright seraphs learn Immanuel's name,
  And try their choicest strains.

7 O may I bear some humble part
  In that immortal song!
Wonder and joy shall tune my heart,
  And love command my tongue.
  Isaac Watts. 1706.

23 C.M.
The invisible things of Him from the creation of the world are clearly seen, being understood by the things that are made.
Romans i. 20.

THERE is a book who runs may read,
  Which heavenly truth imparts;
And all the lore its scholars need,
  Pure eyes and Christian hearts.

2 The works of God above, below,
  Within us, and around,
Are pages in that book to show
  How God Himself is found.

3 The glorious sky, embracing all,
  Is like the Maker's love,
Wherewith encompassed, great and small
  In peace and order move.

4 One name, above all glorious names,
  With its ten thousand tongues,
The everlasting sea proclaims,
  Echoing angelic songs.

5 The raging fire, the roaring wind,
  Thy boundless power display;
But in the gentler breeze we find
  Thy Spirit's viewless way.

6 Thou, who hast given me eyes to see
  And love this sight so fair,
Give me a heart to find out Thee,
  And read Thee everywhere.
  John Keble. 1827.

HIS PROVIDENCE.

24 C.M.
He called the name of that place Bethel.—Genesis xxviii. 19.

O GOD of Bethel! by whose hand
  Thy people still are fed;
Who, through this earthly pilgrimage,
  Hast all our fathers led;

2 Our fervent prayers we now present
  Before Thy throne of grace;
God of our fathers! be the God
  Of their succeeding race.

3 Through each perplexing path of life
  Our wandering footsteps guide;
Give us each day our daily bread,
  And raiment fit provide.

4 O spread Thy covering wings around,
  Till all our wanderings cease;
And at our Father's loved abode
  Our souls arrive in peace.

5 Now, with the humble voice of prayer,
  Thy mercy we implore;
Then, with the grateful voice of praise,
  Thy goodness we'll adore. Amen.
  Philip Doddridge. 1737.
  Alt. by J. Logan. 1781.

25 C.M.
I will bless the Lord at all times; His praise shall continually be in my mouth.—Psalm xxxiv. 1.

THROUGH all the changing scenes of life,
  In trouble and in joy,
The praises of my God shall still
  My heart and tongue employ.

2 O magnify the Lord with me,
  With me exalt His name;
When in distress to Him I called,
  He to my rescue came.

3 The hosts of God encamp around
  The dwellings of the just;
Deliverance He affords to all
  Who on His succour trust.

7

GOD THE FATHER.

 4 O make but trial of His love ;
  Experience will decide
 How blest are they, and only **they**,
  Who **in** His truth confide !

 5 Fear Him, ye saints, and you will then
  Have nothing else to fear ;
 Make you His service your delight,
  Your **wants** shall **be** His **care**.
     Tate and Brady. 1696.

26   7.7.7.7
   Give us day by day
  our daily bread.—Luke xi. 3.

DAY by day the manna fell :
 O to learn this lesson well !
Still by constant mercy fed,
Give me, Lord, my daily bread.

2 Day by day—the promise reads—
 Daily strength **for** daily needs ;
Cast foreboding fears away,
Take the **manna** of to-day.

3 Lord, my times are **in** Thy hand ;
 All my sanguine hopes have planned,
To Thy wisdom I resign,
And would make Thy purpose mine.

4 Thou my daily task shalt give :
 Day by day to Thee I live ;
So shall added years fulfil,
Not my own—my Father's will.

5 Fond ambition, whisper not ;
 Happy is my humble lot ;
Anxious, busy cares away !
I'm provided for to-day.

6 O to live exempt from care
 By **the energy** of prayer ;
Strong **in faith**, with mind subdued,
Yet elate **with** gratitude !
     Josiah Conder. 1836.

27   C.M.
  Thy way is in the sea.
   Psalm lxxvii. 19.

GOD moves in **a** mysterious way,
 His wonders to perform ;
He plants His footsteps in the sea,
 And rides upon the storm.

2 Deep in unfathomable mines
 Of never-failing skill,
He treasures up His bright designs,
 And works His sovereign will.

3 Ye fearful saints, fresh courage take !
 The clouds ye so much dread
Are big with mercy, and shall break
 In blessings on your head.

4 Judge not the Lord by feeble sense,
 But trust Him for His grace ;
Behind a frowning providence
 He hides a smiling face.

 5 His purposes **will** ripen fast,
  Unfolding every hour ;
 The bud may have a bitter taste,
  But **sweet will be the** flower.

 6 **Blind** unbelief is sure to err,
  And scan His work in vain ;
 God is His own interpreter,
  And He will make it plain.
     William Cowper. 1774.

28   L.M.
 God is our refuge and strength,
a very present help in trouble.—Ps. xlvi. 1.

GOD is the refuge of His saints,
 When **storms** of sharp distress invade ;
Ere we can offer our complaints,
Behold Him present with His aid !

2 **Let** mountains from their seats be hurled
 Down to the deep and buried there,
Convulsions shake the solid world,
Our faith shall never yield **to** fear.

3 Loud may the troubled ocean roar ;
 In sacred peace our souls abide ;
While every nation, **every** shore,
Trembles, **and dreads the** swelling tide.

4 **There is a** stream whose gentle **flow**
 Supplies the city of our God,
Life, love, and joy still gliding through,
And watering our divine abode.

5 This sacred stream, Thy living word,
 Thus all our raging fear controls ;
Sweet peace Thy promises afford,
And give new strength to fainting **souls**.

6 **Sion enjoys** her Monarch**'s love**,
 Secure against the threatening hour ;
Nor can her firm foundation move,
Built on His truthfulness and power.
     Isaac Watts. 1719.

29   L.M.
 O taste and see that the Lord
  is good.—Ps. xxxiv. 8.

O TASTE and see that **He** is good,
 The King of heaven, who reigns on high !
His truth through ages firm hath stood,
His mercy reaches to the sky.

2 Good in the sunshine and **the** shower,
 When summer skies are bright and warm ;
Good, when the wintry tempests lower,
Amidst the whirlwind and the storm.

3 O taste and see that He is good,
 The Lord of providence and grace !
He calms the surges and the flood,
And guards us from His holy place.

4 Good, when He smites, and when He heals,
    And when He gives, or takes away;
  Good, when His goodness He conceals,
    In sorrow's dark and cloudy day.

5 O taste and see that He is wise!
    Who chastens sore with grief and pain;
  Then bids the light in darkness rise,
    To cheer the mourner's heart again.

6 O teach us, Lord! to trust Thy love,
    To taste Thy goodness, and adore!
  In clearer light Thy saints above
    Shall see and praise Thee evermore.
              T. R. Birks. 1874.

30
                 8.6. 8.6. 4.4. **8.8.**
    Thy judgments are right.
    Psalm cxix. 75.

WHATE'ER my God ordains is right,
    His will is ever just;
Howe'er He order now my cause,
    I will be still and trust.
      He is my God,
        Though dark my road,
He holds me that I shall not fall,
Wherefore to Him I leave it all.

2 Whate'er **my God** ordains **is** right,
    He never **will** deceive;
  He leads me **by the** proper path,
    And **so to Him** I cleave,
      And take content
        What He hath sent;
His hand can turn my griefs away,
And patiently I wait His day.

3 **Whate'er my God** ordains **is right,**
    He taketh thought for me,
  The cup that my Physician gives
    No poisoned draught can be,
      But medicine due;
        For God is true,
And on **that** changeless truth I build,
And all **my** heart with hope is filled.

4 Whate'er my God ordains is right;
    Though I the cup must drink
That bitter seems to my faint heart,
    I will not fear nor shrink;
      Tears pass away
        With dawn of day,
Sweet comfort yet shall fill my heart,
And pain and sorrow all depart.

5 Whate'er my God ordains is right;
    My Light, my Life is He,
Who cannot will me aught but **good**;
    I trust Him utterly;
      For well I know,
        In joy **or** woe,
We soon shall see, as sunlight clear,
How faithful was our Guardian here.

6 Whate'er my God ordains is right,
    Here will I take my stand;
Though sorrow, need, or death make
    earth

For me a desert land,
    My Father's care
      Is round me there,
He holds me that I shall not fall,
And so to Him I leave it all.
            S. Rodigast. 1675.
    Tr. Catherine Winkworth. 1858.

31
                          S M.
*In all thy ways acknowledge Him,
and He shall direct thy paths.*
    Proverbs iii. 6.

COMMIT thou all thy griefs
    And ways into His hands,
To His sure truth and tender care,
    Who earth and heaven commands.

2 **Who points** the clouds their course,
    Whom **winds and** seas obey,
He shall direct thy wandering feet,
    He shall prepare thy way.

3 **Thou on the Lord rely,**
    So safe shalt thou go on;
Fix on **His** work thy steadfast eye,
    So shall thy work be done.

4 No profit **canst thou gain**
    By self-consuming **care;**
To Him commend **thy cause,** His ear
    Attends the **softest prayer.**

5 Thy everlasting **truth,**
    Father, Thy **ceaseless love,**
Sees all Thy children's wants, and knows
    What best **for each will** prove.

6 **Thou everywhere** hast sway,
    And all things serve Thy might;
Thy every **act pure** blessing **is,**
    Thy path **unsullied** light.

7 When Thou **arisest,** Lord,
    What shall **Thy** work withstand?
Whate'er Thy **children** want, Thou giv'st;
    Who, who **shall** stay Thy hand?
              Paul Gerhardt. 1659.
              Tr. John Wesley. 1539.

32
                          S.M.
He hath done all things well.
    Mark vii. 37.

THOU doest all things well,
    God only wise and true!
My days and nights alternate tell
    Of mercies always new.

2 With daily toil oppressed,
    I sink in welcome sleep;
Or wake in darkness and unrest,
    Yet patient vigil keep.

3 Soon finds each fevered day,
    And each chill night, its bourne;
Nor zeal need droop, nor hope decay,
    Ere rest, or light return.

GOD THE FATHER.

4 But be the night-watch long,
   And sore the chastening rod,
Thou art my health, my sun, my song,
   My glory, and my God!

5 Thy smiling face lights mine;
   If veiled it makes me sad;
Even tears in darkness, starlike, **shine**,
   And morning finds me glad.

6 For weeping, wakeful **eyes**
   Instinctive look above,
And catch, through openings in **the skies**,
   Thy beams, unslumbering **Love!**

7 Hours spent **with pain—and Thee**
   Lost hours **have never seemed**;
No! those are lost, **which but might be**
   From earth for **heaven redeemed.**

8 Its limit, its relief,
   Its hallowed issues, tell,
That, though Thou cause **Thy servant grief**,
   Thou doest **all things well!**
             W. M. Bunting. 1870.

33   8.8. 8.8. 8.8.
He maketh me to lie down in green pastures.—Psalm xxiii. 2.

THE Lord my pasture shall prepare,
   And feed me with a shepherd's care;
His presence shall my wants supply,
   And guard me with a watchful eye;
My noonday walks He shall attend,
   And all my midnight hours defend.

2 When in the sultry glebe I faint,
   Or on the thirsty mountain pant,
To fertile vales and dewy meads
   My weary, wandering steps He leads;
Where peaceful rivers, soft and slow,
   Amid the verdant landscape flow.

3 Though in the **paths of death** I tread,
   With gloomy **horrors** overspread,
My steadfast heart **shall fear no ill**,
   For Thou, O Lord, **art with me still**;
Thy friendly crook shall give me aid,
   And guide **me through the dreadful shade.**

4 Though in **a bare and** rugged way,
   Through devious, lonely wilds **I** stray,
Thy bounty shall my pains beguile;
   The barren wilderness shall smile,
With sudden green and herbage crowned,
   And streams shall murmur all around.
             Joseph Addison. 1712.

34   C.M.
The Lord is my shepherd, I shall not want.—Ps. xxiii. 1.

THE Lord's my Shepherd, I'll not want;
   He makes me down to lie
In pastures green; He leadeth me
   The quiet waters by.

2 My soul He doth restore again;
   And me to walk doth make
Within the paths of righteousness,
   Even for His own name's sake.

3 Yea, though I walk in death's dark vale
   Yet will I fear no ill;
For Thou art with me, and Thy rod
   And staff me comfort still.

4 My **table** Thou hast furnished
   In presence of my foes;
My head Thou dost with **oil** anoint,
   And my cup overflows.

5 Goodness **and** mercy **all my life**
   Shall surely follow **me**;
And in God's house for evermore
   My dwelling-place shall be.
             Francis Rous. 1650.

35   C.M.
I will offer to Thee the sacrifice of thanksgiving.—Psalm cxvi. 17.

WHEN all Thy mercies, O my God,
   My rising soul surveys,
Transported with the view, I'm lost
   In wonder, love, and praise.

2 Unnumbered comforts on my **soul**
   Thy tender care bestowed,
Before my infant heart conceived
   From whom those comforts flowed.

3 **To all my** weak complaints and cries
   Thy mercy lent an ear,
Ere yet my feeble thoughts had learned
   To form themselves in prayer.

4 When in the slippery paths **of youth**
   With heedless steps I ran,
Thine arm **unseen** conveyed me safe,
   And led **me up to man.**

5 **Through hidden dangers,** toils, and deaths,
   It gently cleared my way,
And through the pleasing snares of vice,
   More to be feared than they.

6 Through every period of my life
   Thy goodness I'll pursue,
And after death, in distant worlds,
   The pleasing theme renew.

7 Through all eternity **to Thee**
   A grateful song I'll raise;
But O, eternity's too short
   To utter all Thy praise! Amen.
             Joseph Addison. 1712.

36   L.M.
Ye are blessed of the Lord which made heaven and earth.—Psalm cxv. 15.

HOW do Thy mercies close me round!
   For ever be Thy name adored!
I blush in all things to abound;
   The servant is above his Lord.

HIS MERCY AND GRACE.

2 Inured to poverty and pain,
  A suffering life my Master led;
The Son of God, the Son of Man,
  He had not where to lay His head.

3 But lo! a place He hath prepared
  For me, whom watchful angels keep;
Yea, He Himself becomes my guard,
  He smooths my bed, and gives me sleep.

4 Jesus protects; my fears, be gone!
  What can the Rock of Ages move?
Safe in Thy arms I lay me down,
  Thy everlasting arms of love.

5 While Thou art intimately nigh,
  Who, who shall violate my rest?
Sin, earth, and hell I now defy;
  I lean upon my Saviour's breast.

6 I rest beneath the Almighty's shade;
  My griefs expire, my troubles cease;
Thou, Lord, on whom my soul is stayed,
  Wilt keep me still in perfect peace.

7 Me for Thine own Thou lov'st to take,
  In time and in eternity;
Thou never, never wilt forsake
  A helpless soul that trusts in Thee.
                Wesley. 1740.

37   7.6. 7.6. D.
Although the fig-tree shall not blossom . . . yet I will rejoice in the Lord.
Habakkuk iii. 17, 18.

SOMETIMES a light surprises
  The Christian while he sings:
It is the Lord, who rises
  With healing in His wings.
When comforts are declining,
  He grants the soul again,
A season of clear shining,
  To cheer it after rain.

2 In holy contemplation,
  We gladly then pursue
The theme of God's salvation,
  And find it ever new;
Set free from present sorrow
  We cheerfully can say,
E'en let the unknown morrow
  Bring with it what it may:

3 It can bring with it nothing
  But He will bear us through;
Who gives the lilies clothing,
  Will clothe His people too:
Beneath the spreading heavens
  No creature but is fed;
And He who feeds the ravens
  Will give His children bread.

Though vine nor fig-tree neither,
  Their wonted fruit should bear;
Though all the field should wither,
  Nor flock nor herd be there;

Yet God the same abiding,
  His praise shall tune my voice,
For while in Him confiding,
  I cannot but rejoice.
            William Cowper. 1779.

HIS MERCY AND GRACE.

38   C.M.
The mercy of the Lord is from everlasting to everlasting.—Psalm ciii. 17.

BEGIN, my soul, some heavenly theme,
  And wake my voice to sing
The mighty works, or mightier name,
  Of our eternal King.

2 Tell of His wondrous faithfulness,
  And sound His power abroad;
Sing the sweet promise of His grace,
  And the unchanging God.

3 Proclaim salvation from the Lord,
  For wretched, dying men;
His hand hath writ the sacred word
  With an immortal pen.

4 Engraved as in eternal brass,
  The mighty promise shines;
Nor can the powers of darkness rase
  Those everlasting lines.

5 His every word of grace is strong,
  As that which built the skies;
The voice that rolls the stars along
  Speaks all the promises.

6 How would my fainting heart rejoice
  To know Thy favour sure;
I trust the all-creating voice,
  And faith desires no more.
            Isaac Watts. 1707.

39   L.M.
Like as a father pitieth his children, so the Lord pitieth them that fear Him.—Psalm ciii. 13.

THE Lord, how wondrous are His ways!
  How firm His word, how large His grace!
Goodness and truth surround His throne,
  And thence He makes His mercy known.

2 High as His mighty arm hath spread
  The starry heavens above our head,
His bounteous love exceeds our praise,
  Exceeds the highest hopes we raise.

3 Nor half so far hath nature placed
  The rising morning from the west,
As His forgiving grace removes
  The daily guilt of those He loves.

GOD THE FATHER.

4 How slowly doth His wrath arise!
   On swifter wings salvation flies;
   And if He bids His anger burn,
   How soon His frowns to pity turn!

5 The mighty God, the wise and just,
   Knows that our frame is feeble dust;
   And will no load on us impose
   Beyond the strength that He bestows.

6 For His eternal love is sure
   To all the saints, and shall endure;
   From age to age His truth shall reign,
   Nor children's children hope in vain.
                    Isaac Watts. 1719.

40 *I will trust in the covert of Thy* L. M.
         wings.—Psalm lxi. 4.

FATHER! beneath Thy sheltering wing
   In sweet security we rest,
And fear no evil earth can bring,
   In life, in death supremely blest.

2 For life is good, whose tidal flow
   The motions of Thy will obeys;
   And death is good, that makes us know
   The Life divine, that all things sways.

3 And good it is to bear the cross,
   And so Thy perfect peace to win:
   And nought is ill, nor brings us loss,
   Nor works us harm, save only sin.

4 Redeemed from this we ask no more,
   But trust the love that saves to guide:
   The grace that yields so rich a store,
   Will grant us all we need beside.
                    W. H. Burleigh. 1861.

41   C. M.
   Blessed be Thou, Lord God of
   Israel our father, for ever and ever.
   1 Chronicles xxix. 10.

BLEST be our everlasting Lord,
   Our Father, God, and King!
Thy sovereign goodness we record,
   Thy glorious power we sing.

2 By Thee the victory is given;
   The majesty divine,
   And strength, and might, and earth and
      heaven,
   And all therein, are Thine.

3 The kingdom, Lord, is Thine alone,
   Who dost Thy right maintain,
   And, high on Thine eternal throne,
   O'er men and angels reign.

4 Riches, as seemeth good to Thee,
   Thou dost, and honour, give;
   And kings their power and dignity
   Out of Thy hand receive.

5 Thou hast on us the grace bestowed,
   Thy greatness to proclaim;
   And therefore now we thank our God,
   And praise Thy glorious name.

6 Thy glorious name and nature's powers
   Thou dost to us make known;
   And all the Deity is ours,
   Through Thy incarnate Son.
                    Charles Wesley. 1762.

42   6.6.4. 6.6.4.
   *Mighty to save.—*Is. lxiii. 1.

O STRONG to save and bless,
   My rock and righteousness,
      Draw near to me:
Blessing and joy and might,
Wisdom and love and light,
      Are all with Thee.

2 My refuge and my rest,
   As on a father's breast,
      I lean on Thee:
   From faintness and from fear,
   When foes and ill are near,
      Deliver me.

3 O answer me, my God!
   Thy love is deep and broad,
      Thy grace is near:
   Comfort my soul at last,
   Bring righteousness, and cast
      Away all fear.

4 Descend, Thou mighty Love,
   Descend from heaven above,
      Fill Thou my soul;
   Heal every bruised part,
   Bind up this broken heart,
      And make me whole.   Amen.
                    Horatius Bonar. 1856.

43   7.6. 7.6. 7.8. 7.6.
   O magnify the Lord with me,
   and let us exalt His name together.
         Psalm xxxiv. 3.

GOOD Thou art, and good Thou dost,
   Thy mercies reach to all,
Chiefly those who on Thee trust,
   And for Thy mercy call
New they every morning are;
   As fathers when their children cry,
Us Thou dost in pity spare,
   And all our wants supply

2 Mercy o'er Thy works presides;
   Thy providence displayed,
Still preserves, and still provides
   For all Thy hands have made;
Keeps with most distinguished care
   The man who on Thy love depends;
Watches every numbered hair,
   And all his steps attends.

12

HIS MERCY AND GRACE.

3 Who can sound the depths unknown
  Of Thy redeeming grace?
Grace, that gave Thine only Son
  To save a ruined race!
Millions of transgressors poor
Thou hast for Jesu's sake forgiven,
Made them of Thy favour sure,
  And snatched from hell to heaven.

4 Millions more Thou ready art
  To save, and to forgive;
Every soul and every heart
  Of man Thou wouldst receive:
Father, now accept of mine,
Which now, through Christ, I offer Thee;
Tell me now, in love divine,
  That Thou hast pardoned me! Amen.
                          Charles Wesley. 1763.

44   C.M.
*O the depth of the riches both of
the wisdom and knowledge of God.*
Romans xi. 33.

O GOD: Thy power is wonderful,
  Thy glory passing bright;
Thy wisdom, with its deep on deep,
  A rapture to the sight.

2 Yet more than all, and ever more,
  Should we Thy creatures bless—
Most worshipful of attributes—
  Thine awful holiness.

3 There's not a craving in the mind,
  Thou dost not meet and still;
There's not a wish the heart can have
  Which Thou dost not fulfil.

4 Thy justice is the gladdest thing
  Creation can behold;
Thy tenderness so meek, it wins
  The guilty to be bold.

5 All things that have been, all that are,
  All things that can be dreamed,
All possible creations, made,
  Kept faithful, or redeemed:

6 All these may draw upon Thy power,
  Thy mercy may command;
And still outflows Thy silent sea,
  Immutable and grand.

7 O little heart of mine! shall pain
  Or sorrow make thee moan,
When all this God is all for thee,
  A Father all thine own?
                          F. W. Faber. 1849.

45   L.M.
*The Lord God is a sun and
shield: the Lord will give
grace and glory.*—Ps. lxxxiv. 11.

LORD of all Being! throned afar,
  Thy glory flames from sun and star,
Centre and soul of every sphere;
Yet to each loving heart how near!

2 Sun of our life, Thy wakening ray
Sheds on our path the glow of day;
Star of our hope, Thy softened light
Cheers the long watches of the night.

3 Our midnight is Thy smile withdrawn,
Our noon-tide is Thy gracious dawn,
Our rainbow arch Thy mercy's sign,
All, save the clouds of sin, are Thine!

4 Lord of all life, below, above,
Whose light is truth, whose warmth is
  love;
Before Thy ever-blazing throne
We ask no lustre of our own.

5 Grant us Thy truth to make us free,
And kindling hearts that burn for Thee,
Till all Thy living altars claim
One holy light, one heavenly flame.
                              Amen.
                       Oliver W. Holmes. 1848.

46   C.M.
The love of God.—Jude 21.

THOU Grace divine, encircling all,
  A shoreless, boundless sea,
Wherein at last our souls must fall;
  O Love of God most free.

2 When over dizzy heights we go,
  A soft hand blinds our eyes,
And we are guided safe and slow;
  O Love of God most wise.

3 And though we turn us from Thy face
  And wander wide and long,
Thou hold'st us still in kind embrace;
  O Love of God most strong.

4 The saddened heart, the restless soul,
  The toil-worn frame and mind,
Alike confess Thy sweet control,
  O Love of God most kind.

5 But not alone Thy care we claim,
  Our wayward steps to win;
We know Thee by a dearer name,
  O Love of God within.

6 And filled and quickened by Thy breath,
  Our souls are strong and free,
To rise o'er sin and fear and death,
  O Love of God! to Thee.
                        Eliza Scudder. 1864.

47   7.6. 7.6. 7.8. 7.6.
*Great is the Lord, and
greatly to be praised.*—1 Chronicles xvi. 25.

THOU, the great, eternal Lord,
  Art high above our thought;
Worthy to be feared, adored,
  By all Thy hands have wrought.
None can with Thyself compare;
  Thy glory fills both earth and sky;
We, and all Thy creatures, are
  As nothing in Thine eye.

THE LORD JESUS CHRIST.

2 Of Thy great unbounded power
    To Thee the praise we give,
Infinitely great, and more
    Than heart can e'er conceive:
When Thou wilt to work proceed,
Thy purpose firm none can withstand,
Frustrate the determined deed,
    Or stay the Almighty hand.

3 Thou, O God, art wise alone;
    Thy counsel doth excel;
Wonderful Thy works we own,
    Thy ways unsearchable:
Who can sound the mystery,
Thy judgment's deep abyss explain?
Thine, whose eyes in darkness see
    And search the heart of man!
            Charles Wesley. 1763.

48 *O taste and see that the Lord is good.*—Psalm xxxiv. 8. C.M.D.

THE Lord is rich and merciful,
    The Lord is very kind;
O come to Him, come now to Him,
    With a believing mind.

His comforts they shall strengthen thee,
    Like flowing waters cool;
And He shall for thy spirit be
    A fountain ever full.

2 The Lord is glorious and strong,
    Our God is very high;
O trust in Him, trust now in Him,
    And have security.
He shall be to thee like the sea,
    And thou shalt surely feel
His wind, that bloweth healthily,
    Thy sicknesses to heal.

3 The Lord is wonderful and wise,
    As all the ages tell;
O learn of Him, learn now of Him,
    Then with thee it is well.
And with His light thou shalt be blest,
    Therein to work and live;
And He shall be to thee a rest
    When evening hours arrive.
            T. T. Lynch. 1855.

The Lord Jesus Christ.

HIS DIVINITY AND GLORY.

49 *He is Lord of all.*—Acts x. 36. C.M.

ALL hail the power of Jesus' name,
    Let angels prostrate fall;
Bring forth the royal diadem,
    And crown Him Lord of all.

2 Crown Him, ye martyrs of our God,
    Who from His altar call;
Extol the Stem-of-Jesse's Rod,
    And crown Him Lord of all.

3 Ye chosen seed of Israel's race,
    A remnant weak and small;
Hail Him who saves you by His grace,
    And crown Him Lord of all.

4 Ye Gentile sinners, ne'er forget
    The wormwood and the gall;
Go, spread your trophies at His feet,
    And crown Him Lord of all.

5 Let every kindred, every tribe,
    On this terrestrial ball,
To Him all majesty ascribe,
    And crown Him Lord of all.

6 O that with yonder sacred throng,
    We at His feet may fall,
There join the everlasting song,
    And crown Him Lord of all. Amen.
        Edward Perronet. 1780. *All.*
        Last verse J. Rippon. 1787.

50 *Unto Him that loved us . . . be glory and dominion for ever and ever.* Revelation i. 5, 6. 6.6.8. 6.6.8.

MY heart and voice I raise,
    To spread Messiah's praise;
Messiah's praise let all repeat—
    The universal Lord,
    By whose almighty word
Creation rose in form complete.

2 A servant's form He wore,
    And in His body bore
Our dreadful curse on Calvary;
    He like a victim stood,
    And poured His sacred blood,
To set the guilty captives free.

3 But soon the Victor rose
Triumphant o'er His foes,
And led the vanquished host in chains;
    He threw their empire down,
    His foes compelled to own,
O'er all the great Messiah reigns.

HIS DIVINITY AND GLORY.

4 With mercy's mildest grace,
  He governs all our race
In wisdom, righteousness, and love
  Who to Messiah fly
  Shall find redemption nigh,
And all His great salvation prove.

5 Hail, Saviour, Prince of Peace!
  Thy kingdom shall increase,
Till all the world Thy glory see,
  And righteousness abound,
  As the great deep profound,
And fill the earth with purity! Amen.
  Benjamin Rhodes. 1806.

51 7.7. 7.7. D.
There is none other name under heaven given among men, whereby we must be saved.—Acts iv. 12.

JESUS, lover of my soul,
  Let me to Thy bosom fly,
While the nearer waters roll,
  While the tempest still is high;
Hide me, O my Saviour, hide,
  Till the storm of life be past;
Safe into the haven guide,
  O receive my soul at last!

2 Other refuge have I none,
  Hangs my helpless soul on Thee;
Leave, ah! leave me not alone,
  Still support and comfort me:
All my trust on Thee is stayed,
  All my help from Thee I bring;
Cover my defenceless head
  With the shadow of Thy wing.

3 Thou, O Christ, art all I want,
  More than all in Thee I find:
Raise the fallen, cheer the faint,
  Heal the sick, and lead the blind.
Just and holy is Thy Name,
  I am all unrighteousness;
False and full of sin I am,
  Thou art full of truth and grace.

4 Plenteous grace with Thee is found,
  Grace to cover all my sin;
Let the healing streams abound,
  Make and keep me pure within.
Thou of life the fountain art,
  Freely let me take of Thee;
Spring Thou up within my heart,
  Rise to all eternity. Amen.
  Charles Wesley. 1742.

52 S.M.
Blessed be His glorious name for ever.—Psalm lxxii. 19.

I BLESS the Christ of God;
  I rest on love divine;
And with unfaltering lip and heart,
  I call the Saviour mine.

2 His cross dispels each doubt;
  I bury in His tomb
Each thought of unbelief and fear,
  Each lingering shade of gloom.

3 I praise the God of grace;
  I trust His truth and might;
He calls me His, I call Him mine,
  My God, my joy, my light.

4 In Him is only good,
  In me is only ill;
My ill but draws His goodness forth,
  And me He loveth still.

5 'Tis He who saveth me,
  And freely pardon gives;
I love because He loveth me,
  I live because He lives.

6 My life with Him is hid,
  My death has passed away,
My clouds have melted into light,
  My midnight into day.
  Horatius Bonar. 1863.

53 7.7.7.7.
God hath made that same Jesus, whom ye have crucified, both Lord and Christ.—Acts ii. 36.

JESUS is our common Lord,
  He our loving Saviour is;
By His death to life restored,
  Misery we exchange for bliss;

2 Bliss to carnal minds unknown,
  O 'tis more than tongue can tell!
Only to believers shown,
  Glorious and unspeakable!

3 Chr'st, our Brother and our Friend,
  Shows us His eternal love;
Never shall our triumphs end,
  Till we take our seats above.

4 Let us walk with Him in white,
  For our bridal day prepare,
For our partnership in light,
  For our glorious meeting there!
  Wesley. 1742.

54 7.6. 7.6. D.
Though now ye see Him not, yet believing, ye rejoice with joy unspeakable.
1 Peter i. 8.

O SAVIOUR, precious Saviour,
  Whom yet unseen we love,
O Name of might and favour,
  All other names above:
We worship Thee, we bless Thee,
  To Thee alone we sing;
We praise Thee, and confess Thee
  Our holy Lord and King!

2 O Bringer of salvation,
  Who wondrously hast wrought,
Thyself the revelation
  Of love beyond our thought:
We worship Thee, we bless Thee,
  To Thee alone we sing;
We praise Thee, and confess Thee
  Our gracious Lord and King!

15

THE LORD JESUS CHRIST.

3 In Thee all fulness dwelleth,
   All grace and power divine;
  The glory that excelleth,
   O Son of God, is Thine:
  We worship Thee, we bless **Thee**,
   To Thee alone we sing:
  We praise Thee, and confess **Thee**
   Our glorious Lord and King!

4 O grant the consummation
   Of this our song above,
  In endless adoration,
   And everlasting love:
  Then shall we praise and bless Thee,
   Where perfect praises ring,
  And evermore confess Thee
   Our Saviour and our King! Amen.
             Frances R. Havergal. 1870.

55   7.6. 7.6. D.
That was the true light, which lighteth every man that cometh into the world.—John 1. 9.

O ONE with **God** the Father
   In majesty and might,
  The brightness of His glory,
   Eternal Light of light:
  O'er this our home of darkness
   Thy rays are streaming now;
  The shadows flee before Thee,
   The world's **true Light art** Thou.

2 Yet, Lord, we see but darkly:
   O **heavenly** Light, arise,
  Dispel these mists that shroud us,
   And hide Thee from our eyes!
  We long to track the footprints
   That Thou Thyself hast trod;
  We long to see the pathway
   That leads to Thee, our God.

3 O Jesus, shine around us
   With radiance of Thy grace;
  O Jesus, turn upon us
   The brightness of Thy face.
  We need **no** star to guide **us**,
   As on **our way we** press,
  If Thou **Thy** light vouchsafest,
   O **Sun of** righteousness. Amen.
               Bishop W. W. How. 1871.

56   8.8. 8.8. **8.8.**
Thou art fairer than the children of men.—Ps. xlv. 2.

MY heart **is full of** Christ, and longs
   Its glorious matter to declare!
  Of Him I make **my** loftier songs,
   I cannot from **His** praise forbear:
  My ready **tongue** makes haste to sing
   The hono**urs of my** heavenly King.

2 Fairer than all the earth-born race,
   Perfect in comeliness Thou art;
  Replenished are Thy lips with grace,
   And full of love Thy tender heart.
  God ever blest! we bow the knee,
   And own all fulness dwells in Thee.

---

3 Gird on Thy thigh the Spirit's sword,
   And take to Thee Thy power divine;
  Stir up Thy strength, almighty Lord,
   All power and majesty are Thine;
  Assert Thy worship and renown;
   O all-redeeming God, come down!

4 Come, and maintain Thy righteous cause,
   And let Thy glorious toil succeed;
  Dispread the victory of Thy cross,
   Ride on, and prosper in Thy deed;
  Through earth triumphantly ride on,
   And reign **in every** heart alone. Amen.
                    Wesley. 1743.

57   8.8. 8.8. D. *Anapæstic.*
He shall feed His flock like a shepherd.—Isa. xl. 11.

THOU Shepherd of Israel, and mine,
   The joy and desire of my heart;
  For closer communion I pine,
   I long to reside where Thou art:
  The pasture I languish to find,
   Where all, who their Shepherd obey,
  Are fed, on Thy bosom reclined,
   And screened from the heat of the day.

2 **Ah! show me** that happiest place,
   The place of Thy people's abode,
  Where saints in an ecstasy gaze,
   And hang on a crucified God:
  Thy love for a sinner declare,
   Thy passion and death on the tree;
  My spirit to Calvary bear,
   To suffer and triumph **with Thee.**

3 'Tis there, with the lambs of Thy flock,
   There only I covet to rest,
  To lie at the foot of the rock,
   Or rise to be hid in Thy breast:
  'Tis there I would always abide,
   And never a moment depart;
  Concealed in the cleft of Thy side,
   Eternally held in Thy heart.
                Charles Wesley. 1762.

58   8.8. 8.8. D. *Anapæstic.*
Thou shalt make them drink of the river of Thy pleasures.—Ps. xxvi. 8.

A FOUNTAIN **of Life** and of Grace
   In Christ, our Redeemer, we see;
  For us who His offers embrace,
   For all, it is open and free:
  Jehovah Himself doth invite
   To drink of His pleasures unknown,
  The streams of immortal delight,
   That flow from His heavenly throne.

2 As soon as in Him we believe,
   By faith of His Spirit we take;
  And, freely forgiven, receive
   The mercy for Jesus's sake;

We gain a pure drop of His love,
The life of eternity know,
Angelical happiness prove,
And witness a heaven below.
                    Charles Wesley. 1762.

59 C.M.
Whom having not seen, ye love.
1 Peter i. 8.

JESUS, these eyes have never seen
   That radiant form of Thine;
The veil of sense hangs dark between
   Thy blessed face and mine.

2 I see Thee not, I hear Thee not,
   Yet art Thou oft with me;
And earth has ne'er so dear a spot,
   As where I meet with Thee.

3 Like some bright dream, that comes unsought,
   When slumbers o'er me roll,
Thine image ever fills my thought,
   And charms my ravished soul.

4 Yea, though I have not seen, and still
   Must rest in faith alone,
I love Thee, dearest Lord, and will,
   Unseen but not unknown.

5 When death these mortal eyes shall seal,
   And still this throbbing heart,
The rending veil shall Thee reveal,
   All-glorious as Thou art.
                    Ray Palmer. 1810.

60 7.6, 7.6. D.
*There is a friend that sticketh
closer than a brother.*—Proverbs xviii. 24.

O JESUS, Friend unfailing,
   How dear Thou art to me!
Are cares or fears assailing?
   I find my strength in Thee.
Why should my feet grow weary
   Of this my pilgrim way?
Rough though the path and dreary,
   It ends in perfect day.

2 What fills my soul with gladness?
   'Tis Thine abounding grace;
Where can I look, in sadness,
   But, Jesus, on Thy face?
My all is Thy providing;
   Thy love can ne'er grow cold;
In Thee, my refuge, hiding,
   No good wilt Thou withhold.

3 Why should I droop in sorrow?
   Thou'rt ever by my side;
Why, trembling, dread the morrow?
   What ill can e'er betide?
If I my cross have taken,
   'Tis but to follow Thee;
If scorned, despised, forsaken,
   Nought severs Thee from me.

4 For every tribulation,
   For every sore distress,
In Christ I've full salvation,
   Sure help and quiet rest.
No fear of foes prevailing,
   I triumph, Lord, in Thee:
O Jesus, Friend unfailing,
   How dear art Thou to me!
From the German. Tr. Mrs. H. K. Browne.

61 C.M.
*The Lord descended in a cloud ...
and proclaimed the name of the Lord.*
Exodus xxxiv. 5.

GREAT God! to me the sight afford
   To him of old allowed;
And let my faith behold its Lord
   Descending in a cloud.

2 In that revealing Spirit come down,
   Thine attributes proclaim,
And to my inmost soul make known
   The glories of Thy Name.

3 Jehovah, Christ, I Thee adore,
   Who gav'st my soul to be!
Fountain of being, and of power,
   And great in majesty.

4 The Lord, the mighty God, Thou art;
   But let me rather prove
That name in-spoken to my heart,
   That favourite name of Love.

5 Merciful God, Thyself proclaim
   In this polluted breast;
Mercy is Thy distinguished name,
   Which suits a sinner best.

6 Our misery doth for pity call,
   Our sin implores Thy grace;
And Thou art merciful to all
   Our lost apostate race.
                    Charles Wesley. 1743.

62 7.6, 7.6 D.
*To whom shall we go? Thou
hast the words of eternal life.*—John vi. 68.

TO Thee, O dear, dear Saviour,
   My spirit turns for rest,
My peace is in Thy favour,
   My pillow on Thy breast!
Though all the world deceive me,
   I know that I am Thine,
And Thou wilt never leave me,
   O blessed Saviour mine!

2 In Thee my trust abideth,
   On Thee my hope relies,
O Thou whose love provideth
   For all beneath the skies;
O Thou whose mercy found me,
   From bondage set me free,
And then for ever bound me,
   With threefold cords to Thee.

THE LORD JESUS CHRIST.

3 My grief is in the dulness
  With which this sluggish heart
Doth open to the fulness
  Of all Thou wouldst impart:
My joy is in Thy beauty
  Of holiness divine !
My comfort in the duty
  That binds my life to Thine !

4 Alas, that I should ever
  Have failed in love to Thee,
The only one who never
  Forgot or slighted me !
O for a heart to love Thee
  More truly as I ought,
And nothing place above Thee
  In deed, or word, or thought.

5 O for that choicest blessing
  Of living in Thy love,
And thus on earth possessing
  The peace of heaven above;
O for the bliss that by it
  The soul securely knows,
The holy calm and quiet
  Of faith's serene repose.
                    J. S. B. Monsell. 1862.

63   C.M.
God also hath . . . given Him a name which is above every name.
Philippians ii. 9.

JESUS! the Name high over all,
  In hell, or earth, or sky;
Angels and men before it fall,
  And devils fear and fly.

2 Jesus! the Name to sinners dear,
  The Name to sinners given;
It scatters all their guilty fear,
  It turns their hell to heaven.

3 Jesus the prisoner's fetters breaks,
  And bruises Satan's head;
Power into strengthless souls he speaks,
  And life into the dead.

4 O that the world might taste and see
  The riches of His grace !
The arms of love that compass me,
  Would all mankind embrace !

5 His only righteousness I show,
  His saving truth proclaim;
'Tis all my business here below,
  To cry, ' Behold the Lamb !'

6 Happy, if with my latest breath
  I may but gasp His name;
Preach Him to all, and cry in death,
  ' Behold, behold the Lamb !'
                    Charles Wesley. 1749.

HIS INCARNATION AND ADVENT.

64   C.M.
He hath sent me to heal the broken-hearted, to preach deliverance to the captives.
Luke iv. 18.

HARK, the glad sound! the Saviour comes !
  The Saviour promised long !
Let every heart prepare a throne,
  And every voice a song.

2 On Him the Spirit, largely poured,
  Exerts His sacred fire;
Wisdom, and might, and zeal, and love
  His holy breast inspire.

3 He comes the prisoners to release,
  In Satan's bondage held;
The gates of brass before Him burst,
  The iron fetters yield.

4 He comes, from thickest films of vice,
  To clear the mental ray,
And on the eyes oppressed with night,
  To pour celestial day.

5 He comes the broken heart to bind,
  The bleeding soul to cure,
And with the treasures of His grace
  To enrich the humble poor.

6 Our glad hosannas, Prince of Peace,
  Thy welcome shall proclaim,
And heaven's eternal arches ring
  With Thy beloved name.
                    Philip Doddridge. 1736.

65   7.7. 7.7. 7.7.
When they saw the star, they rejoiced with exceeding great joy.
Matthew ii. 10.

AS with gladness men of old
  Did the guiding star behold,
As with joy they hailed its light,
Leading onward, beaming bright;
So, most gracious Lord, may we
Evermore be led to Thee.

2 As with joyful steps they sped,
Saviour, to Thy lowly bed,
There to bend the knee before
Thee whom heaven and earth adore;
So may we with willing feet
Ever seek the mercy-seat.

3 As they offered gifts most rare
At Thy cradle rude and bare;
So may we with holy joy,
Pure, and free from sin's alloy,
All our costliest treasures bring,
Christ, to Thee, our Heavenly King.

HIS INCARNATION AND ADVENT.

4 Holy Jesus, every day
  Keep us in the narrow way;
  And, when earthly things are past,
  Bring our ransomed souls at last
  Where they need no star to guide,
  Where no clouds Thy glory hide.

5 In the heavenly country bright
  Need they no created light;
  Thou, its Light, its Joy, its Crown,
  Thou its Sun which goes not down;
  There for ever may we sing
  Hallelujahs to our King. Amen.
          W. Chatterton Dix. 1860.

66   8.7. 8.7.
Waiting for the consolation of Israel.—Luke ii. 25.

COME, Thou long-expected Jesus,
  Born to set Thy people free;
From our sins and fears release us,
  Let us find our rest in Thee.

2 Israel's strength and consolation,
  Hope of all the earth Thou art;
The desire of every nation,
  Joy of every contrite heart.

3 Born, Thy people to deliver,
  Born a child, and yet a king;
Born, to reign in us for ever,
  Now Thy gracious kingdom bring.

4 By Thine own Eternal Spirit,
  Rule in all our hearts alone;
By Thine all-sufficient merit,
  Raise us to Thy glorious throne.
          Amen.
          Wesley. 1746.

67   11.10. 11.10. *Anapæst.c.*
Ye shall find the babe wrapped in swaddling clothes, lying in a manger
      Luke ii. 12.

BRIGHTEST and best of the sons of the
  morning!
Dawn on our darkness, and lend us Thine
  aid!
Star of the East, the horizon adorning,
Guide where our infant Redeemer is laid.

2 Cold on His cradle the dew-drops are
  shining,
  Low lies His head with the beasts of the
    stall;
  Angels adore Him in slumber reclining,
  Maker, and Monarch, and Saviour of all.

3 Say, shall we yield Him, in costly devotion
  Odours of Edom, and offerings divine?
  Gems of the mountains, and pearls of the
    ocean,
  Myrrh from the forest, or gold from the
    mine?

4 Vainly we offer each ample oblation,
  Vainly with gifts would His favour
    secure;
  Richer by far is the heart's adoration,
  Dearer to God are the prayers of the
    poor.

5 Brightest and best of the sons of the
    morning!
  Dawn on our darkness, and lend us Thine
    aid!
  Star of the East, the horizon adorning,
  Guide where our infant Redeemer is laid!
          Bishop R. Heber. 1811.

68   6.6. 6.6. **8.8.**
The Lord, whom ye seek, shall suddenly come to His temple.—Malachi iii. 1.

JOIN all the glorious names
  Of wisdom, love, and power,
That ever mortals knew,
  That angels ever bore;
All are too mean to speak His worth,
Too mean to set our Saviour forth.

2 Clothed with our mortal flesh,
  The Covenant-Angel stands,
Holds, with the promises,
  Our pardon in His hands;
Commissioned from His Father's throne
To make His grace to mortals known.

3 Great Prophet of my God,
  My lips shall bless Thy name:
By Thee the joyful news
  Of our salvation came;
The joyful news of sins forgiven,
Of hell subdued, and peace with Heaven.

4 Be Thou my Counsellor,
  My Pattern, Lord, and Guide;
And through this desert land
  Still keep me near Thy side;
O let me never run astray,
Nor follow the forbidden way!

5 I love my Shepherd's voice;
  His watchful eye shall keep
My wandering soul among
  The thousands of His sheep;
He feeds His flock, He calls their names,
Bears in His arms the tender lambs.

6 Jesus, my great High Priest,
  Offered His blood and died!
My guilty conscience seeks
  No sacrifice beside;
His powerful blood did once atone,
And now it pleads before the throne.

7 O Thou almighty Lord,
  My Saviour and my King,
Thy sceptre and Thy sword,
  Thy glorious reign I sing;
Thine is the power; and here I sit
In willing bonds before Thy feet.
          Isaac Watts. 1709.

THE LORD JESUS CHRIST.

69   6.6, 7.7, 7.7.
At the name of Jesus every knee should bow.—Phil. ii. 10.

HIGH above every name,
   Jesus, the Great I AM!
Bows to Jesus every knee,
   Things in heaven, and earth, and hell;
Saints adore Him, demons flee,
   Fiends, and men, and angels feel!

2 He left His throne above,
   Emptied of all but love;
Whom the heavens cannot contain,
   God vouchsafed a worm to appear,
Lord of Glory, Son of Man,
   Poor, and vile, and abject here.

3 His own on earth He sought
   His own received Him not;
Him a sign by all blasphemed,
   Outcast and despised of men,
Him they all a madman deemed,
   Bold to scoff the Nazarene.

4 Hail, Galilean King!
   Thy humble state I sing,
Never shall my triumphs end;
   Hail, derided Majesty!
Jesus, hail! the sinner's Friend,
   Friend of publicans,—and me. Amen.
                              Wesley. 1739.

70   8.7. 8.7. 8.7.
I will not leave you comfortless: I will come to you.—John xiv. 18.

JESUS came—the heavens adoring—
   Came with peace from realms on high;
Jesus came for man's redemption,
   Lowly came on earth to die;
Hallelujah! hallelujah!
   Came in deep humility.

2 Jesus comes again in mercy,
   When our hearts are bowed with care;
Jesus comes again in answer
   To an earnest heart-felt prayer;
Hallelujah! hallelujah!
   Comes to save us from despair.

3 Jesus comes to hearts rejoicing,
   Bringing news of sins forgiven;
Jesus comes in sounds of gladness,
   Leading souls redeemed to heaven;
Hallelujah! hallelujah!
   Now the gate of death is riven.

4 Jesus comes in joy and sorrow,
   Shares alike our hopes and fears;
Jesus comes, whate'er befalls us,
   Glads our hearts, and dries our tears;
Hallelujah! hallelujah!
   Cheering e'en our failing years,

5 Jesus comes on clouds triumphant,
   When the heavens shall pass away;
Jesus comes again in glory;
   Let us then our homage pay;
Hallelujah! ever singing,
   Till the dawn of endless day. Amen.
                        Godfrey Thring. 1866.

71   L.M.D.
I am come that they might have life.
          John x. 10.

THE Lord is come! On Syrian soil,
   The child of poverty and toil;
The Man of sorrows, born to know
Each varying shade of human woe:
His joy, His glory, to fulfil,
In earth and heaven, His Father's will;
On lonely mount, by festive board,
On bitter cross, despised, adored.

2 The Lord is come! Dull hearts to wake,
He speaks, as never man yet spake,
The truth which makes His servants free,
The royal law of liberty.
Though heaven and earth shall pass away,
His living words our spirits stay,
And from His treasures, new and old,
The eternal mysteries unfold.

3 The Lord is come! In Him we trace
The fulness of God's truth and grace;
Throughout those words and acts Divine
Gleams of the eternal splendour shine;
And from His inmost Spirit flow,
As from a height of sunlit snow,
The rivers of perennial life,
To heal and sweeten Nature's strife.

4 The Lord is come! In every heart,
Where truth and mercy claim a part;
In every land where right is might,
And deeds of darkness shun the light;
In every Church, where faith and love
Lift earthward thoughts to things above;
In every holy, happy home,
We bless Thee, Lord, that Thou hast come! Amen.
                      Arthur P. Stanley. d. 1881.

72   C.M.D.
In His days shall the righteous flourish; and abundance of peace so long as the moon endureth.—Ps. lxxii. 7.

IT came upon the midnight clear,
   That glorious song of old,
From angels bending near the earth,
   To touch their harps of gold—
'Peace on the earth, goodwill to men,'
   From heaven's all-gracious King;
The world in solemn stillness lay
   To hear the angels sing.

HIS INCARNATION AND ADVENT.

2 Still through the cloven skies they come,
  With peaceful wings unfurled,
 And still their heavenly music floats
  O'er all the weary world ;
 Above its sad and lowly plains
  They bend on hovering wing,
 And ever o'er its Babel-sounds
  The blessèd angels sing.

3 Yet, with the woes of sin and strife,
  The world has suffered long ;
 Beneath the angel-strain have rolled
  Two thousand years of wrong ;
 And man, at war with man, hears not
  The love-song which they bring ;
 O hush the noise, ye men of strife,
  And hear the angels sing !

4 And ye, beneath life's crushing load,
  Whose forms are bending low,
 Who toil along the climbing way,
  With painful steps and slow,—
 Look now : for glad and golden hours
  Come swiftly on the wing ;
 O rest beside the weary road
  And hear the angels sing !

5 For lo ! the days are hastening on,
  By prophet-bards foretold,
 When with the ever-circling years
  Comes round the age of gold :
 When peace shall over all the earth
  Its ancient splendours fling,
 And the whole world send back the song
  Which now the angels sing.
      E. H. Sears. 1839.

73 C.M.
*And there were . . . shepherds abiding
in the field, keeping watch over their flock
by night.*—Luke ii. 8.

WHILE shepherds watched their flocks
   by night,
 All seated on the ground,
 The angel of the Lord came down,
  And glory shone around.

2 ' Fear not !' said he, for sudden dread
  Had seized their troubled mind,
 ' Glad tidings of great joy I bring
  To you and all mankind.

3 ' To you, in David's town, this day,
  Is born of David's line,
 A Saviour, who is Christ the Lord ;
  And this shall be the sign :

4 ' The heavenly Babe you there shall find,
  To human view displayed,
 All meanly wrapped in swaddling bands,
  And in a manger laid.'

5 Thus spake the seraph ; and forthwith
  Appeared a shining throng
 Of angels praising God on high,
  Who thus addressed their song :

6 ' All glory be to God on high,
  And to the earth be peace ;
 Goodwill henceforth from heaven to
   men,
  Begin and never cease.   Amen
      Nahum Tate. 1700.

74   7.7. 7.7. 7.7.
*The shepherds returned, glorifying
and praising God.*—Luke ii. 20.

SING, O sing, this blessed morn,
  Unto us a child is born,
 Unto us a Son is given,
 God Himself comes down from heaven ;
  Sing, O sing, this blessed morn,
  Jesus Christ to-day is born.

2 God with us, Immanuel,
 Deigns for ever now to dwell,
 And on Adam's fallen race
 Sheds the fulness of His grace ;
  Sing, O sing, this blessed morn,
  Jesus Christ to-day is born.

3 God comes down that man may rise,
 Lifted far above the skies ;
 Christ is Son of Man that we
 Sons of God in Him may be ;
  Sing, O sing, this blessed morn,
  Jesus Christ to-day is born.

4 O renew us, Lord, we pray,
 With Thy Spirit day by day ;
 That we ever one may be
 With the Father and with Thee ;
  Sing, O sing, this blessed morn,
  Jesus Christ to-day is born.

5 Sing, O sing, this blessed morn,
 Jesus Christ to-day is born ;
 Glory to the Father give,
 Praise the Son in whom we live ;
 Glory to the Spirit be,
 Godhead One, and Persons Three. Amen.
      Bishop C. Wordsworth. 1862.

75   8 6.6. 8 6.6.
Unto us a child is born.—Isaiah ix. 6.

ALL my heart this night rejoices,
  As I hear, far and near,
  Sweetest angel voices ;
 ' Christ is born !' their choirs are singing,
  Till the air, everywhere,
  Now with joy is ringing.

2 For it dawns, the promised morrow
  Of His birth, who the earth
  Rescues from her sorrow
 God to wear our form descendeth ;
  Of His grace to our race,
  Here His Son He lendeth.

21

THE LORD JESUS CHRIST.

3 Hark! a voice from yonder manger,
   Soft and sweet, doth entreat—
   'Flee from woe and danger;
  Brethren, come; from all that grieves
     you,
   You are freed; all you need
    I will surely give you.'

4 Ye who pine in weary sadness,
   Weep no more, for the door
    Now is found of gladness:
  Cling to Him, for He will guide you
   Where no cross, pain or loss,
    Can again betide you.

5 Hither come, ye heavy-hearted,
   Who for sin, deep within,
    Long and sore have smarted;
  For the poisoned wounds you're feeling
   Help is near, One is here
    Mighty for their healing.

6 Come then, let us hasten yonder;
   Here let all, great and small,
    Kneel in awe and wonder.
  Love Him who with love is yearning;
   Hail the Star, that from far
    Bright with hope is burning.
             Paul Gerhardt. 1653.
    Tr. *Catherine Winkworth.* 1858.

76   8.7. 8.7. D.
*A multitude of the heavenly host
praising God.*—Luke ii. 13.

HARK! what mean those holy voices
   Sweetly sounding through the
     skies?
Lo! the angelic host rejoices,
   Loudest hallelujahs rise.
Listen to the wondrous story,
   Which they chant in hymns of joy:
'Glory in the highest, glory,
   Glory be to God most high!

2 'Peace on earth, goodwill from heaven,
   Reaching far as man is found;
Souls redeemed, and sins forgiven,
   Loud our golden harps shall sound.
Christ is born, the great Anointed!
   Heaven and earth His glory sing!
Glad receive whom God appointed
   For your Prophet, Priest, and King.

3 'Hasten, mortals, to adore Him,
   Learn His name and taste His joy,
Till in heaven you sing before Him,
   Glory be to God most high!'
Let us learn the wondrous story
   Of our great Redeemer's birth,
Spread the brightness of His glory,
   Till it cover all the earth.
              John Cawood. 1816.

77   10.10. 10.10. 10.10.
*Unto you is born this day . . .
a Saviour, which is Christ the Lord.*
       Luke ii. 11.

CHRISTIANS, awake, salute the happy
    morn
Whereon the Saviour of mankind was born,
Rise to adore the mystery of love,
Which hosts of angels chanted from above;
With them the joyful tidings first begun,
Of God incarnate and the Virgin's Son.

2 Then to the watchful shepherds it was told,
Who heard the angelic herald's voice:
   'Behold,
I bring good tidings of a Saviour's birth
To you and all the nations upon earth;
This day hath God fulfilled His promised
    word,
This day is born a Saviour, Christ the
    Lord.'

3 He spake, and straightway the celestial
    choir
In hymns of joy, unknown before, conspire;
The praises of redeeming love they sang,
And heaven's whole orb with hallelujahs
    rang;
God's highest glory was their anthem still,
Peace upon earth, and unto men goodwill.

4 To Bethlehem straight the enlightened
    shepherds ran,
To see the wonder God had wrought for
    man;
To all the joyful tidings they proclaim,
The first apostles of the Saviour's name,
Then to their flocks, still praising God,
    return,
And their glad hearts with holy rapture
    burn.

5 O may we keep and ponder in our mind
God's wondrous love in saving lost man-
    kind;
Trace we the Babe, who hath retrieved
    our loss,
From the poor manger to the bitter cross;
Tread in His steps, assisted by His grace,
Till man's first heavenly state again takes
    place.

6 Then may we hope, the angelic hosts
    among,
To sing, redeemed, a glad triumphal song;
He that was born upon this joyful day
Around us all His glory shall display;
Saved by His love, incessant we shall sing
Eternal praise to heaven's almighty King.
              John Byrom. 1773.

78 *Irregular.*
Let us now go even unto Bethlehem.—Luke ii. 15.

O COME, all ye **faithful, joyful and triumphant,**
O come ye, O come ye, to Bethlehem;
Born upon earth, behold the King of angels!
   O come, let us adore Him,
   O come, let us adore Him,
O come, let us adore Him, Christ the Lord!

2 He, God **of God, and Light of Light begotten,**
Comes to the world as a maiden's Child;
He, very God, begotten not created:
   O come, let us adore Him,
   O come, let us adore Him,
O come, let us adore Him, Christ the Lord!

3 **Sing, choir of angels, raise your hymn of triumph;**
Sing, ye that stand around the throne on high;
Glory to God, all glory in the highest!
   O come, let us adore Him,
   O come, let us adore Him,
O come, let us adore Him, Christ the Lord!

4 **Thou who didst deign to be born for us this morning,**
Glory to Thee, O Jesus, Lord!
Word of the Eternal Father, now incarnate!
   O come, let us adore Him,
   O come, let us adore Him,
O come, let us adore Him, Christ the Lord!
             Amen.
     From the *Latin*, 18th *Century*.
      Tr. *John Ellerton*. 1871.

79 7.7. 7.7. 7.7. 7.7. **7.7.**
Glory to God in the highest, and on earth, peace, good-will toward men.
Luke ii. 14.

HARK! the herald-angels sing
  'Glory to the new-born King,
Peace on earth, and mercy mild,
God and sinners reconciled.'
Joyful all ye nations rise,
Join the triumphs of the skies;
With the angelic host proclaim,
Christ **is** born **in** Bethlehem.
   Hark! **the** herald-angels sing
   Glory to the new-born King.

2 Veiled **in flesh the Godhead see;**
Hail the incarnate Deity!
Pleased as man with men **to appear,**
Jesus, our Immanuel here.
Mild He lays His glory by,
Born that man no more may die,
Born to raise the sons of earth,
Born to give them second birth.
   Hark! the herald-angels sing
   Glory to the new-born King.

3 Come, Desire of Nations, come,
Fix in us Thy humble home;
Rise, the woman's conquering Seed,
Bruise in us the Serpent's head.
Hail the heaven-born Prince of Peace,
Hail the Sun of Righteousness!
Light and life to all He brings,
Risen with healing in His wings.
   Hark! the herald-angels sing
   Glory to the new-born King.
     Charles Wesley. 1739.

80 8.7. 8.7. 4.7.
Behold, I bring you good tidings of great joy, which shall be to all people.
Luke ii. 10.

ANGELS from the realms of glory,
  Wing your flight o'er all the earth;
Ye, who sang creation's story,
  Now proclaim Messiah's birth:
    Come and worship,
Worship Christ, the new-born King.

2 Shepherds, in the field abiding,
  Watching o'er your flocks by night,
God with man is now residing,
  Yonder shines the infant Light:
    Come and worship,
Worship Christ, the new-born King.

3 Sages, leave your contemplations,
  Brighter visions beam afar;
Seek the great Desire of Nations,
  Ye have seen His natal star:
    Come and worship,
Worship Christ, **the new-born King.**

4 Saints, before the altar bending,
  Waiting long with hope and fear,
Suddenly **the** Lord descending,
  In His temple shall appear:
    Come and worship,
Worship Christ, the new-born King.

5 Sinners, wrung with true repentance,
  Doomed for guilt to endless pains,
Justice now repeals the sentence,
  Mercy calls you, break **your** chains:
    Come **and** worship,
Worship **Christ,** the new-born King.
     James Montgomery. 1819.

81 6.5., 12 *lines.*
Wherefore God also hath highly exalted Him.—Philip. ii. 9.

HARK! the **voice eternal**
  Robed in majesty,
Calling into being
  Earth and sea and sky;
Hark: in countless numbers
  All the angel-throng
Hail Creation's morning
  With one burst of song.
    High in regal glory,
    'Mid eternal light,
    Reign, O King Immortal,
    Holy, Infinite.

THE LORD JESUS CHRIST.

2 Bright the world and glorious,
  Calm both earth and sea,
  Noble in its grandeur
   Stood man's purity:
  Came the great transgression,
  Came the saddening fall,
  Death and desolation
   Breathing over all.
    Still in regal glory,
     'Mid eternal light,
    Reigned the King Immortal,
    Holy, Infinite.

3 Long the nations waited,
  Through the troubled night,
  Looking, longing, yearning
   For the promised light.
  Prophets saw the morning
  Breaking far away,
  Minstrels sang the splendour
   Of that opening day:
    Whilst in regal glory,
     'Mid eternal light,
    Reigned the King Immortal
    Holy, Infinite.

4 Brightly dawned the Advent
  Of the new-born King,
  Joyously the watchers
   Heard the angels sing:
  Sadly closed the evening
  Of His hallowed life,
  As the noontide darkness
   Veiled the last dread strife.
    Lo! again in glory,
     'Mid eternal light,
    Reigns the King Immortal,
    Holy, Infinite.

5 Lo! again He cometh,
  Robed in clouds of light,
  As the Judge Eternal,
   Armed with power and might.
  Nations to His footstool
  Gathered then shall be;
  Earth shall yield her treasures,
   And her dead, the sea.
    Till the trumpet soundeth,
     'Mid eternal light,
    Reign, Thou King Immortal,
    Holy, Infinite.

6 Jesus! Lord and Master,
  Prophet, Priest, and King,
  To Thy feet triumphant
   Hallowed praise we bring.
  Thine the pain and weeping,
  Thine the victory;
  Power, and praise, and honour
   Be, O Lord, to Thee.
    High in regal glory,
     'Mid eternal light,
    Reign, O King Immortal,
    Holy, Infinite.   Amen.
            John Julian. 1880.

HIS EXAMPLE AND TEACHING.

82 *Grace is poured into Thy lips.*   C.M.
    Psalm xlv. 2.

WHAT grace, O Lord, and beauty shone
  Around Thy steps below!
What patient love was seen in all
  Thy life and death of woe!

2 For ever on Thy burdened heart
  A weight of sorrow hung;
  Yet no ungentle, murmuring word
  Escaped Thy silent tongue.

3 Thy foes might hate, despise, revile,
  Thy friends unfaithful prove;
  Unwearied in forgiveness still,
  Thy heart could only love.

4 O, give us hearts to love like Thee,
  Like Thee, O Lord, to grieve
  Far more for others' sins, than all
  The wrongs that we receive.

5 One with Thyself, may every eye,
  In us, Thy brethren, see
  That gentleness and grace which spring
  From union, Lord, with Thee.   Amen.
           Sir E. Denny. 1839.

83 *Lord, it is good for us to be here.*   L.M.D.
    Matthew xvii. 4.

LORD, it is good for us to be
  High on the mountain here with Thee,
Where stand revealed to mortal gaze
The glorious saints of other days,
Who once received, on Horeb's height,
The eternal laws of truth and right,
Or caught the still small whisper, higher
Than storm, than earthquake, or than fire.

2 Lord, it is good for us to be
With Thee, and with Thy faithful three,
Here, where the Apostle's heart of rock
Is nerved against temptation's shock;
Here, where the Son of Thunder learns
The thought that breathes, the word that burns;
Here, where on eagle's wings we move
With Him whose last, best creed is Love.

3 Lord, it is good for us to be
Entranced, enwrapt, alone with Thee,
Watching the glistening raiment glow
Whiter than Hermon's whitest snow,
The human lineaments that shine
Irradiant with a light Divine;
Till we too change from grace to grace,
Gazing on that transfigured face.

HIS EXAMPLE AND TEACHING.

Lord, it is good **for us to** be
Here on the Holy Mount with Thee ;
When darkling in the depths of night,
When dazzled with excess of light,
We bow before the heavenly Voice
That bids bewildered souls rejoice :
Though love wax cold, and faith be dim ;
'This is My Son ! O hear ye Him :'

Arthur P. Stanley. **d.** 1881.

---

84 6.6. 8.6. 10.12.
*In whom are **hid** all the treasures
of wisdom and knowledge.*—Colossians ii. **3.**

O MASTER, **at** Thy feet
I bow in rapture sweet !
Before me, **as in** darkening glass,
Some glorious outlines pass,
Of **love,** and truth, **and** holiness, and
power ;
I own them Thine, **O Christ, and bless Thee**
for this hour.

2 O full of truth and grace,
Smile of Jehovah's face !
O tenderest heart of love untold !
Who may Thy praise unfold ?
Thee, Saviour, Lord of lords and King **of**
kings,
Well may adoring seraphs hymn with veiling wings.

3 **I have no words** to bring
Worthy of Thee, my King,
And yet one **anthem** in Thy praise
I long, I long to raise ;
The heart is full, the eye entranced above,
But words all melt away in silent awe and
love.

4 **How can the lip be dumb,**
The hand all still and numb,
When Thee the heart doth see and own
Her Lord and God alone ?
Tune for Thyself the music **of my days,**
And open **Thou my lips that I may show**
Thy praise.

5 Yea, let my whole life be
One anthem unto Thee.
And let the praise of lip and life
Out-ring all sin and strife.
O Jesus, Master ! be Thy name supreme,
For heaven and earth, **the** one, the grand,
eternal theme. **Amen.**

Frances R. Havergal. **d.** 1879.

---

85 C.M.
I have given you an example.
John xiii. 15.

LORD, as to Thy dear cross we flee,
And plead to be forgiven,
So let Thy life our pattern be,
And form our souls for heaven.

2 Help us, through good report and ill,
Our daily cross to bear ;
Like Thee, to do our Father's will,
Our brethren's griefs to share.

3 Let grace our selfishness expel,
Our earthliness refine ;
And kindness in our bosoms dwell,
As free and true as Thine.

4 Kept peaceful in the midst of **strife,**
Forgiving and forgiven ;
O may we lead the pilgrim's life,
And follow Thee to heaven.

John H. Gurney. 1851.

---

86 8.8. 8.8. 8.8.
*If we suffer, we shall also reign
with Him.*—2 Tim. ii. 12.

SAVIOUR **of all, what hast** Thou done,
What hast Thou suffered on the tree ?
Why didst Thou groan Thy mortal groan,
Obedient unto death for me ?
The mystery of Thy passion show,
The end of all Thy griefs below.

2 Thy soul, **for** sin an offering made,
Hath cleared this guilty soul of mine ;
Thou hast for me a ransom paid,
To change **my** human **to** divine.
To cleanse from **all iniquity,**
And make **the sinner all like Thee.**

3 Pardon, and grace, **and heaven to buy,**
My bleeding Sacrifice expired ;
But didst Thou not my Pattern **die,**
That by Thy glorious spirit **tired,**
Faithful to death I might **endure,**
And make the crown by **suffering sure ?**

4 Thou didst the meek example leave,
That I might in Thy footsteps tread ;
Might, like the Man of Sorrows, grieve,
And groan and bow **with** Thee my head ;
Thy dying **in my** body **bear,**
And all Thy **state of suffering share.**

5 Thy every suffering servant, Lord,
Shall as his perfect Master be ;
To all Thy inward life restored,
And outwardly conformed to Thee,
Out of Thy **grave** the saint shall rise,
And grasp, through death, the glorious
prize.

6 This is the strait and royal way
That leads us to the courts above ;
Here let me ever, ever stay.
Till, **on the** wings of perfect **love.**
I take my last triumphant flight,
From Calvary's to Sion's height. **Amen.**

Charles Wesley. 1746.

---

87 C.M.
*Forasmuch **then as** the children
are partakers of flesh and blood, He at o
Himself likewise took part of the same.*
Hebrews ii. 14.

O! MEAN may seem this house of clay,
Yet 'twas the Lord's abode ;
Our feet may mourn this thorny way,
Yet here Immanuel trod.

THE LORD JESUS CHRIST.

2 This fleshly robe the Lord did wear;
   This watch the Lord did keep;
   These burdens sore the Lord did bear;
   These tears the Lord did weep.

3 Our very frailty brings us near
   Unto the Lord of heaven;
   To every grief, to every tear
   Such glory strange is given.

4 But not this fleshly robe alone
   Shall link us, Lord, to Thee;
   Not only in the tear and groan
   Shall the dear kindred be.

5 We shall be reckoned for Thine own
   Because Thy heaven we share,
   Because we sing around Thy throne,
   And Thy bright raiment wear.

6 O mighty grace, our life to live,
   To make our earth divine!
   O mighty grace, Thy heaven to give,
   And lift our life to Thine!
             Thomas H. Gill. 1846.

88   8.8. 8.8. 8.8.
He would have given thee living water.—John iv. 10.

JESUS, the gift divine I know,
   The gift divine I ask of Thee;
That living water now bestow,
   Thy Spirit and Thyself, on me:
Thou, Lord, of life the fountain art,
Now let me find Thee in my heart.

2 Thee let me drink, and thirst no more
   For drops of finite happiness;
Spring up, O Well, in heavenly power,
   In streams of pure, perennial peace,
In joy, that none can take away,
In life, which shall for ever stay.

3 Father, on me the grace bestow,
   Unblamable before Thy sight,
Whence all the streams of mercy flow;
   Mercy, Thy own supreme delight,
To me, for Jesu's sake, impart,
And plant Thy nature in my heart.

4 Thy mind throughout my life be shown,
   While listening to the mourner's cry,
The widow's and the orphan's groan,
   On mercy's wings I swiftly fly,
The poor and helpless to relieve,
My life, my all, for them to give.

5 Thus may I show the Spirit within,
   Which purges me from every stain;
Unspotted from the world and sin,
   My faith's integrity maintain;
The truth of my religion prove,
By perfect purity and love.   Amen.
             Charles Wesley. 1762.

89   8.8. 8.3.
And He arose, and rebuked the wind, and said unto the sea, Peace, be still.
   Mark iv. 39.

FIERCE raged the tempest o'er the deep,
   Watch did Thine anxious servants keep,
But Thou wast wrapped in guileless sleep,
      Calm and still.

2 'Save, Lord, we perish,' was their cry:
   'O save us in our agony!'
Thy word above the storm rose high,—
      'Peace, be still!'

3 The wild winds hushed; the angry deep
Sank like a little child to sleep,
The sullen billows ceased to leap,
      At Thy will.

4 So, when our life is clouded o'er,
And storm-winds drift us from the shore,
Say, lest we sink to rise no more,
      'Peace, be still!'   Amen.
          Godfrey Thring. 1866.

90   8.5. 8.3.
Come unto Me, all ye that labour and are heavy laden, and I will give you rest.
   Matthew xi. 28.

ART thou weary, art thou languid,
   Art thou sore distrest?
'Come to Me,' saith One, 'and coming,
   Be at rest!'

2 Hath He marks to lead me to Him,
   If He be my Guide?
'In His feet and hands are wound-prints,
   And His side.'

3 Is there diadem, as monarch,
   That His brow adorns?
'Yea, a crown, in very surety,
   But of thorns!'

4 If I find Him, if I follow,
   What His guerdon here?
'Many a sorrow, many a labour,
   Many a tear.'

5 If I still hold closely to Him,
   What hath He at last?
'Sorrow vanquished, labour ended,
   Jordan past!'

6 If I ask Him to receive me,
   Will He say me nay?
'Not till earth, and not till heaven
   Pass away!'

7 Finding, following, keeping, struggling,
   Is he sure to bless?
'Saints, Apostles, Prophets, Martyrs,
   Answer, Yes!'
      Stephen of Saba. 8th Century.
    Tr. and alt. by *J. M. Neale.* 1862.

HIS EXAMPLE AND TEACHING.

91   C.M.D.
*Jesus went unto them walking
on the sea.*—Matthew xiv. 25.

O WHERE is He that trod the sea?
  O, where is He that spake,
And demons from their victims flee,
  The dead from slumber wake?
The palsied rise in freedom strong,
  The dumb men talk and sing,
And from blind eyes, benighted long,
  Bright beams of morning spring.

2 O, where is He that trod the sea?
  'Tis only He can save;
To thousands hungering wearily,
  A wondrous meal He gave:
Full soon, celestially fed,
  Their plenteous food they take;
'Twas springtide when He blest the bread,
  'Twas harvest when He brake.

3 O, where is He that trod the sea?
  My soul! the Lord is here:
Let all thy fears be hushed in thee;
  And leap, and look, and hear.
Thy utmost needs He'll satisfy
  Art thou diseased or dumb?
Or dost thou in thy hunger cry?
  Behold thy Helper come!
                T. T. Lynch. 1855.

92   L.M.
*The Son of Man is come to seek
and to save that which was lost.*
Luke xix. 10.

JESUS, Thy far-extended fame
  My drooping soul exults to hear;
Thy name, Thy all-restoring name,
  Is music in a sinner's ear.

2 Sinners of old Thou didst receive,
  With comfortable words and kind;
Their sorrows cheer, their wants relieve,
  Heal the diseased, and cure the blind.

3 And art Thou not the Saviour still,
  In every place and age the same?
Hast Thou forgot Thy gracious skill,
  Or lost the virtue of Thy name?

4 Faith in Thy changeless name I have,
  The good, the kind Physician, Thou
Art able now our souls to save,
  Art willing to restore them now.

5 Though eighteen hundred years are past
  Since Thou didst in the flesh appear,
Thy tender mercies ever last;
  And still Thy healing power is here!

6 Wouldst Thou the body's health restore,
  And not regard the sin-sick soul?
The sin-sick soul Thou lov'st much more,
  And surely Thou shalt make it whole.

7 All my disease, my every sin,
  To Thee, O Jesus, I confess;
In pardon, Lord, my cure begin,
  And perfect it in holiness.

8 That token of Thine utmost good,
  Now, Saviour, now on me bestow;
And purge my conscience with Thy blood,
  And wash my nature white as snow.
                Amen.
              Charles Wesley. 1749.

93   8.7. 8.7. 7.7.
*And now abideth faith, hope,
charity, these three; but the greatest of these
is charity.*—1 Corinthians xiii. 13.

BLESSÈD Saviour, Thou hast taught us,
  Taught us in Thy word divine,
That our doings are but nothing
  If they be not linked with Thine;
If we be not bound to Thee
With the bond of charity.

2 Though with tongues of men and angels,
  Soaring may our voices rise;
Though we have the gift of knowledge,
  Understanding mysteries;
All will still as nothing be,
If we have not charity.

3 Though with faith, that even mountains
  At our word we may remove,
Though our bodies to be burned
  Yield we, and possess not love,
We have nothing till we be
Bound with bonds of charity.

4 Bind us with the bond that bindeth
  Human hearts to God above,
Bind us with the bond uniting
  Rich and poor with heavenly love.
With the bond that binds to Thee,
Never-failing charity. Amen.
              Godfrey Thring. 1880.

94   L.M.
*It became Him, . . . to make the
Captain of their salvation perfect through
sufferings.*—Hebrews ii. 10.

O THOU through suffering perfect made,
  On whom the bitter cross was laid,
In hours of sickness, grief, and pain,
No sufferer turns to Thee in vain.

2 The halt, the maimed, the sick, the blind
  Sought not in vain Thy tendance kind
Now in Thy poor Thyself we see,
And minister through them to Thee.

3 O loving Saviour, Thou canst cure
  The pains and woes Thou didst endure;
For all who need, Physician great,
  Thy healing balm we supplicate.

THE LORD JESUS CHRIST.

4 But, O! far more, let each keen pain
  And hour of woe be heavenly gain,
  Each stroke of Thy chastising rod
  Bring back the wanderer nearer God.

5 O! heal the bruised heart within;
  O! save our souls all sick with sin;
  Give life and health in bounteous store,
  That we may praise Thee evermore. Amen.
  Bishop W. W. How. 1871.

HIS PASSION AND DEATH.

95   8.7. 8.7. D.
The Lord hath laid on Him the iniquity of us all.—Isaiah liii. 6.

HAIL, Thou once despised Jesus!
  Hail, Thou Galilean King!
Who didst suffer to release us,
  Who didst free salvation bring.
Hail, **Thou** universal Saviour!
  Bearer **of** our sin and shame!
By Thy merits we find favour;
  Life is given through Thy name.

2 Paschal Lamb, by God appointed,
    All our sins on Thee were laid;
  By almighty Love anointed,
    Thou hast full atonement made:
  Every sin may be forgiven,
    Through the virtue of Thy blood;
  Opened is the gate of heaven,
    Peace is made 'twixt man and God.

3 Jesus, hail! enthroned in glory,
    There for ever to abide;
  All the heavenly host adore Thee,
    Seated at Thy Father's side:
  There for sinners Thou art pleading,
    'Spare them yet another year;'
  Thou for saints art interceding,
    Till in glory they appear.

4 Worship, honour, power, and **blessing,**
    Thou art worthy to receive;
  Loudest praises without ceasing,
    Meet it is for us to give.
  Help, ye bright, angelic spirits!
    Bring your sweetest, noblest lays,
  Help to sing the Saviour's merits,
    Help to chant Immanuel's praise.
    Amen.
    John Bakewell. 1760.

96   8.7. 8.7.
God forbid that I should glory, save in the cross of our Lord Jesus Christ.
Galatians vi. 14.

IN the Cross of Christ I glory,
  Towering o'er the wrecks of time:
All the light of sacred story
  Gathers round its head sublime.

2 When the woes of life o'ertake me,
    Hopes deceive and fears annoy,
  Never shall the Cross forsake me:
    Lo! it glows with peace and joy.

3 When the sun of bliss is beaming
    Light and love upon my way,
  From the Cross the radiance streaming
    Adds more lustre to the day.

4 Bane and blessing, pain and pleasure,
    By the Cross are sanctified;
  Peace is there that knows no measure,
    Joys **that through all time** abide.

5 In the Cross of Christ I glory,
    Towering o'er the wrecks of **time:**
  All the light of sacred story
    Gathers round its head sublime.
    Sir John Bowring. 1825.

97   L.M.
They crucified Him.—John xix. 18.

O COME and mourn with me awhile;
  O come ye to the Saviour's side;
O come, together let us mourn:
  Jesus, our Love, is crucified!

2 **Have we no** tears to shed for Him,
    While soldiers scoff, and Jews deride?
  Ah! look how patiently He hangs;
    Jesus, our Love, **is** crucified!

3 Seven times He spake, seven words of love;
    And all three hours His silence cried
  For mercy on the souls of men:
    Jesus, our Love, is crucified!

4 A broken heart, a fount of tears
    Ask, and they will not be denied;
  A broken heart Love's cradle is;
    Jesus, **our** Love, is crucified!

5 O Love of God! O Sin of man!
    In this dread act your strength is tried;
  And victory remains with Love;
    For He, our Love, is crucified!
    F. W. Faber. 1849.

98   L.M.
The righteousness which is of God by faith.—Philippians iii. 9.

JESUS, Thy Blood and Righteousness
  My beauty are, my glorious dress:
'Midst flaming worlds, in these arrayed,
  With joy shall I lift up my head.

2 Bold shall I stand in that great day;
    For who aught to my charge shall lay?
  Fully absolved through these I am,
    From sin and fear, from guilt and shame.

3 The holy, meek, unspotted Lamb,
    Who from the Father's bosom came,
  Who died for me, even me, to atone,
    Now for my Lord and God I own.

HIS PASSION AND DEATH.

4 Lord, I believe Thy precious blood,
　Which, at the mercy-seat of God,
　For ever doth for sinners plead,
　For me, even for my soul, was shed.

5 Lord, I believe, were sinners more
　Than sands upon the ocean shore,
　Thou hast for all a ransom paid,
　For all a full atonement made.

6 When from the dust of death I rise,
　To claim my mansion in the skies,
　Even then, this shall be all my plea,
　Jesus hath lived, hath died for me.
　　　　　Count Zinzendorf. abt. 1736.
　　　　　　Tr. John Wesley. 1740.

99   5.5.11. 5.5.11.
　*Behold and see if there be any
sorrow like unto My sorrow.*—Lament. i. 12.

ALL ye that pass by,
　　To Jesus draw nigh ;
To you is it nothing that Jesus should die ?
　Your ransom and peace,
　Your surety He is :
Come, see if there ever was sorrow like His.

2 For what you have done
　　His blood must atone :
The Father hath punished for you His dear
　　Son.
　The Lord, in the day
　Of His anger, did lay
Your sins on the Lamb, and He bore them
　　away.

3 He answered for all :
　　O come at His call,
And low at His cross with astonishment fall !
　But lift up your eyes
　At Jesus's cries :
Impassive, He suffers ; Immortal, He dies.

4 He dies to atone
　　For sins not His own;
Your debt He hath paid, and your work He
　　hath done.
　Ye all may receive
　The peace He did leave,
Who made intercession, 'My Father, forgive!'

5 For you and for me
　　He prayed on the tree :
The prayer is accepted, the sinner is free.
　That sinner am I,
　Who on Jesus rely,
And come for the pardon God cannot deny.

6 My pardon I claim ;
　　For a sinner I am,
A sinner believing in Jesus's name.
　He purchased the grace
　Which now I embrace :
O Father, Thou know'st He hath died in my
　　place.

7 His death is my plea ;
　　My Advocate see,
And hear the blood speak that hath answered
　　for me.
　My ransom He was
　When He bled on the cross :
And by losing His life He hath carried my
　　cause.
　　　　　　Charles Wesley. 1749.

100   C.M.
　Behold the Lamb of God.
　　　John i. 29.

BEHOLD the saviour of mankind
　Nailed to the shameful tree !
How vast the love that Him inclined
　To bleed and die for thee !

2 Hark, how He groans ! while nature shakes,
　And earth's strong pillars bend ;
The temple's veil in sunder breaks,
　The solid marbles rend.

3 'Tis done ! the precious ransom's paid ;
　'Receive My soul,' He cries :
See where He bows His sacred head :
　He bows His head, and dies !

4 But soon He'll break death's envious chain
　And in full glory shine ;
O Lamb of God : was ever pain,
　Was ever love like Thine?
　　　　　　Samuel Wesley, Sen. 1709.

101   8.8. 8.8. 8.8.
　*Herein is love. . . . God
sent His Son to be the propitiation for our
sins.*—1 John iv. 10.

O LOVE Divine ! what hast Thou done ?
　　The immortal God hath died for me !
The Father's co-eternal Son
Bore all my sins upon the tree :
The immortal God for me hath died !
My Lord, my Love, is crucified.

2 Behold Him, all ye that pass by,
　The bleeding Prince of Life and Peace !
Come, sinners, see your Maker die,
　And say, was ever grief like His?
Come, feel with me His blood applied :
My Lord, my Love, is crucified.

3 Is crucified for me and you,
　To bring us rebels back to God :
Believe, believe the record true,
　Ye all are bought with Jesus's blood ;
Pardon for all flows from His side :
My Lord, my Love, is crucified.

4 Then let us sit beneath His Cross,
　And gladly catch the healing stream ;
All things for Him account but loss,
　And give up all our hearts to Him ;
Of nothing think or speak beside,
My Lord, my Love, is crucified.
　　　　　　　　Wesley. 1742.

THE LORD JESUS CHRIST.

102 7.6. 7.6. D.
When they had platted a crown of thorns, they put it upon His head. Matthew xxvii. 29.

O SACRED Head, once wounded,
  With grief and pain weighed down,
How scornfully surrounded
  With thorns, Thine only crown!
How pale art Thou with anguish,
  With sore abuse and scorn!
How does that visage languish,
  Which once was bright as morn!

2 O Lord of life and glory,
    What bliss till now was Thine!
  I read the wondrous story,
    I joy to call Thee mine.
  Thy grief and Thy compassion
    Were all for sinners' gain;
  Mine, mine was the transgression,
    But Thine the deadly pain.

3 What language shall I borrow
    To praise Thee, Heavenly Friend,
  For this Thy dying sorrow,
    Thy pity without end?
  Lord, make me Thine for ever,
    Nor let me faithless prove;
  O let me never, never,
    Abuse such dying love!

4 Be near me, Lord, when dying,
    O show Thyself to me:
  And, for my succour flying,
    Come, Lord, to set me free:
  These eyes, new faith receiving,
    From Jesus shall not move;
  For he who dies believing,
    Dies safely through Thy love.

Bernard of Clairvaux, 12th Cent., by Paul Gerhardt, 17th Cent. Tr. J. W. Alexander. 1849.

103 9.7. 9.7. 9.9.
Rejoice with me; for I have found my sheep which was lost.—Luke xv. 6.

THERE were ninety and nine that safely lay
  In the shelter of the fold;
But one was out on the hills away,
  Far off from the gates of gold,
Away on the mountains wild and bare,
Away from the tender shepherd's care.

'Lord, Thou hast here Thy ninety and nine;
  Are they not enough for Thee?'
But the Shepherd made answer:—'This of Mine
  Has wandered away from Me;
And, although the road be rough and steep,
I go to the desert to find My sheep.'

3 But **none** of the ransomed ever knew
    How deep were the waters crossed;
  Nor how dark was the night that the Lord passed through
    Ere He found His sheep that was lost,
  Out in the desert He heard its cry,
  Sick, and helpless, and ready to die.

4 'Lord, whence are those blood-drops all the way,
    That mark out the mountain's track?'
  'They were shed for one who had gone astray
    Ere the Shepherd could bring him back.'
  'Lord, whence are Thy hands so rent and torn?'
  'They are pierced to-night by many a thorn.'

5 And all through the mountains thunder-riven,
    And up from the rocky steep,
  There arose a cry to the gate of heaven,
    'Rejoice, I have found My sheep!'
  And the angels echoed around the throne,
  'Rejoice, for the Lord brings back His own!'

Elizabeth C. Clephane. d. 1869.

104 7.7. 7.7. 7.7.
A place called Gethsemane. Matthew xxvi. 36.

GO to dark Gethsemane,
  Ye that feel the tempter's power,
Your Redeemer's conflict see!
  Watch with Him one bitter hour:
Turn not from His griefs away;
Learn of Jesus Christ to pray.

2 Follow to the judgment hall;
    View the Lord of Life arraigned.
  O the wormwood and the gall!
    O the pangs His soul sustained!
  Shun not suffering, shame, or loss:
  Learn of Him to bear the cross.

3 Calvary's mournful mountain climb;
    There, adoring at His feet,
  Mark that miracle of time,
    God's own sacrifice complete.
  'It is finished!' hear Him cry:
  Learn of Jesus Christ to die.

4 Early hasten to the tomb,
    Where they laid His breathless clay;
  All is solitude and gloom:
    Who hath taken Him away?
  Christ is risen. He seeks the skies:
  Saviour, teach us how to rise. Amen.

James Montgomery. 1820.

HIS PASSION AND DEATH.

105 S.M.
It is not possible that the blood of bulls and of goats should take away sins.
Hebrews x. 4.

NOT all the blood of beasts,
  On Jewish altars slain,
Could give the guilty conscience peace,
  Or wash away our stain.

2 But Christ, the heavenly Lamb,
  Takes all our sins away;
A sacrifice of nobler name,
  And richer blood than they.

3 My faith would lay her hand
  On that dear head of Thine,
While like a penitent I stand,
  And there confess my sin.

4 My soul looks back to see
  The burdens Thou didst bear
When hanging on the cursed tree,
  And knows her guilt was there.

5 Believing, we rejoice
  To see the curse remove;
We bless the Lamb with cheerful voice,
  And sing His bleeding love.
            Isaac Watts. 1709.

106 8.8. 8.8. 8.8.
Father, forgive them; for they know not what they do.—Luke xxiii. 34.

WOULD Jesus have the sinner die?
  Why hangs He then on yonder tree?
What means that strange expiring cry?
  Sinners, He prays for you and me:
'Forgive them, Father, O forgive,
  They know not that by Me they live!'

2 Adam, descended from above
  Our loss of Eden to retrieve,
Great God of universal love,
  If all the world through Thee may live,
In us a quickening Spirit be,
  And witness Thou hast died for me!

3 Thou loving, all-atoning Lamb,
  Thee—by Thy painful agony,
Thy bloody sweat, Thy grief and shame,
  Thy cross, and passion on the tree,
Thy precious death and life—I pray,
  Take all, take all my sins away!

4 O let me kiss Thy bleeding feet,
  And bathe and wash them with my tears!
The story of Thy love repeat
  In every drooping sinner's ears:
That all may hear the quickening sound,
  Since I, even I, have mercy found.

5 O let Thy love my heart constrain,
  Thy love for every sinner free;
That every fallen soul of man
  May taste the grace that found out me;
That all mankind with me may prove
  Thy sovereign, everlasting love. Amen.
            Wesley. 1741.

107 L.M.
Christ the power of God, and the wisdom of God.—1 Corinthians i. 24.

WHEN I survey the wondrous Cross
  On which the Prince of Glory died,
My richest gain I count but loss,
  And pour contempt on all my pride.

2 Forbid it, Lord, that I should boast,
  Save in the death of Christ, my God:
All the vain things that charm me most,
  I sacrifice them to His blood.

3 See, from His head, His hands, His feet,
  Sorrow and love flow mingled down:
Did e'er such love and sorrow meet,
  Or thorns compose so rich a crown?

4 Were the whole realm of nature mine,
  That were a present far too small;
Love so amazing, so divine,
  Demands my soul, my life, my all.
            Isaac Watts. 1709.

108 C.M.
In that day there shall be a fountain opened . . . for sin and for uncleanness.—Zechariah xiii. 1.

THERE is a fountain filled with blood
  Drawn from Immanuel's veins;
And sinners, plunged beneath that flood,
  Lose all their guilty stains.

2 The dying thief rejoiced to see
  That fountain in his day;
And there have I, as vile as he,
  Washed all my sins away.

3 Dear dying Lamb, Thy precious blood
  Shall never lose its power,
Till all the ransomed Church of God
  Be saved to sin no more.

4 E'er since, by faith, I saw the stream
  Thy flowing wounds supply,
Redeeming love has been my theme,
  And shall be till I die.

5 Then, in a nobler, sweeter song,
  I'll sing Thy power to save;
When this poor lisping, stammering tongue,
  Lies silent in the grave.
            William Cowper. 1772.

THE LORD JESUS CHRIST.

109   C.M.   *With* **Chorus**.
Who loved me, and gave Himself for me.—Galatians ii. 20.

ALAS! and did my Saviour bleed?
And did my Sovereign die?
Did He devote that sacred head
For sinners such as I?

   Help me, dear Saviour, Thee to own,
    And ever faithful be;
   And when Thou sittest on Thy throne,
    O Lord, remember me.

2 Was it for crimes that I had done
He groaned upon the tree?
Amazing pity! grace unknown!
And love beyond degree!

3 Well might the sun in darkness hide,
And shut his glories in,
When Christ, the great Redeemer died,
For man the creature's sin.

4 Thus might I hide my blushing face
Whilst His dear Cross appears,
Dissolve my heart in thankfulness,
And melt my eyes to tears.

5 But drops of grief can ne'er repay
The debt of love I owe;
Here, Lord, I give myself away,
'Tis all that I can do.
   Isaac Watts. 1709.   *Chorus Anon.*

110   7.7. 7.7. 7.7.
That Rock was Christ.
1 Cor. x. 4.

ROCK of Ages, cleft for me,
Let me hide myself in Thee;
Let the water and the blood,
From Thy wounded side which **flowed**,
Be of sin the double cure,
Cleanse me from its guilt **and power**.

2 Not the labour of my hands
Can fulfil Thy law's demands;
Could my zeal no respite know,
Could my tears for ever flow,
All for sin could not atone;
Thou must save, and Thou alone.

3 Nothing in my hand I bring,
Simply to Thy Cross I cling;
Naked, come to Thee for dress;
Helpless, look to Thee for grace;
Foul, I to the fountain fly;
Wash me, Saviour, or I die.

4 While I draw this fleeting breath,
When mine eyes shall close in death,
When I soar to worlds unknown,
See Thee on Thy judgment throne;
Rock of Ages, cleft for me,
Let me hide myself in Thee.   Amen.
     Augustus M Toplady. 1776.

HIS RESURRECTION AND ASCENSION.

111   7.7. 7.7.   *With Hallelujahs.*
He is not here; for He is risen, as He said.—Matt. xxviii. 6.

CHRIST, the Lord, is risen to-day,
   Hallelujah!
Sons of men and angels say,
   Hallelujah!
Raise your joys and triumphs high,
   Hallelujah!
Sing, ye heavens; thou earth, reply.
   Hallelujah!

2 Love's redeeming work is done,
   Hallelujah!
Fought the fight, the battle won,
   Hallelujah!
Lo! our Sun's eclipse is o'er,
   Hallelujah!
Lo! He sets in blood no more.
   Hallelujah!

3 **Vain the stone,** the watch, the seal,
   Hallelujah!
Christ hath burst the gates of hell,
   Hallelujah!
Death in vain forbids His rise,
   Hallelujah!
Christ hath opened Paradise.
   Hallelujah!

4 **Lives again our** glorious King,
   Hallelujah!
Where, O Death, is now thy sting?
   Hallelujah!
Dying once, He all doth save,
   Hallelujah!
Where's thy victory, boasting grave?
   Hallelujah!

5 **Soar** we now, where Christ hath led,
   Hallelujah!
Following our exalted Head,
   Hallelujah!
Made like Him, like Him we rise,
   Hallelujah!
Ours the cross, the grave, the skies.
   Hallelujah!

6 **King of glory!** Soul of bliss!
   Hallelujah!
Everlasting life is this,
   Hallelujah!
Thee to know, Thy power to prove,
   Hallelujah!
Thus to sing, and thus to love.
   Hallelujah!
     Charles Wesley. 1734.

HIS RESURRECTION.

112 C.M.
To this end Christ both died, and rose, and revived, that He might be Lord both of the dead and living.—Rom. xiv. 9.

AWAKE, glad soul! awake, awake!
  Thy Lord hath risen long:
Go to His grave, and with thee take
  Both tuneful heart and song.

2 Where life is waking all around,
  Where love's sweet voices sing,
The first bright blossoms may be found
  Of an eternal spring.

3 The shade and gloom of life are fled
  This resurrection day;
Henceforth in Christ are no more dead,
  The grave hath no more prey.

4 In Christ we live, in Christ we sleep,
  In Christ we wake and rise;
And the sad tears death makes us weep,
  He wipes from all our eyes.

5 And every bird, and every tree,
  And every opening flower,
Proclaim His glorious victory,
  His resurrection power.

6 The folds are glad, the fields rejoice
  With vernal verdure spread,
The little hills lift up their voice
  And shout that death is dead.

7 Then wake, glad heart! awake, awake!
  And seek thy risen Lord,
Joy in His resurrection take,
  And comfort in His word.

8 And let thy life through all its ways
  One long thanksgiving be,
Its theme of joy, its song of praise,
  Christ died and rose for me.
    J. S. B. Monsell. 1863.

113 L.M.D.
He rose again the third day according to the Scriptures.—1 Cor. xv. 4.

HE dies: the Friend of sinners dies!
  Lo! Salem's daughters weep around:
A solemn darkness veils the skies,
A sudden trembling shakes the ground.
Come, saints, and drop a tear or two
On the dear bosom of your God:
He sheds a thousand drops for you,
A thousand drops of richer blood.

2 Here's love and grief beyond degree,
  The Lord of glory dies for man!
But, lo! what sudden joys I see!
  Jesus, the dead, revives again!
The rising God forsakes the tomb,
The tomb in vain forbids His rise!
Cherubic legions guard Him home,
And shout Him welcome to the skies!

3 Break off your tears, ye saints, and tell
  How high your great Deliverer reigns;
Sing how He spoiled the hosts of hell,
  And led the monster Death in chains:
Say, 'Live for ever, wondrous King!
Born to redeem, and strong to save!'
Then ask the monster, 'Where's thy sting?
And, 'Where's thy victory, boasting grave?'
    Isaac Watts. 1705. Alt. *M. Maclean.* 1760.

114 C.M.
Come, see the place where the Lord lay.—Matthew xxviii. 6.

YE humble souls that seek the Lord,
  Chase all your fears away;
And bow with pleasure down to see
  The place where Jesus lay.

2 Thus low the Lord of Life was brought,
  Such wonders love can do;
Thus cold in death that bosom lay,
  Which throbbed and bled for you.

3 Then raise your eyes, and tune your songs,
  The Saviour lives again;
Not all the bolts and bars of death
  The Conqueror could detain.

4 High o'er the angelic bands He rears
  His once dishonoured head;
And He through endless ages reigns,
  Who dwelt among the dead.

5 With joy like His shall every saint
  His vacant tomb survey;
Then rise with his ascending Lord
  To realms of endless day.
    Philip Doddridge. 1755.

115 7.8. 7.8. 4.
Why seek ye the living among the dead?—Luke xxiv. 5.

JESUS lives! no longer now
  Can thy terrors, Death, appal us;
Jesus lives! by this we know
Thou, O grave, canst not enthral us.
    Hallelujah!

2 Jesus lives! henceforth is death
But the gate of life immortal;
This shall calm our trembling breath,
When we pass its gloomy portal.
    Hallelujah!

3 Jesus lives! for us He died:
Then, alone to Jesus living,
Pure in heart may we abide,
Praise to Him and glory giving.
    Hallelujah!

4 Jesus lives! our hearts know well
Nought from us His love shall sever;
Life, nor death, nor powers of hell,
Part us now from Christ for ever.
    Hallelujah!

THE LORD JESUS CHRIST.

5 Jesus lives! to Him the throne
High o'er heaven and earth is given:
May we go where He is gone,
Rest and reign with Him in heaven.
                    Hallelujah!
                C. F. Gellert. 1757.
            Tr. Frances E. Cox. 1841. alt.

116   8.7. 8.7. D.
*Now is Christ risen from
the dead, and become the firstfruits of them
that slept.*—1 Corinthians xv. 20.

HALLELUJAH! Hallelujah!
  Hearts to heaven and voices raise;
Sing to God a hymn of gladness,
  Sing to God a hymn of praise;
He, who on the cross a victim
  For the world's salvation bled,
Jesus Christ, the King of glory,
  Now is risen from the dead.

2 Christ is risen, Christ the first-fruits
  Of the holy harvest field,
Which will all its full abundance
  At His second coming yield:
Then the golden ears of harvest
  Will their heads before Him wave,
Ripened by His glorious sunshine
  From the furrows of the grave.

3 Christ is risen, we are risen:
  Shed upon us heavenly grace,
Rain, and dew, and gleams of glory
  From the brightness of Thy face;
That we, with our hearts in heaven,
  Here on earth may fruitful be,
And by angel-hands be gathered,
  And be ever, Lord, with Thee.

4 Hallelujah! Hallelujah!
  Glory be to God on high;
Hallelujah! to the Saviour,
  Who has gained the victory;
Hallelujah! to the Spirit,
  Fount of love and sanctity;
Hallelujah! Hallelujah!
  To the Triune Majesty! Amen.
            Bishop C. Wordsworth. 1862.

117   8.7. 8.7. 7.8. 7.4.
*Christ being raised from
the dead, dieth no more; death hath no more
dominion over Him.*—Romans vi. 9.

CHRIST JESUS lay in death's strong
      bands
  For our offences given;
But now at God's right hand He stands,
  And brings us life from heaven;
Wherefore let us joyful be,
And sing to God right thankfully
  Loud songs of Hallelujah!
              Hallelujah!

2 It was a strange and dreadful strife,
  When Life and Death contended;
The victory remained with Life,
  The reign of Death was ended:
Stript of power, no more he reigns,
An empty form alone remains;
  His sting is lost for ever!
              Hallelujah!

3 So let us keep the festival
  Whereto the Lord invites us;
Christ is Himself the joy of all,
  The Sun that warms and lights us;
By His grace He doth impart
Eternal sunshine to the heart;
  The night of sin is ended!
              Hallelujah!

4 Then let us feast this Easter day
  On the true Bread of heaven!
The word of grace hath purged away
  The old and wicked leaven;
Christ alone our souls will feed,
He is our Meat and Drink indeed,
  Faith lives upon no other!
              Hallelujah!
              Martin Luther. 1524.
          Tr. Richard Massie. 1854.

118   7.7. 7.7.
*While He blessed them, He
was parted from them, and carried up into
heaven.*—Luke xxiv. 51.

HAIL the day that sees Him rise
  To His throne above the skies!
Christ, awhile to mortals given,
Re-ascends His native heaven.

2 There for Him high triumph waits;
Lift your heads, eternal gates!
Wide unfold the radiant scene!
Take the King of Glory in!

3 Circled round with angel powers,
Their triumphant Lord and ours,
Conqueror over death and sin,
Take the King of Glory in!

4 Him, though highest heaven receives,
Still He loves the earth He leaves;
Though returning to His throne,
Still He calls mankind His own.

5 See, He lifts His hands above!
See, He shows the prints of love!
Hark! His gracious lips bestow
Blessings on His Church below.

6 Still for us His death He pleads;
Prevalent, He intercedes;
Near Himself prepares our place,
Harbinger of human race.

7 Lord, though parted from our sight,
High above yon azure height,
Grant our hearts may thither rise,
Following Thee beyond the skies.

HIS ASCENSION.

There we shall with Thee remain,
Partners of Thine endless reign ;
There Thy face unclouded see,
Find our heaven of heavens in **Thee.**
Charles Wesley. 1739.

119   8.8.8.8.8.8.
This Man, because He continueth ever, hath an unchangeable priesthood.—Hebrews vii. 24.

ENTERED the holy place above,
  Covered with meritorious scars,
The tokens of His dying love,
  Our great High Priest in glory bears ;
He pleads His passion on the tree,
He shows Himself **to God for me.**

2 Before the throne my Saviour stands,
  My Friend and Advocate appears,
My name is graven on His hands,
  And Him the **Father always** hears ;
While low at Jesus's **cross I bow,**
He hears the **blood of sprinkling now.**

3 This instant now **I may receive**
  The answer of **His powerful prayer ;**
This instant now **by Him I live,**
  His prevalence **with God declare ;**
And soon my spirit, in His hands,
Shall stand where my Forerunner stands.
Charles Wesley. 1762.

120   7.7.7.7. D.
He was taken up ; and a cloud received Him out of their sight.—Acts. i. 9.

HE is gone—**a cloud of light**
  Has **received Him from our sight ;**
High in **heaven, where eye of men**
Follows not, **nor angels' ken ;**
Through the veils **of time and space,**
Passed into **the holiest place ;**
All the toil, **the sorrow done,**
All the battle **fought and won.**

2 He is gone—**towards** their goal,
World and Church must onward roll :
Far behind we leave the past ;
Forward are our glances cast ;
Still His words before us range
Through the ages, as they change :
Wheresoe'er the truth shall lead,
He will give whate'er we need.

3 He is gone—but we once more
Shall behold Him as before ;
In the heaven of heavens the same,
As on earth He went and came.
In the many mansions there,
Place for us He will prepare :
In that world, unseen, unknown,
He and we may yet be one.

4 He is gone—but, not in vain,
Wait, until He comes again ;
He is risen, He is not here,
Far above this earthly sphere ;
Evermore **in** heart and mind,
Where **our** peace in Him we find,
To our **own** Eternal **Friend,**
Thitherward **let us ascend.** Amen.
Arthur P. Stanley. 1859.

121   L.M.
Lift up your heads, O ye gates ; . . . and the King of Glory shall come in.—Psalm xxiv. 9.

OUR Lord is risen from the dead !
  Our Jesus is gone up on high !
The powers of hell are captive led,
  Dragged to the portals of the sky.

2 There His **triumphal chariot** waits,
  And angels **chant the** solemn lay :
Lift up your **heads, ye** heavenly gates,
  Ye everlasting **doors, give** way !

3 Loose all your bars **of** massy light,
  And wide unfold the ethereal scene ;
He claims these mansions as His right ;
  Receive the King of Glory in !

4 **Who is this King of** Glory ? Who ?
  The **Lord** that all our foes o'ercame,
The **world,** sin, death, and hell o'erthrew !
  And Jesus is the Conqueror's name.

5 Lo ! His triumphal chariot waits,
  And angels chant the solemn lay :
Lift up your heads, ye heavenly gates,
  Ye everlasting doors, give way !

6 Who is this King of Glory ? Who ?
  The Lord, of glorious power possessed ;
The King of saints, and angels too,
  God over all for ever blessed.
Wesley. 1741.

122   C.M.
I go to prepare a place for you.
John xiv. 2.

THE golden gates are lifted up,
  The doors **are** opened wide.
The King of Glory **is gone in**
  Unto His Father's **side.**

2 **Thou art gone up before us,** Lord,
  To make for us a place,
That we may be where now Thou art,
  And look upon Thy face.

3 And ever on our earthly path
  A gleam of glory lies,
A light still breaks beyond the cloud,
  That veiled Thee from our eyes.

THE LORD JESUS CHRIST.

4 Lift up our hearts, lift up our minds;
  Let Thy dear grace be given,
  That while we wander here below,
  Our treasure be in heaven.

5 That where Thou art, at God's right hand,
  Our hope, our love may be;
  Dwell Thou in us, that we may dwell
  For evermore in Thee.
  Mrs. Cecil F. Alexander. 1853.

HIS INTERCESSION AND REIGN.

123 6.6. 6.6. 8 4.
When He ascended up on high, He led captivity captive, and gave gifts unto men.—Ephesians iv. 8.

GOD is gone up on high,
  With a triumphant noise;
The clarions of the sky
  Proclaim the angelic joys!
Join all on earth, rejoice and sing,
Glory ascribe to glory's King.

2 God in the flesh below,
  For us He reigns above;
Let all the nations know
  Our Jesus' conquering love!
Join all on earth, rejoice and sing,
Glory ascribe to glory's King.

3 All power to our great Lord
  Is by the Father given;
By angel-hosts adored,
  He reigns supreme in heaven.
Join all on earth, rejoice and sing,
Glory ascribe to glory's King.

4 High on His holy seat,
  He bears the righteous sway;
His foes, beneath His feet,
  Shall sink and die away;
Join all on earth, rejoice and sing,
Glory ascribe to glory's King.

5 His foes and ours are one,
  Satan, the world, and sin;
But He shall tread them down,
  And bring His Kingdom in;
Join all on earth, rejoice and sing,
Glory ascribe to glory's King.

6 Till all the earth, renewed
  In righteousness divine,
With all the hosts of God,
  In one great chorus join,—
Join all on earth, rejoice and sing,
Glory ascribe to glory's King. Amen.
  Charles Wesley. 1746.

---

124 8.7. 8.7. 4.7.
He shall reign for ever and ever.—Rev. xi. 15.

LOOK, ye saints, the sight is glorious,
  See the Man of sorrows now,
From the fight returned victorious;
  Every knee to Him shall bow:
    Crown Him, crown Him,
  Crowns become the Victor's brow.

2 Crown the Saviour, angels, crown Him;
  Rich the trophies Jesus brings;
In the seat of power enthrone Him,
  While the vault of heaven rings:
    Crown Him, crown Him,
  Crown the Saviour, King of kings.

3 Sinners in derision crowned Him,
  Mocking thus the Saviour's claim;
Saints and angels crowd around Him,
  Own His title, praise His name:
    Crown Him, crown Him,
  Spread abroad the Victor's fame.

4 Hark! those bursts of acclamation!
  Hark! those loud triumphant chords!
Jesus takes the highest station,
  O what joy the sight affords;
    Crown Him, crown Him,
  King of kings, and Lord of lords! Amen.
    Thomas Kelly. 1809.

---

125 6.5. 6.5. D. *With Chorus.*
God also hath highly exalted Him.—Philippians ii. 9.

GOLDEN harps are sounding,
  Angel voices ring,
Pearly gates are opened—
  Opened for the King;
Jesus, King of Glory,
  Jesus, King of Love,
Is gone up in triumph
  To His throne above.
    All His work is ended,
      Joyfully we sing,
    Jesus hath ascended!
      Glory to our King!

2 He who came to save us,
  He who bled and died,
Now is crowned with glory
  At His Father's side.
Never more to suffer,
  Never more to die;
Jesus, King of Glory,
  Has gone up on high!

Praying for His ch'ldren,
  In that blessed place,
Calling them to glory,
  Sending them His grace.
His bright home preparing,
  Faithful ones, for you;
Jesus ever liveth,
  Ever loveth too.
    Frances R. Havergal. 1870

126
One is your Master, even Christ.—Matthew xxiii. 8.　C.M.

IMMORTAL Love, for ever full,
　For ever flowing free,
For ever shared, for ever whole,
　A never-ebbing sea !

2 Our outward lips confess the Name
　All other names above ;
Love only knoweth whence it came,
　And comprehendeth love.

3 Blow, winds of God, awake and blow
　The mists of earth away !
Shine out, O Light Divine, and show
　How wide and far we stray !

4 We may not climb the heavenly steeps
　To bring the Lord Christ down ;
In vain we search the lowest deeps,
　For Him no depths can drown.

5 But warm, sweet, tender, even yet
　A present help is He ;
And faith has still its Olivet,
　And love its Galilee.

6 The healing of His seamless dress
　Is by our beds of pain ;
We touch Him in life's throng and press,
　And we are whole again.

7 Through Him the first fond prayers are said
　Our lips of childhood frame ;
The last low whispers of our dead
　Are burdened with His name.

8 O Lord and Master of us all !
　Whate'er our name or sign,
We own Thy sway, we hear Thy call,
　We test our lives by Thine.
　　　　　John G. Whittier. 1847.

127
God hath made that same Jesus, whom ye have crucified, both Lord and Christ.—Acts ii. 36.　6.6. 6.6. 8.8.

REJOICE, the Lord is King !
　Your Lord and King adore,
Mortals, give thanks, and sing,
　And triumph evermore ;
Lift up your heart, lift up your voice,
Rejoice, again I say, rejoice.

2 Jesus the Saviour reigns,
　The God of truth and love ;
When He had purged our stains
　He took His seat above ;
Lift up your heart, lift up your voice,
Rejoice, again I say, rejoice.

3 His kingdom cannot fail,
　He rules o'er earth and heaven ;
The keys of death and hell
　Are to our Jesus given ;
Lift up your heart, lift up your voice,
Rejoice, again I say, rejoice.

4 He sits at God's right hand,
　Till all His foes submit,
And bow to His command,
　And fall beneath His feet ;
Lift up your heart, lift up your voice,
Rejoice, again I say, rejoice.

5 He all His foes shall quell,
　Shall all our sins destroy,
And every bosom swell
　With pure seraphic joy ;
Lift up your heart, lift up your voice,
Rejoice, again I say, rejoice.

6 Rejoice in glorious hope,
　Jesus the Judge shall come,
And take His servants up
　To their eternal home ;
We soon shall hear the archangel's voice,
The trump of God shall sound, 'Rejoice.'
　　　　　Charles Wesley. 1746.

128
On His head were many crowns.—Revelation xix. 12.　S.M.D.

CROWN Him with many crowns,
　The Lamb upon His throne :
Hark ! how the heavenly anthem drowns
　All music but its own :
Awake, my soul, and sing
　Of Him who died for thee,
And hail Him as thy matchless King
　Through all eternity.

2 Crown Him the Lord of Life,
　Who triumphed o'er the grave,
And rose victorious in the strife
　For those He came to save :
His glories now we sing,
　Who died and rose on high,
Who died eternal life to bring,
　And lives that death may die !

3 Crown Him the Lord of Peace,
　Whose power a sceptre sways
From pole to pole, that wars may cease
　And all be love and praise !
His reign shall know no end ;
　And round His pierced feet
Fair flowers of Paradise extend
　Their fragrance ever sweet.

4 Crown Him the Lord of heaven,
　Enthroned in worlds above !
Crown Him the King to whom is given
　The wondrous name of Love ;
All hail, Redeemer, hail !
　For Thou hast died for me ;
Thy praise shall never, never fail
　Throughout eternity ! Amen.
　　　　Matthew Bridges. 1852,
　　　and Godfrey Thring. 1882.

The Holy Spirit.

HIS REGENERATING AND SANCTIFYING GRACE.

129 7.7. 7.7. 7.7.
*He dwelleth with you,
and shall be in you.—John xiv. 17.*

GRACIOUS Spirit, dwell with me!
 I myself would gracious be;
And with words that help and heal,
Would Thy life in mine reveal;
And with actions bold and meek,
Would for Christ, my Saviour, speak.

2 Truthful Spirit, dwell with me!
I myself would truthful be;
And with wisdom kind and clear
Let Thy life in mine appear;
And with actions brotherly
Speak my Lord's sincerity.

3 Tender Spirit, dwell with me!
I myself would tender be;
Shut my heart up like a flower
In temptation's darksome hour;
Open it when shines the Sun,
And His love by fragrance own.

4 Silent Spirit, dwell with me!
I myself would quiet be,
Quiet as the growing blade
Which through earth its way has made;
Silently, like morning light
Putting mists and chills to flight.

5 Mighty Spirit, dwell with me!
I myself would mighty be,
Mighty, so as to prevail,
Where, unaided, man must fail,
Ever, by a mighty hope,
Pressing on and bearing up.

6 Holy Spirit, dwell with me!
I myself would holy be;
Separate from sin, I would
Choose, and cherish all things good;
And, whatever I can be,
Give to Him who gave me Thee. Amen.
T. T. Lynch. 1855.

130 S.M.
*Ye shall be baptized with
the Holy Ghost.—Acts i. 5.*

LORD God, the Holy Ghost!
 In this accepted hour,
As on the day of Pentecost,
Descend in all Thy power.

2 We meet with one accord
In this Thy holy place,
And wait the promise of our Lord,
The Spirit of all grace.

3 Like mighty rushing wind
Upon the waves beneath,
Move with one impulse every mind,
One soul, one feeling breathe.

4 The young, the old inspire
With wisdom from above,
And give us hearts and tongues of fire
To pray, and praise, and love.

5 Spirit of Light! Explore,
And chase our gloom away,
With lustre shining more and more
Unto the perfect day.

6 Spirit of Truth! Be Thou
In life and death our guide:
O Spirit of adoption! Now
May we be sanctified. Amen.
James Montgomery. 1819.

131 S.M.
*No man can say that Jesus
is the Lord, but by the Holy Ghost.*
1 Corinthians xii. 3.

SPIRIT of Faith, come down,
 Reveal the things of God,
And make to us the Godhead known,
And witness with the blood.

2 'Tis Thine the blood to apply,
And give us eyes to see;
Who did for every sinner die,
Hath surely died for me.

3 No man can truly say
That Jesus is the Lord,
Unless Thou take the veil away,
And breathe the living word.

4 Then, only then, we feel
Our interest in His blood,
And cry, with joy unspeakable,
Thou art my Lord, my God!

5 O that the world might know
The all-atoning Lamb!
Spirit of faith! Descend, and show
The virtue of His name.

6 The grace which all may find,
The saving power, impart,
And testify to all mankind,
And speak in every heart.

HIS REGENERATING AND SANCTIFYING GRACE.

7 Inspire the living faith,
   Which whosoe'er receives,
The witness in himself he hath,
   And consciously believes.

8 The faith that conquers all,
   And doth the mountain move,
And saves whoe'er on Jesus call,
   And perfects them in love. Amen.
                              Wesley. 1746.

132   L.M.
    *They were all filled with
    the Holy Ghost.—Acts ii. 4.*

COME, Holy Spirit, raise our songs,
   To reach the wonders of the day
When, with Thy fiery cloven tongues,
Thou didst those glorious scenes display.

2 O 'twas a most auspicious hour,
   Season of grace and sweet delight,
When Thou didst come with mighty power,
   And light of truth divinely bright.

3 By this the blest disciples knew
   Their risen Head had entered heaven,
Had now obtained the promise due,
   Fully by God the Father given.

4 Lord, we believe **to us** and ours
   The apostolic promise given;
We wait the Pentecostal powers,
   The Holy Ghost sent down from heaven.

5 Assembled here with **one accord,**
   Calmly we wait the **promised grace,**
The purchase of our **dying Lord;**
   Come, Holy Ghost, **and fill the place.**

6 If every one that **asks may** find,
   If still Thou dost **on** sinners fall,
Come, as a mighty rushing wind;
   Great grace be now upon us all.

7 Behold, to Thee our souls aspire,
   And languish Thy descent to meet;
Kindle in each the living fire,
   And fix in every heart Thy seat. Amen.
First three verses. R. C. Brackenbury. 1792.
    Remainder, Charles Wesley. 1742.

133   6.6. 6.6. 8.8.
    *Wait for the promise
    of the Father.—Acts i. 4.*

O LORD, with **one** accord
   We gather round Thy throne,
To hear Thy holy word,
   To worship Thee alone.
Now send from heaven **the Holy Ghost,**
Be this another Pentecost.

2 We have **no** strength to meet
   The storms that round us lower;
Keep Thou our trembling feet
   In every trying hour;
More than victorious shall we be
If girded with Thy panoply.

3 Where is the mighty wind
   That shook the holy place,
That gladdened every mind,
   And brightened every face,
And where the cloven tongues of flame
That marked each follower of the Lamb?

4 There is no change in Thee,
   Lord God the Holy Ghost,
Thy glorious majesty
   Is as at Pentecost!
O may our loosened tongues proclaim,
That Thou, our God, art still the same!

5 And may that living wave,
   That issues from on high,
Whose golden waters lave
   Thy throne eternally,
Flow down in power on us to-day,
And none shall go unblessed away! Amen.
               William Pennefather. d. 1873.

134   C.M.
   If any man have **not** *the
   Spirit of Christ, he is* **none** *of His.*
      Romans viii. 9.

SPIRIT Divine, attend our prayers,
   And make this house Thy home;
Descend with all Thy gracious powers,
   O come, great Spirit, come!

2 Come as the light, to us reveal
   Our emptiness and woe;
And lead us in those paths of life
   Where all the righteous go.

3 Come as the fire, and purge our hearts
   Like sacrificial flame;
Let our whole soul an offering be
   To our Redeemer's name.

4 Come as the dew, and sweetly bless
   This consecrated hour;
May barrenness rejoice to own
   Thy fertilizing power.

5 Come as the dove, and spread Thy wings,
   The wings of peaceful love;
And let Thy Church on earth become
   Blest as the Church above.

6 Come as the wind, **with rushing sound,**
   And pentecostal **grace;**
That all of woman **born may see**
   The glory of Thy face.

7 Spirit Divine, attend our prayers,
   Make a lost world Thy home;
Descend with all Thy gracious powers,
   O come, great Spirit, come! Amen.
                   Andrew Reed. 1841.

THE HOLY SPIRIT.

135 C.M.
And there appeared unto them cloven tongues, like as of fire, and it sat upon each of them.—Acts ii. 3.

WHEN God **of old came down from** heaven,
In power and wrath He came ;
Before His feet the clouds were **riven,**
Half **darkness** and half flame.

2 But when He came the second **time,**
He came in power and love ;
Softer than gale at morning prime
Hovered His **Holy** Dove.

3 **The** fires that rushed on Sinai down
In sudden torrents dread,
Now gently light, a glorious crown,
On every sainted head.

4 And, as on Israel's awe-struck ear
The voice exceeding loud,
The trump, that angels quake to hear,
Thrilled from the deep, dark cloud :

5 So, when the Spirit of our God
Came down His flock to find,
A voice from heaven was heard abroad,
A rushing, mighty wind.

6 It fills the Church of God ; **it** fills
The sinful world around ;
Only in stubborn hearts and wills
No place **for** it is found.

7 Come Lord ! come Wisdom, Love, and Power !
Open our ears to hear ;
Let us not miss the accepted hour ;
Save, Lord, by love or fear ! Amen.
John Keble. 1827.

136 8.8. 8.8. 8.8.
Ye are sanctified . . . by the Spirit.—1 Corinthians vi. 11.

CREATOR Spirit, by whose aid
The world's foundations first **were laid,**
Come, visit every humble mind ;
Come, pour Thy joys on all mankind
From sin and sorrow set us free,
And make Thy temples worthy Thee.

2 Thou Strength of His almighty hand,
Whose power does heaven and earth command,
Three **holy Fount,** three holy **Fire,**
Our hearts with heavenly love inspire ;
Come, and Thy sacred unction bring,
To sanctify us while we sing.

3 Plenteous of grace, descend from high,
Rich in Thy sevenfold energy ;
Give us Thyself, that we may see
The Father and the Son by Thee ;
Make us eternal truth receive,
And practise all that **we** believe.

4 Immortal honour, endless fame,
Attend the Almighty Father's name :
The Saviour Son be glorified,
Who for lost man's redemption died :
And equal adoration be,
Eternal Paraclete, to Thee ! Amen.
From the Latin. Tr. John Dryden. 1693.

137 C.M.
I will pray the Father, and He shall give you another Comforter.
John xiv. 16.

SPIRIT of Holiness, descend,
Thy people wait for Thee ;
Thine ear in kind compassion lend,
Let us Thy mercy see.

2 Behold ! **Thy weary Churches** wait
With wistful longing eyes ;
Let us no more be desolate,
O bid Thy light arise !

3 Thy light, that on our **souls hath shone,**
Leads us in hope **to** Thee ;
Let us not feel its rays alone,
Alone Thy people be.

4 O bring our dearest friends to **God,**
Remember those **we** love ;
Fit them on earth for Thine abode,
Fit them for joys above.

5 Spirit of Holiness,'tis **Thine**
To hear our feeble prayer ;
Come, for we wait Thy power divine,
Let us Thy mercy share ! Amen.
S. F. Smith. 1843.

138 7.7.7.7
When He, the Spirit of truth, is come, He will guide you into all truth.
John xvi. 13.

HOLY Spirit, Truth Divine !
Dawn upon this soul of mine ;
Word of God, and inward Light,
Wake my spirit, clear my sight.

2 Holy Spirit, Love Divine !
Glow within this heart of mine,
Kindle every high desire,
Perish self in Thy pure fire !

3 Holy Spirit, Power Divine !
Fill and nerve this will of mine ;
By Thee may I strongly live,
Bravely bear, and nobly strive !

4 Holy Spirit, Right Divine !
King, within my conscience reign ;
Be my Lord, and I shall be
Firmly bound, for ever free.

5 Holy Spirit, Peace Divine !
Still this restless heart of mine,
Speak to calm this tossing sea,
Stayed in Thy tranquillity.

HIS REGENERATING AND SANCTIFYING GRACE.

6 Holy Spirit, Joy Divine!
  Gladden Thou this heart of mine;
  In the desert ways I'll sing,
  Spring, O Well, for ever spring! Amen.
                    Samuel Longfellow. 1846.

139 C.M.
*Come from the four winds,
O breath, and breathe upon these slain, that
they may live.—Ezekiel xxxvii. 9.*

O BREATHE upon this languid frame,
  Spirit of heavenly might!
  Baptize me with the vital flame
  Of purity and light.

2 Descend like heaven's self-kindled fire
  And burn my sin to dust:
  God of my righteousness, inspire
  My soul with hope and trust.

3 Spring up within this barren heart,
  Well-spring of life divine!
  Love to my feeble will impart:
  Light out of darkness shine.

4 O Light and Power! O Life and Love!
  Of every good the source!
  Blow, rushing Wind of God, above,
  And speed me on my course.

5 Then, heavenly Master, come within,
  My every thought control;
  Thy work fulfil, the harbour win,
  Anchor, and keep my soul. Amen.
                    Josiah Conder. 1836.

140 C.M.
*How much more shall your
heavenly Father give the Holy Spirit to them
that ask Him?—Luke xi. 13.*

COME, Holy Spirit, heavenly Dove,
  With all Thy quickening powers;
  Kindle a flame of sacred love
  In these cold hearts of ours.

2 In vain we tune our formal songs,
  In vain we strive to rise,
  Hosannas languish on our tongues,
  And our devotion dies.

3 O Father, shall we ever live
  At this poor dying rate?
  Our love so faint, so cold to Thee,
  And Thine to us so great!

4 Come, Holy Spirit, heavenly Dove,
  With all Thy quickening powers;
  Come, shed abroad the Saviour's love,
  And that shall kindle ours. Amen.
                    Isaac Watts. 1709.

141 C.M.
*God hath sent the Spirit of
His Son into your hearts, crying, Abba,
Father.—Galatians iv. 6.*

WHY should the children of a King
  Go mourning all their days?
  Great Comforter, descend and bring
  The tokens of Thy grace.

2 Dost Thou not dwell in all the saints,
  And seal the heirs of heaven?
  When wilt Thou banish my complaints,
  And show my sins forgiven?

3 Assure my conscience of its part
  In the Redeemer's blood,
  And bear Thy witness with my heart,
  That I am born of God.

4 Thou art the earnest of His love,
  The pledge of joys to come:
  May Thy blest wings, celestial Dove,
  Convey me safely home. Amen.
                    Isaac Watts. 1709.

142 8.8. 8.8. 8.8.
*Ye shall receive power,
after that the Holy Ghost is come upon you.
Acts i. 8.*

COME, Holy Ghost, all-quickening fire,
  Come, and in me delight to rest,
  Drawn by the lure of strong desire,
  O come and consecrate my breast!
  The temple of my soul prepare,
  And fix Thy sacred presence there!

2 If now Thy influence I feel,
  If now in Thee begin to live,
  Still to my heart Thyself reveal,
  Give me Thyself, for ever give;
  A point my good, a drop my store,
  Eager I ask, I pant for more.

3 Eager for Thee I ask and pant;
  So strong the principle divine,
  Carries me out with sweet constraint,
  Till all my hallowed soul is Thine,
  Plunged in the Godhead's deepest sea,
  And lost in Thine immensity.

4 My peace, my life, my comfort Thou,
  My treasure, and my all Thou art;
  True witness of my sonship, now
  Engraving pardon on my heart,
  Seal of my sins in Christ forgiven,
  Earnest of love, and pledge of heaven.

5 Come, then, my God, mark out Thine heir,
  Of heaven a larger earnest give;
  With clearer light Thy witness bear,
  More sensibly within me live,
  Let all my powers Thine entrance feel,
  And deeper stamp Thyself the seal.
                                    Amen.
                    Wesley. 1739.

THE HOLY SPIRIT.

143 8.8. 8.8. 8.8.
And God said, Let there be light: and there was light.—Genesis i. 3.

EXPAND Thy wings, celestial Dove,
  And, brooding o'er my nature's night,
Call forth the ray of heavenly Love,
  Let there in my dark soul be light,
And fill th' illustrated abyss
With glorious beams of endless **bliss.**

2 'Let there be light,' again command,
  And light there in our hearts shall be;
We then through faith shall understand
  Thy great mysterious Majesty,
And, by the shining of Thy grace,
Behold in Christ Thy glorious face.

3 **Father** of everlasting grace,
  Be mindful of Thy changeless word;
We worship toward that Holy Place,
  In which Thou dost Thy name record,
Dost make Thy gracious nature known,
That living Temple of Thy Son.

4 Thou dost with sweet complacence see
  The Temple filled with light divine;
And art Thou not well pleased with me,
  Who, turning to that heavenly Shrine,
Through Jesus to Thy throne apply,
Through Jesus for acceptance cry?

5 With all who **for redemption** groan,
  Father, in Jesu's name I pray;
And still we cry and wrestle on,
  Till mercy take our sins away:
Hear from Thy dwelling-place in heaven,
And now pronounce our sins forgiven.
      Amen.
      Charles Wesley. 1762.

144 L.M.
He shall baptize you with the Holy Ghost, and with fire.—Matt. iii. 11.

FATHER, if justly still we claim
  To us and ours the promise made,
To us be graciously the same,
  And crown with living fire our head.

2 Our claim admit, and from above
  Of holiness the Spirit shower,
Of wise discernment, humble love,
  And zeal, and unity, and power.

3 The Spirit of convincing speech,
  Of power demonstrative, impart;
Such as may every conscience reach,
  And sound the unbelieving heart:

4 The Spirit of refining fire,
  Searching the inmost of the mind,
To purge all fierce and foul desire,
  And kindle life more pure and kind:

5 The Spirit of faith, in this Thy day,
  To break the power of cancelled sin,
Tread down its strength, o'erturn its sway,
  And still the conquest more than win.

6 The Spirit breathe of inward life,
  Which in our hearts Thy laws may write;
Then grief expires, and pain, and strife;
  'Tis nature all, and all delight. Amen.
    Henry More. 1668. *Alt. John Wesley.* 1761.

145 L.M.
He shall come down like rain upon the mown grass.—Psalm lxxii. 6.

ON all **the** earth Thy Spirit shower,
  The earth in righteousness renew;
Thy kingdom come, and hell's o'erpower,
  And to Thy sceptre all subdue.

2 Like mighty winds **or torrents fierce,**
  Let it opposers all o'errun;
And every law of sin reverse,
  That faith and love may make all one.

3 Yea, let **Thy** Spirit in every **place**
  Its richer energy declare;
While lovely tempers, fruits of grace,
  The kingdom of Thy Christ prepare.

4 Grant this, O holy God **and** true!
  The ancient seers Thou didst inspire;
To us perform the promise due,
  Descend, and crown us now with fire!
      Amen.
    Henry More. 1668. *Alt. John Wesley.* 1761.

146 8.8.8.8. **8.8.**
God hath . . . given us the spirit of power, of love, and of a sound mind.—2 Timothy i. 7.

I WANT **the** Spirit of power within,
  Of love, and of a healthful mind;
Of power, to conquer inbred sin;
  Of love, to Thee and all mankind;
Of health, that pain and death defies,
Most vigorous when the body dies.

2 When shall I hear **the** inward voice,
  Which only faithful souls can hear?
Pardon, and peace, **and** heavenly joys,
  Attend the promised Comforter;
O come, and righteousness divine,
And Christ, and all with Christ, are mine.

3 O that **the Comforter** would come,
  Nor **visit us** a transient guest,
But fix **in me** His constant home,
  And take possession of my breast,
And fix in me His loved abode,
The temple of indwelling God.

4 Come, Holy Ghost, my heart inspire;
  Attest that I am born again;
Come, and baptize me now with fire,
  Nor let Thy former gifts be vain:
I cannot rest in sins forgiven;
Where is the earnest of my heaven?

HIS WORK AS TEACHER AND COMFORTER.

5 Where the indubitable seal
   That ascertains the kingdom mine?
The powerful stamp I long to feel,
   The signature of love divine;
O shed it in my heart abroad,
   Fulness of love, of heaven, of God. Amen.
                               Charles Wesley. 1740.

147   S.M.
O Lord, revive Thy work.
Habakkuk iii. 2.

REVIVE Thy work, O Lord,
   Thy mighty arm make bare;
Speak with the voice that wakes the dead,
   And make **Thy** people hear.

2 Revive Thy work, O Lord,
   Disturb this sleep of death;
Quicken the smouldering embers now,
   By Thine almighty breath.

3 Revive Thy work, **O** Lord,
   Create soul-thirst for Thee;
And hungering for the Bread of Life,
   O may **our** spirits be.

4 Revive Thy work, O Lord,
   Exalt Thy precious name;
And, by the Holy Ghost, our love
   For Thee and Thine inflame.

5 Revive Thy work, O Lord,
   And give refreshing showers;
The glory shall be all Thine own,
   The blessing, Lord, be ours. Amen.
                       Albert Midlane. 1861.

HIS WORK AS TEACHER AND COMFORTER.

148   8.7.8.7. D.
Likewise the Spirit also helpeth
our infirmities.—Romans viii. 26.

COME, Thou all-inspiring Spirit,
   Into every longing heart;
Bought for us by Jesu's merit,
   Now Thy blissful self impart:
Sign our uncontested pardon,
   Wash us in the atoning blood;
Make our hearts a watered garden,
   Fill our spotless souls with God.

2 If Thou gav'st the enlarged desire
   Which for Thee we ever feel,
Now our panting souls inspire,
   Now our cancelled sin reveal:
Claim us for Thy habitation,
   Dwell within our hallowed breast;
Seal us heirs of full salvation,
   Fitted for our heavenly rest.

3 Give us quietly to tarry,
   Till for all Thy glory meet,
Waiting, like attentive Mary,
   Happy at the Saviour's feet:
Keep us from the world unspotted,
   From all earthly passions free,
Wholly to Thyself devoted,
   Fixed to live and die for Thee.

4 Wrestling on in mighty prayer,
   Lord, we will not let Thee go,
Till Thou all Thy mind declare,
   All Thy grace **on us** bestow:
Peace, the seal **of** sin forgiven,
   Joy, and perfect love, impart,
Present, everlasting heaven,
   All Thou hast, and all Thou art. Amen.
                       Charles Wesley. 1767.

149   6.6.4. 6.6.6.4.
Wait for **the** *promise of the*
Father.—Acts i. 4.

COME, **Holy** Ghost, in **love,**
   Shed on us from above
Thine own bright ray;
Divinely good Thou art,
Thy sacred gifts impart
To gladden each sad heart;
   O come to-day.

2 Come, tenderest **Friend,** and best,
   Our most delightful **Guest,**
      With soothing power;
Rest which **the** weary know,
Shade 'mid **the** noontide-glow,
Peace when deep griefs o'erflow;
   Cheer us this hour.

3 Come, Light serene **and still,**
   Our inmost bosoms **fill,**
      Dwell in each breast;
We know no dawn but Thine,
Send forth Thy **beams** divine,
On our dark souls to shine,
   And make **us** blest.

4 Exalt our low **desires.**
   Extinguish passion's **fires,**
      Heal every **wound;**
Our stubborn **spirits bend,**
Our icy coldness end,
Our devious steps attend,
   While heavenward bound.

5 Come, **all the faithful** bless;
   Let all who Christ confess
      His praise employ;
Give virtue's rich reward,
Victorious death accord,
And with our glorious Lord
   Eternal joy. Amen.
King Robert II. of France, 11th Century.
                   Tr. Ray Palmer. 1865.

THE HOLY SPIRIT.

150 8.7.8.7.
He shall glorify Me.
John xvi. 14.

COME, Thou everlasting Spirit,
  Bring to every thankful mind
All the Saviour's dying merit,
  All His sufferings for mankind.

2 True Recorder of His passion,
  Now the living faith impart,
Now reveal His great salvation,
  Preach His gospel to **our** heart.

3 Come, Thou witness of His dying,
  Come, Remembrancer divine;
Let us feel Thy power applying
  Christ to every soul—and mine.

4 Let us groan **Thine inward groaning**,
  Look on Him we pierced, and grieve;
All receive **the grace atoning**,
  All the **sprinkled blood receive.** Amen.
            Wesley. 1745.

151 8.7.8.7.
*Singing with grace in your
hearts to the Lord.*—Col. iii. 16.

HOLY Ghost, inspire our praises,
  Shed abroad a Saviour's love;
While we chant the **name of Jesus**,
  Deign on every heart to **move.**

2 Source of sweetest consolation,
  Breathe Thy peace on all below,
Bless, O bless this congregation,
  Bid our hearts with fervour glow.

3 Hail, ye spirits, bright and glorious,
  High exalted round the throne;
Now with you we join in chorus,
  And **your** Lord **we** call our own.

4 God to **us** His Son hath given;
  Saints, your noble anthems raise;
All on earth, and all in heaven,
  Shout the great Jehovah's praise.
                        Amen.
            Joseph Hart. 1759.

152 L.M.
*The Spirit also helpeth our
infirmities.*—Romans viii. 26.

COME, Holy Spirit, calm our minds,
  And fit us to approach our God;
Remove each vain, each worldly thought,
  And lead us to Thy blest abode.

2 Hast Thou imparted to our souls
  A living spark of heavenly fire?
O, kindle now the sacred flame,
  And make us burn with pure desire!

3 Impress upon our wandering hearts
  The love that Christ to sinners bore;
And give a new, a contrite heart,
  A heart the Saviour to adore.

4 A brighter faith and hope impart,
  And let us now Thy glory see;
O, soothe and cheer each burdened heart,
  And bid our spirits rest in Thee. Amen.
            John Stewart. 1835.

153 C.M.
*When the Comforter is come,
… He shall testify of Me.*—John xv. 26.

COME, Holy Ghost, **our hearts** inspire,
  Let us Thine influence prove;
Source of the old prophetic fire,
  Fountain of Light and Love.

2 Come, Holy Ghost, for moved by Thee
  The prophets wrote and spoke;
Unlock the Truth, Thyself the Key,
  Unseal the sacred Book.

3 Expand Thy wings, celestial Dove,
  Brood o'er our nature's night;
On our disordered spirits move,
  And let there now be light.

4 God, through Himself, we then shall know,
  If Thou within us shine;
And sound, with all Thy saints below,
  The depths of love divine. Amen.
            Wesley. 1740.

154 L.M.
*He shall give you another
Comforter, that He may abide with you for
ever.*—John xiv. 16.

JESUS, we on the words depend,
  Spoken by Thee while present here,
'The Father in My name shall send
  The Holy Ghost, the Comforter.'

2 That promise made **to** Adam's race,
  Now, Lord, in us, even us, fulfil,
And give the Spirit of Thy grace,
  To teach us all Thy perfect will:

3 That heavenly Teacher of mankind,
  That Guide infallible impart,
To bring Thy sayings to our mind,
  And write them on our faithful heart.

4 He only can the words apply,
  Through which we endless life possess,
And deal to each His legacy,
  Our Lord's unutterable peace.

5 That peace of God, that peace of Thine,
  O might He now to us bring in,
And fill our souls with power divine,
  And make an end of fear and sin.

44

HIS WORK AS TEACHER AND COMFORTER.

6 The length and breadth of love reveal,
   The height and depth of Deity;
   And all the sons of glory seal,
   And change and make us all like Thee.
                              Amen.
                    Wesley. 1746.

155 *The eternal Spirit.*—Heb. ix. 14.   C.M.

ETERNAL Spirit, by whose power
   Are burst the bands of death,
On our cold hearts Thy blessings shower,
Revive them with Thy breath.

2 Tis Thine to point the heavenly way,
   Each rising fear control,
   And, with a warm, enlivening ray,
   To melt the icy soul.

3 Tis Thine to cheer us when distressed,
   To raise us when we fall,
   To calm the doubting, troubled breast,
   And aid when sinners call.

4 Tis Thine to bring God's sacred word,
   And write it in each heart;
   There its reviving truths record,
   And there its peace impart.

5 Almighty Spirit, visit thus
   Our hearts, and guide our ways;
   Pour down Thy quickening grace on us,
   And tune our lips to praise. Amen.
                    W. H. Bathurst. 1831.

156 *Ye are the temple of God,*   S.M.
and the ... Spirit of God dwelleth in you.
1 Corinthians iii. 16.

HOW shall the mighty God,
   Whom heaven cannot contain,
A temple and a fit abode
Within me ever gain?

2 Come, Spirit of the Lord;
   Teacher and Heavenly Guide;
   Be it according to Thy word,
   In my poor heart reside.

3 Enter, O Holy Ghost!
   Pervade this soul of mine,
   In me renew Thy Pentecost,
   Reveal Thy power divine.

4 Make it my highest bliss
   Thy blessed fruit to bear,
   Thy joy, love, peace, and gentleness,
   Goodness and faith to share.

5 Let me in deepest fear
   Thy holiness to grieve,
   Walk in the Spirit, even here
   And in the Spirit live.

6 Now let me live in Thee
   My inner life of love;
   So best shall I preparing be
   For perfect life above. Amen.
                    George Rawson. 1876.

157 6.5. 6.5. D. With Chorus.
I will pour out My Spirit
upon all flesh.—Joel ii. 28.

HEAR us, Thou that broodest
   O'er the watery deep,
Waking all creation
From its primal sleep;
Holy Spirit, breathing
Breath of life divine,
Breathe into our spirits,
Blending them with Thine.

   Light and life immortal!
   Hear us as we raise
   Hearts, as well as voices,
   Mingling prayer and praise.

2 When the sun ariseth
   In a cloudless sky,
   May we feel Thy presence,
   Holy Spirit, nigh;
   Shed Thy radiance o'er us,
   Keep it cloudless still,
   Through the day before us,
   Perfecting Thy will.

3 When the fight is fiercest
   In the noontide heat,
   Bear us, Holy Spirit,
   To our Saviour's feet,
   There to find a refuge
   Till our work is done,
   There to fight the battle
   Till the battle's won.

4 If the day be falling
   Sadly as it goes,
   Slowly in its sadness
   Sinking to its close,
   May Thy love in mercy
   Kindling, ere it die,
   Cast a ray of glory
   O'er our evening sky.

5 Morning, noon, and evening,
   Whensoe'er it be,
   Grant us, gracious Spirit,
   Quickening life in Thee;
   Life, that gives us, living,
   Life of heavenly love,
   Life, that brings us, dying,
   Life from heaven above. Amen.
                    Godfrey Thring. 1882.

158 7.7. 7.5.
Made partakers of the Holy
Ghost.—Heb. vi. 4.

COME to our poor nature's night,
   With Thy blessed inward light,
Holy Ghost, the Infinite,
Comforter Divine.

THE HOLY TRINITY.

2 We are sinful—cleanse us, Lord,
  Sick and faint—Thy strength afford,
  Lost—until by Thee restored,
    Comforter Divine.

3 Orphans are our souls, **and poor,**
  Give us from Thy heavenly store
  Faith, love, joy, for evermore,
    Comforter Divine.

4 Like the dew Thy peace distil,
  Guide, subdue our wayward will,
  Things of Christ unfolding still,
    Comforter Divine.

5 Gentle, awful, holy Guest,
  Make Thy temple in each breast;
  There Thy presence be confessed,
    Comforter Divine.

6 With us, **for** us, intercede,
  And with voiceless groanings **plead**
  Our unutterable need,
    Comforter Divine.

7 In **us** Abba, Father, **cry**;
  Earnest of the bliss on **high,**
  Seal of immortality,
    Comforter Divine.

8 Search for us the depths of God;
  Upwards, by the starry road,
  Bear us to Thy high abode,
    Comforter Divine.   Amen.
            George Rawson.   1853.

159   8.6.8.4.
*The Comforter, which is
the Holy Ghost.*—John **xiv. 26.**

OUR blest Redeemer, ere He **breathed**
  His tender last farewell,
A Guide, **a** Comforter bequeathed
  With **us to** dwell,

2 He came in semblance of a dove,
  With sheltering wings outspread
  The holy balm of peace and love
    On each to shed.

3 He came in tongues of living flame
    To **teach, convince,** subdue;
  All-powerful as the wind He came—
    As viewless too.

4 He came **sweet** influence to impart,
    A gracious, willing Guest,
  While He can find one humble heart
    Wherein to rest.

5 And His that gentle voice we hear,
    Soft as the breath of even,
  That checks each fault, that calms **each
    fear,**
  And speaks of heaven.

6 And every virtue we possess,
    And every conquest won,
  And every thought of holiness,
    Are His alone.

7 Spirit of purity and grace,
    Our weakness, pitying, see;
  O make our hearts Thy dwelling-place,
    And worthier Thee.

8 O praise the Father; praise **the Son**
    Blest Spirit, praise **to** Thee;
  All praise to God, the Three in One,
    The One in Three.   Amen.
            Harriet Auber.   1829.

The Holy Trinity.

160   11.12. **12.10.**
*Holy, holy, ho'y, Lord God
Almighty.*—Rev. **iv. 8.**

HOLY, Holy, Holy, Lord God Almighty;
  Gratefully adoring, our song shall
      rise to Thee;
Holy, Holy, Holy, merciful and mighty,
God in Three Persons, Blessed Trinity:

Holy, Holy, Holy, all the saints adore Thee,
Casting down their golden crowns around
    the glassy sea;
Cherubim and seraphim falling down
    before Thee,
Which wert, and art, and evermore shalt
    be.

3 Holy, Holy, Holy, though the darkness
    hide Thee,
  Though the eye of sinful man Thy glory
    may not see;
  Only Thou art holy, **there** is none beside
    Thee,
  Perfect **in power, in love,** and purity.

4 Holy, Holy, Holy, Lord God Almighty!
  All Thy works shall praise Thy name in
    earth and sky and sea;
  Holy, Holy, Holy, merciful and mighty,
  God in Three Persons, Blessed Trinity.
                Amen.
            Bishop R. Heber.   1827.

THE HOLY TRINITY.

161 *Glory to God in the highest.* 7.7. 7.7.
Luke ii. 14.

GLORY be to God on high,
   God whose glory fills the sky ;
Peace on earth to man forgiven,
Man, the well-beloved of heaven.

2 Sovereign **Father**, Heavenly King !
Thee we now presume to sing ;
Glad, Thine attributes confess,
Glorious all, and numberless.

3 Hail, by all Thy works adored :
Hail, the everlasting Lord !
Thee, with thankful hearts, we prove
God of power, and God of love.

4 Christ our Lord and God we own,
Christ, the Father's only Son,
Lamb of God for sinners slain,
Saviour of offending man.

5 Bow Thine ear, in mercy bow,
Hear, the world's Atonement, Thou :
Jesus, in Thy name we pray,
Take, O take our sins away.

6 Powerful Advocate with **God**,
Justify **us** by Thy blood ;
Bow Thine ear, in mercy bow,
Hear, the world's **Atonement, Thou.**

7 **Hear, for Thou**, O Christ, alone
Art with Thy great Father one ;
One the Holy Ghost with Thee ;
One supreme, eternal Three. Amen.
                      Wesley. 1739.

162 *Thou art worthy, O Lord,* C.M.
to receive glory and honour and power.
Revelation iv. 11.

A THOUSAND oracles divine
   Their common beams unite,
That sinners may with angels join
To worship God aright :

2 To praise a Trinity adored
By all the hosts above ;
And one thrice-holy God and Lord
Through endless ages Love.

3 Triumphant host ! They never cease
To laud and magnify
The Triune God of Holiness
Whose glory fills the sky :

4 Whose glory to this earth extends,
When God Himself imparts,
And the whole Trinity descends
Into our faithful hearts.

5 By faith the upper **choir we meet,**
And challenge them to sing
Jehovah, on His shining seat,
Our Maker and our King.

6 But God made flesh is wholly ours,
And asks our nobler strain ;
The Father of celestial powers,
The Friend of earth-born man.

7 Ye seraphs, nearest **to the throne**,
With rapturous amaze,
On us, poor ransomed souls, look down
For Heaven's superior praise.

8 The King, whose glorious face **ye see**,
For us His crown resigned ;
That fulness of the Deity,
He died for all mankind !
                Charles Wesley. 1767.

163 *The Lord make His face to* C.M.
shine upon thee, and be gracious unto thee.
Numbers vi. 25.

COME, Father, Son, and Holy Ghost,
   One God in Persons Three,
Bring back the heavenly blessing, lost
By all mankind and me.

2 Thy favour and Thy nature **too**,
To me, to all restore ;
Forgive, and after God **renew**,
And keep us evermore.

3 Eternal Son of **Righteousness**,
Display Thy beams divine,
And cause the glories of Thy face
Upon my heart to shine.

4 Light in Thy light O may I see,
Thy grace and mercy prove,
Revived, and cheered, and blessed by Thee,
The God of pardoning love.

5 Lift up Thy countenance serene,
And let Thy happy child
Behold, without a cloud between,
The Godhead reconciled.

6 That all-comprising peace bestow
On hue, through grace forgiven ;
The joys of holiness below,
And then the joys of heaven. Amen.
                Charles Wesley. 1762.

164 *When ye pray, say, Our* C.M.
Father which art in heaven.—Luke xi. 2.

FATHER of me, and all mankind,
   And all the hosts above,
Let every understanding mind
Unite to praise Thy love :

2 To know Thy nature, and Thy name,
One God in Persons Three ;
And glorify the great I AM,
Through all eternity.

THE HOLY TRINITY.

3 Thy kingdom come, with power and grace,
 To every heart of man;
 Thy peace, and joy, and righteousness,
 In all our bosoms reign.

4 The righteousness that never ends,
 But makes an end of sin,
 The joy that human thought transcends,
 Into our souls bring in;

5 The kingdom of established peace,
 Which can no more remove;
 The perfect power of Godliness,
 The omnipotence of Love. Amen.
 Wesley. 1762.

165 *Who is like Thee, glorious in holiness, fearful in praises, doing wonders?*—Exodus xv. 11. C.M.

HAIL; Father, Son, and Holy Ghost,
 One God in Persons Three;
 Of Thee we make our joyful boast,
 Our songs we make of Thee.

2 Thou neither canst be felt nor seen,
 Thou art a Spirit pure;
 Thou from eternity hast been,
 And always shalt endure.

3 Present alike in every place,
 Thy Godhead we adore;
 Beyond the bounds of time and space,
 Thou dwell'st for evermore.

4 In wisdom infinite Thou **art,**
 Thine eye doth all things see,
 And every thought of every heart
 Is only known to Thee.

5 Whate'er Thou **wilt, in earth below**
 Thou dost, in **heaven** above;
 But chiefly we rejoice to know
 The almighty God of Love.

6 Thou lov'st whate'er Thy hands have made;
 Thy goodness we rehearse,
 In shining characters displayed
 Throughout our universe.

7 Mercy, with love, and endless grace,
 O'er all Thy works doth reign;
 But most Thou dost delight to bless
 Thy favourite creature Man.

8 Wherefore, let every creature give
 To Thee the praise designed;
 But chiefly, Lord, the thanks receive,
 The hearts of all mankind. Amen.
 Charles Wesley. 1763.

166 *Holy, holy, holy, is the Lord of Hosts.*—Isaiah vi. 3. 8.8. 8.8. 8.8.

INFINITE God, to Thee we raise
 Our hearts in solemn songs of praise;
 By all Thy works on earth adored,
 We worship Thee, the common Lord,
 The everlasting Father own,
 And bow our souls before Thy throne.

2 Thee all the choir of angels sings,
 The Lord of hosts, the King of kings;
 Cherubs proclaim Thy praise aloud,
 And seraphs shout the Triune God,
 And, 'Holy, Holy, Holy,' cry,
 'Thy glory fills both earth and sky!'

3 God of the patriarchal race,
 The ancient seers record Thy praise;
 The goodly apostolic band,
 In highest joy and glory stand;
 And all the saints and prophets join
 To extol the Majesty Divine.

4 Head of the martyrs' noble host,
 Of Thee they justly make their boast;
 The Church, to earth's remotest bounds,
 Her heavenly Founder's praise resounds,
 And strives, with those around Thy throne,
 To hymn the mystic Three in One.

5 Father of endless majesty,
 All might and love they render Thee;
 Thy true and only Son adore,
 The same in dignity and power;
 And God the Holy Ghost declare,
 The saints' eternal Comforter.
 Te Deum. From the Latin.
 Tr. Wesley. 1747.

167 *The whole earth is full of His glory.*—Isaiah vi. 3. 8.8. 8.8. 8.8.

MESSIAH, joy of every heart,
 Thou, Thou the King of glory art;
 The Father's everlasting Son,
 Thee, Thee we most delight to own;
 For all our hopes on Thee depend,
 Whose glorious mercies never end.

2 Bent to redeem a sinful race,
 Thou, Lord, with unexampled grace,
 Into a lower world didst come,
 And stoop to a poor virgin's womb;
 Whom all the heavens cannot contain,
 Our God, appeared a child of man!

3 When Thou hadst rendered up Thy breath,
 And dying drawn the sting of death,
 Thou didst from earth triumphant rise,
 And ope the portals of the skies,
 That all who trust in Thee alone,
 Might follow and partake Thy throne.

THE HOLY TRINITY.

4 Seated at God's right hand again,
Thou dost in all His glory reign;
Thou dost, Thy Father's image, shine
In all the attributes Divine;
And Thou in vengeance clad shalt come,
To seal our everlasting doom.

5 Wherefore we **now** for mercy pray;
O Saviour, take our sins away!
Before Thou as our Judge appear,
In dreadful majesty severe,
Appear, our Advocate with God,
And save the purchase of Thy blood.

6 Hallow, and make Thy servants meet,
And with Thy saints in glory seat;
Sustain and bless us by Thy sway,
And keep to that tremendous day,
When all Thy Church shall chant above
The **new** eternal **song of love.** Amen.

Te Deum. From the Latin.
Tr. Wesley. 1747.

168 8.8. 8.8. 8.8.
That they may behold My glory.—John xvii. 24.

SAVIOUR, we now rejoice in hope
That Thou at last wilt take us up;
With daily triumph **we** proclaim,
And bless and magnify Thy name;
And wait Thy greatness to adore
When time and death shall be no more.

2 Till then **with** us vouchsafe **to** stay,
And keep us pure from sin to-day;
Thy great confirming grace bestow,
And guard us all our days below;
And ever nightly defend,
And save, O save us, **to** the **end.**

3 Still let us, **Lord,** with grace be blest,
Who in Thy guardian mercy rest;
Extend Thy mercy's arms to me,
The weakest soul that trusts in Thee;
And never let me lose Thy love,
Till I, even I, am crowned above. Amen.

Te Deum. From the Latin.
Tr. Wesley. 1747.

169 6.6. 6.6. 8.8.
Both young men and maidens; old men and children; let them praise the name of the Lord.—Psalm cxlviii. 12, 13.

YOUNG men and maidens, raise
Your tuneful voices high;
Old men and children, praise
The Lord of earth and sky:
Him Three in One, and One in Three,
Extol to all eternity.

2 The universal King
Let all the world proclaim;
Let every creature sing
His attributes and name;
Him Three in One, and One in Three,
Extol to all eternity.

3 In His great name alone
All excellences meet,
Who sits upon the throne,
And shall for ever sit;
Him Three in One, and **One in Three,**
Extol to all eternity.

4 **Glory to God belongs;**
Glory to God be given,
Above the noblest songs
Of all in earth or heaven:
Him Three in One, and One in Three,
Extol to all eternity. Amen.

Charles Wesley. 1762.

170 8.5. 8.5. 8.4. 3.
Thou hast created all things, and for Thy pleasure they are and were created.—Revelation iv. 11.

ANGEL voices **ever** singing
Round Thy throne of light,
Angel harps for ever ringing,
Rest not day **nor** night:
Thousands only **live** to bless Thee,
And confess Thee,
Lord of might!

2 **Thou, who art beyond the farthest**
Mortal eye can scan,
Can it be that Thou regardest
Songs of sinful man?
Can we know that Thou art near us,
And wilt hear us?
Yea, we can.

3 Yea, we know that Thou rejoicest
O'er each work of Thine;
Thou didst ears, and hands, and voices,
For Thy praise design;
Craftsman's art and music's measure
For Thy **pleasure**
All combine.

4 In Thy house, great God, we offer
Of Thine own to Thee,
And for Thine acceptance proffer
All unworthily,
Hearts, and minds, and hands, and voices,
In our choicest
Psalmody.

5 Honour, glory, might, **and merit,**
Thine shall ever be,
Father, Son, and Holy Spirit,
Blessed Trinity:
Of the best that Thou hast given,
Earth and heaven
Render Thee! Amen.

Francis Pott. 1861.

Divine Worship.

PRAISE AND PRAYER.

171 L.M.
Know ye that the Lord He is God.—Psalm c. 3.

BEFORE Jehovah's awful throne,
 Ye nations, bow with sacred joy
Know that the Lord is God alone,
 He can create, and He destroy.

2 His sovereign power, without our aid,
 Made us of clay, and formed us men;
And when like wandering sheep we strayed,
 He brought us to His fold again.

3 We'll crowd Thy gates with thankful songs,
 High as the heavens our voices raise;
And earth, with her ten thousand tongues,
 Shall fill Thy courts with sounding praise.

4 Wide as the world is Thy command;
 Vast as eternity Thy love;
Firm as a rock Thy truth shall stand,
 When rolling years shall cease to move.
   Isaac Watts. 1719.
   Alt. J. Wesley. 1741.

172 L.M.
Make a joyful noise unto the Lord, all ye lands.—Psalm c. 1.

ALL people that on earth do dwell,
 Sing to the Lord with cheerful voice;
Him serve with mirth, His praise forth tell,
 Come ye before Him and rejoice.

2 Know that the Lord is God indeed;
 Without our aid He did us make;
We are His flock, He doth us feed,
 And for His sheep He doth us take.

3 O enter, then, His gates with praise,
 Approach with joy His courts unto;
Praise, laud, and bless His name always,
 For it is seemly so to do.

4 For why? The Lord our God is good,
 His mercy is for ever sure;
His truth at all times firmly stood,
 And shall from age to age endure.
   William Keth. 1561.

173 8.8. 8.8. 8.8.
Surely the Lord is in this place.—Genesis xxviii. 16.

LO! God is here, let us adore,
 And own how dreadful is this place!
Let all within us feel His power,
 And silent bow before His face;
Who know His power, His grace who prove,
Serve Him with awe, with reverence love.

2 Lo! God is here! Him day and night
 The united choirs of angels sing;
To Him, enthroned above all height,
 Heaven's host their noblest praises bring;
Disdain not, Lord, our meaner song,
Who praise Thee with a stammering tongue.

3 Gladly the toys of earth we leave,
 Wealth, pleasure, fame, for Thee alone;
To Thee our will, soul, flesh, we give;
 O take, O seal them for Thine own!
Thou art the God, Thou art the Lord;
Be Thou by all Thy works adored.

4 Being of beings! May our praise
 Thy courts with grateful fragrance fill,
Still may we stand before Thy face,
 Still hear and do Thy sovereign will;
To Thee may all our thoughts arise,
Ceaseless, accepted sacrifice.

5 As flowers their opening leaves display,
 And glad drink in the solar fire,
So may we catch Thy every ray,
 So may Thy influence thus inspire;
Thou Beam of the eternal Beam,
Thou purging Fire, Thou quickening Flame. Amen.
   Gerhardt Tersteegen. 1731.
    Tr. J. Wesley. 1739.

174 7.7. 7.7. 7.7.
All Thy works shall praise Thee, O Lord, and Thy saints shall bless Thee.—Psalm cxlv. 10.

ALL things praise Thee, Lord most high;
 Heaven and earth and sea and sky,
All were for Thy glory made,
That Thy greatness thus displayed
Should all worship bring to Thee;
All things praise Thee: Lord, may we.

PRAISE AND PRAYER.

2 All things praise Thee ; night to **night**
Sings in silent hymns of light ;
All things praise Thee ; day to day
Chants Thy power, in burning ray ;
Time and space are praising Thee,
All things praise Thee Lord, may wo.

3 All things praise **Thee** ; round her zones
Earth, with her ten thousand tones,
Rolls a ceaseless choral strain ;
Roaring wind and deep-voiced main,
Rustling leaf and humming bee,
All things praise Thee ; Lord, may we.

4 All things praise Thee ; high and low,
Rain and dew and seven-hued bow,
Crimson sunset, fleecy cloud,
Rippling stream and tempest **loud ;**
Summer, winter, all to Thee
Glory render ; Lord, may we.

5 **All things praise Thee; Heaven's high**
shrine
Rings with melody divine ;
Lowly bending at Thy feet,
Seraph and archangel meet ;
This their highest bliss to be
Ever praising : Lord, may we.

6 All things praise Thee ; Gracious Lord,
Great Creator, Powerful Word,
Omnipresent Spirit, now
At Thy feet we humbly bow,
Lift our hearts in praise to Thee ;
All things praise Thee : Lord, may we.
     G. W. Conder. d. 1874.

175   *Praise waiteth for Thee,*   L.M.
   O God, in Zion.—Psalm lxv. 1.

PRAISE, Lord, for Thee in Zion waits :
  Prayer shall besiege Thy temple-gates ;
All flesh shall to Thy throne repair,
And find, through Christ, salvation there.

2 Our spirits faint ; our sins prevail ;
Leave not our trembling hearts to fail ;
O Thou, that hearest prayer, descend,
And still be found the sinner's Friend.

3 How blest Thy saints, how safely led,
How surely kept, how richly fed !
Saviour of all in earth and sea,
How **happy** they who rest in Thee !

4 **Thy hand sets fast the mighty** hills,
Thy voice the troubled ocean stills ;
Evening and morning hymn Thy praise,
And earth Thy bounty wide displays.

5 The year is with Thy goodness crowned ;
Thy clouds drop wealth the world around ;
Through Thee the deserts laugh and sing,
And nature smiles, and owns her King.

6 Lord, on our souls Thine influence pour,
The moral waste within restore ;
O let Thy love our spring-tide be,
And make us all bear fruit to Thee. **Amen.**
     H. F. Lyte. 1834.

176   7.7.7.7.
  O give thanks unto the Lord ;
for He is good : for His mercy endureth for
   ever.—Psalm cxxxvi. 1.

LET us, with **a gladsome mind,**
  Praise the Lord, for He is kind ;
For His mercies **shall endure,**
Ever faithful, **ever sure.**

2 Let us sound His name abroad,
For of gods He is the God ;
For His mercies shall endure,
Ever faithful, ever sure.

3 He, with all-commanding might,
Filled the new-made world with light ;
For His mercies shall endure,
Ever faithful, ever sure.

4 He the golden-tressed sun
Caused all day his course to run ;
For His mercies shall endure,
Ever faithful, ever sure ;

5 And **the moon** to shine by night
'Mong her spangled sisters bright ;
For His mercies shall endure,
Ever faithful, **ever sure.**

6 He His chosen race did b'ess,
In the wasteful wilderness ;
For His mercies shall endure,
Ever faithful, ever sure.

7 He hath, with a piteous eye,
Looked upon our misery ;
For His mercies shall endure,
Ever faithful, ever sure.

8 All things living He doth feed,
His full hand supplies their need ;
For His mercies shall endure,
Ever faithful, ever sure.

9 Let us, then, with gladsome mind,
Praise the Lord, for He is kind ;
For His mercies shall endure,
Ever faithful, ever sure.
     John Milton. 1623.

177   8.8.8. 8.8.8.
  I will sing praises unto my
God while I have any being.—Psalm cxlvi. 2.

I'LL praise my Maker while I've breath ;
  And when my voice is lost in death,
Praise shall employ my nobler powers ;
My days of praise shall ne'er be past,
While life, and thought, and being last,
Or immortality endures.

DIVINE WORSHIP.

2 Happy the man whose hopes rely
 On Israel's God; He made the sky,
  And earth, and seas, with all their train;
 His truth for ever stands secure;
 He saves the oppressed, He feeds the poor,
  And none shall find His promise vain.

3 The Lord pours eyesight on the blind;
 The Lord supports the fainting mind;
  He sends the labouring conscience peace;
 He helps the stranger in distress,
 The widow, and the fatherless,
  And grants the prisoner sweet release.

4 I'll praise Him while He lends me breath;
 And when my voice is lost in death,
  Praise shall employ my nobler powers;
 My days of praise shall ne'er be past,
 While life, and thought, and being last,
  Or immortality endures. Amen.
      Isaac Watts. 1719.

178 8.8.8.4.
He that hath pity upon the poor lendeth unto the Lord.
Proverbs xix. 17.

O LORD of heaven and earth and sea,
 To Thee all praise and glory be;
How shall we show our love to Thee,
 Giver of all?

2 The golden sunshine, vernal air,
 Sweet flowers and fruits Thy love declare,
Where harvests ripen Thou art there,
 Giver of all!

3 For peaceful homes and healthful days,
 For all the blessings earth displays,
We owe Thee thankfulness and praise,
 Giver of all.

4 Thou didst not spare Thine only Son,
 But gav'st Him for a world undone,
And e'en that gift Thou dost outrun,
 And give us all.

5 Thou giv'st the Spirit's blessed dower,
 Spirit of life and love and power,
And dost His sevenfold graces shower
 Upon us all.

6 For souls redeemed, for sins forgiven,
 For means of grace and hopes of heaven,
Father, what can to Thee be given,
 Who givest all?

7 We lose what on ourselves we spend,
 We have as treasure without end
Whatever, Lord, to Thee we lend,
 Who givest all.

8 Whatever, Lord, we lend to Thee,
 Repaid a thousandfold will be;
Then gladly will we give to Thee,
 Giver of all:

9 To Thee, from whom we all derive
 Our life, our gifts, our power to give;
O, may we ever with Thee live,
 Giver of all!
      Bishop C. Wordsworth. 1862.

179 C.M.
I heard the voice of many angels, ... saying, ... Worthy is the Lamb that was slain.—Revelation v. 11, 12.

COME, let us join our cheerful songs
 With angels round the throne;
Ten thousand thousand are their tongues,
 But all their joys are one.

2 'Worthy the Lamb that died,' they cry,
 'To be exalted thus:'
'Worthy the Lamb!' our hearts reply,
 'For He was slain for us.'

3 Jesus is worthy to receive
 Honour and power divine;
And blessings, more than we can give,
 Be, Lord, for ever Thine!

4 The whole creation join in one,
 To bless the sacred name
Of Him that sits upon the throne,
 And to adore the Lamb. Amen.
      Isaac Watts. 1709.

180 L.M.
Unto Him that loved us... be glory and dominion for ever and ever.
Revelation i. 5, 6.

JESUS, Thou everlasting King,
 Accept the tribute which we bring;
Accept Thy well-deserved renown,
 And wear our praises as Thy crown.

2 Let every act of worship be
 Like our espousals, Lord, to Thee;
Like that blest hour when from above
 We first received the pledge of love.

3 The gladness of that happy day,
 O may it ever, ever stay;
Nor let our faith forsake its hold,
 Our hope decline, our love grow cold.

4 Each following moment as it flies,
 Increase Thy praise, improve our joys,
Till we are raised to sing Thy name,
 At the great supper of the Lamb.
      Isaac Watts. 1719.

181 C.M.
Unto you therefore which believe He is precious.—1 Peter ii. 7.

JESUS, I love Thy saving name,
 'Tis music to mine ear;
Fain would I sound it out so loud
 That earth and heaven might hear.

PRAISE AND PRAYER.

2 Yes, Thou art precious to my soul,
  My transport and my trust;
  Jewels to Thee are vanity,
  And gold but sordid dust.

3 All that my largest thoughts can **wish**,
  In Thee doth richly meet;
  Not to mine eyes is light so dear,
  Nor friendship half so sweet.

4 Thy grace still dwells within my heart
  And sheds its fragrance there;
  The noblest balm of all its wounds,
  The cordial of its care.

5 I'll speak the honours of Thy name
  With my last labouring breath;
  And, dying, glory in Thy love,
  The antidote of death.
  Philip Doddridge. 1755.

182   C.M.
I will love Thee, O Lord, my strength.—Psalm xviii. 1.

JESUS, the very thought of Thee
  With sweetness fills my breast;
But sweeter far Thy face to see,
  And in Thy presence rest.

2 Nor voice can sing, nor heart can frame,
  Nor can the memory find
A sweeter sound than Thy blest name,
  O Saviour of mankind!

3 O hope of every contrite heart!
  O joy of all the meek!
To those who fall, how kind Thou art,
  How good to those who seek!

4 But what to those who find? Ah, this—
  Nor tongue nor pen can show;
The love of Jesus—what it is
  None but His loved ones know.

5 Jesus, our **only** joy be Thou,
  As Thou our crown wilt be;
Jesus, be Thou our glory now,
  And through eternity. Amen.
  Bernard of Clairvaux. 12th Century.
  Tr. Edward Caswall. 1849.

183   7.7. 4.4 7. D.
Who shall not fear Thee, O Lord, and glorify Thy name?—Rev. xv. 4.

WORSHIP, and thanks, and blessing,
  And strength ascribe to Jesus!
    Jesus alone
    Defends His own,
When earth and hell oppress us.
Jesus with joy we witness
Almighty to deliver;
    Our seals set to,
    That God is true,
And reigns a King for ever.

2 Omnipotent Redeemer,
  Our ransomed souls adore **Thee**:
    Our Saviour Thou
    We find it now,
  And give Thee all the glory.
  We sing Thine arm unshortened,
  Brought through our sore temptation;
    With heart and voice
    In Thee rejoice,
  The God of our salvation.

3 Thine arm hath safely brought us
  A way no more expected,
    Than when Thy sheep
    Passed through the deep,
  By crystal walls protected:
  Thy glory was our rear-ward,
  Thine hand our lives did cover,
    And we, even we,
    Have passed the sea,
  And marched triumphant over.

4 The world's and Satan's malice,
  Thou, Jesus, hast confounded;
    And, by Thy grace,
    With songs of praise
  Our happy souls resounded:
  Accepting our deliverance,
  We triumph in Thy favour,
    And for the love
    Which now we prove,
  Shall praise Thy name for ever.
    Amen.
  Charles Wesley. 1743.

184   5 5. 5.5. 6.5. 6.5.
O Lord, my God, Thou art very great; Thou art clothed with honour and majesty.—Psalm civ. 1.

O WORSHIP the King,
  All glorious above!
O gratefully sing
  His power and His love!
Our Shield and Defender,
  The Ancient of days,
Pavilioned in splendour,
  And girded with praise.

2 O tell of His might,
  O sing of His grace,
Whose robe is the light,
  Whose canopy, space;
His chariots of wrath,
  Deep thunder-clouds form,
And dark is His path
  On the wings of the storm.

3 The earth, with its store
  Of wonders untold,
Almighty! Thy power
  Hath founded of old,
Hath stablished it fast
  By a changeless decree,
And round it hath cast,
  Like a mantle, the sea.

53

DIVINE WORSHIP.

4 Thy bountiful care
  What tongue can recite?
It breathes in the air,
  It shines in the light,
It streams from the hills,
  It descends to the plain,
And sweetly distils
  In the dew and the rain.

5 Frail children of dust,
  And feeble as frail,
In Thee do we trust,
  Nor find Thee to fail;
Thy mercies how tender,
  How firm to the end,
Our Maker, Defender,
  Redeemer, and Friend!

6 O measureless might!
    ineffable Love!
  While angels delight
    To hymn Thee above,
  The humbler creation,
    Though feeble their lays,
  With true adoration
    Shall lisp to Thy praise. Amen.
            Sir R. Grant. 1833.

---

185 12.1 t. 12.10.
O worship the Lord in the beauty of holiness.—Psalm xcv. 9.

WORSHIP the Lord in the beauty of
    holiness,
Bow down before Him, His glory pro-
    claim;
Gold of obedience, and incense of lowli-
    ness
Bring, and adore Him, the Lord is His
    name;

2 Low at His feet lay thy burden of careful-
    ness,
High on His heart He will bear it for
    thee,
Comfort thy sorrows, and answer thy
    prayerfulness,
Guiding thy steps as may best for thee
    be.

3 Fear not to enter His courts in the slender-
    ness
Of the poor wealth thou wouldst reckon
    as thine;
Truth in its beauty, and love in its tender-
    ness,
These are the offerings to lay on His
    shrine.

4 These, though we bring them in trembling
    and fearfulness,
He will accept for the Name that is dear;
Mornings of joy give for evenings of tear-
    fulness,
Trust for our trembling, and hope for
    our fear.
        54

---

5 Worship the Lord in the beauty of holiness,
  Bow down before him, His glory pro-
    claim;
  Gold of obedience, and incense of lowli-
    ness
  Bring, and adore Him, the Lord is His
    name!
            J. S. B. Monsell. 1837.

---

186 8.4. 8.4. 8.4.
Set your affection on things above.—Colossians iii. 2.

MY God, I thank Thee, who hast made
    The earth so bright;
So full of splendour and of joy,
    Beauty and light;
So many glorious things are here,
    Noble and right.

2 I thank Thee, too, that Thou hast made
    Joy to abound;
So many gentle thoughts and deeds
    Circling us round;
That in the darkest spot of earth
    Some love is found.

3 I thank Thee more that all our joy
    Is touched with pain;
That shadows fall on brightest hours,
    That thorns remain;
So that earth's bliss may be our guide,
    And not our chain.

4 I thank Thee, Lord, that Thou hast kept
    The best in store;
We have enough, yet not too much,
    To long for more
A yearning for a deeper peace
    Not known before.

5 I thank Thee, Lord, that here our souls,
    Though amply blest,
Can never find, although they seek,
    A perfect rest;
Nor ever shall, until they lean
    On Jesu's breast.
        Adelaide A. Procter. 1857.

---

187 C.M.
O the depth of the riches both of the wisdom and knowledge of God! Romans xi. 33.

MY God! how wonderful Thou art,
    Thy majesty how bright!
How beautiful Thy mercy-seat,
    In depths of burning light!

2 How dread are Thine eternal years,
    O everlasting Lord!
By prostrate spirits, day and night,
    Incessantly adored!

PRAISE AND PRAYER.

3 How beautiful, how beautiful
   The sight of Thee must be,
Thine endless wisdom, boundless power,
   And awful purity!

4 O how I fear Thee, living God!
   With deepest, tenderest fears,
And worship Thee with trembling hope,
   And penitential tears.

5 Yet may I love Thee too, O Lord!
   Almighty as Thou art;
For Thou hast stooped to ask of me
   The love of my poor heart.

6 Father of Jesus, Love's Reward!
   What rapture will it be,
Prostrate before Thy throne to lie,
   And gaze and gaze on Thee!
               F. W. Faber. 1849.

2 Praise Him for His grace and favour
   To our fathers in distress;
Praise Him, still the same for ever,
   Slow to chide, and swift to bless;
      Hallelujah!
Glorious in His faithfulness.

3 Father-like, He tends and spares us;
   Well our feeble frame He knows;
In His hands He gently bears us,
   Rescues us from all our foes;
      Hallelujah!
Widely yet His mercy flows!

4 Angels in the height adore Him,
   They behold Him face to face;
All His works bow down before Him,
   Through the boundless realms of space:
      Hallelujah!
Praise with us the God of grace!
               Amen.
              H. F. Lyte. 1864.

188   10.4. 6.6.6.6. 10.4.
Let everything that hath breath, praise the Lord.—Psalm cl. 6.

LET all the world in every corner sing
      My God and King!
The heavens are not too high,
   His praise may thither fly;
The earth is not too low,
   His praises there may grow.
Let all the world in every corner sing
      My God and King!

2 Let all the world in every corner sing
      My God and King!
The Church with psalms must shout,
   No door can keep them out:
But, above all, my heart
   Must bear the longest part.
Let all the world in every corner sing
      My God and King!

3 Let all the world in every corner sing
      My God and King!
The Father, with the Son,
   And Spirit, Three in One,
One everlasting Lord,
   Be evermore adored!
Let all the world in every corner sing
      My God and King! Amen.
        George Herbert. d. 1632. *alt.*

189   8.7. 8.7. 4.7.
Praise ye the Lord from the heavens.—Ps. cxlviii. 1.

PRAISE, my soul, the King of heaven,
   To His feet thy tribute bring;
Ransomed, healed, restored, forgiven,
   Who like thee His praise should sing?
      Hallelujah!
Praise the everlasting King!

190   C.M.
The second man is the Lord from heaven.—1 Corinthians xv. 47.

PRAISE to the Holiest in the height,
   And in the depth be praise;
In all His words most wonderful,
   Most sure in all His ways!

2 O loving wisdom of our God!
   When all was sin and shame,
A second Adam to the fight
   And to the rescue came.

3 O wisest love! that flesh and blood,
   Which did in Adam fail,
Should strive afresh against their foe,
   Should strive and should prevail.

4 O generous love! that He, who smote
   In man for man the foe,
The double agony in man
   For man should undergo;

5 And in the garden secretly,
   And on the cross on high,
Should teach His brethren, and inspire
   To suffer and to die.

6 Praise to the Holiest in the height,
   And in the depth be praise;
In all His words most wonderful,
   Most sure in all His ways. Amen.
              J. H. Newman. 1864.

DIVINE WORSHIP.

191   11.10.11.10. *Iambic.*
*Sing forth the honour of
His name; make His praise glorious.*
Psalm lxvi. 2.

PRAISE ye Jehovah! **Praise the Lord
    most holy,**
Who cheers the contrite, girds with
    strength the weak;
Praise Him who will **with glory crown the
    lowly,**
And with salvation beautify the meek.

2 Praise ye Jehovah! For His lovingkind-
    ness,
And all the tender mercy He hath
    shown;
Praise Him who pardons all our sin and
    blindness,
And calls us sons, and takes us for His
    own.

3 Praise ye Jehovah! Source of all our
    blessing;
Before His **gifts earth's richest boons
    wax dim;**
Resting in Him, His peace and joy
    possessing,
All things **are ours, for we have all in
    Him.**

4 Praise ye the Father! God the Lord, who
    gave us,
With full and perfect love, His only Son;
Praise ye the Son! who died Himself to
    save us;
Praise ye the Spirit! **Praise the Three
    in One!** Amen.
            Lady Mary C. Campbell. 1838.

192   L.M. *With Chorus.*
*Sing praises to God,
sing praises.*—Psalm xlvii. 6.

SING to the Lord a joyful song,
  Lift up your hearts, your **voices raise;**
To us His gracious gifts belong,
  To Him our songs of love and praise:
    For He is Lord of heaven and earth,
    Whom angels serve and saints adore,
    The Father Son, and Holy Ghost,
    To whom be praise for evermore.

2 For life and love, for rest and food,
  For daily help and nightly care,
Sing to the Lord, for He is good,
  And praise His name, for it is fair:

3 For strength to **those** who on Him wait,
  His truth to prove, His will to do,
Praise ye our God, for He is great,
  Trust in His name, for it is true

4 For joys untold that from above,
  Cheer those who love His sweet employ,
Sing to our God, for He is Love,
  Exalt His name, for it is Joy:

5 For life below, with all its bliss,
  And for that life, more pure and high,
That nobler life which after this
  Shall ever shine, and never die:

    Sing to the Lord of heaven and earth,
    Whom angels serve and saints adore,
    The Father, Son, and Holy Ghost,
    To whom be praise for evermore.
              Amen.
        J. S. B. Monsell. 1862.

193   8.8. 8.8. 8.8.
*Rejoice . . . the Lord is at
hand.*—Phil. iv, 4, 5.

LIFT up your heads, ye mighty gates,
  Behold the King of glory waits!
The **King of** kings is drawing near,
The **Saviour** of the world is here;
Life and salvation **doth He** bring,
Wherefore rejoice and gladly sing!

2 The **Lord is just, a** helper **tried,**
Mercy is ever at His side;
His **kingly crown is** holiness;
His sceptre, pity in distress;
The end of all our woe He brings,
Wherefore the earth is glad and sings.

3 O, blest the land, **the** city blest,
  Where Christ the ruler is confest!
O, happy hearts and happy homes,
To whom this King in triumph comes!
The cloudless Sun of joy He is,
Who bringeth pure delight and **bliss.**

4 Fling wide the portals of your heart,
  Make it a temple set apart
From earthly use, for heaven's employ,
Adorned with prayer, and love, and joy;
So shall your Sovereign enter in,
And new and nobler life begin.

5 Redeemer, come, **we** open wide
  Our heart to Thee; here, Lord, abide!
Thine inner presence let us feel,
Thy grace and love in us reveal,
Thy Holy Spirit guide us on,
Until the glorious goal is won! Amen.
            George Weissel. 1635.
    Tr. Catherine Winkworth. 1855.

194   8.7. 8.7. D.
*Hitherto hath the Lord
helped us.*—1 Samuel vii. 12.

COME, thou Fount of every blessing,
  Tune my heart to sing Thy grace;
Streams of mercy never ceasing
  Call for songs of loudest praise:
Teach me, Lord, the rapturous measures
  Sung by flaming hosts above;
Bid me tell the countless treasures
  Of my God's unchanging love.

2 Here I raise my Ebenezer,
   Hither by Thy help I'm come;
And I hope, by Thy good pleasure,
   Safely to arrive at home:
Jesus sought me when a stranger,
   Wandering from the fold of God;
He, to save my soul from danger,
   Interposed His precious blood.

3 O, to grace **how** great a debtor
   Daily I'm constrained to be!
Let that grace break every fetter
   That withholds my heart from Thee:
Prone to wander, Lord, I feel it,
   Prone to **leave** the God I love;
Saviour, take my heart and seal it,
   Seal it for Thy courts above. Amen.
          Robert **Robinson**. 1759.

195 *O give thanks to the Lord*   7.7. 7.7.
of lords: for His mercy endureth for ever.
      Psalm cxxxvi. 3.

PRAISE, O praise our heavenly King,
   Grateful hallelujahs sing;
For His mercies aye endure,
Ever faithful, ever sure.

2 Praise Him, that His love appears
   Crowning our revolving years;
For His mercies aye endure,
Ever faithful, ever **sure.**

3 Praise **Him, that the sun** by day
Pours on all his golden ray;
For His mercies aye endure,
Ever faithful, ever sure.

4 Praise Him, that the moon by night
   Gives the world her silver light;
For His mercies aye endure,
Ever faithful, **ever sure.**

5 Praise **Him,** that the stars appear
   Glittering in the mighty sphere;
For His mercies aye endure,
Ever faithful, ever sure.

6 Praise Him, that the **rain-cloud drops**
   Fatness on the ripening crops;
For His mercies aye endure,
Ever faithful, ever sure.

7 Praise **Him, that the** country round
   Rich with **waving** ears is found;
For His mercies aye endure,
Ever **faithful,** ever sure.

8 Praise **Him, that the** barns contain
   Precious stores **of** gathered grain;
For His mercies aye endure,
Ever faithful, ever sure.

9 Praise Him, that with Living Bread
   Our immortal souls are fed;
For His mercies aye endure,
Ever faithful, ever sure.

10 Praise Him, that He grants in this
   Earnest of eternal bliss;
For His mercies aye endure,
Ever faithful, ever sure.

11 Praise to our all-bounteous King,
   Praise for ever let us sing;
Praise Him, ye angelic host,
Father, Son, and Holy Ghost. **Amen.**
          H. Trend. 1861.

196 *Let them praise the name*   8.7. 8.7.
   of the Lord.—Psalm cxlviii. 5.

PRAISE the Lord, ye heavens, adore
   Him;
Praise Him, angels, in the height;
Sun and moon, rejoice before Him;
Praise Him, all ye stars of light.

2 Praise the Lord, for He hath spoken,
   Worlds His mighty voice obeyed;
Laws which never shall be broken,
   For their guidance He hath made.

3 Praise the Lord, for He **is** glorious,
   Never shall His promise fail;
God hath made His saints victorious,
   Sin and death shall **not** prevail.

4 **Praise the** God of **our** salvation,
   Hosts on high His power proclaim;
Heaven and earth, and all creation,
   Laud and magnify His name. Amen.
          Anon. 1801.

197   *Rejoice in the Lord.*   S.M.
      Phil. iv. 4.

COME, ye that love the Lord,
   And let your joys be known,
Join in a song with sweet accord,
   While ye surround His throne.

2 Let those refuse to sing
   Who never knew our God;
But servants of the Heavenly King
   May speak their joys abroad.

3 The God that rules on high,
   That all the earth surveys,
That rides upon the stormy sky,
   And calms the roaring seas:

4 This mighty God is ours,
   Our Father and our Love;
He will send down His heavenly powers,
   To carry us above.

5 There we shall see His face,
   And never, never sin,
There, from the rivers of His grace,
   Drink endless pleasures in.

6 Yea, and before we rise
  To that immortal state,
The thoughts of such amazing bliss
  Should constant joys create.

7 The men of grace have **found**
  Glory begun below ;
Celestial fruit on earthly ground
  From faith and hope may grow.

8 Then let our songs abound,
  And every tear be dry ;
We're marching through Immanuel's ground
  To fairer worlds on high.
              Isaac Watts. 1709.

198 6.5. 6.5. D.
I press toward the mark for the prize of the high calling of God in Christ Jesus.—Philippians iii. 14.

SAVIOUR, blessed Saviour,
  Listen whilst we sing,
Hearts and voices raising
  Praises to our King:
All we have to offer,
  All we hope to be,
Body, soul, and spirit,
  All we yield to Thee.

2 Nearer, ever nearer,
  Christ, we draw to Thee,
Deep in adoration
  Bending low the knee :
Thou, for our redemption,
  Cam'st on earth to die ;
Thou, that we might follow,
  Hast gone up on high.

3 Great, and ever greater,
  Are Thy mercies here :
True and everlasting
  Are the glories there ;
Where no pain nor sorrow,
  Toil nor care, is known ;
Where the angel-legions
  Circle round Thy throne.

4 Clearer still, and clearer,
  Dawns the light from heaven,
In our sadness bringing
  News of sins forgiven ;
Life has lost its shadows,
  Pure the light within,
Thou hast shed Thy radiance
  On a world of sin.

5 Brighter still, and brighter,
  Glows the western sun,
Shedding all its gladness
  O'er our work that's done ;
Time will soon be over,
  Toil and sorrow past ;
May we, blessed Saviour,
  Find a rest at last !

6 Onward, ever onward,
  Journeying o'er the road
Worn by saints before us,
  Journeying on to God ;
Leaving all behind us,
  May we hasten on,
Backward never looking
  Till the prize is won.

7 Higher then, and higher,
  Bear the ransomed soul,
Earthly toils forgotten,
  Saviour, to its goal ;
Where, in joys unthought of,
  Saints with angels sing,
Never weary, raising
  Praises to their King. Amen.
              Godfrey Thring. 1866.

199 8.7. 8.7. 8.8.7.
Sing unto God, sing praises to His name.—Psalm lxviii. 4.

SING praise to God who **reigns above**,
  The God of all creation,
The God of power, the God of love,
  The God of our salvation ;
With healing balm my soul He fills,
And every faithless murmur stills :
  To God all praise and glory !

2 The angel-host, O King of kings,
  Thy praise for ever telling,
In earth and sky all living things
  Beneath Thy shadow dwelling,
Adore the wisdom which could span,
And power which formed creation's plan :
  To God all praise and glory !

3 What God's almighty power hath made,
  His gracious mercy keepeth ;
By morning glow or evening shade,
  His watchful eye ne'er sleepeth ;
Within the kingdom of His might,
Lo ! all is just and all is right :
  To God all praise and glory !

4 The Lord is never far away ;
  But, through all grief distressing,
An ever-present help and stay,
  Our peace, and joy, and blessing ;
As with a mother's tender hand
He leads His own, His chosen band :
  To God all praise and glory !

5 When every earthly hope has flown
  From sorrow's sons and daughters,
Our Father from His heavenly throne
  Beholds the troubled waters ;
And at His word the storm is stayed,
Which made His children's hearts afraid :
  To God all praise and glory !

PRAISE AND PRAYER.

6 Then all my gladsome way along
  I sing aloud Thy praises,
That men may hear the grateful song
  My voice unwearied raises
Be joyful in the Lord, my heart !
Both soul and body bear your part :
    To God all praise and glory ! Amen.
J. J. Schütz. d. 1690.
Tr. Frances E. Cox. 1864.

200   7.7. 7.7. 7.7.
By Him therefore let us offer the sacrifice of praise to God continually.
      Hebrews xiii. 15.

FOR the **beauty of the earth,**
  For the beauty **of the skies,**
For the love which **from our birth**
Over and around **us lies,**
Father, unto Thee we raise
This, our sacrifice **of** praise.

2 For the beauty of each hour
  Of the day and of the night,
Hill and vale, **and** tree **and** flower,
  Sun and moon, **and** stars of light ;
Father, unto Thee **we raise**
This, our sacrifice **of** praise.

3 For the joy of ear **and eye,**
  For the heart and **mind's delight,**
For the mystic harmony
  Linking sense to sound **and sight ;**
Father, unto Thee **we raise**
This, our sacrifice **of praise.**

4 For the joy of human love,
  Brother, sister, parent, child,
Friends on earth, and friends **above,**
  For all gentle thoughts and **mild ;**
Father, unto Thee we raise
This, our sacrifice **of** praise.

5 **For each perfect gift of Thine**
  To our race so freely given,
Graces human and divine,
Flowers of earth, and buds of heaven ;
Father, unto Thee we raise
This, our sacrifice of praise.

6 **For Thy Church that evermore**
  Lifteth holy hands above,
Offering up on every shore
  Its pure sacrifice of love ;
Father, unto Thee we raise
This, our sacrifice of praise. Amen.
Folliott S. Pierpoint. 1864.

201   6.6.4. 6.6.6.4.
Glory to God in the highest.
       Luke ii. 14.

GLORY to God on high !
  Let praises fill the sky,
Praise ye His name :
Angels His name adore,
Who all our sorrows bore,
And saints cry evermore,
  Worthy the Lamb !

2 All they around the throne
  Cheerfully join in one,
Praising His name :
We who have felt His blood
Sealing our peace with God,
Spread His dear fame abroad ;
  Worthy the Lamb !

3 To Him our hearts we raise,
  None else shall have our praise ;
Praise ye His name :
Him our exalted **Lord,**
Him as below **adored,**
We praise with **one accord,**
  Worthy **the Lamb !**

4 **Join all the** ransomed **race,**
  Our Lord and God to bless,
Praise **ye** His name :
In Him we will rejoice,
Making a cheerful noise,
And say with heart **and voice,**
  Worthy the **Lamb !**

5 **Though we** must change our **place,**
  Our souls will never cease
Praising His name :
To Him we'll tribute **bring,**
Laud Him our gracious **King,**
And, without ceasing, **sing,**
  Worthy the Lamb ! Amen.
J. Allen. 1757.

202   L. M.
O God, Thou art my God.
       Psalm lxiii. 1.

GREAT God, indulge **my humble claim ;**
  Be Thou my hope, **my joy, my rest ;**
The glories that **compose Thy name**
Stand all **engaged to make me blessed.**

2 **Thou great and good, Thou just** and wise,
  Thou art my Father and my God ;
And I am Thine, by sacred ties.
  Thy son, Thy servant, bought with blood.

3 **With heart, and eyes, and** lifted hands,
  For Thee I long, **to Thee** I look,
As travellers **in** thirsty lands
  Pant for the cooling water-brook.

4 **Should I from** Thee, **my** God, remove,
  Life could no lasting joy afford ;
My peace, the sense of pardoning love,
  My guard, the presence of my Lord.

5 I'll lift my hands, I'll raise **my voice,**
  While I have breath to pray or praise ;
This work shall make my heart rejoice,
  And fill the remnant of my days.
Amen.
Isaac Watts. 1709.

DIVINE WORSHIP.

203   8.7.8.7.4.7.
God is love.—1 John iv. 8.

GOD is Love; that anthem olden
   Sing the glorious orbs of light,
In their language, glad and golden,
   Speaking to us day and night
      Their great story,
  God is Love, and God is Might.

2 And the teeming earth rejoices
   In that message from above,
With ten thousand thousand voices
   Telling back, from hill and grove,
      Her glad story,
  God is Might, and God is Love.

3 Through these anthems of creation,
   Mingling in harmonious strife,
Christian songs of Christ's salvation,
   To the world with blessings rife,
      Tell their story,
  God is Love, and God is Life.

4 Through that precious Love He sought us,
   Wandering from His holy ways;
With that precious Life He bought us;
   Then let all our future days
      Tell this story,
  Love is Life, our lives be praise.

5 Gladsome is the theme, and glorious,
   Praise to Christ our gracious Head;
Christ, the risen Christ, victorious,
   Death and hell hath captive led:
      Glory, glory!
  Love lives on, and Death is dead.

6 Up to Him let each affection
   Daily rise, and round Him move
Our whole lives, one resurrection
   To the Life of life above;
      Their glad story,
  God is Life, and God is Love.
          J. S. B. Monsell. 1867.

204   7.7.7.7.
I will sing unto the Lord as long as I live.—Psalm civ. 33.

SONGS of praise the angels sang,
  Heaven with hallelujahs rang,
When Jehovah's work begun,
  When He spake, and it was done.

2 Songs of praise awoke the morn,
  When the Prince of Peace was born;
Songs of praise arose when He
  Captive led captivity

3 Heaven and earth must pass away;
  Songs of praise shall crown that day;
God will make new heavens and earth;
  Songs of praise shall hail their birth.

4 And shall man alone be dumb
Till that glorious kingdom come?
No; the Church delights to raise
Psalms and hymns and songs of praise.

5 Saints below, with heart and voice,
  Still in songs of praise rejoice;
Learning here, by faith and love,
  Songs of praise to sing above.

6 Borne upon their latest breath,
  Songs of praise shall conquer death;
Then, amidst eternal joy,
  Songs of praise their powers employ.
          James Montgomery. 1819.

205   6.6.8.4. D.
Fear not, Abram: I am thy shield.—Genesis xv. 1.

THE God of Abraham praise,
   Who reigns enthroned above,
Ancient of everlasting days,
   And God of Love:
Jehovah, Great I AM,
   By earth and heaven confest;
I bow and bless the sacred name,
   For ever blest.

2 The God of Abraham praise,
   At whose supreme command,
From earth I rise, and seek the joys
   At His right hand;
I all on earth forsake,
   Its wisdom, fame, and power;
And Him my only portion make,
   My shield and tower.

3 The God of Abraham praise,
   Whose all-sufficient grace
Shall guide me all my happy days,
   In all His ways;
He calls a man His friend,
   He calls Himself my God,
And He shall save me to the end,
   Through Jesu's blood.

4 He by Himself hath sworn,
   I on His oath depend;
I shall, on eagles' wings upborne,
   To heaven ascend;
I shall behold His face,
   I shall His power adore,
And sing the wonders of His grace
   For evermore. Amen.
          Thomas Olivers. 1772.

206   6.6.8.4. D.
I am the Lord God of Abraham.—Genesis xxviii. 13.

THOUGH nature's strength decay,
   And earth and hell withstand,
To Canaan's bounds I urge my way,
   At His command;
The watery deep I pass,
   With Jesus in my view,
And through the barren wilderness
   My way pursue.

PRAISE AND **PRAYER.**

2 The goodly land I see,
   With peace and plenty blest ;
A land of sacred liberty
   And endless rest:
There milk and honey flow,
And oil and wine abound,
And trees of life for ever grow,
   With **mercy** crowned.

3 There dwells the Lord our King,
  The Lord our Righteousness,
Triumphant o'er the world and sin,
  The Prince of Peace :
On Sion's sacred height,
  His kingdom still maintains,
And, glorious **with** His saints in light,
  For ever reigns.

4 He keeps His own secure,
  He guards them by His side,
Arrays in garments white and pure
  His spotless **bride :**
With streams **of** sacred bliss,
  With groves of living joys,
With all the fruits of Paradise,
  He still supplies.
         Thomas Olivers. 1772.

207 *Thou art worthy, O Lord.*   6.6.8.4. D.
       Rev. iv. 11.

BEFORE the great Three-One
  Saints all exulting stand,
And tell the wonders He hath done,
  Through **all their** land :
The listening spheres attend,
  And swell the growing fame,
And sing, in songs which never end,
  The **wondrous Name.**

2 **The God** who reigns on high
  The great archangels sing ;
And ' **Holy, holy,** holy, cry,
  ' **Almighty King !**
Who was and is the same,
  And **evermore shall be ;**
Jehovah, **Father, Great I AM,**
  We worship Thee.'

3 **Before the** Saviour's face
  The ransomed nations bow :
O'erwhelmed **at** His almighty grace,
  For **ever new:**
He shows **His** prints of love ;
  They kindle **to a flame,**
And sound, **through all the worlds above,**
  The **slaughtered Lamb.**

4 The whole triumphant host
  Give thanks to God on high ;
' Hail, Father, Son, and Holy Ghost,'
  They ever cry :
Hail, Abraham's God, and mine !
  I join the heavenly lays,
All might and majesty are Thine,
  And endless praise. Amen.
         Thomas Olivers. 1772.

208   S.M.
  The joy of the whole earth
  is Mount Zion.—Psalm xlviii. 2.

GREAT is the **Lord** our God,
  And let His praise be great ;
He makes His churches His abode,
  His most delightful seat.

2 **These temples** of His grace,
  How beautiful they stand :
The honours of our native place,
  And bulwarks of our land.

3 **In Sion God is known**
  A refuge in distress ;
How bright has His salvation shone
  Through all her palaces !

4 **In every new distress**
  We'll to His house repair ;
We'll think upon His wondrous **grace,**
  And seek deliverance there.
         Isaac Watts. 1719.

209   C.M.
  A Name which is above
  every name.—Phil. ii. 9.

HOW sweet the name of Jesus sounds
  In a believer's ear !
It soothes **his** sorrows, heals his wounds,
  And drives away his fear.

2 **It makes the wounded** spirit whole,
  And calms the troubled breast ;
'Tis manna to the hungry soul,
  And to the weary rest.

3 **Dear Name, the Rock on which I build,**
  My Shield and Hiding-place ;
My never-failing Treasury, filled
  With boundless stores of grace.

4 **Jesus, my Shepherd,** Brother, Friend,
  My Prophet, Priest, and King,
My Lord, my Life, my Way, my End ;
  Accept the praise I bring.

5 **Weak is the effort of** my heart,
  And cold my warmest thought ;
But, when I see Thee as Thou art,
  I'll praise Thee as I ought.

6 Till then **I would** Thy love proclaim
  With every fleeting breath ;
And may the music of Thy name
  Refresh **my soul in** death. Amen.
         John Newton. 1779.

210   6.5, 6.5, D. *Anapæstic.*
  Rejoice and sing praise.
    Psalm xcviii. 4.

WITH gladness we worship,
  Rejoice as we sing,
Free hearts and free voices
  How blessed to bring !

DIVINE WORSHIP.

The old thankful **story**
 Shall scale Thine abode,
Thou King of all **glory**,
 Most bountiful **God**!

2 Thy right would we give Thee,
 True homage Thy due,
And honour eternal,
 The universe through
With all **Thy** creation,
 Earth, heaven, and sea,
In one acclamation
 We celebrate Thee.

3 Renewed by Thy Spirit,
 Redeemed by Thy Son,
Thy children revere Thee
 For all Thou hast done;
O Father! returning
 To love and to light,
Thy children are yearning
 To praise Thee aright.

4 Our souls mount aspiring
 To reach the Divine,
Partaking Thy nature
 In Christ—even Thine!
Ascending and soaring,
 With Him in accord,
We triumph adoring,
 We joy in the Lord.

5 We join with the angels,
 And so there is given
From earth, Hallelujah!
 In answer to heaven.
Amen! Be Thou glorious
 Below and above,
Redeeming, victorious,
 And Infinite Love! Amen.
    George Rawson. 1876.

211 S.M.
Stand up and bless the Lord your God.—Nehemiah ix. 5.

STAND up and **bless the Lord**,
 Ye people of **His choice**;
Stand up and bless the **Lord your God**,
 With heart and **soul and voice**.

2 Though high above all **praise**,
 Above all blessing high,
Who would not fear His holy name,
 And laud and magnify?

3 O for **the** living flame
 From His own altar brought,
To touch our lips, our minds inspire,
 And wing to heaven our thought!

4 There, with benign regard,
 Our hymns He deigns to hear;
Though unrevealed to mortal sense
 The spirit feels Him near.

5 God is our strength and song,
 And His salvation ours;
Then be His love in Christ proclaimed
 With all our ransomed powers.

6 Stand up and bless the Lord,
 The Lord your God adore;
Stand up, and bless His glorious name,
 Henceforth for evermore. Amen.
    James Montgomery. 1824.

212 8.8. 8.8. *Anapæstic.*
This God is our God for ever and ever.—Psalm xlviii. 14.

THIS, this is the God we adore,
 Our faithful unchangeable Friend,
Whose love is as great as His power,
 And neither knows measure nor **end**.

2 'Tis Jesus, the First and the Last,
 Whose Spirit shall guide us safe home;
We'll praise Him for all that is past,
 And trust Him for all that's to come.
  Amen.
    Joseph Hart. 1759.

213 L.M.
In all places where I record My Name, I will come unto thee, and I will bless thee.—Exodus xx. 24.

JESUS, where'er Thy people meet,
 There they behold Thy mercy-seat;
Where'er they seek Thee, Thou art found,
 And **every** place is hallowed ground.

2 For Thou, within no walls confined,
 Inhabitest the humble mind;
Such **ever** bring Thee where they come,
 And **going**, take Thee to their home.

3 Dear **Shepherd** of Thy chosen few!
 Thy former mercies here renew;
Here to our waiting hearts proclaim
 The **sweetness** of Thy saving name.

4 Here may we prove the power of prayer
 To strengthen faith, and sweeten care,
To teach **our** faint desires to rise,
 And bring all heaven before our eyes.
   Amen.
    William Cowper. 1769.

214 C.M.
The love of God is shed abroad in our hearts.—Romans v. 5.

BEING of beings, God of love!
 To Thee our hearts we raise;
Thy all-sustaining power we prove,
 And gladly sing Thy praise.

2 Thine, only Thine, we pant to be;
   Our sacrifice receive;
   Made, and preserved, and saved by Thee,
   To Thee ourselves we give.

3 Heavenward our every wish aspires;
   For all Thy mercies' store
   The sole return Thy love requires
   Is, that we ask for more.

4 For more we ask; we open then
   Our hearts to embrace Thy will;
   Turn, and revive us, Lord, again,
   With all Thy fulness fill.

5 Come, Holy Ghost, the Saviour's love
   Shed in our hearts abroad!
   So shall we ever live, and move,
   And be, with Christ, in God.   Amen.
                                    Wesley. 1739.

215   8.4. 4.8. 8.8.
I will bless the Lord at all times.—Ps. xxxiv. 1.

HOW shall we worship Thee, O Lord?
   What shall we bring
      To Thee, our King,
By children and by men adored?
More dear to Thee than prayer and praise
Are loyal deeds and patient days.

2 What can we give? Thou dost desire
   A steadfast will
      Obedient still,
And faithful work that does not tire:
More dear to Thee than prayer and praise
Are loyal deeds and patient days.

3 How easy in the golden light
   Of summer hours,
      Among the flowers,
To bless Thee for a world so bright!
More dear to Thee than prayer and praise
Are loyal deeds and patient days.

4 When sorrow darkens all our sky,
   Life's blossoms lost
      In sudden frost,
And all our courage like to die,
O! help us still Thy name to praise
By loyal deeds and patient days.

5 In life, in death, in joy and pain,
   May we adore
      Thee more and more,
Till love turns all our loss to gain,
And tunes the years to perfect praise
In loyal deeds and patient days.   Amen.
                       Annie Matheson. 1884.

216   7.5. 7.5. 7.5. 7.5. 8.8
Come unto Me, all ye that labour and are heavy laden, and I will give you rest.—Matthew xi. 28.

WHEN the weary, seeking rest,
   To Thy goodness flee;
When the heavy-laden cast
   All their load on Thee;
When the troubled, seeking peace,
   On Thy name shall call;
When the sinner, seeking life,
   At Thy feet shall fall:
Hear then, in love, O Lord, the cry,
In heaven, Thy dwelling-place on high.

2 When the worldling, sick at heart,
   Lifts his soul above;
When the prodigal looks back
   To his Father's love;
When the proud man in his pride
   Stoops to seek Thy face;
When the burdened brings his guilt
   To Thy throne of grace:
Hear then, in love, O Lord, the cry,
In heaven, Thy dwelling-place on high.

3 When the stranger asks a home,
   All his toils to end;
When the hungry craveth food,
   And the poor a friend;
When the sailor on the wave
   Bows the fervent knee;
When the soldier on the field
   Lifts his heart to Thee:
Hear then, in love, O Lord the cry,
In heaven, Thy dwelling-place on high.

4 When the man of toil and care
   In the city crowd,
When the shepherd on the moor
   Names the name of God;
When the learned and the high,
   Tired of earthly fame,
Upon higher joys intent,
   Name the blessed name:
Hear then, in love, O Lord, the cry,
In heaven, Thy dwelling-place on high.

5 When the child, with grave fresh lips,
   Youth, or maiden fair;
When the aged, weak and grey,
   Seek Thy face in prayer;
When the widow weeps to Thee,
   Sad and lone and low;
When the orphan brings to Thee
   All his orphan woe:
Hear then, in love, O Lord, the cry,
In heaven, Thy dwelling-place on high.

6 When creation, in her pangs,
   Heaves her heavy groan;
When Thy Salem's exiled sons
   Breathe their bitter moan;

DIVINE WORSHIP.

When Thy waiting, weeping **Church,**
Looking for a home,
Sendeth up her silent sigh,
'Come, Lord Jesus, come!
Hear then, in love, O Lord, **the cry,**
In heaven, Thy dwelling-place on **high.**
Amen.
Horatius Bonar. 1857.

217   C.M.D.
God is the strength of my
heart, and my portion for ever.
Psalm lxxiii. 26.

MY heart is resting, O my God,—
  I will give thanks and **sing ;**
My heart **is at** the secret **source**
  Of every precious thing.
Now the frail vessel Thou hast **made**
  No hand but Thine shall fill ;
The waters **of** the earth have **failed,**
  And I am thirsty still.

2 I thirst **for springs of heavenly life,**
  And here **all day they rise ;**
I seek the **treasure of Thy love,**
  And close **at hand it ties.**
And a new song is **in my mouth**
  To long-loved **music set ;**
Glory to Thee for **all the grace**
  I have not **tasted yet.**

3 Glory **to** Thee for strength withheld,
  For want and weakness known ;
And fear that sends me to Thyself
  For what is most my **own.**
I have a heritage of joy
  That yet I must not **see ;**
The hand that **bled to make it mine,**
  Is keeping it **for me.**

4 My heart is resting, O my **God,**
  My heart is in Thy care ;
I hear the voice of joy and health
  Resounding everywhere.
' Thou art my portion,' saith my soul,
  Ten thousand voices say ;
The music of their glad Amen
  Will never die away. Amen.
Anna L. Waring. 1852.

218   L.M.
What shall I render unto
the Lord for all His benefits toward me ?
Psalm cxvi. 12.

WHAT shall we offer our good Lord,
  Poor nothings ! for His boundless grace ?
Fain would we **His** great name record,
  And worthily **set** forth His praise.

Great object of our growing love,
  To whom our more than all we owe,
Open the Fountain from above,
  And let it our full souls o'erflow.

3 So shall our lives Thy power proclaim,
  Thy grace for every sinner free ;
Till all mankind shall learn Thy name,
  Shall all stretch out their hands to Thee.

4 Open a door which earth and hell
  May strive to shut, but strive in vain :
Let Thy word richly in us dwell,
  And let our gracious fruit remain.

5 O multiply **the** sower's seed !
  And fruit we every hour shall bear,
Throughout the world Thy Gospel spread,
  Thy everlasting truth declare.

6 We all, in perfect love **renewed,**
  Shall know the greatness **of Thy power,**
Stand in the temple of **our** God
  As pillars, and go out no more.
A. G. Spangenberg. 1734.
Tr. John Wesley. 1742.

219   8.7. 8.7. 4.7.
Let my supplication come
before Thee.—Psalm cxix. 170.

JESUS, Lord **of** life and glory,
  Bend from heaven Thy gracious **ear,**
While **our** waiting souls adore Thee,
  Friend of helpless sinners, hear ;
    By Thy mercy,
O deliver us, good Lord.

2 From the depths of nature's blindness,
  From the hardening power of sin,
From all malice and unkindness,
  From **the** pride that lurks within,
    By **Thy mercy,**
O deliver **us, good Lord.**

3 When temptation sorely presses,
  In the day of Satan's power,
In our times of deep distresses,
  In each dark and trying hour,
    By Thy mercy,
O deliver us, good Lord.

4 When the world around is smiling,
  In the time of wealth and ease,
Earthly joys our hearts beguiling,
  In the day of health and peace,
    By Thy mercy,
O deliver us, good Lord.

5 **In the** weary hours of sickness,
  In the times of grief and pain,
When we feel our mortal weakness,
  When the creature's help is vain,
    By Thy mercy,
O deliver **us, good Lord.**

6 In the solemn hour of dying,
  In the awful judgment day,
May our souls, on Thee relying,
  Find Thee still our hope and stay ;
    By Thy mercy,
O deliver us, good Lord. Amen.
J. J. Cummins. 1839.

PRAISE AND PRAYER

220 8.8.6. 8.8.6.
I will sing with the Spirit.
1 Corinthians xiv. 15.

JESUS, Thou soul of all our joys,
  For whom we now lift up our voice,
And all our strength exert,
Vouchsafe the grace we humbly claim,
Compose into a thankful frame,
  And tune Thy people's heart.

2 While in the heavenly work we join,
  Thy glory be our whole design,—
Thy glory, not our own :
Still let us keep our end in view,
And still the pleasing task pursue,
  To please our God alone.

3 The secret pride, the subtle sin,
  O let it never more steal in,
To offend Thy glorious eyes,
To desecrate our hallowed strain,
And make our solemn service vain,
  And mar our sacrifice.

4 Still let us on **our** guard be found,
  And watch against the **power of sound,**
With sacred jealousy ;
Lest, haply, **sense** should damp our zeal,
And music's charms bewitch and steal
  Our hearts away from Thee.

5 Thee let us praise, our common Lord,
  And sweetly join with one accord
Thy goodness to proclaim :
Jesus, Thyself in us reveal,
And all our faculties shall feel
  Thy harmonizing name.

6 With calmly-reverential joy,
  O let us all our lives employ
In setting forth Thy love ;
And raise in death our triumph higher,
And sing, with all the heavenly choir,
  That endless **song** above ! Amen.
            Charles Wesley. 1749.

221 C.M.
*I will praise Thee, O Lord,
with my whole heart.*—Psalm ix. 1.

FILL Thou my life, O Lord my God,
  In every part, with praise,
That my whole being may proclaim
  Thy being and Thy ways.

2 Not for **the** lip of praise alone,
  Nor even the praising heart
I ask, but for a life made up
  Of praise in every part :

3 Praise in the common words I speak,
  Life's common looks and tones,
In intercourse at hearth or board
  With my beloved ones :

4 Not in the temple crowd alone,
  Where holy voices chime ;
But in the silent paths of earth,
  The quiet rooms of time.

5 Fill every part of me with praise ;
  Let all my being speak
Of Thee and of Thy love, O Lord !
  Poor though I be, and weak.

6 So shalt Thou, Lord, from me, even me,
  Receive the glory due,
And so shall I begin on earth
  The song for ever new.

7 So shall no part of day or night
  From sacredness be free ;
But all my life, in every step,
  Be fellowship with Thee.
          Horatius Bonar. 1867

222 8.8.6. 8.8.6.
*Building up yourselves on
your most holy faith.*—Jude 20.

COME, Wisdom, Power, and Grace
    Divine !
Come, Jesus, in Thy name to join
  A happy, chosen band ;
Who fain would prove Thine utmost will,
And all Thy righteous laws fulfil,
  In love's benign command.

2 If pure essential Love Thou art,
  Thy nature into every heart,
Thy loving self, inspire ;
Bid all our simple souls be one,
United in a bond unknown,
  Baptized with heavenly fire.

3 Still may we to our centre tend,—
To spread Thy praise our common end,
  To help each other on ;
Companions through the wilderness,
To share a moment's pain, and seize
  An everlasting crown.

4 Supply what every member wants ;
To found the fellowship of saints,
  Thy Spirit, Lord, supply ;
So shall we all Thy love receive,
Together to Thy glory live,
  And to Thy glory die. Amen.
            Charles Wesley. 1767.

223 11.10. 11.10. *Anapæstic.*
*We know that all things
work together for good to them that love God.*
Romans viii. 28.

BRIGHTLY, O Father, when morning is
    breaking,
Shed o'er Thy children the beams of Thy
  love,
Scattering the night-clouds of sorrow and
  darkness,
Lifting our spirits to glories above.

DIVINE WORSHIP.

2 Teach us, O Father, to work in the day-
    time.
  Soon, O, too soon, is the night coming
    on ;
  Help us, while earnestly, actively striving,
  To finish our work ere the daylight be
    gone.

3 Bravely, O Father, in life's daily conflict,
  Help us, Thy soldiers, to combat each ill,
  Crushing each foe that impedes our march
    onwards,
  Each impulse within us opposed to Thy
    will.

4 Help us, O Father, in watching or waiting,
  Teach us in all things, Thy way is the
    best ;
  Guide us and keep us throughout our life's
    journey,
  Lead us at last to the mansions of rest.

5 Calmly, O Father, as life's day is closing,
  Bring us in peace to Thy glorious home,
  Where care, and conflict, and labour, and
    watching,
  Darkness, and sorrow, and sin cannot
    come. Amen.
                John Westbury. b. 1838.

224 C.M.
  *We love Him, because He
   first loved us.*—1 John iv. 19.

MY God, I love Thee for Thyself,
  All creature things above ;
Thy glorious works, Thy blessed gifts
  I praise,—but Thee I love.

2 My God, I seek Thee for Thyself,
    Besides, I ask not aught ;
  If Thee, Thyself, I do not find,
    All that I find is nought.

3 If Thou deniest me Thyself,
    Whate'er Thou givest me,
  Empty and void, I languish still,
    And grieve unceasingly.

4 Give me to find, O gracious God,
    Thee, as my final end ;
  To Thee in constancy of love
    Eternally to tend. Amen.
                G. B. Bubier. d. 1869.

225 C.M.
  The Lord is good to all.
      Psalm cxlv. 9.

SWEET is the memory of Thy grace,
  My God, my heavenly King ;
Let age to age Thy righteousness
  In sounds of glory sing.

2 God reigns on high, but not confines
    His goodness to the skies ;
  Through the whole earth His bounty
    shines,
  And every want supplies.

3 With longing eyes the creatures wait
    On Thee for daily food ;
  Thy liberal hand provides them meat,
    And fills their mouths with good.

4 How kind are Thy compassions, Lord !
    How slow Thine anger moves !
  But soon He sends His pardoning word,
    To cheer the souls He loves.

5 Creatures, with all their endless race,
    Thy power and praise proclaim ;
  But we, who taste Thy richer grace,
    Delight to bless Thy name. Amen.
                Isaac Watts. 1719.

226 8.8. 8.8. 8.8.
  *The Author of eternal
   salvation unto all them that obey Him.*
        Hebrews v. 9.

THOU hidden Source of calm repose,
  Thou all-sufficient Love Divine,
My help and refuge from my foes,
  Secure I am, if Thou art mine ;
And lo ! from sin, and grief, and shame,
I hide me, Jesus, in Thy Name.

2 Thy mighty Name salvation is,
    And keeps my happy soul above ;
  Comfort it brings, and power, and peace,
    And joy, and everlasting love ;
  To me, with Thy dear Name, are given,
  Pardon, and holiness, and heaven.

3 Jesus, my all in all Thou art ;
    My rest in toil, my ease in pain,
  The medicine of my broken heart ;
    In war my peace, in loss my gain,
  My smile beneath the tyrant's frown,
  In shame, my glory and my crown ;

4 In want, my plentiful supply,
    In weakness, my Almighty power,
  In bonds, my perfect liberty,
    My light in Satan's darkest hour,
  In grief, my joy unspeakable,
  My life in death, my heaven in hell.
                Charles Wesley. 1749.

227 7.6. 7.6. 7.7. 7.6.
  *Behold, He that keepeth
   Israel shall neither slumber nor sleep.*
        Psalm cxxi. 4.

TO the hills I lift mine eyes,
  The everlasting hills ;
Streaming thence, in fresh supplies,
  My soul the Spirit feels ;
Will He not His help afford ?
  Help, while yet I ask, is given ;
God comes down, the God and Lord
  That made both earth and heaven.

THE LORD'S DAY.

2 Faithful soul, pray always, pray,
   And still in God confide;
He thy feeble steps shall stay,
   Nor suffer thee to slide;
Lean on thy Redeemer's breast,
   He thy quiet spirit keeps,
Rest in Him, securely rest,
   Thy Watchman never sleeps.

3 Neither sin, nor earth, nor hell,
   Thy Keeper can surprise;
Careless slumbers cannot steal
   On His all-seeing eyes;
He is Israel's sure defence;
   Israel all His care shall prove,
Kept by watchful providence,
   And ever-waking love.

4 See the Lord, thy Keeper, stand
   Omnipotently near;
Lo! He holds thee by thy hand,
   And banishes thy fear,
Shadows with His wings thy head,
   Guards from all impending harms;
Round thee and beneath are spread
   The everlasting arms.

5 Christ shall bless thy going out,
   Shall bless thy coming in,
Kindly compass thee about,
   Till thou art saved from sin;
Like thy spotless Master, thou,
   Filled with wisdom, love, and power,
Holy, pure, and perfect, now,
   Henceforth, and evermore.
                      Wesley. 1743.

228   C.M D.
In this was manifested the love of God toward us.—1 John iv. 9.

WE love Thee, Lord, yet not alone,
   Because Thy bounteous hand
Showers down its rich and ceaseless gifts
   On ocean and on land;
Because Thou bidd'st the sun go forth
   Rejoicing in his might,
And kindle earth to glowing life
   And beauty with his light.

2 'Tis not alone because Thy names
   Of wisdom, power, and love,
Are written on the earth beneath,
   The glorious skies above;
For these Thy gifts we praise Thee, Lord,
   Yet not for these alone,
The incense of Thy children's love
   Arises to Thy throne.

3 We love Thee, Lord, because when we
   Had erred and gone astray,
Thou didst recall our wandering souls
   Into the heavenward way;
When helpless, hopeless, we were lost
   In sin and sorrow's night,
Thou didst send forth a guiding ray
   Of Thy benignant light.

4 Because, when we forsook Thy ways,
   Nor kept Thy holy will,
Thou wast not the avenging Judge,
   But gracious Father still:
Because we have forgot Thee, Lord,
   Yet Thou hast not forgot;
Because we have forsaken Thee,
   Yet Thou forsakest not;

5 Because, O Lord, Thou lovedst us
   With everlasting love;
Because Thy Son came down to die,
   That we might live above;
Because, when we were bound by sin,
   Thou gavest hopes of heaven;
Yes; much we love, who much have sinned
   And much have been forgiven.
                    Julia A. Elliott. 1809.

229   7.7. 7.7.
To the Lord . . . belong mercies and forgivenesses.—Daniel ix. 9

LORD, have mercy when we pray
   Strength to seek a better way;
When our wakening thoughts begin
First to loathe our cherished sin;
When our weary spirits fail,
And our aching brows are pale;
When our tears bedew Thy word,
Then, O then, have mercy, Lord!

2 Lord, have mercy when we lie
On the restless bed, and sigh;
Sigh for death, yet fear it still,
From the thought of former ill;
When the dim advancing gloom
Tells us that our hour is come;
When is loosed the silver cord,
Then, O then, have mercy, Lord!

3 Lord, have mercy when we know
First how vain this world below!
When our darker thoughts oppress,
Doubts perplex and fears distress;
When the earliest gleam is given
Of Thy bright but distant heaven;
Then Thy fostering grace afford,
Then, O then, have mercy, Lord! Amen.
                    H. H. Milman. 1827.

THE LORD'S DAY.

230   L.M.
It is a good thing to give thanks unto the Lord.—Psalm xcii. 1.

SWEET is the work, my God, my King,
   To praise Thy name, give thanks and sing,
To show Thy love by morning light,
And talk of all Thy truth at night.

DIVINE WORSHIP.

2 Sweet is the day of sacred rest,
  No mortal cares distract my breast;
  O may my heart in tune be found,
  Like David's harp of solemn sound!

3 My heart shall triumph in the Lord,
  And bless His works, and bless His word;
  Thy works of grace how bright they shine!
  How deep Thy counsels, how divine!

4 Then I shall share a glorious part,
  When grace hath well refined my heart,
  And fresh supplies of joy are shed,
  Like holy oil to cheer my head.

5 Then shall I see, and hear, and know
  All I desired and wished below,
  And every power find sweet employ
  In that eternal world of joy.
  Isaac Watts. 1719.

231   7.6. 7.6. D.
*Call the Sabbath a delight,
the holy of the Lord.*—Isaiah lviii. 13.

O DAY of rest and gladness,
  O day of joy and light,
O balm of care and sadness,
  Most beautiful, most bright!
Thou art a cooling fountain
  In life's dry, dreary sand;
From thee, like Pisgah's mountain
  We view our promised land.

2 On thee, at the creation,
    The light first had its birth;
  On thee, for our salvation,
    Christ rose from depths of earth.
  On thee our Lord victorious
    The Spirit sent from heaven;
  And thus on thee most glorious
    A triple light was given.

3 To-day on weary nations
    The heavenly manna falls;
  To holy convocations
    The silver trumpet calls;
  Where Gospel light is glowing
    With pure and radiant beams;
  And living water flowing
    With soul-refreshing streams.

4 May we new graces gaining
    From this our day of rest,
  Attain the rest remaining
    To spirits of the blest;
  And there our voice upraising
    To Father and to Son
  And Holy Ghost, be praising
    Ever the Three in One. Amen.
    Bishop C. Wordsworth. 1862.

232   7.6. 7.6. D.
*This is the day which the
Lord hath made: we will rejoice and be
glad in it.*—Psalm cxviii. 24.

THE dawn of God's dear Sabbath
  Breaks o'er the earth again,
As some sweet summer morning
  After a night of pain:
It comes as cooling showers
  To some exhausted land;
As shade of clustered palm-trees
  'Mid weary wastes of sand.

2 O day, when earthly sorrow
    Is merged in heavenly joy,
  And trial changed to blessing
    That foes may not destroy:
  When want is turned to fulness,
    And weariness to rest,
  And pain to wondrous rapture,
    Upon the Saviour's breast.

3 Lord, we would bring for offering,
    Though marred with earthly soil,
  A week of earnest labour,
    Of steady faithful toil;
  Fair fruits of self-denial,
    Of strong deep love to Thee,
  Fostered by Thine own Spirit
    In our humility.

4 And we would bring our burden
    Of sinful thought and deed,
  In Thy pure presence kneeling,
    From bondage to be freed;
  Our heart's most bitter sorrow
    For all Thy work undone,—
  So many talents wasted,
    So few bright laurels won!

5 So be it, Lord, for ever;
    O may we evermore,
  In Jesu's holy presence,
    His blessed name adore:
  Upon His peaceful Sabbath,
    Within His temple walls,
  Type of the stainless worship
    In Zion's golden halls;

6 So that, in joy and gladness,
    We reach that home at last;
  When life's short week of sorrow,
    And sin and strife are past:
  When angel-hands have gathered
    The fair ripe fruit for Thee,
  O Father, Lord, Redeemer,
    Most Holy Trinity! Amen.
    Mrs. Ada Cross. 1866.

233   L. M.
*I was in the Spirit on the
Lord's day.*—Rev. i. 10.

AGAIN our weekly labours end,
  And we the Sabbath's call attend;
Improve, our souls, the sacred rest,
And seek to be for ever blest.

THE LORD'S DAY.

2 This day let our devotions rise
　To heaven, a grateful sacrifice;
　And God that peace divine bestow,
　Which none but they who feel it know.

3 This holy calm within the breast
　Prepares for that eternal rest,
　Which for the sons of God remains,
　The end of cares, the end of pains.

4 In holy duties, let the day
　In holy pleasures pass away:
　How sweet the Sabbath thus to spend,
　In hope of that which ne'er shall end!
　　　　　　　　　J. Stennett. 1732.

234　　　　　　　　　　　　C.M.
*Ye shall keep the Sabbath
therefore; for it is holy unto you.*
Exodus xxxi. 14.

THE Lord of Sabbath let us praise,
　In concert with the blest,
Who, joyful, in harmonious lays
　Employ an endless rest.

2 Thus, Lord, while we remember Thee,
　We blest and pious grow;
　By hymns of praise we learn to be
　Triumphant here below.

3 On this glad day a brighter scene
　Of glory was displayed,
　By God, the eternal Word, than when
　This universe was made.

4 He rises, who mankind has bought,
　With grief and pain extreme;
　'Twas great to speak a world from nought;
　'Twas greater to redeem!
　　　　　　Samuel Wesley, jun. 1735.

235　　　　　　　　　8.6. 8.4.
The rest of the Holy Sabbath.
Exodus xvi. 23.

HAIL, sacred day of earthly rest,
　From toil and trouble free;
Hail, day of light, that bringest light
　And joy to me.

2 A holy stillness, breathing calm
　On all the world around,
　Uplifts my soul, O God, to Thee
　Where rest is found.

3 No sound of jarring strife is heard,
　As weekly labours cease;
　No voice, but those that sweetly sing
　Sweet songs of peace.

4 All earthly things appear to fade,
　As, rising high and higher,
　The yearning voices strive to join
　The heavenly choir.

5 For those who sing with saints below
　Glad songs of heavenly love,
Shall sing, when songs on earth have
　　ceased,
　With saints above.

6 Accept, O God, my hymn of praise
　That Thou this day hast given,
　Sweet foretaste of that endless day
　Of rest in heaven. Amen.
　　　　　　　Godfrey Thring. 1870.

236　　　　　　　　　8.8. 8.8.6.
*In Thee, O Lord, do I put
my trust.*—Ps. lxxi. 1.

ON this, the holiest and best
　Of earth's dim days, the day of rest;
O, let my happy portion be
To find supreme delight in Thee—
　In Thee, my God, in Thee!

2 These precious hours I would improve
　In fervent prayer, in sacred love;
From earth's delusive pleasures flee,
To find my every joy in Thee—
　In Thee, my God, in Thee!

3 When, humbly kneeling at Thy throne,
　With deep distress my guilt I own,
O, let my contrite spirit see
What boundless mercy dwells in Thee—
　In Thee, my God, in Thee!

4 When in Thy temple I adore,
　And truth's unfathomed mines explore;
Or trembling, praise the One in Three,
Fresh glories let me ever see
　In Thee, my God, in Thee!

5 Thus on each day of holy rest,
　May I with heavenly joys be blest;
And in a bright eternity
Have my undying bliss in Thee—
　In Thee, my God, in Thee! Amen.
　　　　　　　　　　Anon. 1872.

237　　　　　　　　　S.M.
*The Sabbath of the Lord
thy God.*—Exodus xx. 10.

WELCOME, sweet day of rest,
　That saw the Lord arise;
Welcome to this reviving breast,
　And these rejoicing eyes.

2 The King Himself comes near,
　And feasts His saints to-day;
Here we may sit, and see Him here,
　And love, and praise, and pray.

3 One day amidst the place
　Where Thou, my Lord, hast been,
Is sweeter than ten thousand days
　Of pleasurable sin.

DIVINE WORSHIP.

4 My willing soul would stay
In such a frame as this,
And sit and sing herself away
To everlasting bliss.
Isaac Watts. 1709.

238   *Sing aloud unto God our strength.*—Psalm lxxxi. 1.   S. M.

SING to the Lord, our might,
  With holy fervour sing ;
Let hearts and instruments unite
  To praise our Heavenly King.

2 This is His holy house,
  And this His festal day,
When He accepts the humblest vows
  That we sincerely pay.

3 The Sabbath to our sires
  In mercy first was given ;
The Church her Sabbath still requires
  To speed her on to heaven.

4 We still, like them of old,
  Are in the wilderness ;
And God is still as near His fold,
  To pity and to bless.

5 Then let us open wide
  Our hearts for Him to fill ;
And He that Israel then supplied,
  Will help His Israel still.
H. F. Lyte. 1834.

239   *The first day of the week.*
1 Corinthians xvi. 2.   S. M.

THIS is the day of Light ;
  Let there be light to-day !
O Dayspring, rise upon our night,
  And chase its gloom away.

2 This is the day of Rest
  Our failing strength renew ;
On weary brain and troubled breast
  Send Thou Thy freshening dew.

3 This is the day of Peace ;
  Thy peace our spirits fill ;
Bid Thou the blasts of discord cease,
  The waves of strife be still.

4 This is the day of Prayer :
  Let earth to heaven draw near ;
Lift up our hearts to seek Thee there,
  Come down to meet us here.

5 This is the day of Bread—
  The Bread which Thou wilt give ;
To-day for us Thy feast is spread,
  That hungering souls may live.

6 This is the First of days :
  Send forth Thy quickening breath,
And wake dead souls to love and praise,
  O Vanquisher of Death ! Amen.
John Ellerton. 1867.

240   *God is light.*—1 John i. 5.   7.8. 7.8. 7.7.

LIGHT of light, enlighten me,
  Now anew the day is dawning ;
Sun of grace, the shadows flee,
Brighten Thou my Sabbath morning ;
  With Thy joyous sunshine blest,
  Happy is my day of rest !

2 Fount of all our joy and peace,
  To Thy living waters lead me ;
Thou from earth my soul release,
And with grace and mercy feed me ;
  Bless Thy word that it may prove
  Rich in fruits that Thou dost love.

3 Kindle Thou the sacrifice
That upon my lips is lying ;
  Clear the shadows from mine eyes,
That, from every error flying,
  No strange fire may in me glow
  Which Thine altar doth not know.

4 Let me with my heart to-day,
Holy, Holy, Holy, singing,
  Rapt, awhile from earth away.
All my soul to Thee up-springing,
  Have a foretaste holy given
  How they worship Thee in heaven.

5 Rest in me and I in Thee,
Build a Paradise within me ;
  O reveal Thyself to me,
Blessed Love, who diedst to win me ;
  Fed from Thine exhaustless urn,
  Pure and bright my lamp shall burn.

6 Hence all care and vanity,
For the day to God is holy ;
  Come, Thou glorious Majesty,
Deign to fill this temple lowly ;
  Nought to-day my soul shall move
  Simply resting in Thy love. Amen.
B. Schmolck. 1731.
Tr. *Catherine Winkworth.* 1858.

241   *I was glad when they said unto me, Let us go into the house of the Lord.*
Psalm cxxii. 1.   6.6.8. 6.6.8.

HOW pleased and blest was I
  To hear the people cry,
Come, let us seek our God to-day ;
  Yes, with a cheerful zeal,
  We haste to Zion's hill,
And there our vows and honours pay.

THE LORD'S DAY.

2 Zion, thrice happy place,
   Adorned with wondrous grace,
And walls of strength embrace thee round;
   In thee our tribes appear,
   To pray, and praise, and hear
The sacred gospel's joyful sound.

3 There David's greater Son
   Has fixed His royal throne;
He sits for grace and judgment there:
   He bids the saints be glad,
   He makes the sinner sad,
And humble souls rejoice with fear.

4 May peace attend thy gate,
   And joy within thee wait,
To bless the soul of every guest!
   The man that seeks thy peace,
   And wishes thine increase,
A thousand blessings on him rest!

5 My tongue repeats her vows,
   Peace to this sacred house!
For there my friends and kindred **dwell**;
   And since my glorious God
   Makes thee His blest abode,
My soul shall **ever** love thee well.
             Isaac Watts. 1719.

242   6.6. 6.6. 8.8.
A day in Thy courts is better than a thousand.—Psalm lxxxiv. 10.

LORD of the worlds above!
   How pleasant and how fair
The dwellings of Thy love,
   Thine earthly temples are:
To Thine abode My heart aspires,
With warm desires To see my God.

2 O happy souls that pray
   Where God delights to hear!
O happy men that pay
   Their constant service there!
They praise Thee still; And happy they
Who love the way To Zion's hill.

3 They go from strength to strength,
   Through this dark vale of tears,
Till each o'ercomes at length,
   Till each in heaven appears:
O glorious seat! Thou God, our King,
Shalt thither bring Our willing feet.

4 God is our Sun and Shield,
   Our Light and our Defence;
With gifts His hands are filled,
   We draw our blessings thence:
He shall bestow Upon our race
His saving grace, And glory too.

5 The Lord His people loves;
   His hand no good withholds
From those His heart approves,
   From holy, humble souls:
Thrice happy he, O Lord of Hosts,
Whose spirit trusts Alone in Thee!
             Isaac Watts. 1719.

243   7.7. 7.7. D.
How amiable are Thy tabernacles, O Lord of Hosts.—Ps. lxxxiv. L

PLEASANT are Thy courts above
   In the land of light and love;
Pleasant are Thy courts below
   In this land of sin and woe:
O, my spirit longs and faints
   For the converse of Thy saints,
For the brightness of Thy face,
   For Thy fulness, God of grace.

2 Happy birds that sing and fly
   Round Thy altars, O Most High;
Happier souls that find a rest
   In a heavenly Father's breast;
Like the wandering dove that found
   No repose on earth around,
They can to their ark repair,
   And enjoy it ever there.

3 Happy souls, their praises flow
   In this vale of sin and woe;
Waters in the desert rise,
   Manna feeds them from the skies;
On they go from strength to strength,
   Till they reach Thy throne at length,
At Thy feet adoring fall,
   Who hast led them safe through all.

4 Lord, be mine this prize to win,
   Guide me through a world of sin;
Keep me by Thy saving grace,
   Give me at Thy side a place;
Sun and Shield alike Thou art,
   Guide and guard my erring heart;
Grace and glory flow from Thee;
   Shower, O shower them, Lord, on me.
                  Amen.
             H. F. Lyte. 1834.

244   L.M.
Pray for the peace of Jerusalem.—Psalm cxxii. 6.

SWEET is the solemn voice that calls
   The Christian to the house of prayer;
I love to stand within its walls,
   For Thou, O Lord, art present there.

2 I love to tread the hallowed courts,
   Where two or three for worship meet;
For thither Christ Himself resorts,
   And makes the little band complete.

3 'Tis sweet to raise the common song,
   To join in holy praise and love;
And imitate the blessed throng
   That mingle hearts and songs above.

4 Within these walls may peace abound,
   May all our hearts in one agree;
Where brethren meet, where Christ is found,
   May peace and concord ever be.
             H. F. Lyte. 1834.

DIVINE WORSHIP.

245 L.M.
There remaineth therefore a rest to the people of God.—Heb. iv. 9.

LORD of the Sabbath, hear our vows,
On this Thy day, in this Thy house;
And own as grateful sacrifice,
The songs which from the desert rise.

2 Thine earthly Sabbaths, Lord, we love,
But there's a nobler rest above;
To that our labouring souls aspire,
With ardent pangs of strong desire.

3 No more fatigue, no more distress,
Nor sin, nor hell, shall reach the place;
No groans to mingle with the songs
Which warble from immortal tongues.

4 No rude alarms of raging foes,
No cares to break the long repose,
No midnight shade, no clouded sun,
But sacred, high, eternal noon.

5 O long-expected day! begin,
Dawn on these realms of woe and sin;
Fain would we leave this weary road,
And sleep in death, to rest with God.
Philip Doddridge. 1755.

246 L.M.
Lord, I have loved the habitation of Thy house.—Psalm xxvi. 8.

HOW pleasant, how divinely fair,
O Lord of Hosts, Thy dwellings are!
With strong desire my spirit faints
To meet the assemblies of Thy saints.

2 Blest are the saints that sit on high,
Around the throne of majesty;
Thy brightest glories shine above,
And all their work is praise and love.

3 Blest are the souls that find a place
Within the temple of Thy grace;
There they behold Thy gentle rays,
And seek Thy face, and learn Thy praise.

4 Blest are the men whose hearts are set
To find the way to Sion's gate;
God is their strength, and through the road
They lean upon their helper, God.

5 Cheerful they walk with growing strength,
Till all shall meet in heaven at length,
Till all before Thy face appear,
And join in nobler worship there.
Isaac Watts. 1719.

247 L.M.
My house shall be called the house of prayer.—Matthew xxi. 13.

FAR from my thoughts, vain world, depart,
Make not the house of prayer thy mart;
Lord of the temple and the day,
Drive the intrusive crowd away

2 Fain would I find a calm retreat
From vain distractions near Thy feet,
And, borne above all earthly care,
Be joyful in Thy house of prayer.

3 Lord! in this blest and hallowed hour
Reveal Thy presence and Thy power;
Show to my faith Thy hands and side,
My Lord and God, the Crucified!

4 Or let me, through the opening skies,
Catch one bright glimpse of Paradise;
And realise, with raptured awe,
The vision dying Stephen saw.

5 But, if unworthy of such joy,
Still shall Thy love my heart employ;
For, of Thy favoured children's fare,
'Twere bliss the very crumbs to share.

6 Yet **never** can my soul be fed
With less than Thee, the Living Bread;
Thyself unto my soul impart,
And with Thy presence fill my heart.
Amen.
Isaac Watts. 1709.

248 L.M.
The Lord God is a sun and shield.—Psalm lxxxiv. 11.

GREAT God, attend, while Sion sings
The joy that from Thy presence springs;
To spend one day with Thee on earth
Exceeds a thousand days of mirth.

2 Might I enjoy the meanest place
Within Thy house, O God of grace;
Not tents of ease, nor thrones of power
Should tempt my feet to leave Thy door.

3 God is our sun, He makes our day;
God is our shield, He guards our way
From all the assaults of hell and sin,
From foes without, and foes within.

4 All needful grace will God bestow,
And crown that grace with glory too;
He gives us all things, and withholds
No real good from upright souls.

5 O God, our King, whose sovereign sway
The glorious hosts of heaven obey,
And devils at Thy presence flee,
Blest is the man that trusts in Thee.
Amen.
Isaac Watts. 1719.

249 8.7.8.7.4.7.
Now therefore are we all here present before God.—Acts x. 33.

IN Thy name, O Lord, assembling,
We Thy people now draw near;
Teach us to rejoice with trembling,
Speak, and let Thy servants hear—
Hear with meekness,
Hear Thy word with godly fear.

THE LORD'S DAY.

2 While our days on earth are lengthened,
   May we give them, Lord, to Thee;
Cheered by hope and daily strengthened,
   May we run, nor weary be
      Till Thy glory
      Without clouds in heaven we see.

3 Then in worship, purer, sweeter,
   All Thy people shall adore;
Tasting of enjoyment greater
   Far than thought conceived before;
      Full enjoyment,
      Full, unmixed, and evermore.
              Thomas Kelly. 1815.

250   *It shall be a Sabbath of rest unto you.*—Leviticus xvi. 31.   L.M.

WE rose to-day with anthems sweet,
   To sing before the mercy-seat,
And ere the darkness round us fell,
We bade the grateful vespers swell.

2 Whate'er has risen from heart sincere,
Each upward glance of filial fear,
Each true resolve, each solemn vow,
Jesus, our Lord! accept them now.

3 Whate'er beneath Thy searching eyes
Has wrought to spoil our sacrifice,
'Mid this sweet stillness while we bow,
Jesus, our Lord! forgive us now:

4 And teach us erring souls to win,
And hide their multitude of sin;
To tread in Thy long-suffering way,
And grow more like Thee day by day.

5 So as our Sabbaths hasten past,
And rounding years bring nigh the last;
When sinks the sun behind the hill,
When all the weary wheels stand still;

6 When by our bed the loved ones weep,
And death-dews o'er the forehead creep,
And vain is help or hope from men;
Jesus, our Lord! receive us then.
                Amen.
            W. M. Punshon. 1867.

251   *And at even, when the sun did set, they brought unto Him all that were diseased.*—Mark i. 32.   L.M.

AT even ere the sun was set,
   The sick, O Lord, around Thee lay;
O, in what divers pains they met!
O, with what joy they went away!

2 Once more 'tis eventide, and we,
Oppressed with various ills, draw near;
What if Thy form we cannot see?
We know and feel that Thou art here.

3 O Saviour Christ, our woes dispel;
For some are sick, and some are sad,
And some have never loved Thee well,
And some have lost the love they had;

4 And some have found the world is vain,
Yet from the world they break not free;
And some have friends who give them pain,
Yet have not sought a friend in Thee.

5 O Saviour Christ, Thou too art man;
Thou hast been troubled, tempted, tried;
Thy kind but searching glance can scan
The very wounds that shame would hide;

6 Thy touch has still its ancient power;
No word from Thee can fruitless fall;
Hear in this solemn evening hour,
And in Thy mercy heal us all.   Amen.
            Henry Twells. 1868.

252   *I will trust in the covert of Thy wings.*—Psalm lxi. 4.   C.M.

THE Lord be with us as we bend
   His blessing to receive;
His gift of peace upon us send,
   Before His courts we leave.

2 The Lord be with us as we walk
   Along our homeward road;
In silent thought, or friendly talk,
   Our hearts be still with God.

3 The Lord be with us till the night
   Enfold our day of rest;
Be He of every heart the Light,
   Of every home the Guest.

4 The Lord be with us through the hours
   Of slumber calm and deep;
Protect our homes, renew our powers,
   And guard His people's sleep. Amen.
            John Ellerton. 1870.

253   *The end of the Sabbath.* Matthew xxviii. 1.   8.8.8.6.

THE Sabbath-day has reached its close;
   Yet, Saviour, ere I seek repose,
Grant me the peace Thy love bestows;
   Smile on my evening hour.

2 O heavenly Comforter, sweet Guest!
Hallow and calm my troubled breast;
Weary, I come to Thee for rest;
   Smile on my evening hour.

3 Let not the Gospel seed remain
Unfruitful, or be lost again;
Let heavenly dews descend like rain;
   Smile on my evening hour.

DIVINE WORSHIP.

4 O! ever present, ever nigh,
  Jesus, on Thee I fix mine eye;
  Thou hear'st the contrite spirit's sigh;
  Smile on my evening hour.

5 My only Intercessor, Thou,
  Mingle Thy fragrant incense now
  With every prayer, and every vow;
  Smile on my evening hour.

6 And, O when life's short course shall end,
  And death's dark shades around impend,
  My God, my everlasting Friend,
  Smile on my evening hour. Amen.
  Charlotte Elliott. 1836.

---

254   S.M.
And all the angels stood round about the throne ... and worshipped God.—Rev. vii. 11.

OUR day of praise is done,
  The evening shadows fall;
But pass not from us with the sun,
  True Light that lightenest all.

2 Around the throne on high,
  Where night can never be,
The white-robed harpers of the sky
  Bring ceaseless hymns to Thee.

3 Too faint our anthems here,
  Too soon of praise we tire;
But O, the strains how full and clear
  Of that eternal choir!

4 Yet Lord, to Thy dear will
  If Thou attune the heart,
We in Thine angels' music still
  May bear our lower part.

5 'Tis Thine each soul to calm,
  Each wayward thought reclaim,
And make our life a daily psalm
  Of glory to Thy name.

6 A little while and then
  Shall come the glorious end;
And songs of angels and of men
  In perfect praise shall blend.
  John Ellerton. 1868.

---

255   10.10. 10.10.
The Lord will bless His people with peace.—Psalm xxix. 11.

SAVIOUR, again to Thy dear name we raise
With one accord our parting hymn of praise;
We stand to bless Thee ere our worship cease,
Then lowly kneeling wait Thy word of peace.

2 Grant us Thy peace through this approaching night;
Turn Thou for us its darkness into light;
From harm and danger keep Thy children free,
For dark and light are both alike to Thee.

3 Grant us Thy peace upon our homeward way;
With Thee began, with Thee shall end the day;
Guard Thou the lips from sin, the hearts from shame,
That in this house have called upon Thy name.

4 Grant us Thy peace throughout our earthly life,
Our balm in sorrow, and our stay in strife;
Then, when Thy voice shall bid our conflict cease,
Call us, O Lord, to Thine eternal peace.
  Amen.
  John Ellerton. 1868.

MORNING.

256   L.M.
My voice shalt Thou hear in the morning, O Lord.—Psalm v. 3.

AWAKE, my soul, and with the sun
  Thy daily stage of duty run;
Shake off dull sloth, and early rise
To pay thy morning sacrifice.

2 Thy precious time misspent redeem,
Each present day thy last esteem;
Improve thy talent with due care,
For the great day thyself prepare.

3 In all thy converse be sincere,
In conscience as the noon-day clear;
Think how the all-seeing God surveys
Thy secret thoughts, thy words, and ways.

4 Wake, and lift up thyself, my heart,
And with the angels take thy part,
Who all night long unwearied sing
High glory to the eternal King.

5 Lord, I my vows to Thee renew;
Scatter my sins as morning dew!
Guard my first springs of thought and will,
And with Thyself my spirit fill.

6 Direct, control, suggest, this day,
All I design, or do, or say;
That all my powers, with all their might,
In Thy sole glory may unite. Amen.
  Bishop Ken. 1695.

MORNING.

257 8.4.7. 8.4.7.
*I will sing aloud of Thy
mercy in the morning.*—Psalm lix. 16.

COME, my soul, thou must be waking,
  Now is breaking
O'er the earth another day ;
Come to Him who made this splendour,
  See thou render
All thy feeble strength can pay.

2 Gladly hail the sun returning ;
    Ready burning
  Be the incense of thy powers ;
  For the night is safely ended,
    God hath tended
  With His care thy helpless hours.

3 Pray that He may prosper ever
    Each endeavour,
  When thine aim is good and true ;
  But that He may ever thwart thee,
    And convert thee,
  When thou evil wouldst pursue.

4 Think that He thy ways beholdeth,
    He unfoldeth
  Every fault that lurks within ;
  He the hidden shame glossed over
    Can discover,
  And discern each deed of sin.

5 Mayest thou on life's last morrow,
    Free from sorrow,
  Pass away in slumber sweet ;
  And, released from death's dark sadness,
    Rise in gladness
  That far brighter Sun to greet.

6 Our God's bounteous gifts abuse not,
    Light refuse not,
  But His Spirit's voice obey ;
  Thou with Him shalt dwell, beholding
    Light unfolding
  All things in unclouded day.
    Baron Von Canitz. 17th Century.
        Tr. H. J. Buckoll. 1841.

258 10.10. 10.10.
*The Father of lights, with
whom is no variableness.*—James i. 17.

FATHER of lights, again these new-born rays
That flush the kindling east bespeak Thy praise ;
Shine on our hearts, true Light of Life, that we
May mirror back Thy light and shine for Thee.

2 God of the day ! teach us to walk in light
With guileless hearts, as in our Father's sight ;
To hate the works of darkness, and to be
True to ourselves, our fellow-man, and Thee.

3 God of our time ! Thy latest gift—this day,
We render back to Thee, and humbly lay
Upon Thine altar ; consecrate its hours,
That we may work Thy will with all our powers.

4 God of our home ! we own Thee Master here,
May all be ordered in Thy faith and fear ;
Unseen but felt, O, may Thy presence prove
The bond of peace, the pledge of joy and love.

5 And when at last life's eventide shall come,
And the night gathers round our earthly home,
O, be Thy face unveiled, our morning star,
Herald of dawn in sunnier climes afar.
        W. Hay Aitken. 1872.

259 8.7. 8.7.
*The night is far spent, the
day is at hand.*—Romans xiii. 12.

LO, the golden sun is shining :
  Let us, children of the day,
Cast aside the works of darkness,
  Which have led our souls astray.

2 May the morn, sweet calmness breathing,
    Bring us peace and purity ;
  From our lips all falsehood banish,
    And our thoughts from sin set free.

3 Ever, as the day glides onward,
    Let us keep our tongue from guile,
  Eyes from wandering, feet from sliding,
    Hands from aught that can defile.

4 All day long an Eye is o'er us,
    Which our every secret knows,
  Sees our every step before us,
    From first morn till evening's close.

5 Lord, in holy adoration
    Fix our hearts and eyes on Thee,
  Till we taste Thy blest salvation,
    And unveiled Thy brightness see.

6 Praise unending to the Father,
    To the Son and Spirit Blest,
  Still from age to age ascending,
    Be throughout all worlds addrest.
                    Amen.
From the Latin. Tr. W. J. Copeland. 1847.

260 7.7. 7.7. 7.7.
*O give thanks unto the Lord ;
for He is good.*—Psalm cxxxvi. 1.

O GIVE thanks to Him who made
  Morning light and evening shade,
Source and Giver of all good,
Nightly sleep and daily food ;
Quickener of our wearied powers,
Guard of our unconscious hours.

DIVINE WORSHIP.

2 O give thanks to nature's King,
Who made every breathing thing;
His, our warm and sentient frame,
His, the mind's immortal flame;
O how close the ties that bind
Spirits to the Eternal mind!

3 O give thanks with heart and lip,
For we are His workmanship;
And all creatures are His care;
Not a bird that cleaves the air
Falls unnoticed; but who can
Speak the Father's love to man?

4 O give thanks to Him who came
In a mortal, suffering frame—
Temple of the Deity
Came, for sinful man to die;
In the path Himself hath trod,
Leading back His saints to God.
Josiah Conder. 1836.

261 L.M.
The Lord's mercies . . . are new every morning.—Lam. iii. 22, 23.

O TIMELY happy, timely wise,
Hearts that with rising morn **arise**,
Eyes that the beam celestial view,
Which evermore makes all things new.

2 New, every morning, is the love,
Our wakening and uprising prove;
Through sleep and darkness safely brought,
Restored to life, and **power**, and thought.

3 New mercies, each returning day,
Hover around us while we pray;
New perils past, new sins forgiven,
New thoughts of God, new hopes of heaven.

4 If, on our daily **course**, **our mind**
Be set to hallow **all we find**,
New treasures **still**, **of countless price**,
God will **provide for sacrifice**.

5 Old friends, old scenes will lovelier be,
As more of heaven in each we see;
Some softening gleam of love and prayer
Will dawn on every cross and care.

6 The trivial round, **the common task**
Will furnish all we **ought to ask**;
Room to deny ourselves—a road
To bring us, daily, **nearer God**.

7 Seek we no more,—content with these,
Let present **rapture**, **comfort**, **ease**,
As heaven shall bid them, come or go,—
The secret, **this, of rest below**.

8 Only, O Lord, in Thy dear love,
Fit us for perfect rest above;
And help us, this and every day,
To live more nearly as we pray. Amen.
John Keble. 1827.

262 S.M.
In the morning will I direct my prayer unto Thee, and will look up.
Psalm v. 3.

SWEETLY the holy hymn
Breaks on the morning air;
Before the world with smoke is dim
We meet to offer prayer.

2 While flowers are wet with dews,
Dew of our souls, descend;
Ere yet the sun the day renews,
O Lord, Thy Spirit send!

3 Upon the battle-field,
Before the fight begins,
We seek, O Lord, Thy sheltering shield,
To guard us from our sins.

4 Ere yet our vessel sails
Upon the stream of day,
We plead, O Lord, for heavenly gales
To speed us on our way.

5 On the lone mountain side,
Before the morning's light,
The Man of Sorrows wept and cried,
And rose refreshed with might.

6 O hear us, then, for we
Are very weak and frail;
We make the Saviour's name our plea,
And surely must prevail.
C. H. Spurgeon. 1866.

263 L.M.
He that followeth Me shall not walk in darkness.—John viii. 12.

O JESUS, Lord of light and grace,
Thou brightness of the Father's **face**;
Thou fountain of eternal light,
Whose beams disperse the shades of night.

2 Come, Holy Sun of Heavenly love,
Come in Thy radiance from above,
And to our inward hearts convey
The Holy **Spirit's** cloudless ray.

3 So we the Father's help will claim
And sing the Father's glorious Name,
And His almighty grace implore,
That we may stand, to fall no more.

4 May He our actions deign to bless,
And loose the bonds of wickedness;
From sudden falls our feet defend,
And guide us safely to the end.

5 May faith, deep-rooted in the soul,
Subdue our flesh, our minds control;
May guile depart, and discord cease,
And all within be joy and peace.

MORNING.

6 O hallowed thus be every day;
  Let meekness be our morning ray,
  Our faith like noontide splendour glow,
  Our souls the twilight never know. Amen.
Bishop Ambrose of Milan. 4th Century.
        Tr. John Chandler. 1837.

---

264   C.M.D.
The things which are seen are temporal; but the things which are not seen are eternal.—2 Corinthians iv. 18.

THE roseate hues of early dawn,
  The brightness of the day,
The crimson of the sunset sky,
  How fast they fade away!
O, for the pearly gates of heaven,
  O, for the golden floor,
O, for the Sun of Righteousness,
  That setteth nevermore!

2 The highest hopes we cherish here,
  How fast they tire and faint;
How many a spot defiles the robe
  That wraps an earthly saint!
O, for a heart that never sins,
  O, for a soul washed white,
O, for a voice to praise our King,
  Nor weary day nor night.

3 Here faith is ours, and heavenly hope,
  And grace to lead us higher;
But there are perfectness, and peace,
  Beyond our best desire.
O, by Thy love, and anguish, Lord,
  And by Thy life laid down,
Grant that we fall not from Thy grace,
  Nor cast away our crown. Amen.
        Mrs. Cecil F. Alexander. 1853.

---

265   7.6. 7.6. D.
The heavens declare the glory of God.—Psalm xix. 1.

THY love for all Thy creatures
  What tongue, O God, may tell?
The morning, noon, and evening,
  Alike our praise compel;
The morning, noon, and evening,
  Whene'er they rise or fall,
Unite to hymn Thy praises,
  Great Maker of them all.

2 Behold! the sun in splendour
  Hath lit his fires on high,
The farther on his journey,
  The higher in the sky;
And when again he sinketh
  Beneath the western wave,
A radiant crown of glory
  Shall kindle o'er his grave.

3 May we, to whom in mercy
  A brighter light is given,
The farther on our journey,
  The nearer be to heaven;

And when the shades of evening
  Shall lengthen o'er our heads,
May rays of heavenly glory
  Illume our dying beds.

4 Shine! shine! Thou Sun Eternal,
  And cast a ray divine
On those who hymn Thy praises,
  Both now and ever Thine;
For then no cloud of evening
  Shall gather round the past,
But Thou, O Christ, shalt light us
  Safe Home,—safe Home at last.
                    Amen.
        Godfrey Thring. 1879.

---

266   11.10. 11.10. Iambic.
When I awake, I am still with Thee.—Psalm cxxxix. 18.

STILL, still with Thee, when purple morning breaketh,
  When the bird waketh, and the shadows flee;
Fairer than morning, lovelier than the daylight,
  Dawns the sweet consciousness, I am with Thee.

2 Alone with Thee, amid the mystic shadows,
  The solemn hush of nature newly born;
Alone with Thee, in breathless adoration,
  In the calm dew and freshness of the morn.

3 As in the dawning o'er the waveless ocean,
  The image of the morning star doth rest,
So in this stillness Thou beholdest only
  Thine image in the waters of my breast.

4 Still, still with Thee, as to each new-born morning
  A fresh and solemn splendour still is given,
So doth this blessed consciousness, awaking,
  Breathe, each day, nearness unto Thee and heaven.

5 When sinks the soul, subdued by toil, to slumber,
  Its closing eye looks up to Thee in prayer;
Sweet the repose, beneath Thy wings o'ershadowing,
  But sweeter still to wake and find Thee there.

6 So shall it be at last, in that bright morning
  When the soul waketh, and life's shadows flee;
O! in that hour, fairer than daylight's dawning,
  Shall rise the glorious thought, I am with Thee!
      Mrs. Harriet Beecher Stowe. b. 1814.

DIVINE WORSHIP.

267 S.M.
*With Thee is the fountain
of life.—Psalm xxxvi. 9.*

STILL with Thee, O my God,
  I would desire to be,
By day, by night, at home, abroad,
  I would be still with Thee.

2 With Thee, when dawn comes in,
  And calls me back to care,
Each day returning, to begin
  With Thee, my God, in prayer.

3 With Thee, amid the crowd
  That throngs the busy mart,
To hear Thy voice, 'mid clamour loud,
  Speak softly to my heart.

4 With Thee, when day is done,
  And evening calms the mind,
The setting, as the rising sun,
  With Thee my heart would find.

5 With Thee, when darkness brings
  The signal of repose,
Calm in the shadow of Thy wings
  Mine eyelids I would close.

6 With Thee, in Thee, by faith
  Abiding I would be,
By day, by night, in life, in death,
  I would be still with Thee. Amen.
    James D. Burns. 1856. *alt.*

268 7.6, 7.6, D.
*Be thankful unto Him, and
bless His name.—Psalm c. 4.*

FOR all Thy care we bless Thee,
  O Father, God of might!
For golden hours of morning,
  And quiet hours of night;
Thine is the arm that shields us
  When danger threatens nigh,
And Thine the hand that yields us
  Rich gifts of earth and sky.

2 For all Thy love we bless Thee;
  No mortal lips can speak
Thy comfort to the weary,
  Thy pity for the weak;
By Thee life's path is brightened
  With sunshine and with song;
The heavy loads are lightened,
  The feeble hearts made strong.

3 For all Thy truth we bless Thee;
  Our human vows are frail,
But through the strife of ages
  Thy word can never fail;
The kingdoms shall be broken,
  The mighty ones will fail,
The promise Thou hast spoken
  Shall triumph over all.

4 O teach us how to praise Thee,
  And touch our lips with fire!
Yea, let Thy Dove descending,
  Our hearts and minds inspire;
Thus toiling, watching, singing,
  We tread our desert way,
And every hour is bringing
  Nearer the dawn of day.
    Sarah Doudney. 1871.

EVENING.

269 L.M.
*I will both lay me down
in peace, and sleep.—Psalm iv. 8.*

GLORY to Thee, my God, this night,
  For all the blessings of the light;
Keep me, O keep me, King of kings,
Beneath Thine own almighty wings!

2 Forgive me, Lord, for Thy dear Son,
The ills that I this day have done;
That with the world, myself, and Thee,
I, ere I sleep, at peace may be.

3 O may my soul on Thee repose,
And may sweet sleep mine eyelids close,
Sleep that may me more vigorous make,
To serve my God when I awake.

4 Teach me to live, that I may dread
The grave as little as my bed;
Teach me to die, that so I may
Rise glorious at the judgment day.

5 If in the night I sleepless lie,
My soul with heavenly thoughts supply;
Let no ill dreams disturb my rest,
No powers of darkness me molest.

6 Praise God, from whom all blessings flow,
Praise Him, all creatures here below,
Praise Him above, ye heavenly host,
Praise Father, Son, and Holy Ghost. Amen.
    Bishop Ken. 1695.

270 L.M.
*So He bringeth them unto
their desired haven.—Psalm cvii. 30.*

FATHER of all, again we meet
  With joy to worship at Thy feet;
From home and loved ones parted long
Once more we join their evening song.

2 Thy guiding hand, O Lord, hath been
With us in every changing scene,
And now we bend before Thy throne,
Thy goodness and Thy love to own.

EVENING.

3 Thou know'st the story of the past—
The joys and sorrows that have cast
Their lights and shadows on the way
That we have journeyed day by day.

4 But we would leave the past with Thee,
With all that is, and all to be;
Thy tender care so long hath blest,
We can but trust Thee for the rest.

5 If some we loved have passed away
Through death's dark vale to brighter day,
We would not call them back again
To share with us life's toil and pain:

6 We know that they are safe with Thee,
From every cloud of sorrow free,
And, in a home of light and love,
We all shall meet again above.
H. P. H. 1881.

271 10.10. 10.10.
Abide with us.—Luke xxiv. 29.

ABIDE with me, fast falls the eventide;
The darkness deepens, Lord, with me abide:
When other helpers fail, and comforts flee,
Help of the helpless, O abide with me.

2 Swift to its close ebbs out life's little day,
Earth's joys grow dim, its glories pass away,
Change and decay in all around I see;
O Thou who changest not, abide with me.

3 Not a brief glance I beg, a passing word;
But as Thou dwell'st with Thy disciples, Lord,
Familiar, condescending, patient, free,
Come not to sojourn, but abide with me.

4 I need Thy presence every passing hour;
What but Thy grace can foil the tempter's power?
Who like Thyself my guide and stay can be?
Through cloud and sunshine, Lord, abide with me.

5 I fear no foe, with Thee at hand to bless,
Ills have no weight, and tears no bitterness.
Where is Death's sting? where, Grave, thy victory?
I triumph still, if Thou abide with me.

6 Reveal Thyself before my closing eyes,
Shine through the gloom, and point me to the skies;
Heaven's morning breaks, and earth's vain shadows flee;
In life, in death, O Lord, abide with me.
Amen.
H. F. Lyte. 1847.

272 L.M.
Thy faithfulness every night.
Psalm xcii. 2.

SUN of my soul, Thou Saviour dear,
It is not night if Thou be near;
O may no earth-born cloud arise,
To hide Thee from Thy servant's eyes.

2 When the soft dews of kindly sleep
My wearied eyelids gently steep,
Be my last thought, how sweet to rest
For ever on my Saviour's breast.

3 Abide with me from morn till eve,
For without Thee I cannot live;
Abide with me when night is nigh,
For without Thee I dare not die.

4 If some poor wandering child of Thine
Have spurned to-day the voice Divine,
Now, Lord, the gracious work begin,
Let him no more lie down in sin.

5 Watch by the sick; enrich the poor
With blessings from Thy boundless store;
Be every mourner's sleep to-night,
Like infant's slumbers, pure and light.

6 Come near and bless us when we wake,
Ere through the world our way we take;
Till in the ocean of Thy love
We lose ourselves in heaven above.
Amen.
John Keble. 1820.

273 8.8. 8.8. 8.8.
In blessing I will bless thee.
Genesis xxii. 17.

SWEET Saviour! bless us ere we go;
Thy word into our minds instil;
And make our lukewarm hearts to glow
With lowly love and fervent will.
Through life's long day and death's dark night,
O gentle Jesus! be our light.

2 The day is done, its hours have run,
And Thou hast taken count of all,
The scanty triumphs grace hath won,
The broken vow, the frequent fall.
Through life's long day and death's dark night,
O gentle Jesus! be our light.

3 Grant us, dear Lord! from evil ways
True absolution and release;
And bless us, more than in past days,
With purity and inward peace.
Through life's long day and death's dark night,
O gentle Jesus! be our light.

DIVINE WORSHIP.

4 Do more than pardon; give us joy,
   Sweet fear and sober liberty,
And loving hearts without alloy
   That only long to be like Thee.
Through life's long day and death's dark
     night,
O gentle Jesus! be our light.

5 For all we love, the poor, the sad,
   The sinful, unto Thee we call;
O let Thy mercy make us glad:
   Thou art our Jesus, and our All.
Through life's long day and death's dark
     night,
O gentle Jesus! be our light.   Amen.
                   F. W. Faber. 1861.

274   10.10. 10.10. 10.10.
*The Lord shall be unto thee
an everlasting light, and thy God thy glory.*
      Isaiah lx. 19.

1 THE day is gently sinking to a close,
   Fainter and yet more faint the sun-
     light glows;
O brightness of Thy Father's glory, Thou
Eternal Light of Light, be with us now;
Where Thou art present, darkness cannot
     be,
Midnight is glorious noon, O Lord, with
     Thee.

2 Our changeful lives are ebbing to an end,
Onward to darkness and to death we tend;
O Conqueror of the grave, be Thou our
     Guide,
Be Thou our Light in death's dark even-
     tide;
Then in our mortal hour will be no gloom,
No sting in death, no terror in the tomb.

3 Thou, who in darkness walking didst
     appear
Upon the waves, and Thy disciples cheer,
Come, Lord, in lonesome days, when
     storms assail,
And earthly hopes and human succours
     fall;
When all is dark, may we behold Thee
     high,
And hear Thy voice, 'Fear not, for it is I.'

4 The weary world is mouldering to decay,
Its glories wane, its pageants fade away;
In that last sunset, when the stars shall
     fall,
May we arise, awakened by Thy call,
With Thee, O Lord, for ever to abide
In that blest day which has no eventide!
                       Amen.
          Bishop C. Wordsworth. 1862.

275   7.6. 7.6. 8.8.
*When thou liest down,
thou shalt not be afraid.*—Prov. iii. 24.

1 THE day is past and over;
   All thanks, O Lord, to Thee!
We pray Thee now that sinless
   The hours of dark may be;
O Jesus, keep us in Thy sight,
And save us through the coming night!

2 The joys of day are over;
   We lift our hearts to Thee,
And ask Thee that offenceless
   The hours of dark may be;
O Jesus, make their darkness light,
And save us through the coming night!

3 The toils of day are over;
   We raise our hymn to Thee,
And ask that free from peril
   The hours of dark may be;
O Jesus, keep us in Thy sight,
And guard us through the coming night!

4 Be Thou our soul's preserver,
   For Thou, O God, dost know
How many are the perils
   Awaiting us below;
O loving Jesus, hear our call,
And guard and save us from them all!
                        Amen.
         Anatolius. 5th Century.
         Tr. *J. M. Neale.* 1862.

276   8.8. 8.4.
*And there shall be no night
there.*—Rev. xxii. 5.

1 THE radiant morn hath passed away,
   And spent too soon her golden store;
The shadows of departing day
   Creep on once more.

2 Our life is but an autumn day,
   Its glorious noon how quickly past;
Lead us, O Christ, Thou Living Way,
   Safe home at last.

3 O! by Thy soul-inspiring grace
   Uplift our hearts to realms on high;
Help us to look to that bright place
   Beyond the sky;

4 Where light, and life, and joy, and peace
   In undivided empire reign,
And thronging angels never cease
   Their deathless strain;

5 Where saints are clothed in spotless white,
   And evening shadows never fall,
Where Thou, Eternal Light of light,
   Art Lord of all. Amen.
                Godfrey Thring. 1866.

EVENING.

277 S.M.
The time of my departure is at hand.—2 Timothy iv. 6.

THIS sweetly solemn thought
  Can cheer the evening hour,
I'm nearer to my home to-day
  Than e'er I've been before;

2 Nearer the nightless day,
  Nor sun nor moon to shine;
Nearer the fountains pure and deep,
  Water of life divine:

3 Nearer the pearly gates,
  The city pure as gold;
Nearer the presence of its King,
  To share His love untold:

4 Nearer my Father's house,
  Where many mansions be;
Nearer the glorious great white throne,
  Nearer the crystal sea:

5 Nearer the vale of death,
  To lay my burden down;
To bear the palm and wear the crown,
  And stand before the throne.
    Phœbe Cary. d. 1871.
    And George Gill. 1878.

278 8.8. 8.8. 8.8.
At evening time it shall be light.—Zech. xiv. 7.

AT evening time when day is done,
  Life's little day is near its close,
And all the glare and heat are gone,
  And gentle dews foretell repose;
To crown my faith before the night,
At evening time let there be light!

2 At evening time when labour's past;
  Though storms and toils have marred my day
Mercy has tempered every blast,
  And love and hope have cheered the way;
Now let the parting hour be bright,
At evening time let there be light!

3 God doth send light at evening time,
  And bid the fears, the doubtings flee;
I trust His promises sublime,
  His glory now is risen on me,
His full salvation is in sight,
At evening time, there now is light.
    James Montgomery. 1841.
    Alt. George Rawson. 1857.

279 8.8.7. 8.8.7.
Under the shadow of the Almighty.—Psalm xci. 1.

FATHER, in high heaven dwelling,
  May our evening song be telling,
Of Thy mercy large and free;
Through the day Thy love has fed us,
Through the day Thy care has led us,
  With divinest charity.

2 This day's sins, O, pardon, Saviour!
  Evil thoughts, perverse behaviour,
Envy, pride, and vanity;
From the world, the flesh, deliver,
Save us now, and save us ever,
  O Thou Lamb of Calvary!

3 From enticements of the devil,
  From the might of spirits evil,
Be our shield and panoply;
Let Thy power this night defend us,
And a heavenly peace attend us,
  And angelic company.

4 While the night dews are distilling,
  Holy Ghost, each heart be filling
From Thine own infinity!
Softly let our eyes be closing,
Loving souls on Thee reposing,
  Ever blessed Trinity! Amen.
    George Rawson. 1857.

280 6.6.4. 6.6.6.4.
Now let it please Thee to bless the house of Thy servant.
2 Samuel vii. 29.

FATHER of love and power,
  Guard Thou our evening hour,
    Shield with Thy might;
For all Thy care this day
Our grateful thanks we pay,
And to our Father pray,
    Bless us to-night!

2 Jesus Immanuel!
  Come in Thy love to dwell
    In hearts contrite;
For many sins we grieve,
But we Thy grace receive,
And in Thy word believe;
    Bless us to-night!

3 Spirit of Holiness,
  Gentle transforming grace,
    Indwelling Light;
Soothe Thou each weary breast,
Now let Thy peace possessed
Calm us to perfect rest;
    Bless us to-night! Amen.
    George Rawson. 1857.

281 8.4. 8.4. 8.8.8.4.
There shall no evil befall thee.
Psalm xci. 10.

GOD that madest earth and heaven,
  Darkness and light;
Who the day for toil hast given,
  For rest the night;
May Thine angel-guard defend us,
Slumber sweet Thy mercy send us,
Holy dreams and hopes attend us,
  This livelong night.

2 When we in the morn awaken,
　Guide us Thy way,
Keep our love and truth unshaken
　In work and play;
In our daily task be near us,
In temptation keep and hear us,
And with holy counsel cheer us,
　The livelong day.

3 Guard us waking, guard us sleeping,
　And, when we die,
May we in Thy mighty keeping
　All peaceful lie·
When the last dread call shall wake us,
Do not Thou, our God, forsake us,
But to reign in glory take us
　With Thee on high. Amen.
　　First verse, Bishop R. Heber. 1826.
Third verse, Archbishop Whately. d. 1863.

282　　　　　　　　12.11. 12.11.
　I will be as the dew unto
　Israel.—Hosea xiv. 5.

HOW calmly the evening once more is
　descending,
　As kind as a promise, as still as a prayer;
O wing of the Lord, in Thy shelter be-
　friending,
　May we and our households continue to
　share!

2 The sky, like the kingdom of heaven, is
　open!
　O enter, my soul, at the glorious gates;
The silence and smile of His love are the
　token,
　Who now for all comers invitingly waits.

3 We come to be soothed with His merciful
　healing;
　The dews of the night cure the wounds
　of the day;
We come, our life's worth and its brevity
　feeling,
　With thanks for the past; for the future
　we pray.

4 Lord, save us from folly; be with us in
　sorrow;
　Sustain us in work till the time of our
　rest;
When earth's day is over, may heaven's to-
　morrow
　Dawn on us, of homes long expected
　possessed. Amen.
　　　　　T. T. Lynch. 1855.

283　　　　　　　　11.11. 11.5.
　Thou shalt lie down, and
　none shall make thee afraid.—Job xi. 19.

NOW God be with us, for the night is
　closing;
The light and darkness are of His disposing,
And 'neath His shadow we to rest may
　yield us,
　For He will shield us.

2 Let evil thoughts and spirits flee before us;
　Till morning cometh, watch, O Father,
　o'er us;
In soul and body Thou from harm defend
　us;
　　Thine angels send us.

3 Let holy thoughts be ours when sleep o'er-
　takes us;
Our earliest thoughts be Thine when
　morning wakes us;
All day serve Thee; in all that we are doing
　Thy praise pursuing.

4 We have no refuge; none on earth to aid us,
Save Thee, O Father, who Thine own hast
　made us;
But Thy dear presence will not leave them
　lonely,
　　Who seek Thee only.

5 Father, Thy name be praised, Thy king-
　dom given,
Thy will be done on earth as 'tis in heaven;
Keep us in life, forgive our sins, deliver
　Us now and ever. Amen.
Peter Herbert. 16th Century. 4th verse anon.
　　Tr. Catherine Winkworth. 1858.

284　　　　　　　　8.7. 8.7. D.
　Fear thou not, for I am
　with thee.—Isaiah xli. 10.

SAVIOUR, breathe an evening blessing,
　Ere repose our spirits seal;
Sin and want we come confessing,
　Thou canst save, and Thou canst heal
Though destruction walk around us,
　Though the arrows past us fly,
Angel-guards from Thee surround us;
　We are safe, for Thou art nigh!

2 Though the night be dark and dreary,
　Darkness cannot hide from Thee;
Thou art He who, never weary,
　Watchest where Thy people be:
Should swift death this night o'ertake us,
　And our couch become our tomb,
May the morn in heaven awake us,
　Clad in light, and deathless bloom.
　　　　　　　　　Amen.
　　　　　James Edmeston. 1820.

285　　　　　　　　4.4.7.8.7.
　And the city had no need of the
sun, . . . for the glory of God did lighten it,
and the Lamb is the light thereof.
　　　　Revelation xxi. 23.

THE day departs;
　Our souls and hearts
Long for that better morrow,
　When Christ shall set His people free
　From every care and sorrow,

EVENING.

2 The sunshine bright
  Is lost in night ;
O Lord, Thyself unveiling,
Shine on our souls with beams of love,
  All darkness there dispelling.

3 Be Thou still nigh,
  With sleepless eye,
While all around are sleeping,
And angel-guards, at Thy command,
  Afar all danger keeping.

4 **The land above,**
    Of peace and love,
  No earthly beams need brighten ;
  For all its borders Christ Himself
    Doth with His glory lighten.

5 May we be there,
    That joy to share,
  Glad hallelujahs singing,
  With all the ransomed evermore
    Our joyful praises bringing.

6 Lord Jesus, Thou
    Our Refuge now,
  Forsake Thy servants never ;
  Uphold and guide, that we may stand
  Before Thy throne for ever.   Amen.
          J. A. Freylinghausen. 17th Century.
                      Tr. H. L. L. 1862.

286   L.M.
        Peace be unto you.
          Luke xxiv. 36.

THOU who hast known the careworn
    breast,
  The weary need of sleep's deep balm,
Come, Saviour, ere we go to rest,
  And breathe around Thy perfect calm.

2 Thy presence gives us childlike trust,
    Gladness and hope without alloy,
  The faith that triumphs o'er the dust,
    And gleamings of eternal joy.

3 Stand in **our midst**, dear Lord, and say,
    'Peace be to you this evening hour ;'
  Then all the struggles of the day
    Vanish before Thy loving power.

4 **Blest is the** pilgrimage to heaven,
    A little nearer every night ;
  Christ to our earthly darkness given,
    Till in His glory there is light.
              George Rawson. 1853.

287   9.8. 9.8.
        So He giveth His beloved
          sleep.—Psalm cxxvii. 2.

WE bless Thy name, O holy Jesus,
    For evening hours and silent night,
For day's decline, that gently frees us
    From all the burdens of the light.

2 Thou hast on earth been often weary,
    Pity our weakness from above ;
  The darkness, then no longer dreary,
    Is but the shadow of Thy love.

3 To Thy belovèd, in their sleeping,
    Thou givest rest, sweet rest of heart ;
  Lord ! take us to Thy holy keeping,
    And all Thy peace untold impart.
                                   Amen.
              George Rawson. 1876.

288   6.4. 6.6.
        The lifting up of my hands
    as the evening sacrifice.—Psalm cxli. 2.

THE sun is sinking fast,
    The daylight dies ;
  Let love awake, and pay
    Her evening sacrifice.

2 As Christ upon the **cross**
    His head inclined,
  And to His Father's **hands**
    His parting **soul resigned** ;

3 **So now herself, my soul,**
    Would wholly give
  Into His sacred charge
    In whom all spirits live ;

4 So now beneath **His eye**
    Would calmly **rest**,
  Without a **wish or thought**
    Abiding in the **breast** ;

5 Save that His will **be done**,
    Whate'er betide,
  Dead to herself, and **dead**
    In Him to all beside.

6 **Thus would I live ; yet now**
    Not I, but He,
  In all His power and love,
    Henceforth alive in me.

7 One sacred **Trinity**,
    One Lord **Divine** ;
  May I be ever His,
    And **He for ever mine!** Amen.
                From the Latin.
              Tr. Edward Caswall. 1858.

289   9.8. 9.8.
        The Lord shall reign for ever
          and ever.—Exodus xv. 18.

THE day Thou gavest, Lord, is ended,
    The darkness falls at Thy behest ;
To Thee our morning hymns ascended,
    Thy praise shall sanctify our rest.

83

THE HOLY SCRIPTURES.

2 We thank Thee that Thy **Church unsleep-**
  ing,
  While earth rolls onward **into light,**
  Through all the world her **watch is keep-**
  ing,
  And **rests not now by day or night.**

3 As o'er each continent and island
  The dawn leads on another day,
  The voice of prayer is never silent,
  Nor dies the strain of praise away.

4 The sun that bids us rest is waking
  Our brethren 'neath the western sky,
  And hour by hour fresh lips are making
  Thy wondrous doings heard on high.

5 So be it, **Lord ;** Thy throne shall never,
  Like earth's proud empires, pass away ;
  Thy kingdom stands, and grows for ever,
  Till all Thy creatures own Thy sway.

  John Ellerton. 1870.

The Holy Scriptures.

290 C.M.
  O, how love I Thy law !
  Psalm cxix. 97.

FATHER of mercies, in Thy word
  What endless glory shines !
For ever be Thy name adored
For these celestial lines.

2 Here may the wretched sons of want
  Exhaustless riches find ;
  Riches above what earth can grant,
  And lasting as the mind.

3 Here the fair Tree **of Knowledge grows,**
  And yields a free **repast ;**
  Sublimer sweets **than nature knows,**
  Invite the **longing taste.**

4 Here the Redeemer's **welcome voice**
  Spreads heavenly peace **around ;**
  And life and everlasting joys
  Attend the blissful sound.

5 **Divine Instructor, gracious Lord,**
  Be Thou for ever near !
  Teach me to love Thy sacred word,
  And view my Saviour there.   Amen.

  Anne Steele.   1760.

291 C.M.
  Thy word is a lamp unto my
  feet. — Psalm cxix. 105.

LAMP of our feet, whereby we trace
  Our path when wont to stray ;
Stream from the fount of heavenly grace,
  Brook by the traveller's way ;

2 Bread of our souls whereon we feed,
  True manna from on high ;
  Our guide and chart wherein we read
  Of realms beyond the sky ;

3 Pillar of fire through watches dark,
  And radiant cloud by day ;
  When waves wouldwhelm our tossing bark,
  Our anchor and our stay :

4 Word of the everlasting God,
  Will of His glorious Son,
  Without Thee how could earth be trod,
  Or heaven itself be won ?

5 Lord, grant us all aright to learn
  The wisdom it imparts ;
  And to its heavenly teaching turn
  With simple, childlike hearts !   Amen.

  Bernard Barton   1826.

292 L.M.
  Let the word of Christ dwell
  in you richly in all wisdom.
  Colossians iii. 16.

DWELL in me richly, blessèd word,
  So wise to teach, so safe to guide ;
Come as my counsellor from God,
  And evermore with me abide.

2 I need thy light, for I am dark,
  And prone to go from God astray ;
  Be thou a lamp unto my feet,
  To keep them in the narrow way

3 I need thee when the days are bright,
  And earthly things look fair and gay,
  To point to treasures in the skies,
  That cannot change or fade away

4 I need thee when my aching heart
  Is bowed with sorrow, pain, or care ;
  Through thee I may my Saviour's voice,
  In tones of gentlest comfort, hear.

THE HOLY SCRIPTURES.

5 I need thee when my foes without,
   And inward fightings try me sore,
To tell me of the blessed land
Where conflict shall disturb no more.

6 And when my happy home I reach,
   A gladsome psalm my voice shall raise;
And all thy teachings shall unite
In the new song of thankful praise.
                                        Anon.

293   8.8. 8.8. 8.8.
All Scripture is given by inspiration of God, and is profitable for doctrine.—2 Timothy iii. 16.

INSPIRER of the ancient seers,
   Who wrote from Thee the sacred page,
The same through all succeeding years,
To us, in our degenerate age,
The Spirit of Thy word impart,
And breathe the Life into our heart.

2 While now Thine oracles we read,
   With earnest prayer and strong desire,
O let Thy Spirit from Thee proceed,
Our souls to awaken and inspire,
Our weakness help, our darkness chase,
And guide us by the light of Grace!

3 Whene'er in error's paths we rove,
   The living God through sin forsake,
Our conscience by Thy word reprove,
Convince and bring the wanderers back,
Deep wounded by Thy Spirit's sword,
And then by Gilead's balm restored.

4 The sacred lessons of Thy grace,
   Transmitted through Thy word, repeat,
And train us up in all Thy ways,
To make us in Thy will complete,
Fulfil Thy love's redeeming plan,
And bring us to a perfect man.

5 Furnished out of Thy treasury,
   O may we always ready stand
To help the souls redeemed by Thee,
In what their various states demand,
To teach, convince, correct, reprove,
And build them up in holiest love. Amen.
                     Charles Wesley. 1762.

294   C.M.
Open Thou mine eyes, that I may behold wondrous things out of Thy law.
       Psalm cxix. 18.

FATHER of all, in whom alone
   We live, and move, and breathe,
One bright celestial ray dart down,
And cheer Thy sons beneath.

2 While in Thy word we search for Thee,
   We search with trembling awe!
Open our eyes, and let us see
The wonders of Thy law.

3 Now let our darkness comprehend
   The light that shines so clear;
Now the revealing Spirit send,
And give us ears to hear.

4 Before us make Thy goodness pass,
   Which here by faith we know;
Let us in Jesus see Thy face,
And die to all below. Amen.
                          Wesley. 1740.

295   8.8. 8.8. 8.8.
A prophet shall the Lord your God raise up unto you . . . like unto me; Him shall ye hear in all things.
       Acts iii. 22.

COME, O Thou Prophet of the Lord,
   Thou great Interpreter divine,
Explain Thine own transmitted word;
To teach and to inspire is Thine;
Thou only canst Thyself reveal,
Open the book, and loose the seal.

2 Now, Jesus, now the veil remove,
   The folly of our darkened heart;
Unfold the wonders of Thy love,
The knowledge of Thyself impart;
Our ear, our inmost soul we bow:
Speak, Lord, Thy servants hearken now.
                           Amen.
                          Wesley. 1746.

296   C.M.
Thy testimonies also are my delight and my counsellors.
       Psalm cxix. 24.

HOW precious is the book divine,
   By inspiration given!
Bright as a lamp its glories shine,
To guide our souls to heaven.

2 It sweetly cheers our drooping hearts,
   In this dark vale of tears;
Life, light, and joy, it still imparts,
And quells our rising fears.

3 O'er all the strait and narrow way
   Its radiant beams are cast;
A light whose ever-cheering ray
Grows brightest at the last.

4 O may its lamp, through all the night
   Of life, make plain our way!
Till we behold the clearer light
Of an eternal day. Amen.
                     John Fawcett. 1782.

297   L.M.
Exceeding great and precious promises.—2 Peter i. 4.

LET everlasting glories crown
   Thy head, make Saviour and my Lord;
Thy hands have brought salvation down,
And writ the blessing in Thy word.

THE HOLY SCRIPTURES.

2 In vain the trembling conscience seeks
  Some solid ground to rest upon ;
  With long despair our spirit breaks,
  Till we apply to Christ alone.

3 How well Thy blessèd truths agree !
  How wise and holy Thy command !
  Thy promises, how firm they be !
  How firm our hope and comfort **stand** !

4 Should all the forms that men devise
  Assault my faith with treacherous art,
  I'd call them vanity and lies,
  And bind the Gospel to my heart.
                    Isaac Watts. 1709.

---

298   C.M.
God gave the increase.
1 Corinthians iii. 6.

O GOD, by whom the seed is given,
    By whom the harvest blest ;
Whose word, like manna showered from
    heaven,
Is planted in our breast :

2 Preserve it **from** the passing feet,
  And plunderers of the air ;
  The sultry sun's intenser heat,
  And weeds **of** worldly care.

3 Though buried deep, or thinly strown,
  Do Thou Thy grace supply ;
  The hope in earthly furrows sown
  Shall ripen in the sky.
               Bishop R. Heber. 1827.

---

299   L.M.
*God hath revealed them
unto us by His Spirit.*—1 Cor. ii. 10.

O GOD, who didst Thy will unfold
  In wondrous modes to saints of old,
  By dream, by oracle, or seer ;
  Wilt Thou not still Thy people hear ?

2 What though no answering voice is heard,
  Thine oracles, the written word,
  Counsel and guidance still impart,
  Responsive to the upright heart.

3 What though no more by dreams **is shown**,
  That future things to God are known,
  Enough the promises reveal ;
  Wisdom and love the rest conceal.

4 Faith asks no signal from the skies,
  To show that prayers accepted rise ;
  Our Priest is in the holy place,
  And answers from the throne of grace.

5 No need of prophets to inquire ;
  The Sun is risen ; the stars retire ;
  The Comforter is come, and sheds
  His holy unction on our heads,

6 Lord, with this grace our hearts inspire,
  Answer our sacrifice by fire ;
  And by Thy mighty acts declare,
  Thou art the God who hearest prayer.
                            Amen.
              Josiah Conder. 1836.

---

300   7.6. 7.6. D.
*God . . . hath . . . spoken
unto us by His Son.*—Heb. i. 1, 2.

O WORD of God Incarnate,
    O Wisdom from on high,
O Truth unchanged, unchanging,
    O Light of our dark sky ;
We praise Thee for the radiance
    That from the hallowed page,
A lantern to our footsteps,
    Shines on from age to age.

2 The Church from Thee, her Master,
    Received the gift Divine ;
  And still that light she lifteth
    O'er all the earth to shine.
  It is the golden casket
    Where gems of truth are stored ;
  It is the heaven-drawn picture
    Of Thee, the living Word.

3 It floateth like a banner
    Before God's host unfurled ;
  It shineth like a beacon
    Above the darkling world ;
  It is the chart and compass,
    That, o'er life's surging sea,
  'Mid mists and rocks and quicksands,
    Still guides, O Christ, to Thee.

4 O make **Thy** Church, dear Saviour,
    A lamp of burnished gold,
  To bear before the nations
    Thy true light, as of old.
  O teach Thy wandering pilgrims
    By this their path to trace,
  Till, clouds and darkness ended,
    They see Thee face **to** face. Amen.
              Bishop W. W. How. 1867.

---

301   8.8. 8.8. 8.8.
*Holy men of God spake
as they were moved by the Holy Ghost.*
2 Peter i. 21.

SPIRIT of **Truth**, essential God,
  Who didst Thy ancient saints inspire,
Shed in their hearts Thy love abroad,
  And touch their hallowed lips with
    fire ;
Our God **from** all eternity,
World without end, we worship Thee.

2 Still we believe, Almighty Lord,
  Whose presence fills both earth **and**
    heaven,
  The meaning of the written word
    Is by Thy inspiration given ;
  Thou only dost Thyself explain
  The secret mind of God to man,

THE HOLY SCRIPTURES.

3 Come, then, Divine Interpreter,
   The Scriptures to our hearts apply;
And, taught by Thee, we God revere,
   Him in Three Persons magnify;
In each the triune God adore,
Who was, and is for evermore. Amen.
                    Charles Wesley. 1767.

302   *The entrance of Thy*   C.M.
words giveth light.—Psalm cxix. 130.

A GLORY gilds the sacred page,
   Majestic, like the sun;
It gives a light to every age,
It gives, but borrows none.

2 The Spirit breathes upon the word,
   And brings the truth to sight;
Precepts and promises afford
   A sanctifying light.

3 The hand that gave it still supplies
   The gracious light and heat;
His truths upon the nations rise,
   They rise, but never set.

4 Let everlasting thanks be Thine,
   For such a bright display
As makes a world of darkness shine
   With beams of heavenly day.

5 My soul rejoices to pursue
   The steps of Him I love,
Till glory breaks upon my view
   In brighter worlds above.
                    William Cowper. 1779.

303   C.M.D.
Not as though I had already attained.—Philippians iii. 12.

WE limit not the truth of God
   To our poor reach of mind,
By notions of our day and sect,
   Crude, partial, and confined;
No, let a new and better hope
   Within our hearts be stirred;
The Lord hath yet more light and truth
   To break forth from His word.

2 Who dares to bind to his dull sense
   The oracles of heaven,
For all the nations, tongues, and climes,
   And all the ages given?
That universe, how much unknown!
   That ocean, unexplored!
The Lord hath yet more light and truth
   To break forth from His word.

3 Darkling our great forefathers went
   The first steps of the way;
'Twas but the dawning, yet to grow
   Into the perfect day;

And grow it shall; our glorious Sun
   More fervid rays afford;
The Lord hath yet more light and truth
   To break forth from His word.

4 The valleys passed, ascending still,
   Our souls would higher climb,
And look down from supernal heights
   On all the bygone time;
Upward we press; the air is clear,
   And the sphere-music heard;
The Lord hath yet more light and truth
   To break forth from His word.

5 O Father, Son, and Spirit, send
   Us increase from above,
Enlarge, expand all Christian souls
   To comprehend Thy love;
And make us all go on to know,
   With nobler powers conferred;
The Lord hath yet more light and truth
   To break forth from His word. Amen.
                    George Rawson. 1876.

304   8.8. 8.8. 8.8
His delight is in the law of the Lord.—Psalm i. 2.

WHEN quiet in my house I sit,
   Thy book be my companion still;
My joy Thy sayings to repeat,
   Talk o'er the records of Thy will,
And search the Oracles divine,
Till every heart-felt word be mine.

2 O may the gracious words divine
   Subject of all my converse be;
So will the Lord His follower join,
   And walk and talk Himself with me;
So shall my heart His presence prove,
And burn with everlasting love.

3 Oft as I lay me down to rest,
   O may the reconciling word
Sweetly compose my weary breast!
   While, on the bosom of my Lord,
I sink in blissful dreams away,
And visions of eternal day.

4 Rising to sing my Saviour's praise,
   Thee may I publish all day long!
And let Thy precious word of grace
   Flow from my heart, and fill my tongue.
Fill all my life with purest love,
And join me to the Church above. Amen.
                    Charles Wesley. 1762.

305   C.M.
Give me understanding, and I shall keep Thy law.—Psalm cxix. 34.

OPEN our eyes, O Lord! and show
   The wonders of Thy law;
Thyself reveal, and we shall know
More than the prophets saw.

THE GOSPEL MESSAGE.

2 Thy **word** is truth, each shining page
    Thy countless saints have sung;
  Its promises, from age to age,
    From land to land, have rung.

3 Yet, Lord, we cannot hear aright,
    Until we know Thy voice;
  Nor bear the glory of Thy light,
    Nor in Thy truth rejoice:

4 We scan in vain the mystic roll,
    Sealed with the sevenfold seal:
  Unless Thy Spirit touch our soul,
    And Thy great love **reveal**.

5 That love alone the seal can break,
    Or fix our hearts on Thee:
  Or truths of heavenly wisdom take,
    And bid us come and see.

6 O hope of everlasting life!
    O welcome to the skies!
  Message that calls from earth's **poor strife**,
    To peace that never dies.

7 Such faith Divine, **such** hope we hail,
    The anchor of the soul,
  Reaching to that within the **veil**,
    Faith undefiled and whole.

              W. J. Irons. 1873.

The Gospel Message.

306   *The glorious Gospel of the blessed God.*—1 Timothy i. 11.   C.M.

O FOR a thousand tongues to sing
    My great Redeemer's praise!
The glories of my God and King,
    The triumphs of His grace!

2 My gracious Master, **and my God**,
    Assist me to proclaim,
  To spread through all **the earth abroad**
    The honours of Thy name.

3 Jesus! the name **that charms our fears**,
    That bids **our sorrows cease**;
  'Tis music in **the sinner's ears**,
    'Tis life, **and health, and peace**.

4 He breaks the power of cancelled sin,
    He sets the prisoner free;
  His blood can make the foulest clean,
    His blood availed for me.

5 He speaks, and, listening to His voice,
    New life the dead receive,
  The mournful, broken hearts rejoice,
    The humble poor believe.

6 Hear Him, ye **deaf**; His praise, ye dumb,
    Your loosened tongues employ;
  Ye blind, behold your Saviour come,
    And leap, ye lame, for joy.

7 Look unto Him, ye nations; own
    Your God, ye fallen race;
  Look, and be saved through faith alone,
    Be justified by grace.

8 See all your sins on Jesus laid:
    The Lamb of God was slain,
  His soul was once an offering made
    For every soul of man.

              Charles Wesley. 1739.

---

307   *Salvation to our God which* ***sitteth upon*** *the throne, and unto the Lamb.*   5.5. 5.5. 6.5. **6.**5.
Revelation vii. 10.

YE servants of God,
    Your Master proclaim,
And publish abroad
    His wonderful name;
The name all-victorious
    Of Jesus extol;
His kingdom is glorious,
    And rules **over** all.

2 God ruleth **on high**,
    Almighty to save;
And still He is nigh,
    His presence we have;
The great congregation
    His triumph shall sing,
Ascribing salvation
    To Jesus **our** King.

3 *'Salvation to God
    Who sits on the throne,'
Let all cry aloud,
    And honour the Son
The praises of Jesus,
    The angels proclaim,
Fall down on their faces,
    And worship the Lamb.

4 Then let us adore,
    And give Him His right,
All glory and power,
    All wisdom and might,
All honour and blessing,
    With angels above,
And thanks never ceasing,
    For infinite love. Amen.

              Wesley. 1709.

THE GOSPEL MESSAGE.

308   7.6. 7.6. D.
Come unto Me, all ye that labour and are heavy laden, and I will give you rest.—Matthew xi. 28.

'COME unto Me, ye weary,
   And I will give you rest.'
O blessed voice of Jesus,
  Which comes to hearts oppressed !
It tells of benediction,
  Of pardon, grace, and **peace**,
Of joy that hath **no ending**,
Of love which cannot cease.

2 'Come unto Me, dear children,
   And I will give **you light**.'
O loving **voice** of **Jesus**,
  Which comes to cheer the night :
Our hearts were filled with sadness,
  And we had **lost our** way,
But Thou hast **brought** us gladness,
  And songs **at break of** day.

3 'Come unto Me, ye fainting,
   And I will give you life.'
O peaceful voice of Jesus,
  Which comes to end our strife :
The foe is **stern** and eager,
  The fight **is fierce** and long,
But Thou hast **made** us mighty,
  And stronger **than** the strong.

4 'And whosoever cometh
   I will not cast him out.'
O patient love of Jesus,
  Which drives away our doubt ;
Which calls us very sinners,
  Unworthy though we be
Of love so free and boundless,
  To come, dear Lord, to Thee !
        W. Chatterton Dix.   1867.

309   L.M.
God so loved the world, that He gave His only begotten Son.—John iii. 16.

FATHER, whose everlasting love
  Thy only Son for sinners gave ;
Whose grace to all did freely move,
  And sent Him down the world to save :

2 Help us Thy mercy to extol,
  Immense, unfathomed, unconfined ;
To praise the Lamb who died for all,
  The general Saviour of mankind.

3 Thy undistinguishing regard
  Was cast on Adam's fallen race ;
For all Thou hast in Christ prepared
  Sufficient, sovereign, saving grace.

4 The world He suffered to redeem,
  For all He hath the atonement made :
For those that will not come to Him,
  The ransom of His life was paid.

5 Arise, O God, maintain Thy cause !
  The fulness of the Gentiles call ;
Lift up the standard of Thy cross,
  And all shall own Thou diedst for **all**.
                Amen.
          Wesley.   1741.

310   L.M.
Ho ! every one that thirsteth, come ye to the waters.—Isaiah lv. 1.

HO ! every one that thirsts draw nigh ;
  'Tis God invites the fallen race ;
Mercy and free salvation buy,
  Buy wine, and milk, and gospel grace.

2 Come **to the living** waters, come !
  Sinners, obey your Maker's call ;
Return, ye weary wanderers, home,
  And find My grace **is** free for all.

3 See from the Rock **a fountain rise** !
  For you in healing **streams** it rolls ;
Money ye need not bring, **nor price** ;
  Ye labouring, burdened, **sin-sick souls**.

4 Nothing ye in exchange **shall give** ;
  Leave all you have **and are behind** ;
Frankly the gift of God **receive**,
  Pardon and peace in **Jesus find**.

5 Your willing ear and heart incline,
  My words believingly receive ;
Quickened your souls, by faith divine,
  An everlasting life shall live.
          Wesley.   1740.

311   C.M.D.
Of His fulness have all we received, and grace for grace.—John i. 16.

I HEARD the voice of **Jesus say**,
  '**Come** unto Me, and **rest** ;
Lay down, poor weary one, lay down
  Thy head upon My breast :'
I came to Jesus as I was,
  Weary, and worn, and sad ;
I found in Him **a** resting-place,
  And He has **made** me glad.

2 I heard the voice **of** Jesus **say**,
  'Behold, I freely give
The living water ;—thirsty one,
  Stoop down, and drink, and live :'
I came to Jesus, and I drank
  Of that life-giving stream
My thirst was quenched, my soul revived,
  And **now** I live in Him.

3 I heard the voice of Jesus say,
  'I am this dark world's light ;
Look unto Me, thy morn shall rise,
  And all thy day be bright :'
I looked to Jesus, and I found
  In Him, my Star, my Sun ;
And in that Light of Life I'll walk,
  Till travelling days are done.
         Horatius Bonar.   1857.

THE GOSPEL MESSAGE.

312 C.M.
*The Lord, the Lord God,
merciful and gracious.—Exodus xxxiv. 6.*

THY ceaseless, unexhausted love,
    Unmerited and free,
Delights our evil to remove,
    And help our misery.

2 Thou waitest to be gracious still,
    Thou dost with sinners bear,
That, saved, we may Thy goodness feel,
    And all Thy grace declare.

3 Thy goodness and Thy truth to me,
    To ev'ry soul abound;
A vast, unfathomable sea,
    Where all our thoughts are drowned.

4 Its streams the whole creation reach,
    So plenteous is the store;
Enough for all, enough for each,
    Enough for evermore.

5 Faithful, O Lord, Thy mercies are!
    A Rock that cannot move;
A thousand promises declare
    Thy constancy of love.

6 Throughout the universe it reigns,
    Unalterably sure;
And while the truth of God remains,
    The goodness must endure.
        Charles Wesley. 1762.

313 C.M.
We preach Christ crucified.
1 Corinthians i. 23.

JESUS, Thou all-redeeming Lord,
    Thy blessing we implore;
Open the door to preach Thy word,
    The great effectual door.

2 Gather the outcasts in, and save
    From sin and Satan's power;
And let them now acceptance have,
    And know their gracious hour.

3 Lover of souls! Thou know'st to prize
    What Thou hast bought so dear;
Come, then, and in Thy people's eyes
    With all Thy wounds appear.

4 Appear, as when of old confest
    The suffering Son of God;
And let them see Thee in Thy vest,
    But newly dipt in blood.

5 The hardness from their hearts remove,
    Thou who for all hast died;
Show them the tokens of Thy love,
    Thy feet, Thy hands, Thy side.

6 Thy feet were nailed to yonder tree
    To trample down their sin;
Thy hands stretched out they all may see
    To take Thy murderers in.

7 Thy side an open fountain is
    Where all may freely go,
And drink the living streams of bliss
    And wash them white as snow.

8 Ready Thou art the blood to apply,
    And prove the record true;
And all Thy wounds to sinners cry,
    'I suffered this for you!'
        Charles Wesley. 1749.

314 L.M.
*Thus saith the Lord,
Let not the wise man glory in his wisdom.*
Jeremiah ix. 23.

LET not the wise his wisdom boast;
    The mighty glory in his might;
The rich in flattering riches trust,
    Which take their everlasting flight.

2 The rush of numerous years bears down
    The most gigantic strength of man;
And where is all his wisdom gone,
    When dust he turns to dust again!

3 One only gift can justify
    The boasting soul that knows his God;
When Jesus doth His blood apply,
    I glory in His sprinkled blood.

4 The Lord my Righteousness I praise;
    I triumph in the love divine,
The wisdom, wealth, and strength of grace,
    In Christ to endless ages mine.
        Charles Wesley. 1762.

315 S.M.
*Not by works of righteousness
which we have done, but according to His
mercy He saved us.*—Titus iii. 5.

NOT what these hands have done
    Can save this guilty soul;
Not what this toiling flesh has borne
    Can make my spirit whole.

2 Not what I feel or do
    Can give me peace with God;
Not all my prayers, and sighs, and tears
    Can bear my awful load.

3 Thy work alone, O Christ,
    Can ease this weight of sin;
Thy blood alone, O Lamb of God,
    Can give me peace within.

4 Thy love to me, O God,
    Not mine, O Lord, to Thee,
Can rid me of this dark unrest,
    And set my spirit free.

5 Thy grace alone, O God,
    To me can pardon speak;
Thy power alone, O Son of God,
    Can this sore bondage break.

INVITATION TO THE SINNER.

6 I bless the Christ of God,
I rest on love divine;
And with unfaltering lip and heart,
I call this Saviour mine.
Horatius Bonar. 1857.

316 C.M. *With Chorus.*
The Gospel of your salvation.
Ephesians i. 13.

SALVATION! O the joyful sound!
What pleasure to our ears!
A sovereign balm for every wound,
A cordial for our fears.

Glory, honour, praise, and power
Be unto the Lamb for ever!
Jesus Christ is our Redeemer;
Hallelujah! praise the Lord.

2 Salvation! let the echo fly
The spacious earth around;
While all the armies of the sky
Conspire to raise the sound.

3 Salvation! O Thou bleeding Lamb,
To Thee the praise belongs;
Salvation shall inspire our hearts,
And dwell upon our tongues.
Isaac Watts. 1709.
And W. W. Shirley. 1772.

317 8.7.8.7.
His great love wherewith
He loved us.—Ephesians ii. 4.

WAS there ever kindest shepherd
Half so gentle, half so sweet,
As the Saviour who would have us
Come and gather round His feet?

2 There is welcome for the sinner;
And more graces for the good;
There is mercy with the Saviour,
There is healing in His blood.

3 There is plentiful redemption
In the blood that has been shed;
There is joy for all the members
In the sorrows of the Head.

4 For the love of God is broader
Than the measures of man's mind;
And the heart of the Eternal
Is most wonderfully kind.

5 If our love were but more simple,
We should take Him at His word;
And our lives would be all sunshine
In the sweetness of our Lord.
F. W. Faber. 1849.

Evangelistic Services.

INVITATION TO THE SINNER.

318 L.M.
Come; for all things
are now ready.—Luke xiv. 17.

COME, sinners, to the Gospel feast,
Let every soul be Jesu's guest;
Ye need not one be left behind,
For God hath bidden all mankind.

2 Sent by my Lord, on you I call,
The invitation is to all;
Come all the world, come sinner thou,
All things in Christ are ready now.

3 Come, all ye souls by sin opprest,
Ye restless wanderers after rest;
Ye poor, and maimed, and halt, and blind,
In Christ a hearty welcome find.

4 My message as from God receive,
Ye all may come to Christ, and live;
O let His love your hearts constrain,
Nor suffer Him to die in vain!

5 His love is mighty to compel,
His conquering love consent to feel;
Yield to His love's resistless power,
And fight against your God no more.

6 See Him set forth before your eyes,
That precious bleeding sacrifice!
His offered benefits embrace,
And freely now be saved by grace.

7 This is the time, no more delay,
This is the acceptable day;
Come in, this moment, at His call,
And live for Him who died for all.
Wesley. 1747.

EVANGELISTIC SERVICES.

319 8.7. 8.7. 7.7.
There shall be a fountain opened to the house of David, . . . for sin and for uncleanness.—Zech. xiii. 1.

COME to Calvary's holy mountain,
   Sinners ruined by the fall;
Here a pure and healing fountain
   Flows to you, to me, to all,
In a full perpetual tide,
Opened when the Saviour died.

2 Come, in sorrow and contrition,
   Wounded, impotent, and blind;
Here the guilty free remission,
   Here the troubled peace may find;
Health this fountain will restore,
He that drinks shall thirst no more.

3 He that drinks shall live for ever,
   'Tis a soul-renewing flood;
God is faithful; God will never
   Break His covenant in blood,
Signed when our Redeemer died,
Sealed when He was glorified.
                    James Montgomery. 1819.

320 12.11. 12.11.
Him that cometh to Me I will in no wise cast out.—John vi. 37.

O COME to the merciful Saviour who calls you,
   O come to the Lord who forgives and forgets;
Though dark be the fortune on earth that befalls you,
   There's a bright home above where the sun never sets.

2 O come then to Jesus, whose arms are extended
   To fold His dear children in closest embrace;
O come, for your exile will shortly be ended,
   And Jesus will show you His beautiful face!

3 Yes, come to the Saviour, whose mercy grows brighter
   The longer you look at the depth of His love;
And fear not! 'tis Jesus! and life's cares grow lighter,
   As you think of the home and the glory above.

4 Have you sinned as none else in the world have before you?
   Are you blacker than all other creatures in guilt?
O fear not, and doubt not: the mother who bore you
   Loves you less than the Saviour whose blood you have spilt.

5 O come, then, to Jesus, and say how you love Him,
   And vow at His feet you will keep in His grace;
For one tear that is shed by a sinner can move Him,
   And your sins will drop off in His tender embrace.

6 Come, come to His feet, and lay open your story
   Of suffering and sorrow, of guilt and of shame;
For the pardon of sin is the crown of His glory,
   And the joy of our Lord to be true to His name.
                    F. W. Faber. 1849.

321 8.7. 8.7. 4.7.
I am not come to call the righteous, but sinners to repentance. Matthew ix. 13.

COME, ye sinners, poor and wretched,
   Weak and wounded, sick and sore;
Jesus ready stands to save you,
   Full of pity joined with power:
      He is able;
   He is willing: doubt no more.

2 Ho! ye needy, come and welcome,
   God's free bounty glorify;
True belief and true repentance,
   Every grace that brings us nigh,
      Without money,
   Come to Jesus Christ and buy.

3 Let not conscience make you linger,
   Nor of fitness fondly dream;
All the fitness He requireth
   Is to feel your need of Him:
      This He gives you;
   'Tis the Spirit's rising beam.

4 Come, ye weary, heavy laden,
   Bruised and broken by the fall;
If you tarry till you're better,
   You will never come at all:
      Not the righteous,
   Sinners Jesus came to call.

5 Agonizing in the garden,
   Lo! your Saviour prostrate lies:
On the bloody tree behold Him;
   Hear Him cry before He dies,
      'It is finished!'
   Finished, the great sacrifice.

6 Saints and angels joined in concert,
   Sing the praises of the Lamb;
While the blissful scents of heaven
   Sweetly echo with His name,
      Hallelujah!
   Sinners here may sing the same.
                    Amen.
                    Joseph Hart. 1759.

INVITATION TO THE SINNER.

322   8.7. 8.7. D.
Call the poor, the maimed, the lame, the blind.—Luke xiv. 13.

'CALL them in!' the poor, the wretched,
  Sin-stained wanderers from the fold;
Peace and pardon freely offer,
  Can you weigh their worth with gold?
'Call them in!' the weak, the weary,
  Laden with the doom of sin;
Bid them come and rest in Jesus:
  He is waiting: 'call them in!'

2 'Call them in!' the Jew, the Gentile;
  Bid the stranger to the feast;
'Call them in!' the rich, the noble,
  From the highest to the least.
Forth the Father runs to meet them,
  He hath all their sorrows seen;
Robe, and ring, and royal sandals
  Wait the lost ones: 'call them in!'

3 'Call them in!' the broken-hearted,
  Cowering 'neath the brand of shame;
Speak love's message, low, and tender,
  'Twas for sinners Jesus came.'
See, the shadows lengthen round us,
  Soon the day-dawn will begin;
Can you leave them lost and lonely?
  Christ is coming: 'call them in!'
          Mrs. A. Shipton. 1862.

323   7.7. 7.7.
The Spirit and the bride say, come.—Revelation xxii. 17.

COME, ye weary sinners, come,
  All who groan beneath your load;
Jesus calls His wanderers home,
  Hasten to your pardoning God.

2 Come, ye guilty spirits oppressed,
  Answer to the Saviour's call;
'Come, and I will give you rest,
  Come, and I will save you all.'

3 Jesus, full of **truth** and love,
  We Thy kindest word obey;
Faithful let Thy mercies prove,
  Take our load of guilt away.

4 **Fain we would on Thee** rely,
  Cast on Thee our every care;
To Thine arms of mercy fly,
  Find our lasting quiet there.

5 Burdened with a world of grief,
  Burdened with our sinful load,
Burdened with this unbelief,
  Burdened with the wrath of **God**;

6 Lo! we come **to Thee** for ease,
  True and gracious as Thou art;
Now our groaning souls release,
  Write forgiveness on our heart.
          Wesley. 1747.

324   L.M.
All things are ready; come unto the marriage.—Matthew xxii. 4.

SINNERS, obey the Gospel word,
  Haste to the supper of my Lord,
Be wise to know your gracious day,
  All things are ready, come away!

2 Ready the Father is to own
  And kiss His late-returning Son;
Ready your loving Saviour stands,
  And spreads for **you** His bleeding hands

3 **Ready the Spirit of His Love,**
  Just now the hardest heart to move;
To apply and witness with the blood,
  And wash and seal the sons of God:

4 Ready for you the angels wait
  To triumph in your blest estate;
Tuning their harps they long to praise
  The wonders of redeeming grace.

5 The Father, Son, and Holy Ghost,
  Is ready, with their shining host;
All heaven is ready to resound,
  'The dead's alive! the lost is found!

6 Come, then, ye sinners, to your Lord,
  In Christ to **Paradise restored**;
His proffered **benefits embrace,**
  The plenitude of Gospel grace.
          Charles Wesley. 1749.

325   7.6. 7.6. D.
Standeth before the door.—James v. 9.

O JESUS, Thou art standing
  Outside the fast-closed door,
In lowly patience waiting
  To pass the threshold o'er;
Shame on **us,** Christian brethren,
  His **name and** sign who bear;
O, shame! thrice shame upon us,
  To keep Him standing there.

2 O Jesus, Thou art knocking:
  And lo! that hand is scarred,
And thorns Thy brow encircle,
  And tears Thy face have marred
O love that passeth knowledge,
  So patiently to wait!
O sin that hath no equal,
  So fast to bar the gate!

3 O Jesus, Thou art pleading
  In accents meek and low,
'I died for you, My children,
  And will ye treat Me so?'
O Lord, with shame and sorrow
  We open now the door;
Dear Saviour, enter, enter,
  And leave us never more. Amen.
          Bishop W. W. How. 1867.

EVANGELISTIC SERVICES.

326 7.7.7.7. D.
Why will ye die, O house of Israel?—Ezekiel xviii. 31.

SINNERS, turn, why will ye die?
God, your Maker, asks you why:
God, who did your being give,
Made you with Himself to live;
He the fatal cause demands,
Asks the work of His own hands,
Why, ye thankless creatures, why
Will ye cross His love, and die?

2 Sinners, turn, why will ye die?
God, your Saviour, asks you why:
God, who did your souls retrieve,
Died Himself that ye might live,
Will you let Him die in vain?
Crucify your Lord again?
Why, ye ransomed sinners, why
Will you slight His grace and die?

3 Sinners, turn, why will ye die?
God, the Spirit, asks you why:
He who all your lives hath strove,
Wooed you to embrace His love:
Will you not His grace receive?
Will you still refuse to live?
Why, ye long-sought sinners, why
Will you grieve your God, and die?
Wesley. 1741.

327 7.7.7.7.7.7.
O Israel, return unto the Lord thy God.—Hosea xiv. 1.

WEARY souls that wander wide
From the central point of bliss,
Turn to Jesus crucified,
Fly to those dear wounds of His,
Sink into the purple flood,
Rise into the life of God.

2 Find in Christ the way of peace,
Peace unspeakable, unknown;
By His pain He gives you ease,
Life by His expiring groan;
Else, exalted by His fall,
Find in Christ your all in all.

3 O believe the record true,
God to you His Son hath given!
Ye may now be happy too,
Find on earth the life of heaven,
Live the life of heaven above,
All the life of glorious love.

4 This the universal bliss,
Bliss for every soul designed;
God's original promise this,
God's great gift to all mankind:
Blest in Christ this moment be!
Blest to all eternity!
Wesley. 1747.

328 S.M. With Chorus.
The Master is come, and calleth for thee.—John xi. 28.

I HEAR Thy welcome voice
That calls me, Lord, to Thee,
For cleansing in Thy precious blood
That flowed on Calvary.

I am coming, Lord,
Coming now to Thee!
Wash me, cleanse me, in the blood
That flowed on Calvary.

2 Though coming weak and vile,
Thou dost my strength assure;
Thou dost my vileness fully cleanse,
Till spotless all and pure.

3 'Tis Jesus calls me on
To perfect faith and love,
To perfect hope, and peace, and trust,
For earth and heaven above.

4 'Tis Jesus who confirms
The blessèd work within,
By adding grace to welcomed grace,
Where reigned the power of sin.

5 And He the witness gives
To loyal hearts and free,
That every promise is fulfilled,
If faith but brings the plea.

6 All hail, atoning blood!
All hail, redeeming grace!
All hail, the gift of Christ our Lord,
Our Strength and Righteousness!
Amen.
Mrs. L. Hartsough. 1874.

329 7.6.7.6. D.
Behold, now is the day of salvation.—2 Corinthians vi. 2.

TO-DAY Thy mercy calls us
To wash away our sin,
However great our trespass,
Whatever we have been:
However long from mercy
Our hearts have turned away,
Thy precious blood can cleanse us,
And make us white to-day.

2 To-day Thy gate is open,
And all who enter in
Shall find a Father's welcome,
And pardon for their sin:
The past shall be forgotten,
A present joy be given,
A future grace be promised,
A glorious crown in heaven.

3 To-day our Father calls us;
His Holy Spirit waits;
The blessèd angels gather
Around the heavenly gates:

INVITATION TO THE SINNER.

No question will be asked us
How often we have come;
Although we oft have wandered,
It is our Father's home!

4 O all-embracing mercy!
O ever-open door!
What should we do without Thee
When heart and eye run o'er?
When all things seem against us,
To drive us to despair,
We know one gate is open,
One ear will hear our prayer!

O. Allen. 1862.

330 7.7. 7.7. D.
*Turn ye, turn ye from your
evil ways; for why will ye die?*
Ezekiel xxxiii. 11.

WHAT could your Redeemer do
More than He **hath** done for you?
To procure your peace with God,
Could He more than shed His blood?
After all His waste of love,
All His drawings **from** above,
Why will **you** your Lord deny?
Why will you **resolve** to die?

2 Turn, He cries, ye sinners, turn;
By His life your God hath sworn,
He would have you turn and live,
He would all the world receive:
If your death were His delight,
Would He you to life invite?
Would He ask, beseech, and cry,
Why will you resolve to die?

3 Sinners, turn, while God is near;
Dare not think Him insincere;
Now, even now, your Saviour stands,
All day long He spreads His hands,
Cries, 'Ye will not happy be,
No, ye will not come to Me!
Me, who life to none deny'
Why will you **resolve to die?**'

Wesley. 1741.

331 7.6. 7.6. D. *With Chorus.*
The glorious Gospel of Christ.
2 Corinthians iv. 4.

TELL me the old, old story
Of unseen things above,
Of Jesus and His glory,
Of Jesus and His love.
Tell me the story simply,
As to a little child,
For I am weak and weary,
And helpless and defiled.

Tell **me the old, old story
Of Jesus and His love!**

2 Tell me the story slowly,
That I may take it in;
That wonderful redemption,
God's remedy for sin.

Tell me the story often,
For I forget so soon;
The early dew of morning
Has passed away at noon.

3 Tell me the story softly,
With earnest tones and grave;
Remember, I'm the sinner
Whom Jesus came to save.
Tell me the story always,
If you would really be,
In any time of trouble,
A comforter to me.

4 Tell me the same old story,
When you have cause to fear
That *this* world's empty glory
Is costing me too dear.
Yes, and when *that* world's glory
Is dawning on my soul,
Tell me the old, old story,
Christ Jesus makes thee whole.

Katherine Hankey.

332 7.7.7.
I flee unto Thee to hide me.
Psalm cxliii. 9.

LORD, in this Thy mercy's day,
Ere it pass for aye away,
On our knees we fall and pray.

2 Holy Jesus, grant us tears,
Fill us with heart-searching fears,
Ere that day of doom appears.

3 Lord, on us Thy Spirit pour,
Kneeling lowly at the door,
Ere it close for evermore.

4 By Thy night of agony,
By Thy supplicating cry,
By Thy willingness to die,

5 By Thy tears of bitter woe
For Jerusalem below,
Let us not Thy love forego.

6 Grant us 'neath Thy wings a place,
Lest we lose this day of grace,
Ere we shall behold Thy face.

7 On Thy love we rest alone,
As that love shall then be known
By the pardoned round Thy throne.
Amen.

Isaac Williams. 1842. *alt.*

333 8.8. 8.8. 8.9.
*He heard that it was
Jesus of Nazareth.*—Mark x. 47.

WHAT means this eager, anxious throng,
Which moves with busy haste along,
These wondrous gatherings day by day?
What means this strange commotion, pray?
In accents hushed the throng reply,
'Jesus of Nazareth passeth by.'

EVANGELISTIC SERVICES.

2 Who is this Jesus? Why should He
   The city move so mightily?
   A passing stranger, has He skill
   To move the multitude at will?
   Again the stirring tones reply,
   'Jesus of Nazareth passeth by.'

3 Jesus! 'tis He who once below
   Man's pathway trod 'mid pain and woe;
   And burdened ones, where'er He came,
   Brought out their sick, and deaf, and
      lame:
   The blind rejoiced to hear the cry,
   'Jesus of Nazareth passeth by.'

4 Again He comes! from place to place
   His holy footprints we can trace,
   He pauseth at our threshold—nay,
   He enters—condescends to stay;
   Shall we not gladly raise the cry?
   'Jesus of Nazareth passeth by.'

5 Ho! all ye heavy-laden, come,
   Here's pardon, comfort, rest, and home;
   Ye wanderers from a Father's face,
   Return, accept His proffered grace;
   Ye tempted ones, there's refuge nigh,
   'Jesus of Nazareth passeth by.'

6 But if you still His call refuse,
   And all His wondrous love abuse,
   Soon will He sadly from you turn,
   Your bitter prayer for pardon spurn:
   'Too late! too late!' will be the cry,
   'Jesus of Nazareth has passed by.'
               Etta Campbell. 1863.

---

334   5.5. 5.5. 6.5. 6.5.
*The blind receive their sight,
and the lame walk, . . . and the poor have
the gospel preached to them.*—Matt. xi. 5.

YE neighbours and friends
   Of Jesus, draw near,
His love condescends,
   By titles so dear,
To call and invite you
   His triumph to prove,
And freely delight you
   In Jesus's love,—

2 The Shepherd who died
   His sheep to redeem;
On every side
   Are gathered to Him
The weary and burdened,
   The reprobate race;
And wait to be pardoned
   Through Jesus's grace.

3 The blind are restored
   Through Jesus's name;
They see their dear Lord,
   And follow the Lamb;
The halt they are walking,
   And running their race;
The dumb they are talking
   Of Jesus's grace.

4 The deaf hear His voice,
   And comforting word;
It bids them rejoice
   In Jesu's their Lord:
'Thy sins are forgiven,
   Accepted thou art;'
They listen, and heaven
   Springs up in their heart.

5 The lepers from all
   Their spots are made clean;
The dead by His call
   Are raised from their sin;
In Jesu's compassion
   The sick find a cure;
And gospel salvation
   Is preached to the poor.

6 To us and to them
   Is published the word;
Then let us proclaim
   Our life-giving Lord,
Who now is reviving
   His work in our days,
And mightily striving
   To save us by grace.

7 O Jesus, ride on,
   Till all are subdued;
Thy mercy make known,
   And sprinkle Thy blood;
Display Thy salvation,
   And teach the new song
To every nation,
   And people, and tongue.
               Charles Wesley. 1749.

EXHORTATION TO REPENT.

335   C.M.
*His eyes were as a flame
of fire.*—Rev. i. 14.

THOU Son of God, whose flaming eyes
   Our inmost thoughts perceive,
Accept the evening sacrifice,
   Which now to Thee we give.

2 We bow before Thy gracious throne,
   And think ourselves sincere;
But show us, Lord, is every one
   Thy real worshipper?

3 Is here a soul that knows Thee not,
   Nor feels his want of Thee?
A stranger to the blood which bought
   His pardon on the tree?

4 Convince him now of unbelief,
   His desperate state explain;
And fill his heart with sacred grief,
   And penitential pain.

EXHORTATION TO REPENT.

5 Speak with that voice which wakes the
    dead,
  And bid the sleeper rise !
  And bid his guilty conscience dread
    The death that never dies.

6 Extort the cry, 'What must be done
    To save a wretch like me?
  How shall a trembling sinner shun
    That endless misery ?

7 'I must this instant now begin
    Out of my sleep to awake ;
  And turn to God, and every sin
    Continually forsake :

8 'I must for faith incessant cry,
    And wrestle, Lord, with Thee ;
  I must be born again, or die
    To all eternity.'
        Charles Wesley. 1767.

336   6.6, 6.6, 6.6.
*But first gave their own
selves to the Lord.*—2 Corinthians viii. 5.

I GAVE My life for thee,
  My precious blood I shed,
That thou might'st ransomed be,
  And quickened from the dead :
I gave My life for thee ;
What hast thou given for Me ?

2 I spent long years for thee,
  In weariness and woe,
That an eternity
  Of joy thou mightest know :
I spent long years for thee ;
Hast thou spent one for Me ?

3 My Father's home of light,
  My rainbow-circled throne,
I left for earthly night,
  For wanderings sad and lone :
I left it all for thee ;
Hast thou left aught for Me ?

4 I suffered much for thee,
  More than thy tongue can tell,
Of bitterest agony,
  To rescue thee from hell :
I suffered much for thee ;
What canst thou bear for Me ?

5 And I have brought to thee,
  Down from My home above,
Salvation full and free,
  My pardon and My love :
Great gifts I brought to thee ;
What hast thou brought to Me ?

6 O, let thy life be given,
  Thy years for Me be spent,
World-fetters all be riven,
  And joy with suffering blent :
I gave Myself for thee ;
Give thou thyself to Me.
       Frances R. Havergal. 1859.

H

337   L.M.
*As the Holy Ghost saith, To-
day if ye will hear His voice.*
    Hebrews iii. 7.

O DO not let the word depart,
  And close thine eyes against the light,
Poor sinner, harden not thine heart ;
  Thou would'st be saved ; why not to-
    night ?

2 To-morrow's sun may never rise
  To bless thy long-deluded sight ;
This is the time, O then be wise !
  Thou would'st be saved ; why not to-
    night ?

3 Thy God in pity urges still,
  And wilt thou thus His love requite?
Renounce at length thy stubborn will ;
  Thou would'st be saved ; why not to-
    night ?

4 The world has nothing left to give ;
  No new, no pure, no sure delight ;
Try then the life which Christ will give :
  Thou would'st be saved ; why not to-
    night ?

5 His boundless love refuses none
  Who would to Him their souls unite :
Then be the work of grace begun ;
  Thou would'st be saved ; why not to-
    night ?
       Mrs. Eliza Ann Reed. 1842.

338   S.M.
*Him hath God exalted . . . to
give repentance to Israel, and forgiveness of
sins.*—Acts v. 31.

O THAT I could repent,
  With all my idols part,
And to Thy gracious eyes present
  A humble contrite heart ;

2 A heart with grief opprest,
  For having grieved my God,
A troubled heart, that cannot rest,
  Till sprinkled with Thy blood.

3 Jesus, on me bestow
  The penitent desire ;
With true sincerity of woe
  My aching breast inspire ;

4 With softening pity look,
  And melt my hardness down ;
Strike with Thy love's resistless stroke,
  And break this heart of stone !
             Amen.
       Charles Wesley. 1749.

EVANGELISTIC SERVICES.

339 7.7. 8.7. 8.7.
*Behold, I stand at the door,
and knock.*—Revelation iii. 20.

KNOCKING! knocking! who is there?
  Waiting, waiting, O, how fair!
'Tis a Pilgrim, strange and kingly,
  Never such was seen before;
Ah, my soul, for such a wonder
  Wilt thou not undo the door?

2 Knocking! knocking! still He's there!
  Waiting, waiting, wondrous fair!
But the door is hard to open,
  For the weeds and ivy-vine,
With their dark and clinging tendrils,
  Ever round the hinges twine.

3 Knocking! knocking!—what, still there!
  Waiting, waiting, grand and fair!
Yes, the piercéd hand still knocketh,
  And beneath the crownéd hair
Beam the patient eyes, so tender,
  Of thy Saviour waiting there.
      Mrs. Harriet Beecher Stowe. 1867.
      Alt. P. P. Bliss. 1874.

340 8.6. 8.8. 6.4.
He found nothing but leaves.
Mark xi. 13.

NOTHING but leaves! the Spirit grieves
  Over a wasted life;
O'er sins indulged while conscience slept,
O'er vows and promises unkept;
  And reaps,from years of strife,
    Nothing but leaves!

2 Nothing but leaves! No gathered sheaves
  Of life's fair ripening grain;
We sow our seeds; lo, tares and weeds,
Words, idle words for earnest deeds;
  We reap,with toil and pain,
    Nothing but leaves!

3 Nothing but leaves! Sad memory weaves
  No veil to hide the past;
And as we trace our weary way,
Counting each lost and misspent day,
  Sadly we find at last,
    Nothing but leaves!

4 Ah! who shall thus the Master meet,
  Bearing but withered leaves?
Ah! who shall at the Saviour's feet
Before the awful judgment-seat
  Lay down, for golden sheaves,
    Nothing but leaves?
      Mrs. M. S. Dana. 1869.

SALVATION THROUGH FAITH.

341 C.M.
*If any man hear My voice,
and open the door, I will come in to him.*
Revelation iii. 20.

COME, let us, who in Christ believe,
  Our common Saviour praise;
To Him with joyful voices give
  The glory of His grace.

2 He now stands knocking at the door
  Of every sinner's heart;
The worst need keep Him out no more,
  Or force Him to depart.

3 Through grace we hearken to Thy voice,
  Yield to be saved from sin;
In sure and certain hope rejoice,
  That Thou wilt enter in.

4 Come quickly in, Thou heavenly Guest,
  Nor ever hence remove;
But sup with us, and let the feast
  Be everlasting love. Amen.
      Wesley. 1741.

342 7.6. 7.6. D.
*Unto you . . . which believe,
He is precious.*—1 Peter ii. 7.

I NEED Thee, precious Jesus,
  For I am full of sin;
My soul is dark and guilty,
  My heart is dead within;
I need the cleansing fountain
  Where I can always flee,
The blood of Christ most precious,
  The sinner's perfect plea.

2 I need Thee, precious Jesus,
  For I am very poor;
A stranger and a pilgrim,
  I have no earthly store;
I need the love of Jesus
  To cheer me on my way,
To guide my doubting footsteps,
  To be my strength and stay.

3 I need Thee, precious Jesus,
  I need a friend like Thee;
A friend to soothe and pity,
  A friend to care for me;
I need the heart of Jesus
  To feel each anxious care,
To bear my every burden,
  And all my sorrow share.

4 I need Thee, precious Jesus,
  And hope to see Thee soon,
Encircled with the rainbow,
  And seated on Thy throne;
There, with Thy blood-bought children,
  My joy shall ever be,
To sing Thy praise, Lord Jesus,
  To gaze, my Lord, on Thee.
      F. Whitfield. 1860.

SALVATION THROUGH FAITH.

343 C.M.
Having a form of godliness, but denying the power thereof.
2 Timothy iii. 5.

LONG have I seemed to serve Thee, Lord,
　With unavailing pain ;
Fasted, and prayed, and read Thy word,
　And heard it preached in vain.

2 Oft did I with the assembly join,
　And near Thine altar drew ;
A form of godliness was mine,
　The power I never knew.

3 I rested in the outward law,
　Nor knew its deep design,
The length and breadth I never saw,
　And height, of love divine.

4 To please Thee thus, at length I see,
　Vainly I hoped and strove ;
For what are outward things to Thee,
　Unless they spring from love ?

5 I see the perfect law requires
　Truth in the inward parts,
Our full consent, our whole desires,
　Our undivided hearts.

6 But I of means have made my boast,
　Of means an idol made ;
The spirit in the letter lost,
　The substance in the shade.

7 Where am I now, or what my hope ?
　What can my weakness do ?
Jesus, to Thee my soul looks up,
　'Tis Thou must make it new.
　　　　　　　　Wesley. 1740.

344 7.7. 7.7. D.
Hide Thy face from my sins.
Psalm li. 9.

DEPTH of mercy, can there be
　Mercy still reserved for me ?
Can my God His wrath forbear ?
Me, the chief of sinners, spare ?
I have long withstood His grace,
Long provoked Him to His face,
Would not hearken to His calls,
Grieved Him by a thousand falls.

2 I have spilt His precious blood,
Trampled on the Son of God,
Filled with pangs unspeakable,
I, who yet am not in hell !
Whence to me this waste of love ?
Ask my Advocate above ;
See the cause in Jesu's face,
Now before the throne of grace.

3 Lo ! I cumber still the ground :
Lo ! an Advocate is found :
'Hasten not to cut him down,
Let this barren soul alone :'

Jesus speaks, and pleads His blood ;
He disarms the wrath of God !
Now His tender mercies move,
Justice lingers into love.

4 Kindled His relentings are,
Me He now delights to spare,
Cries, ' How shall I give thee up ?'
Lets the lifted thunder drop :
There for me the Saviour stands,
Shows His wounds, and spreads His hands ;
God is love ! I know, I feel ;
Jesus weeps, and loves me still !
　　　　　　　　Wesley. 1740.

345 7.7. 7.7. *With Chorus.*
Who loved me, and gave Himself for me.—Galatians ii. 20.

I AM coming to the cross,
　I am poor, and weak, and blind,
I am counting all but dross,
　I shall full salvation find.

　I am trusting, Lord, in Thee,
　Blessèd Lamb of Calvary ;
　Humbly at Thy cross I bow,
　Save me, Jesus, save me now.

2 Long my heart has sighed for Thee,
　Long has evil reigned within,
Jesus sweetly speaks to me,
　'I will cleanse thee from all sin.'

3 Here I give my all to Thee,
　Friends, and time, and earthly store,
Soul and body Thine to be,
　Wholly Thine for evermore.

4 In the promises I trust,
　Now I know the blood applied ;
I am prostrate in the dust,
　I with Christ am crucified.

5 Jesus comes ! He fills my soul !
　Perfected in Him I am,
I am every whit made whole,
　Glory, glory to the Lamb !

　Still I'm trusting, Lord, in Thee,
　Blessèd Lamb of Calvary ;
　Humbly at Thy cross I bow,
　Jesus saves me, saves me now.
　　　　　　W. Macdonald. 1874.

346 C.M.
He staggered not at the promise of God through unbelief.
Romans iv. 20.

FATHER of Jesus Christ, my Lord,
　My Saviour, and my Head,
I trust in Thee, whose powerful word
　Hath raised Him from the dead.

EVANGELISTIC SERVICES.

2 Thou know'st for my offence **He died**,
   And rose again for me,
   Fully and freely justified,
     That I might live to Thee.

3 Eternal life to all mankind
   Thou hast in Jesus given ;
   And all who seek, in Him shall find
     The happiness of heaven.

4 O God! Thy record I believe,
   In Abraham's footsteps tread,
   And wait, expecting to receive
     The Christ, the promised Seed.

5 Faith in Thy power Thou seest I have,
   For Thou this faith hast wrought ;
   Dead souls Thou callest from their grave,
     And speakest worlds from nought.

6 In hope, against all human hope,
   Self-desperate, I believe ;
   Thy quickening word shall raise me up,
     Thou shalt Thy Spirit give.

7 The thing surpasses all my thought,
   But faithful is my **Lord** ;
   Through unbelief I stagger not,
     For God hath spoke the word.

8 Faith, mighty faith, the promise sees,
   And looks to that alone ;
   Laughs at impossibilities,
     And cries, 'It shall be done !'
            Wesley. 1742.

---

347   *Lord, I believe ; help Thou mine unbelief.*—Mark ix. 24.   C.M.

HOW sad our state by nature is !
   Our sin, how deep its stains !
   And Satan binds our captive minds
     Fast in his slavish chains.

2 But there's a voice of sovereign grace
   Sounds from the sacred word,
   'Ho, ye despairing sinners, come,
     And trust upon the Lord.'

3 My soul obeys the Almighty's call,
   And runs to this relief ;
   I would believe Thy promise, **Lord**,
     O help **my** unbelief !

4 To the blest fountain of Thy blood,
   Incarnate God, I fly ;
   Here let me wash my spotted soul
     From sins of deepest dye.

5 A guilty, weak, and helpless soul,
   Into Thine arms I fall ;
   Be Thou my strength and righteousness,
     My Saviour, and my all. Amen.
            Isaac Watts. 1709.

---

348   *They that know Thy name will put their trust in Thee.*—Psalm ix. 10.   6.5. 6.5. D.

JESUS, **I will** trust Thee,
   Trust **Thee** with my soul ;
   Guilty, lost, and helpless,
     Thou canst make me whole.
   There is none in heaven
     Or on earth like Thee ;
   Thou hast died **for** sinners,
     Therefore, **Lord, for** me.

2 Jesus, I may trust Thee,
   Name of matchless worth,
   Spoken by the angel
     At Thy wondrous birth,
   Written, and for ever,
     On Thy cross of shame ;
   Sinners, read and worship,
     Trusting in that name.

3 Jesus, I must trust **Thee**,
   Pondering Thy **ways**,
   Full of love and mercy
     All Thine earthly days ;
   Sinners gathered round Thee,
     Lepers sought Thy face,
   None too vile or loathsome
     For **a** Saviour's grace.

4 Jesus, **I can** trust Thee,
   Trust **Thy written** word,
   Though **Thy** voice **of** pity
     I have never heard ;
   When Thy Spirit teacheth,
     To my taste how sweet !
   Only may I hearken,
     Sitting at Thy feet.

5 Jesus, I do trust Thee,
   Trust without a doubt ;
   Whosoever cometh,
     Thou wilt not cast out ;
   Faithful is Thy promise,
     Precious is Thy blood ;
   These my soul's salvation,
     Thou my Saviour God.
            Mrs. Mary Jane Walker. 1864.

---

349   *My strong Rock, for a house of defence.*—Psalm xxxi. 2.   11.11 11.11. *With* **Chorus.**

O SAFE to the Rock that is higher than I,
   My soul in its conflicts and sorrows would fly ;
So sinful, so weary, Thine, Thine would **I** be ;
Thou blest 'Rock of Ages,' I'm hiding in Thee.

     Hiding in Thee, hiding in Thee,
     Thou blest 'Rock of Ages,' I'm hiding in Thee.

REJOICING IN FORGIVENESS.

2 In the calm of the noontide, in sorrow's
      lone hour,
   In times when temptation casts o'er me
      its power;
   In the tempests of life, on its wide, heav-
      ing sea,
   Thou blest 'Rock of Ages,' I'm hiding in
      Thee.

3 How oft in the conflict, when pressed by
      the foe,
   I have fled to my Refuge and breathed out
      my woe;
   How often when trials like sea billows roll,
   Have I hidden in Thee, O Thou Rock of my
      soul.
                                W. O. Cushing.

350 C.M.
*Look unto Me, and be ye
saved, all the ends of the earth.*—Isa. xlv. 22.

JESUS, to Thee I now can fly,
   On whom my help is laid;
Oppressed by sins, I lift my eye,
   And see the shadows fade.

2 Believing on my Lord, I find
   A sure and present aid;
On Thee, O let my constant mind
   Be every moment stayed.

3 Whate'er in me seems wise, or good,
   Or strong, I here disclaim;
I wash my garments in the blood
   Of the atoning Lamb.

4 Jesus, my Strength, my Life, my Rest,
   On Thee will I depend,
Till summoned to the marriage-feast,
   When faith in sight shall end.
                                Wesley. 1742.

351 7.7. 7.7. *With Chorus.*
*Though He slay me, yet will
I trust in Him.*—Job xiii. 15.

SIMPLY trusting every day,
   Trusting through a stormy way;
Even when my faith is small,
Trusting Jesus, that is all.

   Trusting as the moments fly,
   Trusting as the days go by,
   Trusting Him whate'er befall,
   Trusting Jesus, that is all.

2 Brightly doth His Spirit shine
   Into this poor heart of mine;
   While He leads I cannot fall,
   Trusting Jesus, that is all.

3 Singing, if my way is clear;
   Praying, if the path is drear;
   If in danger, for Him call;
   Trusting Jesus, that is all.

4 Trusting Him while life shall last,
   Trusting Him till earth is past,
   Till within the jasper wall;
   Trusting Jesus, that is all.
                                E. Page.

REJOICING IN FORGIVENESS.

352 6.6. 6.6. 8.8.
*God also hath highly exalted
Him.*—Philippians ii. 9.

LET earth and heaven agree,
   Angels and men be joined,
To celebrate with me
   The Saviour of mankind,
To adore the all-atoning Lamb,
And bless the sound of Jesu's name.

2 Jesus, transporting sound!
   The joy of earth and heaven;
No other help is found,
   No other name is given,
By which we can salvation have;
But Jesus came the world to save.

3 Jesus, harmonious name!
   It charms the hosts above;
They evermore proclaim
   And wonder at His love;
'Tis all their happiness to gaze,
'Tis heaven to see our Jesu's face.

4 His name the sinner hears,
   And is from sin set free;
'Tis music in his ears,
   'Tis life and victory;
New songs do now his lips employ,
And dances his glad heart for joy.

5 Stung by the scorpion sin,
   My poor expiring soul
The balmy sound drinks in,
   And is at once made whole;
See there my Lord upon the tree!
I hear, I feel, He died for me.

6 O unexampled love!
   O all-redeeming grace!
How swiftly didst Thou move
   To save a fallen race!
What shall I do to make it known,
What Thou for all mankind hast done?

7 O for a trumpet-voice,
   On all the world to call;
   To bid their hearts rejoice
   In Him who died for all;
For all my Lord was crucified;
For all, for all my Saviour died!
                                Charles Wesley. 1741.

EVANGELISTIC SERVICES.

353 L.M.
My soul thirsteth for God, for the living God.—Psalm xlii. 2.

I THIRST, Thou wounded Lamb of God,
   To wash me in Thy cleansing blood;
To dwell within Thy wounds: then pain
Is sweet, and life or death is gain.

2 Take my poor heart, and let it be
For ever closed to all but Thee:
Seal Thou my breast, and let me wear
That pledge of love for ever there.

3 How blest are they who still abide
Close sheltered in Thy bleeding side!
Who life and strength from thence derive,
And by Thee move, and in Thee live.

4 What are our works but sin and death,
Till Thou Thy quickening Spirit breathe?
Thou giv'st the power Thy grace to move:
O wondrous grace! O boundless love!

5 How can it be, Thou heavenly King,
That Thou should'st us to glory bring,
Make slaves the partners of Thy throne
Decked with a never-fading crown?

6 Hence our hearts melt, our eyes o'erflow,
Our words are lost; nor will we know,
Nor will we think of aught beside,
My Lord, my Love is crucified.

7 Ah, Lord! enlarge our scanty thought,
To know the wonders Thou hast wrought;
Unloose our stammering tongues, to tell
Thy love immense, unsearchable.

8 First-born of many brethren Thou!
To Thee, lo! all our souls we bow;
To Thee our hearts and hands we give;
Thine may we die, Thine may we live!
     Amen.
Count Zinzendorf and John and Anna Nitzchman. 18th Century. Tr. John Wesley. 1740.

354 6.10. 10.6.
Thanks be to God, which giveth us the victory through our Lord Jesus Christ.—1 Cor. xv. 57.

BLESSED be God, our God,
   Who gave for us His well-beloved Son,
His gift of gifts, all other gifts in one,
   Blessed be God, our God!

2 What will He not bestow
Who freely gave this mighty gift, unbought,
Unmerited, unheeded, and unsought—
   What will He not bestow?

3 He spared not His Son!
'Tis this that silences each rising fear,
'Tis this that bids the hard thought disappear,
   He spared not His Son:

4 Who shall **condemn** us now,
Since Christ has **died**, and risen and gone above,
For us to plead at the right hand of **love**,
   Who shall condemn us now?

5 'Tis God that justifies!
Who shall recall the pardon or the grace,
Or who the broken chain of guilt replace?
   'Tis God that justifies!

6 The victory is ours!
For us in might came forth the Mighty One,
For us He fought the fight, the triumph won;
   The victory is ours!
     Horatius Bonar. 1857.

355 8.7. 8.7. 4.7.
Go ye into all the world, and preach the Gospel to every creature.
Mark xvi. 15.

HARK! the Gospel news is sounding,
   Christ hath suffered on the tree;
Streams of mercy are abounding,
   Grace for all is rich and free:
     Now, poor sinner,
Look to Him who died for thee.

2 O! escape to yonder mountain,
   Now begin to watch and pray;
Christ invites you to the fountain,
   Come and wash your sins away:
     Do not tarry,
Come to Jesus while you may.

3 Grace is flowing like a river,
   Millions there have been supplied;
Still it flows as fresh as ever
   From the Saviour's wounded side:
     None need perish,
All may live, for Christ hath died.

4 Christ alone **shall** be our portion,
   Soon we hope **to** meet above;
Then we'll bathe in the full ocean
   Of the great Redeemer's love:
     All His fulness
We shall then for ever prove.
     W. Sanders. 1829.

356 L.M.
Joy shall be in heaven over one sinner that repenteth.—Luke **xv. 7.**

WHO can describe the joys that rise
   Through all the courts of Paradise,
To see a prodigal return,
To see an heir of glory born!

2 With joy the Father doth approve
The fruit of His eternal love;
The Son with joy looks down, and sees
The purchase of His agonies.

REJOICING IN FORGIVENESS.

3 The Spirit takes delight to view
  The contrite soul He forms anew;
  And saints and angels join to sing
  The growing empire of their King.
              Isaac Watts. 1709.

357   *He that believeth on the Son*   S.M.
        of God hath the witness in himself.
        1 John v. 10.

HOW can a sinner know
  His sins on earth forgiven?
How can my gracious Saviour show
  My name inscribed in heaven?

2 What we have felt and seen
    With confidence we tell,
  And publish to the sons of men
    The signs infallible.

3 We who in Christ believe
    That He for us hath died,
  We all His unknown peace receive,
    And feel His blood applied.

4 Exults our rising soul,
    Disburdened of her load,
  And swells unutterably full
    Of glory and of God.

5 We by His Spirit prove
    And know the things of God,
  The things which freely of His love
    He hath on us bestowed.

6 His Spirit to us He gave,
    And dwells in us, we know;
  The witness in ourselves we have,
    And all its fruits we show.

7 Our nature's turned, our mind
    Transformed in all its powers;
  And both the witnesses are joined,
    The Spirit of God with ours.
              Charles Wesley. 1749.

358   *My tongue shall sing aloud*   7.6, 7.6, 7.8, 7.6.
        of Thy righteousness.—Psalm li. 14.

LORD, and is Thine anger gone?
    And art Thou pacified?
  After all that I have done,
    Dost Thou no longer chide?
  Infinite Thy mercies are:
    Beneath the weight I cannot move;
  O! 'tis more than I can bear,
    The sense of pardoning love.

2 Let it still my heart constrain,
    And all my passions sway;
  Keep me, lest I turn again
    Out of the narrow way:
  Force my violence to be still,
    And captivate my every thought;
  Charm, and melt, and change my will,
    And bring me down to nought.

3 See my utter helplessness,
    And leave me not alone;
  O preserve in perfect peace,
    And seal me for Thine own:
  More and more Thyself reveal,
    Thy presence let me always find;
  Comfort, and confirm, and heal
    My feeble, sin-sick mind.

4 As the apple of an eye
    Thy weakest servant keep;
  Help me at Thy feet to lie,
    And there for ever weep:
  Tears of joy mine eyes o'erflow
    That I have any hope of heaven;
  Much of love I ought to know,
    For I have much forgiven.
              Wesley. 1742.

359   11.11. 11.11.   *Anapæstic.*
        I will love Thee, O Lord,
        my strength.—Psalm xviii. 1.

MY Jesus, I love Thee, I know Thou art mine,
For Thee all the pleasures of sin I resign:
My gracious Redeemer, my Saviour art Thou,
If ever I loved Thee, my Jesus, 'tis now.

2 I love Thee because Thou hast first loved me,
  And purchased my pardon on Calvary's tree;
  I love Thee for wearing the thorns on Thy brow,
  If ever I loved Thee, my Jesus, 'tis now.

3 I will love Thee in life, I will love Thee in death,
  And praise Thee as long as Thou lendest me breath;
  And say when the death-dew lies cold on my brow,
  If ever I loved Thee, my Jesus, 'tis now.

4 In mansions of glory and endless delight,
  I'll ever adore Thee in the heaven of light;
  And sing with the glittering crown on my brow,
  If ever I loved Thee, my Jesus, 'tis now.
                                        Amen.

EVANGELISTIC SERVICES.

360   8.8. 8.8. 8.8.
Thanks be unto God for His unspeakable gift.—2 Corinthians ix. 15.

WHAT am I, O Thou glorious God!
  And what my father's house to Thee,
That Thou such mercies hast bestowed
  On me, the chief of sinners, me!
I take the blessing from above,
And wonder at Thy boundless love.

2 Me in my blood Thy love passed by,
  And stopped my ruin to retrieve;
Wept o'er my soul Thy pitying eye,
  Thy goodness yearned, and whispered.
    'Live!'
Dying, I heard the welcome sound,
And pardon in Thy mercy found.

3 Honour, and might, and thanks, and praise,
  I render to my pardoning God;
Extol the riches of Thy grace,
  And spread Thy saving name abroad—
That only name to sinners given,
Which lifts poor dying men to heaven.

4 Jesus, I bless Thy gracious power,
  And all within me shouts Thy name;
Thy name let every soul adore,
  Thy power let every tongue proclaim;
Thy grace let every sinner know,
And find with me their heaven below.
            Amen.
        Charles Wesley. 1749.

361   7.6. 7.6. *With Chorus.*
Present your bodies a living sacrifice.—Romans xii. 1.

MY body, soul, and spirit,
  Jesus, I give to Thee,
A consecrated offering,
  Thine evermore to be.
    My all is on the altar,
    I'm waiting for the fire.

2 O Jesus, mighty Saviour!
  I trust in Thy great name,
I look for Thy salvation,
  Thy promise now I claim.

3 O let the fire descending
  Just now upon my soul,
Consume my humble offering,
  And cleanse and make me whole!

4 O, blissful self-surrender,
  To live, my Lord, by Thee!
Now, Son of God, my Saviour,
  Live out Thy life in me.

5 I'm Thine, O blessed Jesus!
  Washed by Thy precious blood;
Now seal me by Thy Spirit,
  A sacrifice to God.
        Mrs. James.

362   10.7. 10.7. *With Chorus.*
O Lord, truly I am Thy servant.—Psalm cxvi. 16.

I AM Thine, O Lord; I have heard Thy voice,
  And it told Thy love to me;
But I long to rise in the arms of faith,
  And be closer drawn to Thee.
    Draw me nearer, nearer, blessèd Lord
      To the cross where Thou hast died:
    Draw me nearer, nearer, nearer,
      blessèd Lord,
    To Thy precious, bleeding side.

2 Consecrate me now to Thy service, Lord,
  By the power of grace divine;
Let my soul look up with a steadfast hope,
  And my will be lost in Thine.

3 O, the pure delight of a single hour
  That before Thy throne I spend,
When I kneel in prayer, and with Thee, my God,
  I commune as friend with friend.

4 There are depths of love that I cannot know
  Till I cross the narrow sea;
There are heights of joy that I may not reach
  Till I rest in peace with Thee.
      Frances Jane Crosby. b. 1828.

363   5.5.11. 5.5.11.
Whether we live . . . or die, we are the Lord's.—Romans xiv. 8.

MY God, I am Thine,
  What a comfort divine,
What a blessing to know that my Jesus is mine!
  In the heavenly Lamb
  Thrice happy I am,
And my heart it doth dance at the sound of His name.

2 True pleasures abound
  In the rapturous sound,
And whoever hath found it, hath paradise found:
  My Jesus to know,
  And feel His blood flow,
'Tis life everlasting, 'tis heaven below.

3 Yet onward I haste
  To the heavenly feast:
That, that is the fulness; but this is the taste:
  And this I shall prove,
  Till with joy I remove
To the heaven of heavens in Jesus's love.
      Charles Wesley. 1749.

The Christian Life.

CONTRITION AND LONGING FOR GOD.

364 8.7. 8.7. 3.
He shall come down like rain upon the mown grass.—Ps. lxxii. 6.

LORD, I hear of showers of blessing
   Thou art scattering full and free;
Showers the thirsty land refreshing;
   Let some droppings fall on me—Even
     me.

2 Pass me not, O gracious Father,
   Sinful though my heart may be;
Thou might'st leave me, but the rather
   Let Thy mercy light on me—Even me.

3 Pass me not, O tender Saviour,
   Let me live and cling to Thee;
I am longing for Thy favour,
   Whilst Thou'rt calling, call for me—Even
     me.

4 Pass me not, O mighty Spirit;
   Thou canst make the blind to see;
Witnesser of Jesu's merit,
   Speak the word of power to me—Even
     me.

5 Love of God, so pure and changeless!
   Blood of Christ, so rich and free!
Grace of God, so strong and boundless!
   Magnify it all in me—Even me.

6 Pass me not—this lost one bringing,—
   Bind my heart, O Lord, to Thee,
While the streams of life are springing,
   Blessing others, O bless me!—Even me.
                      Amen.
Mrs. Elizabeth Codner. 1860.

365 C.M.
Is not My word like as a fire? saith the Lord.—Jeremiah xxiii. 29.

COME, O Thou all-victorious Lord,
   Thy power to us make known;
Strike with the hammer of Thy word,
   And break these hearts of stone!

2 O that we all might now begin
   Our foolishness to mourn,
And turn at once from every sin,
   And to our Saviour turn!

3 Give us ourselves and Thee to know,
   In this our gracious day;
Repentance unto life bestow,
   And take our sins away.

4 Conclude us first in unbelief,
   And freely then release;
Fill every soul with sacred grief,
   And then with sacred peace.

5 Impoverish, Lord, and then relieve,
   And then enrich the poor;
The knowledge of our sickness give,
   The knowledge of our cure.

6 That blessèd sense of guilt impart,
   And then remove the load;
Trouble, and wash the troubled heart
   In the atoning blood.

7 Our desperate state through sin declare,
   And speak our sins forgiven;
By perfect holiness prepare,
   And take us up to heaven. Amen.
Charles Wesley. 1749.

366 S.M.
I am oppressed; undertake for me.—Isaiah xxxviii. 14.

OPPRESSED with sin and woe,
   A burdened heart I bear;
Opposed by many a mighty foe,
   Yet will I not despair.

2 With this polluted heart
   I dare to come to Thee,
Holy and mighty though Thou art,
   For Thou wilt pardon me.

3 I feel that I am weak,
   And prone to every sin;
But Thou who giv'st to those who seek,
   Wilt give me strength within.

4 I need not fear my foes,
   I need not yield to care,
I need not sink beneath my woes,
   For Thou wilt answer prayer.

5 In my Redeemer's name,
   I give myself to Thee;
And all unworthy as I am,
   My God will welcome me.
Anne Brontë. 1847.

THE CHRISTIAN LIFE.

367 S.M.
*Be not faithless,
but believing.*—John xx. 27.

WHEN shall Thy love constrain,
  And force me to Thy breast?
When shall my soul return again
  To her eternal rest?

2 Ah! what avails my strife,
  My wandering to and fro?
Thou hast the words of endless life;
  Ah! whither should I go?

3 Thy condescending grace
  To me did freely move;
It calls me still to seek Thy face,
  And stoops to ask my love.

4 Lord, at Thy feet I fall,
  I groan to be set free;
I fain would now obey the call,
  And give up all for Thee.

5 To rescue me from woe,
  Thou didst with all things part;
Didst lead a suffering life below,
  To gain my worthless heart.

6 My worthless heart to gain,
  The God of all that breathe
Was found in fashion as a man,
  And died a cursèd death.

7 And can I yet delay
  My little all to give,
To tear my soul from earth away
  For Jesus to receive?

8 Nay, but I yield, I yield,
  I can hold out no more;
I sink, by dying love compelled,
  And own Thee conqueror.
              Wesley. 1740.

368 7.7. 7.7. 7.7.
*Who shall deliver me from
the body of this death?*—Romans vii. 24.

SAVIOUR, cast a pitying eye,
  Bid my sins and sorrows end;
Whither should a sinner fly?
  Art not Thou the sinner's Friend?
Rest in Thee I long to find,
Wretched I, and poor, and blind.

2 Didst Thou ever see a soul
  More in need of help than mine?
Then refuse to make me whole;
  Then withhold the balm divine;
But if I do want Thee most,
Come, and seek, and save the lost.

3 Haste, O haste, to my relief,
  Me from guilt and bondage take;
Rid me of my sin and grief,
  For Thy love and mercy's sake;
Set my heart at liberty,
Show forth all Thy power in me.

4 Jesus, on Thine only name
  For salvation I depend!
In Thy gracious hands I am,
  Save me, save me to the end;
Let the utmost grace be given,
Save me quite from hell to heaven.
                                Amen.
          Charles Wesley. 1749.

369 C.M.
Ask, and it shall be given you.
Matthew vii. 7.

O THAT I could my Lord receive,
  Who did the world redeem;
Who gave His life that I might live
  A life concealed in Him!

2 O that I could the blessing prove,
  My heart's extreme desire;
Live happy in my Saviour's love,
  And in His arms expire!

3 Mercy I ask to seal my peace,
  That, kept by mercy's power,
I may from every evil cease,
  And never grieve Thee more.

4 Now, if Thy gracious will it be,
  Even now, my sins remove;
And set my soul at liberty
  By Thy victorious love.

5 In answer to ten thousand prayers,
  Thou pardoning God, descend:
Number me with salvation's heirs,
  My sins and troubles end.

6 Nothing I ask or want beside,
  Of all in earth or heaven,
But let me feel Thy blood applied,
  And live and die forgiven. Amen.
          Charles Wesley. 1767.

370 S.M.
*Who will have all men to
be saved.*—1 Timothy ii. 4.

AH! whither should I go,
  Burdened, and sick, and faint?
To whom should I my troubles show,
  And pour out my complaint?

2 My Saviour bids me come:
  Ah! why do I delay?
He calls the weary sinner home,
  And yet from Him I stay!

3 What is it keeps me back,
  From which I cannot part,
Which will not let my Saviour take
  Possession of my heart?

4 Some evil thing unknown
  Must surely lurk within,
Some idol, which I will not own,
  Some secret bosom-sin.

CONTRITION AND LONGING FOR GOD.

5 Jesus, the hindrance show,
   Which I have feared to see;
And let me now consent to know
   What keeps me out of Thee.

6 Searcher of hearts, in mine
   Thy trying power display;
Into its darkest corner shine,
   And take the veil away.

7 I now believe, in Thee
   Compassion reigns alone;
According to my faith, to me
   O let it, Lord, be done!

8 In me is all the bar,
   Which Thou would'st fain remove;
Remove it, and I shall declare
   That God is only Love. Amen.
                       Wesley. 1741.

371   7.7, 7.7, 7.7.
*O when will Thou come
unto me?*—Ps. ci. 2.

WHY not now, my God, my God?
   Ready if Thou always art,
Make in me Thy mean abode,
   Take possession of my heart:
If Thou canst so greatly bow,
Friend of sinners, why not now?

2 God of love, in this my day,
   For Thyself to Thee I cry;
Dying, if Thou still delay,
   Must I not for ever die?
Enter now Thy poorest home;
Now, my utmost Saviour, come! Amen.
                      Charles Wesley. 1762.

372   C.M.
*Can any hide himself in
secret places that I shall not see him? saith
the Lord.*—Jeremiah xxiii. 24.

GOD is in this and every place;
   But O, how dark and void
To me—'tis one great wilderness—
   This earth without my God!

2 Empty of Him who all things fills,
   Till He His light impart,
Till He His glorious self reveals,
   The veil is on my heart.

3 O Thou, who seest and know'st my grief,
   Thyself unseen, unknown,
Pity my helpless unbelief,
   And take me for Thine own.

4 Regard me with a gracious eye,
   The long-sought blessing give,
And bid me, at the point to die,
   Behold Thy face and live.

5 Now, Jesus, now, the Father's love
   Shed in my heart abroad;
The middle wall of sin remove,
   And let me into God. Amen.
                      Charles Wesley. 1749.

373   L.M.
*The publican . . . smote
upon his breast, saying, God be merciful to
me a sinner.*—Luke xviii. 13.

WITH broken heart and contrite sigh,
   A trembling sinner, Lord, I cry;
Thy pardoning grace is rich and free;
O God, be merciful to me!

2 I smite upon my troubled breast,
   With deep and conscious guilt opprest,
Christ and His cross my only plea;
O God, be merciful to me!

3 Far off I stand with tearful eyes,
   Nor dare uplift them to the skies;
But Thou dost all my anguish see;
O God, be merciful to me!

4 Nor alms, nor deeds that I have done,
   Can for a single sin atone;
To Calvary alone I flee;
O God, be merciful to me!

5 And when, redeemed from sin and hell,
   With all the ransomed throng I dwell,
My raptured song shall ever be,
God has been merciful to me!
                      Cornelius Elvin. 1852.

374   C.M.
*What things soever ye
desire when ye pray, believe that ye receive
them, and ye shall have them.*—Mark xi. 24.

I ASK the gift of righteousness,
   The sin-subduing power,
Power to believe, and go in peace,
   And never grieve Thee more.

2 I ask the blood-bought pardon sealed,
   The liberty from sin,
The grace infused, the love revealed,
   The kingdom fixed within.

3 Thou hear'st me for salvation pray,
   Thou seest my heart's desire;
Made ready in Thy powerful day,
   Thy fulness I require.

4 My longing soul cries out, opprest,
   Impatient to be freed;
Nor can I, Lord, nor will I rest,
   Till I am saved indeed.

5 Art Thou not able to convert?
   Art Thou not willing too,
To change this old, rebellious heart,
   To conquer and renew?

THE CHRISTIAN LIFE.

6 Thou canst, Thou wilt, I dare believe,
   So arm me with Thy power,
That I to sin shall never cleave,
   Shall never feel it more. Amen.
                    Charles Wesley. 1742.

375   8.8.6. 8.8.6.
Surely He hath borne our griefs, and carried our sorrows.—Is. liii. 4.

O THOU who hast our sorrows borne,
   Help us to look on Thee and mourn,
     On Thee whom we have slain,
Have pierced a thousand, thousand times,
And, by reiterated crimes,
     Renewed Thy mortal pain.

2 Vouchsafe us eyes of faith to see
   The Man transfixed on Calvary,
     To know Thee, who Thou art,
The One Eternal God and True!
And let the sight affect, subdue,
     And break my stubborn heart.

3 Lover of souls, to rescue mine,
Reveal the charity divine,
     That suffered in my stead,
That made Thy soul a sacrifice,
And quenched in death those flaming eyes,
     And bowed that sacred head.

4 The veil of unbelief remove,
And by Thy manifested love,
     And by Thy sprinkled blood,
Destroy the love of sin in me,
And get Thyself the victory,
     And bring me back to God.

5 Now let Thy dying love constrain
My soul to love its God again,
     Its God to glorify;
And, lo! I come Thy cross to share,
Echo Thy sacrificial prayer,
     And with my Saviour die! Amen.
                    Wesley. 1747.

376   C.M.
Give ear to my words, O Lord; consider my meditation.—Ps. v. 1.

MY God, my God, to Thee I cry,
   Thee only would I know;
Thy purifying blood apply,
   And wash me white as snow.

2 Touch me, and make the leper clean,
   Purge my iniquity;
Unless Thou wash my soul from sin,
   I have no part in Thee.

3 But art Thou not already mine?
   Answer, if mine Thou art!
Whisper within, Thou Love divine,
   And cheer my drooping heart.

4 Tell me again my peace is made,
   And bid the sinner live;
The debt's discharged, the ransom's paid,
   My Father must forgive.

5 Behold, for me the Victim bleeds,
   His wounds are opened wide;
For me the blood of sprinkling pleads,
   And speaks me justified.

6 O why did I my Saviour leave,
   So soon unfaithful prove;
How could I Thy good Spirit grieve,
   And sin against Thy love?

7 O could I lose myself in Thee,
   Thy depth of mercy prove;
Thou vast unfathomable sea
   Of unexhausted love!

8 I loathe myself when God I see,
   And into nothing fall;
Content if Thou exalted be,
   And Christ be all in all.
                    Wesley. 1740.

377   8.8. 8.8. 8.8.
Blessed are they that mourn: for they shall be comforted.—Matthew v. 4.

JESUS, if still the same Thou art,
   If all Thy promises are sure,
Set up Thy kingdom in my heart,
   And make me rich, for I am poor:
To me be all Thy treasures given,
The kingdom of an inward heaven.

2 Thou hast pronounced the mourners blest;
   And lo! for Thee I ever mourn:
I cannot, no, I will not rest,
   Till Thou, my only Rest, return;
Till Thou, the Prince of Peace, appear,
And I receive the Comforter.

3 Where is the blessedness bestowed
   On all that hunger after Thee?
I hunger now, I thirst for God;
   See the poor fainting sinner, see,
And satisfy with endless peace,
And fill me with Thy righteousness.

4 Ah, Lord! if Thou art in that sigh,
   Then hear Thyself within me pray;
Hear in my heart Thy Spirit's cry,
   Mark what my labouring soul would say;
Answer the deep, unuttered groan,
And show that Thou and I are one.

5 Shine on Thy work, disperse the gloom,
   Light in Thy light I then shall see;
Say to my soul, 'Thy light is come,
   Glory divine is risen on thee;
Thy warfare's past; thy mourning's o'er
Look up, for thou shalt weep no more.'

CONTRITION AND LONGING FOR GOD.

Lord, I believe the promise sure,
   And trust Thou wilt not long delay;
Hungry, and sorrowful, and poor,
   Upon Thy word myself I stay;
Into Thy hands my all resign,
And wait till all Thou **art** is mine.
                       Wesley. 1740.

378   7.7. 7.7. **7.7.**
Unto you that fear My name shall the Sun of righteousness arise.
   Malachi iv. 2.

O DISCLOSE Thy **lovely face**,
   Quicken all my **drooping powers**;
Gasps my fainting **soul for grace**,
   As a thirsty land **for showers**;
Haste, my Lord, **no more delay**,
Come, my Saviour, **come away**.

2 Christ, whose **glory fills the skies**,
   Christ, the **true, the only Light**,
Sun of righteousness, arise,
   Triumph o'er the shades of night;
Day-spring **from on** high, be near;
Day-star, in **my** heart appear!

3 Dark and cheerless is the morn
   Unaccompanied by Thee;
Joyless is the day's return
   Till Thy mercy's beams I see;
Till Thou inward light impart,
Glad my eyes and warm my heart.

4 Visit then this soul of mine,
   Pierce the gloom of sin and grief;
Fill me, Radiancy Divine;
   Scatter all **my** unbelief;
More and **more** Thyself display,
Shining **to the** perfect day. Amen.
                      Wesley. 1740.

379   8.8. 8.8. **8.8.**
And Jacob was left alone; and there wrestled a man with him until the breaking of the day.—Genesis xxxii. 24.

COME, O Thou Traveller unknown,
   Whom **still** I hold, but cannot see!
My company **before is** gone,
   And I am left **alone** with Thee
With Thee all **night** I mean to stay,
And wrestle **till the** break of day.

2 I need not tell Thee who I am,
   My misery and sin declare;
Thyself hast called me by my name,
   Look on Thy hands, and read it there;
But who, I ask Thee, who art Thou?
Tell me Thy name, and tell me now.

3 In vain Thou strugglest to get **free**,
   I never will unloose my hold;
Art Thou the Man that died for me?
   The secret of Thy love unfold;
Wrestling, I will not let Thee go,
Till I Thy name, Thy nature know.

4 Wilt Thou not yet to me reveal
   Thy new, unutterable name?
Tell me, I still beseech Thee, tell;
   To know it now resolved I am;
Wrestling, I will not let Thee go,
Till I Thy name, Thy nature know.

5 What though my shrinking flesh complain,
   And murmur to contend so long?
I rise superior to my pain;
   When I am weak, then I am strong;
And when my all of strength shall fail,
I shall **with** the God-Man prevail.
                 Charles Wesley. 1742.

380   8.8. 8.8. 8.8.
I will not let Thee go, except Thou bless me.—Genesis xxxii. 26.

YIELD to me **now**, **for I am weak**,
   But confident in self-despair;
Speak to my heart, in blessings speak;
   Be conquered by my instant prayer;
Speak, or Thou never hence shalt move,
And tell me if Thy **name** is Love.

2 'Tis Love! 'tis Love! Thou diedst for me,
   I hear Thy whisper in my heart;
The morning breaks, the shadows flee,
   Pure, universal love Thou art;
To me, to all, Thy mercies move,
Thy nature and Thy name is Love.

3 My prayer hath power with God; the grace
   Unspeakable I now receive;
Through faith I see Thee face to face;
   I see Thee face to face, and live;
In vain I have not wept and strove;
Thy nature and Thy name is Love.

4 I know Thee, Saviour, who Thou art,
   Jesus, the feeble sinner's Friend;
Nor wilt Thou with the night depart,
   But stay and love me to the end;
Thy mercies never shall remove,
Thy nature and Thy name is Love.

5 The Sun **of** Righteousness on me
   Hath **risen** with healing in His wings;
Withered **my** nature's strength, from Thee
   My soul its life and **succour** brings;
My help **is** all laid up **above**,
Thy nature and Thy **name** is **Love.**

6 Contented now upon my thigh
   I halt, till life's short journey **end**;
All helplessness, all weakness, I
   On Thee alone for strength depend;
Nor have I power from Thee to move,
Thy nature and Thy name is Love.

7 **Lame** as I am, I take the prey;
   Hell, earth, and sin, with ease **o'ercome**;
I leap for joy, pursue my way,
   And, as a bounding hart, fly home;
Through all eternity to prove
Thy nature and Thy name is Love.
                 Charles Wesley. 1742.

THE CHRISTIAN LIFE.

381 6.10. 6.10.
The foxes have holes, and the birds of the air have nests; but the Son of man hath not where to lay His head.
Matthew viii. 20.

BIRDS have their quiet nest,
  Foxes their holes, and man his peaceful bed;
All creatures have their rest,
But Jesus had not where to lay His head.

2 And yet He came to give
The weary and the heavy-laden rest;
  To bid the sinner live,
And soothe our griefs to slumber on His breast.

3 I who once made Him grieve,
I who once bid His gentle spirit mourn;
  Whose hand essayed to weave
For His meek brow the cruel crown of thorn:

4 O why should I have peace?
Why—but for that unchanged, undying love,
  Which would not, could not cease,
Until it made me heir of joys above?

5 Yes, but for pardoning grace,
I feel I never should in glory see
  The brightness of that face,
Which once was pale and agonized for me!

6 Let the birds seek their nest,
Foxes their holes, and man his peaceful bed;
  Come, Saviour, in my breast
Deign to repose Thine oft-rejected head.

7 Come! give me rest, and take
The only rest on earth Thou lov'st, within
  A heart, that for Thy sake
Lies bleeding, broken, penitent for sin.
            Amen.
    J. S. B. Monsell. 1857.

382 8.4. 8.4. 8.8.8.
Lo, I am with you alway, even unto the end of the world.
Matthew xxviii. 20.

MY Saviour, 'mid life's varied scene,
  Be Thou my stay;
Guide me, through each perplexing path,
  To perfect day;
In weakness and in sin I stand;
Still faith can clasp Thy mighty hand,
And follow at Thy dear command.

2 My Saviour, I have nought to bring
  Worthy of Thee,
A broken heart Thou wilt not spurn,
  Accept of me:
I need Thy righteousness divine,
I plead Thy promises as mine,
I perish if I am not Thine.

3 My Saviour, wilt Thou turn away
  From such a cry?
My Refuge, wilt Thou me forget,
  And must I die?

110

Faith trembles; but her glance so bright
Has pierced through regions dark as night,
And entered into realms of light.

4 My Saviour, 'mid heaven's glorious throng,
  I see Thee there,
Pleading with all Thy matchless love
  And tender care:
Not for the angel forms around,
But for lost souls in fetters bound,
That they may hear salvation's sound.

5 My Saviour, thus I find my rest
  Alone with Thee;
Beneath Thy wing I have no fear
  Of what may be.
Strengthened with Thy all-glorious might,
I shall be conqueror in the fight,
Then give to Thee my crown of light.
            Amen.
  Mrs. Elizabeth A. Godwin. 1865.

383 C.M.
It is God which worketh in you both to will and to do of His good pleasure.—Philippians ii. 13.

FATHER, to Thee my soul I lift,
  My soul on Thee depends,
Convinced that every perfect gift
  From Thee alone descends.

2 Mercy and grace are Thine alone,
  And power and wisdom too;
Without the Spirit of Thy Son
  We nothing good can do.

3 We cannot speak one useful word,
  One holy thought conceive,
Unless in answer to our Lord,
  Thyself the blessing give.

4 His blood demands the purchased grace;
  His blood's availing plea
Obtained the help for all our race,
  And sends it down to me.

5 Thou all our works in us hast wrought,
  Our good is all divine,
The praise of every virtuous thought,
  And righteous word is Thine.

6 From Thee, through Jesus, we receive
  The power on Thee to call,
In whom we are, and move, and live;
  Our God is all in all!
        Charles Wesley. 1749.

384 C.M.
Jesus of Nazareth passeth by.
Luke xviii. 37.

JESUS, if still Thou art to-day
  As yesterday the same,
Present to heal, in me display
  The virtue of Thy Name.

CONTRITION AND LONGING FOR GOD.

2 If still Thou goest about to do
  Thy needy creatures good,
On me, that I Thy praise may show,
  Be all Thy wonders showed.

3 Now, Lord, to whom for help I call,
  Thy miracles repeat;
With pitying eyes behold me fall
  A leper at Thy feet.

4 Thou seest me deaf to Thy command,
  Open, O Lord, mine ear;
Bid me stretch out my withered hand,
  And lift it up in prayer.

5 Silent, alas! Thou know'st how long,
  My voice I cannot raise;
But, O! when Thou shalt loose my
    tongue,
  The dumb shall sing Thy praise.

6 Blind from my birth to guilt and Thee,
  And dark I am within,
The love of God I cannot see,
  The sinfulness of sin.

7 But Thou, they say, art passing by,
  O let me find Thee near;
Jesus, in mercy, hear my cry,
  Thou Son of David, hear!

8 Behold me waiting in the way
  For Thee, the heavenly Light;
Command me to be brought, and say,
  'Sinner, receive thy sight.' Amen.
                    Wesley. 1761.

385 7.6. 7.6. 7.8. 7.6.
*He cried, saying, Lord,
save me!*—Matthew xiv. 30.

LAMB of God, for sinners slain,
  To Thee I feebly pray;
Heal me of my grief and pain,
  O take my sins away!
From this bondage, Lord, release,
No longer let me be opprest:
  Jesus, Master, seal my peace,
  And take me to Thy breast!

2 Wilt Thou cast a sinner out,
    Who humbly comes to Thee?
  No, my God, I cannot doubt,
    Thy mercy is for me:
  Let me then obtain the grace,
  And be of paradise possest:
    Jesus, Master, seal my peace,
    And take me to Thy breast!

3 Worldly good I do not want,
    He that to others given;
  Only for Thy love I pant,
    My all in earth and heaven;
  This the crown I fain would seize,
  The good wherewith I would be blest:
    Jesus, Master, seal my peace,
    And take me to Thy breast!

4 This delight I fain would prove,
    And then resign my breath;
  Join the happy few whose love
    Was mightier than death.
  Let it not my Lord displease,
  That I would die to be Thy guest:
    Jesus, Master, seal my peace,
    And take me to Thy breast! Amen.
                    Wesley. 1742.

386 L.M.
*Wherewith shall I come
before the Lord?*—Micah vi. 6.

WHEREWITH, O God, shall I draw near,
  And bow myself before Thy face?
How in Thy purer eyes appear?
  What shall I bring to gain Thy grace?

2 Will gifts delight the Lord most high?
  Will multiplied oblations please,
Thousands of rams His favour buy,
  Or slaughtered hecatombs appease?

3 Can these avert the wrath of God?
  Can these wash out my guilty stain?
Rivers of oil, and seas of blood,
  Alas! they all must flow in vain.

4 Whoe'er to Thee themselves approve,
  Must take the path Thy word hath
      showed,
Justice pursue, and mercy love,
  And humbly walk by faith with God.

5 But though my life henceforth be Thine,
  Present for past can ne'er atone;
Though I to Thee the whole resign,
  I only give Thee back Thine own.

6 What have I then wherein to trust?
  I nothing have, I nothing am;
Excluded is my every boast,
  My glory swallowed up in shame.

7 Guilty I stand before Thy face,
  On me I feel Thy wrath abide;
'Tis just the sentence should take place;
  'Tis just;—but O Thy Son hath died!

8 Jesus, the Lamb of God, hath bled,
  He bore our sins upon the tree;
Beneath our curse He bowed His head;
  'Tis finished! He hath died for me!

9 See where before the throne He stands,
  And pours the all-prevailing prayer;
Points to His side, and lifts His hands,
  And shows that I am graven there.

10 He ever lives for me to pray,
  He prays that I with Him may reign;
Amen to what my Lord doth say;
  Jesus, Thou canst not pray in vain.
                    Wesley. 1740.

THE CHRISTIAN LIFE.

387 C.M.
But will God indeed dwell on the earth?—1 Kings viii. 27.

WITH glorious clouds encompassed
  round,
Whom angels dimly see,
Will the Unsearchable be found,
Or God appear to me?

2 Will He forsake His throne above,
Himself to me impart?
Answer, Thou Man of grief and love,
And speak it to my heart!

3 In manifested love explain
Thy wonderful design;
What meant the suffering Son of Man,
The streaming blood divine?

4 Didst Thou not in our flesh appear,
And live and die below,
That I may now perceive Thee near,
And my Redeemer know?

5 Come then, and to my soul reveal
The heights and depths of grace,
The wounds which all my sorrows heal,
That dear disfigured face.

6 Before my eyes of faith confest,
Stand forth a slaughtered Lamb;
And wrap me in Thy crimson vest,
And tell me all Thy name.

7 Jehovah in Thy person show,
Jehovah crucified!
And then the pardoning God I know,
And feel the blood applied:

8 I view the Lamb in His own light,
Whom angels dimly see,
And gaze, transported at the sight,
To all eternity.
Charles Wesley. 1767.

388 C.M.
The word preached did not profit them.—Hebrews iv. 2.

LONG have I sat beneath the sound
  Of Thy salvation, Lord;
But still how weak my faith is found,
And knowledge of Thy word!

2 My glorious Saviour and my God,
How little art Thou known
By all the judgments of Thy rod,
Or blessings of Thy throne.

3 How cold and feeble is my love,
How negligent my fear,
How low my hope of joys above,
How few affections there!

4 Great God! Thy sovereign power impart
To give Thy word success;
Write Thy salvation on my heart,
And make me learn Thy grace.

5 Show my forgetful feet the way
That leads to joys on high,
Where knowledge grows without decay,
And love shall never die. Amen.
Isaac Watts. 1709.

389 6.6. 6.6.
My soul thirsteth for Thee.
Psalm lxiii. 1.

MY spirit longs for Thee
  Within my troubled breast,
Unworthy though I be
Of so divine a guest.

2 Of so divine a guest
Unworthy though I be,
Yet has my heart no rest
Unless it come from Thee.

3 Unless it come from Thee,
In vain I look around;
In all that I can see
No rest is to be found.

4 No rest is to be found
But in Thy blessed love;
O let my wish be crowned,
And send it from above! Amen.
John Byrom. 1773.

390 8.8.6. 8.8.6.
For what I would, that do I not.—Romans vii. 15.

STILL, Lord, I languish for Thy grace
  Reveal the beauties of Thy face,
The middle wall remove;
Appear, and banish my complaint;
Come, and supply my only want,
Fill all my soul with love.

2 O conquer this rebellious will!
Willing Thou art and ready still,
Thy help is always nigh;
The hardness from my heart remove,
And give me, Lord, O give me love,
Or at Thy feet I die.

3 To Thee I lift my mournful eye;
Why am I thus?—O tell me why
I cannot love my God?
The hindrance must be all in me;
It cannot in my Saviour be,
Witness that streaming blood.

4 It cost Thy blood my heart to win,
To buy me from the power of sin,
And make me love again;
Come then, my Lord, Thy right assert,
Take to Thyself my ransomed heart,
Nor bleed, nor die in vain. Amen.
Charles Wesley. 1749.

CONTRITION AND LONGING FOR GOD.

391   7.7. 7.7.
For to me to live is Christ.
Philippians i. 21.

WHEN, my Saviour, shall I be
   Perfectly resigned to Thee?
Poor and vile in my own eyes,
Only in Thy wisdom wise:

2 Only Thee content to know,
   Only serving Thee below,
   Only guided by Thy light,
   Only mighty in Thy might.

3 So I may Thy Spirit know,
   Let Him as He listeth blow;
   Let the manner be unknown,
   So I may with Thee be one.

4 Fully in my life express
   All the heights of holiness,
   Sweetly let my spirit prove
   All the depths of humble love. Amen.
               Charles Wesley. 1742.

392   C.M.
Thine heart was tender,
and thou hast humbled thyself before the
Lord.—2 Kings xxii. 19.

O FOR that tenderness of heart
   Which bows before the Lord,
Acknowledging how just Thou art,
   And trembles at Thy word!

2 O for those humble, contrite tears,
   Which from repentance flow,
That consciousness of guilt, which fears
   The long-suspended blow!

3 Saviour, to me in pity give
   The sensible distress,
The pledge Thou wilt at last receive,
   And bid me die in peace:

4 Wilt from the dreadful day remove,
   Before the evil come;
My spirit hide with saints above,
   My body in the tomb. Amen.
               Charles Wesley. 1762.

393   8.8. 8.8. 8.8.
I will put my Spirit
within you.—Ezekiel xxxvi. 27.

O LOVE, I languish at Thy stay!
   I pine for Thee with lingering smart,
Weary and faint through long delay:
   When wilt Thou come into my heart,
From sin and sorrow set me free,
And swallow up my soul in Thee?

2 Come, O Thou universal Good!
   Balm of the wounded conscience, come!
The hungry, dying spirit's food,
   The weary, wandering pilgrim's home;
Haven to take the shipwrecked in,
My everlasting rest from sin!

3 Be Thou, O Love, whate'er I want;
   Support my feebleness of mind,
Relieve the thirsty soul, the faint
   Revive, illuminate the blind,
The mournful cheer, the drooping lead,
And heal the sick, and raise the dead.

4 Come, O my comfort and delight!
   My strength and health, my shield and
      sun,
My boast, and confidence, and might,
   My joy, my glory, and my crown,
My gospel hope, my calling's prize,
My tree of life, my paradise.

5 The secret of the Lord Thou art,
   The mystery so long unknown,
Christ in a pure and perfect heart,
   The name inscribed in the white stone,
The Life divine, the little leaven,
My precious pearl, my present heaven.
               Wesley. 1742.

394   7.6. 7.6. 7.8. 7.6.
God hath made man
upright.—Ecclesiastes vii. 29.

UPRIGHT, both in heart and will,
   We by our God were made;
But we turned from good to ill,
   And o'er the creature strayed;
Multiplied our wandering thought,
Which first was fixed on God alone;
In ten thousand objects sought
   The bliss we lost in one.

2 From our own inventions vain
   Of fancied happiness,
Draw us to Thyself again,
   And bid our wanderings cease;
Jesus, speak our souls restored
By Love's divine simplicity,
Re-united to our Lord,
   And wholly lost in Thee! Amen.
               Charles Wesley. 1762.

395   8.8. 8.8. 8.8.
I will love Thee, O Lord,
my strength.—Psalm xviii. 1.

THOU hidden love of God, whose height,
   Whose depth unfathomed, no man
      knows,
I see from far Thy beauteous light,
   Inly I sigh for Thy repose;
My heart is pained, nor can it be
At rest, till it finds rest in Thee.

2 Thy secret voice invites me still
   The sweetness of Thy yoke to prove;
And fain I would; but though my will
   Seems fixed, yet wide my passions rove;
Yet hindrances strew all the way;
I aim at Thee, yet from Thee stray.

3 'Tis mercy all that Thou hast brought
   My mind to seek her peace in Thee;
Yet while I seek, but find Thee not,
   No peace my wandering soul shall see;
O when shall all my wanderings end,
And all my steps to Thee-ward tend!

THE CHRISTIAN LIFE.

4 Is there a thing beneath the sun
  That strives with Thee my heart to share?
Ah, tear it thence, and reign alone,
  The Lord of every motion there!
Then shall my heart from earth be free,
  When it hath found repose in Thee.

5 Each moment draw from earth away
  My heart, that lowly waits Thy call;
Speak to my inmost soul, and say,
  'I am thy Love, thy God, thy All!'
To feel Thy power, to hear Thy voice,
  To taste Thy love, be all my choice.
                                Amen.
            Gerhardt Tersteegen. 1731.
                Tr. J. Wesley. 1736.

396 *The cross of Christ.*   8.8.8.6.
        Galatians vi. 12.

DRAWN to the cross which Thou hast blessed
  With healing gifts for souls distressed,
  To find in Thee my Life, my Rest,
        Christ crucified, I come!

2 Stained with the sins which I have wrought
  In word and deed and secret thought,
  For pardon which Thy blood hath bought,
        Christ crucified, I come!

3 Weary of selfishness and pride,
  False pleasures gone, vain hopes denied,
  Deep in Thy wounds my shame to hide,
        Christ crucified, I come!

4 Thou knowest all my griefs and fears,
  Thy grace abused, my misspent years;
  Yet now to Thee, for cleansing tears,
        Christ crucified, I come!

5 I would not, if I could, conceal
  The ills which only Thou canst heal,
  So to the cross, where sinners kneel,
        Christ crucified, I come!

6 Wash me, and take away each stain,
  Let nothing of my sin remain;
  For cleansing, though it be through pain,
        Christ crucified, I come!

7 To be what Thou wouldst have me be,
  Accepted, sanctified in Thee,
  Through what Thy grace shall work in me,
        Christ crucified, I come!
            Genevieve S. Irons. 1881.

397   L.M.
    *He said, It is finished;
    and He bowed His head, and gave up the
        ghost.*—John xix. 30.

O JESUS, let Thy dying cry
  Pierce to the bottom of my heart,
  Its evils cure, its wants supply,
    And bid my unbelief depart.

2 Slay the dire root and seed of sin;
  Prepare for Thee the holiest place;
  Then, O essential Love, come in!
    And fill Thy house with endless praise.

3 Let me, according to Thy word,
  A tender, contrite heart receive,
  Which grieves at having grieved its Lord,
    And never can itself forgive;

4 A heart Thy joys and griefs to feel,
  A heart that cannot faithless prove,
  A heart where Christ alone may dwell,
    All praise, all meekness, and all love.
                                Amen.
              Charles Wesley. 1762.

398   L.M.
    *As many as I love, I
    rebuke and chasten.*—Revelation iii. 19.

O LET us our own works forsake,
  Ourselves, and all we have deny;
  Thy condescending counsel take,
    And come to Thee, pure gold to buy.

2 O might we, through Thy grace, attain
  The faith Thou never wilt reprove,
  The faith that purges every stain,
    The faith that always works by love!

3 O might we see, in this our day,
  The things belonging to our peace,
  And timely meet Thee in Thy way
    Of judgments, and our sins confess!

4 Thy fatherly chastisements own;
  With filial awe revere Thy rod;
  And turn, with zealous haste, and run
    Into the outstretched arms of God.
                                Amen.
                  Wesley. 1742.

FAITH AND CONSECRATION.

399   6.6.4.6.6.6.4.
    *Behold the Lamb of God,
    which taketh away the sin of the world.*
            John i. 29.

MY faith looks up to Thee,
    Thou Lamb of Calvary,
        Saviour divine:
  Now hear me while I pray;
  Take all my guilt away;
  O let me from this day
        Be wholly Thine!

2 May Thy rich grace impart
    Strength to my fainting heart,
        My zeal inspire;
  As Thou hast died for me,
  O may my love to Thee,
  Pure, warm, and changeless, be
        A living fire!

FAITH AND CONSECRATION.

3 While life's dark maze I tread,
And griefs around me spread,
Be Thou my Guide:
Bid darkness turn to day,
Wipe sorrow's tears away,
Nor let me ever stray
From Thee aside.

4 When ends life's transient dream,
When death's cold sullen stream
Shall o'er me roll,
Blest Saviour, then, in love,
Fear and distrust remove;
O bear me safe above—
A ransomed soul! Amen.
Ray Palmer. 1834.

400 *Looking unto Jesus the author and finisher of our faith.* Hebrews xii. 2. L.M.

AUTHOR of faith, Eternal Word,
Whose Spirit breathes the active flame;
Faith, like its Finisher and Lord,
To-day as yesterday the same:

2 To Thee our humble hearts aspire,
And ask the gift unspeakable;
Increase in us the kindled fire,
In us the work of faith fulfil.

3 By faith we **know Thee** strong to save;
Save us, **a** present Saviour Thou!
Whate'er we hope, by faith we have,
Future and past subsisting now.

4 To him that in Thy name believes,
Eternal life with Thee is given;
Into himself he all receives,
Pardon, and holiness, and **heaven.**

5 The things unknown to feeble sense,
Unseen by reason's glimmering ray,
With strong, commanding evidence,
Their heavenly **origin** display.

6 Faith lends its realizing light,
The clouds disperse, the shadows fly;
The invisible appears in sight,
And God is seen by mortal eye.
Wesley. 1740.

401 *Lord, increase our faith.* Luke xvii. 5. C.M.

THOU, who our faithless hearts canst read,
And know'st each weakness there;
Poor, trembling, faint, with Thee we plead,
O turn not from our prayer!

2 We cannot grasp from hour to hour
The truths Thy Gospel saith;
Then aid us by Thy heavenly power,
And so increase our faith:

3 That we may trust Thy guardian care,
When no kind hand we see;
That we may lift our souls in prayer
Undoubtingly to Thee.

4 Help us to gaze on things unseen
By eyes of mortal sight;
To pierce through earth's dark veil, **and** glean
Some beams of heavenly light.

5 Thy glorious presence may we see,
When earth's last tie is riven;
In faith then trust our souls to Thee,
Till we awake in heaven. Amen.
J. Baldwin Brown. 1859.

402 *Surely the Lord is in this place.*—Genesis xxviii. 16. 6.4.6.4.6.6.4.

NEARER, **my** God, to Thee,
Nearer to Thee!
E'en though it be **a cross**
That raiseth me;
Still all my song shall be,
Nearer, my God, to Thee,
Nearer to Thee!

2 Though like **the wanderer,**
The sun gone down,
Darkness be over me,
My rest a stone;
Yet in my dreams I'd be
Nearer, my God, to Thee,
Nearer to Thee!

3 There let the way appear
Steps **unto heaven**;
All that Thou sendest me,
In mercy given;
Angels to beckon me
Nearer, my God, **to Thee,**
Nearer to Thee!

4 Then, with my waking thoughts
Bright with Thy praise,
Out of my stony griefs
Bethel I'll raise;
So by my woes to be
Nearer, my God, to Thee,
Nearer to Thee!

5 Or if on joyful wing
Cleaving the sky,
Sun, moon, and stars forgot,
Upwards I fly;
Still all my song shall be,
Nearer, my God, to Thee,
Nearer to Thee! Amen.
Mrs. Sarah **F. Adams.** 1841.

403 *Have faith in God.* Mark xi. 22. C.M.

O FOR a faith that will not shrink,
Though pressed by many a foe;
That will not tremble on the brink
Of poverty or woe:

THE CHRISTIAN LIFE.

2 That will not murmur nor complain
  Beneath the chastening rod,
  But in the hour of grief or pain
  Can lean upon its God :

3 A faith that shines more bright and clear
  When tempests rage without ;
  That when in danger knows no fear,
  In darkness feels no doubt :

4 A faith that keeps the narrow way
  Till life's last spark is fled,
  And with a pure and heavenly ray
  Lights up the dying bed.

5 Lord, give me such a faith as this,
  And then, whate'er may come,
  I taste e'en now the hallowed bliss
  Of an eternal home. Amen.
              W. H. Bathurst. 1831.

404   8.8.6. 8.8.6.
    Perfect love casteth out fear.
           1 John iv. 18.

O GLORIOUS hope of perfect love !
  It lifts me up to things above,
    It bears on eagles' wings ;
  It gives my ravished soul a taste,
  And makes me for some moments feast
    With Jesu's priests and kings.

2 Rejoicing now in earnest hope,
  I stand, and from the mountain-top
    See all the land below ;
  Rivers of milk and honey rise,
  And all the fruits of Paradise
    In endless plenty grow.

3 A land of corn, and wine, and oil,
  Favoured with God's peculiar smile,
    With every blessing blest ;
  There dwells the Lord our Righteousness,
  And keeps His own in perfect peace,
    And everlasting rest.

4 O that I might at once go up !
  No more on this side Jordan stop,
    But now the land possess ;
  This moment end my legal years,
  Sorrows, and sins, and doubts, and fears,
    A howling wilderness.

5 Now, O my Joshua, bring me in !
  Cast out Thy foes ; the inbred sin,
    The carnal mind, remove ;
  The purchase of Thy death divide !
  And O ! with all the sanctified
    Give me a lot of love ! Amen.
              Wesley. 1742.

405   C.M.
  *If I wash thee not, thou
    hast no part with Me.*—John xiii. 8.

FOR ever here my rest shall be,
  Close to Thy bleeding side ;
  This all my hope, and all my plea,
  For me the Saviour died !

2 My dying Saviour, and my God,
  Fountain for guilt and sin,
  Sprinkle me ever with Thy blood,
  And cleanse, and keep me clean.

3 Wash me, and make me thus Thine own ;
  Wash me, and mine Thou art ;
  Wash me, but not my feet alone,
  My hands, my head, my heart.

4 The atonement of Thy blood apply,
  Till faith to sight improve ;
  Till hope in full fruition die,
  And all my soul be love. Amen.
              Wesley. 1740.

406   7.6. 7.6. D.
    *The Lord hath laid on
  Him the iniquity of us all.*—Isaiah liii. 6.

I LAY my sins on Jesus,
  The spotless Lamb of God !
  He bears them all, and frees us
    From the accursèd load.
  I bring my guilt to Jesus,
    To wash my crimson stains
  White in His blood most precious,
    Till not a spot remains.

2 I lay my wants on Jesus,
    All fulness dwells in Him ;
  He heals all my diseases,
    He doth my soul redeem.
  I lay my griefs on Jesus,
    My burdens and my cares ;
  He from them all releases,
    He all my sorrows shares.

3 I rest my soul on Jesus,
    This weary soul of mine ;
  His right hand me embraces,
    I on His breast recline.
  I love the name of Jesus,
    Immanuel, Christ, the Lord ;
  Like fragrance on the breezes,
    His name abroad is poured.

4 I long to be like Jesus,
    Meek, loving, lowly, mild ;
  I long to be like Jesus,
    The Father's Holy Child.
  I long to be with Jesus,
    Amid the heavenly throng,
  To sing with saints His praises,
    To learn the angels' song.
              Horatius Bonar. 1844.

407   8.8.8. 6.
    Come unto me.—Matt. xi. 28.

JUST as I am—without one plea,
  But that Thy blood was shed for me,
  And that Thou bidd'st me come to Thee,
    O Lamb of God, I come !

2 Just as I am—and waiting not
  To rid my soul of one dark blot,
  To Thee, whose blood can cleanse each spot,
    O Lamb of God, I come !

FAITH AND CONSECRATION.

3 Just as I am—though tossed about
With many a conflict, many a doubt,
Fightings within, and fears without,
O Lamb of God, I come!

4 Just as I am—Thou wilt receive,
Wilt welcome, pardon, cleanse, relieve;
Because Thy promise I believe,
O Lamb of God, I come!

5 Just as I am—Thy love unknown
Has broken every barrier down;
Now to be Thine, yea, Thine alone,
O Lamb of God, I come!

6 Just as I am—of that free love
The breadth, length, depth, and height
to prove,
Here for a season, then above,
O Lamb of God, I come!
Charlotte Elliott. 1836.

408 C.M.
We walk by faith, not by sight.—2 Cor. v. 7.

WE walk by faith, and not by sight;
No gracious words we hear
From Him who spoke as never man,
But we believe Him near.

2 We may not touch His hands and side,
Nor follow where He trod;
But in His promise we rejoice,
And cry, 'My Lord and God!'

3 Help Thou, O Lord, our unbelief;
And may our faith abound,
To call on Thee when Thou art near,
And seek where Thou art found:

4 That when our life of faith is done,
In realms of clearer light
We may behold Thee as Thou art,
With full and endless sight. Amen.
H. Alford. 1844.

409 C.M.
*Thy commandment is
exceeding broad.*—Psalm cxix. 96.

DEEPEN the wound Thy hands have
made
In this weak, helpless soul,
Till mercy, with its balmy aid,
Descends to make me whole.

2 The sharpness of Thy two-edged sword
O! help me to endure;
Till bold to say, My hallowing Lord
Hath wrought a perfect cure.

3 I see the exceeding broad command,
Which all contains in one;
Enlarge my heart to understand
The mystery unknown.

4 O that with all Thy saints I might,
By sweet experience, prove
What is the length, and breadth, and
height,
And depth of perfect love! Amen.
Charles Wesley. 1762.

410 S.M.
*He shall redeem Israel
from all his iniquities.*—Psalm cxxx. 8.

FATHER, I dare believe
Thee merciful and true;
Thou wilt my guilty soul forgive,
My fallen soul renew.

2 Come then for Jesu's sake,
And bid my heart be clean;
An end of all my troubles make,
An end of all my sin.

3 I will, through grace, I will,
I do, return to Thee;
Take, empty it, O Lord, and fill
My heart with purity!

4 For power I feebly pray:
Thy kingdom now restore,
To-day, while it is called to-day,
And I shall sin no more.

5 I cannot wash my heart,
But by believing Thee,
And waiting for Thy blood to impart
The spotless purity.

6 While at Thy cross I lie,
Jesus, Thy grace bestow,
Now Thy all-cleansing blood apply,
And I am white as snow. Amen.
Charles Wesley. 1762.

411 L.M.
*They which be of faith
are blessed with faithful Abraham.*
Galatians iii. 9.

ABRAHAM, when severely tried,
His faith by his obedience showed;
He with the harsh command complied,
And gave his Isaac back to God.

2 His son the father offered up,
Son of his age, his only son,
Object of all his joy and hope,
And less beloved than God alone.

3 O for a faith like his, that we
The bright example may pursue;
May gladly give up all to Thee,
To whom our more than all is due.

4 Now, Lord, to Thee our all we leave,
Our willing soul Thy call obeys;
Pleasure, and wealth, and fame we give,
Freedom, and life, to win Thy grace.

5 Is there a thing than life more dear,
A thing from which we cannot part?
We can; we now rejoice to tear
The idol from our bleeding heart.

6 Jesus, accept our sacrifice;
All things for Thee we count but loss;
Lo! at Thy word our Isaac dies,
Dies on the altar of Thy cross.

THE CHRISTIAN LIFE.

7 For what to Thee, O Lord, we give,
A hundred-fold we here obtain;
And soon with Thee shall all receive,
And loss shall be eternal gain.
Wesley. 1740.

412   7.7. 7.7. D.
*He leadeth me beside the
still waters.*—Psalm xxiii. 2.

HAPPY soul that, free from harms,
Rests within his Shepherd's arms!
Who his quiet shall molest?
Who shall violate his rest?
Jesus doth his spirit bear,
Jesus takes his every care;
He who found the wandering sheep,
Jesus, still delights to keep.

2 O that I might so believe,
Steadfastly to Jesus cleave,
On His only love rely,
Smile at the destroyer nigh;
Free from sin and servile fear,
Have my Jesus ever near,
All His care rejoice to prove,
All His paradise of love!

3 Jesus, seek Thy wandering sheep,
Bring me back, and lead, and keep;
Take on Thee my every care,
Bear me, on Thy bosom bear;
Let me know my Shepherd's voice,
More and more in Thee rejoice,
More and more of Thee receive,
Ever in Thy Spirit live:

4 Live, till all Thy life I know,
Perfect through my Lord below,
Gladly then from earth remove,
Gathered to the fold above,
O that I at last may stand
With the sheep at Thy right hand,
Take the crown so freely given,
Enter in by Thee to heaven! Amen.
Charles Wesley. 1749.

413   10. 10.
*Thou wilt keep him in
perfect peace, whose mind is stayed on Thee.*
Isaiah xxvi. 3.

PEACE, perfect peace, in this dark world
of sin?
The blood of Jesus whispers peace within.

2 Peace, perfect peace, by thronging duties
pressed?
To do the will of Jesus, this is rest.

3 Peace, perfect peace, with sorrows surging
round?
On Jesus' bosom nought but calm is found.

4 Peace, perfect peace, with loved ones far
away?
In Jesus' keeping we are safe, and they.

5 Peace, perfect peace, our future all unknown?
Jesus we know, and He is on the throne.

6 Peace, perfect peace, death shadowing us
and ours?
Jesus has vanquished death and all its
powers.

7 It is enough: earth's struggles soon shall
cease,
And Jesus call us to heaven's perfect
peace.
Bishop E. H. Bickersteth. 1876.

414   8.5. 8.3.
*Believe on the Lord Jesus
Christ, and thou shalt be saved.*
Acts xvi. 31.

I AM trusting Thee, Lord Jesus,
Trusting only Thee,
Trusting Thee for full salvation,
Great and free.

2 I am trusting Thee for pardon,
At Thy feet I bow,
For Thy grace and tender mercy,
Trusting now.

3 I am trusting Thee for cleansing,
In the crimson flood,
Trusting Thee to make me holy,
By Thy blood.

4 I am trusting Thee to guide me,
Thou alone shalt lead,
Every day and hour supplying
All my need.

5 I am trusting Thee for power,
Thine can never fail;
Words which Thou Thyself shalt give me
Must prevail.

6 I am trusting Thee, Lord Jesus,
Never let me fall;
I am trusting Thee for ever,
And for all.
Frances R. Havergal. 1874.

415   7.6. 7.6. D.
*Without Me ye can
do nothing.*—John xv. 5.

I COULD not do without Thee,
O Saviour of the lost!
Whose wondrous love redeemed me
At such tremendous cost;
Thy righteousness, Thy pardon,
Thy precious blood must be
My only hope and comfort,
My glory and my plea.

2 I could not do without Thee,
I cannot stand alone,
I have no strength or goodness,
No wisdom of my own;

FAITH AND CONSECRATION.

But Thou, belovèd Saviour,
Art all in all to me,
And perfect strength in **weakness**
Is theirs who lean on **Thee**.

3 I could not do without Thee,
O Jesus, Saviour dear!
E'en when my eyes are holden,
I know that Thou art near;
How dreary and how lonely
This changeful life would be
Without the sweet communion,
The secret rest with Thee.

4 I could not do without Thee;
No other friend could read
The spirit's strange, deep longings,
Interpreting its need;
No human heart could enter
Each dim recess of mine,
And soothe, and hush, and calm it,
O blessèd Lord, but Thine.

5 I could not do without Thee,
For life is fleeting fast,
And soon in solemn loneness
The river must be passed;
But Thou wilt never leave me,
And though the waves roll high,
I know Thou wilt be with me,
And whisper, 'It is I.'
  Frances R. Havergal. 1873.

416   7.6. 7.6. *With Chorus. Trochaic.*
God forbid that I should glory, save in the cross of our Lord Jesus Christ.—Galatians vi. 14.

JESUS, keep me near the Cross;
There a precious fountain,
Free to all, a healing stream,
Flows from Calvary's mountain.
 In the Cross, in the Cross,
  Be my glory ever;
 Till my raptured soul shall find
  Rest beyond the river.

2 Near the Cross, a trembling soul,
Love and mercy found me;
There the bright and morning star
Shed its beams around me.

3 Near the Cross, O Lamb of God!
Bring its scenes before me;
Make me walk from day to day
With its shadow o'er me.

4 Near the Cross I'll watch and wait,
Hoping, trusting ever,
Till I reach the golden strand,
Just beyond the river.
  Frances Jane Crosby. 1874.

417   7.7. 7.7.
The life was the light of men.
John i. 4.

LIGHT of Life, seraphic fire,
Love Divine! Thyself impart;
Every fainting soul inspire,
Shine in every drooping heart.

2 Every mournful sinner cheer,
Scatter all our guilty gloom,
Son of God, appear, appear!
To Thy human temples come.

3 Come in this accepted hour;
Bring Thy heavenly kingdom in;
Fill us with the glorious power,
Rooting out the seeds of sin.

4 Nothing more can we require,
We will covet nothing less;
Be Thou all **our** heart's desire,
All our joy, and all **our** peace. Amen.
  Charles Wesley. 1749.

418   6.5. 6.5. D.
Looking unto Jesus, the author and finisher of our faith.
Hebrews xii. 2.

LOOKING unto Jesus
With the eye of faith,
Telling Him our troubles,
Hearing what He saith,—
Like the day-spring stealing
Through the shades of night,
Silently it turneth
Darkness into light.

2 Looking unto Jesus,
In a sweet accord
Knitteth the disciple
To the absent Lord:
To our soul's complainings
Jesus giveth heed,
Pouring out His fulness
Over all our need.

3 Looking unto Jesus,
In the stormy day;
'Tis His gracious Spirit
Cheers us on our way:
Looking still to Jesus,
When the storms retreat,
He will be our shelter
From the noontide heat.

4 Looking unto Jesus
From the bed of pain,
As a suffering brother,
Jesus will sustain.
Looking still to Jesus,
In the hour of death,
Lo! the everlasting
Arms are underneath.
  Jane Crewdson. d. 1863.

419   L.M.
Happy is the man that findeth wisdom.—Proverbs iii. 13.

HAPPY the man that finds the grace,
The blessing of God's chosen race,
The wisdom coming from above,
The faith that sweetly works by love.

THE CHRISTIAN LIFE.

2 Happy beyond description he
 Who knows the Saviour died for me,
 The gift unspeakable obtains,
 And heavenly understanding gains.

3 Wisdom divine! Who tells the price
 Of Wisdom's costly merchandise?
 Wisdom to silver we prefer,
 And gold is dross compared to her.

4 Her hands are filled with length of days,
 True riches, and immortal praise,
 Riches of Christ, on all bestowed,
 And honour that descends from God.

5 To purest joys she all invites,
 Chaste, holy, spiritual delights;
 Her ways are ways of pleasantness,
 And all her flowery paths are peace.

6 Happy the man who wisdom gains,
 Thrice happy who his guest retains!
 He owns, and shall for ever own,
 Wisdom, and Christ, and heaven are one.
    Wesley. 1747.

420 C.M.
*There remaineth therefore
a rest to the people of God.*—Hebrews iv. 9.

LORD, I believe a rest remains
 To all Thy people known,
A rest where pure enjoyment reigns,
 And Thou art loved alone;

2 A rest, where all our soul's desire
 Is fixed on things above;
 Where fear, and sin, and grief expire,
 Cast out by perfect love.

3 O that I now the rest might know,
 Believe, and enter in!
 Now, Saviour, now the power bestow,
 And let me cease from sin.

4 Remove this hardness from my heart,
 This unbelief remove;
 To me the rest of faith impart,
 The sabbath of Thy love.

5 I would be Thine, Thou know'st I would,
 And have Thee all my own;
 Thee, O my all-sufficient Good!
 I want, and Thee alone.

6 Thy name to me, Thy nature grant;
 This, only this be given;
 Nothing beside my God I want,
 Nothing in earth or heaven.

7 Come, O my Saviour, come away!
 Into my soul descend;
 No longer from Thy creature stay,
 My Author and my End!

8 Come, Father, Son, and Holy Ghost,
 And seal me Thine abode!
 Let all I am in Thee be lost,
 Let all be lost in God. Amen.
    Wesley. 1740.

421 C.M.
*Blessed are the pure in heart;
for they shall see God.*—Matthew v. 8.

O FOR a heart to praise my God,
 A heart from sin set free;
A heart that always feels Thy blood
 So freely spilt for me!

2 A heart resigned, submissive, meek,
 My great Redeemer's throne,
 Where only Christ is heard to speak,
 Where Jesus reigns alone;

3 A humble, lowly, contrite heart,
 Believing, true, and clean;
 Which neither life nor death can part
 From Him that dwells within;

4 A heart in every thought renewed,
 And full of love divine;
 Perfect, and right, and pure, and good,
 A copy, Lord, of Thine!

5 Thy nature, gracious Lord, impart;
 Come quickly from above,
 Write Thy new name upon my heart,
 Thy new, best name of love. Amen.
    Wesley. 1742.

422 7.7.7.7.
*By whom we have now
received the atonement.*—Romans v. 11.

HOLY Lamb, who Thee receive,
 Who in Thee begin to live,
Day and night they cry to Thee,
As Thou art, so let us be!

2 Jesus, see my panting breast!
 See I long in Thee to rest!
 Gladly would I now be clean,
 Cleanse me now from every sin.

3 Fix, O fix my wavering mind;
 To Thy cross my spirit bind;
 Earthly passions far remove,
 Swallow up my soul in love.

4 Dust and ashes though we be,
 Full of sin and misery,
 Thine we are, Thou Son of God!
 Take the purchase of Thy blood.

5 Who in heart on Thee believes,
 He the atonement now receives,
 He with joy beholds Thy face,
 Triumphs in Thy pardoning grace.

6 Boundless wisdom, power divine,
 Love unspeakable, are Thine;
 Praise by all to Thee be given,
 Sons of earth, and hosts of heaven! Amen.
    Anna Dober. 1735.
    Tr. J. Wesley. 1740.

FAITH AND CONSECRATION.

423 L.M.
Whosoever therefore shall be ashamed of Me ... of him also shall the Son of Man be ashamed.—Mark viii. 38.

LORD Jesus, shall it ever be,
A mortal man ashamed of Thee?
Scorned be the thought by rich and poor!
My soul shall scorn it more and more.

2 Ashamed of Jesus! Sooner far
May evening blush to own a star.
Ashamed of Jesus! Just as soon
May midnight blush to think of noon.

3 Ashamed of Jesus, that dear Friend,
On whom my hopes of heaven depend!
No; when I blush, be this my shame,
That I no more revere His name.

4 Ashamed of Jesus! Yes, I may,
When I've no guilt to wash away,
No tears to wipe, **no** joys to crave,
And **no** immortal soul to save.

5 **Till then, nor is** this boasting vain,
Till then I boast a Saviour slain;
And O, **may this my** glory be,
That **Christ is** not ashamed of me!
Joseph Grigg. 1765.

424 8.8. 8.8. 6.
Be ye ... followers of God, as dear children.—Ephesians v. 1.

O LORD, **Thy** heavenly grace impart,
And fix my frail inconstant heart;
Henceforth my chief desire shall be
To dedicate myself to Thee,
To Thee, **my** God, **to** Thee.

2 Whate'er pursuits my time employ,
One thought shall fill my soul with joy;
That silent, secret thought shall be,
That all my hopes **are** fixed on Thee,
On Thee, my **God,** on Thee.

3 Thy glorious eye pervadeth space;
Thou'rt present, Lord, **in** every place;
And wheresoe'er my lot may be,
Still shall my spirit cleave to Thee,
To Thee, my God, to Thee.

4 Renouncing every **sinful thing,**
Safe 'neath the covert **of Thy** wing,
My sweetest **thought henceforth** shall be,
That all **I want I find in Thee,**
In Thee, **my God, in Thee.**
From the French. abt. 1826.
Tr. Lucy Wilson. 1829.

425 S.M.
I will put My law in their inward parts, and write it in their hearts.
Jeremiah xxxi. 33.

THE thing my God doth hate
That I no more may do,
Thy creature, Lord, again create,
And all my soul renew.

2 My soul shall then, like Thine,
Abhor the thing unclean,
And, sanctified by love divine,
For ever cease from **sin.**

3 That blessèd law of Thine,
Jesus, to me impart;
The Spirit's law of life divine,
O write it in my heart!

4 Implant it deep within,
Whence it may ne'er remove,
The law of liberty from sin,
The perfect law of love.

5 Thy nature be my law,
Thy spotless sanctity,
And sweetly every moment draw
My happy soul to Thee.

6 Soul of my soul remain;
Who didst for all fulfil,
In me, O Lord, fulfil again
Thy heavenly Father's will. Amen.
Charles Wesley. 1762.

426 7.6. 7.6.
We love Him, because He first loved us.—1 John iv. 19.

IN full and glad surrender,
I give myself to Thee,
Thine utterly and only,
And evermore to be.

2 O Son of God who lov'st me,
I will be Thine alone;
And all I have, and am, Lord,
Shall henceforth be Thine own!

3 Reign over me, Lord Jesus!
O make my heart Thy throne!
It shall be Thine, dear Saviour,
It shall be Thine alone.

4 O come and reign, Lord Jesus;
Rule over everything!
And keep me always loyal,
And true to Thee my King. Amen.
Frances R. Havergal. d. 1879.

427 8.7. 8.7. D.
Lo, we have left all, and have followed Thee.—Mark x. 28.

JESUS, I my cross have taken,
All to leave, and follow Thee;
Destitute, despised, forsaken,
Thou, from hence, my all shalt **be:**
Perish **every** fond ambition,
All I've sought, **or** hoped, **or known;**
Yet how rich is my condition,
God and heaven are still my own!

2 Let the world despise and leave me;
They have left my Saviour too;
Human hearts and looks deceive me;
Thou art not, like them, untrue:

THE CHRISTIAN LIFE.

And while Thou shalt smile upon me,
  God of wisdom, love, and might,
Foes may hate, and friends may shun me:
  Show Thy face, and all is bright.

3 Man may trouble and distress me,
  'Twill but drive me to Thy breast;
Life with trials hard may press me,
  Heaven will bring me sweeter rest:
O 'tis not in grief to harm me,
  While Thy love is left to me!
O 'twere not in joy to charm me,
  Were that joy unmixed with Thee!

4 Soul, then know thy full salvation;
  Rise o'er sin, and fear, and care;
Joy to find in every station,
  Something still to do or bear:
Think what Spirit dwells within thee!
  What a Father's smile is thine!
What a Saviour died to win thee!
  Child of Heaven! shouldst thou repine?

5 Haste then on from grace to glory,
  Armed by faith, and winged by prayer,
Heaven's eternal day's before thee,
  God's own hand shall guide thee there:
Soon shall close thy earthly mission,
  Swift shall pass thy pilgrim days,
Hope soon change to glad fruition,
  Faith to sight, and prayer to praise.
          H. F. Lyte. 1824.

428 *According to your faith* C.M.
be it unto you.—Matthew ix. 29.

COME, O my God, the promise seal,
  This mountain, sin, remove;
Now in my gasping soul reveal
  The virtue of Thy love.

2 I want Thy life, Thy purity,
  Thy righteousness brought in;
I ask, desire, and trust in Thee,
  To be redeemed from sin.

3 Anger and sloth, desire and pride,
  This moment be subdued;
Be cast into the crimson tide
  Of my Redeemer's blood.

4 Saviour, to Thee my soul looks up,
  My present Saviour Thou!
In all the confidence of hope,
  I claim the blessing now.

5 'Tis done! Thou dost this moment save,
  With full salvation bless;
Redemption through Thy blood I have,
  And spotless love and peace.
          Charles Wesley. 1762.

429 *Truly I am Thy servant.* 7.7.7.7.
Psalm cxvi. 16.

TAKE my life, and let it be
  Consecrated, Lord, to Thee;
Take my moments and my days,
Let them flow in ceaseless praise.

2 Take my hands, and let them move
  At the impulse of Thy love;
Take my feet, and let them be
Swift and beautiful for Thee.

3 Take my voice, and let me sing
  Always, only for my King;
Take my lips, and let them be
Filled with messages from Thee.

4 Take my silver and my gold,
  Not a mite would I withhold;
Take my intellect, and use
Every power as Thou shalt choose.

5 Take my will, and make it Thine,
  It shall be no longer mine;
Take my heart, it is Thine own,
It shall be Thy royal throne.

6 Take my love, my Lord, I pour
  At Thy feet its treasure-store;
Take myself, and I will be
Ever, only, all for Thee. Amen.
          Frances R. Havergal. 1878.

430 *These were redeemed* 7.7.7.7.
from among men.—Revelation xiv. 4.

THINE for ever! God of love,
  Hear us from Thy throne above;
Thine for ever may we be,
Here and in eternity.

2 Thine for ever! O how blest,
  They who find in Thee their rest!
Saviour, Guardian, Heavenly Friend,
O defend us to the end!

3 Thine for ever! Lord of life,
  Shield us through our earthly strife;
Thou the Life, the Truth, the Way,
Guide us to the realms of day.

4 Thine for ever! Shepherd, keep
  These Thy frail and trembling sheep;
Safe alone beneath Thy care,
Let us all Thy goodness share.

5 Thine for ever! Thou our guide,
  All our wants by Thee supplied;
All our sins by Thee forgiven,
Lead us, Lord, from earth to heaven.
                        Amen.
          Mrs. Mary F. Maude. 1847.

431 *My times are in Thy hand.* C.M.
Psalm xxxi. 15.

LORD, it belongs not to my care,
  Whether I die or live;
To love and serve Thee is my share,
  And this Thy grace must give.

2 If life be long, I will be glad,
  That I may long obey;
If short, yet why should I be sad
  To soar to endless day?

FAITH AND CONSECRATION.

3 Christ leads me through no darker rooms
   Than He went through before;
He who into God's kingdom comes,
   Must enter by this door.

Come, Lord, **when grace hath made me
   meet**
Thy blessèd face to see;
For if Thy work on earth be sweet,
What will Thy glory be?

5 Then shall I end my sad complaints,
   And weary, sinful days;
And join with the triumphant saints,
   Who sing Jehovah's praise.

6 My knowledge of that life is small,
   The eye of faith is dim;
But 'tis enough that Christ knows all,
   And I shall be with Him.
                    Richard Baxter. 1681.

432   S.M.
*Whether we live therefore,
or die, we are the Lord's.*—Romans xiv. 8.

JESUS! I live to Thee,
   The loveliest and best;
My life in Thee, Thy life in me,
   In Thy blest love I rest.

2 Jesus! I die to Thee,
   Whenever death shall come;
To die in Thee is life to me,
   In my eternal home.

3 Whether to live or die,
   I know not which is best;
To live in Thee is bliss to me,
   To die is endless rest.

4 Living or dying, Lord,
   I ask but to be Thine;
My life in Thee, Thy life in me,
Makes heaven for ever mine. Amen.
                    Henry Harbaugh. 1850.

433   6.6. 6.6. 8.8.
*But first gave their own
selves to the Lord.*—2 Corinthians viii. 5.

GOD of my life, to Thee
   My cheerful soul I raise!
Thy goodness bade me be,
   And still prolongs my days;
I see my natal hour return,
And bless the day that I was born.

2 A clod of living earth,
   I glorify Thy name,
From whom alone my birth,
   And all my blessings came:
Creating and preserving grace,
Let all that is within me praise.

3 Long as I live beneath,
   To Thee O let me live!
To Thee my every breath
   In thanks and praises give:
Whate'er I have, whate'er I am,
Shall magnify my Maker's name.

4 My soul, and all its powers,
   Thine, wholly Thine, shall be;
All, all my happy hours
   I consecrate to Thee:
Me to Thine Image now restore,
And I shall praise Thee evermore.

5 I wait Thy will to do,
   As angels do in heaven;
In Christ a creature new,
   Most graciously forgiven,
I wait Thy perfect will to prove,
All sanctified by spotless love.

6 Then, when the work is done,
   The work of faith with power,
Receive Thy favoured son,
   In death's triumphant hour;
Like Moses to Thyself convey,
And bear my raptured soul away. Amen.
                    Charles Wesley. 1742.

434   8.8. 8.8.   *Anapæstic.*
*Thou art the God of my
strength.*—Psalm xliii. 2.

WHAT now is my object and aim?
   What now is my hope and desire?
To follow the heavenly Lamb,
   And after His image aspire:

2 My hope is all centred in Thee,
   I trust to recover Thy love,
On earth Thy salvation to see,
   And then to enjoy it above.

3 I thirst for a life-giving God,
   A God that on Calvary died;
A fountain of water and blood,
   Which gushed from Immanuel's side!

4 I gasp for the stream of Thy love,
   The spirit of rapture unknown,
And then to re-drink it above,
   Eternally fresh from the throne.
                    Charles Wesley. 1762.

435   8.8. 8.8. S.8.
*Let him deny himself, and
take up his cross daily, and follow Me.*
Luke ix. 23.

MASTER! I own Thy lawful claim,
   Thine, wholly Thine, I long to be:
Thou seest, at last, I willing am,
   Where'er Thou goest, to follow Thee
Myself in all things to deny,
Thine, wholly Thine, to live and die.

2 Whate'er my sinful flesh requires,
   For Thee I cheerfully forego;
My covetous and vain desires,
   My hopes of happiness below,
My senses' and my passions' food,
And all my thirst for creature-good.

THE CHRISTIAN LIFE.

3 Pleasure, and wealth, and praise no more
  Shall lead my captive soul astray ;
My fond pursuits I all give o'er,
  Thee, only Thee, resolved to obey ;
My own in all things to resign,
And know no other will but Thine.

4 Wherefore to Thee I all resign ;
  Being Thou art, and Love, and Power,
Thy only will be done, not mine !
  Thee, Lord, let heaven and earth adore !
Flow back the rivers to the sea,
And let our all be lost in Thee !   Amen.
                    Charles Wesley. 1749.

436   If I may but touch His   C.M.
garment, I shall be whole.—Matt. ix. 21.

WHEN in the busy crowd of life
  Too often pressed and thronged,
And in their rude and selfish strife
  Both overlooked and wronged ;

2 How sweet to know faith's lightest touch
    The watchful Saviour feels ;
  And healing, in reply to such,
    Into the sufferer steals.

3 Oft through the world we smoothly go,
    Hiding some secret care,
  Our nearest, dearest, may not know,
    Which God alone can share.

4 We mingle with the busy throng.
    They pass unheeded by ;
  They bear us in their tide along,
    We commune with the sky.

5 Saviour ! it is Thy people's bliss
    To feel Thy care for them ;
  And, while the crowd Thy mercy miss,
    To touch Thy garment's hem.

6 Friends may mistake, or foes may slight,
    Thyself not seem to see ;
  One touch of faith, however light,
    Will find its way to Thee.

7 And Thou wilt give, when sorrow pleads,
    Good comfort to the soul,
  The healing it so sorely needs,
    The faith, which makes it whole.
                    J. S. B. Monsell. 1867.

437   8.7. 8.7. Iambic.
God is faithful, who will not suffer you to be tempted above that ye are able.—1 Corinthians x. 13.

MY Father and my God, behold
  Thy wayward child before Thee ;
And to Thy will my spirit mould,
  I now with tears implore Thee.

2 Without Thee I in plenty pine,
    In throngs of men am lonely ;
  With Thee all earth and heaven are mine,
    With Thee, my Father, only.

3 O search my bosom through and through,
    And strengthen my endeavour,
  And make me always think and do
    What pleases Thee for ever.

4 My love, my life, my all control
    Henceforth by Calvary's story ;
  Stamp here Thy image on my soul,
    And fit me for Thy glory.   Amen.
                    Bishop E. H. Bickersteth. 1883.

438   8.6. 8.6. 8.6. 8.4.
Rest in the Lord, and wait patiently for Him.—Psalm xxxvii. 7.

REST in the Lord ; rest, weary heart,
  With sin and sorrow worn,
And conscience rankling with the smart
  Of pitiless self-scorn ;
O counting all beside but loss,
  Climb Calvary's lowly hill,
And there beneath the bleeding Cross,
  Rest and be still.

2 Rest in the Lord ; what time the storm
    Around thy pathway raves,
  Behold His calm majestic form
    Serenely walks the waves ;
  And hark ! that tranquil voice is heard
    Which winds and waves fulfil ;
  O rest upon His changeless word ;
    Rest and be still.

3 Rest in the Lord ; although the sands
    Of life are running low,
  Though clinging hearts and clasping hands
    May not detain thee now ;
  His hand is on thee ; death's alarms
    Can never work thee ill ;
  Rest on His everlasting arms ;
    Rest and be still.

4 Rest in the Lord ; no conflicts more,
    The latest labour done ;
  The weary strife for ever o'er,
    The crown for ever won.
  Beside the crystal stream, that flows
    From Zion's heavenly hill,
  Rest in Eternal Love's repose ;
    Rest and be still.
                    Bishop E. H. Bickersteth. 1870.

439   6.4. 6.4. 6.6.6.4.
Lord, what wilt Thou have me to do?—Acts ix. 6.

SAVIOUR ! Thy dying love
  Thou gavest me,
Nor should I aught withhold,
  My Lord, from Thee ;
In love my soul would bow,
My heart fulfil its vow,
Some offering bring Thee now,
  Something for Thee.

2 At the blest mercy-seat,
    Pleading for me,
  My feeble faith looks up,
    Jesus, to Thee :

ADOPTION AND SONSHIP.

Help me the cross to bear,
Thy wondrous love declare,
Some song to raise, or prayer,
Something for Thee.

3 Give me a faithful **heart**,
Likeness to Thee,
That each departing day
Henceforth may see
Some work of love begun,
Some deed of kindness done,
Some wanderer sought and won,
Something for Thee.

4 All that I am and have,
Thy gifts so free,
In joy, in grief, through life,
O Lord, for Thee!
And when Thy face I see,
My ransomed soul shall be,
Through all eternity,
Something for Thee. Amen.
S. D. Phelps.

440 *Love the Lord your God with all your heart.*—Deut. xiii. 3. L. M.

MY heart, O God, be wholly Thine,
I would not keep it back from Thee;
Nor wish to shun the grace divine,
Which asks this humble gift of me.

2 O take **it** now, and let Thy love
For evermore within me dwell;
And may Thy Spirit from above
Teach **me** to serve my Master well.

3 Afar be every thought of sin,
Afar be every wish to stray;
Let truth and holiness begin
To lead me up the heavenward **way**.

4 Make this my **only aim and care**,
To seek Thy **praise in all I do**;
To consecrate **each act with** prayer,
As I my **daily work** pursue.

5 More like to Thee, my blessed Lord,
I would be, as my days pass by,
With patience, love, and wisdom stored,
Ready to live, and fit to die. Amen.
W. J. Mathams. 1880.

ADOPTION AND SONSHIP.

441 *Who have fled for refuge to lay hold upon the hope set before us.* Hebrews vi. 18. 8.8. 8.8. 8.8.

NOW I have found the ground wherein
Sure my soul's anchor may remain,
The wounds of Jesus, for my sin,
Before the world's foundation slain;
Whose mercy shall unshaken stay,
When heaven and earth are fled away.

2 Father, Thine everlasting grace
Our scanty thought surpasses far,
Thy heart still melts with tenderness,
Thy arms of love still open are,
Returning sinners to receive,
That mercy they may taste and live.

3 O Love, **Thou** bottomless abyss,
My sins are swallowed **up in Thee**!
Covered is my unrighteousness,
Nor spot of guilt **remains** on me,
While Jesu's blood through earth and skies,
Mercy, free, boundless mercy, cries!

4 With faith I plunge me in this sea,
Here is my hope, my joy, my rest;
Hither, when hell assails, I flee,
I look into my Saviour's breast;
Away, sad doubt, and anxious fear!
Mercy is all that's written there.

5 Though waves and storms go o'er my head,
Though strength, and health, and friends be gone,
Though joys be withered all and dead,
Though every comfort be withdrawn,
On this my steadfast soul relies,
Father, Thy mercy never dies.

6 Fixed on this ground will I remain,
Though my heart fail, and flesh decay;
This anchor shall my soul sustain,
When earth's foundations melt away;
Mercy's full power I then shall prove,
Loved with an everlasting love.
John A. Rothe. 1735.
Tr. J. Wesley. 1740.

442 *By one offering He hath perfected for ever them that are sanctified.* Hebrews x. 14. 6.6. 6.6. 8.8.

ARISE, my soul, arise,
Shake off thy guilty **fears**;
The bleeding sacrifice
In my behalf appears;
Before the throne my Surety stands;
My name is written on His hands.

2 He ever lives above,
For me to intercede,
His all-redeeming love,
His precious blood, to plead;
His blood atoned for all our race,
And sprinkles now the throne of grace.

3 Five bleeding wounds He bears,
Received on Calvary;
They pour effectual prayers,
They strongly speak for me;
'Forgive him, O forgive,' they cry,
'Nor let that ransomed sinner die!'

4 The Father hears Him pray,
His dear Anointed One;
He cannot turn away
The presence of His Son;
His Spirit answers to the blood,
And tells me I am born of God.

THE CHRISTIAN LIFE.

5 My God is reconciled,
  His pardoning voice I hear,
He owns me for His child,
  I can no longer fear,
With confidence I now draw nigh,
And, Father, Abba, Father, cry!
                Wesley. 1742.

443   8.8. 8.8. 8.8.
In whom we have redemption through His blood, the forgiveness of sins.
      Ephesians i. 7.

AND can it be that I should gain
  An interest in the Saviour's blood?
Died He for me, who caused His pain,
  For me, who Him to death pursued?
Amazing love! how can it be
That Thou, my God, shouldst die for me!

2 'Tis mystery all: The Immortal dies!
  Who can explore His strange design!
In vain the first-born seraph tries
  To sound the depths of Love Divine!
'Tis mercy all! let earth adore,
Let angel-minds enquire no more.

3 He left His Father's throne above,
  So free, so infinite His grace!
Emptied Himself of all but love,
  And bled for Adam's helpless race:
'Tis mercy all, immense and free,
For, O my God, it found out me!

4 Long my imprisoned spirit lay
  Fast bound in sin and nature's night:
Thine eye diffused a quickening ray,
  I woke, the dungeon flamed with light;
My chains fell off, my heart was free,
I rose, went forth, and followed Thee.

5 No condemnation now I dread,
  Jesus, and all in Him, is mine;
Alive in Him, my living Head,
  And clothed in righteousness divine,
Bold I approach the eternal throne,
And claim the crown, through Christ, my
  own.
                Wesley. 1739.

444   6.4. 6.4. 10.10.
Thou knowest that I love Thee.
      John xxi. 16.

I LIFT my heart to Thee,
  Saviour Divine,
For Thou art all to me,
  And I am Thine.
Is there on earth a closer bond than this,
That my Beloved's mine, and I am His?

2 Thine am I by all ties;
  But chiefly Thine,
That through Thy sacrifice
  Thou, Lord, art mine.
By Thine own cords of love, so sweetly wound
Around me, I to Thee am closely bound.

3 To Thee, Thou bleeding Lamb,
  I all things owe;
All that I have and am,
  And all I know,
All that I have is now no longer mine,
And I am not mine own, Lord, I am Thine.

4 How can I, Lord, withhold
  Life's brightest hour
From Thee, or gathered gold,
  Or any power?
Why should I keep one precious thing from
  Thee,
When Thou hast given Thine own dear self
  for me?

5 I pray Thee, Saviour, keep
  Me in Thy love,
Until death's holy sleep
  Shall me remove
To that fair realm, where, sin and sorrow
  o'er,
Thou and Thine own are one for evermore.
                Amen.
            C. E. Mudie. b. 1818.

445   L.M.
Thou hast delivered my soul from death, mine eyes from tears, and my feet from falling.—Psalm cxvi. 8.

MY soul, through my Redeemer's care,
  Saved from the second death I feel,
My eyes from tears of dark despair,
  My feet from falling into hell.

2 Wherefore to Him my feet shall run,
  My eyes on His perfections gaze,
My soul shall live for God alone,
  And all within me shout His praise.
            Charles Wesley. 1762.

446   8.8.6. 8.8.6.
I will not leave you comfortless: I will come to you.
      John xiv. 18.

THOU great mysterious God unknown,
  Whose love hath gently led me on,
    Even from my infant days;
Mine inmost soul expose to view,
And tell me, if I ever knew
    Thy justifying grace.

2 If I have only known Thy fear,
And followed, with a heart sincere,
    Thy drawings from above;
Now, now the further grace bestow,
And let my sprinkled conscience know
    Thy sweet forgiving love.

3 Short of Thy love I would not stop,
A stranger to the gospel hope,
    The sense of sin forgiven;
I would not, Lord, my soul deceive,
Without the inward witness live,
    That antepast of heaven.

LOVE AND HOLINESS.

4 If now the witness were in me,
  Would He not testify of Thee
    In Jesus reconciled?
  And should I not with faith draw nigh
  And boldly, Abba, Father, cry,
    And know myself Thy child?

5 Whate'er obstructs Thy pardoning love,
  Or sin, or righteousness, remove,
    Thy glory to display;
  Mine heart of unbelief convince,
  And now absolve me from my sins,
    And take them all away.

6 Father, in me reveal Thy Son,
  And to my inmost soul make known
    How merciful Thou art:
  The secret of Thy love reveal,
  And by Thine hallowing Spirit dwell
    For ever in my heart. Amen.
                    Wesley. 1747.

447   8.8. 8.8. 8.8.
I am come that they might have life, and that they might have it more abundantly.—John x. 10.

O GOD of our forefathers, hear,
  And make Thy faithful mercies known:
To Thee, through Jesus, we draw near,
  Thy suffering, well-beloved Son,
In whom Thy smiling face we see,
In whom Thou art well pleased with me.

2 With solemn faith we offer up,
  And spread before Thy glorious eyes,
That only ground of all our hope,
  That precious, bleeding Sacrifice,
Which brings Thy grace on sinners down,
And perfects all our souls in one.

3 Acceptance through His only name,
  Forgiveness in His blood, we have;
But more abundant life we claim
  Through Him, who died our souls to save,
To sanctify us by His blood,
And fill with all the life of God.

4 Father, behold Thy dying Son!
  And hear the blood that speaks above;
On us let all Thy grace be shown,
  Peace, righteousness, and joy, and love;
Thy kingdom come to every heart,
And all Thou hast, and all Thou art.
                              Amen.
                    Wesley. 1745.

448   C.M.
Because ye are sons, God hath sent forth the Spirit of His Son into your hearts, crying, Abba, Father.
Galatians iv 6.

SOVEREIGN of all the worlds on high,
  Allow my humble claim;
Nor, while unworthy I draw near,
  Disdain a Father's name.

2 My Father God! how sweet the sound,
  How tender and how dear!
Not all the harmony of heaven
  Could so delight the ear.

3 Come, Holy Spirit, seal the grace
  On my expanding heart;
And show that in Jehovah's love
  I share a filial part.

4 Cheered by a witness so divine,
  Unwavering I believe;
And Abba, Father, humbly cry;
  Nor can the sign deceive.
              Philip Doddridge. 1755.

449   C.M.D.
My soul is even as a weaned child.—Psalm cxxxi. 2.

AS helpless as a child who clings
  Fast to his father's arm,
And casts his weakness on the strength
  That keeps him safe from harm;
So I, my Father, cling to Thee,
  And thus I every hour
Would link my earthly feebleness
  To Thine almighty power.

2 As trustful as a child who looks
  Up in his mother's face,
And all his little griefs and fears
  Forgets in her embrace;
So I to Thee, my Saviour, look,
  And in Thy face divine
Can read the love that will sustain
  As weak a faith as mine.

3 As loving as a child who sits
  Close by his parent's knee,
And knows no want while he can have
  That sweet society;
So sitting at Thy feet, my heart
  Would all its love outpour,
And pray that Thou wouldst teach me,
  Lord,
To love Thee more and more. Amen.
                James D. Burns. 1857.

LOVE AND HOLINESS.

450   8.8. 8.8. 8 8.
Filled with all the fulness of God.
Ephesians iii. 19.

JESUS, Thy boundless love to me
  No thought can reach, no tongue declare;
O knit my thankful heart to Thee,
  And reign without a rival there!
Thine wholly, Thine alone, I am;
Be Thou alone my constant flame!

THE CHRISTIAN LIFE.

2 O grant that nothing in my soul
    May dwell, but Thy pure love alone
 O may Thy love possess me whole,
    My joy, my treasure, and my crown!
 Strange flames far from my heart **remove**;
    My **every** act, word, thought, **be love**.

3 O Love, how cheering is Thy ray!
    All pain before Thy presence flies,
 Care, anguish, sorrow, melt away,
    Where'er Thy healing beams arise;
 O Jesus, nothing may I see,
    Nothing desire, or seek, but Thee!

4 Unwearied may I this pursue,
    Dauntless to the high prize aspire;
 Hourly within my soul renew
    This holy flame, this heavenly fire;
 And day and night be all my care,
    To guard the sacred treasure there.
                                Amen.
Paul Gerhardt. 1666.   *Tr. J. Wesley.* 1739.

---

451   8.8. 8.8. 8.8.
*God so loved the world,
that He gave His only begotten Son.*
John iii. 16.

MY Saviour, Thou Thy love to me
    In shame, in want, in pain, hast
      showed;
For me, on the accursèd tree,
    Thou pouredst forth Thy guiltless blood;
 Thy wounds upon my heart impress,
 Nor aught shall the loved stamp efface.

2 More hard than marble is my **heart**,
    And foul with sins of deepest **stain**;
 But Thou the mighty Saviour art,
    Nor flowed Thy cleansing blood **in vain**;
 Ah soften, melt this rock, and may
 Thy blood wash all these stains away!

3 O that I, as a little child,
    May follow Thee, and never rest
 Till sweetly Thou hast breathed Thy mild
    And lowly mind into my breast!
 Nor ever may we parted be,
 And I become **one spirit** with **Thee**.

4 Still let **Thy love** point out my way:
    How **wondrous things Thy love hath
      wrought**!
 Still lead me, lest **I** go astray;
 Direct my word, inspire my thought;
 And if I fall, soon may I hear
 Thy voice, and know that love **is near**.

5 In suffering be Thy love my peace;
    In weakness be Thy love my power;
 And when the storms of life shall cease,
    Jesus, in that important hour,
 In death as life be Thou my guide,
 And save me who for me hast died.
                                Amen.
Paul Gerhardt. 1666.   *Tr. J. Wesley.* 1739.

---

452   8.7. 8.7. D.
*Being rooted and grounded
in love.*—Ephesians iii. 17.

LOVE Divine, all loves excelling,
    Joy of heaven, to earth come down,
Fix in us Thy humble dwelling,
    All Thy faithful mercies crown
Jesus, Thou art all compassion,
    Pure, unbounded love Thou art;
Visit us with Thy salvation,
    Enter **every** trembling heart.

2 Come, almighty to deliver,
    Let us all Thy grace receive;
Suddenly return, **and** never,
    Never more Thy temples leave;
Thee we would be always blessing,
    Serve Thee as Thy hosts above,
Pray, and praise Thee, without ceasing,
    Glory in Thy perfect love.

3 Finish, then, Thy new creation,
    Pure and spotless let us be,
Let us see Thy great salvation,
    Perfectly restored in Thee;
Changed from glory into glory,
    Till in heaven we take our place,
Till we cast our crowns before Thee,
    Lost in **wonder**, love, **and** praise.
                                Amen.
                              Wesley. 1747.

---

453   10.10. 10.10. 4.
*To know the love of Christ,
which passeth knowledge.*—Ephesians iii. **19.**

IT passeth **knowledge**, that dear love **of
    Thine**,
My Saviour, Jesus! Yet **this** soul of mine
Would of Thy love, **in all its** breadth and
    length,
 Its height and **depth**, **and** everlasting
    strength.
    Know more and more.

2 It passeth telling, that dear love of Thine,
My Saviour, Jesus! Yet these lips of mine
Would fain proclaim to sinners far and near
A love which can remove all guilty fear,
    And love beget.

3 **It** passeth praises, that dear love of Thine,
My Saviour, Jesus! Yet this heart of mine
Would sing that love, so full, so rich, so
    free,
Which brings a rebel sinner, such as me,
    Nigh unto God.

4 O, fill me, Saviour, Jesus, with Thy love!
Lead, lead me to the living fount above;
Thither may I, in simple faith draw **nigh**,
And never to another fountain fly,
    But **unto** Thee.

5 And then, when Jesus face to face I see,
When at His lofty throne I bow the knee,
Then of His love, in all its breadth and
    length,
 Its height and depth, its everlasting
    strength,
    My soul shall sing.
                          Mary Shekelton. 1863.

LOVE AND HOLINESS.

454 L.M.
The love of God is shed abroad in our hearts by the Holy Ghost which is given unto us.—Romans v. 5.

COME, Saviour, Jesus, from above!
  Assist me with Thy heavenly grace;
Empty my heart of earthly love,
  And for Thyself prepare the place.

2 O let Thy sacred presence fill,
  And set my longing spirit free!
Which pants to have no other will,
  But day and night to feast on Thee.

3 That path with humble speed I'll seek,
  In which my Saviour's footsteps shine,
Nor will I hear, nor will I speak,
  Of any other love but Thine.

4 Henceforth may no profane delight
  Divide this consecrated soul;
Possess it Thou, who hast the right,
  As Lord and Master of the whole.

5 Thee I can love, and Thee alone,
  With pure delight and inward bliss;
To know Thou tak'st me for Thine own,
  O what a happiness is this!

6 Nothing on earth do I desire,
  But Thy pure love within my breast;
This, only this, will I require,
  And freely give up all the rest.
    From the French of
    Madame Bourignon. 1640.
        Tr. J. Wesley. 1736.

455 C.M.
All things are possible to him that believeth.—Mark ix. 23.

GOD of eternal truth and grace,
  Thy faithful promise seal,
Thy word, Thy oath, to Abraham's race,
  In us, even us, fulfil.

2 Let us, to perfect love restored,
  Thy image here retrieve,
And in the presence of our Lord,
  The life of angels live.

3 That mighty faith on me bestow,
  Which cannot ask in vain,
Which holds, and will not let Thee go,
  Till I my suit obtain.

4 Till Thou into my soul inspire
  The perfect love unknown,
And tell my infinite desire,
  Whate'er thou wilt, be done.

5 But is it possible that I
  Should live and sin no more?
Lord, if on Thee I dare rely,
  The faith shall bring the power.

6 On me that faith divine bestow,
  Which doth the mountain move;
And all my spotless life shall show
  The omnipotence of love. Amen.
        Charles Wesley. 1762.

456 C.M.
The greatest of these is charity.—1 Corinthians xiii. 13.

HAPPY the heart where graces reign,
  Where love inspires the breast;
Love is the brightest of the train,
  And strengthens all the rest.

2 Knowledge, alas! 'tis all in vain,
  And all in vain our fear;
Our stubborn sins will fight and reign,
  If love be absent there.

3 'Tis love that makes our cheerful feet
  In swift obedience move;
The devils know, and tremble too;
  But Satan cannot love.

4 This is the grace that lives and sings,
  When faith and hope shall cease;
'Tis this shall strike our joyful strings
  In the sweet realm of bliss.

5 When joined to that harmonious throng
  That fills the choirs above,
Then shall we raise our noblest song,
  And every note be love.

6 Before we quite forsake our clay,
  Or leave this dark abode,
The wings of love bear us away
  To see our gracious God.
        Isaac Watts. 1709.

457 C.M.
I know that my Redeemer liveth.—Job xix. 25.

I KNOW that my Redeemer lives,
  And ever prays for me;
A token of His love He gives,
  A pledge of liberty.

2 I find Him lifting up my head,
  He brings salvation near,
His presence makes me free indeed,
  And He will soon appear.

3 He wills that I should holy be,
  What can withstand His will?
The counsel of His grace in me
  He surely shall fulfil.

4 Jesus, I hang upon Thy Word;
  I steadfastly believe
Thou wilt return and claim me, Lord,
  And to Thyself receive.

5 Joyful in hope, my spirit soars
  To meet Thee from above,
Thy goodness thankfully adores;
  And sure I taste Thy love.

THE CHRISTIAN LIFE.

  6 When God is mine, and I am His,
    Of paradise possest,
  I taste unutterable bliss,
    And everlasting rest.
              Charles Wesley. 1742.

458   7.7.7.7.
Whom have I in heaven but Thee?—Psalm lxxiii. 25.

JESUS, all-atoning Lamb,
  Thine, and only Thine, I am;
Take my body, spirit, soul;
Only Thou possess the whole.

2 Thou my one thing needful be;
  Let me ever cleave to Thee;
  Let me choose the better part,
  Let me give Thee all my heart.

3 Fairer than the sons of men,
  Do not let me turn again,
  Leave the fountain-head of bliss,
  Stoop to creature-happiness.

4 Whom have I on earth below?
  Thee, and only Thee, I know;
  Whom have I in heaven but Thee?
  Thou art all in all to me.

5 All my treasure is above,
  All my riches is Thy love;
  Who the worth of love can tell?
  Infinite, unsearchable!

6 Thou, O Love, my portion art;
  Lord, Thou know'st my simple heart!
  Other comforts I despise,
  Love be all my paradise.

7 Nothing else can I require,
  Love fills up my whole desire;
  All Thy other gifts remove,
  Still Thou giv'st me all in love.
            Charles Wesley. 1749.

459   C.M.
Believe on the Lord Jesus Christ, and thou shalt be saved.
Acts xvi. 31.

JESUS hath died that I might live,
  Might live to God alone;
In Him eternal life receive,
And be in spirit one.

2 Saviour, I thank Thee for the grace,
  The gift unspeakable!
  And wait with arms of faith to embrace,
  And all Thy love to feel.

3 My soul breaks out in strong desire
  The perfect bliss to prove;
  My longing heart is all on fire
  To be dissolved in love.

4 Give me Thyself; from every boast,
  From every wish set free;
  Let all I am in Thee be lost;
  But give Thyself to me.

  5 Thy gifts, O Lord! can not suffice,
    Unless Thyself be given;
  Thy presence makes my paradise,
    And where Thou art is heaven.
              Charles Wesley. 1742.

460   C.M.
I shall be satisfied, when I awake, with Thy likeness.—Psalm xvii. 15.

JESUS, the all-restoring Word,
  My fallen spirit's hope,
After Thy lovely likeness, Lord,
Ah, when shall I wake up?

2 Thou, O my God, Thou only art
  The Life, the Truth, the Way;
  Quicken my soul, instruct my heart,
  My sinking footsteps stay.

3 Of all Thou hast in earth below,
  In heaven above, to give,
  Give me Thy only love to know,
  In Thee to walk and live.

4 Fill me with all the life of love,
  In mystic union join
  Me to Thyself, and let me prove
  The fellowship divine.

5 Open the intercourse between
  My longing soul and Thee,
  Never to be broke off again
  To all eternity. Amen.
                  Wesley. 1740.

461   C.M.
We love Him, because He first loved us.—1 John iv. 19.

MY God, I love Thee; not because
  I hope for heaven thereby,
Nor yet because who love Thee not
Are lost eternally.

2 Thou, O my Jesus, Thou didst me
  Upon the Cross embrace;
  For me didst bear the nails, and spear,
  And manifold disgrace,

3 And griefs and torments numberless,
  And sweat of agony;
  Yea, death itself; and all for me
  Who was Thine enemy.

4 Then why, O blessed Jesus Christ,
  Should I not love Thee well?
  Not for the sake of winning heaven,
  Nor of escaping hell;

5 Not from the hope of gaining aught,
  Not seeking a reward;
  But as Thyself hast loved me,
  O ever-loving Lord.

6 So would I love Thee, dearest Lord,
  And in Thy praise will sing;
  Solely because Thou art my God,
  And my eternal King. Amen.
         Francis Xavier. 16th Century.
        Tr. *Edward Caswall.* 1849.

LOVE AND HOLINESS.

462 C.M. *To behold the beauty of the Lord.*—Psalm xxvii. 4.

NOW let us see Thy beauty, Lord,
As we have seen before;
And by Thy beauty quicken us
To love Thee and adore.

2 'Tis easy when with simple mind
Thy loveliness we see,
To consecrate ourselves afresh
To duty and to Thee.

3 Our every feverish mood is cooled,
And gone is every load,
When we can lose the love of self,
And find the love of God.

4 'Tis by Thy loveliness we're won
To home and Thee again,
And as we are Thy children true
We are more truly men.

5 Lord, it is coming to ourselves
When thus we come to Thee;
The bondage of Thy loveliness
Is perfect liberty.

6 So now we come to ask again
What Thou hast often given,
The vision of that loveliness
Which is the life of heaven.
Benjamin Waugh. 1886.

463 S.M. *Where the Spirit of the Lord is, there is liberty.*—2 Cor. iii. 17.

O COME, and dwell in me,
Spirit of power within!
And bring the glorious liberty
From sorrow, fear, and sin.

2 The seed of sin's disease,
Spirit of health, remove,
Spirit of finished holiness,
Spirit of perfect love.

3 Hasten the joyful day,
Which shall my sins consume,
When old things shall be passed away,
And all things new become.

4 I want the witness, Lord,
That all I do is right,
According to Thy will and word,
Well-pleasing in Thy sight:

5 I ask no higher state;
Indulge me but in this,
And soon or later then translate
To my eternal bliss. Amen.
Charles Wesley. 1762.

464 C.M. *He shall baptize you with the Holy Ghost and with fire.*—Matt. iii. 11.

MY God! I know, I feel Thee mine,
And will not quit my claim,
Till all I have is lost in Thine,
And all renewed I am.

2 I hold Thee with a trembling hand,
But will not let Thee go,
Till steadfastly by faith I stand
And all Thy goodness know.

3 When shall I see the welcome hour,
That plants my God in me!
Spirit of health, and life, and power,
And perfect liberty!

4 Jesus, Thine all-victorious love
Shed in my heart abroad;
Then shall my feet no longer rove,
Rooted and fixed in God.

5 O that in me the sacred fire
Might now begin to glow,
Burn up the dross of base desire,
And make the mountains flow!

6 O that it now from heaven might fall,
And all my sins consume!
Come, Holy Ghost, for Thee I call,
Spirit of burning, come!

7 Refining fire, go through my heart,
Illuminate my soul;
Scatter Thy life through every part,
And sanctify the whole.

8 My steadfast soul, from falling free,
Shall then no longer move;
But Christ be all the world to me,
And all my heart be love.
Wesley. 1740.

465 C.M. *O the depth of the riches both of the wisdom and knowledge of God!* Romans xi. 33.

WHAT shall I do my God to love,
My loving God to praise?
The length, and breadth, and height to prove,
And depth of sovereign grace?

2 Thy sovereign grace to all extends,
Immense and unconfined;
From age to age it never ends;
It reaches all mankind.

3 Throughout the world its breadth is known,
Wide as infinity!
So wide, it never passed by one,
Or it had passed by me.

4 My trespass was grown up to heaven;
But far above the skies,
In Christ abundantly forgiven,
I see Thy mercies rise!

131

THE CHRISTIAN LIFE.

5 The depth of all-redeeming love,
  What angel-tongue can tell?
 O may I to the utmost prove
  The gift unspeakable!

6 Deeper than hell, it plucked me thence;
  Deeper than inbred sin,
 Jesus's love my heart shall cleanse,
  When Jesus enters in.

7 Assert Thy claim, maintain Thy right,
  Come quickly from above;
 And sink me to perfection's height,
  The depth of humble love. Amen.
        Wesley. 1749.

466   C.M.
Thou shalt call His name Jesus; for He shall save His people from their sins.—Matthew i. 21.

THERE is a name I love to hear,
  I love to speak its worth,
 It sounds like music in mine ear,
  The sweetest name on earth.

2 It tells me of a Saviour's love,
  Who died to set me free;
 It tells me of His precious blood,
  The sinner's perfect plea.

3 It tells of one whose loving heart
  Can feel my deepest woe,
 Who in my sorrow bears a part
  That none can bear below.

4 Jesus! the name I love so well,
  The name I love to hear;
 No saint on earth its worth can tell,
  No heart conceive how dear.

5 His name shall shed its fragrance still
  Along this thorny road;
 Shall sweetly smooth the rugged hill
  That leads me up to God.

6 And there, with all the blood-bought throng,
  From sin and sorrow free,
 I'll sing the new eternal song
  Of Jesus love for me.
        F. Whitfield. 1860.

467   8.8. 8.8. 8.8.
I will love Thee, O Lord, my strength.—Psalm xviii. 1.

THEE will I love, my strength, my tower,
  Thee will I love, my joy, my crown,
 Thee will I love with all my power,
  In all Thy works, and Thee alone;
 Thee will I love, till the pure fire
 Fills my whole soul with chaste desire.

2 Ah, why did I so late Thee know,
  Thee, lovelier than the sons of men!
 Ah, why did I no sooner go
  To Thee, the only ease in pain!
 Ashamed I sigh, and inly mourn,
 That I so late to Thee did turn.

3 In darkness willingly I strayed,
  I sought Thee, yet from Thee I roved;
 Far wide my wandering thoughts were spread,
  Thy creatures more than Thee I loved;
 And now, if more at length I see,
 'Tis through Thy light, and comes from Thee.

4 Give to mine eyes refreshing tears,
  Give to my heart chaste, hallowed fires,
 Give to my soul, with filial fears,
  The love that all heaven's host inspires;
 That all my powers, with all their might,
 In Thy sole glory may unite.

5 Thee will I love, my joy, my crown,
  Thee will I love, my Lord, my God;
 Thee will I love, beneath Thy frown,
  Or smile, Thy sceptre, or Thy rod;
 What though my flesh and heart decay,
 Thee shall I love in endless day!
   John Scheffler. 1657. Tr. *J. Wesley.* 1739.

468   8.7. 8.7. D.
God forbid that I should glory, save in the cross of our Lord Jesus Christ.
        Galatians vi. 14.

SWEET the moments, rich in blessing,
  Which before the cross I spend;
 Life, and health, and peace possessing,
  From the sinner's dying Friend:
 Here I'll sit, for ever viewing
  Mercy's streams, in streams of blood;
 Precious drops! my soul bedewing,
  Plead and claim my peace with God.

2 Truly blessed is this station,
  Low before the cross to lie;
 While I see divine compassion
  Floating in His languid eye;
 Here it is I find my heaven,
  While upon the Lamb I gaze;
 Love I much? I've much forgiven,
  I'm a miracle of grace!

3 Love and grief my heart dividing,
  With my tears His feet I'll bathe;
 Constant, still, in faith abiding,
  Life deriving from His death.
 May I still enjoy this feeling,
  In all need to Jesus go;
 Prove His wounds each day more healing,
  And Himself more deeply know. Amen.
   J. Allen. 1757. and *W. W. Shirley.* 1774.

469   8.8.6. 8.8.6.
For the love of Christ constraineth us.—2 Cor. v. 14.

O LOVE Divine, how sweet Thou art!
  When shall I find my willing heart
   All taken up by Thee?
 I thirst, I faint, I die to prove
 The greatness of redeeming love,
   The love of Christ to me!

LOVE AND HOLINESS.

2 Stronger His love than death or hell;
 Its riches are unsearchable:
 The first-born sons of light
 Desire in vain its depths to see,
 They cannot reach the mystery,
 The length, and breadth, and height.

3 God only knows the love of God:
 O that it now were shed abroad
 In this poor stony heart!
 For love I sigh, for love I pine;
 This only portion, Lord, be mine,
 Be mine this better part!

4 O that I could for ever sit
 With Mary at the Master's feet!
 Be this my happy choice:
 My only care, delight, and bliss,
 My joy, my heaven on earth be this,
 To hear the Bridegroom's voice.

5 O that with humbled Peter I
 Could weep, believe, and thrice reply,
 My faithfulness to prove,
 'Thou know'st, for all to Thee is known,
 Thou know'st, O Lord, and Thou alone,
 Thou know'st that Thee I love!'

6 O that I could, with favoured John,
 Recline my weary head upon
 The great Redeemer's breast!
 From care, and sin, and sorrow free,
 Give me, O Lord, to find in Thee,
 My everlasting rest. Amen.
  Charles Wesley. 1749.

470 *So panteth my soul* L.M.
 after Thee, O God.—Psalm xlii. 1.

O GOD, my God, my all Thou art!
  Ere shines the dawn of rising day,
 Thy sovereign light within my heart,
 Thy all-enlivening power display.

2 For Thee my thirsty soul doth pant,
 While in this desert land I live;
 And hungry as I am, and faint,
 Thy love alone can comfort give.

3 In a dry land, behold, I place
 My whole desire on Thee, O Lord;
 And more I joy to gain Thy grace,
 Than all earth's treasures can afford.

4 More dear than life itself, Thy love
 My heart and tongue shall still employ;
 And to declare Thy praise will prove
 My peace, my glory, and my joy.

5 In blessing Thee with grateful songs
 My happy life shall glide away;
 The praise that to Thy name belongs
 Hourly with lifted hands I'll pay.

6 Abundant sweetness, while I sing
 Thy love, my ravished heart o'erflows;
 Secure in Thee, my God and King,
 Of glory that no period knows.

7 My soul draws nigh and cleaves to Thee;
 Then let or earth or hell assail,
 Thy mighty hand shall set me free;
 For whom Thou sav'st, he ne'er shall fail.
  From the Spanish.
  Tr. J. Wesley. 1735.

471 *Perfecting holiness in* C.M.
 the fear of God.—2 Corinthians vii. 1.

O JESUS, at Thy feet we wait,
  Till Thou shalt bid us rise,
 Restored to our unsinning state,
 To love's sweet paradise.

2 Saviour from sin, we Thee receive,
 From all indwelling sin,
 Thy blood, we steadfastly believe,
 Shall make us throughly clean.

3 Since Thou wouldst have us free from sin,
 And pure as those above,
 Make haste to bring Thy nature in,
 And perfect us in love.

4 The counsel of Thy love fulfil;
 Come quickly, gracious Lord!
 Be it according to Thy will,
 According to Thy word.

5 According to our faith in Thee,
 Let it to us be done;
 O that we all Thy face might see,
 And know as we are known!

6 O that the perfect grace were given,
 The love diffused abroad!
 O that our hearts were all a heaven,
 For ever filled with God! Amen.
  Charles Wesley. 1749.

472 *If any man be in Christ,* 8.8.8.8.8.8.
 he is a new creature.—2 Cor. v. 17.

O JESUS, source of calm repose,
  Thy like nor man nor angel knows,
 Fairest among ten thousand fair!
 Even those whom death's sad fetters bound,
 Whom thickest darkness compassed round,
 Find light and life, if Thou appear.

2 Lord over all, sent to fulfil
 Thy gracious Father's sovereign will,
 To Thy dread sceptre will I bow:
 With duteous reverence at Thy feet,
 Like humble Mary, lo: I sit,
 Speak, Lord, Thy servant heareth now.

3 Renew Thine image, Lord, in me,
 Lowly and gentle may I be;
 No charms but these to Thee are dear:
 No anger may'st Thou ever find,
 No pride in my unruffled mind,
 But faith, and heaven-born peace, be there.

THE CHRISTIAN LIFE.

4 A patient, a victorious mind,
That life and all things casts behind,
Springs forth obedient to Thy call;
A heart that no desire can move,
But still to adore, believe and love,
Give me, my Lord, my Life, my All.
Amen.

J. A. Freylinghausen. 1704.
Tr. J. Wesley. 1739.

473 C.M.
*Search me, O God,
and know my heart.*—Psalm cxxxix. 23.

COME, Thou omniscient Son of Man,
Display Thy sifting power;
Come with Thy Spirit's winnowing fan,
And throughly purge Thy floor.

2 The chaff of sin, the accursèd thing,
Far from our souls be driven;
The wheat into Thy garner bring,
And lay us up for heaven.

3 Look through us with Thy eyes of flame,
The clouds and darkness chase;
And tell me what by sin I am,
And what I am by grace.

4 Whate'er offends Thy glorious eyes,
Far from our hearts remove;
As dust before the whirlwind flies,
Disperse it by Thy love.

5 Then let us all Thy fulness know,
From every sin set free;
Saved, to the utmost, saved below,
And perfectly like Thee. Amen.

Charles Wesley. 1749.

474 C.M.
I will not leave you comfortless: I will come to you.—John xiv. 18.

O JOYFUL sound of gospel grace!
Christ shall in me appear;
I, even I, shall see His face,
I shall be holy here.

2 This heart shall be His constant home;
I hear His Spirit's cry;
'Surely,' He saith, 'I quickly come';
He saith, who cannot lie.

3 The glorious crown of righteousness
To me reached out I view;
Conqueror through Him, I soon shall seize,
And wear it as my due.

4 The promised land, from Pisgah's top,
I now exult to see;
My hope is full, O glorious hope!
Of immortality.

5 With me I know, I feel, Thou art;
But this cannot suffice,
Unless Thou plantest in my heart
A constant paradise.

475 7.6. 7.6. 7.7. 7.6.
*He openeth the ears of men, and
sealeth their instruction.*—Job xxxiii. 16.

OPEN, Lord, my inward ear,
And bid my heart rejoice;
Bid my quiet spirit hear
Thy kind and gentle voice;
Never in the whirlwind found,
Or where earthquakes rock the place,
Still and silent is the sound,
The whisper of Thy grace.

2 From the world of sin, and noise,
And hurry, I withdraw;
For the small and inward voice
I wait with humble awe;
Silent am I now and still,
Dare not in Thy presence move;
To my waiting soul reveal
The secret of Thy love.

3 Thou didst undertake for me,
For me to death wast sold;
Wisdom in a mystery
Of bleeding love unfold;
Teach the lesson of Thy cross,
Let me die with Thee to reign;
All things let me count but loss,
So I may Thee regain.

4 Lord, my time is in Thy hand,
My soul to Thee convert;
Thou canst make me understand,
Though I am slow of heart;
Thine in whom I live and move,
Thine the work, the praise is Thine,
Thou art Wisdom, Power, and Love,
And all Thou art is mine.

Wesley. 1742.

476 C.M.
*They that be wise shall
shine as the brightness of the firmament.*
Daniel xii. 3.

JESUS, the word of mercy give,
And let it swiftly run;
And let Thy ministers believe,
And put salvation on.

2 Clothed with the Spirit of Holiness,
May all Thy people prove
The plenitude of gospel grace,
The joy of perfect love.

3 Jesus, let all Thy lovers shine
Illustrious as the sun;
And, bright with borrowed rays divine,
Their glorious circuit run;

6 Come, O my God, Thyself reveal,
Fill all this mighty void;
Thou only canst my spirit fill;
Come, O my God, my God!

7 Fulfil, fulfil my large desires,
Large as infinity;
Give, give me all my soul requires,
All, all that is in Thee! Amen.

Wesley. 1742.

LOVE AND HOLINESS.

4 Beyond the reach of mortals spread
  Their light where'er they go;
And heavenly influences shed
  On all the world below.

5 As giants may they run their race,
  Exulting in their might;
As burning luminaries, chase
  The gloom of sin's dark night:

6 As the bright Sun of Righteousness,
  Their healing wings display;
And let their lustre still increase
  Unto the perfect day. Amen.
                Charles Wesley. 1749.

477 L.M.
  *Come unto Me, all ye
  that labour.—Matthew xi. 28.*

O THAT my load of sin were gone!
  O that I could at last submit
At Jesu's feet to lay it down,
  To lay my soul at Jesu's feet!

2 Rest for my soul I long to find:
    Saviour of all, if mine Thou art,
  Give me Thy meek and lowly mind,
    And stamp Thine image on my heart.

3 Break off the yoke of inbred sin,
    And fully set my spirit free;
  I cannot rest till pure within,
    Till I am wholly lost in Thee.

4 Fain would I learn of Thee, my God;
    Thy light and easy burden prove,
  Thy cross, all stained with hallowed blood,
    The labour of Thy dying love.

5 I would, but Thou must give the power,
    My heart from every sin release;
  Bring near, bring near the joyful hour,
    And fill me with Thy perfect peace.

6 Come, Lord, the drooping sinner cheer,
    Nor let Thy chariot-wheels delay;
  Appear, in my poor heart appear!
    My God, my Saviour, come away!
                Amen.
                Charles Wesley. 1742.

478 C.M.
  *Teach me to do Thy will.
  Psalm cxliii. 10.*

O THOU who hast Thy servants taught
    That not by words alone,
  But by the fruits of holiness
    The life of God is shown;

2 While in Thy house of prayer we meet,
    And call Thee God and Lord;
  Give us a heart to follow Thee,
    Obedient to Thy word.

3 When we our voices lift in praise,
    Give Thou us grace to bring
  An offering of unfeigned thanks,
    And with the spirit sing.

4 And in the dangerous path of life
    Uphold us as we go;
  That with our lips and in our lives
    Thy glory we may show. Amen.
                H. Alford. 1857.

479 8.8. 8.8. 8 8.
  *Sent Him to bless you, in
  turning away every one of you from his
  iniquities.—Acts iii. 26.*

SAVIOUR from sin, I wait to prove
  That Jesus is Thy healing name;
To lose, when perfected in love,
  Whate'er I have, or can, or am:
I stay me on Thy faithful word,
The servant shall be as his Lord.

2 Answer that gracious end in me,
    For which Thy precious life was given;
  Redeem from all iniquity;
    Restore, and make me meet for heaven;
  Unless Thou purge my every stain,
  Thy suffering and my faith are vain.

3 Didst Thou not in the flesh appear,
    Sin to condemn, and man to save,
  That perfect love might cast out fear,
    That I Thy mind in me might have,
  In holiness show forth Thy praise,
  And serve Thee all my spotless days?

4 Didst Thou not die that I might live
    No longer to myself, but Thee,
  Might body, soul, and spirit give
    To Him who gave Himself for me?
  Come then, my Master, and my God,
  Take the dear purchase of Thy blood.

5 Thy own peculiar servant claim,
    For Thy own truth and mercy's sake;
  Hallow in me Thy glorious name;
    Me for Thine own this moment take,
  And change and throughly purify;
  Thine only may I live and die. Amen.
                Wesley. 1742.

480 L.M.
  *Blessed are they that mourn;
  for they shall be comforted.—Matthew v. 4.*

BLESSED are the humble souls that see
  Their emptiness and poverty;
Treasures of grace to them are given,
And crowns of joy laid up in heaven.

2 Blessed are the men of broken heart,
  Who mourn for sin with inward smart;
  The blood of Christ divinely flows,
  A healing balm for all their woes.

3 Blessed are the souls that pant for grace,
  Hunger and thirst for righteousness;
  They shall be well supplied and fed,
  With living streams, and living bread.

4 Blessed are the pure, whose hearts are clean
  From the defiling power of sin;
  With endless pleasure they shall see
  The God of spotless purity.

THE CHRISTIAN LIFE.

5 Blessed are the sufferers, who partake
Of pain and shame for Jesus' sake;
Their souls shall triumph in the Lord;
Glory and joy are their reward.

6 These are the men, **the pious race**,
Who seek the God of **Jacob's face**;
These shall enjoy the blissful **sight**,
And dwell in everlasting light.
Isaac Watts. 1719.

481   8.8.6. 8.8.6.
*Blessed are the poor in spirit:
for theirs is the kingdom of heaven.*
Matthew v. 3.

SAVIOUR, on me the want bestow,
Which all that feel shall surely know
Their sins on earth forgiven;
Give me to prove the kingdom mine,
And taste, in holiness divine,
The happiness of heaven.

2 Meeken my soul, Thou heavenly **Lamb**,
That I in the new earth may claim
My hundred-fold reward;
My rich inheritance possess,
Co-heir with the great Prince of Peace,
Co-partner with my Lord.

3 Me with that restless thirst inspire,
That sacred, infinite desire,
And feast my hungry heart;
Less than Thyself cannot suffice,
My soul for all Thy fulness cries,
For all Thou hast, and art.

4 **Mercy** who show shall mercy find;
Thy pitiful and tender mind
Be, Lord, on me bestowed;
So shall I still the blessing gain
And to eternal life retain
The mercy of my God.

5 Jesus, the crowning grace **impart**;
Bless me **with** purity of **heart**,
That, now beholding Thee,
I soon may view Thy open face,
On all Thy glorious beauties gaze,
And God for ever see!

6 Called to sustain the hallowed cross,
And suffer for Thy righteous cause,
Pronounce me doubly blest;
And let Thy glorious Spirit, Lord,
Assure me of my great reward,
In heaven's eternal feast. Amen.
Charles Wesley. 1762.

482   C.M.
*That we might be partakers
of His holiness.*—Hebrews xii. 10.

WHAT is our calling's glorious hope,
But inward holiness?
For this to Jesus I look up,
I calmly wait for this.

2 I wait till He shall touch me clean,
Shall life and power impart,
Give me the faith that casts out sin,
And purifies the heart.

3 This is the dear redeeming grace,
For every sinner free;
Surely it shall on me take place,
The chief of sinners, me.

4 **From all** iniquity, from all,
He shall my soul redeem;
In Jesus I believe, and shall
Believe myself to Him.

5 When **Jesus** makes my heart His **home**,
My sin shall all depart;
And, lo! He saith, I quickly come,
To fill and rule thy heart!

6 Be it according **to Thy word**!
Redeem me from **all sin**;
My heart would now receive Thee, Lord,
Come in, my Lord, come in! Amen.
Wesley. 1742.

483   7.7.7.7.
*Let this mind be in you,
which was also in Christ Jesus.*
Philippians ii. 5.

JESUS, shall I never be
Firmly grounded upon Thee?
Never by Thy work abide,
Never in Thy wounds reside?

2 Plant, and root, and fix in me
All the mind that was in Thee;
Settled peace I then shall find;
Jesu's is **a quiet** mind.

3 Anger I no more shall feel,
Always even, always still,
Meekly on my God reclined;
Jesu's is a *gentle* mind.

4 I shall suffer and fulfil
All my Father's gracious will,
Be in all alike resigned;
Jesu's is a *patient* mind.

5 When 'tis deeply rooted here,
Perfect love shall cast out fear;
Fear doth servile spirits bind;
Jesu's is a *noble* mind.

6 When **I feel it** fixed within,
I shall **have no** power to sin;
How shall sin an entrance find?
Jesu's is a *spotless* mind.

7 I shall nothing **know** beside
Jesus, and Him crucified;
Perfectly to Him be joined;
Jesu's is a *loving* mind.

8 I shall fully be restored
To the image of my Lord,
Witnessing to all mankind,
Jesu's is a *perfect* mind.
Wesley. 1742.

LIGHT, GUIDANCE AND GROWTH.

484 7.6. 7.6. 7.8. 7.6.
There shall be showers of blessing.—Ezekiel xxxiv. 26.

US, who climb Thy holy hill,
　A general blessing make,
Let the world our influence feel,
　Our gospel grace partake ;
Grace to help in time of need,
Pour out on sinners from above,
All Thy Spirit's fulness shed
　In showers of heavenly love.

2 Make our souls a fertile field
　　Which God delights to bless ;
　Let us in due season yield
　　The fruits of righteousness :
　Make us trees of paradise,
Which more and more Thy praise may show,
　Deeper sink, and higher rise,
　　And to perfection grow. Amen.
　　　　　　　　　　Charles Wesley. 1762.

3 Thy sanctifying Spirit pour,
　To quench my thirst and make mo clean ;
　Now, Father, let the gracious shower
　Descend, and make me pure from sin.

4 Purge me from every sinful blot ;
　My idols all be cast aside ;
　Cleanse me from every sinful thought,
　From all the filth of self and pride.

5 Give me a new, a perfect heart,
　From doubt, and fear, and sorrow free ;
　The mind which was in Christ impart,
　And let my spirit cleave to Thee.

6 O that I now, from sin released,
　Thy word may to the utmost prove,
　Enter into the promised rest,
　The Canaan of Thy perfect love ! Amen.
　　　　　　　　　　Charles Wesley. 1742.

---

485 C.M.
Your life is hid with Christ in God.—Col. iii. 3.

JESUS, my life ! Thyself apply,
　Thy holy Spirit breathe ;
My vile affections crucify,
　Conform me to Thy death.

2 Conqueror of hell, and earth, and sin,
　Still with Thy rebel strive ;
　Enter my soul, and work within,
　And kill, and make alive.

3 More of Thy life, and more, I have,
　　As the old Adam dies :
　Bury me, Saviour, in Thy grave,
　　That I with Thee may rise.

4 Reign in me, Lord, Thy foes control,
　Who would not own Thy sway ;
　Diffuse Thine image through my soul,
　Shine to the perfect day.

5 Scatter the last remains of sin,
　And seal me Thine abode ;
　O make me glorious all within,
　A temple built by God ! Amen.
　　　　　　　　　　Wesley. 1740.

486 L.M.
I will put My Spirit within you.—Ezek. xxxvi. 27.

GOD of all power, and truth, and grace,
　Which shall from age to age endure,
Whose word, when heaven and earth shall pass,
　Remains and stands for ever sure :

2 That I Thy mercy may proclaim,
　That all mankind Thy truth may see,
　Hallow Thy great and glorious name,
　And perfect holiness in me.

LIGHT, GUIDANCE AND GROWTH.

487 10.4. 10.4. 10.10.
He led them forth by the right way.—Psalm cvii. 7.

LEAD, kindly Light, amid the encircling gloom,
　　Lead Thou me on :
The night is dark, and I am far from home,
　　Lead Thou me on :
Keep Thou my feet ; I do not ask to see
The distant scene ; one step enough for me.

2 I was not ever thus, nor prayed that Thou
　　Shouldst lead me on :
I loved to choose and see my path ; but now
　　Lead Thou me on :
I loved the garish day, and spite of fears,
Pride ruled my will : remember not past years.

3 So long Thy power hath blest me, sure it still
　　Will lead me on,
O'er moor and fen, o'er crag and torrent, till
　　The night is gone,
And with the morn those angel faces smile,
Which I have loved long since, and lost awhile.
　　　　　　　　　　J. H. Newman. 1833.

488 C.M.
Walk in the light, as He is in the Light.—1 John i. 7.

WALK in the light ! so shalt thou know
　That fellowship of love
His Spirit only can bestow,
　Who reigns in light above.

THE CHRISTIAN LIFE.

2 Walk in the light! and thou shalt find
    Thy heart made truly His,
Who dwells in cloudless light enshrined,
    In whom no darkness is.

3 Walk in the light! and thou shalt own
    Thy darkness passed away,
Because that Light hath on thee shone,
    In which is perfect day.

4 Walk in the light! and e'en the tomb
    No fearful shade shall wear;
Glory shall chase away its gloom,
    For Christ hath conquered there.

5 Walk in the light! and thine shall be
    A path, though thorny, bright;
For God, by grace, shall dwell in thee,
    And God Himself is Light.
            Bernard Barton. 1826.

489   8.7. 8.7. D.
The people that walked in darkness have seen a great light.—Is. ix. 2.

LIGHT of those whose dreary dwelling
    Borders on the shades of death,
Come, and by Thy love revealing,
    Dissipate the clouds beneath
The new heaven and earth's Creator,
    In our deepest darkness rise,
Scattering all the night of nature,
    Pouring eyesight on our eyes.

2 Still we wait for Thine appearing;
    Life and joy Thy beams impart,
Chasing all our fears, and cheering
    Every poor benighted heart
Come and manifest the favour
    God hath for our ransomed race;
Come, Thou universal Saviour,
    Come, and bring the gospel grace.

3 Save us in Thy great compassion,
    O Thou mild, pacific Prince!
Give the knowledge of salvation,
    Give the pardon of our sins:
By Thy all-restoring merit
    Every burdened soul release;
Every weary, wandering spirit
    Guide into Thy perfect peace. Amen.
            Charles Wesley. 1716.

490   8.7. 8.7. 4.7.
In the daytime also He led them with a cloud, and all the night with a light of fire.—Psalm lxxviii. 14.

GUIDE me, O Thou great Jehovah,
    Pilgrim through this barren land;
I am weak, but Thou art mighty,
    Hold me with Thy powerful hand:
Bread of heaven,
Feed me till I want no more.

2 Open Thou the crystal fountain,
    Whence the healing streams do flow;
Let the fiery cloudy pillar
    Lead me all my journey through:
Strong deliverer,
Be Thou still my help and shield.

3 When I tread the verge of Jordan,
    Bid my anxious fears subside;
Death of death, and hell's destruction,
    Land me safe on Canaan's side:
Songs of praises
I will ever give to Thee. Amen.
    From the Welsh of W. Williams.
    Tr. W. and P. Williams. 1771.

491   L.M. *With Chorus.*
He leadeth me beside the still waters.—Psalm xxiii. 2.

HE leadeth me! O blessèd thought,
    O words with heavenly comfort fraught!
Whate'er I do, where'er I be,
Still 'tis God's hand that leadeth me.

    He leadeth me! He leadeth me!
    By His own hand He leadeth me!
    His faithful follower I would be,
    For by His hand He leadeth me.

2 Sometimes 'mid scenes of deepest gloom,
Sometimes where Eden's bowers bloom,
By waters calm, o'er troubled sea,
Still 'tis God's hand that leadeth me.

3 Lord, I would clasp Thy hand in mine,
Nor ever murmur or repine;
Content, whatever lot I see,
Since 'tis my God that leadeth me.

4 And when my task on earth is done,
When, by Thy grace, the victory's won,
E'en death's cold wave I will not flee,
Since God through Jordan leadeth me.
            J. H. Gilmore. 1862.

492   7.7. 7.7. 7.7.
Narrow is the way which leadeth unto life.—Matthew vii. 14.

LORD, Thy children guide and keep,
    As with feeble steps they press
On the pathway rough and steep,
    Through this weary wilderness.
Holy Jesus, day by day,
Lead us in the narrow way.

2 There are stony ways to tread;
    Give the strength we sorely lack:
There are tangled paths to thread;
    Light us, lest we miss the track.
Holy Jesus, day by day,
Lead us in the narrow way.

3 There are sandy wastes that lie
    Cold and sunless, vast and drear,
Where the feeble faint and die;
    Grant us grace to persevere.
Holy Jesus, day by day,
Lead us in the narrow way.

4 There are soft and flowery glades,
    Decked with golden-fruited trees,
Sunny slopes and scented shades;
    Keep us, Lord, from slothful ease.
Holy Jesus, day by day,
Lead us in the narrow way.

LIGHT, GUIDANCE AND GROWTH.

5 Upward still to purer heights,
    Onward yet to scenes more blest,
Calmer regions, clearer lights,
    Till we reach the promised rest.
Holy Jesus, day by day,
Lead us in the narrow way. Amen.
            Bishop W. W How. 1854.

493   8,8, 8,8, 8.8.
*A Leader and Commander
to the people.*—Isaiah lv. 4.

CAPTAIN of Israel's host, and Guide
    Of all that seek the land above,
Beneath Thy shadow we abide,
    The cloud of Thy protecting love:
Our strength, Thy grace; our rule, Thy word;
Our end, the glory of the Lord.

2 By Thine unerring Spirit led,
    We shall not in the desert stray;
We shall not full direction need,
    Nor miss our providential way·
As far from danger as from fear,
While love, almighty love is near.

            Charles Wesley. 1749.

494   9.8. 9.8. 8.8.
*Casting all your care upon
Him; for He careth for you.*—1 Peter v. 7.

IF thou but suffer God to guide thee,
    And hope in Him through all thy ways,
He'll give thee strength, whate'er betide thee,
    And bear thee through the evil days;
Who trust in God's unchanging love,
Build on the Rock that nought can move.

2 Only be still, and wait His leisure
    In cheerful hope, with heart content
To take whate'er thy Father's pleasure
    And all-discerning love hath sent;
Nor doubt our inmost wants are known
To Him who chose us for His own.

3 Nor think, amid the heat of trial,
    That God hath cast thee off unheard,
That he whose hopes meet no denial
    Must surely be of God preferred;
Time passes and much change doth bring,
And sets a bound to everything.

4 All are alike before the Highest;
    'Tis easy to our God, we know,
To raise thee up, though low thou liest,
    To make the rich man poor and low;
True wonders still by Him are wrought,
Who setteth up and brings to nought.

5 Sing, pray, and keep His ways unswerving,
    So do thine own part faithfully,
And trust His word, though undeserving,
    Thou yet shalt find it true for thee:
God never yet forsook at need
The soul that trusted Him indeed.
            George Neumarck. 1653.
            Tr. Catherine Winkworth. 1855.

495   8.8.6. 8.8.6.
*Except the Lord build the
house, they labour in vain that build it.*
Psalm cxxvii. 1.

EXCEPT the Lord conduct the plan,
    The best concerted schemes are vain,
    And never can succeed;
We spend our wretched strength for nought;
But if our works in Thee be wrought,
    They shall be blest indeed.

2 Lord, if Thou didst Thyself inspire
Our souls with this intense desire
    Thy goodness to proclaim;
Thy glory if we now intend,
O let our deed begin and end
    Complete in Jesu's name!

3 In Jesu's name behold we meet,
Far from an evil world retreat,
    And all its sinful ways;
One only thing resolved to know,
And mould our useful lives below
    By reason and by grace.

4 Now, Jesus, now Thy love impart,
To govern each devoted heart,
    And fit us for Thy will;
Deep founded in the truth of grace,
Build up Thy rising Church, and place
    The city on the hill.

5 O let our faith and love abound;
O let our lives to all around
    With purest lustre shine;
That all around our works may see,
And give the glory, Lord, to Thee,
    The heavenly Light Divine. Amen.
            Charles Wesley. 1767.

496   C.M.
He knoweth the way that I take.
Job xxiii. 10.

FATHER of love, our Guide and Friend,
    O lead us gently on,
Until life's trial-time shall end,
    And heavenly peace be won.

2 We know not what the path may be,
    As yet by us untrod;
But we can trust our all to Thee,
    Our Father and our God.

3 If called, like Abraham's child, to climb
    The hill of sacrifice,
Some angel may be there in time;
    Deliverance shall arise:

4 Or, if some darker lot be good,
    O teach us to endure
The sorrow, pain, or solitude,
    That makes the spirit pure.

5 Christ by no flowery pathway came,
    And we, His followers here,
Must do Thy will and praise Thy name,
    In hope, and love, and fear.

THE CHRISTIAN LIFE.

6 And till in heaven we sinless bow,
  And faultless anthems raise,
O Father, Son, and Spirit, now
  Accept our feeble praise. Amen.
                              W. J. Irons. 1849.

497 *He led them on safely, so*   10.4.10.4.
that they feared not.—Ps. lxxviii. 53.

I DO not ask, O Lord, that life may be
    A pleasant road :
I do not ask that Thou wouldst take from
    me
        Aught of its load.

2 I do not ask that flowers should always
      spring
        Beneath my feet;
  I know too well the poison and the sting
        Of things too sweet.

3 For one thing only, Lord, dear Lord, I plead:
        Lead me aright,
  Though strength should falter, and though
        heart should bleed,
        Through Peace to Light.

4 I do not ask, O Lord, that Thou shouldst
      shed
        Full radiance here ;
  Give but a ray of peace, that I may tread
        Without a fear.

5 I do not ask my cross to understand,
        My way to see;
  Better in darkness just to feel Thy hand
        And follow Thee.

6 Joy is like restless day : but peace divine
        Like quiet night ;
  Lead me, O Lord, till perfect day shall shine
        Through Peace to Light.
                                    Amen.
              Adelaide A. Procter. d. 1864.

498 *I am the way, the truth,*   S.M.
and the life.—John xiv. 6.

JESUS, my Truth, my Way,
    My sure, unerring Light,
On Thee my feeble steps I stay,
    Which Thou wilt guide aright.

2 My Wisdom and my Guide,
    My Counsellor Thou art ;
  O never let me **leave** Thy side,
    Or from Thy paths depart !

3 I lift my eyes to Thee,
    Thou gracious, bleeding Lamb,
  That I may **now** enlightened be,
    And **never** put to shame.

4 Never will I remove
    Out of Thy hands my cause ;
  But rest in Thy redeeming love,
    And hang upon Thy cross.

5 Teach me the happy art
    In all things to depend
On Thee ; O never, Lord, depart,
    But love me to the end !

6 O make me all like Thee,
    Before I hence remove ;
Settle, confirm, and stablish me,
    And build **me** up in love.

7 **Let** me Thy witness live,
    When sin is all destroyed ;
And then my spotless soul receive,
    And take me home to God. Amen.
                        Charles Wesley. 1749.

499 *For Thy name's sake,*   5.5. 8.8. 5.5.
lead me and guide me.—Psalm xxxi. 3.

JESUS, still lead **on,**
    Till our rest be won :
And, although the way be cheerless,
We will follow, calm and fearless ;
    Guide us by Thy hand
    To **our** Fatherland.

2 If the way be dreary,
    If the foe be near,
  Let not faithless fears o'ertake us,
  Let not love and hope forsake us,
    For, through many a foe,
    To our home we go.

3 **When we seek relief**
    From a long-felt grief,
  When oppressed by new temptations,
  Lord, increase and perfect patience;
    Show us that bright shore
    Where we weep no more.

4 When sweet earth and skies
    Fade before our eyes ;
  When through death we look to heaven,
  And our sins are all forgiven,
    From Thy bright abode,
    Call us home to God.

5 Jesus, still lead **on,**
    Till our rest be won ;
  Heavenly Leader, still direct us,
  Still support, console, protect us,
    Till we safely stand
    In our **Fatherland. Amen.**
                Count Zinzendorf. abt. 1750.
                   Tr. H. L. L. b. 1813.

500 *I am the Lord thy God . . .*   8.7. 8.7. 4.4.7.
which leadeth thee.—Isaiah xlviii. 17.

LEAD us, heavenly Father, lead us
    O'er the world's tempestuous sea ;
Guard us, guide us, keep us, feed us,
    For we have no help but Thee ;
        Yet possessing
        Every blessing,
    If our God our Father be.

LIGHT, GUIDANCE AND GROWTH.

2 Saviour, breathe forgiveness o'er us;
   All our weakness Thou dost know;
  Thou didst tread this earth before us,
  Thou didst feel its keenest woe;
    Lone and dreary,
    Faint and weary,
  Through the desert Thou didst go.

3 Spirit of our God, descending,
   Fill our hearts with heavenly joy;
  Love with every passion blending,
  Pleasure that can never cloy;
    Thus provided,
    Pardoned, guided,
  Nothing can our peace destroy. Amen.
        James Edmeston. 1820.

2 'Mid life's sweetest pleasures, Lord, keep
   me Thine own;
  Lest I should forget Thee, or duty disown:
  When sorrow o'erwhelms me, and gone is
   the light,
  Then shine on me, Father, make Thou my
   way bright.

3 When thought is a burden, when work is
   a care,
  O then let me cherish the sweetness of
   prayer;
  When shadows are falling, when earth's
   day is past,
  O lead me, my Father, to sunshine at last.
           Amen.
        J. Page Hopps. 1873.

501   10.10. 10.10.
  Give ear, O Shepherd of Israel,
  Thou that leadest Joseph like a flock.
       Psalm lxxx. 1.

L EAD us, O Father! in the paths of peace;
   Without Thy guiding hand we go
    astray,
  And doubts appal, and sorrows still
    increase;
  Lead us through Christ, the true and
    living way.

2 Lead us, O Father! in the paths of truth;
  Unhelped by Thee, in error's maze we
    grope,
  While passion stains, and folly dims our
    youth,
  And age comes on uncheered by faith
    and hope.

3 Lead us, O Father! in the paths of right;
  Blindly we stumble when we walk alone;
  Involved in shadows of a darksome night,
  Only with Thee we journey safely on.

4 Lead us, O Father! to Thy heavenly rest,
  However rough and steep the path may
    be,
  Through joy or sorrow, as Thou deemest
    best,
  Until our lives are perfected in Thee.
           Amen.
       W. H. Burleigh. 1858.

502   11.11. 11.11. *Anapæstic.*
  He leadeth me in the
paths of righteousness for His name's sake.
      Psalm xxiii. 3.

O LEAD me, my Father; lead Thou, lest
   I stray;
O lead Thou me onward where Thou wilt
   each day!
All passion be silent, all self-will be still;
And meekly my spirit ask only Thy will.

503   8.8.8. 4.
  Thy right hand upholdeth me.
      Psalm lxiii. 8.

L EANING on Thee, my Guide, my Friend,
  My gracious Saviour, I am blest;
Though weary, Thou dost condescend
  To be my Rest.

2 Leaning on Thee, this darkened room
  Is cheered by a celestial ray;
Thy pitying smile dispels the gloom,
  Turns night to day.

3 Leaning on Thee, with childlike faith
  To Thee the future I confide;
Each step of life's untrodden path
  Thy love will guide.

4 Leaning on Thee, I breathe no moan,
  Though faint with languor, parched with
    heat,
Thy will as now becomes mine own,
  Thy will is sweet.

5 Leaning on Thee, 'midst torturing pain
  With patience Thou my soul dost fill;
Thou whisperest, ' What did I sustain?'
  Then I am still.

6 Leaning on Thee, I do not dread
  The havoc slow disease may make;
Thou, who for me Thy blood hast shed,
  Wilt ne'er forsake.

7 Leaning on Thee, though faint and weak,
  Too weak another voice to hear,
Thy heavenly accents comfort speak,
  'Be of good cheer!'

8 Leaning on Thee, no fear alarms;
  Calmly I stand on death's dark brink;
I feel the everlasting arms,
  I cannot sink.
        Charlotte Elliott. 1836.

THE CHRISTIAN LIFE.

504 L.M.
Speak, Lord; for Thy servant heareth.—1 Samuel iii. 9.

LORD, speak to me, that I may speak
In living echoes of Thy tone;
As Thou hast sought, so let me seek
Thy erring children, lost and lone.

2 O lead me, Lord, that I may lead
The wandering and the wavering feet;
O feed me, Lord, that I may feed
Thy hungering ones with manna sweet.

3 O strengthen me, that while I stand
Firm on the rock and strong in Thee,
I may stretch out a loving hand
To wrestlers with the troubled sea.

4 O teach me, Lord, that I may teach
The precious things Thou dost impart;
And wing my words, that they may reach
The hidden depths of many a heart.

5 O give Thine own sweet rest to me,
That I may speak with soothing power
A word in season, as from Thee,
To weary ones, in needful hour.

6 O fill me with Thy fulness, Lord,
Until my very heart o'erflow
In kindling thought and glowing word,
Thy love to tell, Thy praise to show.

7 O use me, Lord, use even me,
Just as Thou wilt, and when, and where,
Until Thy blessed face I see,
Thy rest, Thy joy, Thy glory share.
Amen.
Frances R. Havergal. 1872.

505 L.M.
Behold, God is my salvation. Isaiah xii. 2.

INTO Thy gracious hands I fall,
And with the arms of faith embrace;
O King of Glory, hear my call,
O raise me, heal me, by Thy grace!

2 Now righteous through Thy wounds I am,
No condemnation now I dread;
I taste salvation in Thy name,
Alive in Thee, my living Head.

3 Still let Thy wisdom be my guide,
Nor take Thy light from me away;
Still with me let Thy grace abide,
That I from Thee may never stray.

4 Let Thy word richly in me dwell;
Thy peace and love my portion be;
My joy to endure and do Thy will,
Till perfect I am found in Thee.

5 Arm me with Thy whole armour, Lord,
Support my weakness with Thy might;
Gird on my thigh Thy conquering sword,
And shield me in the threatening fight.

6 From faith to faith, from grace to grace,
So in Thy strength shall I go on,
Till heaven and earth flee from Thy face,
And glory end what grace begun. Amen.
W. C. Dessler. 1692.
Tr. J. Wesley. 1739.

506 8.8.8.4.
They that know Thy name will put their trust in Thee.—Ps. ix. 10.

WE cannot always trace the way
Where Thou, our gracious Lord, dost move,
But we can always surely say
That Thou art love.

2 When fear its gloomy cloud will fling
O'er earth—our souls to heaven above,
As to their sanctuary, spring;
For Thou art love.

3 When mystery shrouds our darkened path,
We'll check our dread, our doubts reprove;
In this our soul sweet comfort hath,
That Thou art love.

4 Yes, Thou art love; and truth like this
Can every gloomy thought remove,
And turn all tears, all woes to bliss;
Our God is love.
Sir John Bowring. 1821.

507 L.M.
If ye then be risen with Christ, seek those things which are above. Colossians iii. 1.

YE faithful souls, who Jesus know,
If risen indeed with Him ye are,
Superior to the joys below,
His resurrection's power declare.

2 Your faith by holy tempers prove,
By actions show your sins forgiven,
And seek the glorious things above,
And follow Christ, your Head, to heaven.

3 There your exalted Saviour see,
Seated at God's right hand again,
In all His Father's majesty,
In everlasting pomp to reign.

4 To Him continually aspire,
Contending for your native place,
And emulate the angel-choir,
And only live to love and praise.

5 For who by faith your Lord receive,
Ye nothing seek or want beside,
Dead to the world and sin ye live,
Your creature-love is crucified.

6 Your real life, with Christ concealed,
Deep in the Father's bosom lies;
And, glorious as your Head revealed,
Ye soon shall meet Him in the skies.
Charles Wesley. 1762.

THANKFULNESS.

508   6.4. 6.4. 6.6.6.4.
*He shall choose our inheritance
for us.—Psalm xlvii. 4.*

THOU, Lord, my path shalt choose,
  And my Guide be.
What shall I fear to lose
  While I have Thee?
This be my portion blest,
On my Redeemer's breast,
In peaceful trust to rest ;
  He cares for me.

2 This lightens **every cross,**
  Cheers every **ill;**
Suffer I grief or loss,
  It is Thy will,
One who makes no mistake
Chooseth **the** way I take ;
He, who **can** ne'er forsake,
Holds **my** hand still.

3 Sweet words **of** peace **and love**
  Christ whispers me ;
Bearing my soul above
  Life's troubled sea.
This be my portion blest,
On my Redeemer's breast,
In peaceful **trust** to rest ;
  He cares **for** me.

4 Christ died my love to win,
  Christ is my tower ;
He will be with me in
  Each trying hour.
He makes the wounded whole,
He will my heart console,
He will uphold my soul
  By His own power.

5 To Thee, the only wise,
  Whatever be,
I will lift up mine eyes,
  Joyful in Thee.
This be my portion blest,
On my Redeemer's breast,
In peaceful trust to rest ;
  He cares for me.
    From the German. Anon.

509   4.6. 10.10.10. 6.6.
*Lead me in a plain path.
Psalm xxvii. 11.*

HE leads us on
  By paths we did not know ;
Upward He leads us though our steps be
    slow,
Though oft we faint and falter on the way,
Though storms and darkness oft obscure
    the day,
  Yet when the clouds are gone,
  We know He leads us on.

2 He leads us on
Through all the unquiet years ;
Past all our dream-land hopes, and doubts,
    and fears,

He guides our steps through all the tangled
    maze
Of losses, sorrows, and o'erclouded days ;
  We know His will is done,
  And still He leads us on.

3 And He, at last,
  After the weary strife,
After the restless fever we call life,
After the dreariness, the aching pain,
The wayward struggles which have proved
    in vain,
  After our toils are past,
  Will give us rest at last.
    Count Zinzendorf. abt. 1750.
    Tr. H. L. L. b. 1813.

THANKFULNESS.

510   L. M.
*All things work together
for good to them that love God.
Romans viii. 28.*

GOD of my life, whose gracious power
  Through varied deaths my soul hath
    led,
Or turned aside the fatal hour,
  Or lifted up my sinking head ;

2 In all my ways Thy hand I own,
  Thy ruling Providence I see ;
Assist me still my course to run,
  And still direct my paths to Thee.

3 Oft hath the sea confessed Thy power,
  And given me back at Thy command ;
It could not, Lord, my life devour,
  Safe in the hollow of Thine hand.

4 Oft from the margin of the grave
  Thou, Lord, hast lifted up my head ;
Sudden, I found Thee near to save,
  The sickness owned Thy touch, and fled.

5 Whither, O whither should I fly,
  But to my loving Saviour's breast ?
Secure within Thine arms to lie,
  And safe beneath Thy wings to rest.

6 Enlarge my heart to make Thee room,
  Enter, and in me ever stay ;
The crooked then shall straight become ;
  The darkness shall be lost in day.
                  Amen.
    Wesley. 1740.

511   10.10. 10.10.
*All things are yours.
1 Cor. iii. 21.*

WE bless Thee, Lord, for all this common
    life
Can give of rest and joy amidst its strife ;
For earth and trees and sea and clouds
    and springs ;
For work, and all the lessons that it brings ;

THE CHRISTIAN LIFE.

2 For Pisgah gleams of newer, **fairer truth**,
Which ever ripening still **renews** our
youth;
For fellowship with noble **souls** and wise,
Whose hearts **beat time to music of the
skies**;

3 For each achievement **human toil can
reach**;
For all that patriots win, and poets teach;
For the old light that gleams on history's
page,
For the new hope that shines on each new
age.

4 May we to these our lights be ever true,
Find hope and strength and joy for ever
new,
To heavenly visions still obedient prove,
The Eternal Law, writ by the Almighty
Love! Amen.

J. M. White. 1883.

512   7.7. 7.7. 7.7.
*How much owest thou
unto my Lord?*—Luke xvi. 5.

WHEN this passing world is done,
When has sunk yon glaring sun,
When we stand with Christ on high,
Looking o'er life's history,
Then, Lord, shall I fully know,
Not till then, how much I owe.

2 When I stand before **the throne**,
Dressed in beauty **not my own**,
When I see **Thee as Thou art**,
Love Thee with unsinning heart,
Then, Lord, shall I fully know,
Not till then, how much **I owe**.

3 Chosen **not for good in me**,
Wakened up from wrath **to flee**,
Hidden in the Saviour's side,
By the Spirit sanctified,
Teach me, Lord, on earth to show,
By my love, how much I owe.

4 When the praise of heaven **I hear**
Loud as thunders to the ear,
Loud as many waters' noise,
Sweet as harp's melodious voice,
Then, Lord, shalt I fully know,
Not till then, how much I owe.

R. M. McCheyne. 1837.

513   C.M.
*Godliness with contentment
is great gain.*—1 Timothy vi. 6.

SOME murmur when their sky **is clear**
And wholly bright to view,
If one small speck of dark appear
In their great heaven of blue.

2 And some with thankful love are filled,
If but one streak of light,
One ray of God's good mercy gild
The darkness of their night.

3 In palaces are hearts that ask,
In discontent and pride,
Why life is such a dreary task,
And all good things denied.

4 And hearts in poorest huts admire
How Love has in their aid,
The Love that never seems to tire,
Such rich provision made.

Archbishop R. C. Trench. 1839.

514   7.6. 7.6. 7.7. 7.6.
*Let everything that hath
breath praise the Lord.*—Psalm cl. 6.

MEET and right it is to sing,
In every time and place,
Glory to our heavenly King,
The God of Truth and Grace:
Join we then with sweet accord,
All in one thanksgiving join,
Holy, holy, holy Lord,
Eternal praise be Thine!

2 Thee, the first-born sons of light,
In choral symphonies,
Praise by day, day without night,
And never, never cease:
Angels and archangels, all
Praise the mystic Three in One,
Sing, and stop, and gaze, and fall
O'erwhelmed before Thy throne.

3 Vying with that happy choir,
Who chant Thy praise above,
We on eagles' wings aspire,
The wings of faith and love:
There they sing, with glory crowned,
We extol the slaughtered Lamb;
Lower though our voices sound,
Our subject is the same.

4 Father, God, Thy love we praise,
Which gave Thy Son to die;
Jesus, full of truth and grace,
Alike we glorify;
Spirit, Comforter divine,
Praise by all to Thee be given,
Till we in full chorus join,
And earth is turned to heaven.
                       Amen.

Charles Wesley. 1749.

515   C.M.
*If any man be in Christ,
he is a new creature.*—2 Cor. v. 17.

WE praise and bless Thee, gracious
Lord,
Our Saviour, kind and true,
For all the old things passed away,
For all Thou hast made new.

2 New hopes, new purposes, desires,
And joys, Thy grace has given;
Old ties are broken from the earth,
New ties attach to heaven.

AFFLICTION AND RESIGNATION.

3 But yet, how much must be destroyed,
  How much renewed must be,
Ere we can fully stand complete
  In likeness, Lord, to Thee!

4 Thou, only Thou, must carry on
  The work Thou hast begun;
Of Thine own strength Thou must impart,
  In Thine own ways **to run.**

5 Ah! leave us not; from **day to day**
  Revive, restore again;
Our feeble steps do Thou **direct,**
  Our enemies restrain.

6 So shall we faultless stand at last,
  Before Thy Father's throne;
The blessedness for ever ours,
  The glory all Thine own. Amen.
          C. J. P. Spitta. *d.* 1859.
          Tr. *H. L. L.* *b.* 1843.

516 *Every day will I bless Thee.* C. M. D.
       Psalm cxlv. 2.

FOR thousand, thousand mercies **new,**
  At dawn or vesper hour;
The early and the latter dew,
  The sunshine and the flower;
For founts of ever-springing bliss,
  For hope's unclouded ray;
For life's thrice blessed sympathies,
  We bless Thee day by day.

2 For fond affection's richest love,
  For household tones of mirth,
For melodies that hourly pour
  From hearts of kindred birth;
For many a fire-side thrill of love,
  For many a joyous lay;
For peace that emblems peace above,
  We bless Thee day by day.

3 For untold sympathy that dwells
  Enshrined in love's fond breast;
For springs that sorrow most reveals,
  Thrice hallowed and thrice blest;
For waves of blessedness that **steep**
  Our lot in radiant day;
For happiness unknown and deep,
  We bless Thee day by day.

4 For hope of better things above,
  Through Him who died for all;
For love divine—eternal love,
  That raised us from our fall;
For all the Christian's holy dower,
  His anchor, hope, and stay;
For all, our God of love and power,
  We bless Thee day by day.
          Mrs. Sergeant.
T.

AFFLICTION AND RESIGNATION.

517 *In Thee is my trust.* L. M.
       Psalm cxli. 8.

O THOU to whose all-searching sight
  The darkness shineth as the light,
Search, prove my heart, it pants for Thee;
O burst these bonds, and set it free!

2 Wash out its stains, refine its dross,
Nail my affections to the cross;
Hallow each thought; let all within
Be clean, as Thou, my Lord, art clean.

3 If in this darksome wild I stray,
Be Thou my Light, be Thou my Way;
No foes, no violence I fear,
No fraud, while Thou, my God, art near.

4 When rising floods my soul o'erflow,
When sinks my heart in waves of woe,
Jesus, Thy timely aid impart,
And raise my head, and cheer my heart.

5 Saviour, where'er Thy steps I see,
Dauntless, untired, I follow Thee!
O let Thy hand support me still,
And lead me to Thy holy hill!

6 If rough and thorny be the way,
My strength proportion to my day;
Till toil, and grief, and pain shall cease,
Where all is calm, and joy, and peace.
       Count Zinzendorf. abt. 1730.
       Tr. *J. Wesley.* 1739.

518 *My soul thirsteth for God,* L. M.
  for the living God.—Psalm xlii. 2.

THOU Lamb of God, Thou Prince of Peace,
  For Thee my thirsty soul doth pine;
My longing heart implores Thy grace;
O make me in Thy likeness shine!

2 With fraudless, even, humble **mind,**
  Thy will in all things may I **see;**
In love be every wish resigned,
  And hallowed **my whole** heart **to Thee.**

3 When pain o'er **my weak flesh** prevails,
  With lamb-like **patience** arm my breast;
When grief my wounded soul assails,
  In lowly meekness may I rest.

4 **Close by Thy side** still may I keep,
  Howe'er life's various current flow;
With steadfast eye mark every step,
  And follow Thee where'er Thou go.

5 Thou, Lord, the dreadful fight hast won,
  Alone Thou hast the winepress trod;
In me Thy strengthening grace be shown,
  O may I conquer through Thy blood!

THE CHRISTIAN LIFE.

6 So when on Zion Thou shalt stand,
  And all heaven's host adore their King,
Shall I be found at Thy right hand,
  And free from pain Thy glories sing.
                                  Amen.
C. F. Richter. 1700.   *Tr. J. Wesley.* 1739.

519 *Out of the depths have* C.M.
I cried unto Thee.—Psalm cxxx. 1.

OUT of the deep, out of the deep,
  O God, I make my moan;
When I by night, awaked from sleep,
  Do watch with Thee alone.

2 Be not extreme, be not extreme
    To mark what is amiss;
  Forgiveness doth Thee well beseem,
    Lord, be Thou feared in this.

3 My soul doth wait, my soul doth wait
    Till darkness wear away;
  My soul doth flee, I say, to Thee
    Before the breaking day.

4 Trust in the Lord, trust in the Lord,
    Though yet thy dawn be dim;
  He will thee save from out the grave,
    Redemption is with Him.
                              Anon.

520   7.7. 7.7.
Jesus, Thou Son of David,
have mercy on me.—Mark x. 47.

WHEN our heads are bowed with woe,
  When our bitter tears o'erflow,
When we mourn the lost, the dear,
Jesus, Son of David, hear!

2 Thou our throbbing flesh hast worn;
  Thou our mortal grief hast borne;
  Thou hast shed the human tear;
  Jesus, Son of David, hear!

3 Thou hast bowed the dying head;
  Thou the blood of life hast shed;
  Thou hast filled a mortal bier;
  Jesus, Son of David, hear!

4 When the heart is sad within,
  With the thought of all its sin;
  When the spirit shrinks with fear,
  Jesus, Son of David, hear!

5 Thou the shame, the grief hast known;
  Though the sins were not Thine own;
  Thou hast deigned their load to bear!
  Jesus, Son of David, hear!   Amen.
                    H. H. Milman. 1827.

521   11.10. 11.10. 10.10.
Lord, Thou knowest all things.
John xxi. 17.

THOU knowest, Lord, the weariness and sorrow
  Of the sad heart that comes to Thee for rest;
Cares of to-day, and burdens for to-morrow.
  Blessings implored, and sins to be confessed;
We come before Thee at Thy gracious word,
And lay them at Thy feet: Thou knowest, Lord.

2 Thou knowest all the past; how long and blindly
    On the dark mountains the lost wanderer strayed;
  How the Good Shepherd followed, and how kindly
    He bore it home, upon His shoulders laid;
  And healed the bleeding wounds, and soothed the pain,
  And brought back life, and hope, and strength again.

3 Thou knowest all the present, each temptation,
    Each toilsome duty, each foreboding fear;
  All to each one assigned of tribulation,
    Or to beloved ones than self more dear;
  All pensive memories, as we journey on,
  Longings for vanished smiles, and voices gone.

4 Thou knowest all the future; gleams of gladness
    By stormy clouds too quickly overcast;
  Hours of sweet fellowship and parting sadness,
    And the dark river to be crossed at last.
  O! what could hope and confidence afford
  To tread that path, but this, Thou knowest, Lord?

5 Thou knowest—not alone as God all knowing—
    As man, our mortal weakness Thou hast proved;
  On earth with purest sympathies o'erflowing,
    O Saviour, Thou hast wept, and Thou hast loved;
  And love and sorrow still to Thee may come,
  And find a hiding-place, a rest, a home.

6 Therefore we come, Thy gentle call obeying,
    And lay our sins and sorrows at Thy feet;
  On everlasting strength our weakness staying,
    Clothed in Thy robe of righteousness complete;
  Then, rising and refreshed, we leave Thy throne,
  And follow on to know as we are known.
                              H. L. L. 1859.

AFFLICTION AND RESIGNATION.

522 C.M.
Lord, remember me.
Luke xxiii. 42.

O THOU from whom all goodness **flows,**
 I lift my soul to Thee ;
In all my sorrows, conflicts, **woes,**
 Good Lord, remember me.

2 When on my aching, burdened heart
 My sins lie heavily,
Thy pardon speak, new peace impart,
 Good Lord, remember me.

3 When trials sore obstruct my way,
 And ills I cannot flee,
O let my strength be as my day
 Good Lord, remember me.

4 When worn with pain, disease, and grief,
 This feeble body see ;
Grant patience, rest, and kind relief,
 Good Lord, remember me.

5 If, for Thy sake, upon my name
 Shame and reproach shall be,
All hail reproach, and welcome shame,
 Good Lord, remember me.

6 When, in the solemn hour of death,
 I wait Thy just decree,
Be this the prayer of my last breath,
 Good Lord, remember me.

7 And when before Thy throne I stand,
 And lift my soul to Thee,
Then with the saints at Thy right hand,
 Good Lord, remember me. Amen.
  T. Haweis. 1790, *and*
   Thomas Cotterill. 1819.

523 C.M.
*We have not an high priest
which cannot be touched with the feeling of
our infirmities.*—Hebrews iv. 15.

WITH joy we meditate the grace
 Of our High Priest above ;
His heart is made of tenderness,
 And ever yearns with love.

2 Touched **with a sympathy within,**
 He knows **our feeble frame** ;
He knows **what sore temptations mean,**
 For He **hath felt the same.**

3 He **in the days of feeble flesh**
 Poured out His cries and tears ;
And, though **exalted, feels afresh**
 What every **member bears.**

4 He'll never quench the smoking **flax,**
 But raise it to a flame ;
The bruised reed He never breaks,
 Nor scorns **the** meanest name.

5 Then let **our** humble faith address
 His mercy and His power ;
We shall obtain delivering grace
 In the distressing hour.
  Isaac Watts. 1709.

524 C.M.
*I will deliver him, and
honour him.*—Psalm xci. 15.

THEE, Jesus, **full of** truth and grace,
 Thee, Saviour, **we** adore,
Thee in affliction's furnace praise,
 And magnify Thy power.

2 Thy power, in human weakness shown,
 Shall make us all entire ;
We now Thy guardian presence own,
 And walk unharmed in fire.

3 Thee, Son of Man, by faith we see,
 And glory in our Guide ;
Surrounded and upheld by Thee,
 The fiery test abide.

4 The fire our graces shall refine,
 Till, moulded from above,
We bear the character divine,
 The stamp of perfect love.
  Charles Wesley. 1749.

525 L.M.
*I know thy works, and
tribulation, and poverty.*—Rev. ii. 9.

MY sufferings all to Thee are known,
 Tempted in every point like me ;
Regard my grief, regard Thy own,
 Jesus, remember Calvary.

2 Art Thou not touched with human woe ?
 Hath pity left the Son of Man ?
Dost Thou not all my sorrows know,
 And claim a share in all my pain ?

3 Have I not heard, have I not known,
 That Thou, the everlasting Lord,
Whom heaven and earth the r Maker own,
 Art always faithful to Thy word ?

4 Thou wilt not break a bruisèd reed,
 Or quench the smallest spark of grace,
Till through the soul Thy power is spread,
 Thy all-victorious righteousness.

5 The day of small and feeble things
 I know Thou never wilt despise ;
I know with healing in His wings,
 The Sun of Righteousness shall rise.

6 With labour faint Thou wilt not fail,
 Or, wearied, give the sinner o'er,
Till in this earth Thy judgments dwell,
 And, born of God, I sin no more.
  Wesley. 1740.

526 8.8.8.8.8.8.
*Comfort ye, comfort ye
My people, saith your God.*—Isaiah xl. 1.

COMFORT, ye ministers of grace,
 Comfort My people, saith your God ;
Ye soon shall see His smiling face,
 His golden sceptre, not His rod .
And own, when now the cloud's removed,
He only chastened whom He loved.

THE CHRISTIAN LIFE.

2 Who sow in tears, in joy shall reap;
   The Lord shall comfort all that mourn;
Who now go on their way and weep,
   With joy they doubtless shall return,
And bring their sheaves with vast increase,
   And have their fruit to holiness.
                            Wesley. 1742.

527 *Weep with them that weep.* 8.8. 8.8. 8.8
               Romans xii. 15.

LET God, who comforts the distrest,
   Let Israel's Consolation hear:
Hear, Holy Ghost, our joint request,
   And show Thyself the Comforter,
And swell the unutterable groan,
And breathe our wishes to the Throne.

2 We weep for those that weep below,
   And burdened, for the afflicted sigh;
The various forms of human woe
   Excite our softest sympathy,
Fill every heart with mournful care,
And draw out all our souls in prayer.

3 We wrestle for the ruined race,
   By sin eternally undone,
Unless Thou magnify Thy grace,
   And make Thy richest mercy known,
And make Thy vanquished rebels find
Pardon in Christ for all mankind.

4 Father of everlasting Love,
   To every soul Thy Son reveal,
Our guilt and sufferings to remove,
   Our deep, original wound to heal;
And bid the fallen race arise,
And turn our earth to Paradise. Amen.
                            Charles Wesley. 1758.

528 *Hold fast the confidence* 7.6. 7.6. 7.8. 7.6.
*and the rejoicing of the hope firm unto the
         end.*—Hebrews iii. 6.

CAST on the fidelity
   Of my redeeming Lord,
I shall His salvation see,
   According to His word:
Credence to His word I give;
My Saviour in distresses past
Will not now His servant leave,
   But bring me through at last

2 Better than my boding fears
   To me Thou oft hast proved,
Oft observed my silent tears,
   And challenged Thy beloved:
Mercy to my rescue flew,
And death ungrasped his fainting prey,
Pain before Thy face withdrew,
   And sorrow fled away.

3 Now as yesterday the same,
   In all my troubles nigh,
Jesus, on Thy word and name
   I steadfastly rely;
Sure as now the grief I feel,
The promised joy I soon shall have,
   Saved again, to sinners tell
Thy power and will to save.

4 To Thy blessed will resigned,
   And stayed on that alone,
I Thy perfect strength shall find,
   Thy faithful mercies own:
Compassed round with songs of praise,
My all to my Redeemer give,
   Spread Thy miracles of grace,
   And to Thy glory live.
                            Charles Wesley. 1767.

529 *As sorrowful, yet alway* 7.6. 7.6 7.7. 7.6.
rejoicing.—2 Corinthians vi. 10.

FATHER, in the name I pray
   Of Thy incarnate love;
Humbly ask, that as my day
   My suffering strength may prove:
When my sorrows most increase,
   Let Thy strongest joys be given;
Jesus, come with my distress,
   And agony is heaven.

2 Father, Son, and Holy Ghost,
   For good remember me;
Me, whom Thou hast caused to trust
   For more than life on Thee:
With me in the fire remain,
   Till like burnished gold I shine,
Meet, through consecrated pain,
   To see the Face Divine. Amen.
                            Charles Wesley. 1767.

530 L.M.
*Take My yoke upon you,
and learn of Me; for I am meek and lowly
   in heart.*—Matthew xi. 29.

ETERNAL Beam of Light Divine,
   Fountain of unexhausted love,
In whom the Father's glories shine,
   Through earth beneath, and heaven
       above;

2 Jesus, the weary wanderer's rest,
   Give me Thy easy yoke to bear,
With steadfast patience arm my breast,
   With spotless love, and lowly fear.

3 Thankful I take the cup from Thee,
   Prepared and mingled by Thy skill;
Though bitter to the taste it be,
   Powerful the wounded soul to heal.

4 Be Thou, O Rock of Ages, nigh!
   So shall each murmuring thought be
       gone,
And grief, and fear, and care, shall fly,
   As clouds before the mid-day sun.

5 Speak to my warring passions, 'Peace!'
   Say to my trembling heart, 'Be still!'
Thy power my strength and fortress is,
   For all things serve Thy sovereign will.

6 O death! where is thy sting? Where now
   Thy boasted victory, O grave?
Who shall contend with God? or who
   Can hurt whom God delights to save?
                            Wesley. 1739.

AFFLICTION AND RESIGNATION.

531   7.7. 7.7.
Trust in the Lord with all thine heart.—Proverbs iii. 5.

WHEN we cannot see our way,
  Let us trust and still obey;
He who bids us forward go,
Cannot fail the way to show.

2 Though the sea be deep and wide,
Though a passage seem denied,
Fearless, let us still proceed,
Since the Lord vouchsafes to lead.

3 Though it be the gloom of night,
Though we see no ray of light,
Since the Lord Himself is there,
'Tis not meet that we should fear.

4 Night with Him is never night,
Where He is, there all is light;
When He calls us, why delay?
They are happy who obey.

5 Be it ours, then, while we're here,
Him to follow without fear;
Where He calls us, there to go;
What He bids us, that to do.
        Thomas Kelly. 1815.

532   C.M.
Fear not; for I am with thee.
Isaiah xliii. 5.

WE walk on earth, and to its ways
  Our time and thoughts are given,
Yet, amid all its busiest days,
Our hearts may be in heaven.

2 Nothing so lightens the dull load
  Life's urgent claims impose,
As close communion with our God;
It is our best repose.

3 When vexed with ills which we despair
To baffle or control,
The lifting of the heart in prayer
Sheds sunshine on the soul.

4 When disappointed in the love
We leaned on too secure,
What joy it is to look above,
And feel one Friend is sure.

5 When, wearied with life's ebb and flow,
We for 'still waters' sigh;
O how it sweetens change below
To think of rest on high!

6 Thus we in peace our souls possess,
Though all around be fear,
Full of the blessed consciousness
That heaven is sure and near.

7 Dark clouds may o'er us threatening stand,
We can sing on, and smile;
The sunshine of the cloudless land
Lies round us all the while.

8 We can bear any cross, or grief,
If, with their gloom, be given
This one sweet secret of relief,
To keep our thoughts in heaven.
        J. S. B. Monsell. 1867.

533   7.7. 7.7. 7.7.
Be merciful unto me, O God.
Psalm lvii. 1.

GOD! be merciful to me;
  For my spirit trusts in Thee,
And to Thee, her refuge, springs;
Be the shadow of Thy wings
Round my trembling spirit cast,
Till this storm is overpast.

2 From the waterfloods that roll
Deep and deeper round my soul
Take me, O my Saviour, take,
For Thy loving-kindness' sake;
If Thy truth from me depart,
That rebuke will break my heart.

3 Foes increase, they close me round;
Friend nor comforter is found;
Sore temptations now assail;
Hope and strength and courage fail:
Turn not from Thy servant's grief,
Hasten, Lord, to my relief.

4 Poor and sorrowful am I;
Set me, O my God, on high;
Wonders Thou for me hast wrought;
Nigh to death my soul is brought:
Save me, Lord, in mercy save,
Lest I sink below the grave.

5 Hark! He hears me from on high,
'Child of sorrow, it is I!
Thou shalt strive and weep no more,
Come and see My happy shore,
Rest and live and love with Me,
I am thine eternity.'
        James Montgomery. 1853.

534   C.M.
The will of the Lord be done.
Acts xxi. 14

I WORSHIP Thee, sweet Will of God!
  And all Thy ways adore,
And every day I live I seem
To love Thee more and more.

2 Man's weakness waiting upon God
Its end can never miss,
For man on earth no work can do
More angel-like than this.

3 He always wins who sides with God,
To him no chance is lost;
God's will is sweetest to him when
It triumphs at his cost.

4 Ill that He blesses is our good,
All unblest good is ill;
And all is right that seems most wrong
If it be His sweet Will.

THE CHRISTIAN LIFE.

5 When obstacles and trials seem
  Like prison walls to be,
I do the little I can do,
  And leave the rest to Thee.

6 I have no cares, O blessed Will!
  For all my cares are Thine;
I live in triumph, Lord! for Thou
  Hast made Thy triumphs mine.
                     F. W. Faber. 1849.

535   *O My Father, . . . not*   8.8.8.4.
as I will, but as Thou wilt.—Matt. xxvi. 39.

MY God, my Father, while I stray
  Far from my home, on life's rough way,
O teach me from my heart to say,
  Thy will be done!

2 Though dark my path and sad my lot,
  Let me be still and murmur not,
Or breathe the prayer Divinely taught,
  Thy will be done!

3 What though in lonely grief I sigh
  For friends beloved, no longer nigh,
Submissive still would I reply,
  Thy will be done!

4 If Thou shouldst call me to resign
  What most I prize, it ne'er was mine,
I only yield Thee what is Thine;
  Thy will be done!

5 Should grief or sickness waste away
  My life in premature decay,
My Father! still I strive to say,
  Thy will be done!

6 Let but my fainting heart be blest
  With Thy sweet Spirit for its guest,
My God, to Thee I leave the rest;
  Thy will be done!

7 Renew my will from day to day;
  Blend it with Thine and take away
All that now makes it hard to say,
  Thy will be done!

8 Then, when on earth I breathe no more
  The prayer, oft mixed with tears before,
I'll sing upon a happier shore,
  Thy will be done! Amen.
                    Charlotte Elliott. 1836.

536   *I will bring the blind*   8.7.8.7.4.7.
by a way that they knew not.—Isaiah xlii. 16.

MOUNTAINS, by the darkness hidden,
  Are as real as in the day;
Be, then, unbelief forbidden
  In a dreary hour to say,
    'God hath left us;
  O why hath He gone away?'

2 When He folds the cloud about Him,
  Firm within it stands His throne;
Wherefore should His children doubt Him,
  Those to whom His love is known?
    God is with us,
  We are never left alone.

3 Travellers at night, by fleeing,
  Cannot run into the day;
God can lead the blind and seeing,
  On Him wait and for Him stay;
    Be not fearful,
  They who cannot sing can pray.

4 Calm and blest is our composure,
  When the secret is possest,
That our God, in full disclosure,
  Hath to us His heart exprest:
    Thou, O Saviour,
  Hast been given to make us blest.

5 Time and space, O Lord, that show Thee
  Oft in power, veiling good,
Are too vast for us to know Thee
  As our trembling spirits would:
    But in Jesus, yes, in Jesus,
  Father, Thou art understood.
                    T. T. Lynch. 1855.

537   *My times are in Thy hand.*   S.M.
      Psalm xxxi. 15.

MY times are in Thy hand;
  My God, I wish them there;
My life, my soul, my all I leave
  Entirely to Thy care.

2 My times are in Thy hand,
  Whatever they may be;
Pleasing or painful, dark or bright,
  As best may seem to Thee.

3 My times are in Thy hand,
  Why should I doubt or fear?
A Father's hand will never cause
  His child a needless tear.

4 My times are in Thy hand,
  Jesus the crucified!
The hand my many sins have pierced
  Is now my guard and guide.

5 My times are in Thy hand,
  I'll always trust to Thee,
Till I possess the promised land,
  And all Thy glory see.
                    W. F. Lloyd. 1833.

538   *There the wicked cease*   8.7.8.7.
from troubling; and there the weary be at rest.—Job iii. 17.

WHEN the world my heart is rending
  With its heaviest storm of care,
My glad thoughts, to God ascending,
  Find a refuge from despair.

AFFLICTION AND RESIGNATION.

2 There's a hand of mercy near me,
   Though the waves of trouble roar ;
   There's an hour of rest to cheer me,
   When the toils of life are o'er.

3 Happy hour ! when saints are gaining
   That bright crown they longed to wear,
   Not one spot of sin remaining,
   Not one pang of earthly care.

4 O to rest in peace for ever !
   Joined with happy souls above,
   Where no foe my heart can sever
   From the Saviour whom I love.

5 This the hope that shall sustain me
   Till life's pilgrimage be past ;
   Fears may vex, and troubles pain me,
   I shall reach my home at last.
                    Sir John Bowring. 1825.

539 8.8.6. 8.8.6.
Not my wi'l, but Thine, be done.
Luke xxii. 42.

'FATHER ! Thy will, not mine, be done ;'
   So prayed on earth Thy suffering Son ;
The spirit faints, the flesh is weak,
Thy help in agony I seek,
   O take this cup away !

2 If such be not Thy sovereign will,
   Thy wiser purpose then fulfil ;
   My wishes I resign ;
   Into Thy hands my soul commend,
   On Thee for life or death depend ;
   Thy will be done, not mine.   Amen.
                    James Montgomery. 1841.

540 S.M.
I saw that it was from the hand of God.—Ecclesiastes ii. 24.

IT is Thy hand, my God :
   My sorrow comes from Thee ;
I bow beneath Thy chastening rod,
   I know Thou lovest me.

2 I would not murmur, Lord,
   Before Thee I am dumb ;
Lest I should breathe one murmuring word,
   To Thee for help I come.

3 My God, Thy name is Love,
   A Father's hand is Thine ;
With tearful eyes I look above,
   And cry, ' Thy will be mine !'

4 I know Thy will is right,
   Though it may seem severe :
Thy path is still unsullied light,
   Though dark it may appear.

5 Jesus for me hath died,
   Thy Son Thou didst not spare ;
His pierced hands, His bleeding side,
   Thy love for me declare.

6 Here my poor heart can rest ;
   My God, it cleaves to Thee ;
Thy will is love, Thine end is blest ;
   All work for good to me.
                    James G. Deck. 1855.

541 C.M.
Thy will be done.
Matthew xxvi. 42.

FATHER, whate'er of earthly bliss
   Thy sovereign will denies,
Accepted at Thy throne of grace,
   Let this petition rise.

2 Give me a calm, a thankful heart,
   From every murmur free ;
The blessings of Thy grace impart,
   And make me live to Thee.

3 Let the sweet sense that Thou art mine,
   My life and death attend ;
Thy presence through my journey shine,
   And crown my journey's end.   Amen.
                    Anne Steele. 1760.

542 L.M.
We must through much tribulation enter into the kingdom of God.
Acts xiv. 22.

O DEEM not they are blest alone,
   Whose lives a peaceful tenor keep ;
The Power who pities man has shown
   A blessing for the eyes that weep.

2 The light of smiles shall fill again
   The lids that overflow with tears,
And weary hours of woe and pain
   Are promises of happier years.

3 There is a day of sunny rest,
   For every dark and troubled night ;
And grief may bide an evening guest,
   But joy shall come with early light.

4 For God has marked each sorrowing hour,
   And numbered every secret tear ;
And Heaven's long age of love and power
   Grows out of all we suffer here.
                    W. Cullen Bryant. 1836.

543 11.10. 11.10.   Iambic.
Come down ere my child die.
John iv. 49.

ONE touch from Thee, the Healer of
      diseases,
   One little touch would make our brother
      whole ;
And yet Thou comest not ; O blessèd Jesus,
   Send a swift arrow to our waiting soul !

2 Full many a message have we sent, and
      pleaded
   That Thou wouldst haste Thy coming,
      gracious Lord ;
Each message was received and heard and
      heeded,
   And yet we welcome no responsive word.

THE CHRISTIAN LIFE.

3 We know that Thou art **blessing, whilst**
  withholding;
  We know that Thou art **near us, though
  apart;**
  And though we list no answer, Thou art
  folding
  Our poor petitions to Thy smitten heart.

4 A bright and glorious answer is preparing,
  Hid in the heights of love, the depths of
  grace;
  We know that Thou, the Risen, still art
  bearing
  Our cause as Thine, within the Holy
  Place.

5 And so we trust our pleadings to Thy
  keeping;
  So at Thy feet we lay our burden down,
  Content to bear the earthly cross with
  weeping,
  Till at Thy feet we cast the heavenly
  crown.
          Jane Crewdson. d. 1863.

544 8.8. 8.8. 8.8.
*Stand still, and see the
salvation of God.*—Exodus xiv. 13.

PEACE! doubting heart; my God's I am:
  Who formed me man, forbids my fear;
The Lord hath called me by my name;
  The Lord protects, fo ever near;
His blood for me did once atone,
And still He loves and guards His own.

2 When passing through the watery deep,
    I ask in faith His promised aid,
  The waves an awful distance keep,
    And shrink from my devoted head;
  Fearless their violence I dare;
  They cannot harm, for God is there.

3 Still nigh me, O my Saviour, stand!
    And guard in fierce temptation's hour;
  Hide in the hollow of Thy hand,
    Show forth in me Thy saving power,
  Still be Thy arms my sure defence,
  Nor earth nor hell shall pluck me thence.

4 When darkness intercepts the skies,
    And sorrow's waves around me roll,
  When high the storms of passion rise,
    And half o'erwhelm my sinking soul,
  My soul a sudden calm shall feel,
  And hear a **whisper,** 'Peace, be still!'

5 Though in affliction's furnace tried,
    Unhurt on snares and death I'll tread;
  Though sin assail, and hell, thrown wide,
    Pour all its flames upon my head,
  Like Moses' bush, I'll mount the higher,
  And flourish unconsumed in fire.
          Wesley. 1739.

545 7.7. 7.7. 7.7.
*Be in subjection unto the
Father of spirits, and live.*—Heb. xii. 9.

QUIET, Lord, my froward heart;
  Make me teachable and mild,
Upright, simple, free from art;
  Make me as a weaned child,
From distrust and envy free,
Pleased with all that pleases Thee.

2 What Thou shalt to-day provide,
    Let me as a child receive;
  What to-morrow may betide,
    Calmly to Thy wisdom leave;
  'Tis enough that Thou wilt care,
  Why should I the **burden** bear?

3 **As a** little child relies
    On a care beyond his **own,**
  Knows he's neither **strong nor wise,**
    Fears to stir a step alone;
  Let me thus with Thee abide,
  As my Father, Guard, and Guide.

4 Thus preserved from Satan's wiles,
    Safe from dangers, free from fears,
  May I live upon Thy smiles,
    Till the promised hour appears,
  When the sons of God shall prove
  All **their** Father's boundless love. Amen.
          John Newton. 1779.

546 6.5. 6.5. D.
*Our light affliction, which is
but for a moment, worketh for us a far more
exceeding and eternal weight of g'ory.*
2 Corinthians iv. 17.

O LET **him,** whose sorrow
    No relief can find,
  Trust in God, and borrow
    Ease for heart and mind.
  Where the mourner weeping
    Sheds the secret tear,
  God His watch is keeping,
    Though none else be near.

2 **God will never leave thee,**
    All thy wants He knows,
  Feels the pains that grieve thee,
    Sees thy cares and woes.
  Raise thine eyes to heaven
    When thy spirits quail,
  When, by tempests driven,
    Heart and courage fail.

3 When in grief we languish,
    He will dry the tear,
  Who His children's anguish
    Soothes with succour near.
  All our woe and sadness,
    In this world below,
  Balance not the gladness
    We in heaven shall know,

AFFLICTION AND RESIGNATION.

4 Jesus, holy Saviour!
  In the realms above,
  Crown us with Thy favour,
  Fill us with Thy love.
  On Thy truth relying
  In the mortal strife,
  Lord, receive us dying
  To eternal life. Amen.
            H. S. Oswald, d. 1834.
     Tr. Frances E. Cox. 1841.

547   6.5. 6.5. D.
If we suffer, we shall also reign with Him.—2 Timothy ii. 12.

SOMETIME o'er our pathway
  Passing clouds must fail;
Sometime pain and sorrow
  Come to each and all.
God our Father sends us
  Ever what is best;
We in faith and patience
  Find our only rest.

2 If the cup be bitter,
  It is meant to heal,
And our kind Redeemer
  Pities what we feel.
What are all our troubles?
  What our greatest loss?
When we think of Jesus
  Dying on the cross.

3 Then our great Example
  We must learn to find,
When our Father calls us,
  Yielding heart and mind;
So, through joy and sorrow,
  By His Spirit led,
We shall rise in glory,
  With our Royal Head.
          L. Tuttiett. 1863.

548   8.8. 8.8. 8 8.
All things work together for good to them that love God.—Rom. viii. 28.

GOD sendeth sun, He sendeth shower;
  Alike they're needful for the flower;
And joys and tears alike are sent
To give the soul fit nourishment;
As comes to me, or cloud or sun,
Father, Thy will, not mine, be done.

2 Can loving children e'er reprove,
With murmurs, those they trust and love?
Creator! I would ever be
A trusting, loving child to Thee;
As comes to me, or cloud or sun,
Father, Thy will, not mine, be done.

3 O ne'er will I at life repine!
Enough that **Thou** hast made it mine;
When falls **the** shadow cold of death,
I yet will sing with parting breath,
As comes to me, or cloud or sun,
Father, Thy will, not mine, be done.
             Amen.
     Mrs. Sarah F. Adams. 1841.

549   11.10. 11.6.
He that trusteth in the Lord, mercy shall compass him about.
    Psalm xxxii. 10.

STILL will we trust, though earth seem
  dark and dreary,
And the heart faint beneath His chastening rod,
Though rough and **steep our pathway**,
  worn and weary,
    Still will we trust in God.

2 Our eyes see dimly till by faith anointed,
  And our blind choosing brings **us grief**
  and pain;
Through Him **alone**, who hath our way
  appointed,
    We find our peace again.

3 Choose for us, God, nor let our weak preferring
  Cheat our poor souls of good Thou hast
  designed;
Choose for us, God; Thy wisdom is unerring,
    And we are fools and blind.

4 So from our sky the night shall furl her
  shadows,
And day pour gladness through her
  golden gates;
Our rough path leads to flower-enamelled
  meadows,
    Where joy our coming waits.

5 Let us press on: in patient self-denial,
  Accept the hardship, shrink not from the
  loss;
Our **guerdon lies beyond the hour of trial**,
    Our crown beyond the cross.
          W. H. Burleigh. 1868.

550   10.10. 10.10. 10.10.
Return unto thy rest, O my soul.—Psalm cxvi. 7.

BE still, my soul: the Lord is on thy
  side;
Bear patiently thy cross of grief and
  pain;
Leave to thy God to order and provide;
  In every change He faithful will remain.
Be still, my soul: thy best, thy heavenly
  Friend
Through thorny ways leads to a joyful end.

2 Be still, my soul: thy God doth undertake
  To guide the future as He has the past.
Thy hope, thy confidence, let nothing
  shake;
All now mysterious shall be bright at
  last.
Be still, my soul: **the waves and winds**
  shall know
His voice who ruled them while He dwelt
  below.

THE CHRISTIAN LIFE.

3 Be still, my soul: when dearest friends
    depart,
  And all is darkened in the vale of tears,
  Then thou shalt better know His love, His
    heart,
  Who comes to soothe thy sorrow and thy
    fears.
  Be still, my soul: thy Jesus can repay
  From His own fulness all He takes away.

4 Be still, my soul: the hour is hastening on
  When we shall be for ever with the
    Lord;
  When disappointment, grief, and fear are
    gone,
  Sorrow forgot, love's purest joys re-
    stored.
  Be still, my soul: when change and tears
    are past,
  All safe and blessed we shall meet at last.
            H. L. L. b. 1813.

551   8.7 8.7.
*I am thy shield, and thy
exceeding great reward.—Genesis xv. 1.*

THOU art near, yes, Lord, I feel it,
  Thou art near where'er I move,
  And though sense would fain conceal it,
  Faith still whispers it to love.

2 Am I weak? Thine arm will lead me
  Safe through every danger, Lord;
  Am I hungry? Thou wilt feed me
  With the manna of Thy Word.

3 Am I thirsting? Thou wilt guide me
  Where refreshing waters flow;
  Faint or feeble? Thou'lt provide me
  Grace for every want I know.

4 Am I fearful? Thou wilt take me
  Underneath Thy wings, my God!
  Am I faithless? Thou wilt make me
  Bow beneath Thy chastening rod.

5 Am I drooping? Thou art near me,
  Near to bear me on my way;
  Am I pleading? Thou wilt hear me,
  Hear and answer when I pray.

6 Then, my soul, since God doth love thee,
  Faint not, droop not, do not fear;
  Though His heaven is high above thee,
  He Himself is ever near.
            J. S. B. Monsell 1872.

552   10.10. 10.10.6.
*Followers of them who
through faith and patience inherit the
promises.—Hebrews vi. 12.*

WE ask not that our path be always
    bright,
  But for Thine aid to walk therein aright;
  That Thou, O Lord! through all its devious
    way,
  Wilt give us strength sufficient to our day,
  For this, for this we pray;

2 Not for the fleeting joys that earth be-
    stows,
  Not for exemption from its many woes;
  But that, come joy or woe, come good or
    ill,
  With child-like faith we trust Thy guid-
    ance still,
  And do Thy holy will.

3 Teach us, dear Lord, to find the latent
    good
  That sorrow yields when rightly under-
    stood;
  And for the frequent joy that crowns our
    days,
  Help us, with grateful hearts, our hymns
    to raise
  Of thankfulness and praise.

4 Thou knowest all our needs, and wilt
    supply;
  No veil of darkness hides us from Thine
    eye;
  Nor vainly from the depths on Thee we
    call;
  Thy tender love, that breaks the tempter's
    thrall,
  Folds and encircles all.

5 Through sorrow and through loss, by toil
    and prayer,
  Saints won the starry crowns which now
    they wear,
  And by the bitter ministry of pain,
  Grievous and harsh, but oh! not felt in
    vain,
  Found their eternal gain.

6 If it be ours, like them, to suffer loss,
  Give grace, as unto them, to bear our
    cross,
  Till, victors over each besetting sin,
  We, too, Thy perfect peace shall enter in,
  And crowns of glory win.
            W. H. Burleigh. 1863.

553   C.M.
*In the night His song shall
be with me.—Ps. xlii. 8.*

WE praise Thee oft for hours of bliss,
    For days of quiet rest;
  But O! how seldom do we feel
    That pain and tears are best.

2 We praise Thee for the shining sun,
    For kind and gladsome ways;
  When shall we learn, O Lord, to sing
    Through weary nights and days?

3 We praise Thee when our path is plain
    And smooth beneath our feet;
  But fain would learn to welcome pain,
    And call the bitter sweet.

4 Teach Thou our weak and wandering
    hearts
  Aright to read Thy way,
  That Thou with loving hand dost trace
    Our history every day.

AFFLICTION AND RESIGNATION.

5 Then every thorny crown of care
　Worn well in patience now,
Shall grow a glorious diadem
　Upon the faithful brow;

6 And sorrow's face shall be **unveiled**,
　And we at last shall see
Her eyes are eyes of tenderness,
　Her speech but echoes Thee.
　　　　　　J. Page Hopps. 1873.

554　　　　　　　　　　　S.M.
*In all thy ways acknowledge
Him, and He shall direct thy paths.*
Proverbs iii. 6.

GIVE to the winds thy fears;
　Hope, and be undismayed;
God hears thy sighs and counts thy tears,
　God shall lift up thy head.

2 Through waves, and clouds, and storms,
　He gently clears thy way;
Wait thou his time, so shall this night
　Soon end in joyous day.

3 Still heavy is thy heart?
　Still sink thy spirits down?
Cast off the weight, let fear depart,
　Bid every care begone.

4 What though thou rulest not?
　Yet heaven and earth, and hell
Proclaim, God sitteth on the throne,
　And ruleth all things well!

5 Leave to His sovereign sway
　To choose and to command;
So shalt thou wondering own His way,
　How wise, how strong His hand.

6 Far, far above thy thought
　His counsel shall appear,
When fully He the work hath wrought
　That caused thy needless fear.

7 Thou seest our weakness, Lord,
　Our hearts are known to Thee;
O lift thou **up** the **sinking** hand,
　Confirm **the** feeble knee!

8 Let us in life and death
　Thy steadfast truth declare,
And publish with **our** latest breath
　Thy love and guardian care. Amen.
　　　　　　Paul Gerhardt. 1659.
　　　　　　Tr. J. Wesley. 1739.

555　　　　　　　　7.7.7.7.
It is I; be not afraid.
John vi. 20.

WHEN the dark waves round us **roll**,
　And we look in vain for aid,
Speak, Lord, to the trembling soul,
　'It is I; be not afraid.'

2 When we dimly trace Thy form
　In mysterious clouds arrayed,
Be the echoes of the storm,
　'It is I; be not afraid.'

3 When our brightest hopes depart,
　When our fairest visions fade,
Whisper to the fainting heart,
　'It is I; be not afraid.'

4 When we **weep beside the** bier
　Where **some well-loved** form is laid,
O may then **the** mourner hear,
　'It is I; be **not** afraid.'

5 When with wearing, hopeless pain,
　Sinks the spirit sore dismayed,
Breathe Thou **then** the comfort-strain,
　'It is **I**; be **not** afraid.'

6 When we feel the end is near,
　Passing into death's dark shade,
May the voice be strong and clear,
　'It is I; be not afraid.' Amen.
　　　　　　Bishop W. W. How. 1854.

556　　　　　　　　　　L.M.
*Whom the Lord loveth
He chasteneth.*—Hebrews xii. 6.

WHEN gladness **gilds our prosperous**
　　day,
　And hope is by fruition crowned,
'O Lord,' with thankful hearts we say,
　'How doth Thy love to us abound?

2 But is that love less truly **shown**,
　When earthly joys lie cold **and dead**,
And hopes have faded **one** by one,
　Leaving sad memories **in** their stead?

3 **God knows the** discipline **we need**,
　Nor sorrow sends for sorrow's sake;
And though our stricken hearts may
　　bleed,
　His mercy will not let them break.

4 O **teach us to discern the good**
　Thou sendest **in the guise of ill**;
Since all Thou dost, if understood,
　Interpreteth Thy loving will.

5 **For pain is not the end of** pain,
　Not seldom trial comes **to bless**,
And work for us a bundant **gain**,
　The peaceful fruits of righteousness.

6 Then **let us not, with anxious thought**,
　Ask **of to-morrow's joys or woes**,
But, **by His word and Spirit taught**,
　Accept **as best what God bestows**.
　　　　　　W. H. Burleigh. 1868.

557　　　　　　　8.8, 8.8, 8.8.
*In all points tempted like
as we are.*—Hebrews iv. 15.

WHEN gathering clouds around **I**
　　view,
And days are dark and friends are few,
On Him I lean, who, not in vain
Experienced every human pain.
He sees my wants, allays my fears,
And counts and treasures up my tears.

THE CHRISTIAN LIFE.

2 If aught should tempt my soul to stray
From heavenly wisdom's narrow way,
To fly the good I would pursue,
Or do the sin I would not do;
Still He, who felt temptation's power,
Shall guard me in that dangerous hour.

3 If wounded love my bosom swell,
Deceived by those I prized too well,
He shall His pitying aid bestow,
Who felt on earth severer woe;
At once betrayed, denied, or fled,
By those who shared His daily bread.

4 If vexing thoughts within me rise,
And, sore dismayed, my spirit dies;
Still He, who once vouchsafed to bear
The sickening anguish of despair,
Shall sweetly soothe, shall gently dry.
The throbbing heart, the streaming eye.

5 When sorrowing o'er some stone I bend,
Which covers what was once a friend,
And from his hand, his voice, his smile,
Divides me for a little while;
Thou, Saviour, mark'st the tears I shed,
For Thou didst weep o'er Lazarus dead.

6 And O! when I have safely past
Through every conflict but the last;
Still, still unchanging, watch beside
My dying bed, for Thou hast died:
Then point to realms of cloudless day,
And wipe the latest tear away.   Amen.
Sir R. Grant. 1812.

558   C.M.
He shall come down like rain upon the mown grass; as showers that water the earth.—Psalm lxxii. 6.

COME, let us to the Lord our God
   With contrite hearts return:
Our God is gracious, nor will leave
   The desolate to mourn.

2 His voice commands the tempest forth,
   And stills the stormy wave:
And though His arm be strong to smite,
   'Tis also strong to save.

3 Long hath the night of sorrow reigned;
   The dawn shall bring us light;
God shall appear, and we shall rise
   With gladness in His sight.

4 Our hearts, if God we seek to know,
   Shall know Him and rejoice:
His coming like the morn shall be,
   Like morning songs His voice.

5 As dew upon the tender herb,
   Diffusing fragrance round;
As showers that usher in the spring,
   And cheer the thirsty ground:

6 So shall His presence bless our souls,
   And shed a joyful light;
That hallowed morn shall chase away
   The sorrows of the night.
J. Morrison. 1781.

559   11.4. 11.4.
Their works do follow them.—Revelation xiv. 13.

WITH silence only as their benediction,
   God's angels come,
Where, in the shadow of a great affliction,
   The soul sits dumb.

2 Yet would we say what **every heart approveth**,
   Our Father's will,
Calling to Him **the dear ones whom He loveth**,
   Is mercy still.

3 Not upon us or ours the solemn angel
   Hath evil wrought;
The funeral anthem is a glad evangel;
   The good die not!

4 God calls our loved ones, but **we lose not wholly**
   What He has given:
They live on earth in thought and deed, **as truly**
   As in His heaven.
J. G. Whittier. 1847.

560   8.8.6. 8.8.6.
The ransomed of the Lord shall return, and come to Zion with songs.
Isaiah xxxv. 10.

COME on, my partners in distress,
   My comrades through the wilderness,
   Who still your bodies feel;
A while forget your griefs and fears,
And look beyond this vale of tears,
   To that celestial hill.

2 Beyond the bounds of time and space,
Look forward to that heavenly place,
   The saints' secure abode;
On faith's strong eagle-pinions rise,
And force your passage to the skies,
   And scale the mount of God.

3 Who suffer with our Master here,
We shall before His face appear,
   And by His side sit down;
To patient faith the prize is sure,
And all that to the end endure
   The cross, shall wear the crown.

4 Thrice blessèd, bliss-inspiring hope!
It lifts the fainting spirits up,
   It brings to life the dead;
Our conflicts here shall soon be past,
And you and I ascend at last,
   Triumphant with our Head.

5 That great mysterious Deity
We soon with open face shall see;
   The beatific sight
Shall fill heaven's sounding courts with praise,
And wide diffuse the golden blaze
   Of everlasting light.
Charles Wesley. 1749.

CONFLICT AND COURAGE.

561   8.7. 8.7. 6.6.6.6. 7.
God is our refuge and strength.—Psalm xlvi. 1.

A SAFE stronghold our God is still,
  A trusty shield and weapon ;
He'll help us clear from all the ill
That hath us now o'ertaken.
  The ancient prince of hell
  Hath risen with purpose fell :
  Strong mail of craft and power
  He weareth in this hour ;
On earth is not his fellow.

2 With force of **arms we** nothing can,
  Full soon **were we** down-ridden ;
But for us fights the proper Man,
  Whom God Himself hath bidden.
  Ask ye, Who is this same?
  Christ Jesus is His name,
  The Lord Sabaoth's **Son** ;
  He, and no other one,
Shall conquer in the battle.

3 And were this world all devils o'er,
  And watching to devour us,
We lay it **not** to heart so sore ;
  Not they can overpower us.
  And let **the** prince of ill
  Look grim as e'er he will,
  He harms us not a whit ;
  For why? his doom is writ ;
A word shall quickly slay him.

4 God's word, for all their craft and **force**,
  One moment will not linger,
But, spite of hell, shall have its course :
  'Tis written by His finger.
  And, though they take our life,
  Goods, honour, children, wife,
  Yet is their profit small ;
  These things **shall** vanish **all,**
The city of God remaineth.
      Martin Luther. 1521.
      Tr. Thomas Carlyle. 1831.

562   7.6. 7.6. D.
As a good soldier of Jesus Christ.—2 Timothy ii. 3.

STAND up! stand up for Jesus !
  Ye soldiers of the cross ;
Lift high His royal banner,
  It must not suffer loss :
From victory unto victory,
  His army shall He lead,
Till every foe is vanquished,
  And Christ is Lord indeed.

2 Stand up! stand up for **Jesus** !
  The trumpet-call obey ;
Forth to the mighty conflict,
  In this His glorious day ;
Ye that are His, now serve Him,
  Against unnumbered foes ;
Let courage rise with danger,
  And strength to strength oppose.

3 Stand up! stand up for Jesus :
  Stand in His strength alone ;
The arm of flesh will fail you ;
  Ye dare not trust your own :
Put on the gospel **armour,**
  And, watching unto **prayer,**
Where duty calls, **or danger,**
  Be never wanting **there.**

4 **Stand up!** stand up for **Jesus** !
  The strife will not be long ;
This day the noise of battle,
  The next the victor's song :
To him that overcometh,
  A crown of life shall be ;
He with the King of Glory
  Shall reign eternally.
      G. Duffield. 1858.

563   S.M.D.
Put on the whole armour of God.—Ephesians vi. 11.

SOLDIERS of Christ, arise,
  And put your armour on,
Strong in the strength which God supplies
  Through His eternal Son :
Strong in the Lord of Hosts,
  And in His mighty power,
Who in the strength **of** Jesus trusts
  Is more than **conqueror.**

2 Stand **then in** His great might,
  With all His strength endued ;
But take, **to** arm you **for the fight,**
  The panoply of God ;
That having all things done,
  And all your conflicts passed,
Ye may o'ercome through Christ alone,
  And stand entire at last.

3 Stand then against your foes,
  In close and firm array ;
Legions of enemies oppose
  Throughout the evil day :
But meet the sons of night,
  And mock their vain design,
Clad in the arms of heavenly light,
  Of righteousness divine.

4 Leave no unguarded place,
  No weakness of the soul,
Take every **virtue,** every **grace,**
  And fortify **the whole** :
In steadfast union joined,
  To battle all proceed ;
But **arm** yourselves with all the mind
  That was in Christ, your Head.
      Charles Wesley. 1749.

564   S.M.D.
Above all, taking the shield of faith.—Ephesians vi. 16.

SAINTS, above all, lay hold
  On faith's victorious shield ;
Armed with that adamant and gold,
  Be sure to win the field :

THE CHRISTIAN LIFE.

    If faith surround your heart,
      Satan shall be subdued,
    Repelled his every fiery dart,
      And quenched with Jesu's blood.

2 To keep your armour bright,
    Attend with constant care,
Still walking in your Captain's sight,
    And watching unto prayer:
    Ready for all alarms,
      Steadfastly set your face,
And always exercise your arms,
      And use your every grace.

3 Pray, without ceasing pray,
    Your Captain gives the word;
His summons cheerfully obey,
    And call upon the Lord:
    To God your every want
      In instant prayer display;
Pray always; pray, and never faint;
      Pray, without ceasing pray!

4 From strength to strength go on,
    Wrestle, and fight, and pray,
Tread all the powers of darkness down,
    And win the well-fought day:
    Still let the Spirit cry
      In all His soldiers, 'Come,'
Till Christ the Lord descend from high,
      And take the **conquerors** home.
        Charles Wesley. 1749.

565   *Fight the good fight of faith.*   C.M.
      1 Timothy vi. 12.

AM I a soldier of the cross,
    A follower of the Lamb?
And shall I fear to own His cause,
    Or blush to speak His name?

2 Must I be carried to the skies,
    On flowery beds of ease?
While others fought to win the prize,
    And sailed through troubled seas?

3 Are there no foes for me to face?
    Must I not stem the flood?
Is this vile world a friend to grace,
    To help me on to God?

4 Sure I must fight if I would reign;
    Increase my courage, Lord;
I'll bear the toil, endure the pain,
    Supported by Thy word.

5 Thy saints in all this glorious war
    Shall conquer though they die;
They see the triumph from afar,
    And seize it with their eye.

6 When that illustrious day shall rise,
    And all Thine armies shine
In robes of victory through the skies,
    The glory shall be Thine.
        Isaac Watts. 1721.

566   *Looking unto Jesus.*   L.M.
      Hebrews xii. 2.

FIGHT the good fight with all thy might
    Christ is thy strength, in Christ thy right;
Lay hold on life, and it shall be
    Thy joy and crown eternally.

2 Run the straight race, through God's good grace,
Lift up thine eyes, and seek His face;
Life with its way before us lies,
Christ is the way, and Christ the prize.

3 Cast care aside, upon thy Guide
Lean, and His mercy will provide;
Lean, and the trusting soul shall prove
Christ is its life, and Christ its love.

4 Faint not, nor fear, His arm is near,
He changeth not, and thou art dear;
Only believe, and thou shalt see
That Christ is all in all to thee.
        J. S. B. Monsell. 1863.

567   *He teacheth my hands to war.*   S.M.D.
      Psalm xviii. 34.

EQUIP me for the war,
    And teach my hands to fight,
My simple upright heart prepare,
    And guide my words aright;
    Control my every thought,
      My whole of sin remove;
Let all my works in Thee be wrought,
    Let all be wrought in love.

2 O arm me with the mind,
    Meek Lamb! which was in Thee;
And let my knowing zeal be joined
    With perfect charity;
    With calm and tempered zeal
      Let me enforce Thy call,
And vindicate Thy gracious will,
    Which offers life to all.

3 O do not let me trust
    In any arm but Thine!
Humble, O humble to the dust,
    This stubborn soul of mine!
    A feeble thing of nought,
      With lowly shame I own,
The help which upon earth is wrought,
    Thou dost it all alone.

4 O may I love like Thee!
    In all Thy footsteps tread;
Thou hatest all iniquity,
    But nothing Thou hast made.
    O may I learn the art
      With meekness to reprove!
To hate the sin with all my heart,
    But still the sinner love.   Amen.
        Wesley. 1741.

CONFLICT AND COURAGE.

568 6.5. 6.5. D.
Be thou faithful unto death, and I will give thee a crown of life.
Revelation ii. 10.

CHRISTIAN! dost thou see them
  On the holy ground,
How the troops of Midian
  Prowl and prowl around?
Christian! up and smite them,
  Counting gain but loss;
Smite them by the merit
  Of the Holy Cross.

2 Christian! dost thou *feel* them,
  How they work within,
Striving, tempting, luring,
  Goading into sin?
Christian! never tremble;
  Never yield to fear;
Smite them by the virtue
  Of almighty prayer.

3 Christian! dost thou *hear* them,
  How they speak thee fair;
'Always fast and vigil?
  Always watch and prayer?'
Christian! answer boldly:
  'While I breathe I pray,
Peace shall follow battle,
  Night shall end in day.'

4 'Well I know thy troubles,
  O My servant true!
Thou art very weary;
  I was weary too.
But that toil shall make thee
  Some day all Mine own;
And the end of sorrow
  Shall be near My throne.'

Andrew of Crete. 8th Century.
Tr. J. M. Neale. 1862.

569 6.5. 6.5. D. *With Chorus.*
Quit you like men, be strong.
1 Corinthians xvi. 13.

ONWARD, Christian soldiers,
  Marching as to war,
With the Cross of Jesus
  Going on before:
Christ the Royal Master
  Leads against the foe;
Forward into battle,
  See, His banners go!

  Onward, Christian soldiers,
    Marching as to war,
  With the Cross of Jesus
    Going on before.

2 At the sign of triumph
  Satan's host doth flee;
On then, Christian soldiers,
  On to victory!
Hell's foundations quiver
  At the shout of praise;
Brothers, lift your voices,
  Loud your anthems raise.

3 Like a mighty army
  Moves the Church of God;
Brothers, we are treading
  Where the saints have trod.
We are not divided,
  All one body we,
One in hope, in doctrine,
  One in charity.

4 Crowns and thrones may perish,
  Kingdoms rise and wane,
But the Church of Jesus
  Constant will remain:
Gates of hell can never
  'Gainst that Church prevail;
We have Christ's own promise,
  And that cannot fail.

5 Onward, then, ye people,
  Join our happy throng,
Blend with ours your voices
  In the triumph song;
Glory, praise, and honour
  Unto Christ the King;
This through countless ages
  Men and angels sing.

S. Baring-Gould. 1865.

570 8.8.6. 8.8.6.
If any man walk in the day he stumbleth not.—John xi. 9.

ARE there not in the labourer's day
  Twelve hours, in which he safely may
His calling's work pursue?
Though sin and Satan still are near,
Nor sin nor Satan can I fear,
  With Jesus in my view.

2 Not all the powers of hell can fright
A soul that walks with Christ in light,
  He walks and cannot fall;
Clearly he sees, and wins his way,
Shining unto the perfect day,
  And more than conquers all.

3 Light of the world! Thy beams I bless;
On Thee, bright Sun of Righteousness,
  My faith hath fixed its eye;
Guided by Thee, through all I go,
Nor fear the ruin spread below,
  For Thou art always nigh.

4 Ten thousand snares my paths beset;
Yet will I, Lord, the work complete,
  Which Thou to me hast given;
Regardless of the pains I feel,
Close by the gates of death and hell,
  I urge my way to heaven.

Charles Wesley. 1749.

THE CHRISTIAN LIFE.

571   8.8.6. 8.8.6.
In the Lord shall all the seed of Israel be justified, and shall glory.
Isaiah xlv. 25.

LORD, can it be that I should prove
  For ever faithful to Thy love,
  From sin for ever cease?
I thank Thee for the blessed hope;
It lifts my drooping spirits up,
  It gives me back my peace.

2 In Thee, O Lord, I put my trust,
Mighty, and merciful, and just;
  Thy sacred word is passed;
And I, who dare Thy word receive,
Without committing sin shall live,
  Shall live to God at last.

3 I rest in Thine almighty prayer;
The name of Jesus is a tower
  That hides my life above;
Thou canst, Thou wilt my Helper be,
My confidence is all in Thee,
  The faithful God of Love.

4 While still to Thee for help I call,
Thou wilt not suffer me to fall,
  Thou canst not let me sin;
And Thou shalt give me power to pray,
Till all my sins are purged away,
  And all Thy mind brought in.

5 Wherefore, in never-ceasing prayer,
My soul to Thy continual care
  I faithfully commend;
Assured that Thou through life shalt save,
And show Thyself beyond the grave
  My everlasting Friend.
        Charles Wesley. 1749.

572   S.M.T.
King of kings, and Lord of lords.—Revelation xix. 16.

JESUS, the Conqueror, reigns,
  In glorious strength arrayed,
His kingdom over all maintains,
  And bids the earth be glad.
Ye sons of men, rejoice
  In Jesus' mighty love,
Lift up your heart, lift up your voice,
  To Him who rules above.

2 Extol His kingly power,
  Kiss the exalted Son,
Who died, and lives to die no more,
  High on His Father's throne;
Our Advocate with God,
  He undertakes our cause,
And spreads through all the earth abroad,
  The victory of His cross.

3 Urge on your rapid course,
  Ye blood-besprinkled bands;
The heavenly kingdom suffers force,
  'Tis seized by violent hands;
See there the starry crown
  That glitters through the skies!
Satan, the world, and sin, tread down,
  And take the glorious prize.

4 Through much distress and pain,
  Through many a conflict here,
Through blood, ye must the entrance gain;
  Yet, O disdain to fear!
'Courage!' your Captain cries,
  Who all your toil foreknew;
'Toil ye shall have; yet all despise,
  I have o'ercome for you.'

5 The world cannot withstand
  Its ancient Conqueror,
The world must sink beneath the hand
  Which arms us for the war;
This is our victory!
  Before our faith they fall;
Jesus hath died for you and me;
  Believe, and conquer all.
        Charles Wesley. 1749.

573   6 5. 12 *lines.*
Speak unto the children of Israel, that they go forward.—Ex. xiv. 15.

FORWARD! be our watchword,
  Steps and voices joined;
Seek the things before us,
  Not a look behind;
Burns the fiery pillar
  At our army's head;
Who shall dream of shrinking,
  By our Captain led?
    Forward through the desert,
      Through the toil and fight,
    Jordan flows before us,
      Zion beams with light!

2 Forward, when in childhood
  Buds the infant mind;
All through youth and manhood,
  Not a thought behind;
Speed through realms of nature,
  Climb the steps of grace;
Faint not, till in glory
  Gleams our Father's face.
    Forward, all the lifetime,
      Climb from height to height,
    Till the head be hoary,
      Till the eye be light!

3 Glories upon glories
  Hath our God prepared,
By the souls that love Him
  One day to be shared;
Eye hath not beheld them,
  Ear hath never heard;
Nor of these hath uttered
  Thought or speech a word;
    Forward, marching Eastward
      Where the heaven is bright,
    Till the veil be lifted,
      Till our faith be sight!

4 Far o'er yon horizon
  Rise the city towers,
Where our God abideth,
  That fair home is ours;
Flash the streets with jasper,
  Shine the gates with gold;

CONFLICT AND COURAGE.

Flows the gladdening river
  Shedding joys untold.
Thither, onward thither,
  In the Spirit's might;
Pilgrims to your country,
  Forward into light!
      H. Alford. 1859.

574 7.7. 7.7.
Endure hardness as a good soldier of Jesus Christ.—2 Timothy ii. 3.

MUCH in sorrow, oft in woe,
  Onward, Christians, onward go,
Fight the fight, maintain the strife,
Strengthened with the Bread of Life.

2 Onward, Christians, onward go;
  Join the war, and face the foe;
  Faint not! much doth yet remain;
  Dreary is the long campaign.

3 Shrink not, Christians! will ye yield,
  Will ye quit the painful field?
  Will ye flee in danger's hour?
  Know ye not your Captain's power?

4 Let your drooping hearts be glad;
  March, in heavenly armour clad;
  Fight, nor think the battle long;
  Soon shall victory tune your song.

5 Let not sorrow dim your eye,
  Soon shall every tear be dry;
  Let not woe your course impede;
  Great your strength, if great your need.

6 Onward then to battle move;
  More than conquerors ye shall prove;
  Though opposed by many a foe,
  Christian soldiers, onward go.
      H. Kirke White. 1806.
Completed by Frances S. Colquhoun. 1827.

575 S.M.
I have fought a good fight.—2 Timothy iv. 7.

'I THE good fight have fought,'
  O when shall I declare!
The victory by my Saviour got,
  I long with Paul to share.

2 O may I triumph so,
  When all my warfare's past;
  And, dying, find my latest foe
  Under my feet at last!

3 This blessèd word be mine,
  Just as the port is gained,
  'Kept by the power of grace divine,
  I have the faith maintained.'

4 The Apostles of my Lord,
  To whom it first was given,
  They could not speak a greater word,
  Nor all the saints in heaven.
      Charles Wesley. 1762.

576 L.M.
The Captain of their salvation.
Hebrews ii. 10.

JESUS, my King, to Thee I bow,
  Enlisted under Thy command;
Captain of my salvation, Thou
Shalt lead me to the promised land.

2 Thou hast a great deliverance wrought,
  The staff from off my shoulder broke,
  Out of the house of bondage brought,
  And freed me from the Egyptian yoke.

3 O'er the vast barren wilderness,
  To Canaan's bounds Thou hast me led;
  Thou bidd'st me now the land possess,
  And on Thy milk and honey feed.

4 I see an open door of hope,
  Legions of sin in vain oppose;
  Bold I with Thee, my Head, march up,
  And triumph o'er a world of foes.

5 My Lord in my behalf appears;
  Captain, Thy strength-inspiring eye
  Scatters my doubts, dispels my tears,
  And makes the host of aliens fly.

6 Who can before my Captain stand?
  Who is so great a King as mine?
  High over all is Thy right hand,
  And might and majesty are Thine!
      Wesley. 1742.

577 L.M.
They that wait upon the Lord shall renew their strength.
Isaiah xl. 31.

AWAKE, our souls! away, our fears!
  Let every trembling thought be gone;
Awake! and run the heavenly race,
And put a cheerful courage on.

2 True 'tis a strait and thorny road,
  And mortal spirits tire and faint;
  But they forget the mighty God
  That feeds the strength of every saint—

3 The mighty God, whose matchless power
  Is ever new and ever young;
  And firm endures, while endless years
  Their everlasting circles run.

4 From Thee, the ever-flowing Spring,
  Our souls shall drink a fresh supply;
  While such as trust their native strength
  Shall melt away, and droop, and die.

5 Swift as the eagle cuts the air,
  We'll mount aloft to Thine abode;
  On wings of love our souls shall fly,
  Nor tire, while on the heavenly road.
      Isaac Watts. 1709.

THE CHRISTIAN LIFE.

578   8.8.8.8.8.8.
The faith which was once delivered unto the saints. —Jude 3.

FAITH of our fathers, living still
  In spite of dungeon, fire, and sword:
O how our hearts beat high with joy
  Whene'er we hear that glorious word,
Faith of our fathers! holy faith!
We will be true to thee till death.

2 Our fathers, chained in prisons dark,
  Were still in heart and conscience free:
How sweet would be their children's fate,
  If they, like them, could die for thee!
Faith of our fathers! holy faith!
We will be true to thee till death.

3 Faith of our fathers; God's great power
  Shall soon all nations win for thee;
And through the truth that comes from God,
  Mankind shall then indeed be free.
Faith of our fathers! holy faith!
We will be true to thee till death.

4 Faith of our fathers, we will love
  Both friend and foe in all our strife:
And preach thee too, as love knows how,
  By kindly words and virtuous life:
Faith of our fathers! holy faith!
We will be true to thee till death.
            F. W. Faber. 1862.

579   S.M.
There shall no evil befall thee.
Psalm xci. 10.

AWAY, my needless fears,
  And doubts no longer mine;
A ray of heavenly light appears,
  A messenger divine.

2 Thrice comfortable hope,
  That calms my stormy breast;
My Father's hand prepares the cup,
  And what He wills is best.

3 If what I wish is good,
  And suits the will divine;
By earth and hell in vain withstood,
  I know it shall be mine.

4 Still let them counsel take
  To frustrate His decree;
They cannot keep a blessing back,
  By Heaven designed for me.

5 Here then I doubt no more,
  But in His pleasure rest,
Whose wisdom, love, and truth, and power
  Engage to make me blest.

6 To accomplish His design
  The creatures all agree;
And all the attributes divine
  Are now at work for me.
            Charles Wesley. 1749.

580   7.6.7.6.7.7.7.6.
The Eternal God is thy Refuge. —Deut. xxxiii. 27.

NONE is like Jeshurun's God,
  So great, so strong, so high,
Lo! He spreads His wings abroad,
  He rides upon the sky.
Israel is His first-born son;
God, the Almighty God, is thine;
See Him to thy help come down,
  The excellence divine.

2 Thee, the great Jehovah deigns
  To succour and defend;
Thee, the Eternal God sustains,
  Thy Maker and thy Friend:
Israel, what hast thou to dread?
Safe from all impending harms,
Round thee and beneath are spread
  The Everlasting Arms.

3 God is thine; disdain to fear
  The enemy within;
God shall in thy flesh appear,
  And make an end of sin;
God the man of sin shall slay,
Fill thee with triumphant joy;
God shall thrust him out, and say,
  'Destroy them all, destroy!'

4 All the struggle then is o'er,
  And wars and fightings cease,
Israel then shall sin no more,
  But dwell in perfect peace;
All his enemies are gone;
Sin shall have in him no part;
Israel now shall dwell alone,
  With Jesus in his heart.

5 Blest, O Israel, art thou;
  What people is like thee?
Saved from sin, by Jesus, now
  Thou art, and still shalt be;
Jesus is thy seven-fold shield,
Jesus is thy flaming sword;
Earth, and hell, and sin, shall yield
  To God's almighty word.
            Wesley. 1742.

581   8.8.8.8.8.8.
He that believeth on Him is not condemned. —John iii. 18.

SURROUNDED by a host of foes,
  Stormed by a host of foes within,
Nor swift to flee, nor strong to oppose,
  Single against hell, earth, and sin,
Single, yet undismayed, I am;
I dare believe in Jesu's name.

2 What though a thousand hosts engage,
  A thousand worlds, my soul to shake?
I have a shield shall quell their rage,
  And drive the alien armies back;
Portrayed it bears a bleeding Lamb;
I dare believe in Jesu's name.

CONFLICT AND COURAGE.

3 Me to retrieve from Satan's hands,
  Me from this evil world to free,
To purge my sins, and loose my bands,
  And save from all iniquity,
My Lord and God from heaven He came;
I dare believe in Jesu's name.

4 Salvation in His name there is,
  Salvation from sin, death, and hell,
Salvation into glorious bliss,
  How great salvation, who can tell!
But all He hath for mine I claim;
I dare believe in Jesu's name.
                    Charles Wesley. 1749.

582   7.6. 7.6. 7.8. 7.6.
  *By grace are ye saved
  through faith.*—Ephesians ii. 8.

SON of God, if Thy free grace
  Again hath raised me up,
Called me still to seek Thy face,
  And given me back my hope;
Still Thy timely help afford,
And all Thy loving-kindness show:
Keep me, keep me, gracious Lord,
  And never let me go!

2 By me, O my Saviour, stand,
  In sore temptation's hour,
Save me with Thine outstretched hand,
  And show forth all Thy power;
O be mindful of Thy word,
Thy all-sufficient grace bestow:
Keep me, keep me, gracious Lord,
  And never let me go!

3 Give me, Lord, a holy fear,
  And fix it in my heart,
That I may from evil near
  With timely care depart;
Sin be more than hell abhorred,
Till Thou destroy the tyrant foe:
Keep me, keep me, gracious Lord,
  And never let me go!

4 Never let me leave Thy breast,
  From Thee, my Saviour, stray;
Thou art my Support and Rest,
  My true and living Way;
My exceeding great Reward,
In heaven above, and earth below:
Keep me, keep me, gracious Lord,
  And never let me go! Amen.
                    Wesley. 1742.

583   S.M.
  *They that trust in the Lord
  shall be as Mount Zion.*—Psalm cxxv. 1.

WHO in the Lord confide,
  And feel His sprinkled blood,
In storms and hurricanes abide,
  Firm as the mount of God.

2 Steadfast, and fixed, and sure,
  His Sion cannot move;
His faithful people stand secure
  In Jesu's guardian love.

3 As round Jerusalem
  The hilly bulwarks rise,
So God protects and covers them
  From all their enemies.

4 On every side He stands,
  And for His Israel cares;
And safe in His almighty hands
  Their souls for ever bears.

5 But let them still abide
  In Thee, all-gracious Lord,
Till every soul is sanctified,
  And perfectly restored.

6 The men of heart sincere
  Continue to defend;
And do them good, and save them here,
  And love them to the end. Amen.
                    Wesley. 1743.

584   6.4. 6.4.
  *Destitute, afflicted, tormented:
  of whom the world was not worthy.*
  Hebrews xi. 37, 38.

THEIR names are names of kings
  Of heavenly line;
The bliss of earthly things
  They did resign.

2 Chieftains they were, who warred
  With sword and shield;
Victors for God the Lord
  On foughten field.

3 Sad were their days on earth,
  'Mid hate and scorn,
A life of pleasure's dearth,
  A death forlorn;

4 Yet blest that end in woe,
  And those sad days;
Only man's blame below;
  Above—God's praise.

5 A city of great name
  Is built for them,
Of glorious golden fame—
  Jerusalem!

6 Redeemed with precious blood
  From death and sin,
Sons of the Triune God,
  They enter in.

7 So doth the life of pain
  In glory close;
Lord God, may we attain
  Their grand repose! Amen.
                    Samuel J. Stone. 1865.

THE CHRISTIAN LIFE.

585 C.M.
Clouds and darkness are round about Him: righteousness and judgment are the habitation of His throne.
Psalm xcvii. 2.

O IT is hard to work for God,
  To rise and take His part
Upon this battle-field of earth,
  And not sometimes lose heart!

2 He hides Himself so wondrously,
  As though there were no God;
He is least seen when all the powers
  Of ill are most abroad.

3 Or He deserts us at the hour
  The fight is all but lost;
And seems to leave us to ourselves
  Just when we need Him most.

4 It is not so, but so it looks;
  And we lose courage then;
And doubts will come if God hath kept
  His promises to men.

5 Ah! God is other than we think;
  His ways are far above,
Far beyond reason's height, and reached
  Only by childlike love.

6 Thrice blest is he to whom is given
  The instinct that can tell
That God is on the field when He
  Is most invisible.

7 For right is right, since God is God;
  And right the day must win;
To doubt would be disloyalty,
  To falter would be sin.
    F. W. Faber. 1862.

586 C.M.
Without Me ye can do nothing.
John xv. 5.

THE Galilean fishers toil
  All night, and nothing take;
But Jesus comes—a wondrous spoil
  Is lifted from the lake;

2 Lord, when our labours are in vain,
  And vain the help of man,
When fruitless is our care and pain,
  Come, blessèd Jesus, then!

3 The night is dark, the surges fill
  The bark, the wild winds roar;
But Jesus comes; and all is still—
  The ship is at the shore;

4 O Lord, when storms around us howl,
  And all is dark and drear,
In all the tempests of the soul,
  O blessèd Jesus, hear!

5 A frail one, thrice denying Thee,
  Saw mercy in Thine eyes;
The penitent upon the tree
  Was borne to Paradise;

6 In hours of sin and deep distress,
  O show us, Lord, Thy face!
In penitential loneliness,
  O give us, Jesus, grace!

7 The faithful few retire in fear,
  To their closed upper room;
But suddenly, with joyful cheer,
  They see their Master come;

8 Lord, come to us, unloose our bands,
  And bid our terrors cease;
Lift over us Thy blessèd hands,
  Speak, holy Jesus, peace!

9 In days when faith will scarce be found,
  And wolves be in the fold,
When sin and sorrow will abound,
  And charity wax cold;

10 Then hear Thy saints, who to Thee pray
  To bring them to their home;
Hear, when the Bride and Spirit say,
  'Come, blessèd Jesus, come!' Amen.
    Bishop C. Wordsworth. 1862.

WATCHFULNESS AND STEADFASTNESS.

587 6.4. 6.4. 6.7. 6.4.
Continue in prayer, and watch in the same with thanksgiving.
Colossians iv. 2.

HARK! 'tis the watchman's cry,
  Wake, brethren, wake!
Jesus our Lord is nigh;
  Wake, brethren, wake!
Sleep is for sons of night;
Ye are children of the light;
Yours is the glory bright:
  Wake, brethren, wake!

2 Call to each waking band,
  Watch, brethren, watch!
Clear is our Lord's command,
  Watch, brethren, watch!
Be ye as men that wait
Always at the Master's gate,
E'en though He tarry late:
  Watch, brethren, watch!

3 Heed we the Master's call,
  Work, brethren, work!
There's room enough for all;
  Work, brethren, work!
This vineyard of the Lord
Constant labour will afford;
Yours is a sure reward:
  Work, brethren, work!

4 Hear we the Saviour's voice,
  Pray, brethren, pray!
Would ye His heart rejoice?
  Pray, brethren, pray!

WATCHFULNESS AND STEADFASTNESS.

Sin calls for constant fear;
Weakness needs the strong One near;
Long as ye struggle here,
Pray, brethren, pray!

5 Sound now the final chord,
  Praise, brethren, praise!
Thrice holy is our Lord,
  Praise, brethren, praise!
What more befits the tongues,
Soon to join the angels' songs,
While heaven the note prolongs?
  Praise, brethren, praise!
                    Anon. 1859.

588   *Keep the charge of the Lord,*   S.M.
that ye die not.—Leviticus viii. 35.

A CHARGE to keep I have,
    A God to glorify,
A never-dying soul to save,
  And fit it for the sky.

2 To serve the present age,
    My calling to fulfil;
O may it all my powers engage
  To do my Master's will!

3 Arm me with jealous care,
    As in Thy sight to live;
And O! Thy servant, Lord, prepare
  A strict account to give.

4 Help me to watch and pray,
    And on Thyself rely,
Assured, if I my trust betray,
  I shall for ever die.
              Charles Wesley. 1762.

589   *Ye are the salt of the earth.*   L.M.
        Matthew v. 13.

AH, Lord! with trembling I confess,
  A gracious soul may fall from grace:
The salt may lose its seasoning power,
And never, never find it more.

2 Lest this my fearful case should be,
Each moment knit my soul to Thee;
And lead me to the mount above,
Through the low vale of humble love.
                                Amen.
              Charles Wesley. 1762.

590   S.8.8.8.8.8.
  *Walk in the fear of our
God, because of the reproach of the heathen.*
          Nehemiah v. 9.

WATCHED by the world's malignant eye,
  Who load us with reproach and shame,
As servants of the Lord Most High,
  As zealous for His glorious name,
We ought in all His paths to move,
With holy fear and humble love.

2 That wisdom, Lord, on us bestow,
  From every evil to depart;
To stop the mouth of every foe,
  While, upright both in life and heart,
The proofs of godly fear we give,
And show them how the Christians live.
                                Amen.
              Charles Wesley. 1762.

591   8.8.6. 8.8.6.
  *The fear of the Lord,
that is wisdom.*—Job xxviii. 28.

BE it my only wisdom here,
   To serve the Lord with filial fear,
    With loving gratitude;
Superior sense may I display,
By shunning every evil way,
    And walking in the good.

2 O may I still from sin depart!
  A wise and understanding heart,
    Jesus, to me be given;
And let me through Thy Spirit know,
To glorify my God below,
    And find my way to heaven. Amen.
              Charles Wesley. 1762.

592   7.7.7.3.
        Watch and pray.
        Mark xiii. 33.

CHRISTIAN! seek not yet repose,
  Cast thy dreams of ease away,
Thou art in the midst of foes;
            Watch and pray.

2 Principalities and powers,
  Mustering their unseen array,
Wait for thy unguarded hours;
            Watch and pray.

3 Gird thy heavenly armour on,
  Wear it ever night and day,
Ambushed lies the evil one;
            Watch and pray.

4 Hear the victors who o'ercame;
  Still they mark each warrior's way;
All with one sweet voice exclaim,
            Watch and pray.

5 Hear, above all, hear thy Lord,
  Him thou lovest to obey;
Hide within thy heart His word,
            Watch and pray.

6 Watch, as if on that alone,
  Hung the issue of the day;
Pray that help may be sent down;
            Watch and pray.
              Charlotte Elliott. 1859.

593   S.M.
  *Awake, thou that sleepest
... and Christ shall give thee light.*
        Ephesians v. 14.

GRACIOUS Redeemer! shake
   This slumber from my soul;
Say to me now, 'Awake, awake!
  And Christ shall make thee whole.

THE CHRISTIAN LIFE.

2 Lay to Thy mighty hand;
   Alarm me in this hour,
And make me fully understand
   The thunder of Thy power.

3 Give me on Thee to call,
   Always to watch and pray,
Lest I into temptation fall,
   And cast my shield away.

4 For each assault prepared
   And ready may I be,
For ever standing on my guard,
   And looking up to Thee.

5 O do Thou always warn
   My soul of evil near!
When to the right or left I turn,
   Thy voice still let me hear:

6 'Come back! this is the way,
   Come back! and walk herein:
O may I hearken and obey,
   And shun the paths of sin!

7 Myself I cannot save,
   Myself I cannot keep,
But strength in Thee I surely have,
   Whose eyelids never sleep:

8 My soul to Thee alone
   Now therefore I commend;
Thou, Jesus, love me as Thy own,
   And love me to the end. Amen.
                Charles Wesley. 1749.

594   *Keep me as the apple of the eye.*   L.M.
         Psalm xvii. 8.

PIERCE, fill me with a humble fear;
   My utter helplessness reveal!
Satan and sin are always near,
   Thee may I always nearer feel.

2 O that to Thee my constant mind
   Might with an even flame aspire,
Pride in its earliest motions find,
   And mark the risings of desire!

3 O that my tender soul might fly
   The first abhorred approach of ill;
Quick, as the apple of an eye,
   The slightest touch of sin to feel!

4 Till Thou anew my soul create,
   Still may I strive, and watch, and pray,
Humbly and confidently wait,
   And long to see the perfect day. Amen.
                    Wesley. 1742.

595   *God whom I serve ...*   C.M.
with pure conscience.—2 Timothy i. 3.

I WANT a principle within,
   Of jealous, godly fear,
A sensibility of sin,
   A pain to feel it near.

2 I want the first approach to feel
   Of pride, or fond desire;
To catch the wandering of my will,
   And quench the kindling fire.

3 That I from Thee no more may part,
   No more Thy goodness grieve,
The filial awe, the fleshly heart,
   The tender conscience, give.

4 Quick as the apple of an eye,
   O God, my conscience make!
Awake my soul, when sin is nigh,
   And keep it still awake.

5 If to the right or left I stray,
   That moment, Lord, reprove;
And let me weep my life away,
   For having grieved Thy love.

6 O may the least omission pain
   My well-instructed soul,
And drive me to the blood again,
   Which makes the wounded whole!
                          Amen.
                Charles Wesley. 1749.

596   *The Lord hear thee in*   8.8.6.8.8.6.
the day of trouble.—Psalm xx. 1.

HELP, Lord, to whom for help I fly,
   And still my tempted soul stand by,
      Throughout the evil day;
The sacred watchfulness impart,
And keep the issues of my heart,
      And stir me up to pray.

2 My soul with Thy whole armour arm;
   In each approach of sin alarm,
      And show the danger near;
Surround, sustain, and strengthen me,
And fill with godly jealousy,
      And sanctifying fear.

3 Whene'er my careless hands hang down,
   O let me see Thy gathering frown,
      And feel Thy warning eye;
And starting, cry, from ruin's brink,
Save, Jesus, or I yield, I sink,
      O save me, or I die!

4 If near the pit I rashly stray,
   Before I wholly fall away,
      The keen conviction dart;
Recall me by that pitying look,
That kind, upbraiding glance, which broke
      Unfaithful Peter's heart.

5 In me Thine utmost mercy show,
   And make me like Thyself below,
      Unblamable in grace;
Ready prepared, and fitted here,
By perfect holiness to appear
      Before Thy glorious face. Amen.
                Charles Wesley. 1749.

WATCHFULNESS AND STEADFASTNESS.

597   S.M.D.
*Let this mind be in you,
which was also in Christ Jesus.—*Phil. ii. 5.

JESUS, my strength, my hope,
  On Thee I cast my care,
With humble confidence look up,
  And know Thou hear'st my prayer,
Give me on Thee to wait,
  Till I can all things do,
On Thee, almighty to create,
  Almighty to renew.

2 I want a sober mind,
  A self-renouncing will,
That tramples down and casts behind
  The baits of pleasing ill;
A soul inured to pain,
  To hardship, grief, and loss,
Bold to take up, firm to sustain
  The consecrated cross.

3 I want a godly fear,
  A quick discerning eye,
That looks to Thee when sin is near,
  And sees the Tempter fly;
A spirit still prepared,
  And armed with jealous care,
For ever standing on its guard,
  And watching unto prayer.

4 I want a heart to pray,
  To pray and never cease,
Never to murmur at Thy stay,
  Or wish my sufferings less.
This blessing, above all,
  Always to pray, I want,
Out of the deep on Thee to call,
  And never, never faint.

5 I rest upon Thy word;
  The promise is for me;
My succour and salvation, Lord,
  Shall surely come from Thee;
But let me still abide,
  Nor from my hope remove,
Till Thou my patient spirit guide
  Into Thy perfect love. Amen.
                Wesley. 1742.

598   8.7. 8.7. 7.7.
*Neither shall any pluck
them out of My hand.—*John x. 28.

CLOUDS and darkness round about
    Thee
For a season veil Thy face,
Still I trust, and cannot doubt Thee,
  Jesus, full of truth and grace;
Resting on Thy words I stand,
None shall pluck me from Thy hand.

2 O, rebuke me not in anger!
  Suffer not my faith to fail;
Let not pain, temptation, languor,
  O'er my struggling heart prevail:
Holding fast Thy word I stand,
None shall pluck me from Thy hand.

3 In my heart Thy words I cherish,
  Though unseen Thou still art near
Since Thy sheep shall never perish,
  What have I to do with fear?
Trusting in Thy word I stand,
None shall pluck me from Thy hand.
            Charlotte Elliott. 1834.

599   7.7. 7.7. 7.7.
*He restoreth my soul: He
leadeth me in the paths of righteousness for
His name's sake.—*Psalm xxiii. 3.

JESUS, Shepherd of the sheep,
  Pity my unsettled soul;
Guide, and nourish me, and keep,
  Till Thy love shall make me whole;
Give me perfect soundness, give,
Make me steadfastly believe.

2 I am never at one stay,
  Changing every hour I am;
But Thou art as yesterday,
  Now and evermore the same;
Constancy to me impart,
Stablish with Thy grace my heart.

3 Lay Thy weighty cross on me,
  All my unbelief control;
Till the rebel cease to be,
  Keep him down within my soul;
That I never more may move,
Root and ground me fast in love.

4 Give me faith to hold me up,
  Walking over life's rough sea,
Holy, purifying hope,
  Still my soul's sure anchor be:
That I may be always Thine,
Perfect me in love divine. Amen.
            Charles Wesley. 1749.

600   L.M.
*This is the way, walk
ye in it.—*Isaiah xxx. 21.

JESUS, my Saviour, Brother, Friend,
On whom I cast my every care,
On whom for all things I depend,
Inspire, and then accept, my prayer.

2 If I have tasted of Thy grace,
  The grace that sure salvation brings,
If with me now Thy Spirit stays,
  And hovering hides me in His wings;

3 Still let Him with my weakness stay,
  Nor for a moment's space depart,
Evil and danger turn away,
  And keep till He renews my heart.

4 When to the right or left I stray,
  His voice behind me may I hear,
'Return, and walk, in Christ thy way;
  Fly back to Christ, for sin is near.'

5 Jesus, I fain would walk in Thee,
  From nature's every path retreat;
Thou art my Way, my Leader be,
  And set upon the rock my feet.

THE CHRISTIAN LIFE.

6 Uphold me, Saviour, or I fall;
   O reach me out Thy gracious hand!
Only on Thee for help I call;
   Only by faith in Thee I stand. Amen.
                            Wesley. 1742.

601   C.M.
Blessed shalt thou be when thou comest in, and . . . when thou goest out.
Deuteronomy xxviii. 6.

THOU, Lord, hast blest my going out;
   O bless my coming in!
Compass my weakness round about,
   And keep me safe from sin.

2 Still hide me in Thy secret place,
   Thy tabernacle spread;
Shelter me with preserving grace,
   And screen my naked head.

3 To Thee for refuge may I run
   From sin's alluring snare:
Ready its first approach to shun,
   And watching unto prayer.

4 O that I never, never more
   Might from Thy ways depart!
Here let me give my wanderings o'er,
   By giving Thee my heart.

5 Fix my new heart on things above,
   And then from earth release:
I ask not life, but let me love,
   And lay me down in peace. Amen.
                      Charles Wesley. 1740.

602   C.M.
Let us run with patience the race that is set before us, looking unto Jesus.
Hebrews xii. 1, 2.

BEHOLD what witnesses unseen
   Encompass us around!
Men once, like us, with suffering tried,
   But now with glory crowned.

2 Let us, with zeal like theirs inspired,
   Pursue the Christian race,
And, freed from each encumbering weight,
   Their holy footsteps trace.

3 Behold a Witness nobler still,
   Who trod affliction's path!
Jesus, at once the Finisher
   And Author of our faith.

4 He, for the joy before Him set,
   So generous was His love,
Endured the cross, despised the shame,
   And now He reigns above.

5 If He the scorn of wicked men
   With patience did sustain,
Becomes it those for whom He died
   To murmur or complain?

6 Then let our hearts no more despond,
   Our hands be weak no more;
Still let us trust our Father's love,
   His wisdom still adore.
      Anon. 1745. and W. Cameron. 1781.

DECLENSION AND RECOVERY.

603   C.M.
Enoch walked with God.
Genesis v. 22.

O FOR a closer walk with God,
   A calm and heavenly frame;
A light, to shine upon the road
   That leads me to the Lamb!

2 Where is the blessedness I knew
   When first I saw the Lord?
Where is the soul-refreshing view
   Of Jesus and His word?

3 What peaceful hours I once enjoyed!
   How sweet their memory still!
But they have left an aching void
   The world can never fill.

4 Return, O holy Dove, return,
   Sweet messenger of rest!
I hate the sins that made Thee mourn,
   That drove Thee from my breast.

5 The dearest idol I have known,
   Whate'er that idol be,
Help me to tear it from Thy throne,
   And worship only Thee.

6 So shall my walk be close with God;
   Calm and serene my frame;
So purer light shall mark the road
   That leads me to the Lamb.
                    William Cowper. 1772.

604   C.M.
Return unto Me, and I will return unto you.—Malachi iii. 7.

WILT Thou return to me, O Lord,
   If I return to Thee?
O heavenly truth! O gracious word!
   My hope and refuge be.

2 Since from Thy side I dared to roam,
   My soul has found no rest;
Chastised and contrite, back I come,
   To seek it in Thy breast.

3 And dost Thou say Thou wilt receive,
   And call me still Thy own?
My spirit, hear, accept, believe,
   And melt, my heart of stone.

4 Again that gracious word to me,
   O speak that word again!
My guilt is pardoned—can it be?
   And loosed my every chain?

5 No, blessed Lord! not every chain,
   Not every bond, remove:
Let one, at least, unloosed remain,
   The bond of grateful love! Amen.
                              Anon.

DECLENSION AND RECOVERY.

605   7.7.7.7.
Behold, God is my salvation.
Isaiah xii. 2.

DROOPING soul, shake off thy fears,
Fearful **soul**, be strong, be bold ;
Tarry till the **Lord** appears,
Never, **never quit** thy hold !

2 Murmur not at His delay,
Dare not set thy God a time,
Calmly for His coming stay,
Leave it, leave it all to Him.

3 Every **one that** seeks shall find,
Every one that asks shall have
Christ, the Saviour of mankind,
Willing, able, all to save.

4 I shall His salvation see,
I in faith on Jesus call ;
I from sin shall **be** set free,
Perfectly **set free** from all.

5 Lord, my time is in Thine hand,
Weak and helpless as I am,
Surely Thou canst **make** me stand ;
I believe **in** Jesu's name :

6 Saviour in temptation Thou,
Thou hast saved me heretofore,
Thou from sin dost save me now,
Thou shalt save **me** evermore.
                     Wesley. 1742.

606   8.8. 8.8. 8.8.
There is forgiveness with Thee.
Psalm cxxx. 4.

O 'TIS enough, my God, my God !
Here let me give my wanderings o'er,
No longer trample on Thy blood,
And grieve Thy gentleness no more ;
No more Thy lingering anger move,
Or sin against Thy light and love.

2 O Lord, if mercy is with Thee,
Now let it all on me be shown ;
On me, the chief of sinners, me,
Who humbly for Thy mercy groan ;
Me to Thy Father's grace restore,
Nor let me ever grieve Thee more !

3 Fountain of unexhausted love,
Of infinite compassions, hear !
My Saviour and my Prince above,
Once more in my behalf appear ;
Repentance, faith, and pardon give,
O let me turn again and live ! Amen.
                     Wesley. 1741.

607   7.6. 7.6. 7.8. 7.6.
*I will heal their backsliding ;
I will love them freely.*—Hosea xiv. 4.

JESUS, Friend of sinners, hear,
Yet once again I pray ;
From my debt of sin set clear,
For I have nought to pay :
Speak, O speak **the** kind release,
A poor backsliding soul restore ;
Love me freely, seal **my** peace,
And bid **me sin no** more.

2 Though my sins as mountains rise,
And swell and reach to heaven,
Mercy is above the skies,
I may be still forgiven :
Infinite my sins' increase,
But greater is Thy mercy's store ;
Love me freely, seal my peace,
And bid me sin no more.

3 Sin's deceitfulness hath spread
A hardness o'er my heart ;
But if Thou **Thy** Spirit shed,
This **hardness shall** depart :
Shed **Thy love, Thy** tenderness,
And let me feel **Thy** softening power ;
Love me freely, seal my peace,
And bid **me** sin no more.

4 For this only thing I pray,
And this will I require,
Take the power of sin away,
Fill me with chaste desire :
Perfect me in holiness,
Thine image to **my soul restore** ;
Love me freely, seal my peace,
And bid me sin no more. Amen.
                     Wesley. 1742.

608   C.M.
*As the hart panteth after
the water-brooks, so panteth my soul after
Thee, O God.*—Psalm xlii. 1.

AS pants the hart for cooling streams,
When heated in the chase,
So longs my soul, O God, for Thee,
And Thy **refreshing grace.**

2 For Thee, my God, the living God,
My thirsty soul doth pine :
O when shall I behold Thy face,
Thou Majesty divine?

3 I sigh whene'er my musing thoughts
Those happy days present,
When I, with troops of pious friends,
Thy temple did frequent :

4 When **I advanced, with songs of praise,**
My solemn vows to pay ;
And led **the joyful,** sacred throng
That **kept the festal** day

5 Why restless, **why** cast down, my soul ?
Hope still, and thou shalt sing
The praise of Him who is thy God,
Thy health's eternal spring.

6 To Father, Son, and Holy Ghost,
The God whom we adore,
Be glory, as it was, is now,
And shall be evermore. Amen.
                     Tate and Brady. 1696.

THE CHRISTIAN LIFE.

609 7.7. 7.7. 7.7.
Lord, save us: we perish.
Matthew viii. 25.

SAVIOUR, Prince of Israel's race!
See me from Thy lofty throne;
Give the sweet relenting grace,
Soften now this heart of stone,
Stone to flesh, O God, convert;
Cast a look, and break my heart.

2 By Thy Spirit, Lord, reprove,
All my inmost sins reveal;
Sins against Thy light and love,
Let me see, and let me feel;
Sins that crucified my God,
Spilt again Thy precious blood.

3 Jesus, seek Thy wandering sheep,
Make me restless to return;
Bid me look on Thee, and weep,
Bitterly as Peter mourn
Till I say, by grace restored,
'Now, Thou know'st I love Thee, Lord!'

4 Might I in Thy sight appear,
As the Publican distrest;
Stand, not daring to draw near,
Smite on my unworthy breast;
Groan the sinner's only plea,
'God, be merciful to me!'

5 O remember me for good,
Passing through the mortal vale;
Show me the atoning blood,
When my strength and spirit fail;
Give my gasping soul to see
Jesus crucified for me. Amen.
Charles Wesley. 1749.

610 8.8. 8.8. 8.8.
Where sin abounded, grace did much more abound.—Romans v. 20.

WEARY of wandering from my God,
And now made willing to return,
I hear, and bow me to the rod;
For Thee, not without hope, I mourn;
I have an Advocate above,
A Friend before the throne of love.

2 O Jesus, full of truth and grace,
More full of grace than I of sin;
Yet once again I seek Thy face;
Open Thine arms and take me in,
And freely my backslidings heal,
And love the faithless sinner still.

3 Thou know'st the way to bring me back,
My fallen spirit to restore;
O! for Thy truth and mercy's sake,
Forgive, and bid me sin no more;
The ruins of my soul repair,
And make my heart a house of prayer.

4 Give to mine eyes refreshing tears,
And kindle my relentings now;
Fill my whole soul with filial fears,
To Thy sweet yoke my spirit bow;
Bend by Thy grace, O bend or break,
The iron sinew in my neck.

5 Ah! give me, Lord, the tender heart,
That trembles at the approach of sin;
A godly fear of sin impart,
Implant, and root it deep within,
That I may dread Thy gracious power,
And never dare offend Thee more.
Amen.
Charles Wesley. 1749.

611 8.8. 8.8. 8.8.
Verily Thou art a God that hidest Thyself.—Isaiah xlv. 15.

THOU God unsearchable, unknown,
Who still conceal'st Thyself from me,
Hear an apostate spirit groan,
Broke off, and banished far from Thee;
But conscious of my fall I mourn,
And fain I would to Thee return.

2 Send forth one ray of heavenly light,
Of gospel hope, of humble fear,
To guide me through the gulf of night,
My poor desponding soul to cheer,
Till Thou my unbelief remove,
And show me all Thy glorious love.

3 A hidden God indeed Thou art;
Thy absence I this moment feel;
Yet must I own it from my heart,
Concealed, Thou art a Saviour still;
And though Thy face I cannot see,
I know Thine eye is fixed on me.

4 My Saviour Thou, not yet revealed,
Yet will I Thee my Saviour call,
Adore Thy hand, from sin withheld;
Thy hand shall save me from my fall:
Now, Lord, throughout my darkness shine,
And show Thyself for ever mine. Amen.
Charles Wesley. 1762.

612 L.M.
Lord, that I may receive my sight.—Luke xviii. 41.

WHEN, gracious Lord, when shall it be
That I shall find my all in Thee?
The fulness of Thy promise prove;
The seal of Thine eternal Love?

2 Thee, only Thee, I fain would find,
And cast the world and flesh behind;
Thou, only Thou, to me be given,
Of all Thou hast in earth or heaven.

3 Whom man forsakes Thou wilt not leave,
Ready the outcast to receive;
Though all my sinfulness I own,
And all my faults to Thee are known.

4 Ah, wherefore did I ever doubt!
Thou wilt in nowise cast me out,
A helpless soul that comes to Thee,
With only sin and misery.

5 Lord, I am sick,—my sickness cure;
I want,—do Thou enrich the poor;
Under Thy mighty hand I stoop,
O lift the abject sinner up!

HUMILITY.

6 Lord, I am blind,—be Thou my sight ;
  Lord, I am weak,—be Thou my might ;
  A helper to the helpless be,
  And let me find my all in Thee. Amen.
  Wesley. 1742.

613 L.M.
*They rebelled, and vexed
His Holy Spirit.*—Isaiah lxiii. 10.

STAY, Thou insulted Spirit, stay,
  Though I have done Thee such despite,
  Nor cast the sinner quite away,
  Nor take Thine everlasting flight.

2 Though I have steeled my stubborn heart,
  And still shook off my guilty fears,
  And vexed, and urged Thee to depart,
  For many long rebellious years :

3 Though I have most unfaithful been,
  Of all whoe'er Thy grace received ;
  Ten thousand times Thy goodness seen,
  Ten thousand times Thy goodness grieved

4 Yet, O! the chief of sinners spare,
  In honour of my great High Priest ;
  Nor in Thy righteous anger swear
  To exclude me from Thy people's rest.

5 Now, Lord, my weary soul release,
  Upraise me with Thy gracious hand,
  And guide into Thy perfect peace,
  And bring me to the promised land.
                               Amen.
       Charles Wesley. 1749.

HUMILITY.

614 C.M.
*I dwell in the high and
holy place, with him also that is of a contrite
and humble spirit.*—Isaiah lvii. 15.

THY home is with the humble, Lord !
  The simplest are the best :
  Thy lodging is in child-like hearts ;
  Thou makest there Thy rest.

2 Dear Comforter ! Eternal Love !
  If Thou wilt stay with me,
  Of lowly thoughts and simple ways
  I'll build a house for Thee.

3 Thy sweetness hath betrayed Thee, Lord !
  Great Spirit ! It is Thou !
  Deeper and deeper in my heart
  I feel Thee resting now.

4 Who made this beating heart of mine
  But Thou, my heavenly Guest ?
  Let no one have it then, but Thee,
  And let it be Thy rest. Amen.
       F. W. Faber. 1862.

615 8.6. 8.4.
I flee unto Thee to hide me.
Psalm cxliii. 9.

SHOW me myself, O holy Lord ;
  Help me to look within ;
  I will not turn me from the sight
  Of all my sin.

2 Just as it is in Thy pure eyes
  Would I behold my heart,
  Bring every hidden spot to light,
  Nor shrink the smart.

3 Not mine, the purity of heart
  That shall at last see God ;
  Not mine, the following in the steps
  The Saviour trod :

4 Not mine, the life I thought to live
  When first I took His name ;
  Mine, but the right to weep and grieve
  Over my shame.

5 Yet, Lord ; I thank Thee for the sight
  Thou hast vouchsafed to me ;
  And humbled to the dust, I shrink
  Closer to Thee.

6 Unworthy, faithless as it is,
  O let my spirit hide
  Its weakness and its penitence
  In Thy dear side !

7 And if Thy love will not disown
  So frail a heart as mine,
  Chasten and cleanse it as Thou wilt,
  But keep it Thine. Amen.
                          Anon.

616 7.7. 7.7.
*He will be very gracious
unto thee at the voice of thy cry.*
Isaiah xxx. 19.

LORD, that I may learn of Thee,
  Give me true simplicity ;
  Wean my soul, and keep it low,
  Willing Thee alone to know.

2 Let me cast my reeds aside,
  All that feeds my knowing pride ;
  Not to man, but God submit,
  Lay my reasonings at Thy feet.

3 Of my boasted wisdom spoiled,
  Docile, helpless as a child ;
  Only seeing in Thy light,
  Only walking in Thy might.

4 Then infuse the teaching grace,
  Spirit of truth and righteousness ;
  Knowledge, love divine, impart,
  Life eternal, to my heart. Amen.
       Charles Wesley. 1762.

171

THE CHRISTIAN LIFE.

617 C.M.
Blessed are the poor in spirit: for theirs is the kingdom of heaven.
Matthew v. 3.

OUR Father, hear our longing prayer,
And help this prayer to flow,
That humble thoughts, which are Thy care,
May live in us and grow.

2 For lowly hearts shall understand
The peace, the calm delight
Of dwelling in Thy heavenly land,
A pleasure in Thy sight.

3 Give us humility, that so
Thy reign may come within,
And when Thy children homeward go,
We too may enter in.

4 Hear us, our Saviour! ours Thou art,
Though we are not like Thee;
Give us Thy Spirit in a heart
Large, lowly, trusting, free.   Amen.
George Macdonald. 1851.

618 5.4. 5.4. D.
Christ is all, and in all.
Colossians iii. 11.

REST of the weary,
  Joy of the sad,
Hope of the dreary,
  Light of the glad,
Home of the stranger,
  Strength to the end,
Refuge from danger,
  Saviour and Friend!

2 Bosom where lying,
  Love rests its head;
Peace of the dying,
  Life of the dead,
Path of the lowly,
  Prize at the end,
Breath of the holy,
  Saviour and Friend!

3 When my feet stumble,
  I to Thee cry;
Crown of the humble,
  Cross of the high:
When my steps wander
  Over me bend,
Truer and fonder,
  Saviour and Friend!

4 Ever confessing
  Thee, I will raise
Unto Thee blessing,
  Glory, and praise;
All my endeavour,
  World without end,
Thine to be ever,
  Saviour and Friend!   Amen.
J. S. B. Monsell. 1857.

619 7.7.7.7.
Be clothed with humility.
1 Peter v. 5.

LORD, if Thou Thy grace impart,
Poor in spirit, meek in heart,
I shall as my Master be
Rooted in humility.

2 Simple, teachable, and mild,
Humble as a little child,
Pleased with what the Lord provides,
Weaned from all the world besides.

3 Father, fix our souls on Thee,
Every evil let us flee,
Always happy in Thy love,
Looking for our rest above.

4 O that all might seek and find
Every good in Christ combined!
O that all might Him adore,
Trust Him, praise Him evermore!
             Amen.
Wesley. 1741.

620 C.M.
One thing is needful: and Mary hath chosen that good part, which shall not be taken away from her.—Luke x. 42.

AS Jesus sought His wandering sheep,
  With weary toil opprest,
He came to Martha's lowly roof,
  A loved and honoured guest.

2 Blessèd art thou, whose threshold poor
  Those holy feet have trod,
To wait on so divine a Guest,
  And to receive thy God!

3 While Martha serves with busy feet,
  In reverential mood,
Meek Mary sits beside the Judge,
  And feeds on heavenly food.

4 Yea, Martha soon herself shall sit,
  The eternal word to hear,
And shall forget the festal board,
  To feast on holier cheer.

5 Sole rest of all who come to Thee,
  O'er all our works preside,
That we may have in Thee at last
  The part that shall abide.   Amen.
From the Latin. 1686.
Tr. Isaac Williams. 1839.

PRAYER.
(See also Prayer-Meetings.)

621 7.7.7.7
I will therefore that men pray everywhere.—1 Timothy ii. 8.

COME, my soul, thy suit prepare,
Jesus loves to answer prayer;
He Himself has bid thee pray,
Therefore will not say thee, nay.

PRAYER.

2 Thou art coming to a King,
Large petitions with thee bring;
For His grace and power are such,
None can ever ask too much.

3 With my burden I begin,
Lord, remove this load of sin;
Let Thy blood, for sinners spilt,
Set my conscience free from guilt.

4 Lord, I come to Thee for rest,
Take possession of my breast;
There Thy blood-bought right maintain,
And without a rival reign.

5 While I am a pilgrim here,
Let Thy love my spirit cheer;
As my Guide, my Guard, my Friend,
Lead me to my journey's end.

6 Show me what I have to do,
Every hour my strength renew;
Let me live a life of faith,
Let me die Thy people's death. Amen.
John Newton. 1779.

622 C.M.
*If we confess our sins,
He is faithful and just to forgive us our sins.*
1 John i. 9.

LORD, when we bend before Thy throne,
And our confessions pour,
Teach us to feel the sins we own,
And hate what we deplore.

2 Our broken spirit pitying see;
True penitence impart;
Then let a kindling glance from Thee
Beam hope upon the heart.

3 When we disclose our wants in prayer,
May we our wills resign;
Let not a thought our bosoms share,
Which is not wholly Thine.

4 May faith each weak petition fill,
And waft it to the skies,
And teach our hearts 'tis goodness still
That grants it or denies. Amen.
Joseph D. Carlyle. 1802.

623 S.M.
*Thou desirest truth in
the inward parts.*—Psalm li. 6.

HELP me, my God, to speak
True words to Thee each day;
True let my voice be when I praise,
And trustful when I pray.

2 Thy words are true to me;
Let mine to Thee be true,
The speech of my whole heart and soul,
However low and few;

3 True words of grief for sin,
Of longing to be free,
Of groaning for deliverance,
And likeness, Lord, to Thee;

4 True words of faith and hope,
Of godly joy and grief;
Lord, I believe, O hear my cry,
Help Thou my unbelief. Amen.
Horatius Bonar. 1857.

624 C.M.
*Unto Thee lift I up mine
eyes.*—Psalm cxxiii. 1.

I WOULD commune with Thee, my God,
E'en to Thy seat I come;
I leave my joys, I leave my sins,
And seek in Thee my home.

2 I stand upon the mount of God,
With sunlight in my soul;
I hear the storms in vales beneath,
I hear the thunders roll.

3 But I am calm with Thee, my God,
Beneath these glorious skies;
And to the height on which I stand
Nor storms nor clouds can rise.

4 O this is life! O this is joy!
My God, to find Thee so!
Thy face to see, Thy voice to hear,
And all Thy love to know?
G. B. Bubier. 1854.

625 8.8.8.8. 8.8.
*The Spirit also helpeth
our infirmities.*—Romans viii. 26.

JESUS, Thou sovereign Lord of all,
The same through one eternal day,
Attend Thy feeblest followers call,
And O instruct us how to pray!
Pour out the supplicating grace,
And stir us up to seek Thy face.

2 We cannot think a gracious thought,
We cannot feel a good desire,
Till Thou, who call'dst a world from nought,
The power into our hearts inspire;
And then we in Thy Spirit groan,
And then we give Thee back Thine own.

3 Jesus, regard the joint complaint
Of all Thy tempted followers here;
And now supply the common want,
And send us down the Comforter;
The spirit of ceaseless prayer impart,
And fix Thy Agent in our heart.

4 To help our soul's infirmity,
To heal Thy sin-sick people's care,
To urge our God-commanding plea,
And make our hearts a house of prayer,
The promised Intercessor give,
And let us now Thyself receive.

5 Come in Thy pleading Spirit down,
To us who for Thy coming stay;
Of all Thy gifts we ask but one,
We ask the constant power to pray;
Indulge us, Lord, in this request,
Thou canst not then deny the rest. Amen.
Charles Wesley. 1742.

THE CHRISTIAN LIFE.

626   *The hour of prayer.*   8.8.8.4.
Acts iii. 1.

MY God, is any hour so sweet,
  From blush of morn to evening star,
As that which calls me to Thy feet,
    The hour of prayer?

2 Blest is that tranquil hour of morn,
  And blest that solemn hour of eve,
When, on the wings of prayer upborne,
    The world I leave.

3 For then a Day-spring shines on me,
  Brighter than morn's ethereal glow;
And richer dews descend from Thee
    Than earth can know.

4 Then is my strength by Thee renewed;
  Then are my sins by Thee forgiven;
Then dost Thou cheer my solitude
    With hope of heaven.

5 No words can tell what sweet relief
  Here for my every want I find,
What strength for warfare, balm for grief!
    What peace of mind!

6 Hushed is each doubt, gone **every** fear,
  My spirit seems **in** heaven **to stay**;
And e'en the penitential tear
    Is wiped away.

7 Lord, till I reach yon blissful shore,
  No privilege so dear shall be,
As thus my inmost soul to pour
    In prayer to Thee.
         Charlotte Elliott.   1839.

---

627   *Praying always with all prayer.*—Eph. vi. 18.   C.M.

PRAYER is the soul's sincere desire,
  Uttered or unexpressed;
The motion of a hidden fire,
  That trembles in the breast.

2 Prayer is the burden of a sigh,
  The falling of a tear,
The upward glancing of the eye,
  When none but God is near.

3 Prayer is the simplest form of speech
  That infant lips can try;
Prayer the sublimest strains **that reach**
  The Majesty on high.

4 Prayer is the Christian's vital breath,
  The Christian's native air;
His watchword at the gates of death,
  He enters heaven with prayer.

5 Prayer is the contrite sinner's voice,
  Returning from his ways;
While angels in their songs rejoice,
  And cry, Behold, he prays!

6 The saints in prayer appear as one,
  In word, and deed, and mind;
While with the Father and the Son
  Their fellowship **they** find.

7 Nor prayer is made on earth **alone**,
  The Holy Spirit pleads;
And Jesus on the eternal throne
  For sinners intercedes.

8 O Thou by whom **we come** to God,
  The Life, the Truth, the Way,
The path of prayer Thyself hast trod;
  Lord, teach us how to pray! Amen.
         James Montgomery.   1819.

---

628   *Let us . . . come boldly unto the throne of grace.*—Heb. iv. 16.   C.M.

APPROACH, my soul, the mercy-seat,
  Where Jesus answers prayer;
There humbly fall before His feet,
  For none can perish there.

2 Thy promise is my only plea,
  With this I venture nigh;
Thou callest burdened souls to Thee,
  And such, O Lord, am I.

3 Bowed down beneath a load of sin,
  By sorrow sore opprest,
By war without, and fears within,
  I come to Thee for rest.

4 Be Thou my shield and hiding place,
  That, sheltered near Thy side,
I may my fierce accuser face,
  And tell him Thou hast died.

5 O, wondrous love! **to** bleed and **die**,
  To bear the cross and shame,
That guilty sinners, such as I,
  Might plead Thy gracious name.

6 'Poor tempest-tossed soul, be still,
  My promised grace receive;'
'Tis Jesus speaks, I must, I will,
  I can, I do believe.
         John Newton.   1779.

---

629   *I will never leave thee, nor forsake thee.*—Hebrews xiii. 5.   8.7.8.7.

LORD, we know that Thou art near us,
  Though Thou seem'st to hide Thy face;
And are sure that Thou dost hear us,
  Though no answer we embrace.

2 Not one promise shall miscarry;
  Not one blessing come too late;
Though the vision long may tarry,
  Give us patience, Lord, to wait.

3 While withholding, Thou art giving
  In Thine own appointed way;
And while waiting we're receiving
  Blessings suited to our day.

PRAYER.

4 O the wondrous loving-kindness,
   Planning, working out of sight!
   Bearing with us in our blindness,
   Out of darkness bringing light;

5 Weaving blessings out of trials,
   Out of grief evolving bliss;
   Answering prayer by wise denials
   When Thy children ask amiss.

6 And when **faith shall** end in vision,
   And when prayer is lost in praise;
   Then shall love, in full fruition,
   Justify Thy **secret** ways.
             Jane Crewdson. d. 1863.

630   *The cares of this world . . .* L.M.
     choke the word.—Mark iv. 19.

O GOD! who know'st how frail we are,
   How soon the thought of good departs;
We pray that Thou wouldst feed the fount
   Of holy yearning in our hearts.

2 Let not the choking cares of earth
   Their precious springs of life o'ergrow;
   But, ever guarded by Thy love,
   Still purer may their waters flow.

3 To Thee, with sweeter **hope** and trust,
   Be every day our **spirits** given;
   And may we, while **we** walk on earth,
   Walk more **as** citizens of heaven. Amen.
             W. Gaskell. d. 1884.

631   *Lord, help me.*—Matt. xv. 25. C.M.

O HELP us, Lord, each hour of need,
   Thy heavenly succour give;
Help us in thought and word and deed,
   Each hour, on earth, we live.

2 O help us, when our spirits bleed
   With contrite anguish sore;
   And when our hearts are cold and dead,
   O help us, Lord, the more.

3 O help us, through the prayer of faith,
   More firmly to believe;
   For still the more Thy servant hath,
   The more shall he receive.

4 O help us, Saviour, from on high,
   We know no help but Thee;
   O help us so to live and die,
   As Thine in Heaven to be. Amen.
             H. H. Milman. 1827.

632   *The mercy of the Lord is* C.M.
from everlasting to everlasting.—Ps. ciii. 17.

O LORD, turn not Thy face away
   From them that lowly lie,
Lamenting sore their sinful life,
   With tears and bitter cry.

2 Thy mercy-gates are open wide
   To them that mourn their sin;
   O shut them not **against us, Lord,**
   But let **us** enter in.

3 We need not to confess our fault,
   For surely Thou canst tell;
   What we have done, and what we are
   Thou knowest very well.

4 Wherefore, **to beg and** to entreat,
   With tears **we come to** Thee,
   As children that have done amiss
   Fall at their father's knee.

5 And need we then, O Lord, repeat
   The blessing which we crave,
   When Thou dost know, before we speak,
   The thing that we would have?

6 Mercy, O Lord, mercy we ask,
   This is the total sum;
   For mercy, Lord, is all our prayer;
   O let Thy mercy come! Amen.
             John Markant. 1560.
        Alt. by Bishop Heber. 1827.

633   *We ought also to love* L.M.
    one another.—1 John iv. 11.

O THOU, our Saviour, Brother, Friend,
   Behold a cloud of incense rise!
The prayers of saints to heaven ascend,
   Grateful, accepted sacrifice.

2 Regard our prayers for Sion's peace,
   Shed in our hearts Thy love abroad;
   Thy gifts abundantly increase;
   Enlarge, **and fill us** all with God.

3 Before Thy sheep, great Shepherd, go,
   And guide into Thy perfect will;
   Cause us Thy hallowed **name to** know,
   The **work** of faith **in us** fulfil.

4 Help us to make our calling sure;
   O let as all be **saints indeed,**
   And pure as Thou **Thyself art** pure,
   Conformed in **all things to** our Head.

5 Take the dear purchase **of Thy blood;**
   Thy blood shall wash us **white as snow;**
   Present us sanctified to God,
   And perfected in love below.

6 From all iniquity redeem,
   Cleanse **by the water and the word,**
   And free from **every spot** of blame,
   And make **the servant** as his Lord. Amen.
             Charles Wesley. 1749.

634   8.8. 8.8. 8.8.
   The Lord said unto Moses
  . . . Let Me alone.—Exodus xxxii. 9, 10.

O WONDROUS power of faithful prayer,
   What tongue can tell the almighty grace!
God's hands are bound or open are,
   As Moses or Elijah prays.
Let Moses in the spirit groan,
And God cries out, 'Let Me alone!

175

THE CHRISTIAN LIFE.

2 'Let Me alone, that all My wrath
    May rise the wicked to consume !
While justice hears thy praying faith,
    It cannot seal the sinner's doom ;
My Son is in My servant's prayer,
    And Jesus forces Me to spare.'

3 O blessèd word of gospel grace !
    Which now we for our Israel plead,
A faithless and backsliding race,
    Whom Thou hast out of Egypt freed :
O do not then in wrath chastise,
    Nor let Thy whole displeasure rise !

4 Father ! we ask in Jesu's name ;
    In Jesu's power and spirit pray ;
Divert Thy vengeful thunder's aim,
    O turn Thy threatening wrath away !
Our guilt and punishment remove,
    And magnify Thy pardoning love.

5 Father, regard Thy pleading Son !
    Accept His all-availing prayer,
And send a peaceful answer down,
    In honour of our Spokesman there ;
Whose blood proclaims our sins forgiven,
    And speaks Thy rebels up to heaven.
              Amen.
             Wesley. 1747.

635   C.M.
We have not an High Priest which cannot be touched with the feeling of our infirmities.—Hebrews iv. 15.

1 THERE is no sorrow, Lord, too slight
    To bring in prayer to Thee ;
There is no burdening care too light
    To wake Thy sympathy.

2 Thou, who hast trod the thorny road,
    Wilt share each small distress ;
The love which bore the greater load
    Will not refuse the less.

3 There is no secret sigh we breathe
    But meets Thine ear divine ;
And every cross grows light beneath
    The shadow, Lord, of Thine.

4 Life's ills without, sin's strife within,
    The heart would overflow,
But for that love which died for sin,
    That love which wept with woe.
           Jane Crewdson. d. 1863.

636   C.M.
Lord, teach us to pray.
Luke xi. 1.

1 WHEN cold our hearts, and far from Thee
Our wandering spirits stray,
And thoughts and lips move heavily,
    Lord, teach us how to pray !

2 Too vile to venture near Thy throne,
    Too poor to turn away ;
Our only voice Thy Spirit's groan,
    Lord, teach us how to pray !

3 We know not how to seek Thy face,
    Unless Thou lead the way ;
We have no words, unless Thy grace
    Lord, teach us how to pray.

4 Here every thought and fond desire
    We on Thy altar lay ;
And when our souls have caught Thy fire,
    Lord, teach us how to pray ! Amen.
            J. S. B. Monsell. 185.

637   8.8. 8.8. 8.8.
Where two or three are gathered together in My name, there am I in the midst of them.—Matthew xviii. 20.

1 FATHER of omnipresent grace !
    We seem agreed to seek Thy face ;
But every soul assembled here
Doth naked in Thy sight appear ;
Thou know'st who only bows the knee,
And who in heart approaches Thee.

2 Thy Spirit hath the difference made
Betwixt the living and the dead ;
Thou now dost into some inspire
The pure, benevolent desire ;
O that even now Thy powerful call
May quicken and convert us all !

3 The sinners suddenly convince,
O'erwhelmed beneath their load of sins ;
To-day, while it is called to-day,
Awake, and stir them up to pray,
Their dire captivity to own,
And from their burdened conscience groan.

4 Then, then acknowledge and set free
The people bought, O Lord, by Thee,
The sheep for whom their Shepherd bled,
For whom we in Thy Spirit plead ;
Let all in Thee redemption find,
And not a soul be left behind. Amen.
            Charles Wesley. 1767.

SERVICE AND GIVING.

638   S.M.
All things come of Thee, and of Thine own have we given Thee.
1 Chronicles xxix. 14.

1 WE give Thee but Thine own,
    Whate'er the gift may be,
All that we have is Thine alone,
    A trust, O Lord, from Thee.

2 May we Thy bounties thus
    As stewards true receive ;
And gladly, as Thou blessest us,
    To Thee our first-fruits give.

3 O ! hearts are bruised and dead,
    And homes are bare and cold ;
And lambs, for whom the Shepherd bled,
    Are straying from the fold.

SERVICE AND GIVING.

4 To comfort and to bless,
    To find a balm for woe,
To tend the lone and fatherless,
    Is angel's work below.

5 The captive to release,
    To God the lost to bring,
To teach the way of life and peace,
    It is a Christ-like thing.

6 And we believe Thy word,
    Though dim our faith may be;
Whate'er for Thine we do, O Lord,
    We do it unto Thee.
        Bishop W. W. How. 1854.

---

639   C.M.
The Son of man came not to be ministered unto, but to minister. Mark x. 45.

SERVANT of all, to toil for man
    Thou didst not, Lord, refuse;
Thy majesty did not disdain
    To be employed for us.

2 Thy bright example I pursue,
    To Thee in all things rise;
May all I think, or speak, or do,
    Be one great sacrifice.

3 Careless through outward cares I go,
    From all distraction free;
My hands are but engaged below,
    My heart is still with Thee.

4 As done for Thee, do Thou receive
    Each humble work of mine;
Worth to my meanest labour give,
    By joining it to Thine. Amen.
        Wesley. 1739.

---

640   8.8. 8.8, 8.8.
God hath . . . called us . . . unto holiness.—1 Thess. iv. 7.

O GOD, what offering shall I give
    To Thee, the Lord of earth and skies?
My spirit, soul, and flesh receive,
    A holy, living sacrifice;
Small as it is, 'tis all my store;
More shouldst Thou have, if I had more.

2 Now then, my God, Thou hast my soul,
    No longer mine, but Thine I am;
Guard Thou Thine own, possess it whole,
    Cheer it with hope, with love inflame:
Thou hast my spirit, there display
Thy glory to the perfect day.

3 Thou hast my flesh, Thy hallowed shrine,
    Devoted solely to Thy will;
Here let Thy light for ever shine,
    This house still let Thy presence fill;
O Source of Life, live, dwell, and move
In me, till all my life be love!

4 O never in these veils of shame,
    Sad fruits of sin, my glorying be!
Clothe with salvation, through Thy name,
    My soul, and let me put on Thee;
Be living faith my costly dress,
And my best robe Thy righteousness.

5 Send down Thy likeness from above,
    And let this my adorning be;
Clothe me with wisdom, patience, love,
    With lowliness and purity,
Than gold and pearls more precious far,
And brighter than the morning star.

6 Lord, arm me with Thy Spirit's might,
    Since I am called by Thy great name;
In Thee let all my thoughts unite,
    Of all my works be Thou the aim;
Thy love attend me all my days,
And my sole business be Thy praise.
                  Amen.
      Joachim Lange. abt. 1700.
        Tr. J. Wesley. 1739.

---

641   S.M.
Whatsoever ye do, do it heartily, as to the Lord.—Col. iii. 23.

GOD of almighty love!
    By whose sufficient grace
I lift my heart to things above,
    And humbly seek Thy face.

2 Through Jesus Christ the Just,
    My faint desires receive;
And let me in Thy goodness trust,
    And to Thy glory live.

3 Whate'er I say or do,
    Thy glory be my aim;
My offerings all be offered through
    The ever-blessed Name.

4 Jesus, my single eye
    Be fixed on Thee alone;
Thy name be praised on earth, on high;
    Thy will by all be done.

5 Spirit of Faith, inspire
    My consecrated heart;
Fill me with pure, celestial fire,
    With all Thou hast and art. Amen.
        Charles Wesley. 1749.

---

642   7.7. 7.7. 7.7.
Glorify God in your body, and in your spirit, which are God's. 1 Corinthians vi. 20.

FATHER, Son, and Holy Ghost,
    One in Three, and Three in One,
As by the celestial host,
    Let Thy will on earth be done;
Praise by all to Thee be given,
Glorious Lord of earth and heaven!

2 Vilest of the sinful race,
    Lo! I answer to Thy call;
Meanest vessel of Thy grace,
    Grace divinely free for all,
Lo! I come to do Thy will,
All Thy counsel to fulfil.

3 If a sinner such as I
    May to Thy great glory live,
All my actions sanctify,
    All my words and thoughts receive;
Claim me for Thy service, claim
All I have and all I am.

THE CHRISTIAN LIFE.

4 Take my soul and body's powers ;
   Take my memory, mind, and will,
All my goods, and all my hours,
   All I know, and all I feel,
All I think, or speak, or do ;
   Take my heart ;—but make it new.

5 Now, O God, Thine own I am,
   Now I give Thee back Thine own ;
Freedom, friends, and health, and fame,
   Consecrate to Thee alone ;
Thine I live, thrice happy I !
   Happier still if Thine I die.

6 Father, Son, and Holy Ghost,
   One in Three, and Three in One,
As by the celestial host,
   Let Thy will on earth be done ;
Praise by all to Thee be given,
   Glorious Lord of earth and heaven !
                    Amen.
              Wesley. 1745.

643   C.M.
Trust in the Lord and do good.
Psalm xxxvii. 3.

FATHER, into Thy hands alone
   I have my all restored ;
My all, Thy property I own,
   The steward of the Lord.

2 Hereafter, none can take away
   My life, or goods, or fame ;
Ready at Thy demand to lay
   Them down I always am.

3 Confiding in Thy only love,
   Through Jesus strengthening me,
I wait Thy faithfulness to prove,
   And give back all to Thee.

4 Determined all Thy will to obey,
   Thy blessings I restore ;
Give, Lord, or take Thy gifts away,
   I praise Thee evermore.
              Wesley. 1745.

644   C.M.
Be strong . . . and work :
for I am with you, saith the Lord of Hosts.
Haggai ii. 4.

THOUGH lowly here our lot may be,
   High work have we to do ;
In faith and trust to follow Him
   Whose lot was lowly too.

2 Our days of darkness we may bear,
   Strong in a Father's love,
Leaning on His almighty arm,
   And fixed our hopes above.

3 Our lives enriched with gentle thoughts
   And loving deeds may be,
A stream that still the nobler grows
   The nearer to the sea.

4 To duty firm, to conscience true,
   However tried and pressed,
In God's clear sight high work we do,
   If we but do our best.

5 Thus may we make the lowliest lot
   With rays of glory bright ;
Thus may we turn a crown of thorns
   Into a crown of light.
              W. Gaskell. d. 1884.

645   8.7. 8.7.
The barrel of meal wasted
not, neither did the cruse of oil fail.
1 Kings xvii. 16.

IS thy cruse of comfort wasting?
   Haste its scanty drops to share,
And through all the years of famine
   Thou shalt still have drops to spare.

2 Love divine will fill thy storehouse,
   Or thy handful still renew ;
Scanty fare for one will often
   Make a royal feast for two :

3 For the heart grows rich in giving ;
   All its wealth is living grain ;
Seeds which mildew in the garner,
   Scattered, fill with gold the plain.

4 Is thy burden hard and heavy ?
   Do thy steps drag wearily ?
Help to bear thy brother's burden ;
   God will bear both it and thee.

5 Numb and weary on the mountains,
   Wouldst thou sleep amidst the snow ?
Chafe that frozen form beside thee,
   And together both shall glow.

6 Art thou stricken in life's battle ?
   Many wounded round thee moan ;
Lavish on their wounds thy balsams,
   And that balm shall heal thine own.

7 Is thy heart a well left empty ?
   None but God its void can fill ;
Nothing but a ceaseless fountain
   Can its ceaseless longings still.

8 Is thy heart a living power?
   Self-entwined, its strength sinks low ;
It can only live in loving,
   And by serving love will grow.
        Elisabeth Rundle Charles. 1858.

646   L.M.
Go work to-day in My vineyard.
Matthew xxi. 28.

GO, labour on : spend, and be spent,
   Thy joy to do the Father's will ;
It is the way the Master went ;
   Should not the servant tread it still ?

2 Go, labour on : whate'er thy lot ;
   Thy earthly loss is heavenly gain :
Men heed thee, love thee, praise thee not,
   The Master praises : what are men ?

SERVICE AND GIVING.

3 Go, labour on: enough while here
  If He shall praise thee, if He deign
  Thy willing heart to mark and cheer;
  No toil for Him shall be in vain.

4 Go, labour **on**: your hands are weak,
  Your knees are faint, your soul **cast
    down**;
  Yet falter not; the prize you seek
  Is near,—a kingdom and a crown!

5 **Toil on, faint not,** keep watch and pray;
  Be wise the erring soul to win;
  Go forth into the world's highway,
  Compel the wanderer to come in.

6 Toil on, and **in thy toil rejoice**;
  For work comes rest, for exile home;
  Soon shalt **thou hear the Bridegroom's**
    voice.
  The midnight peal, '**Behold I come!**'

  Horatius Bonar. 1857.

647 C.M.
*One is your Master,
even Christ; and all ye are brethren.*
Matthew xxiii. 8.

OUR Friend, our Brother, and our Lord,
  What may Thy service be?
Nor name, nor form, nor ritual word,
  But simply following Thee.

2 Thou judgest us; Thy purity
    Doth all our lusts condemn;
  The love that draws us nearer Thee
    Is hot with wrath to them.

3 Our thoughts lie open to Thy sight;
    And, naked to Thy glance,
  Our secret sins are in the light
    Of Thy pure countenance.

4 Yet weak and blinded though we be,
    Thou dost our service own;
  We bring our varying gifts to Thee,
    And Thou rejectest none.

5 Apart from Thee all gain is loss,
    All labour vainly done;
  The solemn shadow of Thy Cross
    Is better than the sun.

6 Alone, **O Love** ineffable!
    Thy saving **name** is given;
  To turn aside from Thee is hell,
    To walk with Thee is heaven.

7 We faintly hear, we dimly see,
    In differing phrase **we** pray;
  But dim or clear, **we** own in Thee
    The Light, the Truth, the Way!

  J. G. Whittier. 1847.

648 L.M.
*Ye are not your own,
for ye are bought with a price.*
1 Corinthians vi. 19, 20.

FORTH in Thy name, O Lord, I go
  My daily labour to pursue,
Thee, only Thee resolved to know,
  In all I think, or speak, or do.

2 The task Thy wisdom hath assigned,
    O let me cheerfully fulfil;
  In all my works Thy presence find,
    And prove Thy good and perfect will.

3 Thee may I set at my right hand,
    Whose eyes my inmost substance see;
  And labour on at Thy command,
    And offer all my works to Thee.

4 Give me to bear Thy easy yoke,
    And every moment watch and pray,
  And still to things eternal look,
    And hasten to Thy glorious day.

5 For Thee delightfully employ
    Whate'er Thy bounteous grace **hath
      given,**
  And run my course with even joy,
    And closely walk with Thee to heaven.
                                   Amen.
  Charles Wesley. 1749.

649 8.8. 8.8. 8.8.
*The meek will He guide
in judgment.*—Psalm xxv. 9.

BEHOLD the servant of the Lord!
  I wait Thy guiding eye to feel,
To hear and keep Thy every word,
  To prove and do Thy perfect will,
Joyful from my **own** works to cease,
Glad to fulfil all righteousness.

2 Me if Thy grace vouchsafe to use,
    Meanest of all Thy creatures, me,
  The deed, the time, the manner choose,
    Let all my fruit be found of Thee;
  Let all my works in Thee be wrought,
  By Thee to full perfection brought.

3 My every weak, though good design,
    O'errule, or change, as seems Thee meet;
  Jesus, let all my work be Thine!
    Thy work, O Lord, is all complete,
  And pleasing in Thy Father's sight;
  Thou only hast done all things right.

4 **Here then,** to Thee Thy own I leave
    Mould as Thou wilt Thy passive clay,
  But let me all Thy stamp receive,
  But let me all Thy words obey,
  Serve with a single heart and eye,
  And to Thy glory live and die. Amen.
  Charles Wesley. 1749.

650 5.5. 5.11.
By love serve one another.
Galatians v. 13.

COME, let us arise,
    And press to the skies;
  The summons obey,
My friends, my beloved, and hasten away.

2 The Master of all
    For our service doth call,
    And deigns to approve,
With smiles of acceptance, our labour of love.

THE CHRISTIAN LIFE.

3 His burden who bear,
   We alone can declare,
     How easy His yoke,
While to love and good works we each other
      provoke ;

4 By word and by deed,
   The bodies in need,
     The souls to relieve,
And freely as Jesus hath given to give.

5 Then let us attend
   Our heavenly Friend,
     In His members distrest,
By want, or affliction, or sickness opprest ;

6 The prisoner relieve,
   The stranger receive,
     Supply all their wants,
And spend and be spent in assisting His
      saints.

7 Thus while we bestow
   Our moments below,
     Ourselves we forsake,
And refuge in Jesus's righteousness take.

8 His passion alone
   The foundation we own ;
     And pardon we claim,
And eternal redemption, in Jesus's name.
            Charles Wesley. 1749.

---

651   8.8.8.6.
I have given you an example, that ye should do as I have done to you.—John xiii. 15.

O GOD of mercy, God of might,
   In love and pity infinite,
    Teach us, as ever in Thy sight,
      To live our life to Thee.

2 And Thou, who cam'st on earth to die,
   That fallen man might live thereby,
    O hear us, for to Thee we cry,
      In hope, O Lord, to Thee.

3 Teach us the lesson Thou hast taught,
   To feel for those Thy blood hath bought,
    That every word, and deed, and thought
      May work a work for Thee.

4 For all our brethren, far and wide,
   Since Thou, O Lord, for all hast died :
    Then teach us, whatsoe'er betide,
      To love them all in Thee.

5 In sickness, sorrow, want, or care,
   Whate'er it be, 'tis ours to share;
    May we, where help is needed, there
      Give help as unto Thee.

6 And may Thy Holy Spirit move
   All those who live, to live in love,
    Till Thou shalt greet in heaven above
      All those who give to Thee. Amen.
            Godfrey Thring. 1879.

---

652   8.6. 8.6. 8.6.
If any man serve Me, him will My Father honour.—John xii. 26.

DISMISS me not Thy service, Lord,
   But train me for Thy will,
For even I, in fields so broad,
   Some duties may fulfil;
And I will ask for no reward,
   Except to serve Thee still.

2 How many serve, how many more
   May to the service come !
To tend the vines, the grapes to store,
   Thou dost appoint for some :
Thou hast Thy young men at the war,
   Thy little ones at home.

3 All works are good, and each is best
   As most it pleases Thee,
Each worker pleases when the rest
   He serves in charity ;
And neither man nor work unblest,
   Wilt Thou permit to be.

4 Our Master all the work hath done
   He asks of us to-day,
Sharing His service, every one
   Share too His Sonship may ;
Lord, I would serve and be a son :
   Dismiss me not, I pray. Amen.
            T. T. Lynch. 1855.

---

653   8.6. 8.6. 8.6.
Your Father knoweth what things ye have need of.—Matt. vi. 8.

FATHER, I know that all my life
   Is portioned out for me,
The changes that will surely come,
   I do not fear to see :
I ask Thee for a present mind
   Intent on pleasing Thee.

2 I ask Thee for a thoughtful love,
   Through constant watching wise,
To meet the glad with joyful smiles,
   And wipe the weeping eyes ;
A heart at leisure from itself,
   To soothe and sympathise.

3 I would not have the restless will
   That hurries to and fro,
That seeks for some great thing to do,
   Or secret thing to know ;
I would be treated as a child,
   And guided where I go.

4 I ask Thee for the daily strength,
   To none that ask denied,
A mind to blend with outward life,
   While keeping at Thy side,
Content to fill a little space,
   If Thou be glorified.

5 In service which Thy love appoints,
   There are no bonds for me ;
My secret heart is taught the truth
   That makes Thy children free ;
A life of self-renouncing love
   Is one of liberty.
            Anna L. Waring. 1850.

SERVICE AND GIVING.

654 7.7. 7.7.
I beseech you therefore, brethren, by the mercies of God, that ye present your bodies a living sacrifice.
— Romans xii. 1.

GOD of all-redeeming grace,
By Thy pardoning love compelled,
Up to Thee our souls we raise,
Up to Thee **our** bodies yield:

2 Thou **our** sacrifice **receive**,
Acceptable **through Thy Son**,
While to Thee **alone we live**,
While we die **to Thee alone**.

3 Meet it is, and just, and right,
That we should be wholly Thine,
In Thy only will delight,
In Thy blessed service join.

4 O that every **work and word**
Might proclaim **how good Thou art!**
Holiness unto the **Lord**
Still be written **on our heart**. Amen.
Charles Wesley. 1745.

655 7.7.7.7. D.
This is the will of God, even your sanctification. —1 Thess. iv. 3.

HOLY Lamb, **who** Thee confess,
Followers **of Thy** holiness,
Thee they ever keep **in** view,
Ever ask, 'What shall we do?'
Governed by Thy only will,
All Thy words **we** would fulfil,
Would **in** all Thy footsteps go,
Walk as Jesus walked below.

2 While Thou **didst** on earth **appear**,
Servant to **Thy** servants here,
Mindful of **Thy** place above,
All Thy life **was** prayer and love;
Such our whole employment be,
Works of faith and charity;
Works of love on man bestowed,
Secret **intercourse** with God.

3 Early in the temple met,
Let us still our Saviour greet;
Nightly to the mount repair,
Join our praying Pattern there;
There by wrestling faith obtain
Power to work for God again,
Power His image to retrieve,
Power, like Thee, our Lord, to live.

4 Vessels, instruments **of** grace,
Pass we thus our happy days,
'Twixt the mount and multitude,
Doing or receiving good;
Glad to pray and labour on,
Till our earthly course is run,
Till we, on the sacred tree,
Bow the head and die like Thee.
Amen.
Charles Wesley. 1767.

656 C.M.
Thy will be done in earth, as it is in heaven. — Matthew vi. 10.

JESUS, the Life, the Truth, the Way,
In whom I now believe,
As taught by Thee, in faith **I pray**,
Expecting to receive.

2 **Thy** will by me on **earth be done**,
As by the choirs above,
Who always see Thee on Thy **throne**,
And glory in Thy love.

3 I ask in confidence the grace,
That I may do Thy will,
As angels, **who** behold Thy face,
And **all** Thy words fulfil.

4 When Thou the **work** of faith hast wrought,
I shall be pure within,
Nor sin in deed, or word, or thought;
For **angels never sin**.

5 From **Thee** no more shall **I depart**,
No more unfaithful **prove**,
But love Thee with a **constant heart**;
For angels always love.

6 The **graces of my second birth**
To me shall all be given;
And I shall do Thy will on earth,
As angels do in heaven.
Wesley. 1742.

657 C.M.
Ye are Christ's. —1 Cor. iii. 23.

LET Him to whom we now belong
His sovereign right assert,
And take **up** every thankful song,
And **every** loving **heart**.

2 He justly claims us for His own,
Who bought us with a price;
The Christian lives to Christ alone,
To Christ alone he dies.

3 Jesus, Thine own at last receive,
Fulfil our heart's desire,
And let us to Thy glory live,
And in Thy cause expire.

4 Our souls **and** bodies **we resign**;
With joy we render Thee
Our all, no longer **ours**, but Thine
To all eternity. **Amen**.
Wesley. 1745.

658 7.7. 7.7. 7.7.
There are six days in which men ought to work. — Luke xiii. 14.

WORK is sweet, for God has blest
Honest work with quiet rest,
Rest below, and rest above,
In the mansions of His love,
When the work of life is done,
When the battle's fought and won,

THE CHRISTIAN LIFE.

2 Work ye then while yet 'tis day,
Work, ye Christians, while ye may,
Work for all that's great and good,
Working for your daily food,
Working whilst the golden hours,
Health, and strength, and youth are yours:

3 Working not alone for gold,
Nor for work that's bought and sold,
Not the work that worketh strife,
But the working of a life,
Careless both of good or ill,
If ye can but do His will:

4 Working ere the day is gone,
Working till your work is done,
Not as traffickers at marts,
But as fitteth honest hearts,
Working till your spirits rest
With the spirits of the blest.

5 Praise to God, the Father, Son,
Holy Spirit, Three in One,
Who to man beneath the heaven
Happiness in work has given;
And, when work on earth is o'er,
Rest with Him for evermore. Amen.
Godfrey Thring. 1879.

659 *Not slothful in business.* C.M.
Romans xii. 11.

SUMMONED my labour to renew,
And glad to act my part,
Lord, in Thy name my work I do,
And with a single heart.

2 End of my every action Thou,
In all things Thee I see;
Accept my hallowed labour now,
I do it unto Thee.

3 Whate'er the Father views as Thine,
He views with gracious eyes;
Jesus, this mean oblation join
To Thy great sacrifice.

4 Stamped with an infinite desert,
My work He then shall own;
W ll pleased with me, when mine Thou art,
And I His favoured son.
Wesley. 1739.

660 *Let us not be weary in well-* 10.10. 10.10.
doing: for in due season we shall reap, if
we faint not.—Galatians vi. 9.

TEACH me to live! 'Tis easier far to die,
Gently and silently to pass away,
On earth's long night to close the heavy eye,
And waken in the glorious realms of day.

Teach me that harder lesson how to live
To serve Thee in the darkest paths of life;
Arm me for conflict now, fresh vigour give,
And make me more than conqueror in the strife.

3 Teach me to live Thy purpose to fulfil;
Bright for Thy glory let my taper shine;
Each day renew, remould the stubborn will;
Closer round Thee my heart's affections twine.

4 Teach me to live for self and sin no more,
But use the time remaining to me yet;
Not mine own pleasure seeking as before,
Wasting no precious hours in vain regret.

5 Teach me to live! No idler let me be,
But in Thy service hand and heart employ,
Prepared to do Thy bidding cheerfully,
Be this my highest and my holiest joy.

6 Teach me to live, my daily cross to bear,
Nor murmur though I bend beneath its load;
Only be with me, let me feel Thee near;
Thy smile sheds gladness on the darkened road.

7 Teach me to live and find my life in Thee,
Looking from earth and earthly things away;
Let me not falter, but untiringly
Press on, and gain new strength and power each day.

8 Teach me to live! with kindly words for all,
Wearing no cold repulsive brow of gloom,
Waiting with cheerful patience till Thy call
Summons my spirit to its heavenly home. Amen.
Ellen Elizabeth Burman. 1860.

661 *In Thy light shall we see light.* S.M.
Psalm xxxvi. 9.

TEACH me, my God and King,
In all things Thee to see;
And what I do in anything,
To do it as for Thee.

2 A man that looks on glass,
On it may stay his eye;
Or if he pleaseth, through it pass,
And then the heaven espy.

3 All may of Thee partake:
Nothing can be so mean,
Which with this tincture, *for Thy sake,*
Will not grow bright and clean.

4 A servant with this clause
Makes drudgery divine;
Who sweeps a room, as for Thy laws,
Makes that and the action fine.

5 This is the famous stone
That turneth all to gold;
For that which God doth touch and own,
Cannot for less be told.
George Herbert. 1632. *alt.*

SERVICE AND GIVING.

662 S.M.
In the morning sow thy seed.
Ecclesiastes xi. 6.

SOW in the morn thy seed,
 At eve hold not thy hand ;
To doubt and fear give thou no heed,
 Broadcast it o'er the land.

2 Beside all waters sow,
 The highway furrows stock ;
Drop it where thorns and thistles grow,
 Scatter it on the rock.

3 The good, the **fruitful ground,**
 Expect not here **or there ;**
O'er hill and dale by **plots 'tis found,—**
 Go forth, then, **everywhere.**

4 **Thou know'st not which may thrive,**
 The late or early sown ;
Grace keeps the precious germs a'ive,
 When and wherever strewn.

5 **And duly shall** appear,
 In verdure, beauty, strength,
The tender blade, the stalk, the ear,
 And the full corn at length.

6 Thou canst not toil in vain—
 Cold, heat, and moist, and dry
Shall foster and mature the grain,
 For garners in the sky.

7 Thence, when the glorious end,
 The day of God, is come,
The angel reapers shall descend,
 And heaven cry, ' Harvest home.'
   James Montgomery. 1832.

663 L.M.
*I am come to send fire
on the earth.*—Luke xii. 49.

O THOU **who** camest from above,
 The pure celestial fire to impart,
Kindle a flame of sacred love
 On the mean altar of my heart.

2 There let it for Thy glory burn,
 With inextinguishable blaze ;
And trembling to its source return,
 In humble prayer and fervent praise.

3 Jesus, confirm **my** heart's desire
 To work, **and** speak, and think for Thee ;
Still let me guard the holy fire,
 And still stir up Thy gift in me.

4 **Ready for all Thy perfect will,**
 My acts of faith and love repeat,
Till death Thy endless mercies seal,
 And make the sacrifice complete.
      Amen.
   Charles Wesley. 1749.

664 S.M.
*We may boldly say, The
Lord is my helper.*—Hebrews xiii. 6.

SAY not, my soul, ' From whence
 Can God relieve my care ?'
Remember that Omnipotence
 Has servants everywhere.

2 God's help is always sure,
 His methods seldom guessed ;
Delay will make our pleasure pure,
 Surprise will give it zest.

3 His wisdom is sublime,
 His heart profoundly kind ;
God never is before His time,
 And never is behind.

4 Hast thou assumed a load,
 Which few will share with thee,
And art thou carrying it for God,
 And shall He fail to see ?

5 Be comforted at heart,
 Thou art not left alone ;
Now, thou the Lord's companion art ;
 Soon, thou wilt share His throne.
   T. T. Lynch. 1855.

665 8.7.8.7.
*Take therefore no thought
for the morrow.*—Matthew vi. 34.

ONE by one the sands are flowing,
 One by one the moments fall ;
Some are coming, some are going ;
 Do not strive to grasp them all.

2 One by one thy duties wait thee,
 Let thy whole strength go to each,
Let no future dreams elate thee,
 Learn thou first what these can teach.

3 **One by one, bright gifts from heaven,**
 Joys are sent thee here below ;
Take them readily when given,
 Ready, too, to let them go.

4 One by one thy griefs shall meet thee,
 Do not fear an armèd band ;
One will fade as others greet thee ;
 Shadows passing through the land.

5 Do not look on life's long sorrow ;
 See how small each moment's pain ;
God will help thee for to-morrow,
 So each day begin again.

6 Every hour that fleets so slowly
 Has its task to do or bear ;
Luminous the crown, and holy,
 When each gem is set with care.

7 Do not linger with regretting,
 Or for passing hours despond ;
Nor, the daily toil forgetting,
 Look too eagerly beyond.

8 Hours are golden links, God's token,
 Reaching heaven ; but one by one
Take them, lest the chain be broken,
 Ere the pilgrimage be done.
   Adelaide A. Procter. d. 1864.

666 7.6.7.6.
*Thou shalt love thy neighbour
as thyself.*—Lev. xix. 18.

O LORD, Thou art not fickle ;
 Our hope is not in vain ;
The harvest for the sickle
 Will ripen yet again.

THE CHRISTIAN LIFE.

2 But though enough be given
   For all the world to eat,
Sin with Thy love has striven
   Its bounty to defeat.

3 Were men to one another
   As kind as God to all,
Then no man on his brother
   For help would vainly call.

4 On none for idle wasting
   Would honest labour frown;
And none, to riches hasting,
   Would tread his neighbour down.

5 No man enough possesses
   Until he has to spare;
Possession no man blesses
   While self is all his care.

6 For blessings on our labour,
   O then, in hope we pray,
When love unto our neighbour
   Is ripening every day.
                T. T. Lynch. 1855.

667   7.7.7.7.
They that are Christ's have crucified the flesh.—Gal. v. 24.

NEVER further than Thy cross;
   Never higher than Thy feet;
Here earth's precious things seem dross;
   Here earth's bitter things grow sweet.

2 Gazing thus our sin we see,
   Learn Thy love while gazing thus;
Sin which laid the cross on Thee,
   Love which bore the cross for us.

3 Here we learn to serve and give,
   And, rejoicing, self deny;
Here we gather love to live,
   Here we gather faith to die.

4 Symbols of our liberty
   And our service here unite;
Captives by Thy cross set free,
   Soldiers of Thy cross we fight.

5 Pressing onwards as we can,
   Still to this our hearts must tend;
Where our earliest hopes began,
   There our last aspirings end:

6 Till amid the hosts of light,
   We in Thee redeemed complete,
Through Thy cross made pure and white,
   Cast our crowns before Thy feet.
          Elisabeth Rundle Charles. 1859.

668   S.M.
Who then is willing to consecrate his service this day unto the Lord?
1 Chronicles xxix. 5.

LORD, in the strength of grace,
   With a glad heart and free,
Myself, my residue of days,
   I consecrate to Thee.

2 Thy ransomed servant, I
   Restore to Thee Thy own;
And, from this moment, live or die
   To serve my God alone.
                Charles Wesley. 1749.

669   7 6. 7.6. 7.8. 7.6.
Lo, I come to do Thy will,
   O God.—Heb. x. 9.

LO! I come with joy to do
   The Master's blessed will;
Him in outward works pursue,
   And serve His pleasure still:
Faithful to my Lord's commands,
   I still would choose the better part,
Serve with careful Martha's hands
   And loving Mary's heart.

2 Careful without care I am,
   Nor feel my happy toil,
Kept in peace by Jesu's name,
   Supported by His smile;
Joyful thus my faith to show,
   I find His service my reward;
Every work I do below,
   I do it to the Lord.

3 Thou, O Lord, in tender love,
   Dost all my burdens bear!
Lift my heart to things above,
   And fix it ever there:
Calm on tumult's wheel I sit,
   Midst busy multitudes alone,
Sweetly waiting at Thy feet,
   Till all Thy will be done.

4 Thou, O Lord, my portion art,
   Before I hence remove!
Now my treasure and my heart
   Are all laid up above;
Far above all earthly things,
   While yet my hands are here employed,
Sees my soul the King of kings,
   And freely talks with God.

5 O that all the art might know
   Of living thus to Thee!
Find their heaven begun below,
   And here Thy glory see:
Walk in all the works prepared
   By Thee to exercise their grace,
Till they gain their full reward,
   And see Thy glorious face. Amen.
                    Wesley. 1747.

670   6.6. 6.6. 8.8.
He purgeth it, that it may bring forth more fruit.—John xv. 2.

OFT when of God we ask
   For fuller, happier life,
He sets us some new task,
   Involving care and strife:
Is this the boon for which we sought?
Has prayer new trouble on us brought?

HOPE AND JOY.

2 This is indeed the boon,
   Though strange to us it seems;
We pierce the rock, and soon
   The blessing on us streams:
For when we are the most athirst,
Then the clear waters on us burst.

3 We toil as in **a field**
   Wherein, to us unknown,
A treasure lies concealed,
   Which may be all our own:
And shall we **of** the toil complain,
That speedily will bring such gain?

4 We dig the wells of life,
   And God the water gives;
We win our way by strife,
   Then He within us lives:
And only war could make us meet
For peace so sacred and so sweet.
             T. T. Lynch. 1855.

671   *It is good for us to be here.* 10.10.10.10. 10 10.
        Mark ix. 5.

STAY, Master, **stay upon this heavenly**
   hill;
A little longer let us linger still;
With all the mighty ones of old beside,
Near to the awful Presence still abide;
Before the throne of light we trembling
   stand,
And catch a glimpse into the spirit-land.

2 Stay, Master, stay; we breathe **a** purer
   air;
This life is not the life that waits us there;
Thoughts, feelings, flashes, glimpses come
   and go;
We cannot **speak them, nay,** we do not
   know;
Wrapt in this cloud of light we seem to be
The thing we fain would grow—eternally.

3 **No! saith the Lord, the** hour is past, **we**
   go;
Our home, **our** life, our duties lie below,
While here **we** kneel upon the mount **of**
   prayer,
The plough lies **waiting** in the **furrow**
   there;
Here we sought **God that** we might **know**
   His will;
There we **must do it,** serve Him, seek Him
   still.

4 If man aspires **to reach the** throne of God,
O'er the dull **plains of** earth must lie the
   road;
He who best does his lowly duty here,
Shall mount the highest in a nobler sphere;
At God's own feet our spirits seek their
   rest,
And he is nearest Him who serves Him
   best.
             S. Greg. 1867.

HOPE AND JOY.

672   7.7. 4.4. 7. D.
   *In the time of trouble He
shall hide me in His pavilion.*—Ps. xxvii. 5.

HEAD **of** Thy Church triumphant,
   We joyfully adore Thee;
Till Thou appear,
Thy members here
Shall sing like those in glory;
We lift our hearts and voices
With blest anticipation,
   And cry aloud,
   And give to God
The praise of our salvation.

2 While **in affliction's furnace,**
   And passing through **the fire,**
Thy love we praise,
Which knows our days,
And ever brings us nigher;
We clap our hands exulting
In Thine almighty favour;
   The love divine
   Which made us Thine
Shall keep us Thine for ever.

3 Thou dost conduct Thy people
   Through torrents of temptation,
Nor will we fear,
While Thou art near,
The fire of tribulation;
The world with sin and Satan
In vain our march oppose,
   Through Thee we shall
   Break through them all,
And sing the song of Moses.

4 By faith we see the glory
   To which Thou shalt restore us,
The cross despise
For that high prize
Which Thou hast set before us;
And if Thou count us worthy,
We each, as dying Stephen,
   Shall see Thee stand
   At God's right hand,
To take us up to heaven.
             Wesley. 1749.

673   C M.
   *Of whom the whole family
in heaven and earth is named.*—Eph. iii. 15.

HAPPY the souls to Jesus joined,
   And saved by grace alone,
Walking in all His ways, they find
Their heaven on earth begun.

2 The Church triumphant in Thy love,
   Their mighty joys we know;
They sing the Lamb in hymns above,
And we in hymns below.

3 Thee, in Thy glorious realm they praise,
   And bow before Thy throne,
We, in the kingdom of Thy grace;
The kingdoms are but one.

THE CHRISTIAN LIFE.

4 The holy to the holiest leads,
   From thence our spirits rise,
And he that in Thy statutes treads,
   Shall meet Thee in the skies.
                         Wesley. 1747.

674   L.M.
Happy is he that hath the God of Jacob for his help.—Psalm cxlvi. 5.

GOD of my life, through all my days,
   My grateful powers shall sound Thy praise;
My song shall wake with opening light,
And cheer the dark and silent night.

2 When anxious cares would break my rest,
   And griefs would tear my throbbing breast,
Thy tuneful praises, raised on high,
Shall check the murmur and the sigh.

3 When death o'er nature shall prevail,
And all the powers of language fail,
Joy through my swimming eyes shall break,
And mean the thanks I cannot speak.

4 But O, when that last conflict's o'er,
And I am chained to earth no more,
With what glad accents shall I rise
To join the music of the skies!

5 Soon shall I learn the exalted strains
Which echo through the heavenly plains;
And emulate, with joy unknown,
The glowing seraphs round the throne.

6 The cheerful tribute will I give,
Long as a deathless soul shall live
A work so sweet, a theme so high,
Demands and crowns eternity.
                Philip Doddridge. 1755.

675   5.5.5.11. D.
The mercy of the Lord.
Psalm cili. 17.

ALL thanks be to God,
   Who scatters abroad,
Throughout every place,
By the least of His servants, His savour of grace;
Who the victory gave,
The praise let Him have,
For the work He hath done;
All honour and glory to Jesus alone!

2 Our conquering Lord
Hath prospered His word,
Hath made it prevail,
And mightily shaken the kingdom of hell:
His arm He hath bared,
And a people prepared
His glory to show,
And witness the power of His passion below

3 He hath opened a door
To the penitent poor,
And rescued from sin,
Hath admitted the sinners and publicans in:
They have heard the glad sound,
They have liberty found,
Through the blood of the Lamb,
And plentiful pardon in Jesus's name.

4 And shall we not sing
Our Saviour and King?
Thy witnesses, we
With rapture ascribe our salvation to Thee:
Thou, Jesus, hast blessed
And believers increased,
Who thankfully own,
We are freely forgiven through mercy alone.

5 His Spirit revives
His work in our lives,
His wonders of grace,
So mightily wrought in the primitive days:
O that all men might know
His tokens below,
Our Saviour confess,
And embrace the glad tidings of pardon and peace. Amen.
                         Wesley. 1749.

676   8.8.8.8. D. *Anapæstic.*
Glory to God in the highest.
Luke ii. 14.

ALL glory to God in the sky,
   And peace upon earth be restored:
O Jesus, exalted on high,
   Appear our omnipotent **Lord**!
Who, meanly in Bethlehem born,
   Didst stoop to redeem a lost race,
Once more to Thy creatures return,
   And reign in Thy kingdom of grace!

2 When Thou in our flesh didst appear,
   All nature acknowledged Thy birth;
Arose the acceptable year,
   And heaven was opened on earth:
Receiving its Lord from above,
   The world was united to bless
The Giver of concord and love,
   The Prince and the **Author of peace**.

3 O wouldst Thou again be made known,
   Again in Thy Spirit descend,
And set up, in each of Thine own,
   A kingdom that never shall end:
Thou only art able to bless,
   And make the glad nations obey,
And bid the dire enmity cease,
   And bow the whole world to Thy sway.

4 Come then to Thy servants again,
   Who long Thy appearing to know,
Thy quiet and peaceable reign
   In mercy establish below:
All sorrow before Thee shall fly,
   And anger and hatred be o'er;
And envy and malice shall die,
   And discord afflict us no more.

HOPE AND JOY.

5 No horrid alarum of war
    Shall break our eternal repose,
No sound of the trumpet is there,
    Where Jesus's Spirit o'erflows :
Appeased by the charms of Thy grace,
    We all shall in amity join,
And kindly each other embrace,
    And love with a passion like Thine.
              Charles Wesley. 1746.

677   6.6.9. 6.6 9.
I will come again, and receive you unto Myself.—John xiv. 3.

HOW happy are we
    Who in Jesus agree
To expect His return from above !
    We sit under our Vine,
    And delightfully join
In the praise of His excellent love.

2 How pleasant and sweet,
    In His name when we meet,
Is His fruit to our spiritual taste !
    We are banqueting here,
    On angelical cheer,
And the joys that eternally last.

3 Invited by Him,
    We drink of the stream
Ever flowing in bliss from the throne ;
    Who in Jesus believe,
    We the Spirit receive
That proceeds from the Father and Son

4 The unspeakable grace
    He obtained for our race,
And the spirit of faith He imparts ;
    Then, then we conceive
    How in heaven they live,
By the kingdom of God in our hearts.

5 We remember the word
    Of our crucified Lord,
When He went to prepare us a place ;
    'I will come in that day,
    And transport you away,
And admit to a sight of My face.'

6 With earnest desire
    After Thee we aspire,
And long Thy appearing to see ;
    Till our souls Thou receive
    In Thy presence to live,
And be perfectly happy in Thee.
              Charles Wesley. 1767.

678   8.8.6. 8.8.6.
Happy art thou, O Israel.
Deut. xxxiii. 29.

HOW happy, gracious Lord ! are we,
    Divinely drawn to follow Thee,
    Whose hours divided are
Betwixt the mount and multitude ;
    Our day is spent in doing good,
    Our night in praise and prayer.

2 With us no melancholy void,
    No period lingers unemployed,
    Or unimproved, below ;
Our weariness of life is gone,
    Who live to serve our God alone,
    And only Thee to know.

3 The winter's night, and summer's day,
    Glide imperceptibly away,
    Too short to sing Thy praise ;
Too few we find the happy hours,
    And haste to join those heavenly powers
    In everlasting lays.

4 With all who chant Thy name on high,
    And ' Holy, Holy, Holy,' cry,
    A bright harmonious throng ;
We long Thy praises to repeat,
    And restless sing, around Thy seat,
    The new, eternal song.
              Charles Wesley. 1749.

679   5.5. 5.5. 6.5. 6.5.
Rejoice evermore.
1 Thessalonians v. 16.

LET all men rejoice,
    By Jesus restored ;
We lift up our voice,
    And call Him our Lord ;
His joy is to bless us,
    And free us from thrall,
From all that oppress us,
    He rescues us all.

2 Him Prophet, and King,
    And Priest we proclaim,
We triumph and sing
    Of Jesus's name ;
Poor sinners He teaches
    To show forth His praise,
And tell of the riches
    Of Jesus's grace.

3 No matter how dull
    The scholar whom He
Takes into His school,
    And gives him to see ;
A wonderful fashion
    Of teaching He hath,
And wise to salvation
    He makes us through faith.

4 The wayfaring men,
    Though fools, shall not stray,
His method so plain,
    So easy the way ;
The simplest believer
    His promise may prove,
And drink of the river
    Of Jesus's love.

5 Poor outcasts of men,
    Whose souls were despised,
And left with disdain,
    By Jesus are prized :
His gracious creation
    In us He makes known,
And brings us salvation,
    And calls us His own.
              Charles Wesley. 1749.

THE CHRISTIAN LIFE.

680 6.6. 6.6. 8.8.
*He is faithful and just
to forgive us our sins.*—1 John i. 9.

YE ransomed sinners, hear,
　The prisoners of the Lord,
And wait till Christ appear,
　According to His word :
Rejoice in hope, rejoice with me,
We shall from all our sins be free.

2 In God we put our trust ;
　If we our sins confess,
Faithful He is, and just,
　From all unrighteousness
To cleanse us all, both you and me ;
We shall from all our sins be free.

3 Surely in us the hope
　Of glory shall appear ;
Sinners, your heads lift up,
　And see redemption near :
Rejoice in hope, rejoice with me,
We shall from all our sins be free.

4 Who Jesu's sufferings share,
　My fellow-prisoners now,
Ye soon the crown shall wear
　On your triumphant brow :
Rejoice in hope, rejoice with me,
We shall from all our sins be free.

5 The word of God is sure,
　And never can remove,
We shall in heart be pure,
　And perfected in love :
Rejoice in hope, rejoice with me,
We shall from all our sins be free.

6 Then let us gladly bring
　Our sacrifice of praise,
Let us give thanks, and sing,
　And glory in His grace :
Rejoice in hope, rejoice with me,
We shall from all our sins be free.
　　　　　　　　Wesley.　1742.

681 C.M.
*In all these things we are
more than conquerors, through Him that
loved us.*—Romans viii. 37.

WHEN I can read my title clear
　To mansions in the skies,
I bid farewell to every fear,
　And wipe my weeping eyes.

2 Should earth against my soul engage,
　And hellish darts be hurled,
Then I can smile at Satan's rage,
　And face a frowning world.

3 Let cares like a wild deluge come,
　And storms of sorrow fall,
May I but safely reach my home,
　My God, my heaven, my all.

4 There shall I bathe my weary soul
　In seas of heavenly rest,
And not a wave of trouble roll
　Across my peaceful breast.
　　　　　　　Isaac Watts.　1709.

682 5.5. 5.5. 6.5. 6.5.
*I will praise Thee . . .
with my whole heart.*—Psalm ix. 1.

O WHAT shall I do
　　My Saviour to praise,
So faithful and true,
　　So plenteous in grace,
So strong to deliver,
　　So good to redeem
The weakest believer
　　That hangs upon Him !

2 How happy the man
　　Whose heart is set free,
The people that can
　　Be joyful in Thee !
Their joy is to walk in
　　The light of Thy face,
And still they are talking
　　Of Jesus's grace.

3 Their daily delight
　　Shall be in Thy name ;
They shall as their right
　　Thy righteousness claim :
Thy righteousness wearing,
　　And cleansed by Thy blood,
Bold shall they appear in
　　The presence of God.

4 For Thou art their boast,
　　Their glory and power ;
And I also trust
　　To see the glad hour,
My soul's new creation,
　　A life from the dead,
The day of salvation,
　　That lifts up my head.

5 For Jesus, my Lord,
　　Is now my Defence ;
I trust in His word,
　　None plucks me from thence ;
Since I have found favour,
　　He all things will do ;
My King and my Saviour
　　Shall make me anew.

6 Yes, Lord, I shall see
　　The bliss of Thine own,
Thy secret to me
　　Shall soon be made known ;
For sorrow and sadness
　　I joy shall receive,
And share in the gladness
　　Of all that believe.
　　　　　　　　Wesley.　1742.

683 5.5. 5.5. 6.5. 6.5.
*Singing with grace in
your hearts to the Lord.*—Col. iii. 16.

O HEAVENLY King,
　　Look down from above ;
Assist us to sing
　　Thy mercy and love ;
So sweetly o'erflowing,
　　So plenteous the store,
Thou still art bestowing,
　　And giving us more.

2 O God of our life,
　　We hallow Thy name;
　Our business and strife
　　Is Thee to proclaim;
　Accept our thanksgiving
　　For creating grace;
　The living, the living
　　Shall show forth Thy praise.

3 Our Father and Lord,
　　Almighty art Thou;
　Preserved by Thy word,
　　We worship Thee now;
　The bountiful Donor
　　Of all we enjoy;
　Our tongues to Thine honour,
　　And lives we employ.

4 But O! above all,
　　Thy kindness we praise,
　From sin and from thrall
　　Which saves the lost race;
　Thy Son Thou hast given
　　The world to redeem,
　And bring us to heaven,
　　Whose trust is in Him.

5 Wherefore of Thy love
　　We sing and rejoice,
　With angels above
　　We lift up our voice;
　Thy love each believer
　　Shall gladly adore,
　For ever and ever,
　　When time is no more.
　　　　　　Wesley. 1742.

684 7.6.7.6. D.
I will sing of mercy and judgment.—Psalm ci. 1.

MY song shall be of mercy;
　　Come, ye who love the Lord,
　Who know that He is gracious,
　　Who trust His faithful word;
　Tell out His words with gladness,
　　With me exalt His name,
　Whose love endures for ever,
　　To endless years the same.

2 My song shall be of judgment;
　　Ye who His chastenings feel,
　O faint not, nor be weary,
　　He wounds that He may heal;
　Yea, bless the hand that smiteth,
　　And in your grief confess
　That all His ways are wisdom,
　　And truth, and righteousness.

3 Of mercy and of judgment
　　To Thee, O Lord, we sing;
　O Father, Son, and Spirit,
　　O great eternal King!
　For only Thou art holy,
　　For Thou art Lord alone;
　And mercy still and judgment
　　Are pillars of Thy throne.
　　　　　Henry Downton. 1851.

685 C.M.
We also joy in God through our Lord Jesus Christ.—Romans v. 11.

MY God, the spring of all my joys,
　　The life of my delights,
　The glory of my brightest days,
　　And comfort of my nights!

2 In darkest shades, if Thou appear,
　　My dawning is begun;
　Thou art my soul's bright morning star,
　　And Thou my rising sun.

3 The opening heavens around me shine
　　With beams of sacred bliss,
　If Jesus shows His mercy mine,
　　And whispers I am His.

4 My soul would leave this heavy clay
　　At that transporting word;
　Run up with joy the shining way,
　　To see and praise my Lord.

5 Fearless of hell and ghastly death,
　　I'd break through every foe;
　The wings of love, and arms of faith
　　Would bear me conqueror through.
　　　　　　Isaac Watts. 1709.

686 C.M.
In quietness and in confidence shall be your strength.—Isaiah xxx. 15.

MY Father, it is good for me
　　To trust and not to trace,
　And wait with deep humility
　　For Thy revealing grace.

2 Lord, when Thy way is in the sea,
　　And strange to mortal sense,
　I love Thee in the mystery,
　　I trust Thy providence.

3 I cannot see the secret things
　　In this my dark abode;
　I may not reach with earthly wings
　　The heights and depths of God.

4 So, faith and patience, wait awhile!
　　Not doubting, not in fear;
　For soon in heaven my Father's smile
　　Shall render all things clear.

5 Then Thou shalt end time's short eclipse,
　　Its dim uncertain night;
　Bring in the grand apocalypse,
　　Reveal the perfect light.
　　　　　George Rawson. 1876.

687 C.M.
The peace of God which passeth all understanding.—Philippians iv. 7.

WE bless Thee for Thy peace, O God,
　　Deep as the unfathomed sea,
　Which falls like sunshine on the road
　　Of those who trust in Thee.

THE CHRISTIAN LIFE.

2 We ask not, Father, for repose
  Which comes from outward rest,
If we may have through all life's woes
  Thy peace within our breast;

3 That peace which suffers and is strong,
  Trusts where it cannot see,
Deems not the trial-way too long,
  But leaves the end with Thee;

4 That peace which flows serene and deep,
  A river in the soul
Whose banks a living verdure keep,
  God's sunshine o'er the whole.

5 O Father, give our hearts this peace,
  Whate'er the outward be,
Till all life's discipline shall cease,
  And we go home to Thee. Amen.
                              Anon.

688   6.4. 6.4. 6.6.4.
*Enoch walked with God:
and he was not; for God took him.
Genesis v. 24.*

WALKING with Thee, my God,
    Saviour benign,
Daily confer on me
    Converse divine;
Jesus! in Thee restored,
Brother and holy Lord,
  Let it be mine.

2 Walking with Thee, my God,
    Like as a child
Leans on his father's strength,
    Crossing the wild,
And by the way is taught
Lessons of holy thought,
  Faith undefiled.

3 Darkness and earthly mists
    How do they flee
Far underneath my feet,
    Walking with Thee!
Pure is that upper air,
Cloudless the prospect there,
  Walking with Thee!

4 Walking in reverence,
    Humbly with Thee,
Yet from all abject fear
    Lovingly free;
E'en as a friend with friend,
Cheered to the journey's end,
  Walking with Thee!

5 Then Thy companions here
    Walking with Thee
Rise to a higher life—
    Soul liberty;
They are not here to love,
But to the home above
  Taken by Thee.

6 Gently translated, they
    Pass out of sight;
Gone! as the morning stars
    Flee with the night;
Taken to endless day!
So may I fade away
  Into Thy light. Amen.
              George Rawson. 1876.

689   S.M.
*Turn you to the stronghold,
ye prisoners of hope.—Zech. ix. 12.*

PRISONERS of hope, arise,
  And see your Lord appear;
Lo! on the wings of love He flies,
  And brings redemption near.

2 Redemption in His blood
    He calls you to receive;
'Look unto Me, the pardoning God;
  Believe,' He cries, 'believe!'

3 The reconciling word
    We thankfully embrace;
Rejoice in our redeeming Lord,
  A blood-besprinkled race.

4 We yield to be set free;
    Thy counsel we approve;
Salvation, praise, ascribe to Thee,
  And glory in Thy love.

5 Jesus, to Thee we look,
    Till saved from sin's remains;
Reject the inbred tyrant's yoke,
  And cast away his chains.

6 Our nature shall no more
    O'er us dominion have;
By faith we apprehend the power
  Which shall for ever save.
            Charles Wesley. 1749.

690   10.10. 10.10. 10.10.
*The Lord is my portion,
saith my soul.—Lamentations iii. 24.*

LONG did I toil, and knew no earthly rest;
Far did I rove, and found no certain home;
At last I sought them in His sheltering breast,
Who opes His arms, and bids the weary come;
With Him I found a home, a rest divine;
And I since then am His, and He is mine.

2 The good I have is from His stores supplied;
The ill is only what He deems the best;
With Him as Friend I'm rich, with nought beside,
And poor **without Him**, though of all possessed.
Changes may **come**; I take, or I resign;
Content while I am His, while He is mine.

3 Whate'er **may change**, in Him no change is seen;
A glorious sun, that wanes not, nor declines;
Above the clouds and storms He walks serene,
And sweetly on His people's darkness shines.
All may depart; I fret not nor repine,
While I my Saviour's am, while He is mine.

CHARACTER, UNITY AND FELLOWSHIP.

4 While here, alas! I know but half His love,
But half discern Him, and but half adore;
But when I meet Him in the realms above,
I hope to love Him better, praise Him more,
And feel, and tell, amid the choir divine,
How fully I am His, and He is mine.
H. F. Lyte. 1833.

691 L.M.
I am continually with Thee.
Psalm lxxiii. 23.

O THOU by long experience tried,
Near whom no grief can long abide,
My Lord! how full of sweet content
My years of pilgrimage are spent.

2 All scenes alike engaging prove
To souls impressed with sacred love;
Where'er they dwell, they dwell with Thee,
In heaven, in earth, or on the sea.

3 To me remains nor place nor time;
My country is in every clime;
I can be calm and free from care
On any shore, since God is there.

4 While place we seek or place we shun,
The soul finds happiness in none;
But with my God to guide my way,
'Tis equal joy to go or stay.

5 Could I be cast where Thou art not,
That were, indeed, a dreadful lot;
But regions none remote I call,
Secure of finding God in all.

6 Then let me to His throne repair,
And never be a stranger there;
Then love divine shall be my guard,
And peace and safety my reward.
Madame Guion. d. 1717.
Tr. *William Cowper.* 1780.

692 10.4 10.4.10.10.
I am come a light into the world.
John xii. 46.

LIGHT of the world! whose kind and gentle care
Is joy and rest;
Whose counsels and commands so gracious are,
Wisest and best;
Shine on my path, dear Lord, and guard the way,
Lest my poor heart, forgetting, go astray.

2 Lord of my life! my soul's most pure desire,
Its hope and peace;
Let not the faith Thy loving words inspire
Falter, or cease;
But be to me, true Friend, my chief delight,
And safely guide, that every step be right.

3 My blessed Lord! what bliss to feel Thee near,
Faithful and true;
To trust in Thee, without one doubt or fear,
Thy will to do;
And all the while to know that Thou, our Friend,
Art blessing us, and wilt bless to the end.

4 And then, O, then! when sorrow's night is o'er,
Life's daylight come,
And we are safe within heaven's golden door,
At home! at home!
How full of glad rejoicing will we raise,
Saviour, to Thee, our everlasting praise.
Amen.
Henry Bateman. 1862.

The Church of Christ.

CHARACTER, UNITY AND FELLOWSHIP.

693 S.M.
Who redeemeth thy life from destruction.—Psalm ciii. 4.

AND are we yet alive,
And see each other's face?
Glory and praise to Jesus give
For His redeeming grace!

2 Preserved by power divine
To full salvation here,
Again in Jesu's praise we join,
And in His sight appear.

3 What troubles have we seen,
What conflicts have we past,
Fightings without, and fears within,
Since we assembled last!

4 But out of all the Lord
Hath brought us by His love;
And still He doth His help afford,
And hides our life above.

5 Then let us make our boast
Of His redeeming power,
Which saves us to the uttermost,
Till we can sin no more.

191

THE CHURCH OF CHRIST.

6 Let us take up the cross,
  Till we the crown obtain;
And gladly reckon all things loss,
  So we may Jesus gain.
              Charles Wesley. 1749.

694   *Wherefore comfort yourselves together, and edify one another.* C.M.
1 Thessalonians v. 11.

ALL praise to our redeeming Lord,
  Who joins us by His grace,
And bids us, each to each restored,
  Together seek His face.

2 He bids us build each other up,
  And, gathered into one,
To our high calling's glorious hope
  We hand in hand go on.

3 The gift which He on one bestows,
  We all delight to prove;
The grace through every vessel flows,
  In purest streams of love.

4 Even now we think and speak the same,
  And cordially agree;
Concentred all, through Jesu's name,
  In perfect harmony.

5 We all partake the joy of one,
  The common peace we feel;
A peace to sensual minds unknown,
  A joy unspeakable.

6 And if our fellowship below
  In Jesus be so sweet,
What heights of rapture shall we know
  When round His throne we meet!
              Wesley. 1747.

695   *Behold, how good and how pleasant it is for brethren to dwell together in unity.*—Psalm cxxxiii. 1. 6.6. 6.6. 8.8.

BEHOLD, how good a thing
  It is to dwell in peace;
How pleasing to our King,
  This fruit of righteousness;
When brethren all in one agree,
Who knows the joys of unity!

2 When all are sweetly joined,
  True followers of the Lamb,
The same in heart and mind,
  And think and speak the same;
And all in love together dwell;
  The comfort is unspeakable.

3 Where unity takes place,
  The joys of heaven we prove;
This is the gospel grace,
  The unction from above,
The Spirit on all believers shed,
Descending swift from Christ our Head.

4 Where unity is found,
  The sweet anointing grace
Extends to all around,
  And consecrates the place;
To every waiting soul it comes,
And fills it with divine perfumes.

5 Grace every morning new,
  And every night, we feel;
The soft, refreshing dew
  That falls on Hermon's hill;
On Sion it doth sweetly fall;
The grace of one descends on all.

6 Even now our Lord doth pour
  The blessing from above,
A kindly gracious shower
  Of heart-reviving love,
The former and the latter rain,
The love of God and love of man.

7 The riches of His grace
  In fellowship are given
To Sion's chosen race,
  The citizens of heaven;
He fills them with the choicest store,
He gives them life for evermore.
              Wesley. 1742.

696   *The grace of our Lord Jesus Christ be with your spirit.*—Gal. vi. 18. S.M.

AND let our bodies part,
  To different climes repair;
Inseparably joined in heart
  The friends of Jesus are.

2 Jesus, the Corner-stone,
  Did first our hearts unite,
And still He keeps our spirits one,
  Who walk with Him in white.

3 O let us still proceed
  In Jesu's work below;
And, following our triumphant Head,
  To farther conquests go!

4 The vineyard of their Lord
  Before His labourers lies;
And, lo! we see the vast reward
  Which waits us in the skies.

5 O let our heart and mind
  Continually ascend,
That haven of repose to find
  Where all our labours end!

6 Where all our toils are o'er,
  Our sufferings and our pain;
Who meet on that eternal shore
  Shall never part again.

7 O happy, happy place,
  Where saints and angels meet!
There we shall see each other's face,
  And all our brethren greet.

8 The Church of the first-born,
  We shall with them be blest,
And, crowned with endless joy, return
  To our eternal rest.
              Charles Wesley. 1749.

CHARACTER, UNITY AND FELLOWSHIP.

697 *I am the Good Shepherd, and know My sheep.*—John x. 14.   C.M.

JESUS, great Shepherd of the sheep,
  To Thee for help we fly;
Thy little flock in safety keep,
  For, O! the wolf is nigh.

2 He comes, of deadly malice full,
  To scatter, tear, and slay;
He seizes every straggling soul
  As his own lawful prey.

3 Us into Thy protection take,
  And gather with Thy arm;
Unless the fold we first forsake,
  The wolf can never harm.

4 We laugh to scorn his cruel power,
  While by our Shepherd's side;
The sheep he never can devour,
  Unless he first divide.

5 O do not suffer him to part
  The souls that here agree!
But make us of one mind and heart,
  And keep us one in Thee.

6 Together let us sweetly live,
  Together let us die;
And each a starry crown receive,
  And reign above the sky. Amen.
        Charles Wesley. 1749.

698 *Be ye all of one mind, . . . be pitiful, be courteous.*—1 Peter iii. 8.   7.7.7.7.

JESUS, Lord, we look to Thee,
  Let us in Thy name agree:
Show Thyself the Prince of Peace,
Bid our jars for ever cease.

2 By Thy reconciling love,
Every stumbling-block remove;
Each to each unite, endear,
Come, and spread Thy banner here!

3 Make us of one heart and mind,
Courteous, pitiful, and kind,
Lowly, meek, in thought and word,
Altogether like our Lord.

4 Let us for each other care,
Each the other's burden bear,
To Thy Church the pattern give,
Show how true believers live.

5 Free from anger and from pride,
Let us thus in God abide;
All the depths of love express,
All the heights of holiness.

6 Let us then with joy remove
To the family above;
On the wings of angels fly,
Show how true believers die. Amen.
        Charles Wesley. 1749.

699 *By one Spirit are we all baptized into one body.*—1 Cor. xii. 13.   C.M.

JESUS, united by Thy grace,
  And each to each endeared,
With confidence we seek Thy face,
  And know our prayer is heard.

2 Still let us own our common Lord,
  And bear Thine easy yoke;
A band of love, a threefold cord,
  Which never can be broke.

3 Make us into one spirit drink;
  Baptize into Thy name;
And let us always kindly think,
  And sweetly speak the same.

4 Touched by the loadstone of Thy love,
  Let all our hearts agree;
And ever towards each other move,
  And ever move towards Thee.

5 To Thee inseparably joined,
  Let all our spirits cleave;
O may we all the loving mind
  That was in Thee receive!

6 This is the bond of perfectness,
  Thy spotless charity;
O let us, still we pray, possess
  The mind that was in Thee! Amen.
        Charles Wesley. 1742.

700 *Where two or three are gathered together in My name, there am I in the midst of them.*—Matt. xviii. 20.   S.M.

JESUS, we look to Thee,
  Thy promised presence claim;
Thou in the midst of us shalt be,
  Assembled in Thy name;

2 Thy name salvation is,
  Which here we come to prove;
Thy name is life, and health, and peace,
  And everlasting love.

3 Not in the name of pride
  Or selfishness we meet;
From nature's paths we turn aside,
  And worldly thoughts forget.

4 We meet, the grace to take
  Which Thou hast freely given;
We meet on earth for Thy dear sake
  That we may meet in heaven.

5 Present we know Thou art;
  But, O, Thyself reveal!
Now, Lord, let every bounding heart
  The mighty comfort feel.

6 O may Thy quickening voice
  The death of sin remove,
And bid our inmost souls rejoice
  In hope of perfect love! Amen.
        Charles Wesley. 1749.

THE CHURCH OF CHRIST.

701   7.7.7.7.
We ... are one body in Christ.
Romans xii. 5.

PARTNERS of a glorious hope,
  Lift your hearts and voices up ;
Jointly let us rise, and sing
Christ our Prophet, Priest, and King.

2 Monuments of Jesu's grace,
  Speak we by our lives His praise ;
Walk in Him we have received ;
Show we not in vain believed.

3 While we walk with God in light,
  God our hearts doth still unite ;
Dearest fellowship we prove,
Fellowship in Jesu's love.

4 Sweetly each, with each combined,
  In the bonds of duty joined,
Feels the cleansing blood applied,
Daily feels that Christ hath died.

5 Still, O Lord, our faith increase,
  Cleanse from all unrighteousness :
Thee the unholy cannot see ;
Make, O make us meet for Thee !

6 Every vile affection kill ;
  Root out every seed of ill ;
Utterly abolish sin ;
Write Thy law of love within.

7 Hence may all our actions flow ;
  Love the proof that Christ we know ;
Mutual love the token be,
Lord, that we belong to Thee.

8 Love, Thine image, love impart !
  Stamp it on our face and heart !
Only love to us be given !
Lord, we ask no other heaven.   Amen.
                    Wesley. 1746.

702   7.7.7.7.
*One Lord, one faith,
one baptism.*—Ephesians iv. 5.

BUILD us in one body up,
  Called in one high calling's hope ;
One the Spirit whom we claim,
One the pure baptismal flame :

2 One the faith, the common Lord,
  One the Father lives adored,
Over, through, and in us all,
God incomprehensible.

3 Steadfast let us cleave to Thee ;
  Love the mystic union be,
Union to the world unknown,
Joined to God in spirit one :

4 Wait we till the Spouse shall come,
  Till the Lamb shall take us home,
For His heaven the Bride prepare,
Solemnize our nuptials there.
                Charles Wesley. 1749.

RECEPTION OF MEMBERS.

703   L.M.
*I will put My Spirit
within you.*—Ezekiel xxxvi. 27.

UNCHANGEABLE, almighty Lord,
  Our souls upon Thy truth we stay ;
Accomplish now Thy faithful word,
And give, O give us all one way :

2 O let us all join hand in hand,
  Who seek redemption in Thy blood,
Fast in one mind and spirit stand,
And build the temple of our God !

3 Thou only canst our wills control,
  Our wild, unruly passions bind,
Tame the old Adam in our soul,
And make us of one heart and mind.

4 Speak but the reconciling word,
  The winds shall cease, the waves subside,
We all shall praise our common Lord,
Our Jesus, and Him crucified.

5 Giver of peace and unity,
  Send down Thy mild, pacific Dove ;
We all shall then in one agree,
And breathe the spirit of Thy love.

6 O let us take a softer mould,
  Blended and gathered unto Thee ;
Under one Shepherd make one fold,
Where all is love and harmony !

7 Regard Thine own eternal prayer,
  And send a peaceful answer down ;
To us Thy Father's name declare ;
Unite and perfect us in one !

8 So shall the world believe and know
  That God hath sent Thee from above,
When Thou art seen in us below,
And every soul displays Thy love.
                    Wesley. 1742.

704   C.M.
*Come in, thou blessed of
the Lord.*—Genesis xxiv. 31.

COME in, thou blessed of the Lord,
  Stranger nor foe art thou ;
We welcome thee with warm accord,
Our friend, our brother now.

2 The hand of fellowship, the heart
  Of love, we offer thee ;
Leaving the world, thou dost but part
From lies and vanity.

3 The cup of blessing which we bless,
  The heavenly bread we break,
Our Saviour's blood and righteousness,
Freely with us partake.

4 In weal or woe, in joy or care,
  Thy portion shall be ours ;
Christians their mutual burdens bear,
They lend their mutual powers.

RECEPTION OF MEMBERS.

5 Come with us; we will do thee good,
As God to us hath done;
Stand but in Him, as those have stood,
Whose faith the victory won.

6 And when, by turns, we pass away,
As star by star grows dim,
May each, translated into day,
Be lost and found in Him. Amen.
James Montgomery. 1834.

---

705 5.5, 5.5, 6.5, 6.5
*Christ the power of God,
and the wisdom of God.*—1 Corinthians i. 24.

ALL thanks to the Lamb,
  Who gives us to meet;
His love we proclaim,
  His praises repeat;
We own Him our Jesus,
  Continually near
To pardon and bless us,
  And perfect us here.

2 In Him we have peace,
  In Him we have power,
Preserved by His grace
  Throughout the dark hour,
In all our temptations
  He keeps us to prove
His utmost salvation,
  His fulness of love.

3 O what shall we do
  Our Saviour to love?
To make us anew,
  Come, Lord, from above.
The fruit of Thy passion,
  Thy holiness, give,
Give us the salvation
  Of all that believe.

4 Come, Jesus, and loose
  The stammerer's tongue,
And teach even us
  The spiritual song;
Let us without ceasing
  Give thanks for Thy grace,
And glory, and blessing,
  And honour, and praise.

5 Pronounce the glad word,
  And bid us be free;
Ah! hast Thou not, Lord,
  A blessing for me?
The peace Thou hast given
  This moment impart,
And open Thy heaven,
  O Love, in my heart. Amen.
Charles Wesley. 1749.

---

706 C.M.
*Search me, O God, and know
my heart: try me, and know my thoughts.*
Psalm cxxxix. 23.

TRY us, O God, and search the ground
  Of every sinful heart,
Whate'er of sin in us is found,
  O bid it all depart!

2 When to the right or left we stray,
  Leave us not comfortless;
But guide our feet into the way
  Of everlasting peace.

3 Help us to help each other, Lord,
  Each other's cross to bear,
Let each his friendly aid afford,
  And feel his brother's care.

4 Help us to build each other up,
  Our little stock improve;
Increase our faith, confirm our hope,
  And perfect us in love.

5 Up into Thee, our living Head,
  Let us in all things grow,
Till Thou hast made us free indeed,
  And spotless here below.

6 Then, when the mighty work is wrought,
  Receive Thy ready bride;
Give us in heaven a happy lot
  With all the sanctified. Amen.
Charles Wesley. 1742.

RECOGNITION OF MINISTERS.

707 8.8, 8.8, 8.8.
The greatest of these is charity.
1 Corinthians xiii. 13.

GIVE me the faith which can remove
  And sink the mountain to a plain;
Give me the child-like praying love,
  Which longs to build Thy house again;
Thy love let it my heart o'erpower,
And all my simple soul devour.

2 I want an even, strong desire,
  I want a calmly fervent zeal,
To save poor souls out of the fire,
  To snatch them from the verge of hell,
And turn them to a pardoning God,
And quench the brands in Jesu's blood.

3 I would the precious time redeem,
  And longer live for this alone,
To spend, and to be spent, for them
  Who have not yet my Saviour known;
Fully on these my mission prove,
And only breathe, to breathe Thy love.

4 My talents, gifts and graces, Lord,
  Into Thy blessed hands receive;
And let me live to preach Thy word,
  And let me to Thy glory live;
My every sacred moment spend
In publishing the sinner's Friend.

5 Enlarge, inflame, and fill my heart
  With boundless charity divine;
So shall I all my strength exert,
  And love them with a zeal like Thine;
And lead them to Thy open side,
The sheep for whom their Shepherd died.
  Amen.
Charles Wesley. 1749.

THE CHURCH OF CHRIST.

708 C.M.
The Shepherd and Bishop of your souls.—1 Peter ii. 25.

O LORD and Bishop of our souls,
  We bow the lowly knee,
And pray that strength be sent to those
  Who minister for Thee.

O! give them solemn, fearless words
  Which may arouse the old;
Give glowing love, that they may draw
  The lambs within Thy fold.

3 Give lips that burn with heavenly fire,
  From pride and error free;
And earnest hearts to plead with those
  Who never plead with Thee.

4 And grant them, too, a patient zeal,
  A zeal that will not slack;
Nor shun to bear with wayward sheep,
  And bring the wanderer back.

That when at length their work is o'er,
  And rest in heaven is won;
Each faithful servant may receive
  Thy welcome word—'Well done.'
    Amen.
        John P. Hobson. 1881.

709 L.M.
I will also clothe her priests with salvation.—Psalm cxxxii. 16.

LORD, pour Thy Spirit from on high,
  And Thine ordained servants bless,
And grace and gifts to each supply,
  And clothe them all with righteousness.

2 Within Thy temple when they stand,
  To teach the truth as taught by Thee,
Like shining stars in Thy right hand,
  Let all Thy Church's pastors be.

3 True wisdom, firmness, love impart,
  And zeal and meekness from above,
To bear Thy people in their heart,
  And love the souls whom Thou dost love:

4 To love, and pray, and never faint,
  By day and night their guard to keep,
To warn the sinner, form the saint,
  To feed Thy lambs, and tend Thy sheep.

So, when their work is finished here,
  They may in hope their charge resign;
So, when their Master shall appear,
  They may with crowns of glory shine.
    Amen.
        James Montgomery. 1833.

710 8.8.6. 8.8.6.
Prayer was made without ceasing of the Church unto God for him. Acts xii. 5.

LORD of the Church, we humbly pray
  For those who guide us in Thy way,
    And speak Thy holy word;
With love divine their hearts inspire,
And touch their lips with hallowed fire,
  And needful strength afford.

2 Help them to preach the truth of God,
Redemption through the Saviour's blood;
    Nor let the Spirit cease
On all the Church His gifts to shower;
To them a messenger of power,
    To us, of life and peace.

3 So may they live to Thee alone;
Then hear the welcome word, 'Well done!'
    And take their crown above;
Enter into their Master's joy,
And all eternity employ
    In praise, and bliss, and love. Amen.
        Edward Osler. 1836.

711 L.M.
Receive him . . . with all gladness.—Philippians ii. 29.

WE bid thee welcome in the name
  Of Jesus our exalted Head,
Come as a servant: so He came;
  And we receive thee in His stead.

2 Come as a shepherd: guard and keep
  This fold from hell and earth and sin,
Nourish the lambs, and feed the sheep,
  The wounded heal, the lost bring in.

3 Come as a watchman: take thy stand
  Upon thy tower amidst the sky,
And when the sword comes on the land,
  Call us to fight, or warn to fly.

4 Come as an angel: hence to guide
  A band of pilgrims on their way,
That, safely walking at thy side,
  We fail not, faint not, turn, nor stray.

5 Come as a teacher: sent from God,
  Charged His whole counsel to declare,
Lift o'er our ranks the prophet's rod,
  While we uphold thy hands with prayer.

6 Come as a messenger of peace,
  Filled with the Spirit, fired with love;
Live to behold our large increase,
  And die to meet us all above.
        James Montgomery. 1853.

PRAYER MEETINGS.
(See also Prayer.)

712 L.M.
It is good for me to draw near to God.—Psalm lxxiii. 28.

WHAT various hindrances we meet
  In coming to a mercy-seat!
Yet who that knows the worth of prayer
But wishes to be often there?

2 Prayer makes the darkened cloud withdraw,
Prayer climbs the ladder Jacob saw,
Gives exercise to faith and love,
Brings every blessing from above.

3 Restraining prayer, we cease to fight;
  Prayer makes the Christian's armour
      bright;
  And Satan trembles when he sees
  The weakest saint upon his knees.

4 While Moses stood with arms spread wide,
  Success was found on Israel's side;
  But when, through weariness, they failed,
  That moment Amalek prevailed.

5 Have you no words? ah! think again;
  Words flow apace when you complain,
  And fill your fellow-creature's ear
  With the sad tale of all your care;

6 Were half the breath thus vainly spent,
  To heaven in supplication sent,
  Your cheerful song would oftener be,
  Hear what the Lord hath done for me.
                    William Cowper. 1779.

713   C.M.
*He breathed on them,
and saith unto them, Receive ye the Holy
Ghost.*—John xx. 22.

SEE, Jesus, Thy disciples see!
  The promised blessing give;
Met in Thy name, we look to Thee,
  Expecting to receive.

2 Thee we expect, our faithful Lord,
  Who in Thy name are joined;
  We wait, according to Thy word,
  Thee in the midst to find.

3 With us Thou art assembled here;
  But, O, Thyself reveal;
  Son of the living God, appear!
  Let us Thy presence feel.

4 Breathe on us, Lord, in this our day,
  And these dry bones shall live;
  Speak peace into our hearts, and say,
  'The Holy Ghost receive!'

5 Whom now we seek, O may we meet!
  Jesus, the Crucified,
  Show us Thy bleeding hands and feet,
  Thou who for us hast died.

6 Cause us the record to receive,
  Speak, and the tokens show;
  'O be not faithless, but believe
  In Me, who died for you!'
                    Charles Wesley. 1749.

714   S.M.
*The Spirit itself maketh
intercession for us.*—Romans viii. 26.

THE praying Spirit breathe,
  The watching power impart,
From all entanglements beneath
  Call off my anxious heart.

2 My feeble mind sustain,
  By worldly thoughts opprest;
  Appear, and bid me turn again
  To my eternal rest.

3 Swift to my rescue come,
  Thy own this moment seize;
  Gather my wandering spirit home
  And keep in perfect peace.

4 Suffered no more to rove
  O'er all the earth abroad,
  Arrest the prisoner of Thy love,
  And shut me up in God. Amen.
                    Charles Wesley. 1749.

715   C.M.
*The Lord talked with you
face to face.*—Deuteronomy v. 4.

TALK with us, Lord, Thyself reveal,
  While here o'er earth we rove;
Speak to our hearts, and let us feel
  The kindling of Thy love.

2 With Thee conversing, we forget
  All time, and toil, and care;
  Labour is rest, and pain is sweet,
  If Thou, my God, art here.

3 Here then, my God, vouchsafe to stay,
  And bid my heart rejoice;
  My bounding heart shall own Thy sway
  And echo to Thy voice.

4 Thou callest me to seek Thy face;
  'Tis all I wish to seek;
  To attend the whispers of Thy grace,
  And hear Thee inly speak.

5 Let this my every hour employ,
  Till I Thy glory see;
  Enter into my Master's joy,
  And find my heaven in Thee. Amen.
                    Wesley. 1740.

716   C.M.
Pray without ceasing.
1 Thessalonians v. 17.

SHEPHERD Divine, our wants relieve,
  In this our evil day;
To all Thy tempted followers give
  The power to watch and pray.

2 Long as our fiery trials last,
  Long as the cross we bear,
  O let our souls on Thee be cast
  In never-ceasing prayer.

3 The Spirit of interceding grace
  Give us in faith to claim,
  To wrestle till we see Thy face,
  And know Thy hidden name.

4 Till Thou Thy perfect love impart,
  Till Thou Thyself bestow,
  Be this the cry of every heart,
  'I will not let Thee go.'

5 'I will not let Thee go, unless
  Thou tell Thy name to me,
  With all Thy great salvation bless,
  And make me all like Thee.

THE CHURCH OF CHRIST.

6 Then let me on the mountain-top
Behold Thy open face,
Where faith in sight is swallowed up,
And prayer in endless praise. Amen.
Charles Wesley. 1749.

717 C.M.
*Do all in the name of the
Lord Jesus.*—Colossians iii. 17.

BEHOLD us, Lord, a little space
From daily tasks set free,
And met within Thy holy place,
To rest awhile with Thee.

2 Around us rolls the ceaseless tide
Of business, toil, and care ;
And scarcely can we turn aside
For one brief hour of prayer.

3 Yet these are not the only walls
Wherein Thou may'st be sought ;
On homeliest work Thy blessing falls,
In truth and patience wrought.

4 Thine is the loom, the forge, the mart,
The wealth of land and sea ;
The worlds of science and of art,
Revealed and ruled by Thee.

5 Then let us prove our heavenly birth
In all we do and know ;
And claim the kingdom of the earth
For Thee, and not Thy foe.

6 Work shall be prayer, if all be wrought
As Thou wouldst have it done ;
And prayer, by Thee inspired and taught,
Itself with work be one.
John Ellerton. 1870.

718 7.7. 7.7. 7.7.
*Not forsaking the assembling
of ourselves together.*—Hebrews x. 25.

IF 'tis sweet to mingle where
Christians meet for social prayer,
If 'tis sweet with them to raise
Songs of holy joy and praise,
Passing sweet that state must be
Where they meet eternally.

2 Saviour, may these meetings prove
Preparations for above ;
While we worship in this place,
May we go from grace to grace,
Till we each, in his degree,
Meet for endless glory be. Amen.
Ingram Cobbin. 1828.

719 L.M.
*There I will meet with thee,
and I will commune with thee from above
the mercy-seat.*—Exodus xxv. 22.

FROM every stormy wind that blows,
From every swelling tide of woes,
There is a calm, a sure retreat,
'Tis found beneath the mercy-seat.

2 There is a place where Jesus sheds
The oil of gladness on our heads ;
A place than all beside more sweet,
It is the blood-stained mercy-seat.

3 There is a spot where spirits blend,
Where friend holds fellowship with friend ;
Though sundered far, by faith they meet
Around one common mercy-seat.

4 Ah ! whither could we flee for aid,
When tempted, desolate, dismayed ?
Or bow the hosts of hell defeat,
Had suffering saints no mercy-seat ?

5 There, there, on eagle-wing we soar,
And time and sense seem all no more,
And heaven comes down our souls to greet,
And glory crowns the mercy-seat.
Hugh Stowell. 1832.

720 L.M.
*Pray for the peace of
Jerusalem.*—Psalm cxxii. 6.

NOT for a favourite form or name,
But for immortal souls we care ;
Bless, Saviour, our Jerusalem,
That millions may her blessings share.

2 Prosper our Church ; our souls renew ;
Our languid, fainting spirits raise ;
Revive surrounding Churches too,
And spread throughout the earth Thy
praise. Amen.
Anon.

721 8.8.6. 8.8.6.
*The Lord is my strength
and song.*—Psalm cxviii. 14.

NOW have we met that we may ask
Recruited vigour for the task
Of living as we would ;
For we would live by that same word
Which all the honoured men have heard
Who by their faith have stood.

2 Through God alone can man be strong ;
To comfort us He gave this song,
In Jesus Christ we stand ;
Death held Him in His gloomy prison,
He broke the chains and has arisen,
To rule the deathless land.

3 An inner light, an inner calm,
Have they who trust His champion arm,
And hearing do His will ;
For things are not as they appear,
In death is life, in trouble cheer,
So faith is conqueror still.

4 Thus would we live ; and therefore pray
For strength renewed, that we may say,
Our life, It upward tends ;
If we who sing must sometimes sigh—
Yet life, beginning with a cry,
In Hallelujah ends.
T. T. Lynch. 1855.

BAPTISM—THE LORD'S SUPPER.

BAPTISM.

722 C.M.
I will establish My covenant between Me and thee and thy seed after thee.
Genesis **xvii.** 7.

OUR children, **Lord**, in faith and prayer
We now **devote to** Thee;
Let them Thy **covenant** mercies share,
And Thy salvation **see.**

2 Such helpless babes Thou didst **embrace**
While dwelling **here** below;
To us and ours, O God of grace,
The same compassion show.

3 In early days their hearts secure
From worldly snares, we pray,
And let them to the end endure
In every righteous way. Amen.
Anon.

723 C.M.
Suffer the little children to come unto Me.—Mark x. 14.

SEE Israel's gentle Shepherd **stand**
With all-engaging charms;
Hark how He calls the tender lambs,
And folds them in His arms!

2 'Permit them to approach,' **He cries,**
'Nor scorn their humble name;
For 'twas to bless such souls as these,
The Lord of angels came.'

3 We bring them, Lord, in thankful hands,
And yield them up to Thee;
Joyful that we ourselves are Thine,
Thine let our offspring be. Amen.
Philip Doddridge. 1755.

724 S.M.
Of such is the kingdom of God.—Mark x. 14.

TO Thee, O God, in heaven,
These little ones we bring,
Giving to Thee what Thou hast given,
Our dearest offering.

2 To Thee, O God, whose face
Their angels do behold,
We bring them, praying that Thy grace
May keep; Thine arms enfold.

3 To Thee, who children blest
And suffered them to come,
To Thee, who took them to Thy breast,
We bring these infants home.
J. Freeman Clarke. 1844.

THE LORD'S SUPPER.

725 C.M.
This do in remembrance of Me.—Luke xxii. 19.

ACCORDING to Thy gracious word,
In meek humility,
This will I do, **my** dying **Lord,**
I will remember Thee.

2 Thy body broken for my sake
My bread from heaven shall be;
Thy testamental cup I take,
And thus remember Thee.

3 Gethsemane can I forget?
Or there Thy conflict see,
Thine agony and bloody sweat,
And not remember Thee?

4 When to the cross I turn my eyes,
And rest on Calvary,
O Lamb of God, my sacrifice!
I must remember Thee:

5 Remember Thee, and all Thy pains,
And all Thy love to me;
Yea, while a breath, a pulse remains
Will I remember Thee.

6 And when these failing lips grow dumb,
And mind and memory flee,
When Thou shalt in Thy kingdom come,
Jesus, remember me. Amen.
James Montgomery. 1825.

726 S.M.
Take, eat; this is My body, which is broken for you.—1 Cor. xi. 24.

JESUS, we thus obey
Thy last and kindest word;
And, in Thine own appointed way,
We **come** to meet Thee, Lord.

2 **Thus we** remember Thee;
And take this bread and wine
As Thine own dying legacy,
And our redemption-sign.

3 Thy presence makes the feast;
Now let our spirits feel
The glory not to be **expressed,**
The joy unspeakable.

4 With high and heavenly bliss
Thou dost our spirits cheer;
Thy house of banqueting is this,
And Thou hast brought us here.

5 Now let our souls be fed
With manna from above,
And over us Thy banner spread
Of everlasting love. Amen.
Charles Wesley. 1745.

THE CHURCH OF CHRIST.

727   *This cup is the New Testament in My blood.*—1 Cor. xi. 25.   S.M.

COME, all who truly bear
    The name of Christ your Lord,
His last mysterious supper share,
    And keep His kindest word.

2 Hereby your faith approve
    In Jesus crucified ;
'In memory of My dying love,
    Do this,' He said,—and died.

3 The badge and token this,
    The sure confirming seal,
That He is ours, and we are His,
    The servants of His will ;

4 His dear, peculiar ones,
    The purchase of His blood ;
His blood which once for all atones,
    And brings us now to God.

5 Then let us still profess
    Our Master's honoured name ;
Stand forth His faithful witnesses,
    True followers of the Lamb.

6 In proof that such we are,
    His sayings we receive,
And thus to all mankind declare
    We do in Christ believe.
        Wesley. 1745.

728   *His great love wherewith He loved us.*—Ephesians ii. 4.   C.M.

IN memory of the Saviour's love,
    We keep the sacred feast,
Where every humble, contrite heart
    Is made a welcome guest.

2 By faith we take the Bread of Life
    With which our souls are fed,
The cup in token of His blood
    That was for sinners shed.

3 Under His banner thus we sing
    The wonders of His love ;
And thus anticipate by faith
    The heavenly feast above.
      Thomas Cotterill. 1810. *alt.*

729   *Drink the cup of the Lord.* 1 Corinthians x. 21.   C.M.

JESUS, at whose supreme command
    We now approach to God,
Before us in Thy vesture stand,
    Thy vesture dipped in blood !

2 Obedient to Thy gracious word,
    We break the hallowed bread,
Commemorate Thee, our dying Lord,
    And trust on Thee to feed.

3 The tokens of Thy dying love
    O let us all receive !
And feel the quickening Spirit move,
    And sensibly believe.

4 The cup of blessing, blessed by Thee,
    Let it Thy blood impart ;
The bread Thy mystic body be,
    And cheer each languid heart.

5 The Living Bread, sent down from heaven,
    In us vouchsafe to be :
Thy flesh for all the world is given,
    And all may live by Thee.

6 Now, Lord, on us Thy flesh bestow,
    And let us drink Thy blood,
Till all our souls are filled below
    With all the life of God. Amen.
        Wesley. 1742.

730   *Christ our Passover.* 1 Corinthians v. 7.   S.M.

LET all who truly bear
    The bleeding Saviour's name,
Their faithful hearts with us prepare,
    And eat the Paschal Lamb.

2 This Eucharistic feast
    Our every want supplies ;
And still we by His death are blessed,
    And share His sacrifice.

3 Who thus our faith employ,
    His sufferings to record,
Even now we mournfully enjoy
    Communion with our Lord.

4 We too with Him are dead,
    And shall with Him arise ;
The cross on which He bows His head
    Shall lift us to the skies.
        Wesley. 1745.

731   *The table of the Lord.* Malachi i. 12.   L.M.

MY God, and is Thy table spread,
    And does Thy cup with love o'erflow ?
Thither be all Thy children led,
    And let them all its sweetness know.

2 Hail ! sacred feast, which Jesus makes,
    Rich banquet of His flesh and blood ;
Thrice happy he, who here partakes
    That sacred stream, that heavenly food.

3 Why are these emblems still in vain
    Before unwilling hearts displayed ?
Was not for you the victim slain ?
    Are you forbid the children's bread ?

4 O let Thy table honoured be,
    And furnished well with joyful guests ;
And may each soul salvation see,
    That here its sacred pledges tastes.
        Amen.
      Philip Doddridge. 1755. *alt.*

THE LORD'S SUPPER.

732 L. M.
Rejoice in the Lord alway.
Philippians iv. 4.

JESUS, Thou Joy of loving hearts!
Thou Fount of life! Thou Light of men!
From the best bliss that earth imparts,
We turn unfilled to Thee again.

2 Thy truth unchanged hath ever stood;
Thou savest those that on Thee call;
To them that seek Thee, Thou art good,
To them that find Thee, All in all:

3 We taste Thee, O Thou Living Bread,
And long to feast upon Thee still,
We drink of Thee, the Fountain-head,
And thirst our souls from Thee to fill.

4 Our restless spirits yearn for Thee,
Where'er our changeful lot is cast;
Glad, when Thy gracious smile we see,
Blest, when our faith can hold Thee fast.

5 O Jesus, ever with us stay!
Make all our moments calm and bright;
Chase the dark night of sin away,
Shed o'er the world Thy holy light.
Amen.
Bernard of Clairvaux. 12th Century.
Tr. Ray Palmer. 1853.

733 8.10.10.10. 8.6.
Is it not the communion of the blood of Christ? ... Is it not the communion of the body of Christ?—1 Cor. x. 16.

O HOLY Jesus, Prince of Peace!
Thy peace be with us gathering
round Thy board,
Here where the presence of an unseen Lord
Waits to be gracious, charged with full
release
To every heavy-laden soul,
Which here remembers Thee.

2 Once more as in that upper room,
Thou who didst love Thine own unto the
end,
Thou whose dear voice to every sorrowing
friend,
Spoke the great promise through the deepening gloom,
Thou bid'st us, Master of the feast,
To-day remember Thee.

3 And e'en as in our hands we take
This broken bread, this precious cup of love,
Thy dying testament, which from above
Thou deignest ever new and fresh to make,
A fount of grace and life to all;
We do remember Thee.

4 When stung by thoughts of sin and
shame
We scarce can dare to meet our Father's
look,
Through these Thy signs we know that not
rebuke
But pardoning love is ours, as in Thy name
We now present ourselves, and here,
O Christ, remember Thee.

5 Ours is the bond of love divine,
Which knits us each to all and all to each,
That love whose ever-lengthening cords can
reach
From the white choir around Thy heavenly
shrine
To those who come in faith to-day
Here to remember Thee.

6 Thy banquet over, as we go
Strong in the strength of this celestial meat,
To tread the path of life with firmer feet,
To work the works which Thou hast bid us
do,
Abide with us, O Lord, that still
We may remember Thee: Amen.
R. Brown-Borthwick. 1870.

734 C. M.
My flesh is meat indeed, and My blood is drink indeed.
John vi. 55.

O JESUS Christ, the holy One!
I long to be with Thee;
O Jesus Christ, the lowly One!
Come and abide with me.

2 Now, while the symbols of Thy love
Before Thy saints are set,
And Thou, descending from above,
Their yearning hearts hast met;

3 Come, and o'ershadow with Thy power
This lonely heart of mine;
And feed me in this solemn hour
With Thine own bread and wine.

4 My 'meat indeed,' my 'drink indeed'
Art Thou, my gracious Lord;
Help Thou my soul by faith to feed
On this Thy precious word;

5 Till, nourished, strengthened, satisfied,
My glad and thankful heart
Forgets the things Thou hast denied,
In those Thou dost impart. Amen.
Jane E. Saxby. b. 1811.

735 7.7.7.7.7.7.
Ye do shew the Lord's death till He come.—1 Corinthians xi. 26.

'TILL He come!' O, let the words
Linger on the trembling chords;
Let the 'little while' between
In their golden light be seen;
Let us think how heaven and home
Lie beyond that 'till He come.'

2 When the weary ones we love
Enter on their rest above,
Seems the earth so poor and vast,
All our life-joy overcast?
Hush! be every murmur dumb:
It is only 'till He come.'

THE CHURCH OF CHRIST.

3 Clouds and conflicts round us press:
Would we have one sorrow less?
All the sharpness of the cross,
All that tells the world is loss,
Death, and darkness, and the tomb
Only whisper, 'till He come.'

4 See, the feast of love is spread!
Drink the wine and break the bread:
Sweet memorials, till the Lord
Call us round His heavenly board;
Some from earth, from glory some,
Severed only 'till He come.'
Bishop E. H. Bickersteth. 1858.

736 *But when the Comforter* C.M.
is come, . . . He shall testify of Me.
John xv. 26.

COME, Holy Ghost, Thine influence
  shed,
And realize the sign;
Thy life infuse into the bread,
Thy power into the wine.

Effectual let the tokens prove,
And made, by heavenly art,
Fit channels to convey Thy love
To every faithful heart. Amen.
Charles Wesley. 1745.

737 *Our own God shall bless us.* 8.7. 8.7. 4.7.
Psalm lxvii. 6.

NOW in parting, Father, bless us;
  Saviour, still Thy peace bestow;
Gracious Comforter! be with us,
  As we from this table go;
    Bless us, bless us,
Father, Son, and Spirit, now.

2 Bless us here, while still as strangers
  Onward to our home we move;
Bless us with eternal blessings
  In our Father's house above:
    Ever, ever,
Dwelling in the light of love. Amen.
Horatius Bonar. 1882.

LOVEFEAST.

738 *Be ye all of one mind . . .* S.M.
love as brethren.—1 Peter iii. 8.

BLEST be the tie that binds
  Our hearts in Christian love!
The fellowship of kindred minds
  Is like to that above.

2 Before our Father's throne
  We pour our ardent prayers;
Our fears, our hopes, our aims are one,
  Our comforts and our cares.

3 We share our mutual woes,
  Our mutual burdens bear,
And often for each other flows
  The sympathising tear.

4 When we asunder part,
  It gives us inward pain;
But we shall still be joined in heart,
  And hope to meet again.

5 This glorious hope revives
  Our courage by the way,
While each in expectation lives,
  And longs to see the day.

6 From sorrow, toil, and pain,
  And sin, we shall be free,
And perfect love and friendship reign
  Through all eternity.
John Fawcett. 1782.

739 *Then shall ye also appear* 6.6. 6.6. 8.8.
with Him in glory.—Colossians iii. 4.

COME, all whoe'er have set
  Your faces Sion-ward,
In Jesus let us meet,
  And praise our common Lord;
In Jesus let us still go on,
Till all appear before His throne.

2 Nearer, and nearer still,
  We to our country come,
To that celestial hill,
  The weary pilgrim's home,
The new Jerusalem above,
The seat of everlasting love.

3 The ransomed sons of God,
  All earthly things we scorn,
And to our high abode
  With songs of praise return;
From strength to strength we still proceed,
With crowns of joy upon our head.

4 The peace and joy of faith
  Each moment may we feel;
Redeemed from sin and wrath,
  From earth, and death, and hell,
We to our Father's house repair,
To meet our elder Brother there.

5 Our Brother, Saviour, Head,
  Our all in all, is He;
And in His steps who tread,
  We soon His face shall see;
Shall see Him with our glorious friends,
And then in heaven our journey ends.
Charles Wesley. 1749.

740 *Your love-feasts.*—Jude 12. R.V. 7.7.7.7.

COME, and let us sweetly join,
  Christ to praise in hymns divine;
Give we all, with one accord,
Glory to our common Lord;

LOVEFEAST—WATCH-NIGHT SERVICE.

2 Hands, and hearts, and voices raise;
Sing as in the ancient days;
Antedate the joys above;
Celebrate the feast of love.

3 Strive we, in affection strive,
Let the purer flame revive,
Such as in the martyrs glowed,
Dying champions for their God.

4 We, like them, may **live** and love;
Called we are their joys to prove,
Saved with them from future wrath,
Partners of like precious faith.

5 Sing we then **in Jesu's name**,
Now as yesterday the same,
One in every time and place,
Full, for all, of truth and grace.

6 We for **Christ, our** Master, **stand**
Lights in a benighted land;
We our dying Lord confess,
We are Jesu's witnesses.

7 Witnesses that Christ hath died,
We with Him **are** crucified:
Christ hath burst the bands of death,
We His quickening Spirit breathe.

8 Christ is now gone up on high,
Thither all our wishes fly;
Sits at God's right hand above;
There with Him we reign in love!
Wesley. 1740.

741   6.6.9. 6.6.9.
Made us sit together in heavenly places.—Ephesians ii. 6.

COME, let us ascend,
My companion and friend,
To a taste of the banquet above;
If thy heart be as mine,
If for Jesus it pine,
Come up into the **chariot of love.**

2 Who in Jesus confide,
We are bold to outride
The storms of affliction beneath;
With the prophet we soar
To the heavenly shore,
And outfly all the arrows of death.

3 **By faith we are come
To our permanent home;**
By hope **we the rapture improve;**
By love **we still rise,**
And look **down on the skies,**
For the heaven **of heavens is love.**

4 Who on earth can **conceive**
How happy we live,
In the palace of God, the great King?
What a concert of praise,
When our Jesus's grace
The whole heavenly company sing!

5 What a rapturous song,
When the glorified throng
In the spirit of harmony join;
Join all the glad choirs,
Hearts, voices, and lyres,
And the burden is, 'Mercy divine!

6 'Hallelujah,' they cry,
'To the King of the sky,
To the great everlasting I AM;
To the Lamb that was slain,
And liveth again,
Hallelujah to God and the Lamb!

7 'Our foreheads proclaim
His ineffable name;
Our bodies His glory display
A day without night
We feast in His sight,
And eternity seems as a day.'
Wesley. 1749.

WATCH-NIGHT SERVICE.

742   8.7. 8.7. 8.8.7.
Call to remembrance the former days.—Hebrews x. 32.

ACROSS the sky the shades of night
This winter's eve are fleeting;
We come to Thee the Life and Light,
In solemn worship meeting;
And as the year's last hours go **by**
We lift to Thee our earnest cry,
Once more Thy love entreating.

2 Before Thee, Lord, subdued we bow,
To Thee our prayers addressing;
Recounting all Thy mercies now,
And all our sins confessing;
Beseeching Thee, this coming year,
To hold us in Thy faith and fear,
And crown us with **Thy** blessing.

3 **And while we** kneel, we lift our eyes
To dear ones gone before us,
Safe housed with Thee in Paradise,
Their spirits hovering o'er us;
And beg of Thee, when life is past,
To re-unite us all, at last,
And to our lost restore us.

4 We gather up, in this brief hour,
The memory **of** Thy mercies,
Thy wondrous goodness, love, and power,
Our grateful song rehearses;
For Thou hast been **our** strength and Stay
In many a dark and dreary day
Of **sorrow** and reverses.

5 In many an hour, when fear and dread
Like evil spells have bound us,
And clouds were gathering overhead,
Thy Providence hath found us;
In many a night when waves ran high,
Thy gracious Presence drawing nigh
Hath made all calm around us.

THE CHURCH OF CHRIST.

6 Then, O great God, in years to come,
    Whatever fate betide us,
Right onward through our journey home
    Be Thou at hand to guide us;
Nor leave us till, at close of life,
    Safe from all perils, toil, and strife,
    Heaven shall unfold and hide us.
                    Amen.
        James Hamilton. b. 1819.

743   C.M.
*In the night His song
shall be with me.—Psalm xlii. 8.*

JOIN all ye ransomed sons of grace,
    The holy joy prolong,
And shout to the Redeemer's praise
    A solemn midnight song.

2 Blessing, and thanks, and love, and might
    Be to our Jesus given,
Who turns our darkness into light,
    Who turns our hell to heaven.

3 Thither our faithful souls He leads,
    Thither He bids us rise,
With crowns of joy upon our heads,
    To meet Him in the skies.
              Wesley. 1749.

744   5.5.5.11.
*I press toward the mark
for the prize of the high calling of God in
Christ Jesus.—Philippians iii. 14.*

COME, let us anew
    Our journey pursue,
      With vigour arise,
And press to our permanent place in the skies.

2 Of heavenly birth,
    Though wandering on earth
      This is not our place;
But strangers and pilgrims ourselves we confess.

3 At Jesus's call,
    We gave up our all;
      And still we forego
For Jesus's sake, our enjoyments below.

4 No longing we find
    For the country behind;
      But onward we move,
And still we are seeking a country above:

5 A country of joy,
    Without any alloy,
      We thither repair:
Our hearts and our treasure already are there.

6 We march hand in hand
    To Immanuel's land;
      No matter what cheer
We meet with on earth; for eternity's near.

7 The rougher our way,
    The shorter our stay;
      The tempests that rise
Shall gloriously hurry our souls to the skies.

8 The fiercer the blast,
    The sooner 'tis past;
      The troubles that come,
Shall come to our rescue, and hasten us home.
            Charles Wesley. 1749.

745   5.5.5.11.
*Ye know neither the day
nor the hour wherein the Son of Man cometh.*
        Matthew xxv. 13.

COME, let us anew
    Our journey pursue,
Roll round with the year,
And never stand still till the Master appear.

2 His adorable will
    Let us gladly fulfil,
    And our talents improve,
By the patience of hope and the labour of love.

3 Our life is a dream;
    Our time, as a stream
    Glides swiftly away;
And the fugitive moment refuses to stay,

4 The arrow is flown,
    The moment is gone;
    The millennial year
Rushes on to our view, and eternity's here.

5 O that each in the day
    Of His coming may say,
    'I have fought my way through;
I have finished the work Thou didst give me to do.'

6 O that each from his Lord
    May receive the glad word,
    Well and faithfully done;
Enter into my joy, and sit down on My throne.
            Charles Wesley. 1750.

COVENANT SERVICE.

746   C.M.
*Come and let us join
ourselves to the Lord in a perpetual covenant.*
        Jeremiah l. 5.

COME, let us use the grace divine,
    And all, with one accord,
In a perpetual covenant join
    Ourselves to Christ the Lord:

2 Give up ourselves, through Jesu's power,
    His name to glorify;
And promise, in this sacred hour,
    For God to live and die.

3 The covenant we this moment make,
    Be ever kept in mind;
We will no more our God forsake,
    Or cast His words behind.

4 We never will throw off His fear,
    Who hears our solemn vow;
And if Thou art well pleased to hear,
    Come down and meet us now.

DEATH, RESURRECTION AND JUDGMENT.

5 Thee, Father, Son, and Holy Ghost,
   Let all our hearts receive ;
Present with the celestial host,
   The peaceful answer give.

6 To each the covenant blood apply,
   Which takes our sins away ;
And register our names on high,
   And keep us to that day. Amen.
                            Charles Wesley. 1762.

747   8.8. 8.8. 8.8.
*Their sins and iniquities
will I remember no more.—Hebrews x. 17.*

FORGIVE us, for Thy mercy's sake,
   Our multitude of sins forgive,
And for Thine own possession take,
   And bid us to Thy glory live ;
Live in Thy sight, and gladly prove
Our faith by our obedient love.

2 The covenant of forgiveness seal,
   And all Thy mighty wonders show :
Our inbred enemies expel,
   And conquering them to conquer go,
Till all of pride and wrath be slain,
And not one evil thought remain.

3 O put it in our inward parts,
   The living law of perfect love !
Write the new precept in our hearts,
   We shall not then from Thee remove,
Who in Thy glorious image shine,
Thy people, and for ever Thine. Amen.
                            Charles Wesley. 1749.

748   8.8. 8.8. 8.8.
*The Lord is very pitiful,
and of tender mercy.—James v. 11.*

O GOD ! how often hath Thine ear
   To me in willing mercy bowed ;
While worshipping Thine altar near,
   Lowly I wept, and strongly vowed ;
But ah ! the feebleness of man,
Have I not vowed and wept in vain ?

2 Return, O Lord of hosts ! return,
   Behold Thy servant in distress ;
My faithlessness again I mourn ;
   Again forgive my faithlessness ;
And to Thine arms my spirit take,
And bless me for the Saviour's sake.

3 In pity for the soul Thou lov'st,
   Now bid my hateful sin expire ;
Let me desire what Thou approv'st,
   Thou dost approve what I desire ;
And Thou wilt deign to call me Thine,
And I will dare to call Thee mine.

4 This day the covenant I sign,
   The bond of sure and promised peace ;
Nor can I doubt its power divine,
   Since sealed with Jesus blood it is ;
That blood I trust, that blood alone,
And make the covenant peace mine own.

5 But, that my faith no more may know
   Or change, or interval, or end,
Help me in all Thy paths to go,
   And now, as e'er, my voice attend,
And gladden me with answers mild,
And commune, Father, with Thy child.
                                    Amen.
                            W. M. Bunting. 1824.

749   L.M.
*My heart is fixed, O God
. . . I will sing and give praise.—Ps. lvii. 7.*

O HAPPY day that fixed my choice
   On Thee, my Saviour, and my God !
Well may this glowing heart rejoice,
   And tell its raptures all abroad.

2 O happy bond, that seals my vows
   To Him who merits all my love !
Let cheerful anthems fill His house,
   While to that sacred shrine I move.

3 'Tis done, the great transaction's done ;
   I am my Lord's, and He is mine :
He drew me, and I followed on,
   Charmed to confess the voice divine.

4 Now rest, my long-divided heart ;
   Fixed on this blissful centre, rest ;
Nor ever once from Christ depart,
   In Him of every good possest.

5 High heaven that heard the solemn vow,
   That vow renewed shall daily hear,
Till in life's latest hour I bow,
   And bless, in death, a bond so dear.
                            Philip Doddridge. 1755.

Death, Resurrection and Judgment.

750   C.M.
*A thousand years in Thy
sight are but as yesterday when it is past.
Psalm xc. 4.*

O GOD ! our help in ages past,
   Our hope for years to come,
Our shelter from the stormy blast,
   And our eternal home ;

2 Under the shadow of Thy throne,
   Still may we dwell secure ;
Sufficient is Thine arm alone,
   And our defence is sure.

3 Before the hills in order stood,
   Or earth received her frame,
From everlasting Thou art God,
   To endless years the same

DEATH, RESURRECTION AND JUDGMENT.

4 A thousand ages, in Thy sight,
  Are like an evening gone,
Short as the watch that ends the night,
  Before the rising sun.

5 The busy tribes of flesh and blood,
  With all their cares and fears,
Are carried downward by the flood,
  And lost in following years.

6 Time, like an ever-rolling stream,
  Bears all its sons away;
They fly forgotten, as a dream
  Dies at the opening day.

7 O God! our help in ages past,
  Our hope for years to come;
Be Thou our guard while life shall last,
  And our eternal home. Amen.
                    Isaac Watts. 1719.

751 S.M.D.
We spend our years as a tale that is told.—Psalm xc. 9.

A FEW more years shall roll,
  A few more seasons come,
And we shall be with those that rest
  Asleep within the tomb:
    Then, O my Lord, prepare
    My soul for that great day;
  O wash me in Thy precious blood,
    And take my sins away.

2 A few more suns shall set
    O'er these dark hills of time,
  And we shall be where suns are not,
    A far serener clime:
      Then, O my Lord, prepare
      My soul for that blest day;
    O wash me in Thy precious blood,
      And take my sins away.

3 A few more storms shall beat
    On this wild rocky shore,
  And we shall be where tempests cease,
    And surges swell no more:
      Then, O my Lord, prepare
      My soul for that calm day;
    O wash me in Thy precious blood,
      And take my sins away.

4 A few more struggles here,
    A few more partings o'er,
  A few more toils, a few more tears,
    And we shall weep no more:
      Then, O my Lord, prepare
      My soul for that bright day;
    O wash me in Thy precious blood,
      And take my sins away.

5 A few more Sabbaths here
    Shall cheer us on our way,
  And we shall reach the endless rest,
    The eternal Sabbath-day:
      Then, O my Lord, prepare
      My soul for that sweet day;
    O wash me in Thy precious blood,
      And take my sins away.

6 'Tis but a little while
    And He shall come again,
  Who died that we might live, who lives
    That we with Him may reign:
      Then, O my Lord, prepare
      My soul for that glad day;
    O wash me in Thy precious blood,
      And take my sins away. Amen.
                Horatius Bonar. 1856.

752 L.M.
The grass withereth, the flower fadeth.—Isaiah xl. 7.

THE morning flowers display their sweets,
  And gay their silken leaves unfold,
As careless of the noontide heats,
  As fearless of the evening cold.

2 Nipt by the wind's unkindly blast,
    Parched by the sun's directer ray,
  The momentary glories waste,
    The short-lived beauties die away.

3 So blooms the human face divine,
    When youth its pride of beauty shows;
  Fa'rer than spring the colours shine,
    And sweeter than the virgin rose.

4 Or worn by slowly-rolling years,
    Or broke by sickness in a day,
  The fading glory disappears,
    The short-lived beauties die away.

5 Yet these, new rising from the tomb,
    With lustre brighter far shall shine;
  Revive with ever-during bloom,
    Safe from diseases and decline.

6 Let sickness blast, and death devour,
    If heaven must recompense our pains:
  Perish the grass, and fade the flower,
    If firm the word of God remains.
              Samuel Wesley, Jun. 1729.

753 C.M.
Thou turnest man to destruction.—Psalm xc. 3.

THEE we adore, eternal Name!
  And humbly own to Thee,
How feeble is our mortal frame,
  What dying worms we be.

2 Our wasting lives grow shorter still,
    As days and months increase;
  And every beating pulse we tell
    Leaves but the number less.

3 The year rolls round, and steals away
    The breath that first it gave;
  Whate'er we do, where'er we be,
    We are travelling to the grave.

4 Dangers stand thick through all the ground,
    To push us to the tomb;
  And fierce diseases wait around,
    To hurry mortals home.

DEATH, RESURRECTION AND JUDGMENT.

5 Great God! on what a slender **thread**
   Hang everlasting things;
The eternal states of all the dead
   Upon life's feeble strings.

6 Infinite joy, **or** endless woe,
   Attends on every breath;
And yet how unconcerned we go
   Upon the **brink** of death.

7 Waken, O **Lord! our** drowsy sense,
   To walk this dangerous road;
And if **our souls** be hurried hence,
   May they **be found with** God. Amen.
          Isaac Watts. 1709.

754 *So teach us to number our* L.M.
days, that we may apply our hearts unto
wisdom.—Psalm xc. 12.

A LMIGHTY Maker of my frame,
   Teach me the measure of my days,
Teach me to know how frail I am,
   And spend the remnant to Thy praise.

2 My days are shorter than **a** span;
   A little point **my** life appears;
How frail, at best, is dying man!
   How vain are all his hopes and fears!

3 Vain his ambition, noise, and show;
   Vain are the cares which rack his mind;
He heaps up treasures mixed with woe,
   And dies, and leaves them all behind.

4 O be a nobler portion mine!
   My God, I bow before Thy throne;
Earth's fleeting treasures I resign
   And fix my hopes on Thee alone.
          Anne Steele. 1760.

755 *Here have* **we no** *continuing* 7.6. 7.6. D.
city, but we seek **one** *to come.*—Heb. xiii. 14.

B RIEF **life is** here our portion,
   Brief sorrow, short-lived care;
The life **that** knows no ending,
   The tearless life is there.
O happy **retribution!**
   Short **toil, eternal rest;**
For mortals **and for sinners**
   A mansion with the blest!

2 And now we fight the battle,
   And then shall wear the crown
Of full and everlasting
   And passionless renown;
But He, whom now we trust in,
   Shall then **be seen and known;**
And they that know and see Him
   Shall have **Him** for their own.

3 The morning shall awaken,
   The shadows shall decay,
And each true-hearted servant
   Shall shine as does the day.

There God, our King and Portion,
   In fulness of His grace,
Shall we behold for ever,
   And worship face to face.

4 O sweet and blessed **country,**
   The home of God's elect!
O sweet and blessed country,
   That eager hearts expect!
Jesus, in mercy bring us
   To that dear land of rest;
Who art, with God the Father
   And Spirit, ever blest. Amen.
Bernard of *Cluny.* 12th Century.
          Tr *J. M Neale.* 1851.

756 *O death, where is thy sting?* S.M.
       1 Corinthians xv. 55.

I T is not death to die,
   To leave this weary road,
And 'midst the brotherhood on high,
   To be at home with God.

2 It is not death to close
   The eye long dimmed by **tears,**
And wake in glorious repose
   To spend eternal years.

3 It is not death to **bear**
   The wrench that sets us free
From dungeon-chain, to breathe the air
   Of boundless liberty.

4 It is not death to fling
   Aside this mortal dust,
And rise on strong exulting wing,
   To live among the just.

5 Jesus, Thou Prince of Life,
   Thy chosen cannot die:
Like Thee they conquer in the strife,
   To reign with Thee on high.
          C. H. A. Malan. 1826.
          Tr. *G. W. Bethune.* 1847.

757 *Why weepest thou?* C.M.
       John xx. 13.

W HY should our tears in sorrow flow,
   When God recalls His own,
And bids them leave a world of woe
   For an immortal crown?

2 Say, is not death a gain to those
   Whose life to God was given?
Gladly on earth their eyes they close,
   To open them in heaven.

3 Their toils are past, their **work is done,**
   And they are fully blest;
They fought the fight, the victory won,
   And entered into rest.

4 Then let our sorrows cease to flow,
   God has recalled His own;
But let our hearts, in every woe,
   Still say, 'Thy will be done.'
          O. P. 1826.

207

DEATH, RESURRECTION AND JUDGMENT.

758   6.6. 8.6. 8.8.
I will come again, and receive you unto Myself.—John xiv. 3.

FRIEND after friend departs;
  Who hath not lost a friend?
There is no union here of hearts,
  That finds not here an end;
Were this frail world our only rest,
Living or dying, none were blest.

2 Beyond the flight of time,
  Beyond this vale of death,
There surely is some blessed clime
  Where life is not a breath;
Nor life's affections transient fire,
Whose sparks fly upward to expire.

3 There is a world above,
  Where parting is unknown;
A whole eternity of love,
  Formed for the good alone:
And faith beholds the dying here
Translated to that glorious sphere.

4 Thus star by star declines,
  Till all are passed away,
As morning high and higher shines,
  To pure and perfect day;
Nor sink those stars in empty night,
They hide themselves in heaven's own light.

James Montgomery. 1824.

759   8.8.6. 8.8.6.
It is appointed unto men once to die.—Hebrews ix. 27.

AND am I only born to die?
  And must I suddenly comply
With nature's stern decree?
What after death for me remains?
Celestial joy, or dreadful pains,
  To all eternity.

2 How then ought I on earth to live,
While God prolongs the kind reprieve,
  And props the house of clay!
My sole concern, my single care,
To watch, and tremble, and prepare,
  Against the fatal day.

3 No room for mirth or trifling here,
For worldly hope, or worldly fear,
  If life so soon is gone;
If now the Judge is at the door,
And all mankind must stand before
  The inexorable throne.

4 Nothing is worth a thought beneath,
But how I may escape the death
  That never, never dies;
How make mine own election sure,
And, when I fall on earth, secure
  A mansion in the skies.

5 Jesus, vouchsafe a pitying ray;
Be Thou my Guide, be Thou my Way
  To glorious happiness;
Ah, write my pardon on my heart,
And whensoe'er I hence depart,
  Let me depart in peace. Amen.

Charles Wesley. 1763.

760   L.M.
I am going the way of all the earth.—Joshua xxiii. 14.

PASS a few swiftly-fleeting years,
  And all that now in bodies live
Shall quit, like me, the vale of tears,
  Their righteous sentence to receive.

2 But all, before they hence remove,
  May mansions for themselves prepare
In that eternal house above;
  And, O my God, shall I be there?

Charles Wesley. 1762.

761   L.M.
I am a stranger with Thee, and a sojourner.—Psalm xxxix. 12.

SHRINKING from the cold hand of death,
  I too shall gather up my feet,
Shall soon resign this fleeting breath,
  And die, my father's God to meet.

2 Numbered among Thy people, I
  Expect with joy Thy face to see;
Because Thou didst for sinners die,
  Jesus, in death remember me.

3 O that without a lingering groan
  I may the welcome word receive;
My body with my charge lay down,
  And cease at once to work and live!
    Amen.

Charles Wesley. 1762.

762   8.7. 8.7. 8.8.7.
The time of the dead, that they should be judged.—Rev. xi. 18.

GREAT God, what do I see and hear!
  The end of things created!
Behold the Judge of man appear,
  On clouds of glory seated:
The trumpet sounds, the graves restore
The dead, which they contained before;
  Prepare, my soul, to meet Him.

2 The dead in Christ shall first arise,
  At the last trumpet's sounding,
Caught up to meet Him in the skies,
  With joy their Lord surrounding;
No gloomy fears their souls dismay;
His presence sheds eternal day
  On those prepared to meet Him.

3 But sinners, filled with guilty fears,
  Behold His wrath prevailing;
For they shall rise, and find their tears
  And sighs are unavailing;
The day of grace is past and gone,
Trembling they stand before His throne,
  All unprepared to meet Him.

4 Great God, what do I see and hear!
  The end of things created!
Behold the Judge of man appear,
  On clouds of glory seated!
Low at His cross, I view the day
When heaven and earth shall pass away,
  And thus prepare to meet Him.

B. Ringwaldt. 1585. *Tr. Anon.* 1802.
Last three verses by W. B. Collyer. 1812.

DEATH, RESURRECTION AND JUDGMENT.

763 7.6. 7.6. 7.8. 7.6.
*The earth also and the
works that are therein shall be burned up.*
2 Peter iii. 10.

STAND the omnipotent decree !
  Jehovah's will be done !
Nature's end we wait to see,
  And hear her final groan ;
Let this earth dissolve, and blend
In death the wicked and the just,
  Let those ponderous orbs descend,
    And grind us into dust ;

2 Rests secure the righteous man :
  At his Redeemer's beck
Sure to emerge, and rise again,
  And mount above the wreck :
Lo ! the heavenly spirit towers,
Like flame, o'er nature's funeral pyre,
  Triumphs in immortal powers,
    And claps his wings of fire.

3 Nothing hath the just to lose,
  By worlds on worlds destroyed ;
Far beneath his feet he views,
  With smiles, the flaming void ;
Sees the universe renewed,
The grand millennial reign begun ;
  Shouts, with all the sons of God,
    Around the eternal throne.

4 Resting in this glorious hope
  To be at last restored,
Yield we now our bodies up
  To earthquake, plague, or sword ;
Listening for the call divine,
The latest trumpet of the seven,
  Soon our soul and dust shall join,
    And both fly up to heaven.
        Charles Wesley. 1756.

764 6.6. 6.6. 8.8.
*Blessed are they which
are called unto the marriage supper of the
Lamb.*—Revelation xix. 9.

YE virgin souls, arise,
  With all the dead awake !
Unto salvation wise,
  Oil in your vessels take ;
Upstarting at the midnight cry,
' Behold the heavenly Bridegroom nigh !'

2 He comes, He comes, to call
  The nations to His bar,
And raise to glory all
  Who fit for glory are ;
Made ready for your full reward,
Go forth with joy to meet your Lord.

3 Go, meet Him in the sky,
  Your everlasting Friend ;
Your Head to glorify,
  With all His saints ascend ;
Ye pure in heart, obtain the grace
To see, without a veil, His face !

P

4 Ye that have here received
  The unction from above,
And in His Spirit lived,
  Obedient to His love,
Jesus shall claim you for His bride ;
Rejoice with all the sanctified :

5 The everlasting doors
  Shall soon the saints receive,
Above you angel powers,
  In glorious joy to live ;
Far from a world of grief and sin,
With God eternally shut in.

6 Then let us wait to hear
  The trumpet's welcome sound ;
To see our Lord appear,
  Watching let us be found ;
When Jesus doth the heavens bow,
Be found—as, Lord, Thou find'st us now.
        Amen.
        Charles Wesley. 1749.

765 L. M.
*The trumpet shall sound,
and the dead shall be raised incorruptible.*
1 Corinthians xv. 52.

THE great Archangel's trump shall sound,
  While twice ten thousand thunders roar,
Tear up the graves, and cleave the ground,
  And make the greedy sea restore.

2 The greedy sea shall yield her dead,
  The earth no more her slain conceal ;
Sinners shall lift their guilty head,
  And shrink to see a yawning hell.

3 But we, who now our Lord confess,
  And faithful to the end endure,
Shall stand in Jesu's righteousness,
  Stand, as the Rock of Ages, sure.

4 We, while the stars from heaven shall fall,
  And mountains are on mountains hurled,
Shall stand unmoved amidst them all,
  And calmly see a burning world.

5 The earth, and all the works therein,
  Dissolve, by raging flames destroyed ;
While we survey the awful scene,
  And mount above the fiery void.

6 By faith we now transcend the skies,
  And on that ruined world look down ;
By love above all height we rise,
  And share the everlasting throne.
        Charles Wesley. 1749.

766 8.7. 8.7. 4.7.
*Behold, He cometh with
clouds ; and every eye shall see Him.*
Revelation i. 7.

LO ! He comes with clouds descending,
  Once for favoured sinners slain !
Thousand, thousand saints attending,
  Swell the triumph of His train.
    Hallelujah !
God appears on earth to reign.

DEATH, RESURRECTION AND JUDGMENT.

2 Every eye shall now behold Him
    Robed in dreadful majesty;
Those who set at nought and sold Him,
    Pierced and nailed Him to the tree,
      Deeply wailing,
Shall the true Messiah see.

The dear tokens of His passion
    Still His dazzling body bears;
Cause of endless exultation
    To His ransomed worshippers;
      With what rapture
Gaze we on those glorious scars.

4 Yea, Amen! let all adore Thee,
    High on Thy eternal throne;
Saviour, take the power and glory,
    Claim the kingdom for Thine own!
      Jah! Jehovah!
Everlasting God! come down. Amen.
          Charles Wesley. 1758.

---

767   8.8, 8.8, 8.8.
    All live unto Him.—Luke xx. 38.

GOD of the living, in whose eyes
  Unveiled Thy whole creation lies!
All souls are Thine; we must not say
That those are dead who pass away;
From this our world of sense set free,
Our dead are living unto Thee.

2 Released from earthly toil and strife,
With Thee is hidden all their life;
Thine are their thoughts, their works,
    their powers,
All Thine, and yet most truly ours;
For well we know, where'er they be,
Our dead are living unto Thee.

3 Not spilt like water on the ground,
Not wrapped in dreamless sleep profound,
Not wandering in unknown despair,
Beyond Thy voice, Thine arm, Thy care;
Not left to lie like fallen tree;
Not dead, but living unto Thee.

4 Thy word is true, Thy will is just;
To Thee we leave them, Lord, in trust;
And bless Thee for the love which gave
Thy Son to fill a human grave,
That none might fear that world to see
Where all are living unto Thee.

5 O Breather into man of breath,
O Holder of the keys of death,
O Quickener of the life within,
Save us from death, the death of sin;
That body, soul, and spirit be
For ever living unto Thee! Amen.
          John Ellerton. 1867.

---

768   8.8.6. 8.8.6.
   Prepare to meet thy God.
        Amos iv. 12.

THOU God of glorious majesty!
  To Thee, against myself, to Thee,
    A son of earth, I cry;
A half awakened child of man;
An heir of endless bliss or pain;
    A sinner born to die.

2 Lo! on a narrow neck of land,
'Twixt two unbounded seas I stand,
    Secure, insensible;
A point of time, a moment's space,
Removes me to that heavenly place
    Or shuts me up in hell.

3 O God! mine inmost soul convert,
And deeply on my thoughtful heart
    Eternal things impress;
Give me to feel their solemn weight,
And tremble on the brink of fate,
    And wake to righteousness.

4 Before me place, in dread array,
The pomp of that tremendous day,
    When Thou with clouds shalt come,
To judge the nations at Thy bar;
And tell me, Lord, shall I be there,
    To meet a joyful doom?

5 Be this my one great business here,
With serious industry and fear
    Eternal bliss to ensure;
Thine utmost counsel to fulfil,
And suffer all Thy righteous will,
    And to the end endure.

6 Then, Saviour, then, my soul receive
Transported from this vale to live
    And reign with Thee above;
Where faith is sweetly lost in sight,
And hope in full supreme delight,
    And everlasting love. Amen.
          Charles Wesley. 1749.

---

769   S.M.
  *We must all appear before
the judgment seat of Christ.*—2 Cor. v. 10.

THOU Judge of quick and dead,
  Before whose bar severe,
With holy joy, or guilty dread,
  We all shall soon appear!

2 Our cautioned souls prepare
  For that tremendous day;
And fill us now with watchful care,
  And stir us up to pray;

3 To pray, and wait the hour,
  That awful hour unknown,
When, robed in majesty and power,
  Thou shalt from heaven come down.

4 The immortal Son of man,
  To judge the human race,
With all Thy Father's dazzling train,
  With all Thy glorious grace.

5 To damp our earthly joys,
  To increase our gracious fears,
For ever let the Archangel's voice
  Be sounding in our ears;

DEATH, RESURRECTION AND JUDGMENT.

6 The solemn midnight cry,
  'Ye dead, the Judge is come!
Arise, and meet Him in the sky,
  And meet your instant doom!

7 O may we thus be found
  Obedient to His word,
Attentive to the trumpet's sound,
  And looking for our Lord:

8 O may we thus ensure
  A lot among the blest;
And watch a moment to secure
  An everlasting rest!
            Charles Wesley. 1749.

770   8.8. 8.8. 8.8.
*The harvest is the end of
the world.*—Matthew xiii. 39.

THIS is the field, the world below,
  In which the sowers came to sow,
Jesus the wheat, Satan the tares,
For so the word of truth declares;
And soon the reaping time will come,
And angels shout the harvest home.

2 Most awful truth! and is it so,
Must all the world that harvest know,
Is every man or wheat or tare?
Then for that harvest O prepare!
For soon the reaping time will come,
And angels shout the harvest home.

3 To love my sins, a saint to appear,
To grow with wheat, yet be a tare,
May serve me while I live below,
Where tares and wheat together grow;
But soon the reaping time will come,
And angels shout the harvest home.

But all who truly righteous be
Their Father's kingdom then shall see,
And shine like suns for ever there;
He that hath ears, now let him hear;
For soon the reaping time will come,
And angels shout the harvest home.
            Joseph Hinchsliffe. 1787.

771   7.6. 7.6. 7.7. 7.6.
*At midnight there was a cry
made, Behold the bridegroom cometh.*
Matthew xxv. 6.

HEARKEN to the solemn voice,
  The awful midnight cry!
Waiting souls, rejoice, rejoice,
  And see the Bridegroom nigh:
Lo! He comes to keep His word,
  Light and joy His looks impart;
Go ye forth to meet your Lord,
  And meet Him in your heart.

2 Ye who faint beneath the load
  Of sin, your heads lift up;
See your great Redeeming God,
  He comes, and bids you hope:
In the midnight of your grief,
  Jesus doth His mourners cheer;
Lo! He brings you sure relief;
  Believe, and feel Him here.

3 Ye whose loins are girt, stand forth,
  Whose lamps are burning bright,
Worthy in your Saviour's worth,
  To walk with Him in white;
Jesus bids your hearts be clean,
  Bids you all His promise prove;
Jesus comes to cast out sin,
  And perfect you in love.

4 Wait we all in patient hope,
  Till Christ, the Judge, shall come;
We shall soon be all caught up
  To meet the general doom:
In an hour to us unknown,
  As a thief in deepest night,
Christ shall suddenly come down,
  With all His saints in light.

5 Happy he whom Christ shall find
  Watching to see Him come;
Him the Judge of all mankind
  Shall bear triumphant home;
Who can answer to His word?
  Which of you dares meet His day?
'Rise, and come to judgment!'—Lord,
  We rise, and come away.
            Wesley. 1742.

772   7.7. 7.7.
*Where shall the ungodly
and the sinner appear?*—1 Peter iv. 18.

WHEN thy mortal life is fled,
  When the death-shades o'er thee spread,
When is finished thy career,
Sinner, where wilt thou appear?

2 When the world has passed away,
When draws near the judgment-day,
When the awful trump shall sound,
Say, O, where wilt thou be found?

3 When the Judge descends in light,
Clothed in majesty and might,
When the wicked quail with fear,
Where, O where, wilt thou appear?

4 What shall soothe thy bursting heart,
When the saints and thou must part?
When the good with joy are crowned,
Sinner, where wilt thou be found?

5 While the Holy Ghost is nigh,
Quickly to the Saviour fly;
Then shall peace thy spirit cheer,
Then in heaven shalt thou appear.
            S. F. Smith. 1840.

HEAVEN AND THE LIFE HEREAFTER.

Heaven and the Life Hereafter.

773   8.8. 8.8. 8.8.
*Run with patience the race
that is set before us, looking unto Jesus.*
Hebrews xii. 1, 2.

LEADER of faithful souls, and Guide
  Of all that travel to the sky,
Come, and with us, even us, abide,
  Who would on Thee alone rely ;
On Thee alone our spirits stay,
While held in life's uneven way.

2 Strangers and pilgrims here below,
  This earth, we know, is not our place;
But hasten through the vale of woe,
  And, restless to behold Thy face,
Swift to our heavenly country move,
Our everlasting home above.

3 We have no biding city here,
  But seek a city out of sight ;
Thither our steady course we steer,
  Aspiring to the plains of light,
Jerusalem, the saints' abode,
Whose founder is the living God.

4 Patient the appointed race to run,
  This weary world we cast behind ;
From strength to strength we travel on,
  The New Jerusalem to find ;
Our labour this, our only aim,
To find the New Jerusalem.

5 Through Thee, who all our sins hast borne,
  Freely and graciously forgiven,
With songs to Sion we return,
  Contending for our native heaven ;
That palace of our glorious King,
We find it nearer while we sing.

6 Raised by the breath of love Divine,
  We urge our way with strength renewed,
The Church of the first-born to join,
  We travel to the mount of God,
With joy upon our heads arise,
And meet our Captain in the skies.
                  Wesley. 1747.

774   L. M.
*Where I am, there shall
ye be also.*—John xiv. 3.

AS when the weary traveller gains
  The height of some o'erlooking hill,
His heart revives, if, cross the plains,
He sees his home, though distant still.

2 While he surveys the much-loved spot,
He slights the space that lies between ;
His past fatigues are now forgot,
Because his journey's end is seen.

3 Thus, when the Christian pilgrim views,
  By faith, his mansion in the skies,
The sight his fainting strength renews,
  And wings his speed to reach the prize.

4 The thought of home his spirit cheers ;
  No more he grieves for troubles past,
Nor any future trials fears,
  So he may safe arrive at last.

5 'Tis there, he says, I am to dwell
  With Jesus, in the realms of day ;
Then I shall bid my cares farewell,
  And He will wipe my tears away.

6 Jesus, on Thee our hope depends,
  To lead us on to Thine abode ;
Assured our home will make amends
  For all our toil while on the road.
                John Newton. 1779.

775   8.8. 8.8. D. *Anapæstic.*
*I saw a new heaven and
a new earth.*—Revelation xxi. 1.

AWAY with our sorrow and fear !
  We soon shall recover our home,
The city of saints shall appear,
  The day of eternity come :
From earth we shall quickly remove,
  And mount to our native abode,
The house of our Father above,
  The palace of angels and God.

2 Our mourning is all at an end,
  When, raised by the life-giving word,
We see the new city descend,
  Adorned as a bride for her Lord :
The city so holy and clean,
  No sorrow can breathe in the air,
No gloom of affliction or sin,
  No shadow of evil is there.

3 By faith we already behold
  That lovely Jerusalem here ;
Her walls are of jasper and gold,
  As crystal her buildings are clear :
Immovably founded in grace,
  She stands, as she ever hath stood,
And brightly her Builder displays,
  And flames with the glory of God.

4 No need of the sun in that day,
  Which never is followed by night,
Where Jesus's beauties display
  A pure and a permanent light :
The Lamb is their Light and their Sun,
  And, lo ! by reflection they shine,
With Jesus ineffably one,
  And bright in effulgence divine !
                Charles Wesley. 1744.

HEAVEN AND THE LIFE HEREAFTER.

776   S.M.D.
*So shall we ever be with
the Lord.*—1 Thessalonians iv. 17.

   'FOR ever with the Lord!'
     Amen; so let it be!
Life from the dead is in that word,
   'Tis immortality.
Here in the body pent,
   Absent from Him I roam,
Yet nightly pitch my moving tent
   A day's march nearer home.

2 My Father's house on high,
   Home of my soul, how near,
At times, to faith's foreseeing eye,
   Thy golden gates appear!
Ah! then my spirit faints
   To reach the land I love,
The bright inheritance of saints,
   Jerusalem above.

3 'For ever with the Lord!'
   Father, if 'tis Thy will,
The promise of that faithful word,
   Even here to me fulfil.
Be Thou at my right hand,
   Then can I never fail,
Uphold Thou me, and I shall stand,
   Fight, and I must prevail.

4 So when my latest breath
   Shall rend the veil in twain,
By death I shall escape from death,
   And life eternal gain.
Knowing as I am known,
   How shall I love that word,
And oft repeat before the throne,
   'For ever with the Lord!'
            James Montgomery. 1835.

777   8.8. 8.8. 8.8.
*Be thou faithful unto death,
and I will give thee a crown of life.*
Revelation ii. 10.

THOU, Lord, on whom I still depend,
   Shalt keep me faithful to the end:
I trust Thy truth, and love, and power,
Shall save me to the latest hour;
   And, when I lay this body down,
   Reward with an immortal crown.

2 Jesus, in Thy great Name I go
   To conquer death, my final foe;
And when I quit this cumbrous clay,
And soar on angels' wings away,
   My soul the second death defies,
   And reigns eternal in the skies.

3 Eye hath not seen, nor ear hath heard,
   What Christ hath for His saints prepared,
Who conquer through their Saviour's
   might,
Who sink into perfection's height,
   And trample death beneath their feet,
   And gladly die their Lord to meet.

4 Dost thou desire to know and see
What thy mysterious name shall be?
Contending for thy heavenly home,
Thy latest foe in death o'ercome;
Till then thou searchest out in vain,
What only conquest can explain.
            Charles Wesley. 1762.

778   S.M.
*We which have believed
do enter into rest.*—Hebrews iv. 3.

O! WHERE shall rest be found,
   Rest for the weary soul:
'Twere vain the ocean depths to sound
   Or pierce to either pole.

2 The world can never give
   The bliss for which we sigh;
'Tis not the whole of life to live,
   Nor all of death to die.

3 Beyond this vale of tears
   There is a life above,
Unmeasured by the flight of years;
   And all that life is love.

4 Here would we end our quest;
   Alone are found in Thee
The life of perfect love—the rest
   Of immortality.
            James Montgomery. 1819.

779   C.M.
*Blessed are the dead which
die in the Lord.*—Revelation xiv. 13.

HEAR what the voice from heaven
   proclaims
For all the pious dead!
Sweet is the savour of their names,
And soft their dying bed.

2 They die in Jesus, and are blest:
   How calm their slumbers are!
From sufferings and from tears re-
   leased,
And freed from every snare;

3 Till that illustrious morning come,
   When all Thy saints shall rise,
And, decked in full immortal bloom,
   Attend Thee to the skies.

4 Their tongues, great Prince of Life,
   shall join
With their recovered breath,
And all the immortal host ascribe
   Their victory to Thy death.
            Isaac Watts. 1709.

780   *Irregular.*
*Father, I will that they also,
whom Thou hast given Me, be with Me where
I am.*—John xvii. 24.

SOON and for ever,
   Such promise our trust,
Though ashes to ashes,
   And dust be to dust,

HEAVEN AND THE LIFE HEREAFTER.

    Soon and for ever
      Our union shall be
    Made perfect, our glorious
      Redeemer, in Thee;
    When the sins and the sorrows
      Of time shall be o'er,
    Its pangs and its partings
      Remembered no more;
    Where life cannot fail and where
      Death cannot sever,
    Christians with Christ shall be
      Soon and for ever.

2 Soon and for ever
    The breaking of day
  Shall chase all the night-clouds
    Of sorrow away;
  Soon and for ever
    We'll see as we're seen,
  And know the deep meaning
    Of things that have been,
  Where fightings without us
    And conflicts within
  Shall weary no more in
    The warfare with sin,
  Where tears, and where fears, and where
    Death shall be never,
  Christians with Christ shall be
    Soon and for ever.

3 Soon and for ever
    The work shall be done,
  The warfare accomplished,
    The victory won;
  Soon and for ever
    The soldier lay down
  The sword for a harp, and
    His cross for a crown;
  Then droop not in sorrow,
    Despond not in fear,
  A glorious to-morrow
    Is brightening and near,
  When—blessed reward for each
    Faithful endeavour—
  Christians with Christ shall be
    Soon and for ever.

        J. S. B. Monsell. 1837.

781   11.10. 11.10. *Iambic.*
We would see Jesus.
John xii. 21.

'WE would see Jesus:' for the shadows lengthen
  Across the little landscape of our life;
'We would see Jesus,' our weak faith to strengthen
  For the last weariness, the final strife.

2 'We would see Jesus:' for life's hand hath rested,
  With its dark touch, upon both heart and brow;
  And though our souls have many a billow breasted,
  Others are rising in the distance now.

3 'We would see Jesus:' the great rock foundation,
  Whereon our feet were set by sovereign grace;
  Not life, nor death, with all their agitation,
  Can thence remove us if we see His face.

4 'We would see Jesus:' other lights are paling,
  Which for long years we have rejoiced to see;
  The blessings of our pilgrimage are failing,
  We would not mourn them, for we go to Thee.

5 'We would see Jesus:' yet the spirit lingers
  Round the dear objects it has loved so long,
  And earth from earth can scarce unclasp its fingers,
  Our love to Thee makes not this love less strong.

6 'We would see Jesus:' sense is all too blinding,
  And heaven appears too dim, too far away;
  We would see Thee, to gain a sweet reminding
  That Thou hast promised our great debt to pay.

7 'We would see Jesus:' this is all we're needing;
  Strength, joy, and willingness come with the sight;
  'We would see Jesus,' dying, risen, pleading;
  Then welcome day, and farewell mortal night!

    Anon. Christian Treasury. 1854.

782   C.M.
Thine eyes . . . shall behold the land that is very far off.
Isaiah xxxiii. 17

THERE is a land of pure delight,
  Where saints immortal reign;
Infinite day excludes the night,
  And pleasures banish pain.

2 There everlasting spring abides,
  And never-withering flowers:
Death, like a narrow sea, divides
  This heavenly land from ours.

3 Sweet fields beyond the swelling flood
  Stand dressed in living green;
So to the Jews old Canaan stood,
  While Jordan rolled between.

4 But timorous mortals start and shrink
  To cross this narrow sea;
And linger, shivering on the brink,
  And fear to launch away.

5 O could we make our doubts remove,
  Those gloomy thoughts that rise,
And see the Canaan that we love,
  With unbeclouded eyes!

HEAVEN AND THE LIFE HEREAFTER.

6 Could we but climb where Moses stood,
   And view the landscape o'er,
Not Jordan's stream, nor death's cold
    flood,
   Should fright us from the shore.
                  Isaac Watts. 1709.

783 *The Lord said, I will give it you.*—Numbers x. 29.   C.M.

ON Jordan's stormy banks I stand,
   And cast a wistful eye
To Canaan's fair and happy land,
   Where my possessions lie.

2 O, the transporting, rapturous scene
   That rises to my sight!
Sweet fields arrayed in living green,
   And rivers of delight.

3 There generous fruits that never fail,
   On trees immortal grow;
There rocks and hills, and brooks, and
    vales
With milk and honey flow.

4 All o'er those wide extended plains
   Shines one eternal day;
There God, the Sun, for ever reigns,
   And scatters night away.

5 No chilling wind, or poisonous breath,
   Can reach that healthful shore;
Sickness and sorrow, pain and death,
   Are felt and feared no more.

6 When shall I reach that happy place,
   And be for ever blest?
When shall I see my Father's face,
   And in His bosom rest?
           Samuel Stennett. 1787.

784 *That great city, the holy Jerusalem.*—Revelation xxi. 10.   C.M.

JERUSALEM! my happy home!
   Name ever dear to me!
When shall my labours have an end,
   In joy, and peace, and thee?

2 When shall these eyes thy heaven-built
    walls
   And pearly gates behold;
Thy bulwarks, with salvation strong,
   And streets of shining gold?

3 There happier bowers than Eden's bloom,
   Nor sin nor sorrow know;
Blest seats! through rude and stormy
    scenes,
   I onward press to you.

4 O, when, thou city of my God,
   Shall I thy courts ascend,
Where congregations ne'er break up,
   And Sabbaths have no end?

5 Why should I shrink from pain or woe,
   Or feel at death dismay?
I've Canaan's goodly land in view,
   And realms of endless day.

6 Apostles, martyrs, prophets, there
   Around my Saviour stand;
And soon my friends in Christ below
   Will join the glorious band.

7 Jerusalem! my happy home!
   My soul still pants for thee;
Then shall my labours have an end,
   When I thy joys shall see.
                  B. 1801.

785 *I saw the holy city, new Jerusalem . . . prepared as a bride adorned for her husband.*—Revelation xxi. 2.   7.6.7.6. D.

JERUSALEM the golden,
   With milk and honey blessed;
Beneath thy contemplation
   Sink heart and voice oppressed;
The home of fadeless splendour,
   Of flowers that have no thorn;
Where they shall dwell as children
   Who here as exiles mourn.

2 Jerusalem, the only,
   That look'st from heaven below;
In thee is all my glory;
   In me is all my woe;
I strive to win that glory,
   I toil to gain that light;
Send hope before to grasp it,
   Till hope is lost in sight.

3 Jerusalem! exulting,
   On that securest shore,
I hope thee, wish thee, sing thee,
   And love thee evermore!
O happy, holy city,
   The portion of the blest;
True vision of true beauty,
   Sweet balm of all distressed!

4 Thou hast no shore, fair ocean!
   Thou hast no time, bright day!
Dear fountain of refreshment
   To pilgrims far away!
Upon the Rock of Ages
   They raise thy holy tower;
Thine is the victor's laurel,
   And thine the golden dower.

5 The Lamb is all thy splendour,
   The Crucified thy praise;
His laud and benediction
   Thy ransomed people raise.
And He whom now we trust in
   Shall then be seen and known;
And they that know and see Him
   Shall have Him for their own.

6 O sweet and blessed country,
   When shall I see thy face?
O sweet and blessed country,
   When shall I win thy grace?
Exult, O dust and ashes!
   The Lord shall be thy part;
His only, His for ever,
   Thou shalt be, and thou art.
     Bernard of Cluny, 12th Century.
           Tr. *J. M. Neale.* 1851.

HEAVEN AND THE LIFE HEREAFTER.

786   6.6.6.6.4.4.4.4.
He showed me that great city, the holy Jerusalem . . . having the glory of God.—Revelation xxi. 10, 11.

JERUSALEM on high
  My song and city is,
My home whene'er I die,
  The centre of my bliss.

    O happy place!
      When shall I be,
    My God, with Thee,
      To see Thy face?

2 Thy walls, sweet city! thine,
  With pearls are garnished;
Thy gates with praises shine,
  Thy streets with gold are spread.

3 There dwells my Lord, my King,
  Judged here unfit to live;
There angels to Him sing,
  And lowly homage give.

4 The patriarchs of old
  There from their travels cease;
The prophets there behold
  Their longed-for Prince of peace.

5 The Lamb's apostles there
  I might with joy behold;
The harpers I might hear
  Harping on harps of gold.

6 No tears from any **eyes**
  Drop in that holy **choir**;
But death itself there dies,
  And sighs themselves expire.

7 Sweet place; sweet place alone!
  The court of God most high,
The heaven of heavens, the throne
  Of spotless majesty!
        Samuel Crossman. 1664.

787   *Irregular.*
We shall all be changed.
1 Corinthians xv. 51.

NO sorrow, and no sighing,
  O world of peace undying!
There shall true life begin,
No curse, no pain, no sin,
Above, around, within;
    We shall be changed.

2 Transformed, **from** light to light,
  From grace to glory's height;
To more **than** angels knew
Of perfect, **pure, and** true,
For all things **shall be new**;
    We shall be changed.

3 Eternal life, with God,
'Christ's joy' in spheres untrod;
When shall time's shadows fly,
And morning fill the sky,
When shall the Lord draw nigh,
    And we be changed?

4 We shall be like our Lord,
  Our nature all restored,
In Him who is our Head,
The first-born from the dead,
By Him to glory led;
    The same, yet changed.
        W. J. Irons. 1873.

788   8.8.8.8. D. *Anapæstic.*
I would not live alway.
Job vii. 16.

O WHEN shall we sweetly remove?
  O when shall we enter our rest?
Return to the Sion above,
  The mother of spirits distressed;
That city of God the great King,
  Where sorrow and death are no more;
But saints our Immanuel sing,
  And cherub and seraph adore?

2 Not all the archangels can tell
  The joys of that holiest place,
Where Jesus is pleased to reveal
  The light of His heavenly face;
When caught in the rapturous flame,
  The sight beatific they prove,
And walk in the light of the Lamb,
  Enjoying the beams of His love.

3 Thou know'st, in the spirit of prayer,
  We hope Thy appearing to see,
Resigned to the burden we bear,
  But longing to triumph with Thee;
'Tis good at Thy word to be here,
  'Tis better in Thee to be gone,
And see Thee in glory appear,
  And rise to a share in Thy throne.

4 **To** mourn for Thy coming **is sweet**,
  To weep at Thy **longer** delay;
But Thou, whom **we hasten to meet**,
  Shalt chase all **our sorrows** away.
The tears shall be wiped from our eyes,
  When Thee we behold in the cloud,
And echo the joys of the skies,
  And shout to the trumpet of God.
        Charles Wesley. 1744.

789   C.M. *With Chorus.*
The Paradise of God.
Revelation ii. 7.

O PARADISE! O Paradise!
  Who doth not crave for rest?
Who would not seek the happy land
  Where they that loved are blest;
    Where loyal hearts, and true,
      Stand ever in the light,
    All rapture through and through,
      In God's most holy sight?

2 O Paradise! O Paradise!
  The world is growing old;
Who would not be at rest and **free**
  Where love is never cold?

3 O Paradise! O Paradise!
  'Tis weary waiting here;
I long to be where Jesus is,
  To feel, to see Him near.

4 O Paradise! O Paradise!
   I want to sin no more;
   I want to be as pure on earth
     As on Thy spotless shore.

5 O Paradise! O Paradise!
   I greatly long to see
   The special place my dearest Lord
     Is destining for me.
           F. W. Faber. 1861.

790   S.M.
There shall in no wise enter into it anything that defileth.
Revelation xxi. 27.

THERE is no night in heaven;
   In that blest world above
Work never can bring weariness,
   For work itself is love.

2 There is no grief in heaven;
   For life is one glad day,
And tears are of those former things
   Which all have passed away.

3 There is no sin in heaven;
   Behold that blessed throng,
All holy is their spotless robe!
   All holy is their song!

4 There is no death in heaven;
   For they who gain that shore
Have won their immortality,
   And they can die no more.

5 Lord Jesus, be our Guide;
   O lead us safely on,
Till night, and grief, and sin, and death
   Are past, and heaven is won!
         Amen.
      F. Minden Knollis. d. 1863.
      Last verse John Ellerton.

791   10.10.10. 4.
We ... are compassed about with so great a cloud of witnesses.
Hebrews xii. 1.

FOR all the saints, who from their labours rest,
Who Thee by faith before the world confessed,
Thy name, O Jesus, be for ever blest.
     Hallelujah!

2 Thou wast their rock, their fortress, and their might;
Thou, Lord, their Captain in the well-fought fight;
Thou, in the darkness drear, their one true light.
     Hallelujah!

3 O may Thy soldiers, faithful, true, and bold!
Fight as the saints, who nobly fought of old,
And win with them the victor's crown of gold.
     Hallelujah!

4 O blest communion, fellowship divine!
We feebly struggle, they in glory shine;
Yet all are one in Thee, for all are Thine.
     Hallelujah!

5 And, when the strife is fierce, the warfare long,
Steals on the ear the distant triumph-song,
And hearts are brave again, and arms are strong.
     Hallelujah!

6 The golden evening brightens in the west;
Soon, soon to faithful warriors cometh rest;
Sweet is the calm of Paradise the blest.
     Hallelujah!

7 But lo! there breaks a yet more glorious day;
The saints triumphant rise in bright array;
The King of glory passes on His way.
     Hallelujah!

8 From earth's wide bounds, from ocean's farthest coast,
Through gates of pearl streams in the countless host,
Singing to Father, Son, and Holy Ghost.
     Hallelujah! Amen.
       Bishop W. W. How. 1867.

792   7.7. 7.7. D.
What are these which are arrayed in white robes? and whence came they?—Revelation vii. 13.

WHAT are these arrayed in white,
   Brighter than the noon-day sun?
Foremost of the sons of light,
   Nearest the eternal throne?
These are they that bore the cross,
   Nobly for their Master stood;
Sufferers in His righteous cause,
   Followers of the dying God.

2 Out of great distress they came,
   Washed their robes by faith below
In the blood of yonder Lamb,
   Blood that washes white as snow;
Therefore are they next the throne,
   Serve their Maker day and night;
God resides among His own,
   God doth in His saints delight.

3 More than conquerors at last,
   Here they find their trials o'er;
They have all their sufferings past,
   Hunger now and thirst no more:
No excessive heat they feel
   From the sun's directer ray;
In a milder clime they dwell,
   Region of eternal day.

4 He that on the throne doth reign,
   Them the Lamb shall always feed,
With the tree of life sustain,
   To the living fountains lead:
He shall all their sorrows chase,
   All their wants at once remove,
Wipe the tears from every face,
   Fill up every soul with love.
           Wesley. 1745.

HEAVEN AND THE LIFE HEREAFTER.

793 11.10. 11.10. *With Chorus.*
*The voice of many angels
round about the throne.*—Revelation v. 11.

HARK! hark! my soul! angelic songs
   are swelling,
  O'er earth's green fields, and ocean's
   wave-beat shore;
How sweet the truth those blessed strains
   are telling,
  Of that new life when sin shall be no
   more.
    Angels of Jesus, Angels of light,
    Singing to welcome the pilgrims of
     the night!

2 Onward we go, for still we hear them
   singing,
  Come, weary souls, for Jesus bids you
   come!
And, through the dark its echoes sweetly
   ringing,
  The music of the Gospel leads us home.

3 Rest comes at length; though life be long
   and dreary,
  The day must dawn, the darksome night
   be past;
All journeys end in welcomes to the weary,
  And Heaven, the heart's true home, will
   come at last.

4 Cheer up, my soul! faith's moonbeams
   softly glisten
  Upon the breast of life's most troubled
   sea;
And it will cheer thy drooping heart to
   listen
  To those brave songs which angels mean
   for thee.

5 Angels, sing on! your faithful watches
   keeping,
  Sing us sweet fragments of the songs
   above;
While we toil on, and soothe ourselves
   with weeping,
  Till life's long night shall break in endless love.
                 F. W. Faber. 1861.

794 C.M.
*Of whom the whole family
in heaven and earth is named.*
Ephesians iii. 15.

COME, let us join our friends above,
  That have obtained the prize,
And on the eagle wings of love
  To joys celestial rise.

2 Let all the saints terrestrial sing,
  With those to glory gone;
For all the servants of our King,
  In earth and heaven, are one.

3 One family we dwell in Him,
  One Church above, beneath,
Though now divided by the stream,
  The narrow stream of death.

4 One army of the living God,
  To His command we bow;
Part of His host have crossed the flood,
  And part are crossing now.

5 Ten thousand to their endless home
  This solemn moment fly;
And we are to the margin come,
  And we expect to die.

6 His militant embodied host,
  With wishful looks we stand,
And long to see that happy coast,
  And reach the heavenly land.

7 Our old companions in distress
  We haste again to see,
And eager long for our release
  And full felicity.

8 E'en now by faith we join our hands
  With those who went before;
And greet the blood-besprinkled bands
  On the eternal shore.

9 Our spirits too shall quickly join,
  Like theirs with glory crowned;
And shout to see our Captain's sign,
  To hear His trumpet sound.

10 O that we now might grasp our Guide!
  O that the word were given!
Come, Lord of hosts, the waves divide,
  And land us all in heaven! Amen.
                 Wesley. 1759.

795 6.6. 7.7. 7.7.
*I will give thee a crown
of life.*—Revelation ii. 10.

AGAIN we lift our voice,
  And shout our solemn joys;
Cause of highest raptures this,
Raptures that shall never fail,
See a soul escaped to bliss,
Keep the Christian Festival.

2 Our friend is gone before
  To that celestial shore;
He hath left his mates behind,
He hath all the storms outrode,
Found the rest we toil to find,
Landed in the arms of God.

3 And shall we mourn to see
  Our fellow-prisoner free,
Free from doubts, and griefs, and fears,
In the haven of the skies?
Can we weep to see the tears
Wiped for ever from his eyes?

4 No, dear companion, no;
  We gladly let thee go,
From a suffering Church beneath
To a reigning Church above;
Thou hast more than conquered death,
Thou art crowned with life and love.
                 Wesley. 1749.

HEAVEN AND THE LIFE HEREAFTER.

796 L.M.
Awake, awake, put on Thy strength, O arm of the Lord.—Isaiah li. 9.

ARM of the Lord, awake, awake!
Thine own immortal strength put on;
With terror clothed, hell's kingdom shake,
And cast Thy foes with fury down.

2 As in the ancient days appear;
The sacred annals speak Thy fame;
Be now omnipotently near,
To endless ages still the same.

3 Thy arm, Lord, is not shortened now,
It wants not now the power to save;
Still present with Thy people, Thou
Shalt bear them through life's parted wave.

4 By death and hell pursued in vain,
To Thee the ransomed seed shall come;
Shouting, their heavenly Sion gain,
And pass through death triumphant home.

5 The pain of life shall there be o'er,
The anguish and distracting care,
There sighing grief shall weep no more,
And sin shall never enter there.

6 Where pure, essential joy is found,
The Lord's redeemed their heads shall raise,
With everlasting gladness crowned,
And filled with love, and lost in praise.
Charles Wesley. 1739.

797 S.M.
They shall walk with Me in white: for they are worthy.—Rev. iii. 4.

O WHAT a mighty change
Shall Jesu's sufferers know!
While o'er the happy plains they range,
Incapable of woe.

2 No ill-requited love
Shall there our spirits wound,
No base ingratitude above,
No sin in heaven is found.

3 No slightest touch of pain,
Nor sorrow's least alloy,
Can violate our rest, or stain
Our purity of joy.

4 In that eternal day
No clouds nor tempests rise;
There gushing tears are wiped away
For ever from our eyes.
Charles Wesley. 1749.

798 6.6.7.7.7.7.
A house not made with hands, eternal in the heavens.—2 Cor. v. 1.

HOW weak the thoughts, and vain,
Of self-deluding men;
Men, who, fixed to earth alone,
Think their houses shall endure,
Fondly call their lands their own,
To their distant heirs secure.

2 How happy then are we
Who build, O Lord, on Thee!
What can our foundation shock?
Though the shattered earth remove,
Stands our city on a rock,
On the Rock of heavenly Love.

3 A house we call our own,
Which cannot be o'erthrown;
In the general ruin sure,
Storms and earthquakes it defies,
Built immovably secure,
Built eternal in the skies.

4 High on Immanuel's land
We see the fabric stand;
From a tottering world remove,
To our steadfast mansion there;
Our inheritance above
Cannot pass from heir to heir.

5 High on Thy great white throne,
O King of saints! come down;
In the New Jerusalem
Now triumphantly descend;
Let the final trump proclaim
Joys begun, which ne'er shall end.
Amen.
Charles Wesley. 1750.

799 11.11.11.11. *Anapæstic.*
There the weary be at rest. Job iii. 17.

MY rest is in heaven, my rest is not here;
Then why should I murmur when trials are near?
Be hushed, my dark spirit, the worst that can come,
But shortens my journey, and hastens me home.

2 It is not for me to be seeking my bliss,
And building my home in a region like this;
I look for a city which hands have not piled,
I pant for a country by sin undefiled.

3 The thorn and the thistle around me may grow,
I would not lie down upon roses below;
I ask not my portion, I seek not my rest,
Till I find them for ever in Jesus' breast.

4 Afflictions may damp me, they cannot destroy,
One glimpse of His love turns them all into joy;
And the bitterest tears, if He smile but on them,
Like dew in the sunshine, grow diamond and gem.

5 Let doubt then, or danger my progress oppose,
They only make heaven more sweet at the close;
Come joy, or come sorrow, whate'er may befall,
One hour with my God will make up for it all.

HEAVEN AND THE LIFE HEREAFTER.

6 A scrip on my back, and a staff in my hand,
  I march on in haste through an enemy's
    land ;
  The road may be rough, but it cannot be
    long,
  And I'll smooth it with hope, and cheer it
    with song.
                              H. F. Lyte. 1833.

800   C.M.
*Clothed with white robes,
and palms in their hands.*—Rev. vii. 9.

GIVE me the wings of faith to rise
    Within the veil, and see
The saints above, how great their joys,
    How bright their glories be.

2 Once they were mourning here below,
    And poured out cries and tears ;
They wrestled hard as we do now,
    With sins, and doubts, and fears.

3 I ask them whence their victory came ;
    They, with united breath,
Ascribe their conquest to the Lamb,
    Their triumph to His death.

4 They marked the footsteps that He trod,
    His zeal inspired their breast,
And following their incarnate God,
    Possess the promised rest.

5 Our glorious Leader claims our praise
    For His own pattern given :
While the long cloud of witnesses
    Show the same path to heaven.
                            Isaac Watts. 1709.

801   8.8.6, 8.8.6
*Happy art thou, O Israel
. . . O people saved by the Lord.*
Deuteronomy xxxiii. 29.

HOW happy is the pilgrim's lot !
    How free from every anxious thought,
      From worldly hope and fear !
Confined to neither court nor cell,
His soul disdains on earth to dwell,
      He only sojourns here.

2 This happiness in part is mine,
    Already saved from low design,
      From every creature-love ;
Blest with the scorn of finite good,
My soul is lightened of its load,
      And seeks the things above.

3 Nothing on earth I call my own ;
    A stranger, to the world unknown,
      I all their goods despise ;
I trample on their whole delight,
And seek a country out of sight,
      A country in the skies.

4 There is my house and portion fair,
    My treasure and my heart are there,
      And my abiding home ;
For me my elder brethren stay,
And angels beckon me away,
      And Jesus bids me come.

5 I come, Thy servant, Lord, replies,
  I come to meet Thee in the skies,
    And claim my heavenly rest.
Now let the pilgrim's journey end,
Now, O my Saviour, Brother, Friend !
    Receive me to Thy breast. Amen.
                          Wesley. 1747.

802   C.M.D.
*Blessed is he whose trans-
gression is forgiven, whose sin is covered.*
Psalm xxxii. 1.

HOW happy every child of grace,
    Who knows his sins forgiven !
This earth, he cries, is not my place,
    I seek my place in heaven,
A country far from mortal sight ;
    Yet, O ! by faith I see
The land of rest, the saints' delight,
    The heaven prepared for me.

2 To that Jerusalem above
    With singing I repair ;
While in the flesh my hope and love,
    My heart and soul are there :
There my exalted Saviour stands,
    My merciful High Priest,
And still extends His wounded hands
    To take me to His breast.

3 O what a blessèd hope is ours !
    While here on earth we stay,
We more than taste the heavenly powers,
    And antedate that day :
We feel the resurrection near,
    Our life in Christ concealed,
And with His glorious presence here
    Our earthen vessels filled.

4 O would He more of heaven bestow,
    And let the vessel break,
And let our ransomed spirits go
    To grasp the God we seek !
In rapturous awe on Him to gaze,
    Who bought the sight for me ;
And shout, and wonder at His grace,
    Through all eternity.
                    Charles Wesley. 1759.

803   6.6.8. 6.6.8.
*Ye are come unto . . .
the heavenly Jerusalem.*—Hebrews xii. 22.

JERUSALEM divine,
    When shall I call thee mine ?
And to thy holy hill attain,
    Where weary pilgrims rest ;
    And in thy glories blest,
With God Messiah ever reign ?

2 There saints and angels join
    In fellowship divine,
And rapture swells the solemn lay ;
    While all with one accord
    Adore their glorious Lord,
And shout His praise in endless day.

3 May I but find the grace
 To fill an humble place
In that inheritance above;
 My tuneful voice I'll raise
 In songs of loudest praise,
To spread Thy fame, redeeming Love.

4 Mysterious Deity,
 Who ne'er began to be,
To sound Thy endless praise be mine!
 Reign, true Messiah, reign!
 Thy kingdom shall remain,
When stars and sun no more shall shine.
                                   Amen.
               Benjamin Rhodes. 1806.

Christian Missions.

804   7.6. 7.6. D.
He shall have dominion also from sea to sea.—Psalm lxxii. 8.

HAIL to the Lord's Anointed!
  Great David's greater Son;
Hail in the time appointed,
  His reign on earth begun.
He comes to break oppression,
  To set the captive free,
To take away transgression,
  And rule in equity.

2 He shall come down like showers
  Upon the fruitful earth;
Love, joy, and hope, like flowers,
  Spring in His path to birth;
Before Him on the mountains
  Shall peace, the herald, go;
And righteousness, in fountains,
  From hill to valley flow.

3 Arabia's desert ranger
  To Him shall bow the knee;
The Ethiopian stranger
  His glory come to see:
With offerings of devotion,
  Ships from the isles shall meet,
To pour the wealth of ocean
  In tribute at His feet.

4 Kings shall fall down before Him,
  And gold and incense bring;
All nations shall adore Him,
  His praise all people sing:
For He shall have dominion
  O'er river, sea, and shore,
Far as the eagle's pinion,
  Or dove's light wing, can soar.

5 For Him shall prayer unceasing
  And daily vows ascend;
His kingdom still increasing,
  A kingdom without end.
The mountain dew shall nourish
  A seed in weakness sown,
Whose fruit shall spread and flourish,
  And shake like Lebanon.

6 O'er every foe victorious,
  He on His throne shall rest;
From age to age more glorious,
  All blessing and all blest.

The tide of time shall **never**
  His covenant remove;
His name shall stand for ever,
  His great, best name of Love.
                James Montgomery. 1822.

805   7.6. 7.6. D.
All nations shall serve Him.
Psalm lxxii. 11.

FROM Greenland's **icy** mountains,
  From India's **coral** strand,
Where Afric's sunny fountains
  Roll down their golden sand;
From many an ancient river,
  From many a palmy plain,
They call us to deliver
  Their land from error's chain.

2 What though the spicy breezes
  Blow soft o'er Ceylon's isle;
Though every prospect pleases,
  And only man is vile;
In vain, with lavish kindness,
  The gifts of God are strewn;
The heathen, in his blindness,
  Bows down to wood and stone.

3 Shall we, whose souls are lighted
  With wisdom from on high,
Shall we to men benighted
  The lamp of life deny?
Salvation! O Salvation!
  The joyful sound proclaim,
Till each remotest nation
  Has learned Messiah's name.

4 Waft, waft, ye winds, His story;
  And you, ye waters, roll,
Till, like a sea of glory
  It spreads from pole to pole;
Till, o'er our ransomed nature,
  The Lamb for sinners slain,
Redeemer, King, Creator,
  In bliss returns to reign. Amen.
                Bishop R. Heber. 1819.

CHRISTIAN MISSIONS.

806   7.7.7.7. D.
Hallelujah! for the Lord God omnipotent reigneth.—Rev. xix. 6.

HARK! the song of jubilee,
  Loud as mighty thunder's roar,
Or the fulness of the sea
  When it breaks upon the shore:
Hallelujah! for the Lord
  God omnipotent shall reign;
Hallelujah! let the word
  Echo round the earth and main.

2 Hallelujah! Hark! the sound
  From the depths unto the skies,
Wakes above, beneath, around,
  All creation's harmonies:
See Jehovah's banner furled,
  Sheathed His sword; He speaks—
    'tis done,
And the kingdoms of this world
  Are the kingdoms of His Son.

3 He shall reign from pole to pole
  With illimitable sway;
He shall reign when like a scroll
  Yonder heavens have passed away:
Then the end; beneath His rod
  Man's last enemy shall fall;
Hallelujah! Christ in God,
  God in Christ is All in all! Amen.
        James Montgomery.   1819.

807   6.6.6.6.8.8.
Then shalt thou cause the trumpet of the jubilee to sound.
Leviticus xxv. 9.

BLOW ye the trumpet, blow
  The gladly solemn sound;
Let all the nations know,
  To earth's remotest bound,
The year of jubilee is come;
Return, ye ransomed sinners, home.

2 Jesus, our great High Priest,
  Hath full atonement made;
Ye weary spirits rest,
  Ye mournful souls, be glad:
The year of jubilee is come;
Return, ye ransomed sinners, home.

3 Extol the Lamb of God,
  The all-atoning Lamb,
Redemption in His blood
  Throughout the world proclaim.
The year of jubilee is come;
Return, ye ransomed sinners, home.

4 Ye slaves of sin and hell,
  Your liberty receive,
And safe in Jesus dwell,
  And blest in Jesus live.
The year of jubilee is come;
Return, ye ransomed sinners, home.

5 Ye who have sold for nought
  Your heritage above,
Shall have it back unbought,
  The gift of Jesus' love.
The year of jubilee is come;
Return, ye ransomed sinners, home.

6 The gospel trumpet hear,
  The news of heavenly grace,
And, saved from earth, appear
  Before your Saviour's face.
The year of jubilee is come;
Return, ye ransomed sinners, home.
        Charles Wesley.   1750.

808   L.M.
He shall come down like rain upon the mown grass.—Psalm lxxii. 6.

GREAT God, whose universal sway
  The known and unknown worlds obey,
Now give the kingdom to Thy Son,
Extend His power, exalt His throne.

2 The sceptre well becomes His hands;
All heaven submits to His commands;
His justice shall avenge the poor,
And pride and rage prevail no more.

3 With power He vindicates the just,
And treads the oppressor in the dust;
His worship and His fear shall last
Till the full round of time is past.

4 As rain on meadows newly mown,
So shall He send His influence down;
His grace on fainting souls distils,
Like heavenly dew on thirsty hills.

5 The heathen lands that lie beneath
The shades of overspreading death,
Revive at His first dawning light,
And deserts blossom at the sight.

6 The saints shall flourish in His days,
Arrayed in robes of joy and praise;
Peace, like a river, from His throne
Shall flow to nations yet unknown.
        Isaac Watts.   1709.

809   L.M.
He shall reign for ever and ever.
Revelation xi. 15.

JESUS shall reign where'er the sun
  Doth his successive journeys run;
His kingdom stretch from shore to shore,
Till suns shall rise and set no more.

2 For Him shall endless prayer be made,
And praises throng to crown His head;
His name like sweet perfume shall rise
With every morning sacrifice.

3 People and realms of every tongue
Dwell on His love with sweetest song,
And infant-voices shall proclaim
Hosannas to His sacred name.

4 Blessings abound where'er He reigns;
The prisoner leaps to lose his chains;
The weary find eternal rest,
And all the sons of want are blest.

5 Where He displays His healing power,
Death and the curse are known no more;
In Him the tribes of Adam boast
More blessings than their father lost.

CHRISTIAN MISSIONS.

6 Let every creature rise, and bring
  Its grateful honours to our King;
  Angels descend with songs again,
  And earth repeat its loud Amen.
                Isaac Watts. 1719.

810 L.M.
In every place incense shall be offered unto My name, and a pure offering.—Malachi i. 11.

O THOU, to whom in ancient time,
  The lyre of Hebrew bards was strung;
Whom kings adored in songs sublime,
  And prophets praised with glowing tongue;

2 Not now on Zion's height alone,
    Thy favoured worshippers may dwell,
  Nor where at sultry noon Thy Son
    Sat weary by the patriarch's well;

3 From every place below the skies,
    The grateful song, the fervent prayer,
  The incense of the heart may rise
    To heaven, and find acceptance there.

4 To Thee shall age with snowy hair,
    And strength and beauty bend the knee;
  And childhood lisp, with reverent air,
    Its praises and its prayers to Thee.

5 O Thou, to whom, in ancient time,
    The lyre of prophet bards was strung,
  To Thee at last, in every clime,
    Shall temples rise, and praise be sung.
                John Pierpoint. 1840.

811 C.M.
The mountain of the Lord's house.—Isaiah ii. 2.

BEHOLD! The mountain of the Lord,
  In latter days, shall rise
On mountain tops, above the hills,
  And draw the wondering eyes.

2 To this the joyful nations round,
    All tribes and tongues shall flow;
  Up to the hill of God, they'll say,
    And to His house we'll go.

3 The beam that shines from Zion's hill
    Shall lighten every land;
  The King who reigns in Salem's towers
    Shall all the world command.

4 No strife shall vex Messiah's reign,
    Or mar the peaceful years;
  To ploughshares men shall beat their swords,
    To pruning-hooks their spears.

5 No longer hosts encountering hosts
    Their crowds of slain deplore;
  They hang the trumpet in the hall,
    And study war no more.

6 Come, then! O, come from every land,
  To worship at His shrine;
And, walking in the light of God,
  With holy beauties shine.
                Michael Bruce. 1768.

812 6.6. 6.6. 8.8.
That Thy way may be known upon earth, Thy saving health among all nations.—Psalm lxvii. 2.

ARISE, O Lord, and shine
  In all Thy saving might,
And prosper each design
  To spread Thy glorious light;
Let healing streams of mercy flow,
That all the earth Thy truth may know.

2 O bring the nations near,
    That they may sing Thy praise;
  Let all the people hear
    And learn Thy holy ways;
  Reign, Mighty God, assert Thy cause,
  And govern by Thy righteous laws.

3 Put forth Thy glorious power;
    The nations then shall see,
  And earth present her store,
    In converts born to Thee;
  God, our own God, His Church shall bless,
  And earth be filled with righteousness.

4 To God, the Father, Son,
    And Spirit ever Blest,
  Eternal Three in One,
    All worship be addressed;
  Join, all on earth, rejoice and sing,
  All glory give to God our King. Amen.
                W. Hurn. 1813. *alt.*

813 L.M.
O praise the Lord, all ye nations.—Psalm cxvii. 1.

FROM all that dwell below the skies,
  Let the Creator's praise arise;
Let the Redeemer's name be sung,
Through every land, by every tongue.

2 Eternal are Thy mercies, Lord,
  Eternal truth attends Thy word;
  Thy praise shall sound from shore to shore,
  Till suns shall rise and set no more.

3 Praise God, from whom all blessings flow;
  Praise Him, all creatures here below;
  Praise Him above, ye heavenly host;
  Praise Father, Son, and Holy Ghost!
                Isaac Watts. 1719.   Amen.
                Doxology by Bishop Ken. 1695.

814 S.M.
Pray ye . . . the Lord of the harvest, that He will send forth labourers into His harvest.—Matthew ix. 38.

LORD of the harvest, hear
  Thy needy servants' cry;
Answer our faith's effectual prayer,
  And all our wants supply.

CHRISTIAN MISSIONS.

2 On Thee we humbly wait,
  Our wants are in Thy view;
The harvest, truly, Lord, is great,
  The labourers are few.

3 Convert, and send forth more
  Into Thy Church abroad;
And let them speak Thy word of power,
  As workers with their God.

4 Give the pure Gospel word,
  The word of general grace;
Thee let them preach, the common Lord,
  The Saviour of our race.

5 O let them spread Thy name,
  Their mission fully prove,
Thy universal grace proclaim,
  Thy all-redeeming love!

6 On all mankind, forgiven,
  Empower them still to call;
And tell each creature under heaven,
  That Thou hast died for all. Amen.
          Wesley. 1742.

815 S.M.
How beautiful upon the mountains are the feet of him that bringeth good tidings.—Isaiah lii. 7.

HOW beauteous are their feet
  Who stand on Sion's hill;
Who bring salvation in their tongues,
  And words of peace reveal:

2 How rapturous is their voice!
  How sweet the tidings are!
'Sion, behold thy Saviour King;
  He reigns and triumphs here.

3 How favoured are our ears,
  That hear the joyful sound,
Which kings and prophets waited for,
  And sought, but never found!

4 How blessed are our eyes,
  That see this heavenly light!
Prophets and kings desired long,
  But died without the sight.

5 The watchmen join their voice,
  And tuneful notes employ;
Jerusalem breaks forth in songs,
  And deserts learn the joy.

6 The Lord makes bare His arm
  Through all the earth abroad:
Let all the nations now behold
  Their Saviour and their God.
          Isaac Watts. 1709.

816 8.7.8.7.4.7.
To preach the acceptable year of the Lord.—Luke iv. 19.

O'ER the gloomy hills of darkness,
  Look, my soul, be still, and gaze;
All the promises do travail
  With a glorious day of grace;
    Blessed jubilee!
  Let thy glorious morning dawn.

2 Let the Indian, let the negro,
  Let the rude barbarian see
That divine and glorious conquest
  Once obtained on Calvary;
    Let the Gospel
  Loud resound from pole to pole.

3 Kingdoms wide, that sit in darkness,
  Grant them, Lord, Thy glorious light,
And from eastern coast to western
  Let the morning chase the night,
    And Redemption,
  Freely purchased, win the day.

4 Fly abroad, thou mighty Gospel,
  Win and conquer, never cease;
So Immanuel's fair dominions
  Shall extend and still increase,
    Till the kingdoms
  Of the world are all His own.
          W. Williams. 1759.

817 8.7.8.7. D.
So shall He sprinkle many nations.—Isaiah lii. 15.

SAVIOUR, sprinkle many nations,
  Fruitful let Thy sorrows be;
By Thy pains and consolations
  Draw the Gentiles unto Thee:
Of Thy Cross the wondrous story
  Be to all the nations told;
Let them see Thee in Thy glory,
  And Thy mercy manifold.

2 Far and wide, though all unknowing,
  Pants for Thee each mortal breast;
Human tears for Thee are flowing,
  Human hearts in Thee would rest:
Thirsting as for dews of even,
  As the new-mown grass for rain,
Thee they seek, as God of heaven,
  Thee as Man for sinners slain.

3 Saviour, lo, the isles are waiting,
  Stretched the hand, and strained the sight,
For Thy Spirit, now-creating,
  Love's pure flame and wisdom's light.
Give the word, and of the preacher
  Speed the foot and touch the tongue,
Till on earth by every creature
  Glory to the Lamb be sung. Amen.
          Bishop A. C. Coxe. 1851.

818 7.7.7.7. D.
I am come to send fire on the earth.—Luke xii. 49.

SEE how great a flame aspires,
  Kindled by a spark of grace!
Jesu's love the nations fires,
  Sets the kingdoms on a blaze;
To bring fire on earth He came,
  Kindled in some hearts it is,
O that all might catch the flame,
  All partake the glorious bliss!

CHRISTIAN MISSIONS.

2 When He first the work begun,
Small and feeble was His day;
Now the word doth swiftly run,
Now it wins its widening way:
More and more it spreads and grows,
Ever mighty to prevail,
Sin's strongholds it now o'erthrows,
Shakes the **trembling gates** of hell.

3 Sons of God, **your Saviour praise!**
He the **door hath opened wide;**
He hath **given the word of grace,**
Jesus's word **is glorified:**
Jesus, mighty **to redeem,**
He alone the **work hath wrought;**
Worthy is **the work of Him,**
Him **who spake a world from nought.**

4 Saw ye **not the cloud** arise,
Little as a human hand?
Now it spreads along the skies.
Hangs o'er all the thirsty land:
Lo! the promise of a shower
Drops already from above;
But the **Lord** will shortly **pour**
All the **Spirit of** His Love.
Charles Wesley. 1749.

819   8.7. 8.7. **4.7.**
All the ends of the earth shall see the salvation of our God.
Isaiah lii. 10.

YES! we trust the day is breaking:
Joyful times are near at hand;
God, the mighty God, is speaking
By His word in every land;
When He chooses,
Darkness flees at His command.

2 Let us hail the joyful season;
Let us hail the rising ray;
When the Lord appears, there's reason
To expect a glorious day:
At His presence
Gloom and darkness flee away.

3 While the foe becomes more daring,
While he enters like a flood,
God the Saviour is preparing
Means to spread His truth abroad:
Every language
Soon shall tell the love of God.

4 Oh, 'tis pleasant, 'tis reviving
To our hearts, **to hear** each day
Joyful news from **far** arriving,
How the Gospel wins its way;
Those enlightening,
Who in death and darkness lay.

5 God of Jacob, high and glorious!
Let Thy people **see** Thy hand;
Let the Gospel be victorious
Through the world, in every **land:**
And the idols
Perish, Lord, at Thy command. Amen.
Thomas Kelly. 1809.

820   6.6.4. 6.6.6.4.
Let there be light.—Gen. 1. 3.

THOU, whose almighty word,
Chaos and darkness heard,
And took **their** flight,
Hear **us, we** humbly pray;
And where the gospel's day
Sheds not its glorious **ray,**
Let **there** be light.

2 Thou who didst come to bring
On Thy redeeming wing,
Healing and sight,
Health **to the sick in mind,**
Sight to **the inly blind,**
O now, to all mankind,
Let there be light.

3 Spirit **of** truth and love,
Life giving, holy Dove,
Speed forth Thy flight;
Move on the water's face,
Bearing the lamp of grace,
And in earth's darkest place
Let there be light.

4 Blessèd **and holy Three!**
Glorious **Trinity!**
Wisdom! **Love!** Might!
Boundless as ocean's **tide**
Rolling in fullest pride,
Through the world far and wide,
Let there **be** light. Amen.
John Marriott. 1813.

821   7.7.7.7
This gospel of the kingdom shall be preached in all the world.
Matthew xxiv. 14.

SPREAD, O spread, thou mighty word,
Spread the kingdom of the Lord;
Wheresoe'er His breath has given
Life to beings meant for heaven.

2 **Tell them** how the Father's will
Made the world and keeps it still;
How He sent His Son to save
All who help and comfort crave.

3 Tell of our Redeemer's love,
Who for ever doth remove,
By His holy sacrifice,
All the guilt that on us lies.

4 Tell them of the Spirit given
Now to **guide us** up to heaven;
Strong **and holy,** just and true,
Working **both to** will and do.

5 Word of life most pure and strong,
Lo! for thee the nations long;
Spread till, from its dreary night,
All the world awakes to light.

6 Up! the ripening fields ye see,
Mighty shall the harvest be;
But the reapers still are few,
Great the work they have to do.

NEW YEAR.

7 Lord of harvest, let there be
  Joy and strength to work for **Thee**;
  Let the nations far and near
  See Thy light and learn Thy **fear**.
                           Amen.
          J. F. Bahnmaier. d. 1841.
         Tr. Catherine Winkworth. 1858.

Departure of Missionaries.

822   8.7. 8.7. 4.7.
    *Recommended to the grace
    of God for the work which they fulfilled.*
                Acts xiv. 26.

SPEED Thy servants, Saviour, speed
    them,
  Thou art Lord of winds and waves;
They were bound, but Thou hast freed
    them,
  Now they go to free the slaves;
    Be Thou with them:
    'Tis Thine arm alone that saves.

2 Friends and home and all forsaking,
  Lord, they go at Thy command,
As their stay Thy promise taking,
  While they traverse sea and land:
    O be with them!
  Lead them safely by the hand.

3 When they reach the land of strangers,
  And the prospect dark appears,
Nothing seen but toils and dangers,
  Nothing felt but doubts and fears,
    Be Thou with them;
  Hear their sighs, and count their tears.

4 Where no fruit appears to cheer them,
  And they seem to toil in vain,
Then, in mercy, Lord, draw near them,
  Then their sinking hopes sustain;
    Thus supported,
  Let their zeal revive again.

---

5 In the midst of opposition,
  Let them trust O Lord, in Thee;
When success attends their mission,
  Let Thy servants humbler be;
    Never leave them,
  Till Thy face in heaven they see:—

6 There to reap in joy for ever
  Fruit that grows from seed here sown;
There to be with Him who never
  Ceases to preserve His own;
    And with gladness
  Give the praise to Him alone. Amen.
                Thomas Kelly. 1820.

823   L.M.
    *Go ye therefore, and teach
    all nations.*—Matthew xxviii. 19.

GO, messenger of peace and love,
  To nations plunged in shades of
    night;
Like angels sent from fields above,
  Be thine to shed celestial light.

2 Go, to the hungry food impart,
  To paths of peace the wanderer guide;
And lead the thirsty, panting heart
  Where streams of living water glide.

3 On barren rock and desert isle,
  Go, bid the Rose of Sharon bloom;
Till arid wastes around thee smile,
  Bright with the dews of morning's
    womb.

4 From north to south, from east to west,
  Messiah yet shall reign supreme;
His name, by every tongue confest;
  His praise, the universal theme.

5 Then faint not in the day of toil,
  When harvest waits the reaper's hand;
Go, gather in the glorious spoil,
  And joyous in His presence stand.

6 Thy love a rich reward shall find
  From Him who sits enthroned on high;
For they who turn the erring mind
  Shall shine like stars above the sky
                    Balfour. 1828.

New Year.

824   C.M.
    *O give thanks unto the Lord,
    for He is good.*—Psalm cvii. 1.

SING to the Great Jehovah's praise
  All praise to Him belongs;
Who kindly lengthens out our days,
  Demands our choicest songs.

2 His providence has brought us through
  Another varied year;
We all with vows and anthems now,
  Before our God appear.

3 Father, Thy mercies past we own,
  Thy still continued care;
To Thee presenting, through Thy Son,
  Whate'er we have or are.

4 Our lips and lives shall gladly show
  The wonders of Thy love,
While on in Jesu's steps we go
  To see Thy face above.

5 Our residue of days or hours
  Thine, wholly Thine, shall be;
And all our consecrated powers
  A sacrifice to Thee;

NEW YEAR.

6 Till Jesus in the clouds appear
    To saints on earth forgiven,
And bring the grand sabbatic year,
    The Jubilee of heaven.
Charles Wesley. 1750.

825   6.5. 6.5. D. *With Chorus.*
Fear not; for I am with thee.
Isaiah xli. 10.

STANDING at the portal
    Of the opening year,
Words of comfort meet us,
    Hushing every fear,
Spoken through the silence
    By our Father's voice,
Tender, strong, and faithful,
    Making us rejoice.
    Onward, then, and fear not,
      Children of the day!
    For His word shall never,
      Never pass away!

2 'I, the Lord, am with thee,
    Be thou not afraid!
I will help and strengthen,
    Be thou not dismayed!
Yea, I will uphold thee
    With My own right hand;
Thou art called and chosen
    In My sight to stand.'

3 For the year before us,
    O, what rich supplies!
For the poor and needy
    Living streams shall rise;
For the sad and sinful
    Shall His grace abound,
For the faint and feeble
    Perfect strength be found.

4 He will never fail us,
    He will not forsake;
His eternal covenant
    He will never break!
Resting on His promise,
    What have we to fear?
God is all-sufficient
    For the coming year.
Frances R. Havergal. 1873.

826   L.M.
*Thou crownest the year
with Thy goodness.*—Psalm lxv. 11.

ETERNAL Source of every joy,
    Well may Thy praise our lips employ,
While in Thy temple we appear,
Whose goodness crowns the circling year.

2 The flowery spring, at Thy command,
Embalms the air and paints the land;
The summer rays with vigour shine,
To raise the corn and cheer the vine.

3 Thy hand in autumn richly pours
Through all our coasts redundant stores;
And winters, softened by Thy care,
No more a face of horror wear.

4 Seasons, and months, and weeks, and days
Demand successive songs of praise;
Still be the cheerful homage paid
With opening light, and evening shade.

5 Here in Thy house shall incense rise,
As circling Sabbaths bless our eyes;
Still will we make Thy mercies known
Around Thy board, and round our own.

6 O may our more harmonious tongues
In worlds unknown pursue the songs;
And in those brighter courts adore,
Where days and years revolve no more.
    Amen.
Philip Doddridge. 1755.

827   6.6. 6 6. 8.8.
Lord, let it alone this year also.
Luke xiii. 8.

THE Lord of earth and sky,
    The God of ages, praise;
Who reigns enthroned on high,
    Ancient of endless days;
Who lengthens out our trial here,
And spares us yet another year.

2 Barren and withered trees,
    We cumbered long the ground;
No fruit of holiness
    On our dead souls was found;
Yet doth He us in mercy spare
Another and another year.

3 When Justice bared the sword,
    To cut the fig-tree down,
The pity of our Lord
    Cried, 'Let it still alone;
Our gracious God inclines His ear,
And spares us yet another year.

4 Jesus, Thy speaking blood
    From God obtained the grace,
Who therefore hath bestowed
    On us a longer space;
Thou didst in our behalf appear,
And, lo, we see another year!

5 Then dig about our root,
    Break up the fallow ground,
And let our gracious fruit
    To Thy great praise abound;
O let us all Thy praise declare,
And fruit unto perfection bear! Amen.
Wesley. 1749.

828   C.M.D.
*But let us, who are of the
day, be sober, putting on the breast-plate of
faith and love; and for an helmet, the hope
of salvation.*—1 Thess. v. 8.

THE old year's long campaign is o'er;
    Behold a new begun!
Not yet is closed the holy war,
    Not yet the triumph won.
Not yet the end, not yet repose;
    We hear our Captain say,
'Go forth again to meet your foes,
    Ye children of the day!

NEW YEAR.

2 'Go forth, firm faith in every heart,
   Bright hope on every helm ;
Through that shall pierce no fiery dart,
   And this no fear o'erwhelm.
Go in the spirit and the might
   Of Him who led the way ;
Close with the legions of the night,
   Ye children of the day.'

3 So forth we go to meet the strife,
   We will not fear nor fly ;
We love the holy warrior's life,
   His death we hope to die.
We slumber not, that charge in view,
   Toil on while toil ye may,
Then night shall be no night to you,
   Ye children of the day.

4 Lord God, our Glory, Three in One,
   Thine own sustain, defend ;
And give, though dim this earthly sun,
   Thy true light to the end ;
Till morning tread the darkness down,
   And night be swept away,
And infinite sweet triumph crown
   The children of the day. Amen.
           Samuel J. Stone. 1872.

829   C.M.
And now, Lord, what wait I for ? My hope is in Thee.—Psalm xxxix. 7.

THE year is gone beyond recall,
   With all its hopes and fears,
With all its bright and gladdening smiles,
   With all its mournful tears.

2 Thy thankful people praise Thee, Lord,
   For countless gifts received ;
And pray for grace to keep the Faith
   Which saints of old believed.

3 To Thee we come, O gracious Lord,
   The new-born year to bless ;
Defend our land from pestilence ;
   Give peace and plenteousness.

4 Forgive this nation's many sins ;
   The growth of vice restrain ;
And help us all with sin to strive,
   And crowns of life to gain.

5 From evil deeds that stain the past
   We now desire to flee ;
And pray that future years may all
   Be spent, good Lord, for Thee.

6 O Father, let Thy watchful eye
   Still look on us in love,
That we may praise Thee, year by year,
   With angel-hosts above. Amen.
            Meaux Breviary.
     Tr. *Francis Pott.* 1861. Alt.

830   7.7.7.7.
For Thy name's sake lead me and guide me.—Psalm xxxi. 3.

FOR Thy mercy and Thy grace,
   Constant through another year,
Hear our song of thankfulness,
   Jesus, our Redeemer, hear !

2 Lo ! our sins on Thee we cast,
   Thee, our perfect Sacrifice,
And, forgetting all the past,
   Press towards our glorious prize.

3 Dark the future ; let Thy light
   Guide us, Bright and Morning Star ;
Fierce our foes, and hard the fight ;
   Arm us, Saviour, for the war.

4 In our weakness and distress,
   Rock of Strength, be Thou our stay !
In the pathless wilderness
   Be our true and living way.

5 Who of us death's awful road
   In the coming year shall tread ?
With Thy rod and staff, O God,
   Comfort Thou his dying bed.

6 Keep us faithful, keep us pure,
   Keep us evermore Thine own :
Help, O help us to endure ;
   Fit us for the promised crown.

7 So within Thy palace gate
   We shall praise, on golden strings
Thee, the only Potentate,
   Lord of lords, and King of kings !
                     Amen.
        Henry Downton. 1843.

831   7.6.7.6.
I am still with Thee.
Psalm cxxxix. 18.

ANOTHER year is dawning,
   Dear Master, let it be,
In working or in waiting,
   Another year with Thee :

2 Another year of leaning
   Upon Thy loving breast,
Of ever-deepening trustfulness,
   Of quiet, happy rest ;

3 Another year of mercies,
   Of faithfulness and grace ;
Another year of gladness
   In the shining of Thy face ;

4 Another year of progress,
   Another year of praise,
Another year of proving
   Thy presence all the days ;

5 Another year of service,
   Of witness for Thy love ;
Another year of training
   For holier work above.

6 Another year is dawning,
   Dear Master, let it be,
On earth, or else in heaven
   Another year for Thee ! Amen.
     Frances R. Havergal. a. 1879.

SPRING.

832 L.M. *God is my defence, and the God of my mercy.—Psalm lix. 17.*

ANOTHER year has now begun
   With silent pace its course to run ;
Our hearts and voices let us raise
To God, in prayer and songs of praise.

2 Father, Thy bounteous love we bless,
   For gifts and mercies numberless ;
   For life and health, for grace and peace,
   For hope of joys that never cease.

3 O Son of God, in faith and fear
   Teach us to walk as strangers here,
   With hearts in heaven, that we may come
   To where Thou art, our Father's home.

4 Grant us, O Comforter, Thy grace,
   And speed us on our earthly race,
   In body, spirit, and in soul,
   Right onward to the heavenly goal.

5 Thou, Lord, who makest all things new,
   O give us hearts both pure and true ;
   That we, as jewels, ever Thine,
   In New Jerusalem may shine.

6 Blest Three in One, to Thee we pray,
   Defend and guide us on our way ;
   That we at last with joy may see
   The new year of eternity.   Amen.
                    Bishop C. Wordsworth. 1862.

833 8.7, 8 7. D. *Thou shalt guide me with Thy counsel, and afterward receive me to glory.—Psalm lxxiii. 24.*

AT Thy feet, our God and Father,
   Who hast blessed us all our days,
We with grateful hearts would gather,
   To begin the year with praise ;
Praise for light so brightly shining
   On our steps from heaven above ;
Praise for mercies daily twining
   Round us golden cords of love.

2 Jesus, for Thy love most tender,
   On the cross for sinners shown,
   We would praise Thee, and surrender
   All our hearts to be Thine own.
   With so blest a Friend provided,
   We upon our way would go,
   Sure of being safely guided,
   Guarded well from every foe.

3 Every day will be the brighter,
   When Thy gracious face we see ;
   Every burden will be lighter,
   When we know it comes from Thee.
   Spread Thy love's broad banner o'er us,
   Give us strength to serve and wait,
   Till Thy glory break before us,
   Through the city's open gate.   Amen.
                    James D. Burns. 1857.

Seasons of the Year.

Spring.

834 C.M. *Thou visitest the earth, and waterest it.—Psalm lxv. 9.*

THE springtide hour brings leaf and
      flower,
   With songs of life and love ;
And many a lay wears out the day
   In many a leafy grove :

2 Bird, flower, and tree seem to agree
   Their choicest gifts to bring ;
   But this poor heart bears not its part,
   In it there is no spring.

3 Dews fall apace, the dews of grace,
   Upon this soul of sin ;
   And love divine delights to shine
   Upon the waste within :

4 Yet year by year fruits, flowers, appear,
   And birds their praises sing ;
   But this poor heart bears not its part,
   Its winter has no spring.

5 Lord, let Thy love, fresh from above,
   Soft as the south wind blow ;
   Call forth its bloom, wake its perfume,
   And bid its spices flow :

6 And when Thy voice makes earth rejoice,
   And the hills laugh and sing,
   Lord, teach this heart to bear its part,
   And join the praise of spring.   Amen.
                    J. S. B. Monsell. 18 7.

835 8.8. 8.8. 8.8. *The earth is full of the goodness of the Lord.—Psalm xxxiii. 5.*

THOU art, O God, the life and light
   Of all this wondrous world we see ;
Its glow by day, its smile by night,
   Are but reflections caught from Thee :
Where'er we turn, Thy glories shine,
And all things fair and bright are Thine.

2 When day with farewell beam delays
   Among the opening clouds of even,
   And we can almost think we gaze
   Through golden vistas into heaven,
   Those hues that make the sun's decline
   So soft, so radiant, Lord, are Thine.

SEASONS OF THE YEAR.

3 When night with wings of starry gloom
  O'ershadows all the earth and skies,
Like some dark beauteous bird whose
    plume
Is sparkling with unnumbered eyes,
That sacred gloom, those fires divine,
So grand, so countless, Lord, are Thine.

4 When youthful spring around us breathes,
  Thy Spirit warms her fragrant sigh,
And every flower the summer wreathes
  Is born beneath that kindling eye,
Where'er we turn, Thy glories shine,
And all things fair and bright are Thine.

           T. Moore. 1817.

836   *Irregular.*
The flowers appear on the earth; the time of the singing of birds is come.
    Song of Solomon ii. 12.

FOR all Thy love and goodness, so bountiful and free,
    Thy name, Lord, be adored!
On the wings of joyous praise our hearts
   soar up to Thee;
    Glory to the Lord!

2 The springtime breaks all round about,
   waking from winter's night;
    Thy name, Lord, be adored!
The sunshine, like God's love, pours down
   in floods of golden light;
    Glory to the Lord!

3 A voice of joy is in all the earth, a voice is
   in all the air;
    Thy name, Lord, be adored!
All nature singeth aloud to God; there is
   gladness everywhere;
    Glory to the Lord!

4 The flowers are strewn in field and copse,
   on the hill and on the plain;
    Thy name, Lord, be adored!
The soft air stirs in the tender leaves, that
   clothe the trees again;
    Glory to the Lord!

5 The works of Thy hands are very fair; and
   for all Thy bounteous love,
    Thy name, Lord, be adored!
But what, if this world is so fair, is the
   Better Land above?
    Glory to the Lord!

6 O, to awake from death's short sleep, like
   the flowers from their wintry grave!
    Thy name, Lord, be adored!
And to rise all glorious in the day when
   Christ shall come to save;
    Glory to the Lord!

7 O, to dwell in that happy land, where the
   heart cannot choose but sing!
    Thy name, Lord, be adored!
And when the life of the blessèd ones is a
   beautiful endless spring;
    Glory to the Lord! Amen.

    Mrs. Frances J. Douglas. b. 1829,
    And Bishop W. W. How. 1871.

---

837   C.M.
Thou makest it soft with showers; Thou blessest the springing thereof
    Psalm lxv. 10.

THE voices of the spring, O Lord,
   Are wakened by Thy breath;
The winter's cold is past and gone,
   Life triumphs over death.

2 Thy life, through nature throbbing, stirs
   The pulses of the earth;
The meadows laugh beneath Thy smile,
   Thou givest beauty birth.

3 The birds, those feathered minstrels, learn
   Their music, Lord, from Thee;
All nature's chords, touched by Thy hand,
   Resound with melody.

4 The odours of the flowers arise
   Like incense to Thy throne;
Thy goodness makes Thy creatures glad,
   Thy light for them is sown.

5 Thrice holy Lord of earth and sky,
   How beautiful art Thou!
What grace must on Thy servants rest,
   Who in Thy presence bow!

6 O, let Thy love fill all my soul!
   Put in my heart Thy peace;
My footsteps guide to Thy loved home,
   Where praises never cease. Amen.

          Alfred Jones. 1887.

838   5.5. 5.5. D.
I will . . . pour you out a blessing that there shall not be room enough to receive it.—Malachi iii. 10.

O SING to the Lord,
   Whose bountiful hand
Again doth accord
   His gifts to the land.
His clouds have shed down
   Their plenteousness here;
His goodness shall crown
   The hopes of the year;

2 In the clefts of the hills
   The founts He hath burst,
And poureth their rills
   Through valleys athirst;
The river of God
   The pastures hath blest,
The dry, withered sod
   In greenness is dressed.

3 And every fold
   Shall teem with its sheep,
With harvests of gold
   The fields shall be deep;
The vales shall rejoice
   With laughter and song,
And man's grateful voice
   The music prolong.

SUMMER—AUTUMN.

4 So, too, may He pour,
  The Last and the First,
His graces in store
  On spirits athirst,
Till when the great day
  Of harvest hath come,
He takes us away
  To garner at home. Amen.
          R. F. Littledale. 1867.

Summer.

839   6.5.6.5. D.
  *Truly the light is sweet,
and a pleasant thing it is for the eyes to
  behold the sun.*—Eccles. xi. 7.

SUMMER suns are glowing
  Over land and sea,
Happy light is flowing
  Bountiful and free.
Everything rejoices
  In the mellow rays,
All earth's thousand voices
  Swell the psalm of praise.

2 God's free mercy streameth
    Over all the world,
  And His banner gleameth
    Everywhere unfurled.
  Broad and deep and glorious
    As the heaven above,
  Shines in might victorious,
    His eternal Love.

3 Lord, upon our blindness
    Thy pure radiance pour;
  For Thy loving-kindness
    Makes us love Thee more.
  And when clouds are drifting
    Dark across our sky,
  Then, the veil uplifting,
    Father, be Thou nigh.

4 We will never doubt Thee,
    Though Thou veil Thy light;
  Life is dark without Thee;
    Death with Thee is bright.
  Light of Light! shine o'er us
    On our pilgrim way,
  Go Thou still before us
    To the endless day. Amen.
          Bishop W. W. How. 1871.

---

840   6.6.10. 6.6.10.
  *The mercy of the Lord is
from everlasting to everlasting.*—Ps. ciii. 17.

O LORD of heaven and earth,
  Who givest joy and mirth,
Open our lips to show Thy wondrous praise:
  Our hearts are dull and cold,
  We leave Thy love untold;
O give us strength our anthems glad to raise!

2 Each month we sow or reap,
  Each hour we toil or sleep,
Thou givest life and joy, and Thou alone:
  O grant to each and all
  When death's dark shadows fall,
To stand true workers round our Master's throne!

3 So, life's long task-work o'er,
    Set free for evermore,
We shall sit down at Thy great harvest-feast;
    Reaper and sower met,
    The burning heat forget,
And taste God's love, the greatest as the least.

4 Yea, Lord, Thou too dost claim
    The Sower's mystic name;
Thou sendest forth Thy reapers to their hold;
    O be it theirs to bear
    The full corn in the ear,
When Thy true seed its hundred-fold shall yield!

5 Root out the evil tares,
    Earth's vexing griefs and cares,
Bind the hot blasts that wither and destroy;
    And when the hour is come
    To bring the full sheaves home,
Bid men and angels share Thy harvest joy.
                              Amen.
          E. H. Plumptre. 1868.

Autumn.

841   C. M.
  *Seed-time and harvest . . .
shall not cease.*—Genesis viii. 22.

FOUNTAIN of mercy, God of love,
  How rich Thy bounties are!
The changing seasons, as they move,
  Proclaim Thy constant care.

2 When in the bosom of the earth
    The sower hid the grain,
  Thy goodness wrought its secret birth,
    And sent the early rain.

3 The spring's sweet influence, Lord, was Thine,
    The plants in beauty grew;
  Thou gav'st refulgent suns to shine,
    And soft refreshing dew.

4 These various mercies from above
    Matured the swelling grain;
  A yellow harvest crowns Thy love,
    And plenty fills the plain.

5 Seed-time and harvest, Lord, alone
    Thou dost on man bestow;
  Let us not then forget to own
    From whom our blessings flow.

6 Fountain of love! our praise is Thine;
    To Thee our songs we'll raise,
  And all created nature join
    In sweet, harmonious praise.
          Alice Flowerdew. 1811.

SEASONS OF THE YEAR.

842   7.6.7.6.
He . . . gave us rain from heaven and fruitful seasons.—Acts xiv. 17.

THE year is swiftly waning,
    The summer days are past;
And life, brief life, is speeding,
    The end is nearing fast.

2 The ever-changing seasons
    In silence come and go;
But Thou, Eternal Father,
    No time or change canst know.

3 O pour Thy grace upon us,
    That we may worthier be,
Each year that passes o'er us,
    To dwell in heaven with Thee.

4 Behold the bending orchards
    With bounteous fruit are crowned;
Lord, in our hearts more richly
    Let heavenly fruit abound.

5 O, by each mercy sent us,
    And by each grief and pain,
By blessings like the sunshine,
    And sorrows like the rain,—

6 Our barren hearts make fruitful
    With every goodly grace,
That we Thy name may hallow,
    And see at last Thy face. Amen.
        Bishop W. W. How. 1871.

Winter.

843   7.7.7.7.
Thou hast made . . . winter.
    Psalm lxxiv. 17.

WINTER reigneth o'er the land,
    Freezing with its icy breath;
Dead and bare the tall trees stand,
    All is chill and drear as death.

2 Yet it seemeth but a day
    Since the summer flowers were here,
Since they stacked the balmy hay,
    Since they reaped the golden ear.

3 Sunny days are past and gone:
    So the years go, speeding fast,
Onward ever, each new one,
    Swifter speeding than the last.

4 Life is waning; life is brief;
    Death, like winter, standeth nigh
Each one, like the failing leaf,
    Soon shall fade, and fall, and die.

5 But the sleeping earth shall wake,
    And the flowers shall burst in bloom,
And all nature rising break
    Glorious from its wintry tomb.

6 So, the saints from slumber blest,
    Rising shall awake and sing,
And our flesh in hope shall rest,
    Till there breaks the endless spring.
        Bishop W. W. How. 1871.

---

844   L.M.
The end of all things is at hand: be ye therefore sober, and watch unto prayer.—1 Peter iv. 7.

THE tide of time is rolling on,
  And now another year has gone;
The end of all things soon will come,
  O may it bring us to our home.

2 All things around us fade and die;
  All earthly hopes are vanity;
O let our restless hearts be stayed
  On Him whose glories never fade!

3 O Lord of love! let not the past
  Rise up against us at the last;
O Shepherd of our souls! be near
  To guide us through the coming year.

4 Keep us from every evil way,
  Guard and protect us day by day.
Preserve us from the sinner's doom,
  And save us from the wrath to come.

5 And when our spirits take their flight,
  Grant they may live 'mid saints in light;
O guide them to the realms above,
  Where all is joy, and peace, and love!

6 To Thee, O Father, Son, to Thee,
  To Thee, Blest Spirit, glory be;
As ever was in ages past,
  And shall be still while ages last.
        Amen.
        Anon.

---

845   7.7.7.7.
He giveth snow like wool.
He scattereth the hoar frost like ashes.
    Psalm cxlvii. 16.

COLD and cheerless, dark and drear,
    Wintry days and nights appear;
But they all in order stand,
    This is still God's goodly land.

2 Wind, and ice, and shrouding snow,
    At Thy bidding come and go;
Clouds obscure, or planets shine,
    But they serve Thee, and are Thine.

3 Flowers have faded from the plain,
    But their mother-roots remain;
In the chilly earth they lie,
    Waiting for the warmer sky.

4 Leaves, and flowers, and golden grain,
    God will bring all back again;
They shall come in beauty drest,
    This is but their time of rest.

5 Thee we praise, then, Father dear,
    E'en for winter, dark and drear;
All things lie within Thy mind,
    Ever loving, ever kind.
        J. Page Hopps. 1860.

Flower Service

846 *11.10. 11.10. Special.*
Bring an offering, and come into His courts.—Psalm xcvi. 8.

HERE, Lord, we **offer** Thee all **that** is fairest,
 Bloom from the garden, and flowers from the field ;
 Gifts for the stricken ones, knowing Thou carest
  More for the **love than the wealth** that we yield.

2 Send, Lord, **by these to** the sick and the dying,
 Speak to their hearts with a message **of** peace ;
 Comfort the sad, who in weakness are lying,
 Grant the departing a gentle release.

3 Raise, Lord, **to** health **again** those who have sickened,
 Fair be their lives as the roses in bloom ;
 Give of Thy grace to the souls Thou hast quickened,
 Gladness for **sorrow, and brightness for** gloom.

4 **We, Lord, like flowers, must bloom and must wither,**
 We, like these blossoms, must fade and must die ;
 Gather us, Lord, to Thy bosom for ever,
 Grant us a place in Thy home in the sky.
  Amen.
  A. G. W. Blunt. b. 1827.

847 C.M.
He hath made everything beautiful in its time.—Eccles. iii. 11.

GOD might have made the earth bring forth
 Enough **for great and small,**
 The oak tree and the **cedar tree,**
  Without a flower at all.

2 He might have made **enough—enough**
 For every want of **ours,**
 For food and medicine and toil,
  And yet have made **no flowers.**

3 Then wherefore, wherefore had they birth,
 All dyed with rainbow light,
 All fashioned with supremest grace,
  Upspringing day and night ?

4 Springing in valleys green and low,
 And on the mountains high,
 And in the silent wilderness,
  Where no man passeth by ?

5 Our outward life requires them not,
 Then wherefore had they birth ?
 To minister delight to man,
  And beautify the earth.

6 To whisper hope, to comfort man,
 Whene'er his faith is dim ;
 For He who careth for the flowers
  Will care much more for him.
  Mrs. Mary Howitt. d. 1888.

848 S.M.
Mountains and all hills ; fruitful trees, and all cedars : . . . young men, and maidens ; old men, and children : let them praise the Name of the Lord.
Psalm cxlviii. 9, 12, 13.

GREAT Giver of all good,
 To Thee our thanks we yield,
For all the beauties of the wood,
 Of hill, and dale, and field.

2 Ten thousand various flowers
 To Thee sweet offerings bear,
And joyous birds in woodland bowers
 Sing forth Thy tender care.

3 The fields on every side,
 The trees on every hill,
The glorious sun, the rolling tide
 Proclaim Thy wonders still.

4 But trees, **and** fields, and skies
 Still praise a God unknown ;
For gratitude and love **can rise**
 From living hearts alone.

5 These living hearts **of** ours
 Thy holy Name would bless ;
The blossoms of **a** thousand flowers
 Would please the Saviour less.

6 While earth itself decays,
 Our souls can never die ;
O, tune them all to sing Thy praise
 In better songs on high. Amen.
  Asa Fitz. 1864.
  Alt. by Godfrey Thring. 1879.

849 *11.11. 11.11. Anapæstic.*
All things come of Thee, and of Thine own have we given Thee.
1 Chronicles xxix. 14.

THINE, Lord, are **the** blossoms of forest and field,
And the loveliest gems which the gardens yield,
The heath **of the** uplands, the ferns of the glen,
And the flowers that gladden the dwellings of men.

2 **Thy** wisdom and love bid the seed in the earth,
And watched o'er its growth from its secret birth,
Once mantled with snows from the wintry blast,
Till the call of the springtide was heard at last.

HARVEST THANKSGIVING.

3 Thine, Lord, were the dews and the showers
  of heaven,
So eagerly longed for, so lovingly given;
The breath of the morning, the sunshine of
  noon,
The sweetness of May, and the glory of
  June.

4 Thou dwellest in beauty no tongue can
    express,
  The beauty and glory of holiness;
  But the flowers are glimpses of Thee and
    Thine,
  And in them bright gleams of Thy good-
    ness shine.

5 We meet in Thy temple to worship and
    pray;
  But we think of Thy suffering children to-
    day;
  Grant, Lord, that these gifts of Thy bounty
    may shed
  The glow of Thy smiles on their weary bed.

6 We offer Thee, Lord, in these fruits and
    flowers,
  No fabric of man's, no fashion of ours;
  But Thy need in Thy needy ones here we
    see,
  And now of Thine own have we given
    Thee.

Bishop E. H. Bickersteth. 1883.

850 8.8. 8.8. 8.8.
O sing praises unto the Lord.
Psalm lxviii. 32.

WHEN buds appear in early spring,
  And flowers their light and sweet-
    ness bring;
When meads are clothed in freshest green,
And beauty everywhere is seen,
Let songs ascend to God above,
For all His wisdom, power, and love.

2 When rosy summer throws her light,
  And makes the landscape fair and bright;
  When woods their richest hues display,
  And song-birds tune their cheerful lay;
  Let praise be given to God above,
  For these sweet tokens of His love.

3 And when the golden corn is high,
  And harvest time is drawing nigh;
  When ripe and mellow fruit is seen,
  Amid the foliage bright and green;
  Let songs ascend to God above,
  For all His tender care and love.

4 And when, O God, our course is run,
  And all our earthly work is done;
  Matured and perfect may we be,
  Prepared by grace Thy face to see;
  Then songs shall rise to God above,
  And endless praise for all His love.

Alfred Winfield. 1888.

Harvest Thanksgiving.

851 7.7.7.7. D.
*They joy before Thee ac-
cording to the joy in harvest.*—Isaiah ix. 3.

COME, ye thankful people, come,
  Raise the song of harvest-home;
All is safely gathered in,
Ere the winter storms begin;
God our Maker doth provide
For our wants to be supplied;
Come to God's own temple, come,
Raise the song of harvest-home.

2 We ourselves are God's own field,
  Fruit unto His praise to yield;
  Wheat and tares together sown,
  Unto joy or sorrow grown;
  First the blade, and then the ear,
  Then the full corn shall appear;
  Grant, O harvest Lord, that we
  Wholesome grain and pure may be.

3 For the Lord our God shall come,
  And shall take His harvest home;
  From His field shall in that day
  All offences purge away;
  Give His angels charge at last
  In the fire the tares to cast;
  But the fruitful ears to store
  In His garner evermore.

4 Then, thou Church triumphant, come,
  Raise the song of harvest-home;
  All are safely gathered in,
  Free from sorrow, free from sin;
  There for ever purified,
  In God's garner to abide;
  Come, ten thousand angels, come,
  Raise the glorious harvest-home.

H. Alford. 1844.

852 6.6.4. 6.6.6.4.
*The valleys also are covered
over with corn; they shout for joy, they also
sing.*—Psalm lxv. 13.

THE God of harvest praise,
  In loud thanksgivings raise
    Hand, heart, and voice;
  The valleys laugh and sing,
  Forests and mountains ring,
  The plains their tribute bring,
    The streams rejoice.

2 Garden and orchard ground
  Autumnal fruits have crowned,
    The vintage glows;
  Here plenty pours her horn;
  There the full tide of corn,
  Swayed by the breath of morn,
    The land o'erflows.

HARVEST THANKSGIVING.

3 The wind, the rain, the sun,
  Their genial work have done;
    Wouldst thou be fed?
  Man, to thy labour bow,
  Thrust in the sickle now,
  Reap where thou once didst plough,
    God sends thee bread.

4 A few seeds scattered wide
  God's hand hath multiplied:
    Here thou may'st find
  Christ's miracle renewed;
  With self-producing food
  He feeds a multitude,
    He feeds mankind.

5 The God of harvest praise;
  Hands, hearts, and voices raise
    With one accord:
  From field to garner throng,
  Bearing your sheaves along;
  And in your harvest song
    Bless ye the Lord!
            James Montgomery. 1810.

853 7.6. 7.6. D.
He reserveth unto us the appointed weeks of ... harvest.
            Jeremiah v. 24.

SING to the Lord of harvest,
  Sing songs of love and praise;
With joyful hearts and voices
  Your hallelujahs raise:
By Him the rolling seasons
  In fruitful order move,
Sing to the Lord of harvest
  A song of happy love.

2 By Him the clouds drop fatness,
  The deserts bloom and spring,
The hills leap up in gladness,
  The valleys laugh and sing;
He filleth with His fulness
  All things with large increase,
He crowns the year with goodness,
  With plenty and with peace.

3 Heap on His sacred altar
  The gifts His goodness gave,
The golden sheaves of harvest,
  The souls He died to save:
Your hearts lay down before Him,
  When at His feet ye fall,
And with your lives adore Him,
  Who gave His life for all.
            J. S. B. Monsell. 1872.

854 L.M.
The husbandman waiteth for the precious fruit of the earth.
            James v. 7.

GREAT God, as seasons disappear,
  And changes mark the rolling year,
Thy favour still has crowned our days,
And we would celebrate Thy praise.

2 The harvest-song would we repeat;
  Thou givest us the finest wheat;
  The joys of harvest we have known;
  The praise, O Lord, is all Thine own.

3 Our tables spread, our garners stored,
  O give us hearts to bless Thee, Lord;
  Forbid it, Source of light and love,
  That hearts and lives should barren prove.

4 Another harvest comes apace;
  Ripen our spirits by Thy grace,
  That we may calmly meet the blow
  The sickle gives to lay us low:

5 That so, when angel-reapers come
  To gather sheaves to Thy blest home,
  Our spirits may be borne on high
  To Thy safe garner in the sky.   Amen.
            Edmund Butcher. d. 1822.

855 10.10. 7
He ... shall ... come again with rejoicing, bringing his sheaves with him.—Psalm cxxvi. 6.

GREAT Giver of all good, to Thee again
  We humbly now present, in joyous strain,
    Our Harvest-tide thanksgiving.

2 To Thee, in whom we live and move, we come,
  To praise Thee for the sheaves brought safely home,
    With Harvest-tide thanksgiving.

3 Thou dost prepare our corn, and year by year
  Before Thine altar, Lord, will we appear
    With Harvest-tide thanksgiving.

4 Thine was the former and the latter rain,
  Enriching earth, and calling forth again
    The Harvest-tide thanksgiving.

5 Thou openest wide, great God, Thy bounteous hand,
  And far and wide ascends from all the land
    Glad Harvest-tide thanksgiving.

6 Thou fillest all that live with plenteousness;
  They, in return, Thy sacred name all bless,
    In Harvest-tide thanksgiving.

7 Thy clouds drop fatness on the teeming earth;
  Accept these festal songs of reverent mirth,
    This Harvest-tide thanksgiving.

8 The year is crowned with goodness, Lord, by Thee;
  Then meet it is that we should offer Thee
    The Harvest-tide thanksgiving.

HARVEST THANKSGIVING.

9 On every side, the little hills rejoice,
  On every side sounds forth the grateful
    voice
  Of Harvest-tide thanksgiving.

10 The valleys thick with corn do laugh and
    sing;
  Let all, who sow and reap, together bring
    Their Harvest-tide thanksgiving.
          S. Childs-Clarke. 1863.

856   8.8.8.8.4.4.8.
*The earth is satisfied with
the fruit of Thy works.*—Psalm civ. 13.

LORD of the harvest! Thee we hail;
  Thine ancient promise doth not fail,
The varying seasons haste their round,
With goodness all our years are crowned:
      Our thanks we pay
      This holy day;
O let our hearts in tune be found!

2 If spring doth wake the song of mirth,
  If summer warms the fruitful earth;
  When winter sweeps the naked plain,
  Or autumn yields its ripened grain;
      Still do we sing
      To Thee, our King;
  Through all the changes Thou dost reign.

3 But chiefly when Thy liberal hand
  Scatters new plenty o'er the land,
  When sounds of music fill the air,
  As homeward all their treasures bear;
      We too will raise
      Our hymn of praise,
  For we Thy common bounties share.

4 Lord of the harvest, all is Thine!
  The rains that fall, the suns that shine,
  The seed once hidden in the ground,
  The skill that makes our fruits abound.
      New, every year,
      Thy gifts appear;
  New praises from our lips shall sound.
          John H. Gurney. 1851.

857   8.8.8.8.8.8.
*The harvest is the end of
the world: and the reapers are the angels.*
          Matthew xiii. 39.

LORD of the harvest, once again
  We thank Thee for the ripened
    grain;
For crops, safe carried, sent to cheer
Thy servants through another year;
For sweet and holy thoughts supplied
By seed-time, and by harvest-tide.

2 The bare dry grain, in autumn sown,
  Its robe of vernal green puts on;
  Glad from its wintry grave it springs,
  Fresh garnished by the King of kings:
  So, Lord, to those who sleep in Thee
  Shall new and glorious bodies be.

3 Nor vainly of Thy word we ask
  A lesson from the reaper's task;

So shall Thine angels issue forth;
The tares be burnt; the just of earth,
To wind and storm exposed no more,
Be gathered to their Father's store.

4 Daily, O Lord, our prayer is said,
  As Thou hast taught, for daily bread;
  But not alone our bodies feed,
  Supply our fainting spirits' need;
  O Bread of Life, from day to day,
  Be Thou their Comfort, Food, and Stay
            Amen.
          Joseph Anstice. 1836. alt.

858   7.6.7.6. D.
*The fields ... are white
already to harvest.*—John iv. 35.

LORD of the living harvest,
  That whitens o'er the plain,
Where angels soon shall gather
  Their sheaves of golden grain;
Accept these hands to labour,
  These hearts to trust and love,
And deign with them to hasten
  Thy kingdom from above.

2 As labourers in Thy vineyard,
    Send us out, Christ, to be
  Content to bear the burden
    Of weary days for Thee;
  We ask no other wages,
    When Thou shalt call us home,
  But to have shared the travail
    Which makes Thy kingdom come.

3 Come down, Thou Holy Spirit!
    And fill our souls with light,
  Clothe us in spotless raiment,
    In linen clean and white;
  Within Thy sacred temple
    Be with us, where we stand,
  And sanctify Thy people
    Throughout this happy land.

4 Be with us, God the Father!
    Be with us, God the Son!
  And God, the Holy Spirit!
    O Blessèd Three in One!
  Make us a Royal Priesthood,
    Thee rightly to adore,
  And fill us with Thy fulness,
    Now, and for evermore. Amen.
          J. S. B. Monsell. 1872.

859   8.7.8.7. D. Iambic.
*We have thought of Thy
loving kindness, O God.*—Psalm xlviii. 9.

TO Thee, O Lord, our hearts we raise
    In hymns of adoration,
To Thee bring sacrifice of praise
  With shouts of exultation;
Bright robes of gold the fields adorn,
  The hills with joy are ringing,
The valleys stand so thick with corn
  That even they are singing.

2 And now, on this our festal day,
    Thy bounteous Hand confessing,
  Upon Thine altar, Lord, we lay
    The first-fruits of Thy blessing;

MARRIAGE.

By Thee the souls of men are fed
 With gifts of grace supernal,
Thou, who dost give us earthly bread,
 Give us the Bread Eternal.

3 We bear the burden of the day,
 And often toil seems dreary;
But labour ends with sunset ray,
 And rest comes for the weary;
May we, the angel-reaping o'er,
 Stand at the last accepted,
Christ's golden sheaves for evermore
 To garners bright elected.

4 O, blessèd is that land of God,
 Where saints abide for ever;
Where golden fields spread far and broad,
 Where flows the crystal river:
The strains of all its holy throng
 With ours to-day are blending;
Thrice blessed is that harvest-song
 Which never hath an ending.
  W. Chatterton Dix. 1867.

860 7.6.7.6. D. *With Chorus.*
  *He . . . filleth thee with
  the finest of the wheat.*—Psalm cxlvii. 14.

WE plough the fields, and scatter
  The good seed on the land,
But it is fed and watered
  By God's almighty hand;

He sends the snow in winter,
 The warmth to swell the grain,
The breezes, and the sunshine,
 And soft, refreshing rain.

 All good gifts around us
  Are sent from heaven above;
 Then thank the Lord, O thank the Lord
  For all His love!

2 He only is the Maker
 Of all things near and far;
He paints the wayside flower,
 He lights the evening star;
The winds and waves obey Him,
 By Him the birds are fed;
Much more to us His children
 He gives our daily bread.

3 We thank Thee, then, O Father,
 For all things bright and good,
The seed-time and the harvest,
 Our life, our health, our food;
Accept the gifts we offer
 For all Thy love imparts,
And, what Thou most desirest,
 Our humble, thankful hearts.
  Matthias Claudius. 1800. *alt.*
  Tr. Jane M. Campbell. 1861.

Special Occasions.

MARRIAGE.

861 7.6.7.6.
  And God blessed them.
  Genesis i. 28.

THE voice that breathed o'er Eden,
  That earliest wedding day,
The primal marriage blessing,
 It hath not passed away:

2 Still in the pure esponsal
 Of Christian man and maid,
The Holy Three are with us,
 The threefold grace is said.

3 For dower of blessèd children,
 For love and faith's sweet sake,
For high mysterious union
 Which nought on earth may break;

4 Be present, loving Father,
 To give away this bride,
As Eve Thou gav'st to Adam,
 Out of his own piercèd side;

5 Be present, holy Saviour,
 To join their loving hands,
As Thou did'st bind two natures
 In Thine eternal bands;

6 Be present, gracious Spirit,
 To bless them as they kneel,
As Thou for Christ, the Bridegroom,
 The heavenly spouse dost seal.

7 O spread Thy pure wing o'er them,
 Let no ill power find place,
When onward through life's journey,
 The hallowed path they trace.

8 To cast their crowns before Thee,
 In perfect sacrifice,
Till to the home of gladness
 With Christ's own bride they rise.
  Amen.
  John Keble. 1857.

862 7.6.7.6. D.
  *And both Jesus was called,
  and His disciples, to the marriage.*
  John ii. 2

CROWN with Thy benediction
  This sacrament of love;
And make this hallowed union
 Foretaste of heaven above;
Let pure and perfect gladness,
 Let pure and perfect rest,
And peace, that knows no sadness,
 Thy presence, Lord, attest.

SPECIAL OCCASIONS.

2 As once in Eden's springtime,
  As once at Cana's feast,
So consecrate this bridal,
  Be Thou its Guest and Priest:
With sunshine wreathe the altar,
  Chase every cloud away,
Nor let their voices falter
  Who plight their truth to-day.

3 God bless the bride and bridegroom,
  And fill with joy their life;
Keep them, through all its changes,
  True husband, faithful wife:
If Thou wilt smile upon them,
  They shall not need the sun:
This thought their hearts rejoicing—
  Henceforth, not twain but one.

4 With Thy great love befriend them,
  The love that casts out fear;
And make a rainbow round them
  For every falling tear:
Till, all their sheaves well-garnered,
  Heaven's harvest-home they raise,
Where love, that knows no ending,
  Inspires more perfect praise. Amen.
  John B. Greenwood. 1883.

LAYING FOUNDATION AND MEMORIAL STONES.

863 6.5.6.5. D.
I have set my affection to the house of my God.—1 Chronicles xxix. 3.

CHRIST is the Foundation
  Of the house we raise;
Be its walls salvation,
  And its gateways praise:
May its threshold lowly
  To the Lord be dear;
May the hearts be holy
  That shall worship here.

2 On the Rock of Ages,
    Resting broad and deep,
  When life's tempest rages,
    Here let passion sleep;
  Here may prayers and praises
    Never cease to rise,
  Till through Christ they raise us
    Nearer to the skies.

3 Here the vow be sealed
    By Thy Spirit, Lord;
  Here the sick be healed,
    And the lost restored;
  Here the broken-hearted
    Thy forgiveness prove;
  Here the friends long parted
    Be restored to love.

4 Here may every token
    Of Thy presence be;
  Here may chains be broken,
    Prisoners here set free;

Here may light illumine
  Every soul of Thine,
Lifting up the human
  Into the divine.

5 Here may God the Father,
    Christ the Saviour—Son,
  With the Holy Spirit,
    Be adored as One;
  Till the whole creation
    At Thy footstool fall,
  And in adoration
    Own Thee Lord of all! Amen.
    J. S. B. Monsell. 1863.

864 L.M.
Except the Lord build the house, they labour in vain that build it. Psalm cxxvii. 1.

EXCEPT the Lord the temple build,
  In vain their toil the workmen yield;
Except the Lord shall guard the bounds,
In vain the watchman's voice resounds.

2 O Lord, the Master-builder Thou,
  Make us Thy fellow-workers now;
  Builders of souls here may we be,
  And living shrines be raised for Thee.

3 Give to our teachers words of fire,
  To kindle every high desire;
  And form in all the constant mind
  To serve their God and serve mankind.

4 Watch Thou within, lest we should spoil
  Thy work, or fail in earnest toil;
  May Thine abiding presence keep
  Our hearts from strife, our souls from sleep.

5 Thus may we train, in Thy blest will,
  Young ardent souls to serve Thee still,
  To bear, in bright and eager hands,
  The torch that leaves our drooping hands.
    Amen.
    E. S. A. 1887.

865 L.M.
The glory of Lebanon shall come unto thee, the fir tree, the pine tree, and the box together, to beautify the place of My sanctuary.—Isaiah lx. 13.

O LORD of hosts, whose glory fills
  The bounds of the eternal hills,
Who yet vouchsafes, in Christian lands,
To dwell in temples made with hands;

2 Grant that all we, who here to-day
  Rejoicing this foundation lay,
  May be in very deed Thine own,
  Built on the precious Corner-stone.

3 The heads that guide endue with skill,
  The hands that work preserve from ill,
  That we who these foundations lay,
  May raise the topstone in its day.

4 Both now and ever, Lord, protect
  The temple of Thine own elect;
  Be Thou in them, and they in Thee,
  O ever-blessed Trinity! Amen.
    J. M. Neale. 1844.

OPENING SERVICES.

866 L.M.
*We shall be satisfied with
the goodness of Thy house.*—Psalm lxv. 4.

THIS stone to Thee in faith we lay ;
  To Thee this temple, Lord, we build ;
Thy power and goodness here display,
  And be it with Thy presence filled.

2 Here, when Thy people seek Thy face,
  And dying sinners pray to live,
Hear Thou, in heaven, Thy dwelling-place,
  And when Thou hearest, O forgive !

3 Here, when Thy messengers proclaim
  The blessed Gospel of Thy Son,
Still by the power of His great name
  Be mighty signs and wonders done.

4 Hosanna ! to their heavenly King,
  When children's voices raise that song ;
Hosanna ! let their angels sing,
  And heaven with earth the strain prolong.

5 But will indeed Jehovah deign
  Here to abide, no transient guest ?
Here will the world's Redeemer reign ?
  And here the Holy Spirit rest ?

6 That glory never hence depart ;
  Yet choose not, Lord, this house alone,
Thy kingdom come to every heart,
  In every bosom fix Thy throne. Amen.
        James Montgomery. 1822.

OPENING SERVICES.

867 7.6.7.6.D.
*Behold, heaven and the
heaven of heavens cannot contain Thee.*
2 Chronicles vi. 18.

O THOU whose hand has brought us
    Unto this joyful day,
  Accept our glad thanksgivings,
    And listen as we pray ;
  And may our preparation
    For this day's service be
  With one accord to offer
    Ourselves, O Lord, to Thee.

2 For this new house we praise Thee,
    Reared by Thine own command,
  For every generous bosom,
    And every willing hand ;
  And now within Thy temple
    Thy glory let us see,
  For all its strength and beauty
    Are nothing without Thee.

3 And oft as here we gather,
    And hearts in worship blend,
  May truth reveal its power,
    And fervent prayer ascend ;
  Here may the busy toiler
    Rise to the things above ;
  The young, the old, be strengthened,
    And all men learn Thy love.

4 And as the years roll over,
    And strong affections twine,
  And tender memories gather
    About this sacred shrine,
  May this, its chief distinction,
    Its glory ever be,
  That multitudes within it
    Have found their way to Thee.

5 Lord God : our fathers' helper,
    Our joy and hope and stay,
  Grant now a gracious earnest
    Of many a coming day :
  Our yearning hearts Thou knowest,
    We wait before Thy throne,
  O come, and by Thy presence
    Make this new house Thine own !
          Amen.
        F. W. Goadby. 1880.

868 L.M.
*I will glorify the house
of my glory.*—Isaiah lx. 7.

BE with us, gracious Lord, to-day ;
  This house we dedicate to Thee :
O, hear Thy servants as they pray,
  And let Thine ear attentive be.

2 Within these walls let holy peace,
  Let love and truth be always found ;
May burdened hearts find sweet release,
  And souls with richest grace be crowned.

3 May here be heard the suppliant's sigh,
  The weary enter into rest ;
Here may the contrite to Thee cry,
  And waiting souls be richly blest.

4 Here, when the Gospel sound is heard,
  And here proclaimed the saving Name,
May hearts be quickened, moved, and stirred,
  And souls be kindled into flame.

5 Here may the dead be made to live,
  The dumb to sing, the deaf to hear ;
And do Thou to the humble give
  Pardon and peace instead of fear.

6 Make this, O Lord, Thine own abode ;
  Thy presence in these courts be given ;
Be this, indeed, the house of God,
  And this in truth the gate of heaven.
          Amen.
        Anon.

869 L.M.
All Thine own.
1 Chronicles xxix. 16.

ALL things are Thine : no gift have we,
  Lord of all gifts ! to offer Thee ;
And hence with grateful hearts to-day,
  Thine own before Thy feet we lay.

2 Thy will was in the builders' thought ;
  Thy hand unseen amidst us wrought ;
Through mortal motive, scheme and plan,
  Thy wise eternal purpose ran.

213

SPECIAL OCCASIONS.

3 No lack Thy perfect fulness knew;
From human needs and longings grew
This house of prayer, this home of rest,
Where Thy great name shall be confessed.

4 In weakness and in want we call
On Thee for whom the heavens are small:
Thy glory is Thy children's good,
Thy joy Thy tender Fatherhood.

5 O Father! deign these walls to bless;
Fill with Thy love their emptiness:
And let their door a gateway be
To lead us from ourselves to Thee. Amen.
J. G. Whittier. 1847.

870 L.M.
*And of Zion it shall be
said, This and that man was born in her.*
Psalm lxxxvii. 5.

GREAT God, Thy watchful care we bless,
Which guards these sacred courts in peace;
Nor dare tumultuous foes invade,
To fill Thy worshippers with dread.

2 And will the great eternal God
On earth establish His abode?
And will He, from His radiant throne,
Avow our temples for His own?

3 We bring the tribute of our praise,
And sing that condescending grace,
Which to our notes will lend an ear,
And call such sinful mortals near.

4 These walls we to Thy honour raise,
Long may they echo to Thy praise;
And Thou, descending, fill the place
With choicest tokens of Thy grace.

5 Here let the great Redeemer reign,
With all the virtues of His train;
While power divine His word attends
To conquer foes, and cheer His friends.

6 And in the great decisive day,
When God the nations shall survey,
May it before the world appear,
That crowds were born to glory here.
Amen.
Philip Doddridge. 1755. *alt.*

871 C.M.
*That Thine eyes may be
open upon this house day and night.*
2 Chronicles vi. 20.

O THOU, whose own vast temple stands
Built over earth and sea,
Accept the walls that human hands
Have raised to worship Thee.

2 Lord, from Thine inmost glory send,
Within these courts to abide,
The peace that dwelleth, without end,
Serenely by Thy side.

3 May erring minds that worship here
Be taught the better way;
And they who mourn, and they who fear,
Be strengthened as they pray.

4 May faith grow firm, and love grow warm,
And pure devotion rise;
While, round these hallowed walls, the storm
Of earth-born passion dies. Amen.
W. Cullen Bryant. 1835.

872 C.M.
*The glory of the Lord
filled the house.*—2 Chronicles vii. 1.

LIGHT up this house with glory, Lord;
Enter, and claim Thine own;
Receive the homage of our souls,
Erect Thy temple-throne.

2 We rear no altar, Thou hast died;
We deck no priestly shrine;
What need have we of creature-aid?
The power to save is Thine.

3 We ask no bright shekinah-cloud
To glorify the place;
Give, Lord, the substance of that sign,
A plenitude of grace.

4 No rushing, mighty wind, we ask;
No tongues of flame desire;
Grant us the Spirit's quickening light,
His purifying fire.

5 Light up this house with glory, Lord;
The glory of that love
Which forms and saves a Church below,
And makes a heaven above. Amen.
John Harris. 1859.

873 C.M.
*Teaching them to observe
all things whatsoever I have commanded
you.*—Matthew xxviii. 20.

GREAT Shepherd of Thy people, hear;
Thy presence now display;
As Thou hast given a place for prayer,
So give us hearts to pray.

2 Show us some token of Thy love
Our feeble hope to raise,
And pour Thy blessing from above,
That we may render praise.

3 Within these walls let holy peace,
And love, and concord dwell;
Here give the troubled conscience ease,
The wounded spirit heal.

4 The hearing ear, the watchful eye,
The contrite heart bestow,
And shine upon us from on high,
To make our graces grow.

5 May we in faith receive Thy word,
In faith address our prayers,
And in the presence of the Lord
Unbosom all our cares.

6 And may the gospel's joyful sound,
Enforced by grace divine,
Awaken many sinners round,
And bend their wills to Thine. Amen.
John Newton. 1779.

HOSPITAL SUNDAY.

874 *I have hallowed this house which thou hast built.*—1 Kings ix. 3. 7.7.7.7.

LORD of hosts, to Thee we raise
Here a house of prayer and praise;
Thou Thy people's hearts prepare,
Here to meet for praise and prayer

2 Let Thy children here be fed
With Thy word, the heavenly bread;
Here, with richest mercy blest,
May the weary soul find rest.

3 Here to Thee a temple stand,
While the sea shall gird the land;
Here reveal Thy mercy sure,
While the sun and moon endure.

4 Hallelujah! earth and sky
To the joyful sound reply;
Hallelujah! hence ascend
Prayer and praise till time shall end.
          Amen.
James Montgomery. 1825.

Opening of an Organ.

875 *Praise Him with stringed instruments and organs.*—Psalm cl. 4. C.M.

ALL nature's works His praise declare,
  To whom they all belong;
There is a voice in every star,
In every breeze a song.

2 Sweet music fills the world abroad
With strains of love and power;
The stormy sea sings praise to God,
The thunder and the shower.

3 To God the tribes of ocean cry,
And birds upon the wing;
To God the powers that dwell on high
Their tuneful tribute bring.

4 Like them, let man the throne surround,
With them loud chorus raise,
While instruments of loftier sound
Assist his feeble praise.

5 Great God, to Thee we consecrate
Our voices and our skill;
We bid the pealing organ wait
To speak alone Thy will.

6 O teach its rich and swelling notes
To lift our souls on high,
And while the music round us floats,
Let earth-born passions die. Amen.
          H. Ware, jun. d. 1843.

Opening of a Bazaar.

876 *The wise and their works are in the hand of God.*—Ecclesiastes ix. 1. L.M.

THOU God of glory, truth, and love,
  Lord over all beneath, above!
Our thoughts and hearts to Thee we raise,
And with our lips proclaim Thy praise.

2 Creation rose at Thy command,
The seas, the floods, the solid land;
And at Thy wisdom's high behest,
In beauteous robes Thy works were drest.

3 Thy goodness doth to men impart
The fount of every useful art,
The skilful hand, the inventive thought,
By which new forms of grace are wrought.

4 Behold, O Lord, before Thee stand
Our works of thought, of heart, and hand;
We humbly bring them to Thy throne,
And render back with joy Thine own.
          Edward Doaden. 1889.

HOSPITAL SUNDAY AND BENEVOLENT INSTITUTIONS.

877 *They .. brought unto Him all that were diseased; . . . and as many as touched were made perfectly whole.*
Matthew xiv. 35, 36. C.M.D.

THINE arm, O Lord, in days of old,
  Was strong to heal and save;
It triumphed o'er disease and death,
O'er darkness and the grave.
To Thee they went, the blind, the dumb,
The palsied and the lame,
The leper with his tainted life,
The sick with fevered frame.

2 And lo! Thy touch brought life and health,
Gave speech, and strength, and sight;
And youth renewed, and frenzy calmed
Owned Thee, the Lord of light:
And now, O Lord, be near to bless,
Almighty as of yore,
In crowded street, by restless couch,
As by Gennesareth's shore.

3 Be Thou our great Deliverer still,
Thou Lord of life and death;
Restore and quicken, soothe and bless,
With Thine almighty breath:
To hands that work, and eyes that see,
Give wisdom's heavenly lore,
That whole and sick, and weak and strong,
May praise Thee evermore. Amen.
          E. H. Plumptre.

SPECIAL OCCASIONS.

878   8.7. 8.7. 7.7.
I was sick, and ye visited me.
Matthew xxv. 36.

THOU to whom the sick and dying
  Ever came, nor came in vain,
Still with healing words replying
  To the wearied cry of pain;
Hear us, Jesus, as we meet
Suppliants at Thy mercy-seat.

2 Every care, and every sorrow,
  Be it great, or be it small,
Yesterday, to-day, to-morrow,
  When, where'er it may befall,
Lay we humbly at Thy feet,
Suppliants at Thy mercy-seat.

3 Still the weary, sick, and dying
  Need a brother's, sister's care;
On Thy higher help relying
  May we now their burden share,
Bringing all our offerings meet,
Suppliants at Thy mercy-seat.

4 May each child of Thine be willing,
  Willing both in hand and heart;
All the law of love fulfilling,
  Ever comfort to impart,
Ever bringing offerings meet,
Suppliant to Thy mercy-seat.

5 So may sickness, sin, and sadness,
  To Thy healing power yield,
Till the sick and sad in gladness,
  Rescued, ransomed, cleansed, healed,
One in Thee together meet,
Pardoned at Thy judgment-seat.
    Amen.
Godfrey Thring. 1866.

879   C.M.
Inasmuch as ye have done it unto one of the least of these My brethren, ye have done it unto Me.—Matt. xxv. 40.

O FOUNT of good, to own Thy love
  Our thankful hearts incline;
What can we render, Lord, to Thee,
  When all the worlds are Thine?

2 But Thou hast needy brethren here,
  Partakers of Thy grace;
Whose names Thou wilt Thyself confess
  Before the Father's face.

3 In each sad accent of distress
  Thy pleading voice is heard;
In them Thou may'st be clothed and fed,
  And visited, and cheered.

4 Help us then, Lord, Thy yoke to wear,
  With joy to do Thy will;
Each other's burdens gladly bear,
  And love's sweet law fulfil.

5 Thy face with reverence and with love
  We in Thy poor would see;
And while we minister to them,
  Would do it as to Thee.

6 Do Thou, O Lord, our alms accept,
  And with Thy blessing speed;
Bless us in giving; greatly bless
  Our gifts to them that need.

7 To Father, Son, and Holy Ghost,
  The God whom we adore,
Be glory, as it was, is now,
  And shall be evermore. Amen.
Philip Doddridge. 1755. alt.

880   7.5. 7.5.
Ye have the poor with you always.—Mark xiv. 7.

THINE are all the gifts, O God!
  Thine the broken bread;
Let the naked feet be shod,
  And the starving fed.

2 Let Thy children, by Thy grace,
  Give as they abound,
Till the poor have breathing-space,
  And the lost are found.

3 Wiser than the miser's hoards
  Is the giver's choice;
Sweeter than the song of birds
  Is the thankful voice.

4 Welcome smiles on faces sad
  As the flowers of spring;
Let the tender hearts be glad
  With the joy they bring.
J. G. Whittier. 1847.

BURIAL OF THE DEAD.

881   7.7. 7.7. D.
Blessed are the dead which die in the Lord.—Rev. xiv. 13.

HARK! a voice divides the sky—
  Happy are the faithful dead!
In the Lord who sweetly die,
  They from all their toils are freed,
Them the Spirit hath declared
  Blest, unutterably blest;
Jesus is their great Reward,
  Jesus is their endless Rest.

2 Followed by their works, they go
  Where their Head hath gone before;
Reconciled by grace below,
  Grace hath opened mercy's door;
Justified through faith alone,
  Here they knew their sins forgiven;
Here they laid their burden down,
  Hallowed, and made meet for heaven.

3 Who can now lament the lot
  Of a saint in Christ deceased?
Let the world, who know us not,
  Call us hopeless and unblessed;
When from flesh the spirit freed,
  Hastens homeward to return,
Mortals cry, 'A man is dead!'
  Angels sing, 'A child is born!'

BURIAL OF THE DEAD.

4 Born into the world above,
  They our happy brother greet;
Bear him to the throne of love,
  Place him at the Saviour's feet;
Jesus smiles, and says, 'Well done,
  Good and faithful servant thou;
Enter, and receive thy crown;
  Reign with Me triumphant now.'

5 Angels catch the approving sound,
  Bow, and bless the just award;
Hail the heir with glory crowned,
  Now rejoicing with his Lord;
Fuller joys ordained to know,
  Waiting for the general doom,
When the archangel's trump shall blow,
  'Rise, ye dead, to judgment come!'
                    Wesley. 1742.

882   7.7.7.7.
*They .. rest from their
labours; and their works do follow them.
Revelation xiv. 13.*

1 O! a voice from heaven hath said,
  Henceforth blessèd are the dead
Dying in their risen Lord,
  Trusting His redeeming word.

2 Blessèd! for their work is done;
  Home they went at set of sun;
They were weary, it was best
  To lie down and take their rest.

3 Blessèd ones! they calmly sleep,
  Leaving us to wake and weep,
Still to bear our fleshly pains,
  Sins and doubts and spirit-chains.

4 Blessèd! they have done with tears,
  Sickness, darkness, death, and fears;
And the soul's long conflict past,
  Victory is theirs at last.

5 Theirs is the eternal peace,
  Growing with divine increase;
Theirs—eternal rest above,
  Rest in the Eternal Love.

6 Dwelling in the Light of Light,
  They possess the Infinite;
Every mystery unsealed,
  And the glory all revealed.
              George Rawson. 1876.

883   8.7.8.7. D. Iambic.
*There remaineth therefore
a rest to the people of God.—Hebrews iv 9.*

1 THE journey done, the rest begun,
    The day of death now ended;
To life above, on wings of love,
    The freed one hath ascended;
What we do weep, the Christ doth keep,
    He died that He might save it;
The body trust we to the dust,
    The soul to God who gave it.

2 Our tears must fall at loss of all
    That time cannot restore us;
But to the skies we'll lift our eyes,
    And think of what's before us;

There, safe above, with Him whose love
    For all its want provideth,
The spirit blest, in changeless rest
    Of Paradise, abideth.

3 Your muffled chime, ye bells of time,
    Ring out with chastened gladness;
The happy soul needs not your toil,
    As if it dwelt in sadness;
Toll for the dead who, living, tread
    Earth's sinful ways, hard-hearted;
But a bright chime, ye bells of time,
    Ring out for Christ's departed.

4 Their warfare o'er, now never more
    Shall sin or sorrow grieve them;
Against that day, not far away,
    In quiet earth we leave them:
What we do weep, the Christ doth keep,
    He died that He might save it;
The body trust we to the dust,
    The soul to God who gave it.
              J. S. B. Monsell. 1872.

884   7.7.7.7.
*The Lord gave, and the Lord
hath taken away; blessed be the name of the
Lord.—Job I. 21.*

1 CHRIST will gather in His own
  To the place where He is gone,
Where their heart and treasure lie,
Where our life is hid on high.

2 Day by day the Voice saith, 'Come,
Enter thine eternal home:'
Asking not if we can spare
This dear soul it summons there.

3 Had He asked us, well we know
We should cry, 'O, spare this blow!
Yea, with streaming tears should pray,
'Lord, we love him, let him stay!'

4 But the Lord doth nought amiss,
And since He hath ordered this,
We have nought to do but still
Rest in silence on His will.

5 Many a heart no longer here,
Ah! to us was all too dear;
Yet, O Love, 'tis Thou dost call,
Thou wilt be our All in all.
        Bohemian Brethren. 1531.
    Tr. Catherine Winkworth. 1858.

885   C.M.
*Him that overcometh will
I make a pillar in the temple of my God.
Revelation iii. 12.*

1 CAPTAIN and Saviour of the host
  Of Christian chivalry,
We bless Thee for our comrade true
  Now summoned up to Thee.

2 We bless Thee for his every step,
  In faithful following Thee;
And for his good fight fought so well,
  And crowned with victory

TRAVELLERS BY LAND AND SEA.

3 We thank Thee that the wayworn sleeps
   The sleep in Jesus blest ;
The purified and ransomed soul
   Hath entered into rest.

4 We bless Thee that his humble love
   Hath met with such regard :
We bless Thee for his blessedness,
   And for his rich reward.
                George Rawson. 1857.

886   7.7. 7.7. 8.8.
Into Thine hand I commit my spirit.—Psalm xxxi. 5.

NOW the labourer's task is o'er ;
   Now the battle day is past ;
Now upon the farther shore
   Lands the voyager at last.
Father, in Thy gracious keeping
Leave we now Thy servant sleeping.

2 There the tears of earth are dried ;
   There its hidden things are clear ;
There the work of life is tried
   By a juster Judge than here.
Father, in Thy gracious keeping
Leave we now Thy servant sleeping.

3 There the Shepherd bringing home
   Many a lamb forlorn and strayed,
Shelters each, no more to roam,
   Where the wolf can ne'er invade.
Father, in Thy gracious keeping
Leave we now Thy servant sleeping.

4 There the penitents who turn
   To the Cross their dying eyes,
All the love of Jesus learn
   At His feet in Paradise.
Father, in Thy gracious keeping
Leave we now Thy servant sleeping.

5 There no more the powers of hell
   Can prevail to mar their peace ;
Christ the Lord shall guard them well,
   He who died for their release.
Father, in Thy gracious keeping
Leave we now Thy servant sleeping.

6 'Earth to earth, and dust to dust,'
   Calmly now the words we say,
Left behind, we wait in trust
   Till the resurrection-day.
Father, in Thy gracious keeping
Leave we now Thy servant sleeping.
                John Ellerton. 1871.

887   8.8. 8.8. D. *Anapæstic.*
To die is gain.
Philippians i. 21.

REJOICE for a brother deceased,
   Our loss is his infinite gain ;
A soul out of prison released,
   And free from his bodily chain :
With songs let us follow his flight,
   And mount with his spirit above,
Escaped to the mansions of light,
   And lodged in the Eden of love.

2 Our brother the haven hath gained,
   Out-flying the tempest and wind ;
His rest he hath sooner obtained,
   And left his companions behind,
Still tossed on a sea of distress,
   Hard toiling to make the blest shore,
Where all is assurance and peace,
   And sorrow and sin are no more.

3 There all the ship's company meet,
   Who sailed with the Saviour beneath ;
With shouting each other they greet,
   And triumph o'er trouble and death :
The voyage of life's at an end,
   The mortal affliction is past ;
The age that in heaven they spend,
   For ever and ever shall last.
                Charles Wesley. 1744.

Travellers by Land and Sea.

888   8.8. 8.8. 8.8.
He maketh the storm a calm, so that the waves thereof are still.
Psalm cvii. 29.

ETERNAL Father, strong to save,
   Whose arm doth bind the restless wave,
Who bidd'st the mighty ocean deep
   Its own appointed limits keep ;
O hear us when we cry to Thee
For those in peril on the sea.

2 O Saviour, whose almighty word
   The winds and waves submissive heard,
Who walkedst on the foaming deep,
   And calm amid its rage didst sleep ;

O hear us when we cry to Thee
For those in peril on the sea.

3 O sacred Spirit, who didst brood
   Upon the chaos dark and rude,
Who bad'st its angry tumult cease,
   And gavest light, and life, and peace ;
O hear us when we cry to Thee
For those in peril on the sea.

4 O Trinity of love and power,
   Our brethren shield in danger's hour,
From rock and tempest, fire and foe,
   Protect them wheresoe'er they go ;
And ever let there rise to Thee
Glad hymns of praise from land and sea.
                    Amen.
               William Whiting. 1860.

TRAVELLERS BY LAND AND SEA.

889   7.7.7.7.
*Be of good cheer : it is I ;
be not afraid.*—Mark vi. 50.

ON the waters dark and drear,
  Jesus, Saviour, Thou art near,
With our ship where'er it roam,
As with loving friends at home.

2 Thou hast walked the heaving wave,
  Thou art mighty still to save ;
With one gentle word of peace
Thou canst bid the tempest cease.

3 Safely from the boisterous main
  Bring us back to port again ;
In our haven we shall be,
Jesus, if we have but Thee.

4 Only by Thy power and love
  Fit us for the port above ;
Still the deadly storm within,
Gusts of passion, waves of sin.

5 So, when breaks the glorious dawn
  Of the resurrection morn,
When the night of toil is o'er,
We shall see Thee on the shore.

6 Holy Father, Holy Son,
  Holy Spirit, Three in One,
Praise unending unto Thee,
Now and evermore shall be. Amen.
        W. Chatterton Dix. 1870.

890   L.M.
*Thou rulest the raging
of the sea.*—Psalm lxxxix. 9.

LORD of the sea ! afar from land
  We still within Thy presence stand,
Now grant us grace to worship Thee,
And keep our Sabbath on the sea.

2 Be banished care, be vanquished fear ;
  Our hearts into calm waters steer ;
So may they rest although we roam,
And on the deep be still at home ;

3 Be calm without and calm within,
  And all our worship free from sin ;
And as of Thee Thy servants hear,
O let us feel that Thou art near !

4 Thy blessing, gracious Lord, we crave ;
  Thou oft didst sail the Hebrew wave ;
Sail with us now that, joyful, we
May keep our Sabbath on the sea.

5 Thine is the sea, as Thine the land ;
  We still within Thy presence stand ;
In Thy blest Spirit's light may we
Find mercy's gate upon the sea. Amen.
        George T. Coster. 1884.

891   L.M.
*Which stilleth the noise
of the seas, the noise of their waves.*
Psalm lxv 7.

ALMIGHTY Father, hear our cry,
  As o'er the trackless deep we roam,
Be Thou our haven always nigh,
On homeless waters Thou our home.

2 O Jesus, Saviour, at whose voice
  The tempest sank to perfect rest,
Bid Thou the fearful heart rejoice,
And cleanse and calm the troubled breast.

3 O Holy Ghost, beneath whose power
  The ocean woke to life and light,
Command Thy blessing in this hour,
Thy fostering warmth, Thy quickening might.

4 Great God of our salvation, Thee
  We love, we worship, we adore ;
Our Refuge on time's changeful sea,
Our Joy on heaven's eternal shore. Amen.
        Bishop E. H. Bickersteth. 1870.

892   8.8. 8.8. 8.8.
*When the waves thereof
arise, Thou stillest them.*—Psalm lxxxix. 9.

GREAT Ruler of the land and sea,
  Almighty God, we come to Thee,
Able to succour and to save
From perils of the wind and wave :
Keep by Thy mighty hand, O keep
The dwellers on the homeless deep !

2 Smooth the rough ocean's troubled face,
  And bid the hurricane give place
To the soft breeze that waits the barque
Safely alike through light and dark ;
Keep by Thy mighty hand, O keep
The dwellers on the homeless deep !

3 In storm or battle, with Thine arm,
  Shield Thou the mariner from harm,
From foes without, from ills within,
From deeds and words and thoughts of sin :
Keep by Thy mighty hand, O keep
The dwellers on the homeless deep !

4 O Son of God, in days of ill,
  Say to each sorrow, ' Peace, be still ; '
In hours of weakness be Thou nigh,
Heal Thou the sickness, hear the cry ;
Keep by Thy mighty hand, O keep
The dwellers on the homeless deep !

5 When hidden is each guiding star,
  Flash out the beacon's light afar ;
From mist and rock and shoal and spray
Protect the sailor on his way ;
Keep by Thy mighty hand, O keep
The dwellers on the homeless deep !

6 Good Pilot of the awful main,
  Let us not plead Thy love in vain ;
Jesus, draw near with kindly aid,
Say, ' It is I, be not afraid ;'
Keep by Thy mighty hand, O keep
The dwellers on the homeless deep ! Amen.
        Horatius Bonar. 1866.

TRAVELLERS BY LAND AND SEA.

893 6.6. 6.6. 8.8.
*Trust thou in the Lord:
He is their help and their shield.*
Psalm cxv. 9.

FATHER, who art alone
  Our helper and our stay,
O, hear us! as we plead
  For loved ones far away;
And shield with Thine Almighty hand
Our wanderers by sea and land.

2 For Thou, our Father-God,
  Art present everywhere,
And bendest low Thine ear
  To catch the faintest prayer;
Waiting rich blessings to bestow
On all Thy children here below.

3 O, compass with Thy love
  The daily path they tread!
And may Thy light and truth
  Upon their hearts be shed;
That, one in all things with Thy will,
Heaven's peace and joy their souls may fill.

4 Guard them from every harm,
  When dangers shall assail,
And teach them that Thy power
  Can never, never fail;
We cannot with our loved ones be,
But trust them, Father, unto Thee.

5 We all are travellers here
  Along life's various road,
Meeting and parting oft
  Till we shall mount to God;
At home at last, with those we love,
Within the Fatherland above.
            E. J. 1885.

894 8.8. 8.8. 8.8. 8.7.
*Who art the confidence of
all the ends of the earth, and of them that are
afar off upon the sea.*—Psalm lxv. 5.

O MIGHTY God, Creator, King,
  Who rulest over sea and land,
And dost the ocean deeps sustain
  Within the hollow of Thine hand;
O hear us as we cry to Thee
For those who traverse land and sea,
That they may now and ever be
  Safe in Thy holy keeping.

2 And Thou who cam'st on earth to breathe
  The breath of peace o'er heath and hill,
Didst walk upon the angry wave,
  And bid the troubled sea be still;
O hear us as we cry to Thee
For those who traverse land and sea,
That they may now and ever be
  Safe in Thy holy keeping.

3 Wherever danger threatens, then,
  O Holy Spirit, be Thou there,
And breathe into each trembling heart
  The will and power of fervent prayer;
That we and all who cry to Thee,
With those who traverse land and sea,
Both now and evermore may be
  Safe in Thy holy keeping. Amen.
            Godfrey Thring. 1879.

895 L.M.
*The sea is His, and He
made it.*—Psalm xcv. 5.

LORD of the wide-extended main,
  Whose power the wind, the sea, controls,
Whose hand doth earth and heaven sustain,
  Whose Spirit leads believing souls:

2 For Thee we leave our native shore,
  We whom Thy love delights to keep,
In other climes Thy works explore,
  And see Thy wonders in the deep.

3 'Tis here Thine unknown paths we trace,
  Which dark to human eyes appear:
While through the mighty waves we pass,
  Faith only sees that God is here.

4 Throughout the deep Thy footsteps shine,
  We own Thy way is in the sea,
O'erawed by majesty divine,
  And lost in Thy immensity.

5 Thy wisdom here we learn to adore,
  Thine everlasting truth we prove;
Amazing heights of boundless power,
  Unfathomable depths of love.
            Wesley. 1739.

896 8.8. 8.8. 8.8.
*The Lord our God shall
deliver us.*—2 Chronicles xxxii. 11.

NOW weigh the anchor, hoist the sail,
  Launch out upon the pathless deep,
Resolved, however veers the gale,
  The destined port in mind to keep;
Through all the dangers of the way,
Deliver us, good Lord, we pray.

2 When tempests mingle sea and sky,
  And winds like lions rage and rend,
Ships o'er the mountain-waters fly,
  Or down unfathomed depths descend,
Though skill avail not, strength decay,
Deliver us, good Lord, we pray.

3 If lightnings from embattled clouds
  Strike, or a spark in secret burst,
From stem to stern, o'er masts and shrouds
  Like doomsday's conflagration burst,
Amid the fire Thy power display,
Deliver us, good Lord, we pray.

4 Through yielding planks, should ocean urge
  Rude entrance, flooding all below,
Speak, ere we founder in the surge,
  'Thus far, nor farther shall ye go;
Here, ye proud waves, your fury stay:'
Deliver us, good Lord, we pray.

5 With cordage snapt, and canvas riven,
  Through straits thick-strown with rock and shoal,
Along some gulf-stream darkly driven,
  Fast wedged 'midst icebergs at the pole,
Or on low breakers cast away,
Deliver us, good Lord, we pray.

TRAVELLERS BY LAND AND SEA.

6 Save, or we perish; calms or storms,
  By day, by night, at home, afar,
Death walks the waves in all his forms,
  And shoots his darts from every star;
Want, pain, and woe man's path waylay,
Deliver us, good Lord, we pray. Amen.
James Montgomery. 1853.

897 *In His hand are the deep* C.M.
  places of the earth.—Psalm xcv. 4.

HOW are Thy servants blest, O **Lord**!
  How sure is their defence!
Eternal Wisdom is their guide,
  Their help Omnipotence.

2 In foreign realms, and lands remote,
    Supported by Thy care,
  Through burning climes they pass unhurt,
    And breathe in tainted air.

3 When by the dreadful tempest borne,
    High on the broken wave,
  They know Thou art not slow to hear,
    Nor impotent to save.

4 The storm is laid, the **winds retire**,
    Obedient to Thy will;
  The sea, that roars **at Thy command**,
    At Thy command **is still**.

5 In midst of dangers, fears, and **deaths**,
    Thy goodness we'll adore;
  We'll praise Thee for Thy mercies past,
    And humbly **hope** for more.

6 Our life, while Thou preserv'st that life,
    Thy sacrifice shall be;
  And death, when death shall be **our lot**,
    Shall join o**u**r souls to Thee.
Joseph Addison. 1712.

898 *The Lord on high is mightier* S.M.
  than the noise of many waters.
  Psalm xciii. 4.

O GOD, **whose love is** near,
  Although **it seem** to stay,
Be with us through our voyage here,
  And smooth the ocean way.

2 Though on a foreign sea,
    We sail not far from home;
  And nearer to the port of peace
    We every moment come.

3 When loud the surges rise,
    And calms delay to be,
  The storm is blest and kind the waves
    That drive us nearer Thee.

4 And when the winds are hushed,
    And on the deep is peace,
  And we behold the land where lies
    Our haven of release;

5 With soft and gentle winds
    O waft us smooth along;
  While fastened deep within the veil,
    Hope is our anchor strong.

6 Wait till all tempests flee,
    Wait thy appointed hour!
  Wait till the Master of thy soul
    Reveal His love with power.

7 Tarry His leisure then!
    Although He seem to stay;
  For heaven's harbourage with Him
    All storms shall overpay.
Augustus M. Toplady. 1776.
And S. A. Brooke. 1881.

899 *The wind and the* C.M.
  sea obey Him.—Mark iv. 41.

O LORD, be with us when **we sail**
  Upon the lonely deep,
Our guard when on the silent deck
  The nightly watch we keep.

2 We need not fear, though all around,
    'Mid rising winds, we hear
  The multitude of waters surge;
    For Thou, O God, art near.

3 The **calm**, the breeze, the gale, the storm,
    The ocean and the land,
  All, all are Thine, and held within
    The hollow of Thine hand.

4 As when on blue Gennesaret
    Rose high the angry wave,
  And Thy disciples quailed in dread,
    One word of Thine could save;

5 So when the fiercer storms arise,
    From man's unbridled will,
  Be Thou, Lord, **present** in our hearts
    To whisper, 'Peace, be still!'

6 Across this troubled tide of life
    Thyself our Pilot be,
  Until we reach that better land,
    The land that knows no sea.

7 To Thee the Father, Thee the Son,
    Whom earth and heaven adore,
  Thee, Spirit, moving **on** the deep,
    Be praise for evermore. Amen.
Edward A. Dayman. b. 1807.

900 *These see the works of* 7.7.7.7.
  the Lord, and His wonders in the deep.
  Psalm cvii. 24.

LORD, whom winds and seas obey,
Guide us through the watery way;
In the hollow of Thy hand
Hide, and bring us safe to land.

247

TRAVELLERS BY LAND AND SEA.

2 Jesus, let our faithful mind
Rest, on Thee alone reclined ;
Every anxious thought repress,
Keep our souls in perfect peace.

3 Keep the souls whom now we leave,
Bid them to each other cleave,
Bid them walk on life's rough sea,
Bid them come by faith to Thee.

4 Save, till all these tempests end,
All who on Thy love depend ;
Waft our happy spirits o'er,
Land us on the heavenly shore. Amen.
Charles Wesley. 1872.

901 L.M.
*He . . . rebuked the wind,
and said unto the sea, Peace, be still.*
Mark iv. 39.

THE billows swell, the winds are high ;
Clouds overcast my wintry sky ;
Out of the depths to Thee I call,
My fears are great, my strength is small.

2 O Lord ! the pilot's part perform,
And guide and guard me through the storm ;
Defend me from each threatening ill ;
Control the waves ; say 'Peace, be still.

3 Amid the roaring of the sea,
My soul still hangs her hope on Thee ;
Thy constant love, Thy faithful care,
Is all that saves me from despair.

4 Though tempest-tossed and half a wreck,
My haven through the floods I seek ;
Let neither winds nor stormy main
Force back my shattered bark again.
Amen.
William Cowper. 1779.

902 8.7.8.7. D.
*He was in the hinder
part of the ship, asleep on a pillow.*
Mark iv. 38.

TOSSED upon life's raging billow,
Sweet it is, O Lord, to know
Thou hast pressed a sailor's pillow,
And canst feel a sailor's woe ;
Never slumbering, never sleeping,
Though the night be dark and drear,
Thou the faithful watch art keeping,
'All is well !' Thy constant cheer.

2 And though loud the wind is howling,
Fierce though flash the lightnings red,
Though the storm-clouds dark are scowling,
O'er the sailor's anxious head ;
Thou canst calm the raging ocean,
All its noise and tumult still,
Hush the billows' wild commotion,
At the bidding of Thy will.

3 Thus our hearts the hope will cherish,
While to heaven we lift our eyes ;
Thou wilt save us ere we perish,
Thou wilt hear our faintest cries :
And, though mast and sail be riven,
Life's short voyage soon is o'er ;
Safely moored in heaven's wide haven,
Storms and tempests vex no more.
G. W. Bethune. 1847.

903 12.12.12.12.
Lord, save us : we perish.
Matthew viii. 25.

WHEN through the torn sail the wild tempest is streaming,
When o'er the dark wave the red lightning is gleaming,
Nor hope lends a ray the poor seaman to cherish,
We fly to our Maker :—'Save, Lord, or we perish.'

2 O Jesus, once tossed on the breast of the billow,
Aroused by the cry of despair from Thy pillow,
Now seated in glory, the mariner cherish,
Who cries in his danger, 'Save, Lord, or we perish.'

3 And, O ! when the whirlwind of passion is raging,
When sin in our hearts its wild warfare is waging,
Arise in Thy grace, Thy redeemèd to cherish ;
Rebuke the destroyer :—'Save, Lord, or we perish.' Amen.
Bishop R. Heber. 1827.

904 C.M.
*Why are ye fearful,
O ye of little faith ?*—Matthew viii. 26.

WHILE lone upon the furious waves,
Where danger fiercely rides,
There is a Hand, unseen, that saves,
And through the ocean guides.

2 Almighty Lord of land and sea,
Beneath Thine eye we sail ;
And if our hope be fixed on Thee,
Our hearts can never quail.

3 Though tempests shake the angry deep,
And thunder's voice appal ;
Serene we wake, and calmly sleep,
Our Father governs all.

4 Still prove Thyself through all the way,
The Guardian and the Friend ;
Cheer with Thy presence every day,
And every night defend. Amen.
Ebenezer E. Jenkins. 1876.

Parents and Family Worship.

905 7.7.7.7.
As obedient children.
1 Peter i. 14.

GOD of mercy, hear our prayer
For the children Thou hast given;
Let them all Thy blessings share,
Grace on earth, and bliss in heaven!

2 In the morning of their days
May their hearts be drawn to Thee;
Let them learn to lisp Thy praise
In their earliest infancy.

3 Cleanse their souls from every stain,
Through the Saviour's precious blood;
Let them all be born again,
And be reconciled to God.

4 For this mercy, **Lord, we cry;**
Bend Thine **ever-gracious ear;**
While on **Thee our souls rely,**
Hear our **prayer, in mercy hear!**
Amen.
Thomas Hastings. 1834.

906 8.8.8.8.8.8.
*I and the children which
God hath given me.*—Hebrews ii. 13.

CAPTAIN **of our salvation,** take
The souls **we here** present to **Thee,**
And fit for Thy great service make
These heirs of immortality;
And let them **in** Thine image rise,
And then transplant **to** Paradise.

2 Unspotted from the world and pure,
Preserve them for Thy glorious cause,
Accustomed daily to endure
The welcome burden of Thy cross;
Inured to toil and patient pain,
Till all Thy perfect mind they gain.

3 Our sons henceforth be wholly Thine,
And serve and love Thee all their days;
Infuse the principle divine
In all who here expect Thy grace;
Let each improve the grace bestowed,
Rise every child **a** man of God!

4 Train up Thy hardy soldiers, Lord,
In all their Captain's steps to tread!
Or send them **to** proclaim Thy word,
Thy Gospel through the world to spread;
Freely as they receive **to** give,
And preach the death **by** which we live!
Amen.
Charles Wesley. 1763.

907 8.8.8.8.8.8.
*As for me and my house,
we will serve the Lord.*—Joshua xxiv. 15.

COME, Father, Son, and Holy Ghost,
To whom we for our children cry;
The good desired and wanted most,
Out of Thy richest grace supply;
The sacred discipline be given,
To train and bring them up for heaven.

2 Answer on them the end **of** all
Our cares, and pains, and studies here;
On them, recovered from their fall,
Stamped with the humble character,
Raised by the nurture of the Lord,
To all their Paradise **restored.**

3 Error and ignorance remove,
Their blindness both of heart and mind;
Give them the wisdom from above,
Spotless, and peaceable, and kind;
In knowledge pure their minds renew,
And store with thoughts divinely true.

4 Unite the pair so oft disjoined,
Knowledge and vital piety;
Learning and holiness combined,
And truth and love, let all men see,
In those whom up to Thee we give,
Thine, wholly Thine, to die and live.

5 Father! accept them through Thy Son,
And ever by Thy Spirit guide;
Thy wisdom in their lives be shown,
Thy name confessed and glorified;
Thy power and love diffused abroad,
Till all the earth is filled with God.
Amen.
Charles Wesley. 1749.

908 C.M.
*Train up a child in the
way he should go.*—Proverbs xxii. 6.

GOD only wise, almighty, good,
Send forth Thy truth and light,
To point us out the narrow road,
And guide our steps aright.

2 **To** steer our dangerous course between
The rocks on either hand,
And fix us in the golden mean,
And bring our charge to land.

3 Made apt, by Thy sufficient grace,
To teach as taught by Thee,
We come to train in all Thy ways
Our rising progeny.

4 Their selfish will in time subdue,
And mortify their pride;
And lend their youth a sacred clue
To find the Crucified.

5 We would in every step look up,
By Thy example taught
To alarm their fear, excite their hope,
And rectify their thought.

6 We would persuade their hearts to obey,
With mildest zeal proceed;
And never take the harsher way,
When love will do the deed.

SERVICES FOR THE YOUNG.

7 For this we ask, in faith sincere,
　The wisdom from above,
To touch their hearts with filial fear,
　And pure, ingenuous love:

8 To watch their will, to sense inclined;
　Withhold their hurtful food;
And gently bend their tender mind,
　And draw their souls to God.
　　　　　　Charles Wesley. 1767.

909　　　　　　8.8.6. 8.8.6.
*I will walk within my
house with a perfect heart.*—Psalm ci. 2.

HOW shall I walk my God to please,
　And spread content and happiness
O'er all beneath my care?
A pattern to my household give,
And as a guardian angel live,
　As Jesus's messenger?

2 The opposite extremes I see,
　Remissness and severity,
　　And know not how to shun
The precipice on either hand,
While in the narrow path I stand,
　And dread to venture on.

3 Shall I, through indolence supine,
Neglect, betray my charge divine,
　My delegated power?
The souls I from my Lord receive,
Of each I an account must give,
　At that tremendous hour.

4 Lord over all, and God most high!
Jesus, to Thee for help I fly,
　For constant power and grace:
That, taught by Thy good Spirit and led,
I may with confidence proceed,
　And all Thy footsteps trace.

5 O teach me my first lesson now!
And, while to Thy sweet yoke I bow,
　Thy easy service prove,
Lowly and meek in heart, I see
The art of governing like Thee
　Is governing by love.
　　　　　　Charles Wesley. 1767.

910　　　　　　C.M.
*The Angel which redeemed
me from all evil, bless the lads.*
Genesis xlviii. 16.

THE great redeeming Angel, Thee,
　O Jesus, we confess!
Do Thou our great Deliverer be,
　And all our offspring bless.

2 Early discipled to the Lord,
　May they be taught of Thee;
And, made to know and trust Thy word,
　Wise to salvation be.

3 Thou who hast borne our sins away,
　Our children's sins remove;
And bring them through their evil day,
　To sing Thy praise above.

4 Partakers of our nature, make
　Partakers of Thy grace;
And then the heirs of glory take
　To dwell before Thy face. Amen.
　　　　　　Charles Wesley. 1762.

911　　　　　　L.M.
*Thou shalt see thy
children's children.*—Psalm cxxviii. 6.

IN this glad hour, when children meet,
　And home with them their children
　　bring,
Our hearts with one affection beat,
　One song of praise our voices sing.

2 For all the faithful, loved and dear,
　Whom Thou so kindly, Lord, hast given,
For those who still are with us here,
　And those who wait for us in heaven;

3 For every past and present joy,
　For honour, competence, and health,
For hopes which time may not destroy
　Our soul's imperishable wealth.

4 For all, accept our humble praise;
　Still bless us, Father, by Thy love;
And when are closed our mortal days,
　Unite us in one home above. Amen.
　　　　　　H. Ware, Jun. d. 1843.

Services for the Young.

*Hymns suitable for Children's Services will be found in all parts of
this Hymnal. See Special Index.*

912　8.7. 8.7. *With Chorus. Iambic.*
Rejoice in the Lord alway.
Philippians iv. 4.

A GLADSOME hymn of praise we sing,
　And thankfully we gather,
To bless the love of God above,
　Our everlasting Father.

　　In Him rejoice with heart and voice,
　　　Whose glory fadeth never,
　　Whose providence is our defence,
　　Who lives and loves for ever.

2 From shades of night, He calls the light,
　And from the soil the flower;
From every cloud His blessings break,
　In sunshine, or in shower.

3 Full in His sight His children stand,
　By His strong arm defended;
And He, whose wisdom guides the world,
　Our footsteps hath attended.

4 For nothing falls unknown to Him,—
　Or care, or joy, or sorrow;
And He whose mercy ruled the past,
　Will be our stay to-morrow.

SERVICES FOR THE YOUNG.

5 Then praise the Lord with one accord,
  To His great name give glory,
  And of His never-changing love
  Repeat the wondrous story.
          A. N. Blatchford.

913   7.7.7.7. D.
*I laid me down and slept ;
I awaked ; for the Lord sustained me.*
      Psalm iii. 5.

GOD of mercy and of love,
  Listen from the heaven above,
While to Thee my voice I raise
In a morning hymn of praise ;
It was Thine almighty arm
Kept me all night long from harm ;
It is only, Lord, by Thee
That another morn I see.

2 Lo ! the happy light of day
  Drives the shadows all away ;
  Lo ! it brings again to sight
  All things beautiful and bright :
  White clouds sailing in the air,
  Little flowers so fresh and fair,
  Greenest fields, and rippling streams,
  Glitter in the morning beams

3 Father, keep me all day long
  From all hurtful things and wrong ;
  Make me an obedient child,
  Make me loving, gentle, mild ;
  Hark ! the birds are singing gay ;
  Let me sing, as well as they,
  Praise to Him who is above
  For His mercies and His love.   Amen.
          Anon.

914   C.M.D.
*Young men, and maidens ;
old men, and children ; let them praise the
name of the Lord.*—Psalm cxlviii. 12, 13.

O LORD of all, we bring to Thee
   Our sacrifice of praise,
To Thee with glad and thankful hearts
  Our festal hymn we raise ;
We are but children here on earth,
  And Thou art high above,
But yet we dare to come to Thee,
  Because Thy name is Love.

2 We praise Thee now for life, and health,
    And earthly happiness,
  For all the sacred human love
    That still our lives doth bless,
  For Thy dear Son whom Thou hast sent,
    Whose kind and tender voice
  Bids the young children come to Thee,
    And in Thy love rejoice.

3 What shall we render Thee, O Lord ?
    What tribute shall we bring ?
  O let us give our hearts, our lives,
    In thankful offering.
  Although we are but children, yet
    Thou dost our service ask,
  And each in Thy great work may find
    His own appointed task.

4 O make us watchful, lest by sin
    Our hearts be overborne ;
  O make us true in word and work,
    Though all the world should scorn ;
  O make us willing here to serve,
    In lowliness and love,
  For Him who in a **servant's** form
    Came down from **heaven** above.

5 The night of sin must wane at last,
    The morn of joy begin,
  When Christ in every human heart
    His royal throne must win ;
  O let us give Him now in youth
    Our ardour and our strength,
  Work for His glorious kingdom here,
    And share His joy at length !

6 Already breaks the early dawn
    Of that great day of God ;
  Already sounds the Master's voice
    Through all the earth abroad.
  Then cast the works of night away,
    Gird on the arms of light,
  And on the side of Christ our King
    Stand ready for the fight.
          E. S. A. 1887.

915   C.M.
Ye are of God, little children.
    1 John iv. 4.

COME, let us join the hosts above,
   Now in our youngest days ;
Remember our Creator's love,
  And lisp our Father's praise.

2 His majesty will not despise
    The day of feeble things ;
  Grateful the songs of children rise,
    And please the King of kings.

3 He loves to be remembered thus,
    And honoured for his grace ;
  Out of the mouths of babes like us,
    His wisdom perfects praise.

4 Glory to God, and praise, and power,
    Honour and thanks be given ;
  Children and cherubim adore
    The Lord of earth and heaven.
              Amen.
        Charles Wesley. 1763.

916   6.5. 6.5. D.   *With Chorus.*
*Who is this King of glory ?
The Lord of hosts, He is the King of glory.*
        Psalm xxiv. 10.

JESUS, King of glory,
   Throned above the sky,
Jesus, tender Saviour,
  Hear Thy children cry :
Pardon our transgressions,
  Cleanse us from our sin ;
By Thy Spirit help us
  Heavenly life to win.

    Jesus, King of glory,
      Throned above the sky,
    Jesus, tender Saviour,
      Hear Thy children cry.

251

SERVICES FOR THE YOUNG.

2 On this day of gladness,
  Bending low the knee
In Thine earthly temple,
  Lord, we worship Thee;—
Celebrate Thy goodness,
  Mercy, grace, and truth;
All Thy loving guidance
  Of our heedless youth;

3 For the little children
    Who have come to Thee;
  For the glad, bright spirits
    Who Thy glory see;
  For the loved ones resting
    In Thy dear embrace;
  For the pure and holy
    Who behold Thy face;

4 For Thy faithful servants
    Who have entered in;
  For Thy fearless soldiers
    Who have conquered sin;
  For the countless legions
    Who have followed Thee,
  Heedless of the danger,
    On to victory.

5 Help us ever steadfast
    In the faith to be;
  In Thy Church's conflicts
    Fighting valiantly;
  Loving Saviour, strengthen
    These weak hearts of ours,
  Through Thy cross to conquer
    Crafty evil powers.

6 When the shadows lengthen,
    Show us, Lord, Thy way;
  Through the darkness lead us
    To the heavenly day;
  When our course is finished,
    Ended all the strife,
  Grant us with the faithful
    Palms and crowns of life. Amen.
                        W. H. Davison. b. 1827.

917   C.M.
   *When they were come to the
   place, which is called Calvary, there they
   crucified Him.*—Luke xxiii. 33.

THERE is a green hill far away
    Without a city wall,
  Where the dear Lord was crucified,
    Who died to save us all.

2 We may not know, we cannot tell
    What pains He had to bear,
  But we believe it was for us
    He hung and suffered there.

3 He died that we might be forgiven,
    He died to make us good,
  That we might go at last to heaven,
    Saved by His precious blood.

4 There was no other good enough
    To pay the price of sin;
  He only could unlock the gate
    Of heaven, and let us in.
252

5 O dearly, dearly has He loved,
    And we must love Him too,
  And trust in His redeeming blood,
    And try His works to do.
              Mrs. Cecil F. Alexander. 1848.

918   S.M.D.
   *Dwelling in the light
   which no man can approach unto.*
                    1 Timothy vi. 16.

ABOVE the clear blue sky,
    Beyond our feeble sight,
  The God of glory dwells on high,
    In everlasting light.
  Around His glorious throne
    The holy angels stand;
  In songs of praise their King they own,
    Or fly at His command.

2 And we may praise Him too,
    And serve Him here below;
  He stoops to mark what children do,
    Their inmost thoughts to know;
  And though He reigns above,
    Where angels ceaseless praise,
  He will accept our humble love,
    And lead us in His ways.

3 O, may we humbly seek
    To do His holy will,
  And try with thankful hearts, and meek,
    To sing His praises still;
  And then for Jesu's sake,
    Who came for us to die,
  Our happy spirits He will take
    To praise Him in the sky.
              Mrs. M. Bourdillon. 1849.

919   6.6. 6.6. 4.4. 4.4.
   *Out of the mouth of babes
   and sucklings Thou hast perfected praise.*
                    Matthew xxi. 16.

ABOVE the clear blue sky,
    In heaven's bright abode,
  The angel-host on high
    Sing praises to their God:
      Hallelujah!
    They love to sing
  To God their King
    Hallelujah!

2 But God from infant tongues
    On earth receiveth praise;
  We then our cheerful songs
    In sweet accord will raise:
      Hallelujah!
    We too will sing
  To God our King
    Hallelujah!

3 O blessèd Lord, Thy truth
    To us Thy babes impart,
  And teach us in our youth
    To know Thee as Thou art.
      Hallelujah!
    Then shall we sing
  To God our King
    Hallelujah!

SERVICES FOR THE YOUNG.

4 O, may Thy holy word
  Spread all the world around;
  And all with one accord
    Uplift the joyful **sound**,
      Hallelujah!
  All then shall sing
  To God their King
    Hallelujah! Amen.
        John Chandler. 1841.

920   7.6.7.6. D. *Special.*
They brought young children to Him, that He should touch them.
Mark x. 13.

THERE'S a Friend for little children,
  Above the bright blue sky,
A Friend who never changes,
  Whose love will never die:
Unlike our friends by nature,
  Who change with changing years,
This Friend is always worthy
  Of that dear name He bears.

2 There's a rest for little children,
  Above the bright blue sky,
Who love the blessèd Saviour,
  And to His Father cry;
A rest from every trouble,
  From sin and danger free,
Where every little pilgrim
  Shall rest eternally.

3 There's a **home** for little children,
  Above the bright blue sky,
Where Jesus reigns in glory,
  A home of **peace** and joy.
No home **on earth** is like it,
  Nor can **with it** compare;
For every **one is happy**,
  Nor **could be happier**, there.

4 There's a crown for little children,
  Above the bright blue sky,
And all who look for Jesus
  Shall wear it by-and-by;
A crown of brightest glory,
  Which He will then bestow
On those who love the Saviour,
  And walk with Him below.

5 There's **a song for little children,**
  Above the **bright blue sky,**
A song that **will not weary,**
  Though **sung continually,**
A song which **even angels**
  Can **never, never sing;**
They know not **Christ as Saviour,**
  But **worship Him as King.**

6 There's **a** robe for little children,
  Above **the** bright blue sky,
And a harp **of** sweetest music,
  And palms of victory
All, all above **is** treasured,
  And found in Christ alone;
O come, dear little children,
  That all may be your own.
        Albert Midlane. 1867.

921   8.5.8.5.8.4.3.
The children crying in the temple, and saying, Hosanna to the Son of David.—Matthew xxi. 15.

LORD, Thy children lowly **bending**
  Bow before Thy Throne;
Praise from youthful lips ascending
  Wilt Thou deign **to own?**
Wilt Thou hear **us while we bless Thee,**
  And confess **Thee**
    God alone?

2 While the heavens declare **Thy glory**
  To the listening earth,
While the angels sing the story
  Of creation's birth,
Wilt Thou hear **our** child-notes swelling,
  Gladly telling
    Jesus's worth?

3 Yes, Thou wilt; for Thou dost love us,
  Cam'st for us to die;
Bending from Thy throne above us
  With a pitying eye,
Well we know that Thou art near us,
  And wilt hear **us**
    When **we** cry.

4 Then our humble praises bringing,
  We will seek Thy face,
Hymns with grateful voices singing
  In this hallowed place,
We will dare to come before Thee,
  And adore Thee,
    Lord **of grace.**
        Anon.

922   7.6.7.6. D.
Consider the lilies of the field.—Matthew vi. 28.

I KNOW who makes the **daisies,**
  And paints them starry bright;
I know who clothes the lilies,
  So sweet, and soft, and white
And surely needful raiment
  He will for **me** provide,
Who know Him as my Jesus,
  And in His love confide.

2 I know who feeds the sparrow,
  And robin, red and gay;
I know who makes the skylark
  Soar up to greet the day.
And me much more He cares for,
  And feeds with daily bread,
Whom He has taught to love Him,
  And trust what He has said.

3 The daisy and the lily
  Obey Him as they can;
The robin and the skylark
  Fulfil His perfect plan;
And I, to whom are given
  A heart, and mind, and will,
Must try to serve Him better,
  And all His laws fulfil.

4 The daisies, they must perish,
  The lark and robin die;
But I shall live for ever,
  Above the bright blue sky;
Dear Jesus, Thou wilt help me
  To love Thee more and more,
Until in heaven I see Thee,
  Am like Thee, and adore.
          C. Newman Hall. 1878.

923   7.6. 7.6. *Special.*
  *God saw everything that
He had made, and, behold, it was very good.*
            Genesis i. 31.

ALL things bright and beautiful,
  All creatures, great and small,
All things wise and wonderful,
  The Lord God made them all.

2 Each little flower that opens,
  Each little bird that sings,
He made their glowing colours,
  He made their tiny wings.

3 The purple-headed mountain,
  The river running by,
The sunset, and the morning
  That brightens up the sky;

4 The cold wind in the winter,
  The pleasant summer sun,
The ripe fruits in the garden,
  He made them every one.

5 The tall trees in the greenwood,
  The meadows where we play,
The rushes by the water
  We gather every day;

6 He gave us eyes to see them,
  And lips that we might tell
How great is God Almighty
  Who has made all things well.
        Mrs. Cecil F. Alexander. 1848.

924   6.5. 12 *lines.*
    Who is on the Lord's side?
          Exodus xxxii. 26.

WHO is on the Lord's side?
  Who will serve the King?
Who will be His helpers
  Other lives to bring?
Who will leave the world's side?
  Who will face the foe?
Who is on the Lord's side?
  Who will for Him go?
    By Thy call of mercy,
    By Thy grace divine,
  We are on the Lord's side,
    Saviour, we are Thine!

2 Not for weight of glory,
  Not for crown and palm,
Enter we the army,
  Raise the warrior's psalm;
But for love that claimeth
  Lives for whom He died,
He whom Jesus nameth
  Must be on His side,

254

    By Thy love constraining,
    By Thy grace divine,
  We are on the Lord's side,
    Saviour, we are Thine!

3 Jesus, Thou hast bought us,
  Not with gold or gem,
But with Thine own life-blood,
  For Thy diadem.
With Thy blessing filling
  Each who comes to Thee,
Thou hast made us willing,
  Thou hast made us free.
    By Thy grand redemption,
    By Thy grace divine,
  We are on the Lord's side,
    Saviour, we are Thine!
        Frances R. Havergal. 1877.

925   7.6. 7.6. D.
    *Remember now thy Creator
in the days of thy youth.*—Ecclesiastes xii. 1.

REMEMBER thy Creator
  In childhood's happy days,
He from the mouths of infants
  Knows how to perfect praise.
The Lord took little children
  Within His kind embrace,
And they who seek Him early
  Shall surely find His face.

2 Remember thy **Creator**
  In youth's rejoicing years:
Ere yet thy steps have entered
  Life's shadowed vale of tears:
Thus save thy heart from sorrows
  That sadden after days,
And keep thy feet from straying
  In sin's destructive ways.

3 Remember thy Creator
  In manhood's active prime,
And render to His service
  The first-fruits of thy time.
Seek not to find thy treasure
  In things that must decay,
But lay up store in heaven
  Which shall not pass away.

4 Remember thy Creator
  In age's eventide,
They ne'er shall be forsaken
  Who in His love confide:
Thy failing heart He'll strengthen,
  Thy weary spirit cheer;
With Him, in death's dark valley
  No evil shalt thou fear.

5 Remember thy **Creator**
  Whate'er thy need may be,
In gladness or in sorrow
  He will remember thee;
Will guide thee with His counsel,
  Uphold thee by His grace,
Then take thee to His glory
  With joy to see His face.
          T. A. Stowell. 1887.

SERVICES FOR THE YOUNG.

926   8.7. 8. 7. 7. 7.
*Unto you is born this day
in the city of David, a Saviour.*
Luke ii. 11.

ONCE, in royal David's city,
  Stood a lowly cattle shed,
Where a mother laid her baby,
  In a manger for His bed :
    Mary was that mother mild,
    Jesus Christ her little child.

2 He came down to earth from heaven,
  Who is God and Lord of all,
And His shelter was a stable,
  And His cradle was a stall :
    With the poor and mean and **lowly**
    Lived on earth our Saviour holy.

3 And through all His wondrous childhood
  He would honour, and obey,
Love, and watch the lowly mother
  In whose gentle **arms** he lay :
    Christian children all must **be**
    Mild, obedient, good as He.

4 For **He is our** childhood's pattern,
  Day by day like us He grew,
He was little, weak, and helpless,
  Tears and smiles like us He knew :
    And He feeleth for our sadness,
    And He shareth in our gladness.

5 And our eyes at last shall see Him,
  Through His own redeeming love,
For that child, so dear and gentle,
  Is our Lord in heaven above :
    And He leads His children **on**
    To the place where He is gone.

6 Not in that poor lowly stable,
  With the oxen standing by,
We shall see Him, but in heaven,
  Set at God's right hand on high ;
    When like stars His children crowned,
    All in white shall wait around.

Mrs. Cecil F. Alexander. 1848.

927   C.M.
*Hold up my goings in Thy
paths, that my footsteps slip not.*
Psalm xvii. 5.

BE Thou my Guardian and my Guide,
  And hear me when I call ;
Let not my slippery footsteps slide,
  And hold me lest I fall.

2 The world, **the** flesh, and Satan dwell
  Around the path I tread ;
O save me from the snares of hell,
  Thou Quickener of the dead.

3 And if I tempted am to sin,
  And outward things are strong,
Do Thou, O Lord, keep watch within,
  And save my soul from wrong.

4 Still let me ever watch and pray,
  And feel that I am frail :
That if the tempter cross my way,
  Yet he may not prevail.

5 Then in the last and loneliest hour
  I shall have no alarms,
But underneath me feel in power
  Thine everlasting arms.

Isaac Williams. 1842.

928   C.M.
*We will remember the name
of the Lord our God.* —Psalm xx. 7.

O LORD, while life **and hope are young,**
  And all are kind **to me,**
While strains of pleasure **fill my** tongue,
  Let me remember Thee.

2 Where'er my wayward footsteps turn,
  Whate'er mine eyes may see,
May I Thy power, Thy love discern,
  And thus remember Thee.

3 And when to man's estate I grow,
  Though rich or poor I be,
May all my feelings heavenward flow
  And I remember Thee.

4 And O, when evil **days shall fall,**
  And health and comfort flee,
Midst sorrow's cloud **and suffering's** thrall,
  May I remember **Thee.**

5 And thus, till life itself shall end,
  And I from sin am free,
Creator, Father, Guardian, Friend,
  May I remember Thee. Amen.

Anon.

929   6.5. 6.5. D.
*He shall gather the lambs
with His arm, and carry them in His bosom.*
Isaiah xl. 11.

JESUS is **our** Shepherd,
  Wiping every tear ;
Folded in His bosom,
  What have we to fear ?
Only let us follow
  Whither He doth lead,
To the thirsty desert,
  Or the dewy mead.

2 Jesus is our Shepherd,
  Well we know His voice,
How its gentlest whisper
  Makes our heart rejoice ;
Even when He chideth,
  Tender is its tone,
None but He shall guide us,
  We are His alone.

3 Jesus is our Shepherd ;
  For the sheep He bled,
Every lamb is sprinkled
  With the blood He shed ;
Then on each He setteth
  His own secret sign ;
'They that have My Spirit,
  These,' saith He, 'are Mine.'

SERVICES FOR THE YOUNG.

4 Jesus is our Shepherd;
  Guarded by His arm,
Though the wolves may raven,
  None can do us harm;
When we tread death's valley,
  Dark with fearful gloom,
We will fear no evil,
  Victors o'er the tomb.
                Hugh Stowell. 1849.

930   8.7. 8.7. 8.7.
He took them up in His arms, . . . and blessed them.—Mark x. 16.

GRACIOUS Saviour, gentle Shepherd,
  Little ones are dear to Thee;
Gathered with Thine arms, and carried
  In Thy bosom may we be;
Sweetly, fondly, safely tended;
  From all want and danger free.

2 Tender Shepherd, never leave us
  From Thy fold to go astray;
By Thy look of love directed,
  May we walk the narrow way;
Thus direct us, and protect us,
  Lest we fall an easy prey.

3 Let Thy holy word instruct us,
  Guide us daily by its light;
Let Thy love and grace constrain us
  To approve whate'er is right,
Take Thine easy yoke, and wear it,
  Strengthened by Thy heavenly might.

Taught to lisp the holy praises
  Which on earth Thy children sing,
Both with lips and hearts unfeigned,
  May we our thank-offerings bring;
Then with all the saints in glory,
  Join to praise the Shepherd-King.
                          Amen.
Jane Leeson. 1842. *Alt. by John Keble* 1857.

931   6.5. 6.5.
Hear, O Lord, and have mercy upon me.—Psalm xxx. 10.

JESUS, high in glory,
  Lend a listening ear;
When we bow before Thee,
  Children's praises hear.

2 Though Thou art so holy,
  Heaven's Almighty King,
Thou wilt stoop to listen
  When Thy praise we sing.

3 We are little children,
  Weak and apt to stray;
Saviour, guide and keep us
  In the heavenly way.

4 Save us, Lord, from sinning;
  Watch us day by day;
Help us now to love Thee;
  Take our sins away.

5 Strengthen us for duty,
  While on earth we live;
May we to Thy service
  Our best talents give.

6 Then when Jesus calls us
  To our heavenly home,
We would gladly answer,
  'Saviour, Lord, we come.'
                     Anon. 1847.

932   6.5. 6.5
The Spirit also helpeth our infirmities.—Romans viii. 26.

HOLY Spirit! hear us;
  Help us while we sing;
Breathe into the music
  Of the praise we bring.

2 Holy Spirit! prompt us
  When we kneel to pray;
Nearer come, and teach us
  What we ought to say.

3 Holy Spirit! shine Thou
  On the Book we read;
Gild its holy pages
  With the light we need.

4 Holy Spirit! give us
  Each a lowly mind;
Make us more like Jesus,
  Gentle, pure and kind.

5 Holy Spirit! brighten
  Little deeds of toil;
And our playful pastimes
  Let no folly spoil.

6 Holy Spirit! keep us
  Safe from sins which lie
Hidden by some pleasure,
  From our youthful eye.

7 Holy Spirit! help us
  Daily by Thy might,
What is wrong to conquer,
  And to choose the right. Amen.
                    W. H. Parker. 1880.

933   8.8. 8.4. 8.4.
Our Father which art in heaven.—Matthew vi. 9.

THE child leans on its parent's breast,
  Leaves there its cares, and is at rest;
The bird sits singing by his nest,
  And tells aloud
His trust in God, and so is blest
  'Neath every cloud.

2 He has no store, he sows no seed;
Yet sings aloud, and doth not heed;
By flowing stream or grassy mead
  He sings to shame
Men, who forget, in fear of need,
  A Father's Name.

3 The heart that trusts for ever sings,
And feels as light as it had wings;
A well of peace within it springs;
  Come good or ill,
Whate'er to-day, to-morrow brings,
  It is His will!
                    Isaac Williams. 1842.

SERVICES FOR THE YOUNG.

934 *Irregular.*
Thy Holy Child Jesus,
whom Thou hast anointed.—Acts iv. 27.

THERE came a little Child to earth
    Long ago ;
And the angels of God proclaimed His
    birth,
    High and low.

2 Out on the night, so calm and still,
    Their song was heard ;
For they knew that the Child on Bethle-
    hem's hill
    Was Christ the Lord.

3 Far away in a goodly land,
    Fair and bright,
Children with crowns of glory stand,
    Robed in white.

4 In white more pure than the spotless snow ;
    And their tongues unite
In the psalm which the angels sang long
    ago
    On that still night.

5 They sing how the Lord of that world so
    fair
    A Child was born,
And that they might a crown of glory wear
    Wore a crown of thorn ;

6 And in mortal weakness, in want and pain,
    Came forth to die,
That the children of earth might for ever
    reign
    With Him on high.

7 He has put on His kingly apparel now,
    In that goodly land ;
And He leads to where fountains of water
    flow
    That chosen band ;

8 And for evermore, in their robes most fair
    And undefiled,
Those ransomed children His praise declare
    Who was once a Child.
        Emily E. S. Elliott. 1873.

935 8.8.8.4.
I love them that love Me.
Proverbs viii. 17.

DEAR Master, what can children do ?
    The angels came from heaven above
To comfort Thee ; may children too
    Give Thee their love ?

2 No more, as on that night of shame,
    Art Thou in dark Gethsemane,
Where, worshipping, an angel came
    To strengthen Thee.

3 But Thou hast taught us that Thou art
    Still present in the crowded street,
In every lonely, suffering heart
    That there we meet.

4 And not one simple, loving deed,
    That lessens gloom, or lightens pain,
Or answers some unspoken need,
    Is done in vain ;

5 Since every passing joy we make,
    For men and women that we see,
If it is offered for Thy sake,
    Is given to Thee.

6 O God, our Master, help us then
    To bless the weary and the sad,
And, comforting our fellow-men,
    To make Thee glad. Amen.
        Annie Matheson. 1884.

936 7.7. 8.8.7.
I must be about My
Father's business.—Luke ii. 49.

O WHAT can little hands do
    To please the King of heaven ?
The little hands some work may try
To help the poor in misery ;
    Such grace to mine be given !

2 O what can little lips do
    To please the King of heaven ?
The little lips can praise and pray,
And gentle words of kindness say ;
    Such grace to mine be given !

3 O what can little hearts do
    To please the King of heaven ?
Our hearts, if God His Spirit send,
Can love and trust their Saviour-Friend ;
    Such grace to mine be given !

4 Though small is all that we can do
    To please the King of heaven ;
When hearts and hands and lips unite
To serve the Saviour with delight,
    Then perfect grace is given.
        Mrs. Hinsdale.

937 8.6. 8 6. 8.6.
Behold the fowls of the
air.—Matt. vi. 26.

O LITTLE birds that all day long
    Carol in every tree,
What is the secret of your song,
    The meaning of your glee
You are so very, very glad ;
    How loving God must be !

2 Dear flowers that blossom round my feet,
    It fills my heart to see
Your smiling faces, when you meet
    God's wind upon the lea ;
You seem to laugh for happiness ;
    How loving God must be !

3 And all day long our hearts rejoice,
    God cares for you and me ;
We are but children, yet our voice
    May praise Him merrily ;
And we can sing like all the birds,
    How loving God must be !

SERVICES FOR THE YOUNG.

4 God's men and women sometimes look
　　Less full of joy than we,
　Yet He their suffering nature took
　　As Son of Man, and He
　Poured out His life to heal them all:
　　How loving God must be!
　　　　　　　Annie Matheson. 1880.

938　　　　　6.5, 6.5. D.
*Man goeth forth unto his
work and to his labour until the evening.*
Psalm civ. 23.

WHILE the sun is shining
　　Brightly in the sky,
Ere his rays declining
　Tell that night is nigh;
Ere the shadows falling
　Lengthen on thy way,
Hark! a voice is calling,
　Work while it is day.

2 Work for God in heaven;
　　Seek the Saviour's face,
　Plead to be forgiven,
　　Strive to grow in grace;
　Watch against temptation,
　　Watch and fight and pray:
　Each in his own station
　　Work while it is day.

3 Work, but not in sadness,
　　For our Lord above;
　He will make it gladness
　　With His smile of love:
　When that Lord returning
　　Knocketh at the gate,
　Let your lights be burning,
　　Be like men who wait.

4 Happy then the meeting,
　　When we see His face;
　Welcome then the greeting
　　From the throne of grace:
　'Good and faithful servants
　　Of My Father blest,
　Now your work is ended,
　　Enter into rest.'
　　　　　　　T. A. Stowell. 1869.

939　　11.11. 11.11. *Anapæstic.*
The Lord is among them.
Psalm lxviii. 17.

THERE is out of sight the fair land of
　　the blest,
Which Jesus has made for His followers'
　　rest;
He calls us to come, and invites us to
　　stay;
Then march to the land of the blest, march
　　away!

2 No sorrow is felt, for our Saviour is there,
　'Tis sinless and joyful, a land, O, how
　　fair!
　Where darkness is lost in all-glorious
　　day;
　Then march to the land of the blest, march
　　away!

3 Our Saviour is good; but no words can
　　express
　The depths of His love or the heights of
　　His grace;
　He bids us come to Him, then let us obey,
　And march to the land of the blest, march
　　away!

4 Come, children, don't tarry, for Jesus now
　　stands,
　His arms opened wide, and His merciful
　　hands
　Extended to touch you, and bless you for
　　aye;
　Then march to the land of the blest, march
　　away!
　　　　　　　Anon.

940　　　　　　　　　C.M.
*It is God which worketh
in you both to will and to do of His good
pleasure.*—Philippians ii. 13.

GOD make my life a little light
　Within the world to glow;
A little flame that burneth bright,
　Wherever I may go.

2 God make my life a little flower,
　That giveth joy to all,
　Content to bloom in native bower,
　Although the place be small.

3 God make my life a little song
　That comforteth the sad,
　That helpeth others to be strong,
　And makes the singer glad.

4 God make my life a little staff,
　Whereon the weak may rest,
　That so what health and strength I have
　May serve my neighbours best.

5 God make my life a little hymn
　Of tenderness and praise,
　Of faith, that never waxeth dim,
　In all His wondrous ways. Amen.
　　　　　　M. Betham-Edwards. 1872.

941　　　　　6.5. 6.5.
*Even the night shall be
light about me.*—Psalm cxxxix. 11.

NOW the day is over,
　Night is drawing nigh;
Shadows of the evening
　Steal across the sky.

2 Jesus, grant the weary
　Calm and sweet repose;
　With Thy tenderest blessing
　May our eyelids close.

3 Grant to little children
　Visions bright of Thee;
　Guard the sailors tossing
　On the deep blue sea.

SERVICES FOR THE YOUNG.

4 Comfort every sufferer
  Watching late in pain;
Those who plan some evil
  From their sin restrain.

5 Through the long night watches,
  May Thine angels spread
Their white wings above me,
  Watching round my bed.

6 When the morning wakens,
  Then may I arise,
Pure, and fresh, and sinless,
  In Thy holy eyes.

7 Glory to the Father,
  Glory to the Son,
And to Thee, blest Spirit,
  Whilst all ages run. Amen.
      S. Baring-Gould. 1865.

942 8.7. 8.7. 4.7.
*The blessing of the Lord,
it maketh rich.—Proverbs x. 22.*

FATHER, let Thy benediction,
  Gently falling as the dew,
And Thy ever gracious presence
  Bless us all our journey through;
    May we ever
  Keep the end of life in view.

2 Young in years, we need the wisdom
  Which can only come from Thee:
In the morn of our existence
  Let us Thy salvation see;
    Changed in spirit,
  Then shall we Thy children be.

3 When temptations shall assail us,
  When we falter by the way,
Let Thine arm of strength defend us,
  Saviour, hear us when we pray;
    Thou art mighty,
  Be Thou then our Rock and Stay.

4 Praise and blessing, power and glory,
  Will we render, Lord, to Thee;
For the news of Thy salvation
  Shall extend from sea to sea;
    All the nations
  Joyfully shall worship Thee. Amen.
      Mrs. M. E. Shelly. 1844.

943 7.6. 7.6. D.
*The shadows of the
evening are stretched out.—Jeremiah vi. 4.*

THE hours of day are over,
  The evening calls us home;
Once more to Thee, O Father,
  With thankful hearts we come,
For all Thy countless blessings
  We praise Thy holy Name,
And own Thy love unchanging,
  Through days and years the same.

2 For life, and health, and shelter
  From harm throughout the day,
The kindness of our teachers,
  The gladness of our play;
For all the dear affection
  Of parents, brothers, friends,
To Thee our thanks we render,
  Who these, and all things, sends.

3 But these, O Lord, can show us
  Thy goodness but in part;
Thy love would lead us onward
  To know Thee as Thou art;
Thy Son came down from heaven
  To take away our sin,
Thy Spirit dwells among us
  To make us clean within.

4 For this, O Lord, we bless Thee,
  For this we thank Thee most—
The cleansing of the sinful,
  The saving of the lost;
The Teacher ever present,
  The Friend for ever nigh,
The home prepared by Jesus
  For us beyond the sky.

5 Lord, gather all Thy children
  To meet Thee there at last,
When earthly tasks are ended,
  And earthly days are past;
With all our dear ones round us
  In that eternal home,
Where death no more shall part us,
  And night shall never come! Amen.
      John Ellerton. 1856.

944 8.7. 8.7. 7.7.
*Speak, Lord; for Thy
servant heareth.—1 Samuel iii. 9.*

MASTER, speak! Thy servant heareth,
  Waiting for Thy gracious word,
Longing for Thy voice that cheereth;
  Master! let it now be heard.
I am listening, Lord, for Thee:
What hast Thou to say to me?

2 Speak to me by name, O Master,
  Let me know it is to me
Speak, that I may follow faster,
  With a step more firm and free,
Where the Shepherd leads the flock,
In the shadow of the Rock.

3 Master, speak! though least and lowest,
  Let me not unheard depart;
Master, speak! for O, Thou knowest
  All the yearning of my heart;
Knowest all its truest need;
Speak! and make me blest indeed.

4 Master, speak! and make me ready,
  When Thy voice is truly heard,
With obedience glad and steady
  Still to follow every word.
I am listening, Lord, for Thee:
Master, speak, O, speak to me! Amen.
      Frances R. Havergal. 1874.

Private Devotion.

945   C.M.
*Go forth into the plain,
and I will there talk with thee.*
Ezekiel iii. 22.

FAR from the world, O Lord, I flee;
  From strife and tumult far;
From scenes where Satan wages still
  His most successful war.

2 The calm retreat, the silent shade,
  With prayer and praise agree;
And seem by Thy sweet bounty made
  For those who follow Thee.

3 There, if Thy spirit touch the soul,
  And grace her mean abode,
O with what peace, and joy, and love,
  She communes with her God!

4 There, like the nightingale, she pours
  Her solitary lays;
Nor asks a witness of her song,
  Nor thirsts for human praise.

5 Author and Guardian of my life!
  Sweet source of light divine!
And, all harmonious names in one,
  My Saviour! Thou art mine.

6 What thanks I owe Thee, and what love,
  A boundless, endless store,
Shall echo through the realms above,
  When time shall be no more!
         William Cowper. 1779.

946   7 7. 7. 6.
*I will not leave you comfortless:
I will come to you.*—John xiv. 18.

IN the dark and cloudy day,
  When earth's riches flee away,
And the last hope will not stay,
  My Saviour, comfort me.

2 When the hoard of many years
Like a fleet cloud disappears,
And the future's full of fears,
  My Saviour, comfort me.

3 When the secret idol's gone
That my poor heart yearned upon—
Desolate, bereft, alone,
  My Saviour, comfort me.

4 Thou who wast so sorely tried,
In the darkness crucified,
Bid me in Thy love confide;
  My Saviour, comfort me.

5 Comfort me, I am cast down,
'Tis my Heavenly Father's frown;
I deserve it all, I own:
  My Saviour, comfort me.

6 In these hours of sad distress
Let me know He loves no less,
Bid me trust His faithfulness:
  My Saviour, comfort me.

7 Not unduly let me grieve,
Meekly the kind stripes receive,
Let me humbly still believe:
  My Saviour, comfort me.

8 So, it shall be good for me
Much afflicted now to be,
If Thou wilt but tenderly,
  My Saviour, comfort me. Amen.
         George Rawson. 1857.

947   8.8. 8.8. *Anapæstic.*
*Behold, He that keepeth
Israel shall neither slumber nor sleep.*
Psalm cxxi. 4.

INSPIRER and Hearer of prayer,
  Thou Shepherd and Guardian of Thine,
My all to Thy covenant care
  I, sleeping and waking, resign.

2 If Thou art my shield and my sun,
  The night is no darkness to me,
And, fast as my moments roll on,
  They bring me but nearer to Thee.

3 Thy ministering spirits descend,
  To watch while Thy saints are asleep;
By day and by night they attend,
  The heirs of salvation to keep.

4 Their service no interval knows,
  Their fervour is still on the wing;
And, while they protect my repose,
  They chant to the praise of my King.

5 I too, at the season ordained
  Their chorus for ever shall join;
And love, and adore without end,
  Their faithful Creator and mine.
         Augustus M. Toplady. 1770.

948   C.M.
*When thou prayest, enter
into thy inner chamber.*—Matt. vi. 6.

FATHER of Jesus Christ, my Lord,
  I humbly seek Thy face,
Encouraged by the Saviour's word
  To ask Thy pardoning grace.

2 Entering into my closet, I
  The busy world exclude,
In secret prayer for mercy cry,
  And groan to be renewed.

3 Far from the paths of men, to Thee
  I solemnly retire;
See, Thou who dost in secret see,
  And grant my heart's desire.

PRIVATE DEVOTION.

4 Thy grace I languish to receive,
The Spirit of love and power,
Blameless before Thy face to live,
To live and sin no more.

5 Fain would I all Thy goodness feel,
And know my sins forgiven,
And do on earth Thy perfect will,
As angels do in heaven.

6 O Father, glorify Thy Son,
And grant what I require;
For Jesu's sake the gift send down,
And answer me by fire.

7 Kindle the flame of love within,
Which may to heaven ascend,
And now the work of grace begin,
Which shall in glory end. Amen.
Wesley. 1747.

949 S.M.
I give myself unto prayer.
Psalm cix. 4.

I GIVE myself to prayer;
Lord, give Thyself to me,
And let the time of my request
Thy time of answer be.

2 My thoughts are like the reeds,
And tremble as they grow,
In the sad current of a life
That darkly runs and slow.

3 I am as if asleep,
Yet conscious that I dream;
Like one who vainly strives to wake
And free himself, I seem.

4 The loud distressful cry
With which I call on Thee,
Shall wake me, Lord, to find that Thou
Canst give me liberty.

5 I give myself to prayer;
Lord, give Thyself to me;
And in the time of my distress,
O haste and succour me!

6 Then be my heart, my world,
Rehallowed unto Thee,
And Thy pervading glory, Lord,
O let me feel and see! Amen.
T. T. Lynch. 1855.

950 8.8. 8.8. 8.8.
My soul waiteth for the Lord
more than they that watch for the morning.
Psalm cxxx. 6.

FATHER, to Thee I lift mine eyes,
My longing eyes, and restless heart;
Before the morning watch I rise,
And wait to taste how good Thou art,
To obtain the grace I humbly claim,
The saving power of Jesu's name.

2 This slumber from my soul, O shake!
Warned by Thy Spirit's inward call;
Let me to righteousness awake,
And pray that I no more may fall,
Or give to sin or Satan place,
But walk in all Thy righteous ways.

3 O wouldst Thou, Lord, Thy servant guard
'Gainst every known or secret foe;
A mind for all assaults prepared,
A sober, vigilant mind bestow,
Ever apprised of danger nigh,
And when to fight, and when to fly.

4 O never suffer me to sleep
Secure within the verge of hell!
But still my watchful spirit keep
In lowly awe and loving zeal;
And bless me with a godly fear,
And plant that guardian-angel here.

5 Attended by the sacred dread,
And wise from evil to depart,
Let me from strength to strength proceed,
And rise to purity of heart;
Through all the paths of duty move,
From humble faith to perfect love. Amen.
Charles Wesley. 1749.

951 7.6. 7.6. D.
Hear my prayer, O Lord;
give ear to my supplications.—Ps. cxliii. 1.

I'M kneeling at the threshold,
Aweary, faint, and sore;
I'm waiting for the dawning,
The opening of the door;
I'm waiting till the Master
Shall bid me rise and come
To the glory of His presence,
The gladness of His home.

2 A weary path I've travelled,
'Mid darkness, storm, and strife,
And bearing many a burden,
Contending for my life;
But now the morn is breaking,
My toil will soon be o'er,
I'm kneeling at the threshold,
My hand is on the door.

3 Methinks I hear the voices
Of the blessed as they stand,
Sweet singing in the sunshine
Of that unclouded land;
O would that I were with them,
Amid the shining throng,
Uniting in their worship,
Rejoicing in their song!

4 The friends that started with me
Have entered long ago;
Ah! one by one they left me,
To struggle with the foe;
Their pilgrimage was shorter,
Their triumph sooner won;
How lovingly they'll hail me,
When once my work is done!

5 With them the blessed angels,
That know nor grief nor sin,
I see them at the portals,
Prepared to let me in;
O Lord, I wait Thy pleasure,
Thy time and way are best;
I'm wasted, worn, and weary,
My Father, bid me rest. Amen.
W. L. Alexander. d. 1884.

PRIVATE DEVOTION.

952 C.M.D.
As ye are partakers of the sufferings, so shall ye be also of the consolation.—2 Corinthians i 7.

I HOPED that with the brave and strong,
 My portioned task might lie ;
To toil amid the busy throng,
 With purpose pure and high ;
But God has fixed another part,
 And He has fixed it well ;
I said so with my breaking heart,
 When first this trouble fell.

These weary hours will not be lost,
 These days of misery,
These nights of darkness, anguish-tossed,
 Can I but turn to Thee :
With secret labour to sustain
 In patience every blow,
To gather fortitude from pain,
 And holiness from woe.

3 If Thou shouldst bring me back to life,
 More humble I should be,
More wise, more strengthened for the strife,
 More apt to lean on Thee :
Should death be standing at the gate,
 Thus should I keep my vow ;
But, Lord ! whatever be my fate,
 O let me serve Thee now ! Amen.
    Anne Bronte. 1847.

953 C.M.
When I remember these things, I pour out my soul in me.
Psalm xlii. 4.

THOUSANDS, O Lord of hosts ! this day
 Around Thine altar meet ;
And tens of thousands throng to pay
 Their homage at Thy feet.

2 They see Thy power and glory there,
 As I have seen them too ;
They read, they hear, they join in prayer,
 As I was wont to do.

3 They sing Thy deeds, as I have sung,
 In sweet and solemn lays ;
Were I among them, my glad tongue
 Might learn new themes of praise.

4 For Thou art in their midst to teach,
 When on Thy name they call ;
And Thou hast blessings, Lord, for each,
 Hast blessings, Lord, for all.

5 I, of such fellowship bereft,
 In spirit turn to Thee ;
O hast Thou not a blessing left,
 A blessing, Lord, for me ?

6 The dew lies thick on all the ground ;
 Shall my poor fleece be dry ?
The manna rains from heaven around ;
 Shall I of hunger die ?

7 Behold Thy prisoner ; loose my bands,
 If 'tis Thy gracious will ;
If not, contented in Thy hands,
 Behold Thy prisoner still.

8 I may not to Thy courts repair ;
 Yet here Thou surely art ;
Lord ! consecrate a house of prayer
 In my surrendered heart.

9 To faith reveal the things unseen ;
 To hope, the joys untold ;
Let love, without a veil between,
 The glory now behold.

10 O make Thy face on me to shine,
 That doubt and fear may cease !
Lift up Thy countenance benign
 On me,—and give me peace. Amen.
    James Montgomery. 1832.

954 6.6.9. 6.6.9.
O, how great is Thy goodness.
Psalm xxxi. 19.

AWAY with our fears !
 The glad morning appears,
When an heir of salvation was born !
 From Jehovah I came,
 For His glory I am,
And to Him I with singing return.

2 Thee, Jesus, alone,
 The Fountain I own,
Of my life and felicity here ;
 And cheerfully sing
 My Redeemer and King,
Till His sign in the heavens appear.

3 With thanks I rejoice
 In Thy fatherly choice
Of my state and condition below ;
 If of parents I came
 Who honoured Thy name,
'Twas Thy wisdom appointed it so.

4 I sing of Thy grace,
 From my earliest days,
Ever near to allure and defend ;
 Hitherto Thou hast been
 My Preserver from sin,
And I trust Thou wilt save to the end.

5 O the infinite cares,
 And temptations, and snares,
Thy hand hath conducted me through ;
 O the blessings bestowed
 By a bountiful God,
And the mercies eternally new !

6 What a mercy is this,
 What a heaven of bliss,
How unspeakably happy am I !
 Gathered into the fold,
 With Thy people enrolled,
With Thy people to live and to die !

TEMPERANCE SERVICES.

7 O the goodness of God,
　　Employing a clod
His tribute of glory to raise!
　　His standard to bear,
　　And with triumph declare
His unspeakable riches of grace!

8 O the fathomless love,
　　That has deigned to approve
And prosper the work of my hands;
　　With my pastoral crook
　　I went over the brook,
And, behold, I am spread into bands!

9 Who, I ask in amaze,
　　Hath begotten me these?
And inquire from what quarter they
　　　came?
　　My full heart it replies,
　　They are born from the skies,
And gives glory to God and the Lamb.

10 All honour and praise
　　To the Father of grace,
To the Spirit, and Son, I return!
　　The business pursue,
　　He hath made me to do,
And rejoice that I ever was born.

11 In a rapture of joy
　　My life I employ,
The God of my life to proclaim;
　　'Tis worth living for this,
　　To administer bliss
And salvation in Jesus's name.

12 My remnant of days
　　I spend in His praise,
Who died the whole world to redeem:
　　Be they many or few,
　　My days are His due,
And they all are devoted to Him.

　　　　　　Charles Wesley. 1749.

Temperance Services.

955　　　*Lord, what wilt Thou have*　　L.M.
　　　　　me to do?—Acts ix. 6.

HERE, Lord, assembled in Thy name,
Thy work to do, Thy help we claim,
And pray for grace that we may be
Inspired by purest love to Thee.

2 Not might, nor power, Thyself hast said,
Can vice destroy, or virtue spread;
Thy Spirit, Lord, this work must do,
Who only can our hearts renew.

3 Come then, to us reveal Thy love,
And pour the Spirit from above,
That we, with holy motives, may
The impulse of His will obey.

4 O! touch our lips that we may speak
To guard the tempted, help the weak,
And guide the wandering to retrace
Their steps, and seek a Father's face.

5 **With Christ-like** sympathy may we
The sorrows of our brethren see,
Who, captive led by love of drink,
Beneath a load of evil sink.

6 With ready hands **and** willing feet,
By methods wise **and** actions meet,
Guided by Thee, **O may we run**
To seek and **save the erring one:**

7 And while sobriety we teach,
Let us the heart and conscience reach,
And by a power through Christ bestowed
Make sober men Thy sons, O God.
　　　　　　　　　　　　Amen.

　　　　　Edward Boaden. 1889.

956　　　*I must work the works of*　　6.5. **6.5.**
　　　　　Him that sent Me, while it is day.
　　　　　　John ix. 4.

CHRISTIAN, work for Jesus,
　Who on earth for thee
Laboured, wearied, suffered,
　Died upon the **tree.**

2 Work with eye that rangeth
　Over sin's great deep;
Where lie thousands drifting,
　Rocked to fatal sleep.

3 Work with hands that Jesus
　Maketh strong to bring
Souls to Him, their Saviour,
　Trustfully to cling.

4 Work with feet untiring,
　By the Master led,
Help to free the drunkards
　From their bondage dread.

5 Work with lips so fervid
　That thy words may prove
Thou hast brought a message
　From the God of love.

6 Work with heart that **burneth**
　Humbly at His feet;
Priceless gems to offer,
　For His crown made meet.

7 Work with prayer unceasing,
　Borne on faith's strong wing,
Earnestly beseeching
　Trophies for the King.

TEMPERANCE SERVICES.

8 Work while strength endureth,
Until death draw near;
Then thy Lord's sweet welcome
Thou in heaven shalt hear.
M. Haslock. 1881.

957 8.8.6. 8.8.6.
When He had fasted forty days and forty nights, He was afterward an hungred.—Matthew iv. 2.

O THOU who on the mountain heights,
For forty days and forty nights,
Didst keep a solemn fast :
Grant us such abstinence to know,
That we may daily fitter grow
For Thy blest courts at last.

2 Strong drink makes many to offend,
We therefore on Thine arm depend
To help us to abstain ;
Confirm our good resolves, we pray,
That we may boldly, day by day,
From its dread power refrain.

3 Vouchsafe to us Thy strengthening grace ;
Help us, dear Lord, in every place
To put our trust in Thee ;
So shall we confidently stand,
Assured that Thy protecting hand
Will make the tempter flee.

4 We sing with all the ransomed host,
'To Father, Son, and Holy Ghost
Be glory evermore ;'
Our thankful hearts shall daily raise
A joyful strain of grateful praise,
Unceasingly adore. Amen.
Frederick Sherlock. 1879.

958 S. M.
Wine is a mocker.
Prov. xx. 1.

BEHOLD, O Lord our God,
A foe within Thy gates
Thy goodly heritage despoils,
Thy Zion desolates.

2 This raging, guileful foe
Assumes a friend's disguise,
Ensnares Thy watchmen, and deceives
The simple and the wise.

3 Through wine and through strong drink
Prophet and priest have erred :
Guides, counsellors have gone astray,
And preachers of Thy word.

4 The young, Thy Church's hope,
So greatly loved by Thee,
Are by his wiles betrayed, and led
Into captivity.

5 Arouse Thy Church, O God,
This mocker to assail,
To drive him forth beyond her walls,
And o'er his rage prevail.

6 Come forth Thyself, appear
Thy servants' zeal to own ;
And let the foe be everywhere
And utterly o erthrown. Amen.
Edward Ibsden. 1867.

959 6.5. 10. D. *With Chorus.*
Others save with fear, pulling them out of the fire.—Jude 23.

RESCUE the perishing,
Care for the dying,
Snatch them in pity from sin and the grave,
Weep o'er the erring one,
Lift up the fallen,
Tell them of Jesus, the mighty to save.
  Rescue the perishing,
  Care for the dying ;
  Jesus is merciful, Jesus will save.

2 Though they are slighting Him,
Still He is waiting,
Waiting the penitent child to receive,
Plead with them earnestly,
Plead with them gently ·
He will forgive if they only believe.

3 Down in the human heart,
Crushed by the tempter,
Feelings lie buried that grace can restore ;
Touched by a loving heart,
Wakened by kindness,
Chords that were broken will vibrate once more.

4 Rescue the perishing ;
Duty demands it,
Strength for thy labour the Lord will provide ;
Back to the narrow way,
Patiently win them,
Tell the poor wanderer a Saviour has died.
Frances Jane Crosby. b. 1823.

960 8.8. 8.8. 8.8.
Bear ye one another's burdens, and so fulfil the law of Christ.
Galatians vi. 2.

O THOU whose chosen place of birth
Was 'mid the humblest scenes of earth,
Who didst all scorn and pain endure,
To save the lost and bless the poor ;
Our duty in Thy life we see,
And pray for grace to follow Thee.

2 Thou who hast taught us by Thy word,
The servant's not above his lord,
Give us the courage which we need
To follow Thee in word and deed ;
The highest honour that we crave
Be this, the lost to seek and save.

3 Where'er the wine-cup's deadly blight
Has shrouded hearts in sorrow's night,
Our eyes to all its evils ope,
Inspire our souls with faith and hope,
And may our charity extend
As Thine, alike to foe and friend.

4 Where'er a tempted brother falls,
Make quick our ear to hear his calls,
Make swift our feet to reach the spot,
Make true our hearts to leave him not,
Make strong and willing every hand,
To lift him up and help him stand.
W. S. Peterson.

National Hymns.

961 6.6.4. 6.6.6.4.
Righteousness exalteth a nation.—Proverbs xiv. 34.

GOD bless our native land!
May heaven's protecting hand
  Still guard our shore;
May peace her power extend,
Foe be transformed to friend,
And Britain's power depend
  On war no more.

2 O Lord, our monarch bless
With strength and righteousness
  Long may she reign!
Her heart inspire and move
With wisdom from above;
And in a nation's love
  Her throne maintain.

3 May just and righteous laws
Uphold the public cause,
  And bless our isle!
Home of the brave and free,
The land of liberty!
We pray that still on thee
  Kind heaven may smile.

4 And not this land alone,
But be Thy mercies known
  From shore to shore.
Lord, make the nations see
That men should brothers be,
And form one family,
  The wide world o'er! Amen.
          W. E. Hickson. 1855.

962 8.8.6. 8.8.6.
When He giveth quietness, who then can make trouble?—Job xxxiv. 29.

A NATION God delights to bless,
  Can all our raging foes distress,
    Or hurt whom they surround?
Hid from the general scourge we are,
Nor see the bloody waste of war,
    Nor hear the trumpet's sound.

2 O might we, Lord! the grace improve,
By labouring for the rest of love,
    The soul-composing power!
Bless us with that internal peace,
And all the fruits of righteousness,
    Till time shall be no more. Amen.
          Charles Wesley. 1762.

963 C.M.
Our fathers have told us, what work Thou didst in their days.
Psalm xliv. 1.

GREAT God of hosts, our ears have heard,
  Our fathers oft have told,
What wonders Thou hast done for them,
  Thy glorious deeds of old.

2 Not by their might was safety wrought,
  Nor victory by their sword;
But Thou didst guard the chosen race
  Who Thy great Name adored.

3 Great God of hosts! their God and ours;
  Our only Lord and King;
Let that right arm which fought for them
  To us salvation bring.

4 To Thee the glory we'll ascribe,
  By whom the conquest came,
And, in triumphant songs of praise,
  Will celebrate Thy Name. Amen.
          Edward Osler. 1836.

964 C.M.
Blessed be the Lord, that hath given rest unto His people.
1 Kings viii. 56.

LORD, while for all mankind we pray,
  Of every clime and coast,
O hear us for our native land,
  The land we love the most.

2 Our fathers' sepulchres are here
  And here our kindred dwell;
Our children, too; how should we love
  Another land so well?

3 O guard our shores from every foe,
  With peace our borders bless;
With prosperous times our cities crown,
  Our fields with plenteousness.

4 Unite us in the sacred love
  Of knowledge, truth, and Thee;
And let our hills and valleys shout
  The songs of liberty.

5 Here may religion, pure and mild,
  Upon our Sabbaths smile;
And piety and virtue reign,
  And bless our native isle.

6 Lord of the nations, thus to Thee
  Our country we commend;
Be Thou her Refuge and her Trust,
  Her everlasting Friend. Amen.
          J. R. Wreford. 1837.

965 8.6. 8.6. 8.8.
The Prince of Peace.
Isaiah ix. 6.

THROUGH centuries of sin and woe
  Hath streamed the crimson flood,
While man, in concert with the foe,
  Hath shed his brother's blood:
Now lift Thy banner, Prince of Peace,
And let the cruel war-cry cease.

2 In vain, 'mid clamours loud and rude,
  Thy servants seek repose,
See, day by day, the strife renewed,
  And brethren turned to foes;
Then lift Thy banner, Prince of Peace,
Make wrongs among Thy subjects cease.

265

NATIONAL HYMNS.

3 Still to the heavens the weak will pour
  Their loud unanswered cry ;
Still wealth doth heap its secret store,
  And want forgotten lie :
Lift high Thy banner, Prince of Peace,
Let hatred die, and love increase.

4 Thy gospel, Lord, is grace and love ;
  O send it all abroad,
Till every heart submissive prove,
  And bless the reigning God :
Come lift Thy banner, Prince of Peace,
And give the weary world release.
                              Amen.
        John H. Gurney.   1838.

966   8.7.8.7.8.8.7.
    Our fathers trusted in Thee.
        Psalm xxii. 4.

WE come unto our fathers' God ;
   Their Rock is our Salvation ;
The Eternal Arms, their dear abode,
   We make our habitation :
We bring Thee, Lord, the praise they
   brought ;
We seek Thee as Thy saints have sought
   In every generation

2 Unto Thy people we belong,
   Elect, redeemed, renewed ;
We join the blessed pilgrim throng
   With Thine own strength endued :
Our hands their task divine essay ;
Our feet pursue the heavenly way
   Their steadfast feet pursued.

3 The Fire Divine, their steps that led,
   Still goeth bright before us ;
The Heavenly Shield, around them spread,
   Is still high holden o'er us :
The grace those sinners that subdued,
The strength those weaklings that renewed,
   Doth vanquish, doth restore us.

4 The cleaving sins that brought them low
   Are still our souls oppressing ;
The tears that from their eyes did flow
   Fall fast, our shame confessing ;
As with Thee, Lord, prevailed their cry,
So our strong prayer ascends on high,
   And bringeth down Thy blessing.

5 Their precious things on us bestowed
   The same dear Lord discover ;
The joy wherewith their souls o'erflowed
   Makes our glad hearts run over ;
Their fire of love in us doth burn ;
As yearned their hearts, our hearts do
   yearn
   After the Heavenly Lover.

6 Their joy unto their Lord we bring ;
   Their song to us descendeth :
The Spirit who in them did sing
   To us His music lendeth ;
His song in them, in us, is one ;
We raise it high, we send it on,
   The song that never endeth.

7 Ye saints to come, take up the strain,
   The same sweet theme endeavour !
Unbroken be the golden chain ;
   Keep on the song for ever :

Safe in the same dear dwelling-place,
Rich with the same eternal grace,
   Bless the same boundless Giver.
        Thomas H. Gill.   1869.

967   7.6.7.6. D.   Special.
   *And pray unto the Lord for
   it : for in the peace thereof shall ye have
   peace.*—Jeremiah xxix. 7.

NOW pray we for our country,
   That England long may be
The holy and the happy,
   And the gloriously free.
Who blesseth her is blessed !
   So peace be in her walls ;
And joy in all her palaces,
   Her cottages and halls.
        Bishop A. C. Coxe.   1848.

968   C.M.D.
   *O Lord, correct me, but
   with judgment.*—Jeremiah x. 24.

GREAT King of nations, hear our prayer,
   While at Thy feet we fall,
And humbly, with united cry,
   To Thee for mercy call.
The guilt is ours, but grace is Thine ;
   O, turn us not away,
But hear us from Thy lofty throne,
   And help us when we pray.

2 Our fathers' sins were manifold,
   And ours no less, we own ;
Yet wondrously from age to age
   Thy goodness hath been shown :
When dangers, like a stormy sea,
Beset our country round,
   To Thee we looked, to Thee we cried,
   And help in Thee was found.

3 With one consent we meekly bow
   Beneath Thy chastening hand,
And, pouring forth confession meet,
   Mourn with our mourning land :
With pitying eye behold our need,
   As thus we lift our prayer,
' Correct us with Thy judgments, Lord ;
   Then let Thy mercy spare.'   Amen.
        John H. Gurney.   1838.

969   6.6.4.6.6.6.4.
   *And all the people shouted,
   and said, God save the king.*—1 Sam. x. 24.

GOD save our gracious Queen,
   Long live our noble Queen,
   God save the Queen.
Send her victorious,
Happy and glorious,
Long to reign over us,
   God save the Queen.

2 Thy choicest gifts in store,
   On her be pleased to pour,
   Long may she reign.
May she defend our laws,
And ever give us cause
To sing with heart and voice,
   God save the Queen.
        Henry Carey.   d. 1743.

Dismissal Hymns and Doxologies.

970 *Ye are all one in Christ Jesus.*
Galatians iii. 28.   C.M.

BLEST be the dear uniting love,
That will not let us part:
Our bodies may far off remove,
We still are one in heart.

2 Joined in one spirit to our Head,
Where He appoints we go;
And still in Jesu's footsteps tread,
And show His praise below.

3 O may we ever walk in Him,
And nothing know beside;
Nothing desire, nothing esteem,
But Jesus Crucified.

4 Closer and closer let us cleave
To His beloved embrace;
Expect His fulness to receive,
And grace to answer grace.

5 Partakers of the Saviour's grace,
The same in mind and heart,
Nor joy, nor grief, nor time, nor place,
Nor life, nor death can part.

6 But let us hasten to the day
Which shall our flesh restore,
When death shall all be done away,
And bodies part no more.
Wesley. 1742.

971 *The things which are not seen are eternal.*—2 Corinthians iv. 18.   6.6. 6.6. 8.8.

JESUS, accept the praise
That to Thy name belongs;
Matter of all our lays,
Subject of all our songs;
Through Thee we now together came,
And part exulting in Thy name.

2 In flesh we part awhile,
But still in spirit joined,
To embrace the happy toil
Thou hast to each assigned;
And while we do Thy blessed will,
We bear our heaven about us still.

3 O let us thus go on
In all Thy pleasant ways,
And, armed with patience, run
With joy the appointed race;
Keep us, and every seeking soul,
Till all attain the heavenly goal.

4 There we shall meet again,
When all our toils are o'er,
And death, and grief, and pain,
And parting are no more;
We shall with all our brethren rise,
And soar with them above the skies.

5 Then let us wait the sound
That shall our souls release;
And labour to be found
Of Him in spotless peace,
In perfect holiness renewed,
Adorned with Christ, and meet for God.
Wesley. 1747.

972 *Your life is hid with Christ in God.*—Colossians iii. 3.   C.M.

GOD of all consolation! take
The glory of Thy grace:
Thy gifts to Thee we render back
In ceaseless songs of praise.

2 Through Thee we now together came
In singleness of heart;
We met, O Jesus, in Thy name,
And in Thy name we part.

3 We part in body, not in mind;
Our minds continue one;
And, each to each in Jesus joined,
We hand in hand go on.

4 Our life is hid with Christ in God;
Our life shall soon appear,
And shed His glory all abroad
In all His members here.

5 Our souls are in His mighty hand,
And He shall keep them still;
And you and I shall surely stand
With Him on Sion's hill.

6 Him eye to eye we there shall see,
Our face like His shall shine;
O what a glorious company,
When saints and angels join!

7 O what a joyful meeting there!
In robes of white arrayed;
Palms in our hands we all shall bear
And crowns upon our head.

8 Then let us lawfully contend,
And fight our passage through;
Bear in our faithful minds the end,
And keep the prize in view.
Wesley. 1747.

973 *Stand fast in one spirit.*
Philippians i. 27.   6.6. 6.6. 8.8.

LORD, we Thy will obey,
And in Thy pleasure rest;
We, only we, can say,
'Whatever is, is best;'
Joyful to meet, willing to part,
Convinced we still are one in heart.

2 Hereby we sweetly know
Our love proceeds from Thee,
We let each other go,
From every creature free,
And cry, in answer to Thy call,
'Thou art, O Christ, our All in all.'

267

DISMISSAL HYMNS AND DOXOLOGIES.

3 Our Saviour, Brother, Friend,
   Our Counsellor Divine !
    Thy chosen ones depend
     On no support but Thine ;
   Our everlasting Comforter !
   We cannot want, if Thou art here.

4 Still let us, gracious Lord,
    Sit loose to all below ;
   And to Thy love restored,
    No other portion know ;
   Stand fast in glorious liberty,
   And live and die wrapt up in Thee.
                    Amen.
                 Wesley. 1749.

Departure of Friends.

974   6.6.8.4.
*Being recommended by
the brethren unto the grace of God.*
Acts xv. 40.

WITH the sweet word of peace
   We bid our brethren go ;
Peace, as a river, to increase
   And ceaseless flow.

2 With the calm word of prayer
   We earnestly commend
Our brethren to Thy watchful care,
   Eternal Friend !

3 With the dear word of love
   We give our brief farewell ;
Our love below, and Thine above,
   With them shall dwell.

4 With the strong word of faith
   We stay ourselves on Thee ;
That Thou, O Lord, in life and death
   Their help shall be.

5 Then the bright word of hope
   Shall on our parting gleam,
And tell of joys beyond the scope
   Of earth-born dream.

6 Farewell ! in hope, and love,
   In faith, and peace, and prayer ;
Till He whose home is ours above
   Unite us there.
            George Watson. b. 1816.

975   8.7.8.7.4.7.
*He lifted up His hands,
and blessed them.*—Luke xxiv. 50.

LORD ! dismiss us with Thy blessing,
   Fill our hearts with joy and peace ;
Let us all, Thy love possessing,
   Triumph in redeeming grace ;
    O refresh us
Travelling through this wilderness.

2 Thanks we give, and adoration,
   For Thy gospel's joyful sound ;
Let the fruits of Thy salvation
   In our hearts and lives abound ;
    Ever faithful
To the truth may we be found.

3 So whene'er the signal's given,
   Us from earth to call away,
Borne on angels' wings to heaven,
   Glad the summons to obey,
    May we ever
Reign with Christ in endless day.
                    Amen.
  Anon. Shawbury Collection. 1773.

976   8.7.8.7.
Thou art worthy, O Lord.
Revelation iv. 11.

WORSHIP, honour, glory, blessing,
   Lord, we offer unto Thee ;
Young and old, Thy praise confessing,
   In glad homage bend the knee.

2 As the saints in heaven adore Thee,
   We would bow before Thy throne ;
As Thine angels serve before Thee,
   So on earth Thy will be done. Amen.
             Edward Osler. 1836.

977   7.7.7.7.
*Jesus . . . stood in the midst,
and saith . . . Peace be unto you.*
John xx. 19.

PART in peace ! Christ's life was peace,
   Let us live our life in Him ;
Part in peace ! Christ's death was peace ;
   Let us die our death in Him.

2 Part in peace ! Christ promise gave
   Of a life beyond the grave,
Where all mortal partings cease ;
   Holy brethren, part in peace !
        Mrs. Sarah F. Adams. 1841.

978   8.7.8.7.
*The grace of the Lord
Jesus Christ . . . be with you all.*
2 Corinthians xiii. 14.

MAY the grace of Christ our Saviour,
   And the Father's boundless love,
With the Holy Spirit's favour,
   Rest upon us from above !

2 Thus may we abide in union
   With each other in the Lord ;
And possess, in sweet communion,
   Joys which earth can ne'er afford.
                    Amen.
            John Newton. 1779.

979   L. M.

BE present at our table, Lord ;
   Be here and everywhere adored ;
Thy creatures bless, and grant that we
May feast in Paradise with Thee.
            John Cennick. 1741.

980   L. M.

WE thank Thee, Lord, for this our food,
   But more because of Jesu's blood ;
Let manna to our souls be given,
The bread of Life sent down from heaven.
            John Cennick. 1741.

PSALMS AND CANTICLES.

EXPLANATORY NOTE.

THERE is no portion of the Old Testament Scriptures so helpful to the strengthening of the spiritual life as the Book of Psalms. Many of these inspired songs were expressly written for use in public worship. There is little doubt that some of them were sung by Christ Himself, and by His apostles. Through succeeding ages the psalms have also been sung by devout Christians of every land; and it is a matter for thankfulness that, during the last few years, their use has become general in public worship.

As the psalms were not written in regular metres, they require to be pointed for chanting. Good chanting is little more than good reading with a musical tone; and after some practice, congregations will find no greater difficulty in chanting a psalm than in singing a metrical hymn. In reading the psalms, even well-educated persons do not always emphasize the same words, or group together the same parts of a sentence; so, in chanting, there are scarcely two collections of 'Psalms and Canticles' which are pointed exactly alike. For this reason, the Hymn-book Committee deemed it best that the psalms they had selected should be pointed by persons of the highest authority. Arrangements were therefore made with the eminent firm of Novello, Ewer, & Co., by which the Committee received permission to use the pointing adopted in 'The Bible Psalter.' The psalms, in this copyright work, were pointed for chanting by the Rev. J. Troutbeck, D.D., Minor Canon of Westminster, on the same principle as that adopted in 'The Cathedral Psalter, which was prepared by S. Flood Jones, M.A., Precentor of Westminster; James Turle, late Organist of Westminster; J. Stainer, Mus. Doc., Organist of St. Paul's; Joseph Barnby, Precentor of Eton; and Dr. Troutbeck. Higher authority than this there is none. In the musical edition of the 'Psalms and Canticles' the Preface to 'The Bible Psalter'—which contains various important directions in relation to chanting—will be published. The following explanation of the principal marks employed is all that at present need be given:

1. The words, from the commencement of each verse and half-verse up to the accented syllable, are called the Recitation. On reaching the accented syllable, and beginning with it, the *music* of the chant commences.

2. An asterisk (*) is a direction to take breath. Other stops, such as comma and semi-colon (, ;), must be attended to as in good reading.

3. [2 *pt*] directs the choir to repeat the second half of a double chant at the verse to which it is prefixed.

4. Sometimes the first bar contains an accented asterisk (*), with a word unaccented following it. In this case the first bar must be regarded as beginning with a minim rest, *e.g.*—

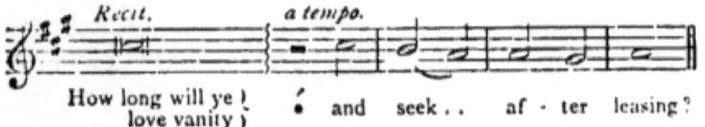

How long will ye love vanity   *   and   seek ..   af - ter   leasing?

It will be found to be a sufficient observance of the minim rest, in practice, to take breath at the asterisk which follows the Recitation, and to pronounce the next word quickly, without dwelling on it.

☞ *At the end of each Psalm may be sung:*

Glory be to the Fáther, | and · to the | Son : ǎnd | to the | Holy | Ghost :
As it was in the beginning * is nów, and | ever | shall be : wórld without | end. |
A · | -men.

PSALMS.

[By permission of NOVELLO, EWER, & CO., *the Pointing in this Collection is the same as in 'The Bible Psalter.'*]

981   PSALM I.

BLESSED is the man that walketh not in the counsel of the ungodly ∗ nor stand- eth in the | way of | sinners : nor sitteth in the | seat | of the | scornful.
2 But his delight is in the law | of the | **Lord** ; and in His law doth he | **medi** - tate | day and | night.
3 And he shall be like a **tree** planted by the rivers of water ∗ that bringeth forth his fruit | in his | season : his leaf also shall not wither ∗ and whatsoever he | doeth | shall | **prosper**.
4 The ungodly | are not | so : but are like the chaff which the | wind | dri - veth a- | -way.
5 Therefore the ungodly shall not stand | in the | judgment ; nor sinners in the congre- | -gation | of the | righteous.
6 For the Lord knoweth the way | of the | righteous : but the way of the un- godly | shall | perish.

982   PSALM VIII.

O LORD our **Lord** ∗ how excellent is Thy name in | all the | earth : who hast set Thy | glo - **ry a-** | -bove the | heavens
2 Out of the **mouths** of babes and sucklings hast Thou ordained strength ∗ because of Thine | enemies : that Thou mightest still the | ene - my | and - the a- | -venger.
3 When I consider Thy **heavens** ∗ the work of Thy | fingers : the moon and the stars | which Thou | hast or- | -dained ;
4 What is man, that **Thou** art | mindful of | him : and the **son** of **man** | that Thou | visit - est | him ?
5 For Thou hast made him a little lower | than the | angels : and hast crowned | him with | glory - **and** | honour.
6 Thou madest him to **have** dominion over the works | of Thy | hands : Thou hast put | all things | under ∗ his | feet ;
7 All | sheep and | oxen : yea and the | beasts | of the | field ;
8 The fowl of the air, and the fish | of the | sea : and whatsoever passeth through the | paths | of the | seas.
9 [2 pt.] O Lord | our | Lord : how excellent is Thy | name in | all the | earth !

983   PSALM XVI.

PRESERVE | me O | God : for in Thee | do I | put my | trust.
2 I have said unto the **Lord** ∗ Thou art my | **Lord** ; I have no | good be- | -yond | Thee.
3 As for the saints that are in the | earth : they are the excellent ∗ in whom is | all | my de- | -light.
4 Their sorrows shall be multiplied ∗ that hasten after an- | -other | god : their drink offerings of blood will | not offer ∗ nor take up their | names | into - my | lips.
5 The Lord is the portion of mine inherit- ance ∗ and | of my | cup : Thou main- | -tainest | my | lot.
6 The lines are fallen unto me in | pleasant | places : yea I | have a | goodly | heri- tage.
7 I will bless the Lord who hath | given | me | counsel : my reins also instruct me | in the | night | seasons.
8 I have set the Lord | always be- | -fore me : because He is at my right hand I | shall | not be | moved.
9 Therefore my heart is glad ∗ and my | glory - re- | -joiceth : my flesh | also | shall | rest in | hope.
10 For Thou wilt not leave my | soul in | hell : neither wilt Thou suffer Thine Holy | One to | see cor- | -ruption.
11 [2 pt.] Thou wilt shew me the | path of | life : in Thy presence is fulness of joy ∗ at Thy right hand there are | pleasures - for | ever - | -more.

984   PSALM XIX.

THE heavens declare the | glory - of | God : and the firmament | sheweth - His | handy- | -work.
2 Day unto day | utter - eth | speech : and night unto | night | sheweth | know- ledge.
3 There is no | speech nor | language : where their | voice | is not | heard.
4 Their line is gone out through all the earth ∗ and their words to the end | of the | world : in them hath He set a | taber - nacle | for the | sun

PSALMS.

5 Which is as a bridegroom cóming | out of · his | chamber : and rejoiceth as a stróng | man to | run a | race.
6 His going forth is from the end of the heaven * and his circuit unto the | ends of | it : and there is nothing hid | from the | heat there- | -of.
7 The law of the Lord is perfect * con- | verting - the | soul : the testimony of the Lord is súre * | making | wise the | simple.
8 The statutes of the Lord are right * re- | joicing - the | heart : the commandment of the Lórd is | pure, en- | -lightening · the | eyes.
9 The fear of the Lord is clean * en- | during - for | ever : the judgments of the Lord are true * and | righteous | alto- | -gether.
10 More to be desired are they than gold * yéa than | much fine | gold : sweeter also than hóney | and the | honey- | comb.
11 Moreover by thém is Thy | servant | warned : and in keeping of thém | there is | great re- | -ward.
12 Who can únder- | -stand his | errors : cleánse Thou | me from | secret | faults.
13 Keep back Thy servant also from pre- sumptuous sins * let them not have dominion | over | me : then shall | be úpright * and I shall be innocent | from the | great trans- | -gression.
14 Let the words of my mouth, and the meditation of my heart * be accept- able | in Thy | sight : O Lórd my | strength and | my re- | -deemer.

985 PSALM XXIII.

THE Lórd | is my | shepherd : I | shall | not | want.
2 He maketh me to lie dówn in | green | pastures : He leadeth mé be- | -side the | still | waters.
3 Hé re- | -storeth my | soul : He leadeth me in the paths of righteousness * | for His | name's | sake.
4 Yea, though I walk through the valley of the shadow of death * I | will | fear no | evil : for Thou art with me * Thy ród and Thy | staff, they | comfort | me.
5 Thou preparest a table before me * in the présence | of mine | enemies : Thou anointest my head with oil * my | cup | runneth | over.
6 Surely goodness and mercy shall follow me * all the dáys | of my | life : and I will dwéll in the | house - of the | Lord for | ever.

986 PSALM XXIV.

THE earth is the Lórd's and the | fulness | there- | -of : the world, and | they that | dwell there- | -in.
2 For He hath founded it up- | -on the | seas : and established | it up- | -on the | floods.

3 Who shall ascend into the híll | of the | Lord : or who shall stánd | in His | holy | place?
4 He that hath clean hánds and a | pure | heart : who hath not lifted up his soul unto vanity * nor | sworn | —de- | -ceit- fully.
5 He shall receive the blessing from the | Lord : and righteousness from the | God of | his sal- | -vation.
6 This is the generation of | them that | seek Him : that | seek Thy | face O | Jacob.
7 Lift up your heads, O ye gates * and be ye lift up, ye éver- | -lasting | doors : and the King of | glory | shall come | in
8 Whó is this | King of | glory : The Lord strong and mighty * the Lórd | mighty | in | battle.
9 Lift up your heads, O ye gates * even lift them up, ye éver- | -lasting | doors : and the King of | glory | shall come | in.
10 Whó is this | King of | glory : The Lord of hósts | He | is the | King of | glory.

987 PSALM XXV.

UNTO | Thee O | Lord : do I | lift | up my | soul.
2 O my God, I trust in Thee * let me not be a- | -shamed : let not mine enemies | triumph | over | me.
3 Yea, let none that wait on Thée | be a- | -shamed : let them be ashamed * which trans- | -gress with- | -out | cause.
4 Shów me Thy | ways O | Lord : téach | me | Thy | paths.
5 Lead me in Thy trúth and | teach | me : for Thou art the God of my salvation * on Thée do I | wait | all the | day.
6 Remember, O Lord, Thy tender mercies * and Thy | loving- | -kindnesses : for they have | been | ever - of | old.
7 Remember not the sins of my youth nor | my trans- | -gressions : according to Thy mercy remember Thou me * for Thy goodness' | sake O | Lord.
8 Good and úpright | is the | Lord : there- fore will He téach | sinners | in the | way.
9 All the paths of the Lórd are | mercy - and | truth : unto such as keep His | cove - nant | and His | testimonies.
10 What man is hé that | feareth - the | Lord : him shall He teach in the | way that | He shall | choose.
11 His soul shall | dwell at | ease : and his seed - shall in- | -herit - the | earth.
12 The secret of the Lórd is with | them that | fear Him : and Hé will | shew | them His | covenant.
13 Let integrity and úpright- | -ness pre- | serve me : for I | wait | on | Thee.
14 Redeem Ísrael | O | God : out of | all | his | troubles.

272

PSALMS.

988 PSALM XXVII.

1 THE Lord is my light and my salvation * whom | shall I | fear : the Lord is the strength of my life * of whom | shall I | be a- | -fraid ?
2 When the wicked, even mine enemies and my foes * came upon me to eat | up my | flesh : they | stumbled | and | fell.
3 Though an host should encamp against me * my heart | shall not | fear : though war should rise against me * in | this will | I be | confident.
4 One thing have I desired of the Lord * that will I | seek | after that I may dwell in the house of the Lord all the days of my life * to behold the beauty of the Lord * and to en- | -quire | in His | temple.
5 For in the time of trouble He shall hide me in | His pa- | -vilion : in the secret of His tabernacle shall He hide me * He shall set me | up up- | -on a | rock.
6 And now shall mine head be lifted up * above mine enemies | round a- | -bout me : therefore will I offer in His taber- nacle sacrifices of joy * I will sing, yea, I will sing | praises | unto - the | Lord.
7 Hear, O Lord, when I cry* | with my | voice : have mercy also up- | -on * me and | answer | me.
8 When Thou saidst, Seek | ye My | face : my heart said unto Thee, Thy | face Lord | will I | seek.
9 Hide not Thy face far from me * put not Thy servant a- | -way in | anger : Thou hast been my help *, leave me not, neither forsake me * O | God of | my sal- | -vation.
10 When my father and my | mother - for- | sake me : then the | Lord will | take me | up.
11 Teach me Thy | way O | Lord : and lead me in a plain path be- | -cause | of mine | enemies.
12 Deliver me not over unto the will | of mine | enemies : for false witnesses are risen up against me * and | such as | breathe out | cruelty.
13 I had fainted * unless I had believed to see the goodness | of the | Lord : In the | land | of the | living.
14 Wait on the Lord, be of good courage * and He shall | strengthen * thine | heart wait, I | say, | on the | Lord.

989 PSALM XXXII.

1 BLESSED is he whose transgression | is for- | -given : whose | sin | is | covered.
2 Blessed is the man unto whom the Lord imputeth | not in- | -iquity : and in whose | spirit - there | is no | guile.
3 When I kept silence * my bones | waxed | old : through my | roaring | all the | day long.
4 For day and night Thy hand was | heavy - up- | -on me : my moisture is turned - into - the | drought of | summer.

5 I acknowledged my sin unto Thee * and mine iniquity I have I - not | hid : I said, I will confess my transgressions unto the Lord * and Thou forgavest the in- | -iqui - ty | of my | sin.
6 For this shall every one that is godly pray unto Thee * in a time when Thou | mayest - be | found : surely in the floods of great waters * they shall not come | nigh - unto | him.
7 Thou art my hiding place * Thou shalt preserve | me from | trouble : Thou shalt compass me about with | songs | of de- | -liverance.
8 I will instruct thee and teach thee in the way which | thou shalt | go : I will | guide thee | with Mine | eye.
9 Be ye not as the horse, or as the mule * which have no | under- | -standing : whose mouth must be held in with bit and bridle * lest they | come | near unto | thee.
10 Many sorrows shall be | to the | wicked : but he that trusteth in the Lord * mercy shall | compass | him a- | -bout.
11 [2 pt.] Be glad in the Lord and re- | -joice ye | righteous : and shout for joy, all ye that are | upright | in | heart.

990 PSALM XXXIV.

1 I WILL bless the Lord at | all | times : His praise shall continually | be | in my | mouth.
2 My soul shall make her boast | in the | Lord : the humble shall hear there- | -of | and be | glad.
3 O magnify the | Lord with | me : and let us ex- | -alt His | name to- | -gether.
4 I sought the Lord | and He | heard me : and delivered | me from | all my | fears.
5 They looked unto Him | and were | light- ened : and their | faces - were | not a- | shamed.
6 This poor man cried and the | Lord | heard him : and saved him | out of | all his | troubles.
7 The angel of the Lord encampeth round about | them that | fear Him : and | — de- | -liver- -eth | them.
8 O taste and see that the | Lord is | good : blessed is the | man that | trusteth - in | Him.
9 O fear the Lord | ye His | saints : for there is no | want to | them that | fear Him.
10 The young lions do lack and | suffer | hunger : but they that seek the Lord shall | not want | any - good | thing
11 Come, ye children, hearken | unto | me : I will teach you the | fear | of the | Lord.
12 What man is he that de- | -sireth | life : and loveth many days that | he may | see | good?
13 Keep thy | tongue from | evil : and thy | lips from | speaking | guile.
14 Depart from evil and | do | good : seek | peace | and pur- | -sue it.

15 The eyes of the Lord are up- | -on the | righteous: and His ears are | open | un- to · their | cry.
16 The face of the Lord is against them that | do | evil : to cut off the remembrance | of them | from the | earth.
17 The righteous cry" and the | Lord | hear- eth : and delivereth them | out of | all their | troubles.
18 The Lord is nigh unto them that are of a | broken | heart : and saveth such as | be - of a | contrite | spirit.
19 Many are the afflictions | of the | right- eous : but the Lord de- | -livereth · him : out of · them | all.
20 The Lord redeemeth the soul | of His | servants : and none of them that trust in | Him | shall be | desolate.

991 PSALM XXXIX.

I SAID, I will take heed to my ways * that I sin not | with my | tongue : I will keep my mouth with a bridle * while the | wicked | is be- | -fore me.
2 I was dumb with silence * I held my peace | even · from | good : and my | sorrow | was | stirred.
3 My heart was hot within me * while I was musing the | fire | burned : then | spake I | with my | tongue,
4 Lord, make me to know mine end * and the measure of my days | what it | is : that I" may | know how | frail I | am.
5 Behold, Thou hast made my days as an handbreadth * and mine age is as noth- ing be- | -fore | Thee : verily every man at his best state is | alto- | -gether | vanity.
6 Surely **every man** walketh in a vain shew * **surely** they are disquiet- | -ed in | vain : **he** heapeth up riches, **and** knoweth **not** | who shall | gather | them.
7 And now, Lord what | wait I | for : my" hope | is in | Thee.
8 Deliver me from all | my trans- | -gres- sions : make me not the re- | -proach | of the | foolish.
9 I was dumb, I opened | not my | mouth : be- | -cause | Thou | didst it.
10 Remove Thy stroke a- | -way | from me : I am consumed by" the | blow | of Thine | hand.
11 When Thou with rebukes dost correct man for iniquity * Thou makest his beauty to consume away | like a | moth : surely | ever - y | man is | vanity.
12 Hear my prayer, O Lord, and give ear unto my cry * hold not Thy peace | at my | tears : for I am a stranger with Thee, and a sojourner * as | all my | fathers | were.
13 [2 pt.] O spare me, that I" may re- | -cover | strength : before I go | hence and | be no | more.

992 PSALM XLII.

A S the hart panteth after the | water- | brooks : so panteth my soul | after | Thee O | God.
2 My soul thirsteth for God * for the | living | God : when shall I come **and** ap- | -pear be- | -fore | God?
3 My tears have been my meat | day and | night : while they continually say **unto** me, | Where | is thy | God?
4 When I remember these things * I pour out my | soul | in me : for I had gone with the multitude * I went with them to the house of God * with the voice of joy and praise * with a multitude that | kept | holy | day.
5 Why art thou cast down, O my soul * and why **art** thou disquiet- | -ed | in me hope thou in God * for I shall yet praise Him for the | help | of His | counten- ance.
6 O my God, my soul is cast | down with- | in me : therefore will I remember Thee from the land of Jordan, and of the Hermonites * | from the | hill | Mizar
7 Deep calleth unto deep at the noise of Thy | water- | -spouts : all Thy waves and Thy billows are | gone | over | me.
8 **Yet** the Lord will command His loving- kindness | in the | daytime : and in the night His song shall be with me * and my prayer unto the | God | of my | life.
9 I will say unto God my rock * Why hast Thou for- | -gotten | me : why go | mourning because of the op- | -pression | of the | enemy?
10 As with a sword **in** my bones * mine ene- | -mies re- | -proach me : while they say daily **unto** me, | Where | is thy | God?
11 [2 pt.] Why art thou cast down, O my soul * and why art thou disquiet- | -ed with- | -in me : hope thou in God ; for I shall yet praise Him * who is the health of my | counte - nance | and my | God.

993 PSALM XLVI.

G OD is our | refuge · and | strength : a very | present | help in | trouble.
2 Therefore will not we fear * though the earth | be re- | -moved : and though the mountains be carried into the | midst | of the | sea ;
3 Though the waters thereof roar | and be | troubled : though the mountains shake | with the | swelling · there- | -of.
4 There is a river * the streams whereof shall make glad the | city - of | God : the holy place of the tabernacles | of the | most | High.
5 God is in the midst of her * she shall | not be | moved : God shall | help · her and | that right | early.
6 The heathen raged, the | kingdoms · were | moved : He uttered His | voice, the | earth | melted.

PSALMS.

7 The Lórd of | hosts is | with us : **the Gód** of | Jacob | is our | refuge.
8 Come, behold the wórks | of **the | Lord** : what desolations He hath **| made | in** the | earth.
9 He maketh wars to cease unto the **énd |** of the | earth : **He** breaketh the bow, and cutteth the spear in sunder • **He** búrneth the | chari - ot | in the | fire.
10 Be still, and knów that | I am | God : I will be exalted among the heathen • I' will be ex- | -alted | in the | earth.
11 [2 pf.] The Lórd of | hosts is | with us : the Gód of | Jacob | **is** our | refuge.

994   PSALM LI.

HAVE mercy upon me, O **God** • accórding to Thy | loving- | -kindness : accórding unto the multitude of Thy **tender** mércies • | blot out | my trans- | -gres- sions.
2 Wash me throughly from **| mine** in- | iquity : ánd | cleanse me | **from my |** sin.
3 For I acknowledge | my trans- | -gres- sions : ánd my | sin is | ever - be- | -fore me.
4 Against Thee, **Thee** only, have I sinned • and done this **évil** | in Thy | sight : that Thou mightest **be** justified when Thou speakest • ánd **be** | clear | when Thou | judgest.
5 Híde Thy fáce | from my | sins : and blót out | all | **mine** in- | -iquities.
6 Create in me a cléan | heart O | God : and renéw **a** | right | spirit with- | -in **me**.
7 Cast me not awáy | from Thy | presence : and táke not Thy | Holy | Spirit | from me.
8 Restore **unto** me **the jóy of | Thy | sal-** | vation : and **uphóld me | with Thy |** free | Spirit.
9 **Then** will I téach trans- | -gressors - **Thy** : ways : and sinners shall bé con- | -vert- ed | unto | Thee.
10 Deliver me from blood-guiltiness, O God • Thou God of | my sal- | -vation : and my tongue shall sing a- | -loud | of Thy | righteousness.
11 O Lord, ópen | Thou my | lips **: and my** mouth shall | shew | forth Thy | praise.
12 For Thou desirest not sacrifice • else | would I | give it : Thou delightest | not in | burnt | offering.
13 [2 pf.] The sacrifices of Gód are a | broken | spirit : a broken and a contrite heart, O Gód | Thou wilt | not de- | -spise.

995   PSALM LXIII.

O GOD, Thou art my God • éarly | will I | seek Thee : my soul thirsteth for Thee, my flesh longeth for Thee • in a dry and thirsty lánd where | no | water | is ;
2 To sée Thy pówer | and Thy | glory : so as I have | seen Thee | in the | sanctuary.

3 Because Thy loving-kindness is | better - than | life : my' | lips shall | praise | Thee.
4 Thus will I bléss Thee | while I | live ; I will lift úp my | hands | in Thy | name.
5 My soul shall be satisfied • as with marrow - and | fatness : and my mouth shall práise | Thee with | joyful | lips :
6 When I remember Thée up | -on my | bed : and meditate on Thée | in the | night | watches.
7 Because Thou hast | been my | help : therefore in the shadow of Thy | wings will | I re- | -joice.
8 My soul followeth hárd | after | Thee . **Thy** right | hand up- | -holdeth | me.

996   PSALM LXV.

PRAISE waiteth for Thée O | God in | Sion : and unto Thée shall the | **vow** | be per- | formed.
2 O Thóu that | hearest | prayer : únto | Thee shall | all flesh | come.
3 Iniquities pre- | -vail a- | -gainst me : as for our transgressions • Thou shalt | purge | them a- | -way.
4 Blessed is the man whom Thou choosest, and causest to approach unto Thee • that he may dwéll | in Thy | courts : we shall be satisfied with the goodness of Thy house • éven | of Thy | holy | temple.
5 By terrible things **in** righteousness wilt Thou answer us • O Gód of | our sal- vation : who art the confidence of all the ends of the earth • and of them that are afár | off up- | -on the | sea :
6 Which by His stréngth setteth | fast the mountains being | girded | with | power :
7 Which stilleth the **nóise !** of the | seas the noise of their **waves •** ánd the | tu- mult | of the | people.
8 They also that dwell **in** the uttermost parts are afraid | at Thy | tokens : Thou makest the outgoings of the mórning and | evening | to re- | -joice.
9 Thou visitest the earth, and waterest it • Thou greatly enrichest it with the river of God • which is | full of | water : Thou preparest them corn • when Thou hast | so pro- | -vided | for it.
10 Thou waterest the ridges thereof abun- dantly • Thou séttlest the | furrows there- | -of : Thou makest it soft with showers • Thóu | blessest - the | spring- ing - there- | -of.
11 Thou crownest the yéar | with Thy | goodness : ánd Thy | paths | drop | fat- ness.
12 They drop upon the pástures | of the | wilderness : and the little hills re- joice on | ever - y | side.
13 [2 pf.] The pastures are | clothed - with flocks ; the valleys also are covered over with corn • they shout for | joy they | also | sing.

PSALMS.

997   PSALM LXVII.

GOD be merciful únto | us and | bless us : | and cáuse His | fáce to | shíne up- | -on us ;

2 That Thy way may be knówn up- | -on | earth : Thy sáving | health a- | -mong all | nations.

3 Let the people práise | Thee O | God : let | all the | people | praise Thee.

4 O let the nations be glád and | sing for | joy : for Thou shalt júdge the people righteously ✻ and góvern the | na‧tions up- | -on | earth.

5 Let the people práise | Thee O | God : let | all the | people | praise Thee.

6 Then shall the éarth | yield her | íncrease : and God, éven our | own | God shall | bless us.

7 [2 pt.] Gód | shall | bless us : and all the énds of the | earth shall | fear | Him.

998   PSALM LXXII.

GIVE the king Thy | júdgments · O | God : and Thy ríghteousness | unto · the | king's | son.

2 He shall júdge Thy | people · with | ríghteousness : ánd Thy | poor | with | júdgment.

3 The mountains shall bring péace | to the | people : ánd the | little | hills by | ríghteousness.

4 He shall júdge the poor | of the | people : He shall save the chíldren of the néedy ✻ and shall bréak in | pieces | the op- | pressor.

5 They shall fear Thée as long as the sún and | moon en- | -dúre : thrōughout | all | gener- | -ations.

6 He shall come dówn like rain upón the | mown | grass : ás | showers · that | water · the | earth.

7 In His dáys shall the | righteous | flóurish : and abundance of péace so | long · as the | moon en- | -dúreth.

8 He shall have dóminion álso from | sea to | sea : and from the river únto the | ends | of the | earth.

9 They that dwéll in the wílderness shall | bow be- | -fore Him : ánd His | enemies shall | lick the | dust.

10 The kings of Társhish and of the Isles shall | bring | présents : the kings of Shéba and | Seba · shall | offer | gifts.

11 Yea, all kíngs shall fáll | down be- | -fore Him : áll | nations | shall | serve Him.

12 For He shall deliver the néedy | when he | críeth : the poor also ✻ and | him that | hath no | helper.

13 He shall spáre the | poor and | néedy : and shall sáve the | souls | of the | needy.

14 He shall redéem their sóul from de- | -céit and | víolence : and précious shall their | blood be | in His | sight.

15 And He shall líve ✻ and to Him shall be gíven of the | gold of | Shéba : prayer álso shall be made for Him contínually ✻ and | daily · shall | He be | praised.

276

16 There shall be an hándful of córn in the | earth ✻ upon the | tóp | of the | móuntains : the frúit thereof shall sháke like Lébanon ✻ and they of the cíty shall flóurish like | grass | of the | earth.

17 His náme shall endúre for éver ✻ His name shall be contínued as lóng | as the | sun : and men shall be bléssed in Him ✻ áll | nations · shall | call Him | blessed.

18 Blessed be the Lord Gód the | God of | Israel : who ónly | doeth | wondrous | things.

19 [2 pt.] And blessed be His glórious | name for | ever : and let the whóle earth be filled with His glóry ✻ A- | -men, and | A- | -men.

999   PSALM LXXXIV.

HOW amíable are Thy | taber- | -nacles : | O | Lord | of | Hosts !

2 My sóul longeth, yea, even fáinteth ✻ for the cóurts | of the | Lord : my heart and my flesh críeth óut | for the | living | God.

3 Yea, the spárrow hath found an hóuse ✻ and the swállow a nest for hersélf ✻ where she may | lay her | young : even Thíne altars, O Lord of hosts ✻ my | King | and my | God.

4 Blessed are they that dwéll | in Thy | house : they will be | still | praising | Thee.

5 Blessed is the man whose stréngth | is in | Thee : in whose heart are the | híghways to | Zion.

6 Passing through the válley of Wéeping ✻ they máke it a | place of | springs : yea, the early ráin | covereth | it with | blessings.

7 They gó from | strength to | strength : every one of them appéareth be- | -fore | God in | Zion.

8 O Lord God of hósts | hear my | prayer : give | ear, O | God of | Jacob.

9 Behóld O | God our | shield : and look upón the | face of | Thine an- | -ointed.

10 For a dáy in Thy cóurts is bétter | than a | thousand : I had rather be a doorkeeper in the house of my Gód ✻ than to | dwell in the | tents of | wickedness.

11 For the Lord Gód is a | sun and | shield : the Lord will give grace and glóry ✻ no good thing will He withhóld from | them that | walk | uprightly.

12 O | Lord of | hosts : blessed is the | man that | trusteth · in | Thee.

1000   PSALM LXXXIX.

I WILL sing of the mércies of the | Lord for | ever : with my mouth will I make known Thy fáithfulness ✻ to | all | gener- | -ations.

2 For I have said, Mércy shall be búilt | up for | ever : Thy fáithfulness shalt Thou estáblish | in the | very | heavens.

PSALMS.

3 I have made a covenant | with My | chosen : I' have | sworn · unto | David · My | servant.
4 Thy seed will I' e- | -stablish · for | ever : and build up thy throne to | all | gener- | -ations.
5 And the heavens shall praise Thy | won- ders · O | Lord ; Thy faithfulness also in the congre- | -gation | of the | saints.
6 For who in the heaven can be compared | unto · the | Lord : who among the sons of the mighty can be | likened | unto · the | Lord?
7 God is greatly **to be feared in the assembly** | of the | saints ; and to be had in rever- ence of all | them that | are a- | -bout Him.
8 O Lord God of hosts * who is a strong Lord | like · unto | Thee : or to Thy | faithful · ness | round a- | -bout Thee?
9 Thou rulest the raging | of the | sea : when the waves thereof a- | -rise Thou | stillest | them.
10 Thou hast broken Rahab in pieces as | one that · is | slain : Thou hast scattered Thine enemies | with Thy | strong | arm.
11 The heavens are Thine * the earth | also · is | Thine : as for the world and the fulness thereof * | Thou hast | founded | them.
12 The north and the south, Thou hast cre- | -ated | them : Tabor and Hermon shall re- | -joice | in Thy | name.
13 Thou hast a | mighty | arm ; strong is Thy hand * and high | is Thy | right | hand.
14 Justice and judgment are the habitation | of Thy | throne : mercy and truth shall | go be- | -fore Thy | face.
15 Blessed is the people that know the | joy- ful | sound : they shall walk, O Lord in the | light | of Thy | countenance.
16 In Thy name shall they rejoice | all the | day : and in Thy righteousness | shall they | be ex- | -alted.
17 For Thou art **the glory** | of their | strength : and in Thy favour our | horn shall | be ex- | -alted.
18 For the Lord is | our de- | -fence : and the Holy One of | Isra · el | is our | King.

1001   PSALM XC.

LORD, Thou hast been our | dwelling- | place : in | all | gene- | -rations.
2 Before the mountains were brought forth * or ever Thou hadst formed the earth | and the | world : even from ever- lasting to ever- | -lasting | Thou art | God.
3 Thou turnest man | to de- | -struction : and sayest, Re- | -turn ye | children | of | men.
4 For a thousand years in Thy sight * are but as yesterday | when it · is | past : and as a | watch | in the | night.
5 Thou carriest them away as with a flood * they are | as a | sleep : in the morning they are like | grass which | groweth | up

6 In the morning it flourisheth and | grow- eth | up : in the evening, it is | cut | down and | withereth.
For we are consumed | by Thine | anger : and by' Thy | wrath | are we | troubled.
8 Thou hast set our iniquit- | -ies be- | -fore Thee : our secret sins in the | light | of Thy | countenance.
9 For all our days are passed away | in Thy wrath : we bring our years to an end * as a | tale | that is | told.
10 The days of our years are threescore years and ten * and if by reason of strength they be | fourscore | years : yet is their strength labour and sorrow * for it is soon cut off | and we | fly a- | way.
11 Who knoweth the power | of Thine | anger : even according to Thy fear | so is Thy | wrath.
12 So teach us to number · our | days : that we may apply' our | hearts | unto | wisdom.
13 Return O | Lord how | long : and let it re- pent Thee con- | -cerning | Thy | servants.
14 O satisfy us early | with Thy | mercy : that we may rejoice and be | glad | all our | days.
15 Make us glad * according to the days wherein Thou hast af- | -flicted | us : and the years where- | -in · we have | seen | evil.
16 Let Thy work appear | unto · Thy | ser- vants : and Thy | glory | unto · their | children.
17 [2 p.] And let the beauty of the Lord our God | be up- | -on us : and establish Thou the work of our hands upon us * yea, the work of our hands e- | -stablish | Thou | it.

1002   PSALM XCI.

HE that dwelleth in the secret place of the | most · High : shall abide under the | shadow | of · the Al- | -mighty.
2 I will say of the Lord * He is my refuge | and my | fortress : my God in | Him | will I | trust.
3 Surely He shall deliver thee from the snare | of the | fowler : and | from the noisome | pestilence.
4 He shall cover thee with His feathers * and under His wings shalt thou trust : His truth shall | be thy | shield and | buckler.
5 Thou shalt not be afraid for the | terror by | night : nor for the | arrow · that flieth · by | day.
6 Nor for the pestilence that | walketh · in | darkness : nor for the de- | -struction · that | wasteth · at | noonday.
7 Because thou hast made the Lord which | is my | refuge : even the most | High · thy | habi- | -tation ;
8 There shall no | evil · be- | -fall thee : neither shall any | plague come | nigh thy | dwelling.

277

PSALMS.

9 For He shall give His angels charge | over | thee : to keep | thee in | all thy | ways.
10 They shall bear thee up | in their | hands : lest thou dash thy | foot a- | -gainst a | stone.
11 Thou shalt tread upon the | lion · and | adder : the young lion and the dragon shalt thou | trample | under | feet.
12 Because he hath set his love upon Me ✻ therefore will I° de- | -liver | him : I will set him on high ✻ because | he hath | known My | name.
13 He shall call upon Me ✻ and I° will | answer | him : I will be with him in trouble ✻ I will deliver | him and | honour | him.
14 With long life will I | satis · fy | him : and | shew him | My sal- | -vation.

1003 PSALM XCV.

O COME, let us sing | unto · the | Lord : let us make a joyful noise to the | rock of | our sal- | -vation.
2 Let us come before His presence with | thanks- | -giving : and make a joyful noise | unto | Him with | psalms.
3 For the Lord is a | great | God : and a great | King a- | -bove all | gods.
4 In His hand are the deep places | of the | earth : the strength of the | hills is | His | also.
5 The sea is His | and He | made it : and His hands | formed · the | dry | land.
6 O come, let us worship and | bow | down : let us kneel be- | -fore the | Lord our | maker.
7 [2 pt.] For He | is our | God : and we are the people of His pasture, and the | sheep of | His | hand.

1004 PSALM XCVI.

O SING unto the Lord a | new | song : sing unto the | Lord | all the | earth.
2 Sing unto the Lord | bless His | name : shew forth His sal- | -vation · from | day to | day.
3 Declare His glory a- | -mong the | heathen : His | won · ders a- | -mong all | people.
4 For the Lord is great ✻ and greatly | to be | praised : He is to be feared a- | -bove | all | gods.
5 For all the gods of the | nations · are | idols : but the | Lord | made the | heavens.
6 Honour and majesty | are be- | -fore Him : strength and | beauty · are | in His | sanctuary.
7 Give unto the Lord, O ye kindreds | of the | people : give unto the Lord | glory | and | strength.
8 Give unto the Lord the glory due | unto · | His | name : bring an offering ✻ and | come | into | His | courts.

9 O worship the Lord in the | beauty · of | holiness : fear be- | -fore Him | all the | earth.
10 Say among the heathen that the | Lord | reigneth : the world also shall be established that it shall not be moved ✻ He shall | judge the | people | right- eously.
11 Let the heavens rejoice ✻ and let the | earth be | glad : let the sea roar | and the | fulness · there- | -of.
12 Let the field be joyful ✻ and all that | is there- | -in : then shall all the trees of the wood re- | -joice be- | -fore the | Lord :
13 [2 pt.] For He cometh, for He cometh to | judge the | earth : He shall judge the world with righteousness ✻ and the | people | with His | truth.

1005 PSALM XCVIII.

O SING unto the Lord a new song ✻ for He hath done | marvel · lous | things : His right hand and His holy arm hath | gotten | Him the | victory.
2 The Lord hath made known | His sal- | vation : His righteousness hath He openly shewed in the | sight | of the | heathen.
3 He hath remembered His mercy and His truth toward the | house of | Israel : all the ends of the earth have seen the sal- | vation | of our | God.
4 Make a joyful noise unto the Lord | all the | earth : make a loud noise and re- | joice and | sing | praise.
5 Sing unto the Lord | with the | harp : with the harp and the | voice | of a | psalm.
6 With trumpets and | sound of | cornet : make a joyful noise be- | -fore the | Lord the | King.
7 Let the sea roar and the | fulness · there- | -of : the world and | they that | dwell there- | -in.
8 Let the floods | clap their | hands : let the hills be joyful to- | -gether · be- | -fore the | Lord :
9 [2 pt.] For He cometh to | judge the | earth : with righteousness shall He judge the world ✻ and the | people | with | equity.

1006 PSALM C.

MAKE a joyful noise unto the Lord | all ye | hands : serve the Lord with glad- ness ✻ come be- | -fore His | presence · with | singing.
2 Know ye that the Lord | He is | God : it is He that hath made us, and not we our- selves ✻ we are His people, and the | sheep of | His | pasture.
3 Enter into His gates with thanksgiving ✻ and into His | courts with | praise : be

278

PSALMS.

thankful unto | **Him and** | bless His | name.
4 For the Lord is good ∗ His mercy is | ever- | -lasting : and His truth endureth to | all | gener- | -ations.

1007 PSALM CIII.

BLESS **the Lord** | **O** my | **soul** : and all that **is within me** | bless His | holy | name.
2 Bless the Lord | O my | soul : **and for-** | get not | all His | benefits :
3 Who forgiveth all | thine in- | -iquities : who healeth | all | thy dis- | -eases ;
4 Who redeemeth thy life | from de- | struction : who crowneth thee with loving- | -kindness ∙ and | tender | mercies ;
5 Who satisfieth thy mouth with | good | things : so that thy youth is re- | newed | like the | eagle's.
6 **The** Lord executeth righteous- | -ness and | judgment : for | all that | are op- | pressed.
7 He made **known His ways** | **unto** | **Moses** : His acts | unto ∙ the | **children ∙ of** | Israel.
8 The Lord is merci- | -ful and | gracious : slow to | anger ∙ **and** | plenteous ∙ in | mercy.
9 He will **not** | always | chide : neither will He | keep His | anger ∙ for | ever.
10 **He** hath not dealt with **us** | after ∙ **our** | sins : nor rewarded us ac- | -cording ∙ to | our in- | -iquities.
11 For as the heaven is high a- | -bove the | earth : so great is His mercy | toward | them that | fear Him.
12 As far as the east is | from **the** | **west : so** far hath He removed | **our trans-** | gressions | from us.
13 Like as a father | pitieth ∙ his | children : so the Lord | piti ∙ eth | them that | fear Him.
14 For He | knoweth ∙ our | frame : He re- | membereth | that we | are | dust.
15 As for man, his days | are as | grass : as a flower of the | field | so he | flourisheth.
16 For the wind passeth over it | and ∙ it is | gone : and the place thereof shall | know it | no | more.
17 But the mercy of the Lord is from ever- | lasting to everlasting ∗ upon | them that | fear Him : and His righteous- ness | unto | children's | children ;
18 To such as | keep His | **covenant** : and **to** those that remember | **His com-** | -**mand-** ments ∙ to | do them.
19 The Lord hath **prepared His throne** | in the | heavens : **and His kingdom** | ruleth | over | all.
20 Bless the Lord, ye His angels ∗ that **ex-** | cel in | strength : that do His command- ments ∗ hearkening unto the | voice | of | His | word.
21 Bless ye the Lord all | ye His | hosts : ye ministers of | His that | do His | pleasure.

22 Bless the Lord, all His works ∗ in all places of | His do- | -minion : bless the Lord | O my | soul.

1008 PSALM CXV.

NOT unto us, O Lord, not unto us ∗ but unto Thy name | give | glory : for Thy mercy and | for Thy | truth's | sake.
2 Wherefore should the | heathen | say Where is | now | their | God?
3 But our God is | in the | heavens : He hath done whatso- | -ever | He hath | pleased.
4 The Lord hath been mindful of us ∗ He will | bless | us : He will bless the house of Israel ∗ He will | bless the | house of | Aaron.
5 He will bless them that | **fear the** | **Lord** : both | small | and | great.
6 The Lord shall increase you | more and | **more** : you | and | your | children.
7 Ye are blessed | of the | Lord which | made | heaven ∙ and | earth.
8 The heaven, even the heavens | are the | Lord's : but the earth hath He given to the | children ∙ of | men.
9 **The** dead praise | not the | Lord : neither any that go | down | into | silence.
10 **But we** will bless the Lord ∗ from this time forth and for | ever- | -more ; Praise | — | — the | Lord.

1009 PSALM CXVI.

I LOVE | — the | Lord : because He hath heard my voice | and my | suppli- | -cations.
2 Because He hath inclined His ear | unto | me therefore will I call upon Him as | long | as I | live.
3 Gracious is the | Lord and | righteous : yea our | God is | merci- | -ful.
4 Return unto thy rest | O my | soul : for the Lord hath dealt | bounti- | -fully | with thee.
5 What shall I render | unto ∙ the | Lord : for all His | bene- | -fits toward | me?
6 I will take the cup of | sal- | -vation : and call upon the | name | of the | Lord.
7 I will pay my vows | unto ∙ the | Lord : now in the | presence | of | all His | people.
8 Precious in the sight | of the | Lord : is the | death | of His | saints.
9 O Lord, truly | I am ∙ Thy | servant : I am Thy servant, Thou hast | loosed | my | bonds.
10 I will offer to Thee the sacrifice of thanks- | -giving : and will call upon the | name | of the | Lord.
11 I will pay my vows | unto ∙ the | Lord : now in the | presence ∙ of | all His | people.
12 In the courts of the Lord's house ∗ in the midst of thee | O Je- | -rusalem . Praise | — | ye the | Lord.

PSALMS.

1010 Psalm CXVIII. 14-29.

THE Lórd is my | strength and | song : and ís he- | -come | my sal- | -vation.
2 The voice of rejoicing and salvation ✱ is in the tábernacles | of the | ríghteous : the right hánd of the | Lord | doeth | valiantly.
3 The right hand of the Lórd | is ex- | alted : the right hánd of the | Lord doeth | valiantly.
4 I shall not | die but | líve : and declare the | works of the | Lord.
5 The Lórd hath | chástened ⸱ me | sore : but He hath not given me | over | unto | death.
6 Open to mé the | gates of | righteousness : I will go into them ✱ and | I will | praise the | Lord :
7 This gáte | of the | Lord : into which the | ríghteous | shall | enter.
8 I' will | praise | Thee : for Thou hast heard me ✱ and árt be- | -come | my sal- | -vation.
9 The stóne which the | builders ⸱ re- | fused : is become the | head stone | of the | corner.
10 This is the | Lord's | doing : it is | márvel ⸱ lous | in our | eyes.
11 This is the dáy which the | Lord hath | made : we will rejóice | and be | glad in | it.
12 Save now, I beséech | Thee O | Lord : O Lord, I beséech Thee | send | now pros- | -perity.
13 Blessed be he that cometh in the náme | of the | Lord : we have blessed you out of the | house | of the | Lord.
14 God is the Lórd which hath | shewed ⸱ us | light : bind the sacrifice with cords, even únto the | horns | of the | altar.
15 Thou art my Gód and | I will | praise Thee : Thou art my | God I | will ex- | -alt Thee.
16 O give thanks unto the Lórd for | He is | good : for His | mercy ⸱ en- (-dureth ⸱ for | ever.

1011 Psalm CXXI.

I WILL lift up mine éyes | unto ⸱ the | hills : from | whence | cometh ⸱ my | help.
2 My help cómeth | from the | Lord : which | made | heaven ⸱ and | earth.
3 He will not súffer thy fóot | to be | moved : He that | keepeth ⸱ thee | will not | slumber.
4 Behold, Hé that | keepeth | Israel : shall neither | slumber | nor | sleep.
5 The Lórd | is thy | keeper : the Lord is thy sháde up- | -on thy | right | hand.
6 The sun shall not smíte ⸱ thee by | day : nor the | moon | by | night.
7 The Lord shall presérve thee from | all | evil : He | shall pre- | -serve thy | soul.
8 The Lord shall preserve thy going out and thy | coming | in : from this time forth and | even ⸱ for | ever- | -more.

1012 Psalm CXXII.

I WAS glad when they sáid | unto | me : Let us gó into the | house | of the | Lord.
2 Our feet shall stánd with- | -in thy | gates : O | — Jer- | -usa- | -lem.
3 Jerusalem is buílded | as a | city : that | is com- | -pact to- | -gether :
4 Whither the tribes go up ✱ the tríbes | of the | Lord : unto the testimony of Israel ✱ to give thánks unto the | name | of the | Lord.
5 For there are sét | thrones of | judgment : the thrónes | of the | house of | David.
6 Pray for the péace | of Je- | -rusalem : they shall | prosper ⸱ that | love | thee.
7 Péace be with- | -in thy | walls : and pros- | -per- ⸱ ty with- | -in thy | palaces.
8 For my bréthren and com- | -panions' | sakes : I will now sáy, | Peace | be with- | -in thee.
9 [2 pt.] Because of the house of the | Lord our | God : I' will | seek | thy | good.

1013 Psalm CXXXVI.

O GIVE thanks unto the Lórd for | He is | good : for His | mercy ⸱ en- | -dureth ⸱ for | ever.
2 O give thánks unto the | God of | gods : for His | mercy ⸱ en- | -dureth ⸱ for | ever.
3 O give thanks to the | Lord of | lords : for His | mercy ⸱ en- | -dureth ⸱ for | ever.
4 To Him who alóne doeth | great | wonders : for His | mercy ⸱ en- | -dureth ⸱ for | ever.
5 To Him that by wisdom | made the | heavens : for His | mercy ⸱ en- | -dureth ⸱ for | ever.
6 To Him that stretcheth out the eárth a- | -bove the | waters : for His | mercy ⸱ en- | -dureth ⸱ for | ever.
7 To Him that máde | great | lights : for His | mercy ⸱ en- | -dureth ⸱ for | ever.
8 The sún to | rule by | day : for His | mercy ⸱ en- | -dureth ⸱ for | ever.
9 The moon and stars to | rule by | night : for His | mercy ⸱ en- | -dureth ⸱ for | ever.
10 Who remembered ús in our | low e- | -state : for His | mercy ⸱ en- | -dureth ⸱ for | ever.
11 And hath redéemed us | from our | enemies : for His | mercy ⸱ en- | -dureth ⸱ for | ever.
12 Who giveth fóod to | all | flesh : for His | mercy ⸱ en- | -dureth ⸱ for | ever.
13 [2 pt.] O give thánks unto the | God of | heaven : for His | mercy ⸱ en- | -dureth ⸱ for | ever.

1014 Psalm CXXXIX.

O LORD, Thóu hast | searched | me : And | — | known | me.
2 Thou knowest my downsítting and | mine up- | -rising : Thou understándest my | thought a- | -far | off.

PSALMS.

3 Thou compassest my páth and my | lying | down : and árt ac- | -quainted - with | all my | ways.
4 For there is not a wórd | in my | tongue : but lo, O Lórd Thou | knowest it | alto- | -gether
5 Thou hast beset me behind | and be- | fore : and | laid Thine | hand up- | -on me.
6 Such knowledge is too wónder- | -ful for me : it is high, I cánnot at- | -tain unto | it.
7 Whither shall I gó | from Thy | Spirit : or whither sháll I | flee | from Thy | presence?
8 If I ascend up into héaven | Thou art | there if I make my bed in héll be- | hold | Thou art | there.
9 If I take the wings | of the | morning : and dwell in the úttermost | parts | of the | sea ;
10 Even thére shall | Thy hand | lead me : and | Thy right | hand shall | hold me.
11 If I say, Surely the dárkness shall | cover | me * even the night | shall be | light a- | -bout me.
12 Yea, the darkness hídeth not from Thee * but the night shíneth | as the | day : the darkness and the light are | both a- | -like to | Thee.
13 How precious also are Thy thoughts un- to | me O | God : how gréat | is the | sum of | them !
14 If I should count them * they are more in número | than the | sand : when I awake | I am | still with | Thee.
15 Search me, O Gód and | know my | heart : try' me and | know | my | thoughts :
16 And see if there be any wícked | way | in me : and lead me in the | way | ever- | lasting.

1015   PSALM CXLV.

I WILL extól Thee my | God O | King : and I will bléss Thy | name for | ever - and | ever
2 Every dáy | will I | bless Thee : and I will praise Thy | name for | ever - and | ever.
3 Great is the Lord, and gréatly | to be | praised and His | greatness | is un- | searchable.
4 One generation shall praise Thy wórks | to an- | -other : and shall de- | -clare Thy | mighty | acts.
5 I will speak of the glorious hónour | of Thy | majesty : and | of Thy | won- drous | works.
6 And men shall speak of the might of Thy | terri - ble | acts : and I' will de- clare | Thy | greatness.
7 They shall abúndantly utter the me- mory * of Thy | great | goodness : and shall | sing | of Thy | righteousness.
8 The Lord is gracious, and fúll | of com- | passion : slow to ánger | and of | great | mercy.
9 The Lórd is | good to | all : and His tender mércies are | over | all His | works.

10 All Thy works shall práise | Thee O | Lord : And Thy | saints | shall | bless Thee.
11 They shall speak of the glóry | of Thy | kingdom : and | talk | of Thy | power :
12 To make known to the sons of mén His | mighty | acts : and the glórious | maj- jes - ty | of His | kingdom.
13 Thy kingdom is an éver- | -lasting | king- dom : and Thy dominion endureth throughout | all | gener- | -ations.
14 The Lord uphóldeth | all that | fall : and raiseth up all thóse | that be | bowed | down.
15 The eyes of áll | wait up - on | Thee ; and Thou gívest them their | meat in | due | season.
16 Thou ópenest | Thine | hand : and sat- isfiest the desíre of | ever - y | living | thing.
17 The Lord is rígteous in | all His | ways : and | holy - in | all His | works.
18 The Lord is nigh unto all thém that | call up- | -on Him : to áll that call up- | -on Him - in | truth.
19 He will fulfil the desíre of | them that | fear Him : He also will héar their | cry | and will | save them.
20 The Lord presérveth all | them that | love Him : but áll the | wicked - will | He de- | -stroy.
21 [2 pt.] My mouth shall speak the práise | of the | Lord : and let all flesh bless His hóly | name for | ever - and | ever.

1016   PSALM CXLVI.

PRAISE | ye the | Lord : Praise the | Lord | O my | soul.
2 While I live will I | praise the | Lord : I will sing praises unto my God * while I | have | any | being.
3 Put not your trust in princes * nor in the | son of | man : in whóm | there is | no | help.
4 His breath goeth forth * he retúrneth | to his | earth : in that véry | day his | thoughts | perish.
5 Happy is he that hath the God of Jácob for his | help : whose hópe is | in the | Lord his | God
6 Which made heaven and earth * the sea and áll that | therein | is : which | keep- eth | truth for | ever :
7 Which executeth judgment for the op- pressed * which gíveth food | to the | hungry : Thé | Lord | looseth the prisoners :
8 The Lord openeth the eyes of the blínd * the Lord raiseth thém that are | bowed down : thé | Lord | loveth - the | right- eous :
9 The Lord preserveth the strangers * He relieveth the fáther- | -less and | widow : but the way of the wícked He | turneth | upside | down.
10 The Lord shall reign for ever, even thy God, O Zíon * unto áll | gener- | -ations : Práise | — | ye the | Lord.

CANTICLES.

1017   1 CHRONICLES XXIX. 10-13.

BLESSED be Thou, Lord God of I'srael | our | father : fór | ever | and | ever.
2 Thine, O Lord is the greatness * and the pówer | and the | glory : ánd the | victory | and the | majesty :
3 For all that is | in the | heaven : ánd | in the | earth is | Thine.
4 Thine is the | kingdom · O | Lord : and Thou art exálted as | head a- | -bove | all.
5 Both riches and hónour | come of | Thee : and Thóu | reignest | over | all.
6 And in Thine hánd is | power and | might : and in Thine hand it is to make great * and to give | strength | unto | all.
7 [2 pt.] Now therefore our | God we | thank Thee : ánd | praise Thy | glorious | name.

1018   ISAIAH XII.

O LÓRD | I will | praise Thee : though Thou wast angry with me * Thine anger is turned awáy | and Thou | comfortedst | me.
2 Behold, Gód is | my sal- | -vation : I will trúst and | not | be a- | -fraid.
3 For the Lord Jehovah is my stréngth | and my | song ; He also is be- | -come | my sal- | -vation.
4 Therefore with jóy shall | ye draw | water : óut of the | wells | of sal- | -vation.
5 And in that dáy | shall ye | say : Praise the Lórd, | call up- | -on His | name.
6 Declare His dóings a- | -mong the | people : make mention thát His | name | is ex- | -alted.
7 Sing unto the Lord, for He hath dóne | excellent | things : this is | known in | all the | earth.
8 Cry out and shout, thou inhábi- | -tant of | Zion : for great is the Holy One of I'srael | in the | midst of | thee.

1019   ISAIAH XXV. 1-9.

O LÓRD, Thou | art my | God : I will exált Thee, | I will | praise Thy | name.
2 For Thou hast dóne | wonderful | things : Thy counsels of óld are | faithful- | -ness and | truth.
3 For Thou hast made of a city an heap * of a defénced | city · a | ruin : a palace of strangers to be no city * it shall | never | be | built.
4 Therefore shall the strong péople | glorify | Thee : the city of the térrible | nations · shall | fear | Thee.
5 For Thou hast been a stréngth | to the poor : a strength to the | needy · in his dis- | -tress.

6 A refuge from the storm * a shádow | from the | heat : when the blast of the terrible ones is ás a | storm a- | -gainst the | wall.
7 Thou shalt bring dówn the | noise of strangers : as the héat | in a | dry | place.
8 Even the heat with the shádow | of a | cloud the branch of the terrible ónes | shall be | brought | low.
9 And in this mountain shall the Lord of Hosts make unto all people a feast of fat things * a feast of wínes | on the | lees : of fat things full of marrow * of wines on the | lees | well re- | -fined.
10 And He will destroy in this mountain the face of the covering * cást over | all | people : and the véil that is | spread · over | all | nations.
11 He will swallow up | death in | victory : and the Lord God will wipe away | tears from | off all | faces ;
12 And the rebuke of His people shall He take away from off | all the | earth : fór the | Lord hath | spoken | it.
13 And it shall be said in that day * Lo, this is | our | God : we have wáited for | Him and | He will | save us.
14 This is the Lord, wé have | waited | for Him : we will be glád and re- | -joice in | His sal- | -vation.

1020   ISAIAH XL. 1-11.

COMFORT ye, comfort ye My péople | saith your | God : spéak ye | comfort · ably | to Je- | -rusalem,
2 And cry unto her, that her wárfare | is ac- | -complished : thát her in- | -iqui- | -ty is | pardoned.
3 The voice of him that crieth | In the | wilderness : prepáre ye the | way | of the | Lord,
4 Make stráight | in the | desert : á | highway | for our | God.
5 Every válley shall | be ex- | -alted : and every mountain and híll | shall be | made | low ;
6 And the crooked shall be | made | straight : ánd the | rough | places | plain.
7 And the glory of the Lord shall be revealed * and all flésh shall | see it · to- | -gether : for the mouth of the | Lord hath | spoken | it.
8 The vóice | said, | Cry : and he sáid, | What | shall I | cry ?
9 All | flesh is | grass : and all the goodliness thereof is ás the | flower | of the | field.
10 The grass withereth á | the | flower | fadeth : because the spirit of the Lord bloweth upon it * súrely the | people | is | grass.

CANTICLES.

11 The grass withereth * the | flower | fad-
eth : but the word of our | God shall |
stand for | ever.
12 O Zion that | bringest - good | tidings |
get thee up | into - the | high | moun-
tain.
13 O Jerúsalem that | bringest - good |
tidings ; lift | up thy | voice with |
strength.
14 Lift it up, bé | not a- | -fraid : say unto
the cities of Judah * be- | -hold | your |
God.
15 Behold, the Lord God will cóme with
strong | hand : ánd His | arm shall |
rule | for Him.
16 Behold, His re- | -ward is | with Him ;
and | — His | work be- | -fore Him.
17 He shall feed His flock | like a | shepherd :
He shall gáther the | lambs | with His |
arm,
18 And cárry them | in His | bosom : and
shall gently léad | those that | are with |
young.

1021   ISAIAH LII. 7-10.

HOW béautiful up- | -on the | mountains |
are the feet of him that | bringeth |
good | tidings.
2 That publisheth peace * that bringeth
good | tidings - of | good : that pub-
lisheth salvation * that sáith unto |
Zion - thy | God | reigneth.
3 Thy watchmen shall lift | up the | voice |
with the vóice to- | -gether | shall they |
sing.
4 For they shall sée | eye to | eye : when
the Lórd shall | bring a- | -gain | Zion.
5 Break forth into jóy, | sing to- | -gether :
ye wáste | places | of Je- | -rusalem.
6 For the Lord hath cómfort- | -ed His |
people : Hé | hath re- | -deemed - Je- |
rusalem.
7 The Lord hath made báre His | holy |
arm : in the | eyes of | all the | nations.
8 And áll the | ends - of the | earth : shall
sée the sal- | -vation | of our | God.

1022   ISAIAH LIII. 3-12.

HE is despísed and re- | -jected of | men :
a man of sórrows, | and ac- | -quainted -
with | grief ;
2 And we hid as it wére our | faces | from
Him : He was despísed and | we es- |
teemed Him | not.
3 Surely Hé hath | borne our | griefs : ánd |
carried | our | sorrows ;
4 Yét we did es- | -teem Him | stricken :
smitten of | God | and af- | -flicted.
5 But He was wounded for | our trans- |
gressions : Hé was | bruised - for | our
in- | -iquities ;
6 The chastisement of our peace | was up- |
on Him : and with His | stripes | we
are | healed.
7 All we like sheep have | gone a- | -stray :
we have turned évery one | to his |
own | way ;

8 And the Lórd hath | laid on | Him : the
in- | -iqui- ty | of us | all
9 He was oppressed, and He | was af- |
flicted : yét He | opened | not His |
mouth :
10 He is brought as a lámb | to the | slaughter ;
and as a sheep before her shearers is
dumb * só He | openeth | not His |
mouth.
11 He was taken from prison | and from |
judgment : and whó shall de- | -clare
His | gener- | -ation?
12 For He was cut óff out of the lánd | of
the | living : for the transgréssion of
My | people | was He | stricken.
13 And He made His gráve | with the |
wicked : and with the | rich | in His
death ;
14 Becáuse He had | done no | violence :
neither was ány de- | -ceit | in His |
mouth.
15 Yet it pléased the | Lórd to | bruise Him :
yéa He hath | put | Him to | grief ;
16 When Thou shalt make His sóul an |
offering - for | sin : He shall see His
seed * Hé | shall pro- | -long His | days.
17 And the pléasure | of the | Lord : shall |
prosper | in His | hand.
18 He shall see of the trávail | of His | soul :
ánd | shall be | satis- | -fied ;
19 By His knowledge shall my ríghteous
sérvant | justify | many : for Hé shall |
bear | their in- | -iquities.
20 Therefore will | divide Him a pórtion |
with the | great : and He shall divide
the | spoil | with the | strong ;
21 Because He hath poured out His sóul |
unto | death : And Hé was | numbered |
with the | trans- | -gressors ;
22 And He báre the | sin of | many : and
máde inter- | -cession | for the - trans- |
gressors.

1023   ISAIAH LV.

HO, every one that thirsteth, cóme ye | to
the | waters : and he that hath no
móney | come ye | buy and | eat ;
2 Yea cóme buy | wine and | milk : without
móney | and with- | -out | price.
3 Wherefore do ye spend money for thát
which | is not | bread : and your labour
for thát which | satis- | -fieth | not?
4 Hearken diligently unto me, and éat ye |
that which | is good : and let your sóul
de- | -light it- | -self in | fatness.
5 Incline your ear, and cóme | unto | me ;
héar | and your | soul shall | live :
6 And I will make an everlasting cóve- |
nant with | you . éven the | sure |
mercies of | David.
7 Behold, I have given him for a witness
to the | people : a léader and com-
mander | to the | people.
8 Behold, thou shalt call a nation thát thou |
knowest | not : and nations that knew
not thée shall | run | unto | thee,
9 Becáuse of the Lord thy Gód * and for
the Hóly | One - of | Israel : for Hé hath
glori- | -fied | thee.

283

CANTICLES.

10 Seek ye the Lord while He | may be | found : call ye upon Him | while | He is | near:
11 Let the wicked for- | -sake his | way : ánd the un- | -righteous | man his | thoughts:
12 And let him return unto the Lord ✱ and He will have | mercy • up- | -on him: and to our God ✱ for He will a- | -bundant- | -ly | pardon.
13 For my thoughts áre not | your | thoughts: neither are your ways | My ways | saith the | Lord.
14 For as the heavens are higher | than the | earth : so are My ways higher than your ways ✱ and My" | thoughts than | your | thoughts.
15 For as the rain cometh down, ánd the | snow from | heaven : and returneth not thither ✱ but | water- | -eth the | earth,
16 And maketh it bring | forth and | bud : that it may give seed to the sower ✱ and | bread | to the | eater :
17 So shall My word be that goeth fórth out of • My | mouth : it shall not return • unto | Me | void,
18 But it shall accomplish | that which • I | please ; and it shall prósper in the thing where- | -to I | sent it.
19 For ye shall gó | out with | joy : ánd be | led | forth with | peace :
20 The mountains and the hills shall break forth befóre you | into | singing : and all the trées of the | field shall | clap their | hands.
21 Instead of the thórn sha'l come | up the | fir tree : and instead of the brier shall | come | up the | myrtle tree :
22 And it shall be to the Lórd | for a | name : for an everlasting sign that shall | not be | cut | off.

1024 ISAIAH LX. 1, 2, 3 ; IX. 2, 6, 7.

ARISE, shine ✱ fór thy | light is | come : and the glóry of the | Lord is | risen • up- | -on thee.
2 For behold, the dárkness shall | cover • the | earth : and gróss | dark- | -ness the | people.
3 But the Lórd shall a- | -rise up- | -on thee : and His glóry | shall be | seen up- | on thee.
4 And the Gentiles shall cóme | to thy | light and kings to the | brightness | of thy | rising.
5 The péople that | walked in | darkness | have | seen a | great | light.
6 They that dwell in the lánd of the | shadow • of | death : upon thém | hath the | light | shined.
7 For unto us a Child is born, unto ús a | Son is | given : and the government shall | be up | -on His | shoulder :
8 And His name shall be called Wonderful, Counsellor, ✱ the | mighty | God : the everlasting Father ✱ the | Prince | of | Peace.

9 Of the increase of His government and péace there shall | be no | end : upon the throne of David ✱ and upón His | kingdom • to | order | it.
10 And to estáblish | it with | judgment : and with jústice from | henceforth | even • for | ever.

1025 LAMENTATIONS III. 22-27, 31-33, 39-41.

IT is of the Lord's mercies that we áre | not con- | -sumed : becáuse | His com- | passions | fail not.
2 They are nów | every | morning : great | is Thy | faithful | -ness.
3 The Lord is my pórtion, | saith my | soul : thérefore | will I | hope in | Him.
4 The Lord is good unto thém that | wait for | Him : tó the | soul that | seeketh | Him.
5 It is good that a man should both hópe and | quietly | wait : fór the sal- | -vation | of the | Lord.
6 It is góod | for a | man : that he béar the | yoke | in his | youth.
7 For the Lord will not cást | off for | ever : but though He cause grief, yet will He have compassion ✱ according to the | multitude | of His | mercies.
8 For He doth not af- | -flict | willingly : nór | grieve the | children • of | men.
9 Wherefore doth a líving | man com- | plain : a mán for the | punishment | of his | sins?
10 Let us séarch and | try our | ways : and túrn a- | -gain | to the | Lord :
11 [2 pt.] Let us lift up our héart | with our | hands : únto | God | in the | heavens.

1026 HABAKKUK III. 2-6, 10, 11, 13, 17, 18.

O LORD, I have heard Thy speech ✱ and | was a- | -fraid : O Lord, revive Thy wórk in the | midst | of the | years,
2 In the midst of the | years make | known : in | wrath re- | -member | mercy.
3 Gód | came from | Teman : ánd the | Holy One | from mount | Paran.
4 His glóry | covered • the | heavens : and the éarth was | full | of His | praise.
5 And His brightness was | as the | light : He had rays coming forth from His hand ✱ and thére was the | hiding | of His | power.
6 Before Him | went the | pestilence : and burning cóals went | forth | at His | feet.
7 He stóod and | measured • the | earth : He behéld ✱ and | drove a- | -sunder • the | nations.
8 And the everlasting mountains were scattered ✱ the perpétual | hills did | bow ; his | ways are | ever- | -lasting.
9 The mountains sáw Thee, | and they trembled : the overflówing of the | water | passed | by :

SELECTIONS FROM THE NEW TESTAMENT.

10 The deep | uttered · his | voice : and
lifted | up his | hands on | high
11 The sun and moon stood still in their |
habi- | -tation: at the light of Thine |
arrows they went * and at the shining |
of Thy | glittering | spear.
12 Thou wentest forth for the salvation | of |
Thy | people : even for salvation | with |
Thine an- | -ointed.

13 Although the fig tree | shall not | blossom |
neither shall | fruit be | in the | vines.
14 The labour of the | olive · shall | fail : and
the | fields shall | yield no | meat.
15 The flock shall be cut off | from the |
fold : and there shall be no | herd | in
the | stalls.
16 Yet I will rejoice | in the | Lord : I will
joy in the | God of | my sal- | -vation.

SELECTIONS FROM THE NEW TESTAMENT.

1027   Matthew V. 3-12.

BLÉSSED are **the** | poor in | spirit : for
théirs **| is the |** kingdom of | heaven.
2 Bléssed are | they that | mourn : fór | they |
shall be | comforted.
3 Bléssed | **are** the | meek : for théy | **shall**
in- | -hérit · the | earth.
4 Blessed are they which do hunger and
thirst | after | righteousness: fór | they |
shall be | filled.
5 Bléssed | are the | merciful : **for théy |**
shall ob- | -tain | mercy.
6 Bléssed are the | pure in | **heart : fór |**
they shall | see | God.
7 Bléssed | are the | peacemakers : for they
shall be cálled the | children | of | God
8 Blessed are they which are persecuted *
for righteous- · -ness | sake : for theirs |
is the | kingdo- of | heaven.
9 Bléssed **are** ye, when men shall **revile**
you * and | perse · cute | you : and
shall say all manner **of** evil agáinst you |
falsely | for My | sake.
10 Rejoice and be ex- | -ceeding | glad : for
great is **your re- | -ward in |** heaven.

1028   Romans VIII. 31-39.

IF | God be | **for us :** whó | - can | be
a- | -gainst us?
2 He that spared not His **own Son** * but
delivered Him up | for **us | all |** how
shall He not with Him also **| freely |**
give us | all things?
3 Who shall lay anything to the chárge of |
God's e- | -lect : It is God that justifieth *
who is · he | that con- | -demneth?
4 It is Christ that died * yea rather that
is | risen - a- | -gáin : who is even at the
right hand of God * who also máketh |
inter- | -cession | for us.
5 Who shall separate us from the | love of |
Christ : shall tribulation, or distress, or
persecution * or famine or nakedness *
or | peril, | or | sword?
6 As it is written, For Thy sake we are
killed | all the · day | long : we are ac-
cóunted as | sheep | for the | slaughter :

7 Nay, in **all these** things we **are |** more
than | conquerors : through | Him that |
loved | us.
8 For I am persuaded, that néither | death
nor | life ; nor angels, nor principalities,
nor powers * nor things | present ·
nor | things to | come,
9 [2 pt.] Nor height, **nor** depth * nor any |
other | creature : shall be able to separ-
ate us from the **love** of God * which is in
Christ | Jesus **| our |** Lord.

1029   I Corinthians XV. 20-23, 51-57.

NOW is Christ risen | from the | dead :
and become the | first · fruits of | them
that | slept.
2 For since by | man came | death : **by man**
came also the resur- | -rection | of the |
dead.
3 **For as in Ádam | all | die : even so in
Christ shall | all be |** made a- | -live.
4 **But every mán in** his **own | order :
Christ the** first-fruits * **afterward théy**
that are **| Christ's | at His | coming.**
5 Behold, I shéw | you a | **mystery : wé |**
shall not | all | sleep,
6 But we shall | all be | changed : **in a**
moment, in the twinkling of an **éye |**
at the | last | trump :
7 For the trúmpet | shall | sound | : and the
dead shall be raised incorruptible *
and | we | shall be | changed
8 For this corruptible must put on | incor- |
ruption : and this mortal must put |
on | immor- | -tality.
9 So when this corruptible shall have put
ón | incor- | -ruption : and this mortal
shall have put | on | immor- | -tality.
10 Then shall be brought to pass the sáying |
that is | written : death is | swallowed |
up in | victory.
11 O death, whére | is thy | sting O gráve, |
where | is thy | victory?
12 The sting | of déath | is | sin : and the
strength of | sin | is the | law.
13 [2 pt.] But thánks | be to | God : which
giveth us the victory * through our |
Lord | Jesus | Christ.

ANCIENT HYMNS OF THE CHURCH.

1030 1 COR. V. 7-8; ROM. VI. 9-11;
          1 COR. XV. 20-22.

CHRIST our passover is sacri- | -ficed · for | us : therefore | let us | keep the | feast.
2 Not with the old leaven ∗ neither with the leaven of | malice · and | wicked- ness : but with the unleavened bread of sin- | -cer- | -ty and | truth.
3 Christ being raised from the dead | dieth · no | more : death hath no more do- | minion | over | Him.
4 For in that He died ∗ He died unto | sin | once : but in that He liveth ∗ He | liv- eth | unto | God.
5 Likewise reckon ye also yourselves to be dead indeed | unto | sin : but alive unto God through | Jesus | Christ our | Lord.
6 Now is Christ risen | from the | dead : and become the | first · fruits of | them that | slept.
7 For since by | man came | death : by man came also the resur- | -rection | of the | dead.
8 For as in Adam | all | die : even so in Christ shall | all be | made a- | -live.

1031 EPHESIANS III. 14-21.

I BOW my knees unto the Father of our Lord | Jesus | Christ : of whom the whole family in | heaven and | earth is | named.
2 That He would grant you ∗ according to the riches | of His | glory : to be strengthened with might by His Spirit in the | inner | man ;
3 That Christ may dwell in your | hearts by | faith : that ye, being rooted and | grounded | in | love,

4 May be able to comprehend with | all | saints : what is the breadth and | length and | depth and | height ;
5 And to know the love of Christ which | passeth | knowledge : that ye might be filled with | all the | fulness · of | God.
6 Now unto Him that is able to do exceed- ing abundantly ∗ above all that we | ask or | think : according to the | power that | worketh | in us,
7 [2 pt.] Unto Him be glory in the Church by Christ Jesus ∗ through- | -out all | ages : world without | end. A- | -men.

1032 REVELATION I. 5-8 ; IV. 8, 11.

UNTO | Him that | loved us : and washed us from our sins | in His | own | blood,
2 And hath made us kings and priests unto God | and His | Father : to Him be glory and dominion ∗ for ever and | ever. | A- | -men.
3 Behold He | cometh · with | clouds ; and | every | eye shall | see Him,
4 And they also which | pierced | Him : and all kindreds of the earth shall | wail be- | -cause of | Him.
5 I am | Alpha · and | Omega : the begin- ning and the ending | saith | the | Lord,
6 Which is | and which | was : and which is to | come | the Al- | -mighty.
7 Holy | Holy, | Holy : Lord | God | Al- | mighty,
8 Which was | and | is : and | is | to | come.
9 Thou art | worthy · O | Lord : to receive | glory · and | honour · and | power ;
10 For Thou hast cre- | -ated | all things : and for Thy pleasure they | are, and | were cre- | -ated.

ANCIENT HYMNS OF THE CHURCH.

1033 TE DEUM LAUDAMUS.

WE praise | Thee O | God : we acknow- ledge | Thee to | be the | Lord.
2 All the earth doth | worship | Thee ; the | Father | ever- | -lasting.
3 To Thee all Angels | cry a- | -loud : the Heavens, and | all the | Powers there- | -in.
4 To Thee Cherubin and | Seraph- | -in : con- | -tinual- | -ly do | cry,
5 Holy | Holy | Holy : Lord | God of | Saba- | -oth.
6 Heaven and earth are full of the | Ma- jes- | -ty : of | Thy | Glo- | -ry.
7 The glorious company | of · the | A- | postles : praise | — | — | Thee.

8 The goodly fellowship | of the | Prophets : praise | — | — | Thee.
9 [2 pt.] The noble | army · of | Martyrs : praise | — | — | Thee.
10 The holy Church throughout | all the | world : doth ac- | -know- | -ledge | Thee ;
11 The | Fa- | -ther : of an | Infinite | Ma- jes- | -ty ;
12 Thine honour- | -able, | true : and | on- | -ly | Son ;
13 Also the | Holy | Ghost : the | Com- | fort- | -er.
14 Thou art the | King of | Glory : O | — | — | Christ.
15 Thou art the ever- | -lasting | Son : of | — | the | Fa- | -ther.
16 When Thou tookest upon Thee to de- | liver | man : Thou didst not ab- | -hor the | Virgin's | womb.

ANCIENT HYMNS OF THE CHURCH.

17 When Thou hadst overcóme the | sharpness · of | death : Thou didst open the Kingdom of | Heaven to | all be- | lievers.
18 Thou sittest **at the** right | hand **of** | God : in the | Glory | **of** the | Father.
19 We believe that | **Thou** shalt | come : tó | be | our | Judge.
20 We therefore pray **Thee** | help Thy | servants : **whom Thou** hast redeemed | with Thy | precious | blood.
21 Make them **to be** númbered | with **Thy** | Saints : in | **glory** | **ever-** | -lasting.
22 O Lórd | **save Thy** | **people** : ánd | bless Thine | herit- | -age.
23 Góv- | -ern | them : ánd | lift them | up for | ever.
24 Dáy | **by** | day : wé | magni- | -fy | Thee ;
25 **Ánd** we | worship · Thy | Name : éver | world with- | -out | end.
26 Vóuch- | -safe O | Lord : to keep us **this** | day with- | -out | sin.
27 O Lórd have | mercy · up- | -on us : háve | mer- | -cy up- | -on us.
28 O Lord let **Thy** mércy | lighten · **up-** | -on us : ás our | trust | is in | Thee.
29 O **Lord in Thée** | have I | trusted : let me , **never** | be con- | -founded.

Bishop Ambrose of Milan. 4th Century.

1034 MAGNIFICAT. LUKE I. 46-55.

MY soul doth mágni- | -fy the | Lord : and my spirit hath re- | -joiced · in | God my | Saviour.
2 Fór He | hath re- | -garded : the lówliness | of His | hand- | -maiden.
3 Fór be- | -hold from | henceforth : áll gener- | -ations · shall | call me | blessed.
4 For He that is mighty hath | magnified | me : ánd | holy | is His | Name.
5 And His mércy is **on** | them that | fear Him : throughóut | all | gener- | -ations.
6 He hath shewed strength | with His | arm . He hath scattered the proud in the imágin- | -ation | of their | hearts.
7 He hath put down the mighty | from their | seat : and háth **ex-** | -alted · **the** | humble and | meek.
8 He hath filled the húngry with | good | things : and the rích He hath | sent empty · **a-** | -way.
9 [2 *pt*.] He remembering His mercy hath hólpen His | servant | Israel : as He promised to our forefathers ✱ Ábraham | and his | seed for | ever.

1035 BENEDICTUS. LUKE I. 68-79.

BLESSED **be the Lórd** | **God of** | Israel : for He hath **visited** | **and re-** | -deemed His | people ;
2 And hath raised up a mighty sal- | -vation | for us : in the hóuse | of His | servant | David ;
3 As He spake by the móuth of His | holy | Prophets : which have béen | since the | world be- | -gan ;
4 That we should be sáved | from our | enemies : and fróm the | hands of | all that | hate us ;
5 To perform the mercy prómised | to our | forefathers : ánd to re- | -member · His | holy | Covenant ;
6 To perform the **oath which** He sware to our | forefather | **Abraham** : thát | He would | give | us ;
7 That we being delivered out of the hánd | of our | enemies : might sérve | Him with- | -out | fear ;
8 In holiness and ríghteous- | -ness be- | fore Him : áll the | days | of our | life.
9 And thou Child shalt be called the Próphet | of the | Highest . for thou shalt go before the **face of** the | Lórd | to pre- | pare His | ways ;
10 To give knowledge **of** salvátion | unto · His | people : fór the re- | -mission | of their | sins,
11 Through the ténder mércy | of our | God : whereby the day-spring fróm on | high hath | visited | us ;
12 To give light to them that sit in dárkness ✱ and in the | shadow | of | death : and to guide our féet | into | the | way of | peace.

1036 NUNC DIMITTIS. LUKE II. 29-32.

LORD, now lettest Thou Thy sérvant de- | -part in | peace, ác- | -cording | to Thy | word.
2 Fór mine | eyes have | **seen : Thy*** | — sal- | -va- | -tion,
3 Whích Thou | hast pre- | -pared : befóre the | face of | all | people ;
4 Tó be a light to | lighten · the | Gentiles : and to be the glóry | of Thy | people | Israel.

1037 GLORIA IN EXCELSIS.

GLORY bé to | God on | high : and on earth peace ✱ good | will | towards | men.
2 We praise Thee, we bless Thee, we worship Thee ✱ we glóri- | -fy | Thee : we give thanks to Thée | for Thy | great | glory.
3 O Lord Gód | **Heavenly** | **King** : Gód the | Father | **Al-** | -mighty.
4 O Lord, the only begotten Són | Jesus | Christ : O Lord God, Lamb of Gód, | Son | of the | Father.
5 Thou that takest away the síns, | of the | world : háve | mer- | -cy up- | -on us.
6 Thou that takest away the síns | of the | world : háve | mer- | -cy up- | -on us.
7 Thou that takest away the síns | of the | world : re- | -ceive | our | prayer.
8 Thou that sittest at the right hánd of | God the | Father : háve | mer- | -cy up- | on us.

ANCIENT HYMNS OF THE CHURCH.

9 For Thóu | only - art | holy : Thóu | only |
   art the | Lord.
10 Thou only, O Christ, with the | Holy |
   Ghost : art most high in the glory of
   God the | Father. | A- | -men.

1038 *All Thy works shall praise Thee, O Lord.*—Psalm cxlv. 10.

THE strain upraise of joy and praise.
                      Hallelujah !

2 To the glory of their King
   Shall the ransomed people sing
                      Hallelujah !

3 And the choirs that dwell on high
   Shall re-echo through the sky
                      Hallelujah !

4 They in the rest of Paradise who dwell,
   The blessed ones with joy the chorus
   swell
                      Hallelujah !

5 The planets glittering on their heavenly
   way,
   The shining constellations, join and say
                      Hallelujah !

6 Ye clouds that onward sweep,
   Ye winds on pinions light,
   Ye thunders, echoing loud and deep,
   Ye lightnings, wildly bright,
   In sweet consent unite your Hallelujah !

7 Ye floods and ocean billows,
   Ye storms and winter snow,
   Ye days of cloudless beauty,
   Hoar frost and summer glow,
   Ye groves that wave in spring,
   And glorious forests, sing   Hallelujah !

8 First let the birds, with painted plumage
   gay,
   Exalt their great Creator's praise, and say
                      Hallelujah !

9 Then let the beasts of earth, with varying strain,
   Join in creation's hymn, and cry again
                      Hallelujah !

10 Here let the mountains thunder forth
   sonorous   Hallelujah !
   There let the valleys sing in gentler
   chorus   Hallelujah !

11 Thou jubilant abyss of ocean, cry
                      Hallelujah !
   Ye tracts of earth and continents, reply
                      Hallelujah !

12 To God, who all creation made,
    The frequent hymn be duly paid :
                      Hallelujah !

13 This is the strain, the eternal strain, the
    Lord Almighty loves;   Hallelujah !
    This is the song, the heavenly song, that
    Christ Himself approves : Hallelujah !

14 Wherefore we sing, both heart and voice
   awaking,   Hallelujah !
   And children's voices echo, answer
   making,   Hallelujah !

15 Now from all men be outpoured
   Hallelujah to the Lord ;
   With Hallelujah evermore
   The Son and Spirit we adore.

16 Praise be done to the Three in One.
   Hallelujah ! Hallelujah ! Hallelujah !
              Godescalcus, 10th Century.
              Tr. J. M. Neale. 1851.

1039   10.10.7.
A great voice of much people in heaven, saying Hallelujah.
Revelation xix. 1.

SING Hallelujah forth in duteous praise,
   Ye citizens of heaven ; O sweetly raise
               An endless Hallelujah.

2 Ye powers who stand before the Eternal
   Light,
   In hymning choirs re-echo to the height
               An endless Hallelujah.

3 The Holy City shall take up your strain,
   And with glad songs resounding wake
   again   An endless Hallelujah.

4 In blissful antiphons ye thus rejoice
   To render to the Lord with thankful voice
               An endless Hallelujah.

5 Ye who have gained at length your palms
   in bliss,
   Victorious ones, your chant shall still be
   this,   An endless Hallelujah.

6 There, in one grand acclaim, for ever ring
   The strains which tell the honour of your
   King,   An endless Hallelujah.

7 This is sweet rest for weary ones brought
   back,
   This is glad food and drink which ne'er
   shall lack,   An endless Hallelujah.

8 While Thee, by whom were all things
   made, we praise
   For ever, and tell out in sweetest lays
               An endless Hallelujah.

9 Almighty Christ, to Thee our voices sing
   Glory for evermore ; to Thee we bring
            An endless Hallelujah. Amen.
        Mozarabic Breviary, 5th Century.
          Tr. John Ellerton. 1865.

1040   DIES IRÆ.   8.8.8.
The Lord grant unto him that he may find mercy of the Lord in that day !
2 Timothy 1. 18.

DAY of wrath, O Day of mourning !
   See once more the cross returning,
   Heaven and earth in ashes burning.

THE COMMANDMENTS.

2 O what fear man's bosom rendeth!
When from heaven the Judge descendeth,
On whose sentence all dependeth.

3 Wondrous sound the trumpet flingeth,
Through earth's sepulchres it ringeth,
All before the Throne it bringeth.

4 Death is struck, and nature quaking,
All creation is awaking,
To its Judge an answer making.

5 Lo the Book, exactly worded,
Wherein all hath been recorded,
Thence shall judgment be awarded.

6 When the Judge His seat attaineth,
And each hidden deed arraigneth,
Nothing unavenged remaineth.

7 What shall I, frail man, be pleading?
Who for me be interceding,
When the just are mercy needing?

8 **King of majesty tremendous,
Who dost free salvation send us,
Fount of Pity, then befriend us.**

9 Think, kind Jesus, my salvation
Caused Thy wondrous incarnation,
Leave me not to reprobation!

10 Faint and weary Thou hast sought me,
On the cross of suffering bought me;
Shall such grace be vainly brought me?

11 Righteous Judge of retribution,
Grant Thy gift of absolution,
Ere that reckoning-day's conclusion.

12 Guilty now I pour my moaning,
All my shame with anguish owning,
Spare, O God, Thy suppliant groaning!

13 Thou the sinful woman savest;
Thou the dying thief forgavest,
And to me a hope vouchsafest.

14 **Worthless are my** prayers and sighing,
Yet, good Lord, in grace complying,
Rescue me from fires undying.

15 **With Thy favoured** sheep, O place me!
Nor among the goats abase me,
But to Thy right hand upraise me.

16 While the wicked are confounded,
Doomed to flames of woe unbounded,
Call me, with Thy saints surrounded.

17 Low I kneel, with heart-submission,
See, like ashes, my contrition,
Help me, in my last condition.

18 Ah that Day of tears and mourning!
From the dust of earth returning,
Man for judgment must prepare him;
Spare, O God, in mercy spare him!

19 Lord, all pitying, **Jesus** blest,
Grant us Thine eternal rest. Amen.
From the Latin. Tr. W. J. Irons, 1848.
Verse nineteen Tr. Isaac Williams. 1839.

SANCTUS.

1041 HOLY, holy, holy, Lord God of hosts; heaven and earth are full of Thy glory.
Glory be to Thee, O Lord most high.

THE COMMANDMENTS.

1042 EXODUS XX. 1–17.

GOD spake all these words, saying,

I. I am the Lord thy God, which have brought thee out of the land of Egypt, out of the house of bondage. Thou shalt have no other gods before me.
Lord, have mercy upon us, and incline our hearts to keep this law.

II. Thou shalt not make unto thee any graven image, or any likeness of anything that is in heaven above, or that is in the earth beneath, or that is in the water under the earth: thou shalt not bow down thyself to them, nor serve them: for I the Lord thy God am a jealous God, visiting the iniquity of the fathers upon the children unto the third and fourth generation of them that hate Me; and shewing mercy unto thousands of them that love Me, and keep My commandments.
Lord, have mercy upon us, and incline our hearts to keep this law.

THE COMMANDMENTS.

III. Thou shalt not take the name of the Lord thy God in vain; for the Lord will not hold him guiltless that taketh His name in vain.
Lord, have mercy upon us, and incline our hearts to keep this law.

IV. Remember the sabbath-day, to keep it holy. Six days shalt thou labour, and do all thy work: but the seventh day is the sabbath of the Lord thy God: in it thou shalt not do any work, thou, nor thy son, nor thy daughter, thy man-servant, nor thy maid-servant, nor thy cattle, nor thy stranger that is within thy gates: for in six days the Lord made heaven and earth, the sea, and all that in them is, and rested the seventh day: wherefore the Lord blessed the sabbath-day, and hallowed it.
Lord, have mercy upon us, and incline our hearts to keep this law.

V. Honour thy father and thy mother: that thy days may be long upon the land which the Lord thy God giveth thee.
Lord, have mercy upon us, and incline our hearts to keep this law.

VI. Thou shalt not kill.
Lord, have mercy upon us, and incline our hearts to keep this law.

VII. Thou shalt not commit adultery.
Lord, have mercy upon us, and incline our hearts to keep this law.

VIII. Thou shalt not steal.
Lord, have mercy upon us, and incline our hearts to keep this law.

IX. Thou shalt not bear false witness against thy neighbour.
Lord, have mercy upon us, and incline our hearts to keep this law.

X. Thou shalt not covet thy neighbour's house, thou shalt not covet thy neighbour's wife, nor his man-servant, nor his maid-servant, nor his ox, nor his ass, nor anything that is thy neighbour's.
Lord, have mercy upon us, and write all these Thy laws in our hearts, we beseech Thee.

ALPHABETICAL INDEX TO HYMNS.

	HYMN
A charge to keep I have	588
A few more years shall roll	751
A fountain of life and of grace	58
A gladsome hymn of praise	912
A glory gilds the sacred page	302
A nation God delights to	962
A safe stronghold our God	561
A thousand oracles divine	162
Abide with me, fast falls the	271
Above the clear blue sky, Be-	918
Above the clear blue sky, In	919
Abraham when severely tried	411
According to Thy gracious	725
Across the sky the shades of	742
Again our weekly labours end	232
Again we lift our voice	795
Ah, Lord, with trembling I	589
Ah, whither should I go	370
Alas! and did my Saviour	109
All glory to God in the sky	676
All hail the power of Jesus'	49
All my heart this night	75
All nature's works His praise	873
All people that on earth do	172
All praise to our redeeming	684
All thanks be to God	675
All thanks to the Lamb, who	705
All things are Thine; no gift	869
All things bright and	923
All things praise Thee, Lord	174
All ye that pass by, To Jesus	99
Almighty Father, hear our	891
Almighty Maker of my frame	754
Am I a soldier of the Cross	565
And am I only born to die	759
And are we yet alive	693
And can it be that I should	443
And let our bodies part	696
Angels from the realms of	80
Angel voices ever singing	170
Another year has now begun	832
Another year is dawning	831
Approach, my soul, the mercy-	628
Are there not in the labourer's	570
Arise, my soul, arise	442
Arise, O Lord, and shine	812
Arm of the Lord, awake	796
Art thou weary, art thou	90

	HYMN
As helpless as a child who	449
As Jesus sought His wandering	620
As pants the hart for cooling	608
As when the weary traveller	774
As with gladness men of old	65
At even ere the sun was set	254
At evening time when day is	278
At Thy feet, our God and	833
Author of faith, Eternal Word	460
Awake, glad soul! awake	112
Awake, my soul, and with the	256
Awake, our souls! away, our	577
Away, my needless fears	579
Away with our fears, the glad	954
Away with our sorrow and	775
Before Jehovah's awful throne	171
Before the great Three-One	207
Begin my soul some heavenly	38
Behold how good a thing	695
Behold, O Lord our God	958
Behold! the mountain of the	811
Behold the Saviour of	100
Behold the servant of the Lord	649
Behold us, Lord, a little space	717
Behold what witnesses unseen	602
Being of beings, God of love!	214
Be it my only wisdom here	591
Be present at our table, Lord	979
Be still my soul: the Lord is	559
Be Thou my guardian and	927
Be with us, gracious Lord	868
Birds have their quiet nest	361
Blessed are the humble souls	480
Blessed be God our God	354
Blessed Saviour, Thou hast	93
Blest be our everlasting Lord	41
Blest be the dear uniting love	970
Blest be the tie that binds	738
Blow ye the trumpet, blow	807
Brief life is here our portion	755
Brightest and best of the sons	67
Brightly, O Father, when	223
Build us in one body up	702
Call them in, the poor and	322
Captain and Saviour of the	885
Captain of Israel's host and	493
Captain of our salvation	906

ALPHABETICAL INDEX TO HYMNS.

	HYMN		HYMN
Cast on the fidelity	528	Come, ye thankful people	851
Christ is the foundation	863	Come ye that love the Lord	197
Christ Jesus lay in death's	117	Come, ye weary sinners, come	323
Christ, the Lord, is risen	111	Comfort, ye ministers of grace	526
Christ will gather in His own	834	Commit thou all thy griefs	31
Christian! dost thou see them	568	Creator Spirit, by whose aid	136
Christian, work for Jesus	956	Crown Him with many crowns	128
Christian, seek not yet repose	592	Crown with Thy benediction	842
Christians, awake, salute the	77		
Clouds and darkness round	598	Day by day the manna fell	26
Cold and cheerless, dark and	815	Day of wrath, O day of	1010
Come, all whoe'er have set	739	Dear Master, what can	935
Come, all who truly bear	727	Deepen the wounds Thy	409
Come, and let us sweetly join	740	Depth of mercy, can there be	344
Come, Father, Son, and Holy	907	Dismiss me not Thy service	652
Come, Father, Son, and Holy	163	Drawn to the cross which	396
Come, Holy Ghost, all-quick-	142	Drooping soul, shake off thy	605
Come, Holy Ghost, in love	149	Dwell in me richly, blessed	292
Come, Holy Ghost, our hearts	153		
Come, Holy Ghost, Thine	736	Entered the holy place above	119
Come, Holy Spirit, calm our	152	Equip me for the war	567
Come, Holy Spirit, heavenly	140	Eternal beam of Light Divine	530
Come, Holy Spirit, raise our	132	Eternal Father, strong to save	888
Come in, thou blessed of the	704	Eternal light! Eternal light	10
Come, let us anew our journey	744	Eternal Power, whose high	1
Come, let us anew our journey	745	Eternal source of every joy	826
Come, let us arise, and press	650	Eternal Spirit! by whose	155
Come, let us ascend, my	741	Except the Lord conduct the	495
Come, let us join our cheerful	179	Except the Lord the temple	864
Come, let us join our friends	794	Expand Thy wings, celestial	143
Come, let us join the hosts	915		
Come, let us to the Lord our	558	Faith of our fathers, living	578
Come, let us use the grace	746	Far from my thoughts, vain	217
Come, let us who in Christ	311	Far from the world, O Lord	915
Come, my soul, thou must be	257	Father, beneath Thy sheltering	40
Come, my soul, thy suit	621	Father, how wide Thy glory	22
Come, O my God, the promise	428	Father, I dare believe	410
Come, O Thou all-victorious	365	Father, I know that all my	653
Come, O Thou Prophet of	295	Father, if justly still we claim	144
Come, O Thou Traveller	379	Father, in high heaven	279
Come on, my partners in	560	Father, in the name I pray	529
Come, Saviour Jesus, from	454	Father, into Thy hands alone	643
Come, sinners, to the Gospel	318	Father, let Thy benediction	942
Come, sound His praise abroad	16	Father of all, again we meet	270
Come, Thou all-inspiring	148	Father of all, in whom alone	294
Come, Thou everlasting Spirit	150	Father of Jesus Christ, my	918
Come, Thou fount of every	194	Father of Jesus Christ, my	346
Come, Thou long-expected	66	Father of lights, again these	258
Come, Thou omniscient Son	473	Father of love and power	280
Come to Calvary's holy	319	Father of love, our guide and	496
Come to our poor nature's	158	Father of me and all mankind	164
Come unto Me, ye weary	308	Father of mercies, in Thy	280
Come wisdom, power and	222	Father of omnipresent grace	637
Come, ye sinners, poor and	321	Father, Son and Holy Ghost	612

ALPHABETICAL INDEX TO HYMNS.

	HYMN		HYMN
Father, Thy will, not mine	539	God of the living, in whose	767
Father, to Thee I lift mine	940	God only wise, almighty, good	908
Father, to Thee my soul I lift	383	God save our gracious Queen	919
Father, whate'er of earthly	541	God sendeth sun, He sendeth	518
Father, who art alone	803	God the Lord is King! before	2
Father, whose everlasting love	369	God that madest earth and	281
Fierce raged the tempest o'er	89	Golden harps are sounding	135
Fight the good fight with all	566	Good Thou art and good	43
Fill Thou my life, O Lord	221	Gracious Redeemer, shake	593
For all the saints, who from	791	Gracious Saviour, gentle	939
For all Thy care we bless	268	Gracious Spirit, dwell with me	129
For all Thy love and goodness	836	Great Giver of all good	848
For ever here my rest shall	405	Great Giver of all good to	855
For ever with the Lord	776	Great God, as seasons	854
For the beauty of the earth	200	Great God attend while Zion	248
For thousand, thousand	516	Great God, indulge my	292
For Thy mercy and Thy grace	830	Great God of hosts, our ears	963
Forgive us for Thy mercies'	747	Great God, Thy watchful care	870
Forth in Thy name, O Lord	618	Great God! to me the sight	61
Forward! be our watchword	573	Great God! what do I see	762
Fountain of mercy, God of	841	Great God, whose universal	808
Friend after friend departs	753	Great is the Lord our God	248
From all that dwell below the	813	Great King of nations, hear	968
From every stormy wind that	719	Great Ruler of the land and	892
From Greenland's icy mountains	805	Great Shepherd of Thy people	873
		Guide me, O Thou great	490
Give me the faith which can	707		
Give me the wings of faith to	840	Hail Father, Son, and Holy	165
Give to the winds thy fears	354	Hail sacred day of earthly	235
Glory be to God on high	161	Hail the day that sees Him	118
Glory to God on high	201	Hail, Thou once despised	95
Glory to Thee, my God, this	209	Hail to the Lord's anointed	804
Go labour on; spend and be	616	Hallelujah! hallelujah!	116
Go, messengers of peace	623	Happy man whom God doth	21
Go to dark Gethsemane	104	Happy soul that free from	412
God! be merciful to me	533	Happy the heart where graces	456
God bless our native land	941	Happy the man that finds the	419
God is gone up on high	123	Happy the souls to Jesus	673
God is in this and every place	372	Hark, a voice divides the sky	841
God is love, that anthem	203	Hark! hark! my soul, angelic	793
God is the refuge of His	28	Hark, the glad sound: the	64
God make my life a little	940	Hark! the Gospel news is	335
God might have made the	817	Hark, the herald angels sing	79
God moves in a mysterious	27	Hark the song of jubilee	808
God of all consolation, take	972	Hark! the voice eternal	81
God of all power, and truth	486	Hark, 'tis the watchman's cry	587
God of all-redeeming grace	654	Hark, what mean those holy	76
God of almighty love	641	Head of Thy Church triumphant	672
God of eternal truth and	455	Hearken to the solemn voice	771
God of mercy, hear our	505	Hear us Thou that broodest	157
God of mercy and of love	915	Hear what the voice from	779
God of my life, through all	674	He dies: the Friend of sinners	113
God of my life, to Thee	433	He is gone—a cloud of light	120
God of my life, whose	510	He leadeth me! O blessed	491

ALPHABETICAL INDEX TO HYMNS.

Hymn	HYMN	Hymn	HYMN
He leads us on, by paths we	509	I would commune with Thee	624
Help, Lord, to whom for help	596	I'll praise my Maker while	177
Help me, my God, to speak	623	If thou but suffer God to	494
Here, Lord, assembled in Thy	955	If 'tis sweet to mingle where	718
Here, Lord, we offer Thee all	836	I'm kneeling at the threshold	951
High above every name	69	Immortal love, for ever full	126
Ho! every one that thirsts	310	In all my vast concerns with	11
Holy Ghost, inspire our praises	151	In full and glad surrender	426
Holy, holy, holy, Lord God	160	In memory of the Saviour's	728
Holy Lamb, who Thee confess	655	In the cross of Christ I glory	96
Holy Lamb, who Thee receive	422	In the dark and cloudy day	946
Holy Spirit! hear us	932	In this glad hour when children	911
Holy Spirit, truth divine	138	In Thy name, O Lord	249
How are Thy servants blest	897	Infinite God, to Thee we raise	166
How beauteous are their feet	815	Inspirer and hearer of prayer	947
How calmly the evening once	282	Inspirer of the ancient seers	293
How can a sinner know	357	Into Thy gracious hands I	505
How do Thy mercies close	36	Is thy cruse of comfort	645
How happy are we, who in	677	It came upon the midnight	72
How happy every child of	802	It is not death to die	736
How happy, gracious Lord!	678	It is Thy hand, my God	540
How happy is the pilgrim's	801	It passeth knowledge, that	453
How pleasant, how divinely	246		
How pleased and blest was I	241	Jerusalem divine	803
How precious is the book	296	Jerusalem, my happy home	784
How sad our state by nature	347	Jerusalem on high	786
How shall I walk my God to	909	Jerusalem the golden	785
How shall the mighty God	156	Jesus, accept the praise	971
How shall we worship Thee	215	Jesus, all-atoning Lamb	458
How sweet the name of Jesus	209	Jesus, at whose supreme	729
How weak the thoughts and	798	Jesus came, the heavens	70
		Jesus, friend of sinners, hear	607
I am coming to the cross	345	Jesus, great Shepherd of the	697
I am Thine, O Lord; I have	362	Jesus hath died that I might	459
I am trusting Thee, Lord	414	Jesus, high in glory	931
I ask the gift of righteousness	374	Jesus, if still the same Thou	377
I bless the Christ of God	52	Jesus, if still Thou art to-day	384
I could not do without Thee	415	Jesus! I live to Thee	432
I do not ask, O Lord, that	497	Jesus, I love Thy saving name	181
I gave My life for thee	336	Jesus, I my cross have taken	427
I gave myself to prayer	949	Jesus, I will trust Thee	348
I heard the voice of Jesus say	311	Jesus is our common Lord	53
I hear Thy welcome voice	328	Jesus is our Shepherd	929
I hoped that with the brave	952	Jesus, keep me near the cross	416
I know that my Redeemer	457	Jesus, King of glory	916
I know who makes the daisies	922	Jesus lives! no longer now	115
I lay my sins on Jesus	406	Jesus, Lord of life and glory	219
I lift my heart to Thee	441	Jesus, Lord, we look to Thee	698
I need Thee, precious Jesus	342	Jesus, lover of my soul	51
I the good fight have fought	575	Jesus, my King, to Thee I	576
I thirst, Thou wounded Lamb	353	Jesus, my life! Thyself apply	485
I want a principle within	595	Jesus, my Saviour, brother	600
I want the spirit of power	146	Jesus, my strength, my hope	597
I worship Thee, sweet Will of	534	Jesus, my truth, my way	498
294			

ALPHABETICAL INDEX TO HYMNS.

Hymn	HYMN		HYMN
Jesus, shall I never be	483	Lo! a voice from heaven hath	802
Jesus shall reign where'er the	809	Lo! God is here! let us	173
Jesus, Shepherd of the sheep	599	Lo! He comes with clouds	746
Jesus, still lead on	499	Lo! I come with joy to do	669
Jesus, the all-restoring word	460	Lo! the golden sun is shining	279
Jesus, the Conqueror, reigns	572	Long did I toil, and knew no	690
Jesus, the gift divine I know	88	Long have I sat beneath the	388
Jesus, the Life, the Truth, the	653	Long have I seemed to serve	343
Jesus, the name high over all	63	Looking unto Jesus	418
Jesus, the very thought of	182	Look, ye saints, the sight is	124
Jesus, the word of mercy give	476	Lord, and is Thine anger	358
Jesus, these eyes have never	59	Lord, as to Thy dear cross we	87
Jesus, Thou all-redeeming	313	Lord, can it be that I should	571
Jesus, Thou everlasting King	180	Lord, dismiss us with Thy	975
Jesus, Thou joy of loving	732	Lord God, by whom all	3
Jesus, Thou soul of all our	220	Lord God, the Holy Ghost	130
Jesus, Thou sovereign Lord	625	Lord, have mercy when we	729
Jesus, Thy blood and	98	Lord, I believe a rest remains	420
Jesus, Thy boundless love to	470	Lord, I hear of showers of	364
Jesus, Thy far-extended fame	92	Lord, if Thou Thy grace	619
Jesus, to Thee I now can fly	350	Lord, in the strength of grace	668
Jesus, united by Thy grace	699	Lord, in this Thy mercy's day	332
Jesus, we look to Thee	700	Lord, it belongs not to my	431
Jesus, we on the words depend	154	Lord, it is good for us to be	83
Jesus, we thus obey	726	Lord Jesus, shall it ever be	423
Jesus, where'er Thy people	213	Lord of all being, throned	47
Join all the glorious names	68	Lord of earth, Thy forming	15
Join all ye ransomed sons of	743	Lord of hosts, to Thee we	874
Just as I am, without one plea	407	Lord of the Church, we	710
		Lord of the harvest, hear	814
Knocking! knocking! who is	339	Lord of the harvest, once	857
		Lord of the harvest! Thee	836
Lamb of God, for sinners	385	Lord of the living harvest	858
Lamp of our feet, whereby	291	Lord of the Sabbath, hear our	245
Leader of faithful souls and	773	Lord of the sea: afar from	890
Lead, kindly Light, amid the	487	Lord of the wide-extended	895
Lead us, heavenly Father	500	Lord of the worlds above	212
Lead us, O Father, in the	501	Lord, pour Thy Spirit from	709
Leaning on Thee, my guide	503	Lord, speak to me, that I	501
Let all men rejoice, by Jesus	679	Lord, that I may learn of	616
Let all the world in every	188	Lord, Thy children guide and	492
Let all who truly bear	730	Lord, Thy children lowly	921
Let earth and heaven agree	372	Lord, we know that Thou art	679
Let everlasting glories crown	297	Lord, we Thy will obey	973
Let God, who comforts the	527	Lord, when we bend before	622
Let Him to whom we now	657	Lord, while for all mankind	961
Let not the wise his wisdom	314	Lord, whom winds and seas	900
Let us with a gladsome mind	176	Love divine, all loves excelling	452
Lift up your heads, ye mighty	193		
Light of life, seraphic fire	417	Master, I own Thy lawful	435
Light of light, enlighten me	240	Master, speak! Thy servant	944
Light of the world! whose	692	May the grace of Christ our	973
Light of those, whose dreary	489	Meet and right it is to sing	514
Light up this house with	872	Messiah, joy of every heart	167

ALPHABETICAL INDEX TO HYMNS.

	HYMN		HYMN
Mountains, by the darkness	536	O come and mourn with me	97
Much in sorrow, oft in woe	574	O come to the merciful	320
My body, soul and spirit	361	O day of rest and gladness	231
My faith looks up to Thee	399	O deem not they are blest	542
My Father and my God	437	O disclose Thy lovely face	378
My Father, it is good for me	686	O do not let the word depart	337
My God, and is Thy table	731	O for a closer walk with God	603
My God, how wonderful	187	O for a faith that will not	403
My God, I am Thine, what a	363	O for a heart to praise my	421
My God, I know, I feel Thee	464	O for a thousand tongues to	306
My God, I love Thee for	224	O for that tenderness of heart	392
My God, I love Thee; not	461	O Fount of good, to own Thy	879
My God, I thank Thee, who	186	O give thanks to Him who	260
My God, is any hour so sweet	626	O glorious hope of perfect	404
My God, my Father, while I	535	O God, by whom the seed is	298
My God, my God, to Thee I	376	O God, how often hath Thine	748
My God, my King, Thy	5	O God, my God, my all Thou	470
My God, the spring of all my	685	O God of Bethel, by whose	24
My heart and voice I raise	50	O God of good the unfathomed	4
My heart is full of Christ	56	O God of mercy, God of	651
My heart is resting, O my	217	O God of our forefathers hear	447
My heart, O God, be wholly	440	O God! our help in ages past	750
My Jesus I love Thee, I know	359	O God, the Rock of Ages	12
My rest is in heaven, my rest	799	O God, Thou bottomless abyss	6
My Saviour, 'mid life's varied	382	O God, Thy power is	44
My Saviour, Thou Thy love	451	O God, what offering shall I	640
My song shall be of mercy	684	O God! who didst Thy will	299
My soul, through my	445	O God! who know'st how	630
My spirit longs for Thee	389	O God, whose love is near	898
My sufferings all to Thee are	525	O happy day that fixed my	749
My times are in Thy hand	537	O heavenly King, look down	683
		O help us Lord! each hour	631
Nearer, my God, to Thee	402	O Holy Jesus, Prince of Peace	733
Never further than Thy cross	667	O, it is hard to work for God	585
No sorrow, and no sighing	787	O Jesus at Thy feet we wait	471
None else but Thee	13	O Jesus Christ, the holy one	734
None is like Jeshurun's God	590	O Jesus, Friend unfailing	60
Not all the blood of beasts	195	O Jesus, let Thy dying cry	397
Not for a favourite form or	729	O Jesus, Lord of light and	263
Not what these hands have	315	O Jesus, source of calm repose	472
Nothing but leaves! the	340	O Jesus, Thou art standing	325
Now God be with us, for the	283	O joyful sound of Gospel	474
Now have we met that we	721	O lead me, my Father; lead	502
Now I have found the ground	411	O let him whose sorrow	516
Now in parting, Father, bless	737	O let us our own works	398
Now let us see Thy beauty	462	O little birds that all day long	937
Now pray we for our country	967	O Lord and Bishop of our	708
Now the day is over	911	O Lord be with us when we	899
Now the labourer's task is o'er	886	O Lord of all, we bring to	944
Now weigh the anchor, hoist	896	O Lord of heaven and earth and	178
		O Lord of heaven and earth	840
O breathe upon this languid	139	O Lord of hosts, whose glory	865
O come, all ye faithful	78	O Lord, Thou art not fickle	666
O come and dwell in me	465	O Lord, Thy heavenly grace	424

ALPHABETICAL INDEX TO HYMNS.

	HYMN		HYMN
O Lord, turn not Thy face	632	Open, Lord, my inward ear	475
O Lord, with one accord	133	Open our eyes, O Lord! and	305
O Lord, while life and hope	928	Oppressed with sin and woe	366
O love Divine, how sweet	469	Our blest Redeemer, ere He	159
O love Divine: what hast	101	Our children, Lord, in faith	722
O love, I languish at Thy stay	393	Our day of praise is done	254
O Master, at Thy feet	84	Our Father, hear our longing	617
O mean may seem this house	87	Our friend, our brother, and	647
O mighty God, Creator, King	894	Our Lord is risen from the	121
O one with God the Father	55	Out of the deep, out of the	519
O paradise! O paradise	789		
O sacred head once wounded	102	Parent of good, Thy	9
O safe to the Rock that is	349	Part in peace! Christ's life	977
O Saviour, precious Saviour	54	Partners of a glorious hope	701
O sing to the Lord, whose	838	Pass a few swiftly fleeting	760
O strong to save and bless	42	Peace: doubting heart; my	544
O taste and see that He	29	Peace, perfect peace, in this	413
O that I could my Lord	369	Pierce, fill me with humble	594
O that I could repent	338	Pleasant are Thy courts	243
O that my load of sin were	477	Praise, Lord, for Thee in Zion	175
O Thou by long experience	691	Praise, my soul, the King of	189
O Thou from whom all	522	Praise, O praise our heavenly	195
O Thou, our Saviour, Brother	633	Praise the Lord, ye heavens	196
O Thou to whom in ancient	810	Praise to the Holiest in the	190
O Thou to whose all-searching	517	Praise ye Jehovah! praise	191
O Thou through suffering	94	Praise ye the Lord, 'tis good	14
O Thou who camest from	663	Prayer is the soul's sincere	627
O Thou who hast Thy	478	Prisoners of hope, arise	689
O Thou who hast our sorrows	375		
O Thou who on the mountain	957	Quiet, Lord, my froward	543
O Thou whose chosen place	969		
O Thou whose hand has	867	Rejoice for a brother deceased	887
O Thou whose own vast	871	Rejoice, the Lord is King	127
O timely happy, timely wise	261	Remember thy Creator	925
O 'tis enough, my God, my	606	Rescue the perishing, care	959
O what a mighty change	797	Rest in the Lord, rest weary	438
O what can little hands do	936	Rest of the weary, joy of the	618
O what shall I do, my Saviour	682	Revive Thy work, O Lord	147
O when shall we sweetly	788	Rock of Ages, cleft for me	110
O where is He that trod the	91		
O where shall rest be found	778	Saints, above all, lay hold	564
O wondrous power of faithful	634	Salvation! O the joyful sound	316
O Word of God incarnate	500	Saviour, again to Thy dear	255
O worship the King, all	184	Saviour, blessed Saviour	198
O'er the gloomy hills of	816	Saviour, breathe an evening	284
Oft when of God we ask	670	Saviour, cast a pitying eye	368
On all the earth Thy Spirit	145	Saviour from sin, I wait to	479
On Jordan's stormy banks I	783	Saviour of all, what hast	86
On the waters dark and drear	889	Saviour, ou me the want	481
On this, the holiest and best	236	Saviour, Prince of Israel's	609
Once in royal David's city	926	Saviour, sprinkle many nations	817
One by one the sands are	645	Saviour: Thy dying love	439
One touch from Thee, the	543	Saviour, we now rejoice in	168
Onward, Christian soldiers	569	Say not, my soul, from whence	664

ALPHABETICAL INDEX TO HYMNS.

	HYMN		HYMN
See how great a flame aspires	818	Talk with us, Lord, Thyself	715
See Israel's gentle Shepherd	723	Teach me, my God and King	661
See, Jesus, Thy disciples see	713	Teach me to live, 'tis easier	660
Servant of all, to toil for man	639	Tell me the old, old story	331
Shepherd Divine, our wants	716	The billows swell, the winds	901
Show me myself! O holy Lord	615	The child leans on its parents'	953
Shrinking from the cold hand	761	The dawn of God's dear	232
Simply trusting every day	351	The day departs : our souls	285
Sing hallelujah forth in	1039	The day is gently sinking to	274
Sing, O sing, this blessed morn	74	The day is past and over	275
Sing praise to God who reigns	199	The day Thou gavest, Lord	289
Sing to the great Jehovah's	824	The Galilean fishers' toil	586
Sing to the Lord a joyful	192	The God of Abraham praise	205
Sing to the Lord of harvest	853	The God of harvest praise	852
Sing to the Lord our might	238	The God of nature and of	17
Sinners, obey the gospel word	321	The golden gates are lifted	122
Sinners, turn, why will ye die	326	The great archangel's trump	765
Soldiers of Christ arise	563	The great redeeming angel	910
Some murmur when their sky	513	The heavens declare Thy	19
Sometimes a light surprises	37	The hours of day are over	943
Sometime o'er our pathway	547	The journey done, the rest	883
Songs of praise the angels	204	The Lord be with us as we	252
Son of God, if Thy free	582	The Lord, how wondrous are	39
Soon and forever, such	780	The Lord is come, on Syrian	71
Sovereign of all the worlds	448	The Lord is rich and	48
Sow in the morn thy seed	662	The Lord Jehovah reigns	20
Speed Thy servants, Saviour	822	The Lord my pasture shall	33
Spirit Divine! attend our	134	The Lord of earth and sky	827
Spirit of faith, come down	131	The Lord of Sabbath let us	234
Spirit of holiness, descend	137	The Lord's my Shepherd, I'll	34
Spirit of truth, essential God	301	The morning flowers display	752
Spread, O spread, thou	821	The old year's long campaign	828
Standing at the portal	825	The praying Spirit breathe	714
Stand the omnipotent decree	763	The radiant morn hath passed	276
Stand up and bless the Lord	211	The roseate hues of early	264
Stand up! stand up for Jesus	562	The Sabbath day has	253
Stay, Master, stay upon this	671	The spacious firmament on	18
Stay, thou insulted Spirit	613	The springtide hour brings	834
Still, Lord, I languish for Thy	390	The sun is sinking fast	288
Still, still, with Thee when	266	The strain upraise of joy and	1038
Still will we trust, though	519	The thing my God doth hate	425
Still with Thee, O my God	267	The tide of time is rolling	844
Summer suns are glowing	839	The voices of the spring, O	837
Summoned my labour to	659	The voice that breathed o'er	861
Sun of my soul! Thou	272	The year is gone beyond	829
Surrounded by a host of foes	581	The year is swiftly waning	842
Sweet is the memory of Thy	225	Thee, Jesus, full of truth and	524
Sweet is the solemn voice	214	Thee we adore, eternal name	753
Sweet is the work, my God	230	Thee will I love, my strength	467
Sweet Saviour, bless us ere	273	Their names are names of	584
Sweet the moments rich in	468	There came a little child to	934
Sweetly the holy hymn	262	There is a book who runs	23
		There is a fountain filled	108
Take my life and let it be	429	There is a green hill far away	917

294

ALPHABETICAL INDEX TO HYMNS.

	HYMN		HYMN
There is a land of pure delight	782	To the hills I lift mine eyes	227
There is a name I love to hear	466	Tossed upon life's raging	992
There is no night in heaven	790	Try us, O God, and search	706
There is no sorrow, Lord	635		
There is out of sight the fair	939	Unchangeable, Almighty	703
There's a friend for little	920	Upright both in heart and will	334
There were ninety and nine	103	Us, who climb Thy holy hill	484
Thine are all the gifts, O God	880		
Thine arm, O Lord, in days	877	Walking with Thee, my God	688
Thine for ever! God of love	430	Walk in the light! so shalt	468
Thine, Lord, are the blossoms	819	Was there ever kindest	317
This, this is the God we adore	212	Watched by the world's	380
This is the day of Light	239	We ask not that our path be	592
This is the field, the world	770	We bid thee welcome in the	711
This stone to Thee in faith we	866	We bless Thee for Thy peace	687
This sweetly solemn thought	277	We bless Thee, Lord, for all	511
Thou art near, yes, Lord, I feel	551	We bless Thy name, O holy	287
Thou art, O God, the life	855	We cannot always trace the	596
Thou doest all things well	32	We come unto our fathers'	996
Thou God of glorious majesty	768	We give Thee but Thine own	638
Thou God of glory, truth and	876	We limit not the truth of God	303
Thou God unsearchable	611	We love Thee, Lord, yet not	228
Thou grace divine, encircling	46	We plough the fields and	859
Thou great mysterious God	416	We praise and bless Thee	515
Thou hidden love of God	395	We praise Thee oft for hours	553
Thou hidden source of calm	226	We rose to-day with anthems	259
Thou Judge of quick and	789	We thank Thee, Lord, for	989
Thou knowest, Lord, the	521	We walk by faith, and not by	408
Thou Lamb of God, Thou	518	We walk on earth and to its	532
Thou, Lord, hast blest my	601	'We would see Jesus'—for	781
Thou, Lord, my path shall	508	Weary of wandering from my	610
Thou, Lord, on whom I still	777	Weary souls that wander	327
Thou Shepherd of Israel, and	57	Welcome, sweet day of rest	237
Thou Son of God, whose	335	What am I, O thou glorious	390
Thou, the great eternal Lord	47	What are these arrayed in	792
Thou, to whom the sick and	878	What could your Redeemer	330
Thou true and only God	8	Whate'er my God ordains is	30
Thou, whose almighty word	820	What grace, O Lord, and	82
Thou, who hast known the	286	What is our calling's	482
Thou, who our faithless hearts	401	What means this eager	333
Though lowly here our lot	644	What now is my object and	434
Though nature's strength	206	What shall I do my God to	465
Thousands, O Lord of hosts	953	What shall we offer our good	218
Through all the changing	25	What various hindrances we	712
Through centuries of sin and	965	When all Thy mercies, O my	35
Thy ceaseless, unexhausted	312	When buds appear in early	820
Thy hand, O God, Thy	7	When cold our hearts and far	636
Thy home is with the humble	614	When gathering clouds	557
Thy love for all Thy creatures	265	When gladness gilds our	556
'Till He come!' O let the	735	When God of old came down	135
To-day Thy mercy calls us	329	When, gracious Lord, when	612
To Thee, O dear, dear Saviour	62	When I can read my title	681
To Thee, O God, in heaven	724	When in the busy crowd of	436
To Thee, O Lord, our hearts	859	When I survey the wondrous	107

INDEX OF AUTHORS AND TRANSLATORS.

	HYMN
When, my Saviour, shall I be	391
When our heads are bowed	520
When quiet in my house I sit	304
When shall Thy love constrain	362
When the dark waves around	555
When the weary seeking rest	216
When the world my heart	538
When this passing world is	512
When through the torn sail	903
When thy mortal life is fled	772
When we cannot see our way	531
Wherewith, O God, shall I	386
While lone upon the furious	904
While shepherds watched	73
While the sun is shining	938
Who can describe the joys	356
Who in the Lord confide	583
Who is on the Lord's side	924
Why not now, my God	371
Why should the children	141
Why should our tears in	757
Wilt Thou return to me	691

	HYMN
Winter reigneth o'er the land	843
With broken heart and	373
With gladness we worship	210
With joy we meditate the	523
With glorious clouds	387
With silence only as their	559
With the sweet word of peace	974
Work is sweet, for God has	658
Worship and thanks and	183
Worship, honour, glory	976
Worship the Lord in the	185
Would Jesus have the sinner	106
Ye faithful souls, who Jesus	507
Ye humble souls that seek	114
Ye neighbours and friends of	334
Ye ransomed sinners, hear	680
Ye servants of God, your	307
Ye virgin souls arise	764
Yes, we trust the day is	819
Yield to me now, for I am	380
Young men and maidens	169

INDEX OF AUTHORS AND TRANSLATORS.

b = born : d = died : p = published.
When two dates in brackets are found, the first is the date of birth,
and the second of death.

Adams (née Flower), Sarah (1805—1848) 402, 548, 977.
Addison, Joseph (1672—1719), 18, 33, 35, 897.
Aitken, William M. H. Hay (p 1872), 258.
Alexander (née Humphreys), Cecil Frances (b 1823), 122, 264, 917, 923, 926.
Alexander, James Waddell (1804—1859), 102.
Alexander, William Lindsay (1808—1884), 951.
Alford, Henry, Dean (1810—1871), 408, 478, 573, 851.
Allen, James (1734—1804), 201, 468 part.
Allen, Oswald (p 1862), 329.
Ambrose, Bishop of Milan (340—397), 263, 1033.
Anatolius (5th Century), 275.
Andrew of Crete (660—732), 568.
Anonymous, 196, 236, 292, 373, 508, 519, 587, 612, 614, 615, 687, 720, 722, 770, 781, 844, 868, 913, 921, 928, 931, 936, 939, 975.
Anstice, Joseph (1808—1836), 857.
Auber, Harriet, (1773—1862), 159.

B. (*pub.* 1801), 784.

Bahnmaier, Jonathan Friedrich (1774—1841), 821.
Bakewell, John (1721—1819), 95.
Balfour, 823.
Baring-Gould, Sabine (b 1834), 569, 941.
Barton, Bernard (1784—1849), 291, 488.
Bateman, Henry (1802—1872), 692.
Bathurst, William Hiley (1796—1877), 155, 463.
Baxter, Richard (1615—1691), 431.
Bernard of Clairvaux (1091—1153), 102, 182, 732.
Bernard of Cluny (12th Century), 755, 785.
Betham-Edwards, Matilda (p 1872), 940.
Bethune, George William (1805—1862), 756, 902.
Bickersteth, Edward Henry, Bishop (b 1825), 12, 413, 437, 438, 735, 849, 894.
Binney, Thomas (1798—1874), 10.
Birks, Thomas Rawson (1810—1883), 29.
Blatchford, A. N., 912.
Blunt, Abel Gerald Wilson (b 1827), 846.
Boaden, Edward (b 1827), 876, 955, 958.
Bohemian Hymn, (p 1531) 884.

INDEX OF AUTHORS AND TRANSLATORS.

Bonar, Horatius (1808—1889), 42, 52, 216, **221**, 311, 315, 354, 406, 623, 646, 737, 751, 862, 918.
Bourdillon (née Cotterill), Mary (1819—1879), 918.
Bourignon, Antoinette (1616—1680), 454.
Bowring, Sir John (1792—1872), 96, 506, 538.
Brady, Nicholas (1659—1726), 25, 608.
Brackenbury, Robert Carr (1752—1818), 132.
Bridges, Matthew (b 1800), 128.
Brontë, Anne (1820—1849), 396, 952.
Brooke, Stopford A. (p 1881), 898.
Brown-Borthwick, Robert (b 1840), 733.
Brown, James Baldwin (1821—1884), 401.
Browne, H. K., 60.
Bruce, Michael (1746—1767), 811.
Bryant, William Cullen (1794—1879), **542**, 871.
Butler, **George** Burden (1823—1869), 224, **624**.
Buckoll, **Henry** James (1803—1871), 257.
Bunting, **William** Maclardie (1805—1866), 32, 748.
Burleigh, Wm. **Henry (1812—1871), 40, 501**, 549, 552, 556.
Burman, Ellen E. (p 1860), 660.
Burns, James Drummond (1823—1864), **267**, 449, 833.
Butcher, Edmund (1757—1822), 854.
Byrom, John (1691—1763), 77, 389.

Cameron, William (1751—1811), 602.
Campbell, Etta (p 1868), 333.
Campbell, Jane Montgomery **(1817—1878)**, 860.
Campbell (née Malcolm), **Lady Margaret** Cockburn (p 1838), 191.
Canitz, Baron von F. R. L. **(1654—1699)**, 257.
Carey, Henry (d 1743), 969.
Carlyle, Joseph D. (1758—1804), **622**.
Carlyle, Thomas (1795—1881), 561.
Cary, Phoebe (1824—1871), 277.
Caswall, Edward (1814—1878), 182, **288, 461**.
Cawood, John **(1775—1852)**, 76.
Cennick, John **(1717— 1755)**, 979, **980**.
Chandler, John **(1806—1876)**, 263, 919.
Charles (née **Rundle**), Elisabeth (p 1850), **645**, 667.
Childs-Clarke, Samuel (b 1821), 835.
Clarke, James Freeman, (1810—1888), 724.
Claudius, Matthias (1740—1815), 860.
Clephane, Elizabeth Cecilia (1830—1869), 103.
Cobbin, Ingram (1777—1851), 718.
Codner, Elizabeth (p 1860), 364.
Collyer, Wm. Bengo (1782—1854), 762.
Colquhoun (née Fuller Maitland) Frances Sara (1809—1877), 574.
Conder, Geo. William (1821—1874), 174.
Conder, Josiah (1789—1855), 26, 139, 260, 292.
Copeland, William John (1804—1885), 259.
Coster, George Thomas (b 1835), 830.
Cotterill, Thomas (1779—1823), 522, 728.
Cowper, Wm. (1731—1800), 27, 37, 108, **213**, 302, 603, 691, 712, 901, 945.
Cox, Frances Elizabeth, 115, 199, 546.
Coxe, Arthur Cleveland, Bishop (b 1818), **817**, 967.
Crewdson (née **Fox**), **Jane (1809—1863), 418**, 543, 629, 635.
Crosby, Frances Jane (b 1823), 362, 416, 959.
Cross, (née Cambridge), Ada (b 1844), 232.
Crossman, Samuel (1624—1683), 786.
Cummins, John James (d 1857), 219.

Cushing, William O., 349.

Dana, Mrs. M. S. (p 1860), 340.
Davison, W. H. (b 1827), 916.
Dayman, Edward Arthur (b 1807), **899**.
Deck, James George (b 1802), 540.
Denny, Sir Edward (b 1796), 82.
Dessler, Wolfgang Christoph **(1660—1722)**, 505.
Dix, William **Chatterton** (b 1837), 65, 308, 879, 889.
Dober, **(née Schindler), Anna (1713—1739)**, 422.
Doddridge, Philip (1702—1751), 24, 64, 114, 181, 245, 448, 674, 723, 731, 749, 826, 870, 873.
Doudney, Sarah (p 1871), 258.
Douglas, Frances Jane (b 1829), 826.
Downton, Henry (1818—1885), 684, 830.
Dryden, John (1631—1700), 136.
Duffield, George (b 1818), 562.

Edmeston, **James (1791—1867), 284, 500**.
E. J., 893.
Ellerton, John (b 1826), 78, 239, 252, 254, 255, 289, 717, 767, 886, 943, 1039.
Elliott, Charlotte (1789—1871), 253, 407, 503, 535, 592, 598, 626.
Elliott, Emily Elizabeth Steele (p 1873), 934.
Elliott (née Marshall), Julia Anne (d 1841), 228.
E. S. **A., 864, 914**.
Elvin, **Cornelius (1797—1873), 373**.

Faber, Frederick Wm. (1815—1863), 44, 87, 187, 273, 317, 320, 534, 578, 585, 614, 789, 793.
Fawcett, John (1739—1817), 296, 738.
Fitz, Asa (p 1854), 848.
Flowerdew, Alice (1759—1830), 841.
Freylinghausen, John Anastasius **(1670—1729)**, 285, 472.
French, From the, **424**.

Gaskell, **Wm. (1805—1884), 630, 644**.
Gellert, **Christian Furchtegott (1715—1769)**, 115.
Gerhardt, **Paul (1606—1676), 31, 75**, 102, 450, 451, 554.
German, From the, 60, 508.
Gill, Thomas Hornblower (b 1819), 3, 87, 277, 966.
Gilmore, J. H. (p 1862), 461.
Goadby, Fredk. William (1845—1880), 867.
Godescalcus (10th Century), 1038.
Godwin, Elizabeth Aytoun (p 1865), 362.
Grant, Sir Robert (1787—1838), 15, 184, 557.
Gregg, Samuel (1804—1877), 671.
Greenwood, John Broo e (b 1828), 862.
Grigg, Joseph (d 1768), 423.
Guion, Jeanne Marie Bouvière de la Mothe (1648—1717), 691.
Gurney, **John** Hampden (1802—1862), 85, 856, 965, 968.

Hall, Christopher Newman (b 1816), 922.
Hamilton, James (b 1819), 742.
Hankey, Katherine, 331.
H. P. H. (p 1881), 270.
Harbaugh, Henry (1816—1867), 482.
Harris, John (1802—1856), 872.
Hart, Joseph (1712—1768), 151, 212, 321.
Hartsough, Mrs. Lydia (p 1874), 328.

301

INDEX OF AUTHORS AND TRANSLATORS

Haslock, Mary (*p* 1881), 956.
Hastings, Thomas (1784—1872), 905.
Havergal, Frances Ridley (1836—1879), 54, 84, 125, 336, 414, 415, 426, 429, 504, 825, 831, 924, 944.
Hawels, Thomas (1734—1820), 522.
Heber, Reginald, Bishop (1783—1826), **67, 160**, 281, 298, 805, 903.
Herbert, George (1593—1632), 188, 661.
Herbert, Peter (*d* 1571), 283.
Hickson, William Edward (*p* 1855), 961.
Hinchsliffe, Joseph (1760—1807), 770.
Hinsdale, Mrs , 936.
H. L. L. (*b* 1813), 285, 499, 509, 515, 521, 550.
Hobson, John P. (*p* 1881), 708.
Holmes, Oliver Wendell (*b* 1809), 45.
Hopps, John Page (*b* 1834), 502, 553, 845.
How, Wm. Walsham, Bishop (*b* 1823), 55, 94, 300, 325, 492, 555, 638, 791, 836, 839, 842, 843.
Howitt, Mary (1804—1888), 847.
Hurn, Wm. (1754—1829), 812.

Irons, Geneviève S. (*p* 1881), 396.
Irons, Wm. Joseph, D.D. (1812—1883), 305, 496, 787, 1036.

James, Mrs., 361.
Jenkins, Ebenezer E. (*p* 1876), 904.
Jones, Alfred (*b* 1834), 837.
Julian, John (*b* 1839), 81.

Keble, John (1792—1866), 23, 135, 261, 272, 861, 930.
Kelly, Thos. (1769—1855), 124, 249, 531, 819, 822.
Ken, Thos., Bishop (1637—1711), 256, 269.
Kethe, Wm. (*p* 1560), 172.
Knollys, F. Minden (1815—1863), 790.

Lange, Ernst (1650—1727), 6, 7, 8, 9, 640.
Latin, from the, 78, 136, 166, 167, 168, 259, 288, 620.
Leeson, Jane Elizabeth (*p* 1842), 930.
Littledale, Richard Frederick (*b* 1833), 838.
Logan, John (1748—1788), 24.
Longfellow, Samuel (*b* 1819), 138.
Lloyd, Wm. Freeman (1791—1853), 537.
Luther, Martin (1483—1546) 124, 561.
Lynch, Thos. Toke (1818—1871), 48, 91, 129, 282, 536, 652, 664, 666, 670, 721, 949.
Lyte, Henry Francis (1793—1847), **5, 175, 189**, 238, 243, 244, 271, 427, 690, 799.

Macdonald, George (*b* 1824), 617.
Macdonald, Wm. (*p* 1874), 345.
Madan, Martin (1726—1790), 113.
Malan, Cæsar, H. A. (1787—1864), **756**.
Markant, John (16th Century) 632.
Marriott, John (1780—1825), 820.
Massie, Richard (*b* 1800), 117.
Mathams, Walter John (*b* 1853), 440.
Matheson, Annie (*b* 1853), 215, 935, **937**.
Maude (née Hooper), Mary Fawler (*p* 1847), 434.
M'Cheyne, Robt. Murray (1813—1843), **512**.
Meaux Breviary, 829.
Midlane, Albert (*b* 1825), 147, 920.
Milman, Henry Hart, Dean (1791—1868), 229, 789, 631.
Milton, John (1608—1674), 176.

Monsell, John Samuel Bewley (1811—1875), 62, 112, 185, 192, 203, 381, 436, 532, 551, 566, 618, 636, 780, 834, 853, 858, 863, 883.
Montgomery, James (1771—1854), 17, 80, 104, 130, 204, 211, 278, 319, 535, **539**, 627, 662, 704, 709, 711, 725, 758, 776, 778, **804**, 806, 852, 866, 874, 896, 953.
Moore, Thos. (1779—1852), 835.
More, Henry (1614—1687), 144, **145**.
Morrison, John (1749—1798), 558.
Mudie, Charles Edward (*b* 1818), 444.

Neale, John Mason (1818—1866), 90, 275, 368, 755, 785, 865, 1038.
Neumarck, George (1621—1681), 424.
Newman, John Henry, Cardinal (*b* 1801), 190, 487.
Newton, John (1725—1807), 209, 545, 621, 628, 774, 873, **974**.
Nitzchman, John and Anna (18th Century), 353.

Olivers, Thos. (1725—1799), 205, 206, 207.
O. P. (*p* 1826), 757.
Osler, Edward (1798—1863), 710, 963, 976.
Oswald, Henry Siegmund (1751—1834), 546.

Page, E., 351.
Palmer, Ray (1808—1887), 59, **149, 399, 732**.
Parker, W H. (*p* 1880), 932.
Pennefather, Wm. 1816—1873), 133.
Perronet, Edward (1726—1792), 49.
Peterson, W. S., 960.
Phelps, S. D., 439.
Pierpoint, Folliott Sandford (*b* 1835), 290.
Pierpoint, John (1785—1866), 810.
Plumptre, Edwd. Hayes, Dean (*b* 1821), 840, 877.
Pott, Francis (*b* 1832), 170, 829.
Procter, Adelaide Anne (1825—1864), 186, 497, 665.
Punshon, Wm. Morley (1824—1881), 270.

Rawson, George (1807—1889), 2, 156, 158, 210, 278, 279, 280, 286, 287, 303, 686, 688, 882, 885, 946.
Reed, Mrs. Eliza Ann (*p* 1842), 337.
Reed, Andrew (1787—1862), 134.
Rhodes, Benjamin (1743—1815), 50, **803**.
Richter, C. F. (1676—1711), 518.
Ringwaldt, Bartholomew (1530—1598), 762.
Rippon, John (*p* 1787), 49.
Robert II., King of France (972—1031), **149**.
Robinson, Robert (1735—1790), 194.
Rodigast, Samuel (1649—1708), 30.
Rous, Francis (*p* 1650), 34.
Rothe, Johann Andreas (1688—1758), 441.

Sanders, William (*p* 1829), 355.
Saxby (née Browne), Jane Euphemia (*b* 1811), 734.

Scheffler, John (1624—1677), 4, 467.
Schmolck, Benjamin (1672—1737), 210.
Schutz, John Jacob (1646—1690), 199.
Scudder, Eliza (*b* 1821), 46.
Sears, Edmund Hamilton (1810—1876), **72**.
Sergeant, Mrs., 516.
Shekelton, Mary (*p* 1863), 453.
Shelly, Mrs. M. E. (*p* 1844), 942.
Sherlock, Frederick (*p* 1879), 957.
Shipton, Anna (*p* 1862), 322.

INDEX OF AUTHORS AND TRANSLATORS.

Shirley, Walter **William** (1725—1786), **316**, 468.
Smith, Samuel Francis (b 1808), 137, **772**.
Spangenberg, A. G. (1704—1792), 218.
Spanish, from the, 479.
Spitta, Carl John Philip (1801—1859), 515.
Spurgeon, Charles Haddon (b 1834), 262.
Stanley, Arthur Penrhyn, Dean (1815—1881), 71, 83, 120.
Steele, Anne (1716—1778), 260, 541, 754.
Stennett, Joseph (1663—1713), 233.
Stennett, Samuel (1721—1795), 783.
Stephen, the Sabaite (725—794), 90.
Stewart, John (p 1835), 152.
Stone, Samuel John (b 1839), 13, 584, 828.
Stowe (née Beecher), Harriet (b 1814), 266, 339.
Stowell, Hugh (1799—1865), **719**, **929**.
Stowell, Thomas Alfred (b **1831**), **925**, **938**.

Tate, Nahum (1652—1715), 73.
Tate and Brady (p 1696), 25, 608.
Tersteegen, Gerhardt (1697—1769), 173, 395.
Thring, Godfrey (b 1823), 70, 89, 93, 128, 157, 198, 235, 265, 276, 651, 658, 848, 878, 894.
Toplady, Augustus Montague (1740—1778), 110, 898, 947.
Trench, Richard Chenevix, **Archbishop (1807**—1885), 513.
Trend, Henry (**p** 1861), 195.
Tuttiett, Lawrence (b 1825), **547**.
Twells, Henry (b 1823), 251.

Walker (*née* Deck), Mrs. Mary Jane (*p* 1864), 348.
Ware, **Henry**, jun. (1794—1843), 875, 911.
Waring, Anna Letitia (b 1820), 217, 653.
Watson, George (b 1816), 704.
Watts, Isaac (1674—1748), 1, **11**, **14**, **16**, **19**, **20**, 22, 28, 38, 39, 68, 105, 107, 109, **113**, **149**, **141**, 171, 177, 179, 180, 197, 202, **208**, **225**, **230**, **237**, 241, 242, 246, 247, 248, 257, **316**, **347**, **356**, **388**, 476, 480, 523, 565, 577, 681, **685**, **750**, **753**, **779**, 782, 800, 808, 809, 813, 815.
Waugh, Benjamin (*p* 1886), **462**.
Weiszel, George (1590—1635), **193**.
Wesley (not certain whether John or Charles), 36, 53, 56, **66**, 69, 101, 106, 121, 131, 142, 150, 153, 154, 161, 164, 166, 167, 168, 214, 227, 294, 295, 307, 309, 310, 318, 323, 326, 327, 330, 341, 343, 344, 346, 350, 358, 367, 373, 376, 377, 378, 384, 385, 386, 393, 398, 400, **404**, 405, 411, 419, 420, 421, 442, 443, 446, 447, **452**, 460, 461, 465, 474, 475, 479, 482, 483, 485, **510**, 525, 526, 530, **544**, **567**, **576**, 580, 582, 583, **594**, 597, 600,
605, 606, 607, **612**, **619**, 634, 639, 642, 643, 656, 657, 659, 669, **672**, **673**, 675, 680, 682, 683, 694, 695, 701, 703, **715**, **727**, 729, 730, 740, 741, 743, 771, 773, 792, **794**, **795**, 801, 814, 827, 881, 895, 948, 970, **971**, **972**, **973**.
Wesley, Charles (**1708—1788**), **21**, 41, 43, **47**, 51, 57, **58**, **61**, **63**, 79, **86**, **88**, **92**, 99, 111, **118**, 119, **123**, **127**, **132**, **143**, **146**, **148**, 162, 163, **165**, 169, **183**, 220, **222**, **226**, **293**, **301**, 304, 306, **312**, 313, **314**, 324, **334**, **335**, **338**, **352**, 357, 360, **363**, 365, 368, 369, **371**, **372**, **374**, **379**, 380, **383**, **387**, 390, 391, 392, 394, **397**, **409**, **410**, **412**, 417, 423, 428, 433, 434, 435, **445**, **455**, **457**, **458**, 459, 463, 469, **471**, **473**, **476**, **477**, **481**, **484**, **486**, 489, 493, **495**, **498**, **507**, **514**, **524**, **527**, **528**, **529**, 560, 563, **564**, **570**, **571**, **572**, **575**, **579**, **541**, **586**, 569, 590, **591**, **593**, **595**, **596**, **599**, **601**, **609**, **610**, **611**, 613, **616**, **625**, **633**, **637**, **641**, 646, **649**, **670**, 654, 655, **663**, **668**, **676**, **677**, **678**, **679**, **689**, **693**, 696, 697, **658**, **699**, **700**, **702**, **705**, **706**, **707**, **713**, 714, 716, **726**, **736**, **739**, **744**, **745**, **746**, **747**, **759**, 760, 761, **763**, **764**, **765**, **766**, **768**, **774**, **775**, **777**, 788, 796, **797**, **798**, **802**, **807**, **818**, **824**, **887**, **890**, 896, 907, **908**, **909**, **910**, **915**, 970, **954**, **962**.
Wesley, **John** (**1703—1791**), **4**, **6**, **7**, 8, 9, 31, 98, **144**, **145**, **173**, **218**, **353**, **395**, **422**, 441, 450, 451, **454**, **467**, **470**, **472**, **505**, **517**, **518**, 554, 640. All translations.
Wesley, Samuel, jun. (1690—1739), 224, 752.
Wesley, Samuel, sen. (1662—1735), 169.
Westbury, John (b 1838), 223.
Whately, **Richard**, **Archbishop (1787—1863)**, 281.
White, Henry Kirke (1785—1806), 574.
White, J. M (p 1883), 511.
Whitfield, Frederick (p 1869), 342, 466.
Whiting, Wm. (1825—1878), 888.
Whittier, John Greenleaf (b 1808), **126**, **350**, 647, 869, **890**.
Williams, **Isaac** (**1802—1865**), **332**, 620, 937, 953.
Williams, **Peter** (1722—1796), 490.
Williams, Wm. (1717—1791), 490, 816.
Wilson (née Atkins), Lucy (p 1829), 424.
Winfield, Alfred (p 1896), 830.
Winkworth, Catherine (1827—1878), 30, 75, 193, 240, 283, 494, 821, 884.
Wordsworth, Christopher, Bishop (1807—1885), 74, 116, 178, 231, 274, 586, 832.
Wreford, John Reynall (p 1837), 964.

Xavier, Francis (1506—1552), 461.

Zinzendorf, Count von Nicolaus Ludwig (1700—1760), 98, 353, 499, 509, 517.

303

INDEX OF TEXTS OF SCRIPTURE
PREFIXED TO THE HYMNS.

Chap.	Ver.	Hymn.	Chap.	Ver.	Hymn.	Chap.	Ver.	Hymn.
GENESIS.			**1 SAMUEL.**			**PSALMS.**		
i.	3	143, 820	iii.	9	504, 944	ix.	10	348, 506
i.	28	861	vii.	12	194	xvii.	5	927
i.	31	923	x.	24	969	xvii.	8	594
v.	22	603				xvii.	15	460
v.	24	688	**2 SAMUEL.**			xviii.	1	182, 359, 395, 467
viii.	22	841	vii.	29	280			
xv.	1	205, 551				xviii.	31	567
x.ii.	7	722	**1 KINGS.**			xix.	1	18, 19, 265
xxii.	17	273	vii.	27	387	xx.	1	596
xxiv.	31	704	viii.	56	964	xx.	7	928
xxviii.	13	206	ix.	3	874	xxii.	4	966
xxviii.	16	173, 402	xvii.	16	645	xxiii.	1	34
xxviii.	19	24				xxiii.	2	33, 412, 491
xxxii.	24	379	**2 KINGS.**			xxiii.	3	502, 599
xxxii.	26	380	xxii.	19	392	xxiv.	9	121
xlviii.	16	910				xxiv.	10	916
			1 CHRONICLES.			xxv.	9	649
EXODUS.			xvi.	25	47	xxvi.	8	246
xiv.	13	544	xxix.	3	863	xxvii.	4	462
xiv.	15	573	xxix.	5	668	xxvii.	5	672
xv.	11	6, 165	xxix.	10	41	xxvii.	11	509
xv.	18	289	xxix.	11	9	xxix.	11	255
xvi.	23	235	xxix.	14	638, 849	xxx.	10	931
xx.	10	237	xxix.	16	869	xxxi.	2	349
xx.	24	213				xxxi.	3	499, 830
xxv.	22	719	**1 CHRONICLES.**			xxxi.	5	886
xxxi.	14	234	vi.	18	867	xxxi.	15	431, 537
xxxii.	9, 10	634	vi.	30	871	xxxi.	19	954
xxxii.	26	924	vii.	1	872	xxxii.	1	802
xxxiv.	5	61	xxxii.	11	896	xxxii.	10	549
xxxiv.	6	312				xxxiii.	5	835
			NEHEMIAH.			xxxiii.	6	7
LEVITICUS.			v.	9	590	xxxiv.	1	25, 215
viii.	35	588	ix.	5	211	xxxiv.	3	43
xvi.	31	259				xxxiv.	8	29, 48
xix.	18	695	**JOB.**			xxxvi.	8	58
xxv.	9	807	i.	21	884	xxxvi.	9	267, 661
			iii.	17	538, 799	xxxvii.	3	643
NUMBERS.			vii.	16	788	xxxvii.	7	438
vi.	25	163	xi.	19	283	xxxix.	7	829
x.	29	783	xiii.	15	351	xxxix.	12	761
			xix.	25	457	xliii.	1	470, 608
DEUTERONOMY.			xxiii.	10	416	xliii.	2	353, 518
iv.	35	13	xxviii.	28	591	xliii.	4	953
v.	4	715	xxxiii.	16	475	xliii.	8	553, 743
xiii.	3	440	xxxiv.	29	962	xliii.	2	434
xxvii.	6	691				xliv.	1	963
xxxiii.	27	580	**PSALMS.**			xlv.	2	56, 83
xxxiii.	29	678, 801	i.	2	304	xlvi.	1	28, 561
			iii.	5	913	xlvii.	4	508
JOSHUA.			iv.	8	269	xlvii.	6	192
xxiii.	14	760	v.	1	376	xlviii.	2	208
xxiv.	15	907	v.	3	256, 262	xlviii.	9	859
			ix.	1	221, 682	xlviii.	14	212
						li.	6	623
						li.	9	344

INDEX OF TEXTS OF SCRIPTURE.

Chap.	Ver.	Hymn.	Chap.	Ver.	Hymn.	Chap.	Ver.	Hymn.
PSALMS.			**PSALMS.**			**PSALMS.**		
li.	14	358	c.	1	172	cxiii.	10	478
lvii.	1	533	c.	3	171	cxiv.	2	516
lvii.	7	719	c.	4	268	cxiv.	9	225
lvii.	8	5	ci.	1	684	cxlv.	10	174, 1034
lix.	16	257	ci.	2	371, 909	cxlvi.	2	177
lix.	17	832	cii.	27	12	cxlvi.	5	674
lxi.	4	40, 252	ciii.	4	693	cxlvii.	1	14
lxiii.	1	202, 389	ciii.	13	39	cxlvii.	14	860
lxiii.	8	503	ciii.	17	38, 632, 675, 846	cxlvii.	16	845
lxv.	1	175				cxlviii.	1	180
lxv.	4	864	civ.	1	184	cxlviii.	5	186
lxv.	5	894	civ.	13	854	cxlviii. 9, 12, 13		818
lxv.	7	891	civ.	23	938	cxlviii.	12, 13	169, 914
lxv.	9	834	civ.	33	204	cl.	4	875
lxv.	10	837	cvii.	1	824	cl.	6	188, 514
lxv.	11	826	cvii.	7	487			
lxv.	13	852	cvii.	24	900	**PROVERBS.**		
lxvi.	2	191	cvii.	29	888	iii.	5	521
lxvii.	2	812	cvii.	30	270	iii.	6	31, 554
lxvii.	6	737	cix.	4	919	iii.	13	419
lxviii.	4	199	cxv.	9	893	iii.	24	277
lxviii.	17	939	cxv.	15	36	viii.	17	937
lxviii.	32	850	cxvi.	7	550	x.	22	942
lxxi.	1	256	cxvi.	8	443	xiv.	34	961
lxxii.	6	145, 364, 558, 808	cxvi.	12	218	xviii.	24	61
			cxvi.	16	362, 429	xix.	17	174
lxxii.	7	72	cxvi.	17	35	xx.	1	958
lxxii.	8	804	cxvii.	1	813	xxii.	6	908
lxxii.	11	805	cxviii.	1	4			
lxxii.	19	52	cxviii.	14	721	**ECCLESIASTES.**		
lxxiii.	23	691	cxviii.	24	232	ii.	24	540
lxxiii.	24	833	cxix.	18	294	iii.	11	847
lxxiii.	25	15, 458	cxix.	24	296	vii.	29	394
lxxiii.	26	217	cxix.	34	305	ix.	1	876
lxxiii.	28	712	cxix.	75	30	xi.	6	662
lxxiv.	17	843	cxix.	96	409	xi.	7	839
lxxvii.	19	27	cxix.	97	290	xii.	1	925
lxxviii.	14	490	cxix.	105	291			
lxxviii.	53	497	cxix.	130	302	**SONG OF SOLOMON.**		
lxxx.	1	501	cxix.	170	219	ii.	12	836
lxxxi.	1	236	cxxi.	4	227, 947			
lxxxiv.	1	243	cxxii.	1	241	**ISAIAH.**		
lxxxv.	10	242	cxxii.	6	244, 720	ii.	2	811
lxxxiv.	11	45, 248	cxxiii.	1	624	vi.	3	1, 166, 167
lxxxvi.	10	8	cxxv.	1	583	ix.	2	489
xxxvii.	5	870	cxxvi.	6	855	ix.	3	851
lxxxix.	9	890, 892	cxxvi.	1	495, 864	ix.	6	75, 265
xc.	3	753	cxxvii.	2	287	xii.	2	505, 605
xc.	4	750	cxxviii.	6	911	xxvi.	3	413
xc.	9	751	cxxx.	1	519	xxx.	15	646
xc.	12	754	cxxx.	4	606	xxx.	19	616
xci.	1	279	cxxx.	6	940	xxx.	21	690
xci.	10	281, 579	cxxx.	8	410	xxxiii.	17	782
xci.	15	524	cxxxi.	2	449	xxxv.	10	569
xcii.	1	230	cxxxii.	16	709	xxxviii.	14	396
xcii.	2	272	cxxxiii.	1	695	xl.	1	526
xciii.	4	838	cxxxvi.	1	176, 260	xl.	7	752
xcv.	1	16	cxxxvi.	3	195	xl.	11	57, 929
xcv.	4	807	cxxxix.	1	11	xl.	26	17
xcv.	5	895	cxxxix.	11	941	xl.	31	577
xcvi.	8	846	cxxxix.	18	266, 831	xlii.	10	204, 825
xcvi.	9	185	cxxxix.	23	473, 706	xlii.	16	596
xcvii.	1	20	cxli.	2	288	xliii.	5	532
xcvii.	2	585	cxli.	8	517	xlv.	15	611
xcviii.	4	210	cxliii.	1	951	xlv.	22	350
xcix.	3	2	cxliii.	9	332, 613			

INDEX OF TEXTS OF SCRIPTURE.

Chap.	Ver.	Hymn.	Chap.	Ver.	Hymn.	Chap.	Ver.	Hymn.
ISAIAH.			**HAGGAI.**			**MATTHEW.**		
xlv.	25	571	ii.	4	644	xxvii.	29	102
xlviii.	17	500				xxviii.	1	253
li.	9	796	**ZECHARIAH.**			xxviii.	6	111, 114
lii.	7	815	ix.	12	689	xxviii.	19	823
lii.	10	819	xiii.	1	108, 319	xxviii.	20	382, 873
lii.	15	817	xiv.	7	278			
liii.	4	375				**MARK.**		
liii.	6	95, 406	**MALACHI.**			i.	32	251
iv.	1	310	i.	11	810	iv.	19	630
iv.	4	493	i.	12	731	iv.	38	902
lvii.	15	614	iii.	1	68	iv.	39	89, 901
lviii.	13	231	iii.	7	604	iv.	41	899
lx.	7	868	iii.	10	838	vi.	50	889
lx.	13	865	iv.	2	378	vii.	37	32
lx.	19	274				viii.	38	423
lxiii.	1	42	**MATTHEW.**			ix.	5	671
lxiii.	10	613	i.	21	466	ix.	23	455
			ii.	10	65	ix.	24	347
JEREMIAH.			iii.	11	144, 464	x.	13	920
v.	24	853	iv.	2	957	x.	14	723, 724
vi.	4	943	v.	3	481, 617	x.	16	920
ix.	23	314	v.	4	377, 480	x.	28	427
x.	24	1468	v.	8	421	x.	45	639
xxii.	24	372	v.	13	589	x.	47	333, 720
xxiii.	29	285	vi.	6	948	xi.	13	340
xxix.	7	867	vi.	8	633	xi.	22	403
xxxi.	33	425	vi.	9	933	xi.	24	374
l.	5	746	vi.	10	656	xiii.	33	592
			vi.	26	937	xiv.	7	880
LAMENTATIONS.			vi.	28	922	xvi.	15	355
i.	12	99	vi.	34	665			
iii.	22, 23	261	vii.	7	369	**LUKE.**		
iii.	24	690	vii.	14	492	ii.	8	73
			viii.	20	381	ii.	10	80
EZEKIEL.			viii.	25	609, 903	ii.	11	77, 926
iii.	22	945	viii.	26	904	ii.	12	67
xviii.	31	326	ix.	13	321	ii.	13	76
xxxiii.	11	330	ix.	21	436	ii.	14	79, 161, 201, 676
xxxiv.	26	484	ix.	29	428			
xxxvi.	27	393, 486, 703	ix.	38	814	ii.	15	78
xxxvii.	9	139	xi.	5	334	ii.	20	74
			xi.	28	90, 216, 308, 407, 477	ii.	25	66
DANIEL.						ii.	49	936
ix.	9	229	xi.	29	530	iv.	18	64
xii.	3	476	xiii.	39	770, 857	iv.	19	816
			xiv.	25	91	ix.	23	435
HOSEA.			xiv.	30	385	x.	42	620
xiv.	1	327	xiv.	35, 36	877	xi.	1	636
xiv.	4	607	xv.	27	631	xi.	2	164
xiv.	5	282	xvii.	4	83	xi.	3	26
			xviii.	20	637, 700	xi.	13	140
JOEL.			xxi.	13	247	xii.	49	663, 818
ii.	28	157	xxi.	15	921	xiii.	8	827
			xxi.	16	919	xiii.	14	658
AMOS.			xxi.	28	646	xiv.	13	322
iv.	12	768	xxii.	4	324	xiv.	17	318
			xxiii.	8	126, 647	xv.	6	103
MICAH.			xxiv.	14	821	xv.	7	356
vi.	6	386	xxv.	6	771	xvi.	5	512
			xxv.	13	745	xvii.	5	401
HABAKKUK.			xxv.	36	878	xviii.	13	573
iii.	2	147	xxv.	40	879	xviii.	37	584
iii.	17, 18	37	xxvi.	36	104	xviii.	41	612
		306	xxvi.	39	535	xix.	10	92
			xxvi.	42	541	xx.	38	707

INDEX OF TEXTS OF SCRIPTURE.

Chap.	Ver.	Hymn.	Chap.	Ver.	Hymn.	Chap.	Ver.	Hymn.
LUKE.			**ACTS.**			**1 CORINTHIANS.**		
xxii.	19	725	i.	9	120	xiii.	13	93, 456, 707
xxii.	42	539	ii.	3	135	xiv.	15	220
xxiii.	33	917	ii.	4	132	xv.	4	113
xxiii.	34	106	ii.	36	53, 127	xv.	20	116
xxiii.	42	522	iii.	1	626	xv.	47	190
xxiv.	5	115	iii.	22	295	xv.	51	787
xxiv.	29	274	iii.	26	479	xv.	52	765
xxiv.	36	286	iv.	12	51	xv.	55	756
xxiv.	50	975	iv.	27	934	xv.	57	854
xxiv.	51	118	v.	31	338	xvi.	2	229
			ix.	6	439, 955	xvi.	13	569
JOHN.			x.	33	240			
i.	4	417	x.	36	49	**2 CORINTHIANS.**		
i.	9	55	xii.	5	710	i.	7	972
i.	16	311	xiv.	17	842	iii.	17	463
i.	29	100, 399	xiv.	22	542	iv.	4	331
ii.	2	862	xiv.	26	822	iv.	17	546
iii.	16	309, 451	xv.	40	974	iv.	18	264, 971
iii.	18	581	xvi.	31	414, 459	v.	1	798
iv.	10	88	xxi.	14	534	v.	7	408
iv.	35	858				v.	10	760
iv.	49	543	**ROMANS.**			v.	14	469
vi.	20	555	i.	20	23	v.	17	472, 515
vi.	37	320	iv.	20	346	vi.	2	329
vi.	55	734	v.	5	214, 454	vi.	10	529
vi.	68	62	v.	11	422, 685	vii.	1	474
viii.	12	263	v.	20	610	viii.	5	336, 453
ix.	4	956	vi.	9	117	ix.	15	390
x.	10	71, 447	vii.	15	390	xliii.	14	978
x.	14	697	vii.	24	368			
x.	28	508	viii.	9	134	**GALATIANS.**		
xi.	9	570	viii.	26	148, 152, 625, 714, 932	ii.	20	109, 345
xi.	28	328				iii.	9	411
xii.	21	781	viii.	28	223, 510, 548	iii.	28	970
xii.	26	652	viii.	37	681	iv.	6	144, 448
xii.	46	602	xi.	33	44, 187, 465	v.	13	650
xiii.	8	405	xii.	1	364, 654	v.	24	667
xiii.	15	85, 651	xii.	5	701	vi.	2	960
xiv.	2	122	xii.	11	659	vi.	9	660
xiv.	3	677, 758, 774	xii.	15	527	vi.	12	396
xiv.	6	498	xiii.	12	259	vi.	14	96, 416, 468
xiv.	16	137, 154	xiv.	8	363, 432	vi.	18	696
xiv.	17	129	xiv.	9	112			
xiv.	18	70, 446, 474, 946				**EPHESIANS.**		
xiv.	26	159	**1 CORINTHIANS.**			i.	7	443
xv.	2	670	i.	23	313	i.	13	346
xv.	5	415, 586	i.	24	107, 705	ii.	4	317, 728
xv.	26	153, 736	ii.	10	259	ii.	6	741
xvi.	13	138	iii.	6	298	ii.	8	582
xvi.	14	150	iii.	16	156	iii.	15	673, 794
xvii.	24	168, 780	iii.	21	511	iii.	17	4, 2
xix.	18	97	iii.	23	657	iii.	19	450, 453
xix.	30	397	v.	7	730	iv.	5	702
xx.	13	757	vi.	11	136	iv.	8	123
xx.	19	977	vi.	19, 20	648	v.	1	424
xx.	22	713	vi.	20	642	v.	14	593
xx.	27	367	x.	4	110	vi.	11	533
xxi.	16	444	x.	13	437	vi.	16	564
xxi.	17	521	x.	16	733	vi.	18	627
			x.	21	729			
ACTS.			xi.	24	726	**PHILIPPIANS.**		
i.	4	133, 149	xi.	25	727	i.	21	391, 887
i.	5	130	xi.	26	735	i.	27	973
i.	8	142	xii.	3	131	ii.	5	483, 597
			xii.	13	699			

INDEX OF TEXTS OF SCRIPTURE.

Chap.	Ver.	Hymn.	Chap.	Ver.	Hymn.	Chap.	Ver.	Hymn.
PHILIPPIANS.			**HEBREWS.**			**1 JOHN.**		
ii.	9	63, 81, 125, 209, 352	i.	1, 2	300	i.	5	10, 240
ii.	10	69	ii.	10	94, 576	i.	7	488
ii.	13	383, 940	ii.	13	906	i.	9	622, 680
ii.	29	711	ii.	14	87	iv.	4	915
iii.	9	98	iii.	6	528	iv.	8	203
iii.	12	303	iii.	7	337	iv.	9	228
iii.	14	198, 744	iv.	2	388	iv.	10	101
iv.	4	197, 732, 912	iv.	3	778	iv.	11	633
iv.	4, 5	193	iv.	9	245, 420, 883	iv.	18	404
iv.	7	687	iv.	15	523, 557, 635	iv.	19	224, 426, 461
			iv.	16	628	v.	10	357
COLOSSIANS.			v.	9	226			
			vi.	4	158	**JUDE.**		
ii.	3	84	vi.	12	552		3	578
iii.	1	507	vi.	18	441		12	740
iii.	2	186	vii.	24	119		20	222
iii.	3	3, 485, 972	ix.	14	155		21	46
iii.	4	739	ix.	27	759		23	959
iii.	11	618	x.	4	105			
iii.	16	131, 292, 683	x.	9	669	**REVELATION.**		
iii.	17	717	x.	14	442			
iii.	23	641	x.	17	747	i.	5, 6	50, 180
iv.	2	587	x.	25	718	i.	7	766
			x.	32	742	i.	10	233
1 THESSALONIANS.			xi.	37, 38	584	i.	14	335
			xii.	1	791	ii.	7	789
iv.	3	655	xii.	1, 2	773	ii.	9	525
iv.	7	610	xii.	2	400, 418, 566, 602	ii.	10	568, 777, 795
iv.	17	776				iii.	4	797
v.	8	828	xii.	6	556	iii.	12	885
v.	11	691	x i.	9	545	iii.	19	398
v.	16	679	xii.	10	482	iii.	20	339, 341
v.	17	716	xii.	22	803	iv.	8	160
			xiii.	5	629	iv.	11	162, 170, 207, 976
1 TIMOTHY.			xiii.	6	664			
i.	11	306	xiii.	14	755	v.	11	793
ii.	4	370	xiii.	15	200	v.	11, 12	179
ii.	8	621				vii.	9	800
iii.	16	22	**JAMES.**			vii.	10	307
vi.	6	513	i.	17	21, 258	vii.	11	264
vi.	12	565	v.	7	854	vii.	13	792
vi.	16	918	v.	9	325	xi.	15	124, 809
			v	11	748	xi.	18	762
2 TIMOTHY.			**1 PETER.**			xiv.	4	430
i.	3	595	i.	8	54, 59	xiv.	13	559, 779, 881, 882
i.	7	146	i.	14	905	xv.	4	183
i.	18	1040	ii.	7	181, 342	xix.	1	1039
ii.	3	562, 574	ii.	25	708	xix.	6	806
ii.	12	86, 647	iii.	8	698, 738	xix.	9	764
iii.	5	343	iv.	7	844	xix.	12	128
iii.	16	293	iv.	18	772	xix.	16	572
iv.	6	277	v.	5	619	xxi.	1	775
iv.	7	575	v.	7	494	xxi.	2	785
						xxi.	10	784
TITUS.			**2 PETER.**			xxi.	10, 11	786
			i.	4	297	xxi.	23	285
iii.	5	315	i.	21	301	xxi.	27	790
			iii	10	763	xxii.	5	276
						xxii.	17	323

GENERAL INDEX TO THE SUBJECTS OF THE HYMNS.

The Figures refer to the Numbers of the Hymns.

When subjects that form Sections of this Hymnal are given they are printed in small capitals.

For Hymns appropriate to the Seasons of the Year, and to Special Services, readers are referred to the Special Index.

Acceptance with God. See Forgiveness, and Holy Spirit.
ADOPTION AND SONSHIP, 437, 441-449, 545.
Adoration. See Christ, and God, Adoration of.
Advent. See Christ, Incarnation of, and Second Coming.
AFFLICTION AND RESIGNATION, 27, 30-32, 36, 37, 40, 126, 274, 402, 405, 487, 491, 494, 496, 503, 508, 517-590, 629, 635, 949, 952, 953, 1025.
All in All, Christ. See Christ.
Angels, 5, 170, 189, 514, 539, 793.
Armour, Spiritual. See Conflict and Courage.
Atonement. See Christ, Passion and Death of, Christ our Redeemer, and Christ our Saviour.
Attributes. See God.
Backsliding. See Declension and Recovery.
BAPTISM, 702, 722-724, 905, 919. See Holy Spirit.
Battle, Life a. See Conflict and Courage.
Beatitudes, The, 377, 480, 481.
Beauty of the Lord, The, 187, 462, 837, 847, 849.
Believers. See Church, Happiness, and Patience.
Bible, The. See Holy Scriptures.
Birth, the New. See Holy Spirit, and Regeneration.
Blessedness of Christians. See Happiness.
Blessing of God. See God, Goodness of.
Blood of Christ, The. See Christ, Passion and Death of.
BURIAL OF THE DEAD, 881-887. See Death.
Business Life, 267, 436, 437, 562, 601, 629, 630, 648, 658, 659, 661. See Presence of God.
Calvary. See Christ, Passion and Death of.
Charity, Christian. See Love.
Children of God. See Adoption, and Father, God our.
—— Prayer for, 905-910.
—— Hymns for, 912-944.
CHRIST, THE LORD JESUS, 49-128.
—— adoration of, 49, 84, 95, 179, 180, 183, 198, 390, 705.
—— all in all, 68, 209, 226, 273, 382, 414, 444, 458, 618.
—— Captain, our. See Conflict and Courage.
—— DIVINITY AND GLORY OF, 49-63, 68, 69, 118, 122, 125, 128, 878.
—— EXAMPLE AND TEACHING OF, 82-94, 381, 547, 639, 655, 678.
—— INCARNATION AND ADVENT OF, 64-81, 676, 934, 1034-1036.

—— INTERCESSION AND REIGN OF, 49, 50, 69, 81, 84, 95, 115, 123-128, 289, 344, 382, 442, 804, 808, 809, 816, 818, 827.
—— Love of, to sinners, 325, 339, 341, 360, 441, 443, 453.
—— Miracles of, 89, 91, 92, 94, 251, 384, 612, 877, 888.
—— Offices of, 64, 68, 209, 295.
—— PASSION AND DEATH OF, 95-110, 288, 309, 313, 330, 353, 375, 396, 416, 443, 461, 468, 520, 917.
—— Redeemer, our, 183, 190, 305, 309, 312, 313, 317, 336, 354, 375, 376, 405-407, 442, 465, 807, 1022, 1037.
—— Refuge, our, 51, 89, 227, 275.
—— RESURRECTION AND ASCENSION OF, 50, 111-122, 507, 1029.
—— Saviour, our, 53, 54, 58, 63, 90-92, 103, 181, 182, 209, 219, 308, 311, 316, 317, 320, 321, 327, 350, 352, 415, 417, 441, 443, 453, 459.
—— Second Coming of, 676, 755, 764, 771, 1032.
—— Shepherd, a, 33, 34, 57, 412, 599, 633, 697, 929, 930, 985.
—— Sympathy of, 286, 287, 521, 523-525, 635, 691.
—— Transfiguration of, 83, 671.
—— Unchangeableness of, 60, 92, 115, 118, 120, 122, 126, 212, 213, 349, 377, 384, 441, 523, 525, 528, 530.
CHRISTIAN LIFE, THE, 364-692.
—— —— Disinterestedness, of 224, 393, 434, 458, 459, 461.
—— —— Freedom of, 45, 46, 71, 226, 303, 425, 457, 463, 464, 578, 653, 667, 689.
—— —— Growth of, 198, 484, 492, 505, 507, 569, 570, 573, 574, 577, 649, 842.
—— —— Pilgrimage of, 85, 569, 773, 774.
—— —— Voyage of, 901, 903.
—— —— Warfare of. See Conflict and Courage.
CHRISTIAN MISSIONS, 19, 49, 50, 56, 63, 72, 123, 124, 127, 128, 134, 145, 164, 165, 169, 172, 188, 218, 289, 306, 307, 309, 312, 316, 322, 334, 489, 569, 651, 662, 675, 676, 679, 804-822, 997, 998, 1004, 1005, 1023, 1024.
CHURCH, THE CHRISTIAN, 289, 500, 693-749.
—— CHARACTER, UNITY AND FELLOWSHIP OF THE, 222, 693-702, 738, 740, 791, 794.
—— Dismission of members of the, 970-978.
—— RECEPTION OF MEMBERS OF THE, 703-706.
Comforter. See Holy Spirit.
Comfort in Trouble. See Affliction and Resignation.

300

INDEX TO SUBJECTS.

Communion. Holy. See Lord's Supper
—— with Christ. See Christ, Sympathy of, and Prayer.
CONFLICT AND COURAGE, 20, 28, 56, 123 127, 128, 403, 561-586, 592 672. 796, 800 924. 963, 993.
Conscience, 594-597
Consecration, 84, 256-259, 263, 288, 353, 361. 362, 391, 399-440, 444, 454, 458, 459, 640-643, 648 657, 663, 668, 669, 1031. See Holiness
Contentment, 513, 532, 534, 535. See Affliction, and Praise.
CONTRITION AND LONGING FOR GOD. 319. 323, 335, 344, 364-398, 609, 610, 622, 632.
Conversion. See Holy Spirit.
Conviction of Sin. See Contrition.
COVENANT SERVICES, 142, 198, 221 288 353, 361, 362, 399, 405, 424-427, 429-432, 435, 437, 440, 454, 458, 640-642, 654, 657, 663, 668, 690. 746-749 See Consecration.
Cross-bearing. 85, 86, 288, 423, 427, 435, 517, 565, 639, 660, 667. See Conflict and Consecration.
DEATH, RESURRECTION AND JUDGMENT, 750-772, 1040.
—— of friends, 555, 559, 758, 795.
—— of the righteous, 757, 779, 800, 881-887.
—— of the young, 752.
—— Preparation for, 277, 431 560. 573, 674, 681, 753, 759-761.
—— Victory over, 756, 777
DECLENSION AND RECOVERY, 603-613, 636, 950.
Dedication. See Consecration.
Delay, Warnings against, 321, 324, 325, 329, 332, 335, 337, 339, 341, 350, 355, 365, 367, 370, 398, 401, 407, 410, 428, 446, 467, 751, 759, 768, 928.
DISMISSAL AND DOXOLOGIES, 970-979.
DIVINE WORSHIP, 171-289. See Public Worship.
Divinity of Christ. See Christ, Divinity of.
Domestic Blessings. See Parents and Family Worship.
Eternity. See God, Eternity of.
EVANGELISTIC SERVICES, 38, 42, 48-54, 57, 58, 63, 85, 92, 95-110, 129-159, 179-182, 194, 197, 209, 221, 277, 297, 306-440, 442, 445, 452, 453, 463, 466, 468, 473, 476, 487, 569, 573, 578, 587- 589, 592, 598, 603-613, 627, 628, 641, 657, 662, 668, 673, 675, 681-683, 685, 705, 706, 713-716, 719, 749, 762, 766, 770, 776, 780, 782, 796, 797, 799, 800, 802, 807, 924.
EXHORTATION TO REPENT, 335-340. See Contrition.
FAITH AND CONSECRATION, 399-440. See Holiness.
—— 270, 741-351, 355, 357, 379, 380, 399, 403, 407, 408, 411, 414, 431, 447, 449, 497, 498, 507, 528, 549, 554, 561, 566, 576-579, 581, 583, 584, 664, 690, 707, 912, 933.
Faithfulness of God. See God, Faithfulness of.
—— of Christians 571, 575, 577, 588, 589, 591, 596, 597, 680.
—— of ministers, 708-711.
Family Worship. See Parents.
FATHER, GOD THE, 1-48, 223. See God, Goodness of.
—— NATURE AND PERFECTIONS OF, 1-13

—— WORKS IN CREATION OF 14-23.
—— PROVIDENCE OF, 24-37.
—— MERCY AND GRACE OF, 38-48.
Fellowship of Saints. See Church.
—— with Christ, 460, 461, 468, 469. See Christ, Sympathy of, and Prayer.
Fire, The baptism of, 130, 132-134, 138, 139, 142, 144, 146, 152. 464 663. See Holy Spirit, and Revivals.
Following Christ, 498 499. 504, 659. See Christ, Example of.
Forgiveness, 39, 43, 52. 61, 86, 95, 98, 106, 163, 354-358, 365-370, 373, 374, 376, 386, 396, 407, 414, 442, 447, 500, 519, 989, 994, 1007, 1018, 1025 See Contrition.
Formalism, 140, 343, 388, 623.
Freedom. See Christian Life, Freedom of the.
Fruitfulness. See Christian Life. Growth of the.
Gifts of the Holy Spirit. See Holy Spirit.
Giving. See Service.
Glory of Christ. See Christ, Divinity and Glory of.
—— of God. See God, Glory of.
God. See Father, God the.
—— Adoration of, 47, 172, 173 184, 185, 187 201-207, 210, 218
—— Creator, 7, 14-23 174, 176, 184, 195, 196, 200, 203, 260.
—— Eternity of, 1, 3, 6, 12, 47, 187, 750.
—— Faithfulness of, 38, 546, 550.
—— Glory of, 2, 5, 10, 16, 17, 19, 20, 22, 41, 44, 45, 48, 184, 187, 193, 918, 1026.
—— Goodness of, 4, 9, 21, 29, 35-48, 186, 189, 191, 192, 194, 195, 199, 260, 207, 228, 260, 265, 268, 270, 278, 309, 312, 354, 379, 380, 411, 465, 469, 506, 551, 683, 684, 693, 824, 828, 835-839, 847, 849, 850, 852, 853, 855, 856, 857, 859, 860, 937, 943, 1016.
—— Government of, 2, 5, 16, 20, 41, 171, 225, 534, 551, 808, 1017, 1019.
—— Holiness of, 44, 187, 190, 240, 1011.
—— Infinity of, 1, 4, 6, 13, 44, 187.
—— Omnipotence of, 7, 23, 47, 171, 184, 199, 207.
—— Omnipresence of, 15, 165, 173, 213, 266, 267, 572, 424, 691, 1014.
—— Omniscience of, 7, 11, 27, 427. 473, 517, 1014.
—— Providence of, 24-37, 189, 268, 281-284, 492, 506, 510, 547, 548, 825, 892, 897. See Mystery of Providence.
—— Righteousness of, 22, 30, 42, 202, 215.
—— Teacher, a, 19, 23. 48, 153-156, 290-305, 475, 487-489, 491-498, 501, 502, 504, 508, 509, 511, 536, 616, 619, 620, 653, 660, 661, 679, 708-710, 907, 930, 932, 987.
—— Unchangeableness of, 3, 12, 13, 38, 212 666, 691.
—— Will of, 299, 534, 535, 539, 540, 579, 656.
—— Wisdom of, 7, 8, 11, 14, 18, 19, 32, 290.
GOSPEL MESSAGE, THE, 306-317, 815.
Gospel Feast, The, 318, 322, 324.
—— Freeness of the, 309, 310, 312, 319, 321 355.
—— Power of the, 306, 311, 352, 357.
—— Success of the, 354, 675, 676, 818, 819.
Grace. See God, Goodness of, and Salvation by Grace.

310

INDEX TO SUBJECTS.

Gratitude. See God, **Goodness of, Praise,** and Thankfulness.
Growth in Grace. See **Christian Life, Growth of the,** and Light.
Guidance. See Light.
Happiness of Christians, 197, 282, 353, 357, 412, 419, 431, 456, 468, 491, 508, 580, 624, 775, 981, 983, 990, 1002, 1008, 1009, 1011, 1027. See Heaven, Hope and Joy, and Praise.
Healing of Spiritual Diseases. See Christ, Miracles of.
Hearing the Word. See Holy Scriptures.
HEAVEN AND THE LIFE HEREAFTER, 197, 245, 277, 285, 431, 546, 560, 674, 681, 696, 741, 755, 773-803. See Death, and Burial of the Dead.
Help, Prayer for, 504, 586, 596, 631, 633. See Contrition, and Prayer.
High Priesthood of Christ. See Christ, Intercession and Reign of, and Passion and Death of.
Holiness, 214, 221, 224, 264, 374, 397, 450-486, 580, 588, 594, 595, 640, 673. See Consecration.
HOLY SCRIPTURES, THE, 3, 9, 28, 38, 144, 153-155, 196, 268, 290-305, 331, 388, 486, 511, 815, 821, 984.
HOLY SPIRIT, THE, 129-159, 293, 294, 301, 364, 463, 47 486, 527, 613, 614, 625, 637, 713, 858, 932.
HOPE AND JOY, 515, 575, 672-692, 992. See Happiness and Heaven.
HUMILITY, 614-620.
Image of God. See Consecration and Holiness.
Incarnation. See Christ, Incarnation of.
Inspiration of the Bible. See Holy Scriptures.
Intercession of Christ. See Christ, Intercession of.
—— of Christians. See Prayer.
INVITATION TO THE SINNER, 308, 310, 311, 318-334.
Jesus. See Christ.
—— Name of, 63, 68, 69, 181, 182, 306, 352, 406, 581.
—— Voice of, 308, 311, 328, 587.
Joy. See Happiness, and Hope and Joy.
Judgment. See Death, Resurrection and Judgment.
Justification. See Forgiveness.
King, or Queen, Prayer for, 961, 969.
Kingdom of Christ. See Christ, Intercession and Reign of, Church and Missions.
Lamb of God, 385, 655. See Christ, Passion and Death of.
Leaning on Christ, 503. See Faith, and Rest.
Life, Brevity and frailty of, 274, 276, 284, 750-755, 759-761.
—— Greatness of, 429, 584, 638, 639, 644, 651, 652, 659, 660, 661, 669, 670.
—— Vicissitudes of, 502, 538, 541-543, 547, 548.
LIGHT, GUIDANCE AND GROWTH, 83, 257-259, 261, 263, 265, 266, 290-305, 378, 417, 487-509, 567, 570, 576, 585, 600, 601, 649, 653, 692.
Likeness to God. See Consecration, and Holiness.
Litanies, 216, 219, 229, 280, 332, 492, 520, 522, 535, 896, 946.
LONGING FOR GOD, 202, 364-398, 402. See Contrition.
Looking to Jesus, 418, 781. See Faith.

LORD'S DAY, THE, 230-255. See Christ, Resurrection of.
—— SUPPER, THE, 95-110, 353, 468, 520, 523, 725-737, 977, 1030. See Christ, Passion and Death of.
LOVE AND HOLINESS, 450-486. See Consecration, and Holiness.
Love to Christ, 359, 378, 393, 395, 404, 415, 421, 427, 434, 467.
—— to one another, 93, 456, 645, 647, 650, 651, 693-706.
LOVEFEASTS, 180, 197, 341, 465, 467, 469, 483, 682, 683, 694, 701, 705, 706, 732, 738-741.
Mediator, Christ the, 10, 387. See Christ, Intercession and Reign of.
Meditation, 37, 257, 261, 266, 267, 282, 301, 462, 475, 532, 606, 671, 691, 945, 949, 951, 952.
Members of the Church. See Church.
Mercy. See God, Goodness of.
—— Prayer for. See Evangelistic Services.
—— Seat, 65, 98, 439, 624, 628, 712, 719.
Mind of Christ, 483. See Christ, Example and Teaching of.
Missions. See Christian Missions.
Mystery of Providence, The, 27, 536, 585, 664, 670, 686. See God, Providence of.
—— of Redemption, The, 441, 443, 446, 611. See Christ, our Redeemer.
Nation, Thanksgivings and Prayers for the, 41, 189, 193, 561, 578, 681, 808, 961-969, 993, 998, 1000, 1003, 1008, 1013-1017, 1019.
Nativity of Jesus, The. See Christ, Incarnation of.
Nazareth, Jesus of, 333.
New birth, The. See Holy Spirit, and Regeneration.
Obedience to God, 411, 425, 429, 435, 472, 478, 492-502, 531, 534, 535, 539, 655.
Omnipotence. See God, Omnipotence of.
Omnipresence. See God, Omnipresence of.
Omniscience. See God, Omniscience of.
OPENING SERVICES, 867-876.
Paradise. See Heaven.
Pardon. See Forgiveness.
PARENTS AND FAMILY WORSHIP, 24, 26, 200, 229, 275, 276, 287, 516, 905-911.
Patience, 215, 463, 483, 494, 499, 503, 518, 522, 534, 535, 537, 539, 540, 545, 602, 603. See Affliction and Resignation.
Peace, 26, 30-34, 40, 46, 158, 159, 164, 226, 277, 235, 239, 240, 245, 282, 286, 327, 358, 413, 508, 532, 538, 541, 542, 544, 550, 687.
—— Meetings, 72, 79, 676, 811, 961, 962, 965, 967.
Penitence. See Contrition.
Perfect Love. See Consecration, and Love and Holiness.
Perseverance. See Watchfulness and Steadfastness.
Physician, Christ a. See Christ, Miracles of.
Pleasantness of Religion. See Happiness.
PRAISE AND PRAYER, 171-229. See God the Father, and Worship.
PRAYER MEETINGS, 213, 244, 601, 617, 621-637, 663, 700, 712-721. See Evangelistic Services.
Preachers. See Ministers.
Presence of God, The, 59, 266, 267, 271, 281, 283, 286, 402, 691, 700, 713, 715. See Business-Life, and God, Omnipresence of.

311

INDEX TO SUBJECTS.

Priesthood of Christ. See Christ, Offices of, Intercession of, and Passion and Death of.
PRIVATE DEVOTION, 11, 26, 32, 35, 59, 60, 62, 138, 156, 256, 257, 277, 304, 449, 497, 508, 626, 688, 945-954.
Providence. See God, Providence of, and Mystery of Providence.
PUBLIC WORSHIP, 171-289, 1033, 1038, 1053.
— Beginning of, 1-3, 6, 7, 9, 14, 16, 22, 25, 35, 38, 43, 50, 54, 64, 160, 161, 166, 172-176, 178, 183, 184, 185, 187, 189, 190, 195, 200, 201, 203-205, 210, 211, 214, 230-249, 256, 259, 260-268, 313, 352, 354, 386, 514, 515, 621, 637, 683, 685, 773, 808, 810, 912, 914, 1033.
— Conclusion of, 12, 13, 24, 36, 40, 42, 44, 48, 52, 155, 159, 177, 183, 186, 191, 194, 196, 212, 221, 250-255, 269, 271-280, 298, 302, 305, 308, 320, 321, 324, 329, 332, 337, 339, 399, 402, 429, 452, 466, 468, 490, 500, 512, 516, 663, 665, 673, 674, 751, 753-755, 782-781, 970-978.
Queen, Prayer for. See King, or Queen.
Ransom, Christ a. See Christ, our Redeemer.
Reception of Members. See Church.
Redemption. See Christ, our Redeemer.
Refuge, God our, 28, 533, 561, 580, 583, 719, 750, 902-904. See God, Providence of.
Regeneration, 353, 357, 442, 443, 445. See Holy Spirit.
Reign of Christ. See Christ, Intercession and Reign of.
Rejoicing in Forgiveness, 352-363. See Forgiveness.
Religion, Excellence of. See Happiness.
Repentance. See Contrition.
Resignation. See Affliction.
Rest, God our, 217, 541, 542, 544, 545, 550.
Rest in Christ, 282, 381, 389, 420, 438, 503, 508, 538, 618, 690, 692.
— of the Sabbath. See Lord's Day.
Restoration. See Declension and Recovery.
Resurrection of Christ. See Christ, Resurrection of.
— of the Dead. See Death.
Revivals, 130, 132, 133, 137, 139, 140, 144, 145, 147, 155, 214, 364, 378, 384, 393, 545, 603-605, 818.
Sabbath. See Lord's Day.
Sacraments. See Baptism, and Lord's Supper.
Sacrifice of Christ, The. See Christ, Passion and Death of.
— of Christians. See Conflict, Consecration, and Cross Bearing.
Sailors. See Travellers by Land and Sea.
Salvation by Grace, 38, 39, 43, 51, 58, 63, 71, 86, 194, 304, 310, 312, 315, 318, 324, 347, 353, 355, 358, 367, 383, 386, 387, 428, 465, 619, 673.
— through Faith. See Faith.
Sanctification. See Consecration, Holiness, and Holy Spirit.
Satan, 561, 569, 570, 672, 697.
Saviour. See Christ, our Saviour.
Scriptures. See Holy Scriptures, and Holy Spirit.
SEA, FOR THOSE AT. See Travellers.
Self-denial. See Cross-Bearing.

SERVICE AND GIVING, 620, 638-671.
Shepherd, The Good. See Christ, a Shepherd.
Simplicity, 394, 458, 616, 619.
Sin, 92, 109, 249, 251, 279, 319, 321, 322, 326, 330, 338, 340, 344, 407, 425, 473, 477, 479, 595, 607, 615. See Contrition and Forgiveness.
Sincerity, 129, 256, 623, 627, 647. See Consecration, and Holiness.
Soldiers of Christ. See Conflict and Courage.
Sowing and Reaping, 228, 340, 526, 548, 652, 662, 770, 814, 821-823, 827, 834, 838, 840, 842, 851, 854, 857-859.
Spirit. See Holy Spirit.
Stability. See Watchfulness and Steadfastness.
Strength, Spiritual. See Conflict and Courage.
Sympathy of Christ. See Christ, Sympathy of.
— of Christians, 527, 638, 645, 650, 651, 653, 656, 694, 698, 699, 706, 738.
Teacher, God a. See God.
Temptation, 219, 366, 370, 492, 528, 568, 570, 581, 582, 592, 593, 595-597, 600, 691.
THANKFULNESS, 510-516. See Praise, and Worship.
Transfiguration. See Christ, Transfiguration of.
TRAVELLERS BY LAND AND SEA, 89, 91, 438, 491, 509, 514, 691, 888-904.
Trials. See Affliction, and Temptation.
TRINITY, THE HOLY, 160-170, 280, 1033.
Trust. See Faith.
Unchangeableness. See Christ, and God, Unchangeableness of.
Unity. See Church.
Vows. See Consecration, and Covenant Services.
War. See Peace Meetings.
WATCHFULNESS AND STEADFASTNESS, 403, 412, 424, 430, 560, 568, 570, 572, 574, 585, 587 602, 1028. See Consecration.
WATCH-NIGHT SERVICES, 12, 24, 35, 487, 510, 521, 537, 587, 665, 742-745, 750, 754 753-755, 764, 768, 771, 843.
Will of God. See God, Will of.
Will, Freedom of the, 326, 330, 359, 429, 467.
Wisdom. See God, Wisdom of.
Witness. See Holy Spirit.
Witnesses to the truth, 578, 602, 791, 792, 794, 890.
Word of God, The. See Holy Scriptures.
Work, 26, 224, 256, 261, 267, 436, 504, 938, 956. See Service.
Worship, 171-289. See Public Worship.
Wrestling with God, 147, 224, 367, 370, 377, 379, 380, 446, 527, 613, 632, 634, 716.
YOUNG, SERVICES FOR THE, 21, 29, 48, 51, 64, 67, 73, 74, 82, 103, 110, 141, 122, 125, 130, 134, 156, 159, 174, 176, 178, 179, 182, 184, 186, 192, 194, 195, 197, 198, 200, 210, 221, 223, 252, 255, 256, 259, 261, 269, 271-273, 275, 277, 279-284, 281, 290, 291, 294, 311, 316, 317, 321, 333, 339, 349, 351, 359, 364, 406, 407, 416, 419, 426, 429, 430, 437, 440, 449, 452, 461, 466, 487, 491, 492, 513, 516, 537, 541, 542, 545, 548, 562, 569, 573, 578, 584, 614, 618, 623, 627, 644, 652, 658, 663, 685, 749, 751, 752, 770, 776, 782, 785, 790, 793, 799, 805, 809, 811, 815, 824, 825, 831, 832, 838, 839, 812, 843, 845, 846-869, 880, 912-944, 959.
Zeal. See Baptism of Fire, Holy Spirit, and Service.

www.ingramcontent.com/pod-product-compliance
Lightning Source LLC
Chambersburg PA
CBHW030754230426
43667CB00007B/960